POLITICS

Palgrave Foundations

A series of introductory texts across a wide range of subject areas to meet the needs of today's lecturers and students

Foundations texts provide complete yet concise coverage of core topics and skills based on detailed research of course requirements suitable for both independent study and class use – the firm foundations for future study.

Published

A History of English Literature (second edition)
Biology
British Politics (second edition)
Chemistry (fourth edition)
Communication Studies
Contemporary Europe (third edition)
Economics
Economics for Business
European Union Politics
Foundations of Marketing
Global Politics
Modern British History
Nineteenth-Century Britain
Philosophy
Physics (third edition)
Politics (fourth edition)
Theatre Studies

POLITICS

Fourth Edition

ANDREW HEYWOOD

palgrave
macmillan

First edition 1997
Second edition 2002
Third edition 2007
Fourth edition 2013

Published by
PALGRAVE MACMILLAN

Palgrave Macmillan in the UK is an imprint of Macmillan Publishers Limited, registered in England, company number 785998, of Houndmills, Basingstoke, Hampshire RG21 6XS.

Palgrave Macmillan in the US is a division of St Martin's Press LLC, 175 Fifth Avenue, New York, NY 10010.

Palgrave Macmillan is the global academic imprint of the above companies and has companies and representatives throughout the world.

Palgrave® and Macmillan® are registered trademarks in the United States, the United Kingdom, Europe and other countries

ISBN 978–0–230–36337–3   hardback
ISBN 978–0–230–36338–0   paperback

This book is printed on paper suitable for recycling and made from fully managed and sustained forest sources. Logging, pulping and manufacturing processes are expected to conform to the environmental regulations of the country of origin.

A catalogue record for this book is available from the British Library.

Library of Congress Cataloging-in-Publication Data
Heywood, Andrew.
Politics / Andrew Heywood. – 4th ed.
p. cm.
ISBN 978-0-230-36338-0
1. Political science.   I. Title.
JA66.H45 2013
320–dc23   2012024723

10 9 8 7 6 5 4 3 2 1
22 21 20 19 18 17 16 15 14 13

Printed and bound in China

Brief Contents

Contents

List of Illustrative Material

Concepts

Key ideas

Featured thinkers

Figures

For Mark and Robin

Preface to the Fourth Edition

This book provides a comprehensive and up-to-date introduction to the study of politics. It is designed to be of use to students taking courses in any field of the discipline, as well as general readers with an interest in the subject.

The book has been substantially revised and restructured in its fourth edition to take account of changes in the ever-evolving field of politics, but especially those changes that have led to a growing interdependence between domestic, international and global political developments. Instead of, as in earlier editions, attempting to address the international dimension of politics substantially through a single chapter, the current edition acknowledges the declining relevance of the disciplinary divide between politics and international relations, and of the domestic/international divide, upon which it is based. There are, therefore, new chapters on issues such as political economy and globalization, multi-level politics, security, and global governance and world order. A new final chapter focuses on the increasingly pressing notion that politics is in crisis, and, in the process, draws together themes that have been addressed at various points in the book. The previous organization of the book into five central themes has also been dropped, thereby acknowledging the arbitrary nature of such divisions and the essentially holistic nature of political analysis. Nevertheless, the organization of the book does follow an unfolding logic, and this is explained in 'Using this book' on pp. xviii–xix. This fourth edition also contains several new features, whose chief purpose is to encourage readers to develop critical awareness as well as their own views. A 'Guide to the key features' can be found on pp. xx–xxi.

I would like to express my sincere gratitude to John Greenaway, Wyn Grant, Chris Brown and Gerry Stoker, who commented on earlier editions, and to Jonathon Moses, who commented on the current draft. Their advice and criticism, and that of the publisher's many other reviewers, have been both constructive and insightful, and undoubtedly improved the book at a number of points. Discussions with colleagues and friends, particularly Karon and Doug Woodward, also helped to sharpen the ideas and arguments developed here. My publisher, Steven Kennedy, was closely involved in planning this fourth edition, while Helen Caunce showed just the right balance of support, encouragement and patience in overseeing the project on behalf of Palgrave Macmillan. Thanks should also go to Keith Povey and Ian Wileman for their contribution to the production process. My most heartfelt thanks, however, go, as ever, to my wife Jean. Not only did she take sole responsibility for the preparation of the typescript of this book, but she also offered advice on both style and content, which was especially useful when I was in danger of lapsing into incoherence.

2013   ANDREW HEYWOOD

Using This Book

Politics is, by its nature, an overlapping and interlocking field. The material encountered in this book therefore stubbornly resists compartmentalization, which is why, throughout, there is regular cross-referencing to related discussions that occur in other chapters and particularly to relevant boxed material found elsewhere. Nevertheless, the book develops by considering what can be thought of as a series of broad issues or themes.

The first group of chapters is designed to provide a background understanding for the study of politics by considering a range of key conceptual and theoretical issues.

- Chapter 1 reflects on the nature of politics, provides an introduction to contrasting approaches to political analysis and considers how and why globalizing tendencies have reshaped our understanding of the subject.
- Chapter 2 examines political ideas from the perspective of the major ideological traditions, looking at how they offer competing 'lenses' on the political world.
- Chapter 3 considers the importance of the state in politics, examining debates about both the nature and the desirable role of the state, as well as whether the state is losing its central importance in politics.
- Chapter 4 discusses the nature and significance of political legitimacy, considering, in particular, the relationship between legitimacy and democracy, especially in the light of contrasting models of democratic governance and debates about how democracy operates in practice.
- Chapter 5 examines the key theories of nationalism, seeking both to understand the forces that underpin national identity and to reflect on the breadth of nationalist traditions, including their often quite different political implications.

The next group of chapters discusses the dynamics of political interaction by reflecting on the relationship between politics and economics, culture and society, and by examining the mechanisms through which societal pressures gain political expression.

- Chapter 6 discusses the linkages between economics and politics, focusing especially on the nature and different forms of capitalism, and on the dynamics and implications of economic globalization.
- Chapter 7 considers the relationship between politics and society, and reflects on the rise of identity politics, the different forms it has taken, and its implications.
- Chapter 8 discusses the nature and significance of political culture, and examines the growing political importance of the media, especially in relation to its implications for democracy and governance.

- Chapter 9 looks at the nature of representation, the role of elections, including debates and controversies about electoral systems, and how voting behaviour can best be understood.
- Chapter 10 examines the key role played in politics by political parties, and also discusses the nature and significance of different party systems.
- Chapter 11 discusses the nature of group politics, including debates about the impact of groups on the distribution of political power, and the rise and implications of social movements.

The following group of chapters considers the machinery of government and the processes through which public policy is formulated and implemented.

- Chapter 12 provides an introduction to the machinery of government by considering how systems of government are classified and examining the range of political regimes that exist in the modern world.
- Chapter 13 addresses the role of political executives, where power lies within the executive and, more broadly, the significance of political leadership and the forms it can take.
- Chapter 14 examines the role of assemblies or legislatures, considering also the significance of their internal organization and the factors that affect their impact on policy-making.
- Chapter 15 considers the nature and purpose of constitutions, and examines the relationship between politics and law, notably in terms of the role and importance of the judiciary.
- Chapter 16 focuses on public policy, reflecting both on how decisions are made and the stages through which policy is developed; it also considers the link between bureaucracies and the policy process, as well as wider political developments.

The next group of chapters focuses on various issues that highlight overlaps between the domestic realm and the international realm, paying particular attention to the growing significance of global politics.

- Chapter 17 discusses multilevel politics, examining the territorial configuration of politics at a domestic level and at a transnational level, especially through regionalism.
- Chapter 18 focuses on the issue of security, examining the maintenance of order and security in the domestic realm, as well as debates about security in its national, international and global forms.
- Chapter 19 looks at the changing shape of twenty-first-century world order, reflecting on its significance for peace and stability, and also examines the nature and effectiveness of the emerging framework of global governance.

The final chapter attempts to draw together strands and themes that have featured in earlier chapters through a discussion of the merits and demerits of politics.

- Chapter 20 reflects on the issue of growing disenchantment with formal politics and, despite this, how politics can be defended; it also considers the different ways in which the performance of political systems can be evaluated.

GUIDE TO THE KEY FEATURES

The pedagogical features found in this book allow important events, concepts and theoretical issues to be examined in greater depth or detail, whilst also maintaining the flow of the main body of the text. They are, moreover, designed to encourage readers to think critically and independently about the key issues in political analysis.

Each chapter starts with a **Preview** that outlines the major themes and a series of questions that highlight the central themes and issues addressed in the chapter. At the end of each chapter there is a **Summary** of its major points, a list of **Questions for discussion**, and suggestions for **Further reading**. Additional material is provided throughout the text in the form of glossary panels and boxed information. These boxes are comprehensively cross-referenced throughout the text. The most significant features are the following:

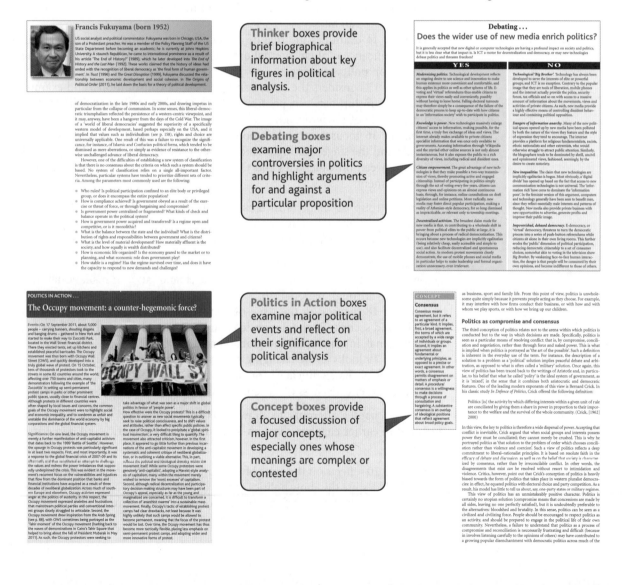

Thinker boxes provide brief biographical information about key figures in political analysis.

Debating boxes examine major controversies in politics and highlight arguments for and against a particular proposition

Politics in Action boxes examine major political events and reflect on their significance for political analysis

Concept boxes provide a focused discussion of major concepts, especially ones whose meanings are complex or contested

Focus on . . .
Why do revolutions occur?

Why do regimes collapse? Should revolutions be understood primarily in political terms, or are they more a reflection of deeper economic or social developments? Contrasting theories of revolution have been advanced by Marxists and non-Marxists. In Marxist theory, revolution emerges out of contradictions that exist at a socio-economic level. Marx (see p. 41) believed that revolution marks the point at which the class struggle develops into open conflict, leading one class to overthrow and displace another. Just as the French Revolution was interpreted as a 'bourgeois' revolution, the Russian Revolution was later seen as a 'proletarian' revolution that set in motion a process that would culminate in the establishment of socialism and, eventually, full communism. However, revolutions have not come about as Marx forecast. Not only have they tended to occur in relatively backward societies, not (as he predicted) in the advanced capitalist countries, but Marxist revolutions were often *coup d'états* rather than popular revolutions.

A variety of non-Marxist theories of revolution have been advanced. Systems theorists have argued that

revolution results from 'disequilibrium' in the political system, brought about by economic, social, cultural or international changes to which the system itself is incapable of responding – the 'outputs' of government become structurally out of line with the 'inputs'. The idea of a 'revolution of rising expectations' suggests that revolutions occur when a period of economic and social development is abruptly reversed, creating a widening gap between popular expectations and the capabilities of government. The classic statement of this theory is found in Ted Gurr's *Why Men Rebel* (1970), which links rebellion to 'relative deprivation'.

The social-structural theory of revolution implies that regimes usually succumb to revolution when, through international weakness and/or domestic ineffectiveness, they lose their ability, or the political will, to maintain control through the exercise of coercive power. Theda Skocpol (1979) explained the outbreak of the French, Russian and Chinese revolutions in these terms, but they could equally be applied to the swift and largely bloodless collapse of the Eastern European communist regimes in the autumn and winter of 1989 (see p. 44).

Focus boxes provide either further insight into a theoretical issue or additional information about the topic

ent as the UK, France, Spain, Australia and New Zealand have accommodated themselves to broadly similar goals and values. As this happened, a political culture that once emphasized social justice, welfare rights and public responsibilities gave way to one in which choice, enterprise, competition and individual responsibility are given prominence.

However, legitimation crises may have more dramatic consequences. When faltering support for a regime can no longer be managed by adjustments in public policy or a change in leadership, legitimacy may collapse altogether, leading either to a resort to repression, or to revolution. While evolutionary change is usually thought of as reform, revolution involves root-and-branch change. Revolutions recast the political order entirely, typically bringing about an abrupt and often violent break with the past. Although there is considerable debate about the causes of revolution, there is little doubt that revolution has played a crucial role in shaping the modern world. The American Revolution (1776) led to the creation of a constitutional republic independent from Britain and gave practical expression to the principle of representation. The French Revolution (1789) set out to destroy the old order under the banner of 'liberty,

● **Revolution:** A popular uprising, involving extra-legal mass action, which brings about fundamental change (a change in the political system itself) as opposed to merely a change of policy or governing elite.

● **Reform:** Change brought about within a system, usually by peaceful and incremental measures; reform implies improvement.

Marginal definitions briefly explain the meaning of key terms in political analysis

● **Behaviouralism:** The belief that social theories should be constructed only on the basis of observable behaviour, providing quantifiable data for research.

● **Bias:** Sympathies or prejudices that (often unconsciously) affect human judgement; bias implies distortion (see 'political bias', p. 183).

Oxford, Paris and Columbia, and by 1906 the *American Political Science Review* was being published. However, enthusiasm for a science of politics peaked in the 1950s and 1960s with the emergence, most strongly in the USA, of a form of political analysis that drew heavily on behaviouralism. For the first time, this gave politics reliably scientific credentials, because it provided what had previously been lacking: objective and quantifiable data against which hypotheses could be tested. Political analysts such as David Easton (1979, 1981) proclaimed that politics could adopt the methodology of the natural sciences, and this gave rise to a proliferation of studies in areas best suited to the use of quantitative research methods, such as voting behaviour, the behaviour of legislators, and the behaviour of municipal politicians and lobbyists. Attempts were also made to apply behaviouralism to IR, in the hope of developing objective 'laws' of international relations.

Behaviouralism, however, came under growing pressure from the 1960s onwards. In the first place, it was claimed that behaviouralism had significantly constrained the scope of political analysis, preventing it from going beyond what was directly observable. Although behavioural analysis undoubtedly produced, and continues to produce, invaluable insights in fields such as voting studies, a narrow obsession with quantifiable data threatens to reduce the discipline of politics to little else. More worryingly, it inclined a generation of political scientists to turn their backs on the entire tradition of normative political thought. Concepts such as 'liberty', 'equality', 'justice' and 'rights' were sometimes discarded as being meaningless because they were not empirically verifiable entities. Dissatisfaction with behaviouralism grew as interest in normative questions revived in the 1970s, as reflected in the writings of theorists such as John Rawls (see p. 45) and Robert Nozick (see p. 68).

Moreover, the scientific credentials of behaviouralism started to be called into question. The basis of the assertion that behaviouralism is objective and reliable is the claim that it is 'value-free': that is, that it is not contaminated by ethical or normative beliefs. However, if the focus of analysis is observable behaviour, it is difficult to do much more than describe the existing political arrangements, which implicitly means that the status quo is legitimized. This conservative value bias was demonstrated by the fact that 'democracy' was, in effect, redefined in terms of observable behaviour. Thus, instead of meaning 'popular self-government' (literally, government by the people), democracy came to stand for a struggle between competing elites to win power through the mechanism of popular election. In other words, democracy came to mean what goes on in the so-called democratic political systems of the developed West.

Rational-choice theory

Amongst recent theoretical approaches to politics is what is called 'formal political theory', variously known as 'rational-choice theory', 'public-choice theory' (see p. 252) and 'political economy' (see p. 129). This approach to analysis draws heavily on the example of economic theory in building up models based on procedural rules, usually about the rationally self-interested behaviour of the individuals involved. Most firmly established in the USA, and associated in particular with the so-called Virginia School, formal political theory provides at

The **companion website** at **www.palgrave.com/foundations/heywood** contains a variety of resources for lecturers and students.

For lecturers:
● **Exam questions**
● **PowerPoint slides**
● **Figures and tables**

For students:
● **Case studies**
● **A searchable glossary**
● **Profiles on featured thinkers**
● **Multiple-choice questions**
● **Chapter notes**
● **Web links**

Acknowledgements

The author and publishers would like to thank the following who have kindly given permission for the use of pictorial copyright material:

Press Association, pp. 7, 11, 37, 41, 43, 44, 47, 50, 51, 54, 61, 77, 84, 88, 99, 114, 116, 136, 137, 138, 155, 161, 164, 168, 181, 184, 198, 263, 238, 262, 280, 297, 301, 304, 312, 327, 369, 381, 410, 414, 440, 450; Getty, pp. 5, 6, 13, 31, 59, 68, 82, 96, 97, 169, 175, 199, 214, 227, 245, 319, 348, 372; Alamy, pp. 36, 42, 110; Library of Congress, p. 130; The Library of the London School of Economics and Political Science, p. 177; Robert Putnam, p. 176; Yale University, p. 250; Francis Fukuyama, p. 271; Saltzman Institute for War and Peace Studies, Columbia University, p. 409; Jon Chase/Harvard Staff Photographer, p. 425; Naomi Klein, p. 261; Woodrow Wilson School of Public and International Affairs, Princeton University, p. 434; Jean Bethke Elshtain, p. 413; European Union 2012, p. 394; Schumacher Society, p. 141

Every effort has been made to contact all copyright-holders, but if any have been inadvertently omitted the publishers will be pleased to make the necessary arrangement at the earliest opportunity.

CHAPTER 1

What is Politics?

'Man is by nature a political animal.'

ARISTOTLE, *Politics*, 1

PREVIEW

Politics is exciting because people disagree. They disagree about how they should live. Who should get what? How should power and other resources be distributed? Should society be based on cooperation or conflict? And so on. They also disagree about how such matters should be resolved. How should collective decisions be made? Who should have a say? How much influence should each person have? And so forth. For Aristotle, this made politics the 'master science': that is, nothing less than the activity through which human beings attempt to improve their lives and create the Good Society. Politics is, above all, a social activity. It is always a dialogue, and never a monologue. Solitary individuals such as Robinson Crusoe may be able to develop a simple economy, produce art, and so on, but they cannot engage in politics. Politics emerges only with the arrival of a Man (or Woman) Friday. Nevertheless, the disagreement that lies at the heart of politics also extends to the nature of the subject and how it should be studied. People disagree about what it is that makes social interaction 'political', whether it is where it takes place (within government, the state or the public sphere generally), or the kind of activity it involves (peacefully resolving conflict or exercising control over less powerful groups). Disagreement about the nature of politics as an academic discipline means that it embraces a range of theoretical approaches and a variety of schools of analysis. Finally, globalizing tendencies have encouraged some to speculate that the disciplinary divide between politics and international relations has now become redundant.

KEY ISSUES

- What are the defining features of politics as an activity?
- How has 'politics' been understood by various thinkers and traditions?
- What are the main approaches to the study of politics as an academic discipline?
- Can the study of politics be scientific?
- What roles do concepts, models and theories play in political analysis?
- How have globalizing trends affected the relationship between politics and international relations?

DEFINING POLITICS

Politics, in its broadest sense, is the activity through which people make, preserve and amend the general rules under which they live. Although politics is also an academic subject (sometimes indicated by the use of 'Politics' with a capital P), it is then clearly the study of this activity. Politics is thus inextricably linked to the phenomena of **conflict** and **cooperation**. On the one hand, the existence of rival opinions, different wants, competing needs and opposing interests guarantees disagreement about the rules under which people live. On the other hand, people recognize that, in order to influence these rules or ensure that they are upheld, they must work with others – hence Hannah Arendt's (see p. 7) definition of political power as 'acting in concert'. This is why the heart of politics is often portrayed as a process of conflict resolution, in which rival views or competing interests are reconciled with one another. However, politics in this broad sense is better thought of as a *search* for conflict resolution than as its achievement, as not all conflicts are, or can be, resolved. Nevertheless, the inescapable presence of diversity (we are not all alike) and scarcity (there is never enough to go around) ensures that politics is an inevitable feature of the human condition.

Any attempt to clarify the meaning of 'politics' must nevertheless address two major problems. The first is the mass of associations that the word has when used in everyday language; in other words, politics is a 'loaded' term. Whereas most people think of, say, economics, geography, history and biology simply as academic subjects, few people come to politics without preconceptions. Many, for instance, automatically assume that students and teachers of politics must in some way be biased, finding it difficult to believe that the subject can be approached in an impartial and dispassionate manner (see p. 19). To make matters worse, politics is usually thought of as a 'dirty' word: it conjures up images of trouble, disruption and even violence on the one hand, and deceit, manipulation and lies on the other. There is nothing new about such associations. As long ago as 1775, Samuel Johnson dismissed politics as 'nothing more than a means of rising in the world', while in the nineteenth century the US historian Henry Adams summed up politics as 'the systematic organization of hatreds'.

The second and more intractable difficulty is that even respected authorities cannot agree what the subject is about. Politics is defined in such different ways: as the exercise of power, the science of government, the making of collective decisions, the allocation of scarce resources, the practice of deception and manipulation, and so on. The virtue of the definition advanced in this text – 'the making, preserving and amending of general social rules' – is that it is sufficiently broad to encompass most, if not all, of the competing definitions. However, problems arise when the definition is unpacked, or when the meaning is refined. For instance, does 'politics' refer to a particular way in which rules are made, preserved or amended (that is, peacefully, by debate), or to all such processes? Similarly, is politics practised in all social contexts and institutions, or only in certain ones (that is, government and public life)?

From this perspective, politics may be treated as an 'essentially contested' concept, in the sense that the term has a number of acceptable or legitimate meanings (concepts are discussed more fully later in the chapter). On the other

● **Conflict**: Competition between opposing forces, reflecting a diversity of opinions, preferences, needs or interests.

● **Cooperation**: Working together; achieving goals through collective action.

	Politics as an arena	Politics as a process
Definitions of politics	The art of government Public affairs	Compromise and consensus Power and the distribution of resources
Approaches to the study of politics	Behaviouralism Rational-choice theory Institutionalism	Feminism Marxism Post-positivist approaches

Figure 1.1   Approaches to defining politics

hand, these different views may simply consist of contrasting conceptions of the same, if necessarily vague, concept. Whether we are dealing with rival concepts or alternative conceptions, it is helpful to distinguish between two broad approaches to defining politics (Hay, 2002; Leftwich, 2004). In the first, politics is associated with an *arena* or location, in which case behaviour becomes 'political' because of where it takes place. In the second, politics is viewed as a *process* or mechanism, in which case 'political' behaviour is behaviour that exhibits distinctive characteristics or qualities, and so can take place in any, and perhaps all, social contexts. Each of these broad approaches has spawned alternative definitions of politics, and, as discussed later in the chapter, helped to shape different schools of political analysis (see Figure 1.1). Indeed, the debate about 'what is politics?' is worth pursuing precisely because it exposes some of the deepest intellectual and ideological disagreement in the academic study of the subject.

Politics as the art of government

'Politics is not a science . . . but an art', Chancellor Bismarck is reputed to have told the German Reichstag. The art Bismarck had in mind was the art of government, the exercise of control within society through the making and enforcement of collective decisions. This is perhaps the classical definition of politics, developed from the original meaning of the term in Ancient Greece.

The word 'politics' is derived from **polis**, meaning literally 'city-state'. Ancient Greek society was divided into a collection of independent city-states, each of which possessed its own system of government. The largest and most influential of these city-states was Athens, often portrayed as the cradle of democratic government. In this light, politics can be understood to refer to the affairs of the *polis* – in effect, 'what concerns the *polis*'. The modern form of this definition is therefore 'what concerns the state' (see p. 57). This view of politics is clearly evident in the everyday use of the term: people are said to be 'in politics' when they hold public office, or to be 'entering politics' when they seek to do so. It is also a definition that academic political science has helped to perpetuate.

In many ways, the notion that politics amounts to 'what concerns the state' is the traditional view of the discipline, reflected in the tendency for academic

● **Polis**: (Greek) City-state; classically understood to imply the highest or most desirable form of social organization.

CONCEPT

Authority

Authority can most simply be defined as 'legitimate power'. Whereas power is the *ability* to influence the behaviour of others, authority is the *right* to do so. Authority is therefore based on an acknowledged duty to obey rather than on any form of coercion or manipulation. In this sense, authority is power cloaked in legitimacy or rightfulness. Weber (see p. 82) distinguished between three kinds of authority, based on the different grounds on which obedience can be established: *traditional* authority is rooted in history; *charismatic* authority stems from personality; and *legal–rational* authority is grounded in a set of impersonal rules.

● **Polity**: A society organized through the exercise of political authority; for Aristotle, rule by the many in the interests of all.

● **Anti-politics**: Disillusionment with formal or established political processes, reflected in non-participation, support for anti-system parties, or the use of direct action.

study to focus on the personnel and machinery of government. To study politics is, in essence, to study government, or, more broadly, to study the exercise of authority. This view is advanced in the writings of the influential US political scientist David Easton (1979, 1981), who defined politics as the 'authoritative allocation of values'. By this, he meant that politics encompasses the various processes through which government responds to pressures from the larger society, in particular by allocating benefits, rewards or penalties. 'Authoritative values' are therefore those that are widely accepted in society, and are considered binding by the mass of citizens. In this view, politics is associated with 'policy' (see p. 352): that is, with formal or authoritative decisions that establish a plan of action for the community.

However, what is striking about this definition is that it offers a highly restricted view of politics. Politics is what takes place within a **polity**, a system of social organization centred on the machinery of government. Politics is therefore practised in cabinet rooms, legislative chambers, government departments and the like; and it is engaged in by a limited and specific group of people, notably politicians, civil servants and lobbyists. This means that most people, most institutions and most social activities can be regarded as being 'outside' politics. Businesses, schools and other educational institutions, community groups, families and so on are in this sense 'non-political', because they are not engaged in 'running the country'. By the same token, to portray politics as an essentially state-bound activity is to ignore the increasingly important international or global influences on modern life, as discussed in the next main section.

This definition can, however, be narrowed still further. This is evident in the tendency to treat politics as the equivalent of party politics. In other words, the realm of 'the political' is restricted to those state actors who are consciously motivated by ideological beliefs, and who seek to advance them through membership of a formal organization such as a political party. This is the sense in which politicians are described as 'political', whereas civil servants are seen as 'non-political', as long as, of course, they act in a neutral and professional fashion. Similarly, judges are taken to be 'non-political' figures while they interpret the law impartially and in accordance with the available evidence, but they may be accused of being 'political' if their judgement is influenced by personal preferences or some other form of bias.

The link between politics and the affairs of the state also helps to explain why negative or pejorative images have so often been attached to politics. This is because, in the popular mind, politics is closely associated with the activities of politicians. Put brutally, politicians are often seen as power-seeking hypocrites who conceal personal ambition behind the rhetoric of public service and ideological conviction. Indeed, this perception has become more common in the modern period as intensified media exposure has more effectively brought to light examples of corruption and dishonesty, giving rise to the phenomenon of **anti-politics** (as discussed in Chapter 20). This rejection of the personnel and machinery of conventional political life is rooted in a view of politics as a self-serving, two-faced and unprincipled activity, clearly evident in the use of derogatory phrases such as 'office politics' and 'politicking'. Such an image of politics is sometimes traced back to the writings of Niccolò Machiavelli, who, in *The Prince* ([1532] 1961), developed a strictly realistic account of politics that drew attention to the use by political leaders of cunning, cruelty and manipulation.

Niccolò Machiavelli (1469–1527)

Italian politician and author. The son of a civil lawyer, Machiavelli's knowledge of public life was gained from a sometimes precarious existence in politically unstable Florence. He served as Second Chancellor (1498–1512), and was despatched on missions to France, Germany and throughout Italy. After a brief period of imprisonment and the restoration of Medici rule, Machiavelli embarked on a literary career. His major work, *The Prince*, published in 1532, drew heavily on his first-hand observations of the statecraft of Cesare Borgia and the power politics that dominated his period. It was written as a guide for the future prince of a united Italy. The adjective 'Machiavellian' subsequently came to mean 'cunning and duplicitous'.

CONCEPT

Power

Power, in its broadest sense, is the ability to achieve a desired outcome, sometimes seen as the 'power *to*' do something. This includes everything from the ability to keep oneself alive to the ability of government to promote economic growth. In politics, however, power is usually thought of as a relationship; that is, as the ability to influence the behaviour of others in a manner not of their choosing. This implies having 'power *over*' people. More narrowly, power may be associated with the ability to punish or reward, bringing it close to force or manipulation, in contrast to 'influence'. (See 'faces' of power, p. 9 and dimensions of global power, p. 428.)

Such a negative view of politics reflects the essentially liberal perception that, as individuals are self-interested, political power is corrupting, because it encourages those 'in power' to exploit their position for personal advantage and at the expense of others. This is famously expressed in Lord Acton's (1834–1902) aphorism: 'power tends to corrupt, and absolute power corrupts absolutely'. Nevertheless, few who view politics in this way doubt that political activity is an inevitable and permanent feature of social existence. However venal politicians may be, there is a general, if grudging, acceptance that they are always with us. Without some kind of mechanism for allocating authoritative values, society would simply disintegrate into a civil war of each against all, as the early social-contract theorists argued (see p. 62). The task is therefore not to abolish politicians and bring politics to an end but, rather, to ensure that politics is conducted within a framework of checks and constraints that guarantee that governmental power is not abused.

Politics as public affairs

A second and broader conception of politics moves it beyond the narrow realm of government to what is thought of as 'public life' or 'public affairs'. In other words, the distinction between 'the political' and 'the non-political' coincides with the division between an essentially public sphere of life and what can be thought of as a private sphere. Such a view of politics is often traced back to the work of the famous Greek philosopher Aristotle. In *Politics*, Aristotle declared that 'man is by nature a political animal', by which he meant that it is only within a political community that human beings can live the 'good life'. From this viewpoint, then, politics is an ethical activity concerned with creating a 'just society'; it is what Aristotle called the 'master science'.

However, where should the line between 'public' life and 'private' life be drawn? The traditional distinction between the public realm and the private realm conforms to the division between the state and civil society. The institutions of the state (the apparatus of government, the courts, the police, the army, the social security system and so forth) can be regarded as 'public' in the sense that they are responsible for the collective organization of community life. Moreover, they are funded at the public's expense, out of taxation. In contrast,

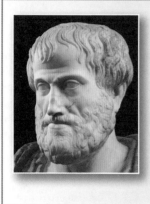

Aristotle (384–322 BCE)

Greek philosopher. Aristotle was a student of Plato (see p. 13) and tutor of the young Alexander the Great. He established his own school of philosophy in Athens in 335 BCE; this was called the 'peripatetic school' after his tendency to walk up and down as he talked. His 22 surviving treatises, compiled as lecture notes, range over logic, physics, metaphysics, astronomy, meteorology, biology, ethics and politics. In the Middle Ages, Aristotle's work became the foundation of Islamic philosophy, and it was later incorporated into Christian theology. His best-known political work is *Politics*, in which he portrayed the city-state as the basis for virtue and well-being, and argued that democracy is preferable to oligarchy (see p. 267–9).

CONCEPT

Civil society

Civil society originally meant a 'political community'. The term is now more commonly distinguished from the state, and is used to describe institutions that are 'private', in that they are independent from government and organized by individuals in pursuit of their own ends. Civil society therefore refers to a realm of autonomous groups and associations: businesses, interest groups, clubs, families and so on. The term 'global civil society' (see p. 106) has become fashionable as a means of referring to nongovernmental organizations (NGOs) (see p. 248) and transnational social movements (see p. 260).

civil society consists of what Edmund Burke (see p. 36) called the 'little platoons', institutions such as the family and kinship groups, private businesses, trade unions, clubs, community groups and so on, that are 'private' in the sense that they are set up and funded by individual citizens to satisfy their own interests, rather than those of the larger society. On the basis of this 'public/private' division, politics is restricted to the activities of the state itself and the responsibilities that are properly exercised by public bodies. Those areas of life that individuals can and do manage for themselves (the economic, social, domestic, personal, cultural and artistic spheres, and so on) are therefore clearly 'non-political'.

An alternative 'public/private' divide is sometimes defined in terms of a further and more subtle distinction; namely, that between 'the political' and 'the personal' (see Figure 1.2). Although civil society can be distinguished from the state, it nevertheless contains a range of institutions that are thought of as 'public' in the wider sense that they are open institutions, operating in public, to which the public has access. One of the crucial implications of this is that it broadens our notion of the political, transferring the economy, in particular, from the private to the public realm. A form of politics can thus be found in the workplace. Nevertheless, although this view regards institutions such as businesses, community groups, clubs and trade unions as 'public', it remains a restricted view of politics. According to this perspective, politics does not, and should not, infringe on 'personal' affairs and institutions. Feminist thinkers in particular have pointed out that this implies that politics effectively stops at the front door; it does not take place in the family, in domestic life, or in personal relationships (see p. 11). This view is illustrated, for example, by the tendency of politicians to draw a clear distinction between their professional conduct and their personal or domestic behaviour. By classifying, say, cheating on their partners or treating their children badly as 'personal' matters, they are able to deny the political significance of such behaviour on the grounds that it does not touch on their conduct of public affairs.

The view of politics as an essentially 'public' activity has generated both positive and negative images. In a tradition dating back to Aristotle, politics has been seen as a noble and enlightened activity precisely because of its 'public' character. This position was firmly endorsed by Hannah Arendt, who argued in *The*

Hannah Arendt (1906–75)

German political theorist and philosopher. Hannah Arendt was brought up in a middle-class Jewish family. She fled Germany in 1933 to escape from Nazism, and finally settled in the USA, where her major work was produced. Her wide-ranging, even idiosyncratic, writing was influenced by the existentialism of Heidegger (1889–1976) and Jaspers (1883–1969); she described it as 'thinking without barriers'. Her major works include *The Origins of Totalitarianism* (1951), which drew parallels between Nazi Germany and Stalinist Russia, her major philosophical work *The Human Condition* (1958), *On Revolution* (1963) and *Eichmann in Jerusalem* (1963). The final work stimulated particular controversy because it stressed the 'banality of evil', by portraying Eichmann as a Nazi functionary rather than as a raving ideologue.

Public	Private
The state: apparatus of government	Civil society: autonomous bodies – businesses, trade unions, clubs, families, and so on

Public	Private
Public realm: politics, commerce, work, art, culture and so on	Personal realm: family and domestic life

Figure 1.2   Two views of the public/private divide

Human Condition (1958) that politics is the most important form of human activity because it involves interaction amongst free and equal citizens. It thus gives meaning to life and affirms the uniqueness of each individual. Theorists such as Jean-Jacques Rousseau (see p. 97) and John Stuart Mill (see p. 198) who portrayed political participation as a good in itself have drawn similar conclusions. Rousseau argued that only through the direct and continuous participation of all citizens in political life can the state be bound to the common good, or what he called the 'general will'. In Mill's view, involvement in 'public' affairs is educational, in that it promotes the personal, moral and intellectual development of the individual.

In sharp contrast, however, politics as public activity has also been portrayed as a form of unwanted interference. Liberal theorists, in particular, have exhibited a preference for civil society over the state, on the grounds that 'private' life is a realm of choice, personal freedom and individual responsibility. This is most clearly demonstrated by attempts to narrow the realm of 'the political', commonly expressed as the wish to 'keep politics out of' private activities such

CONCEPT

Consensus

Consensus means agreement, but it refers to an agreement of a particular kind. It implies, first, a broad agreement, the terms of which are accepted by a wide range of individuals or groups. Second, it implies an agreement about fundamental or underlying principles, as opposed to a precise or exact agreement. In other words, a consensus permits disagreement on matters of emphasis or detail. A *procedural* consensus is a willingness to make decisions through a process of consultation and bargaining. A *substantive* consensus is an overlap of ideological positions that reflect agreement about broad policy goals.

as business, sport and family life. From this point of view, politics is unwholesome quite simply because it prevents people acting as they choose. For example, it may interfere with how firms conduct their business, or with how and with whom we play sports, or with how we bring up our children.

Politics as compromise and consensus

The third conception of politics relates not to the arena within which politics is conducted but to the way in which decisions are made. Specifically, politics is seen as a particular means of resolving conflict: that is, by compromise, conciliation and negotiation, rather than through force and naked power. This is what is implied when politics is portrayed as 'the art of the possible'. Such a definition is inherent in the everyday use of the term. For instance, the description of a solution to a problem as a 'political' solution implies peaceful debate and arbitration, as opposed to what is often called a 'military' solution. Once again, this view of politics has been traced back to the writings of Aristotle and, in particular, to his belief that what he called 'polity' is the ideal system of government, as it is 'mixed', in the sense that it combines both aristocratic and democratic features. One of the leading modern exponents of this view is Bernard Crick. In his classic study *In Defence of Politics*, Crick offered the following definition:

> Politics [is] the activity by which differing interests within a given unit of rule are conciliated by giving them a share in power in proportion to their importance to the welfare and the survival of the whole community. (Crick, [1962] 2000)

In this view, the key to politics is therefore a wide dispersal of power. Accepting that conflict is inevitable, Crick argued that when social groups and interests possess power they must be conciliated; they cannot merely be crushed. This is why he portrayed politics as 'that solution to the problem of order which chooses conciliation rather than violence and coercion'. Such a view of politics reflects a deep commitment to liberal–rationalist principles. It is based on resolute faith in the efficacy of debate and discussion, as well as on the belief that society is characterized by consensus, rather than by irreconcilable conflict. In other words, the disagreements that exist *can* be resolved without resort to intimidation and violence. Critics, however, point out that Crick's conception of politics is heavily biased towards the form of politics that takes place in western pluralist democracies: in effect, he equated politics with electoral choice and party competition. As a result, his model has little to tell us about, say, one-party states or military regimes.

This view of politics has an unmistakeably positive character. Politics is certainly no utopian solution (compromise means that concessions are made by all sides, leaving no one perfectly satisfied), but it is undoubtedly preferable to the alternatives: bloodshed and brutality. In this sense, politics can be seen as a civilized and civilizing force. People should be encouraged to respect politics as an activity, and should be prepared to engage in the political life of their own community. Nevertheless, a failure to understand that politics as a process of compromise and reconciliation is neccessarily frustrating and difficult (because in involves listening carefully to the opinions of others) may have contributed to a growing popular disenchantment with democratic politics across much of the developed world. As Stoker (2006) put it, 'Politics is designed to disappoint'; its outcomes are 'often messy, ambiguous and never final'. This is an issue to which we will return in the final chapter of the book.

Politics as power

The fourth definition of politics is both the broadest and the most radical. Rather than confining politics to a particular sphere (the government, the state or the 'public' realm), this view sees politics at work in all social activities and in every corner of human existence. As Adrian Leftwich proclaimed in *What is Politics? The Activity and Its Study* (2004), 'politics is at the heart of *all* collective social activity, formal and informal, public and private, in *all* human groups, institutions and societies'. In this sense, politics takes place at every level of social interaction; it can be found within families and amongst small groups of friends just as much as amongst nations and on the global stage. However, what is it that is distinctive about political activity? What marks off politics from any other form of social behaviour?

Focus on . . .

'Faces' of power

Power can be said to be exercised whenever A gets B to do something that B would not otherwise have done. However, A can influence B in various ways. This allows us to distinguish between different dimensions or 'faces' of power:

- **Power as decision-making**: This face of power consists of conscious actions that in some way influence the content of decisions. The classic account of this form of power is found in Robert Dahl's *Who Governs? Democracy and Power in an American City* (1961), which made judgements about who had power by analysing decisions in the light of the known preferences of the actors involved. Such decisions can nevertheless be influenced in a variety of ways. In *Three Faces of Power* (1989), Keith Boulding distinguished between the use of force or intimidation (the stick), productive exchanges involving mutual gain (the deal), and the creation of obligations, loyalty and commitment (the kiss).
- **Power as agenda setting**: The second face of power, as suggested by Bachrach and Baratz (1962),

is the ability to prevent decisions being made: that is, in effect, 'non-decision-making'. This involves the ability to set or control the political agenda, thereby preventing issues or proposals from being aired in the first place. For instance, private businesses may exert power both by campaigning to defeat proposed consumer-protection legislation (first face), and by lobbying parties and politicians to prevent the question of consumer rights being publicly discussed (second face).
- **Power as thought control**: The third face of power is the ability to influence another by shaping what he or she thinks, wants, or needs. This is power expressed as ideological indoctrination or psychological control. This is what Lukes (2004) called the 'radical' view of power, and it overlaps with the notion of 'soft' power (see p. 428). An example of this would be the ability of advertising to shape consumer tastes, often by cultivating associations with a 'brand'. In political life, the exercise of this form of power is seen in the use of propaganda and, more generally, in the impact of ideology (see p. 28).

At its broadest, politics concerns the production, distribution and use of resources in the course of social existence. Politics is, in essence, power: the ability to achieve a desired outcome, through whatever means. This notion was neatly summed up in the title of Harold Lasswell's book *Politics: Who Gets What, When, How?* (1936). From this perspective, politics is about diversity and conflict, but the essential ingredient is the existence of scarcity: the simple fact that, while human needs and desires are infinite, the resources available to satisfy them are always limited. Politics can therefore be seen as a struggle over scarce resources, and power can be seen as the means through which this struggle is conducted.

Advocates of the view of politics as power include feminists and Marxists. The rise of the women's liberation movement in the 1960s and 1970s, bringing with it a growing interest in feminism, stimulated more radical thinking about the nature of 'the political'. Not only have modern feminists sought to expand the arenas in which politics can be seen to take place, a notion most boldly asserted through the radical feminist slogan 'the personal is the political', but they have also tended to view politics as a process, specifically one related to the exercise of power over others. This view was summed by Kate Millett in *Sexual Politics* (1969), in which she defined politics as 'power-structured relationships, arrangements whereby one group of persons is controlled by another'.

Marxists, for their part, have used the term 'politics' in two senses. On one level, Marx (see p. 41) used 'politics' in a conventional sense to refer to the apparatus of the state. In the *Communist Manifesto* ([1848] 1967), he (and Engels) thus referred to political power as 'merely the organized power of one class for oppressing another'. For Marx, politics, together with law and culture, are part of a 'superstructure' that is distinct from the economic 'base' that is the real foundation of social life. However, he did not see the economic 'base' and the legal and political 'superstructure' as entirely separate. He believed that the 'superstructure' arose out of, and reflected, the economic 'base'. At a deeper level, political power, in this view, is therefore rooted in the class system; as Lenin (see p. 99) put it, 'politics is the most concentrated form of economics'. As opposed to believing that politics can be confined to the state and a narrow public sphere, Marxists can be said to believe that 'the economic is political'. From this perspective, civil society, characterized as Marxists believe it to be by class struggle, is the very heart of politics.

Views such as these portray politics in largely negative terms. Politics is, quite simply, about oppression and subjugation. Radical feminists hold that society is patriarchal, in that women are systematically subordinated and subjected to male power. Marxists traditionally argued that politics in a capitalist society is characterized by the exploitation of the proletariat by the bourgeoisie. On the other hand, these negative implications are balanced against the fact that politics is also seen as an emancipating force, a means through which injustice and domination can be challenged. Marx, for instance, predicted that class exploitation would be overthrown by a proletarian revolution, and radical feminists proclaim the need for gender relations to be reordered through a sexual revolution. However, it is also clear that when politics is portrayed as power and domination it need not be seen as an inevitable feature of social existence. Feminists look to an end of 'sexual politics' achieved through the construction of a nonsexist society, in which people will be valued according to personal worth, rather than on the basis of gender. Marxists believe that 'class politics' will end with the

POLITICS IN ACTION ...

The rise of Women's Liberation: making politics personal?

Events: Although an organized women's movement first emerged in the mid-nineteenth century, focused on the campaign for female suffrage, it was not until the 1960s that it was regenerated through the birth of the Women's Liberation Movement. Often viewed as the 'second wave' of feminism, this reflected the belief that redressing the status of women required not just political reform, but a process of radical, and particularly cultural, change, brought about by 'consciousness raising' amongst women and the transformation of family, domestic and personal life. Protests designed to challenge conventional stereotypes of 'femininity' took place: for example, at the Miss America pageants in 1968 and 1969 (where, by throwing stiletto shoes and other symbols of oppression into a 'freedom trashcan', demonstrators claimed a great deal of publicity and also acquired a false reputation for bra burning), and at the 1970 Miss World beauty competition (where, in front of millions of television viewers worldwide, about fifty women and a few men started to throw flour bombs, stink bombs, ink bombs and leaflets at the stage). This radical phase of feminist activism subsided from the early 1970s onwards, but the women's movement nevertheless continued to grow and acquired an increasingly prominent international dimension.

Significance: The 'first wave' of feminist activism, in the nineteenth and early twentieth centuries, was framed within a largely conventional notion of 'politics'. As the primary goal of feminism during this period was 'votes for women', it complied with the idea that politics takes place within a 'public' sphere of government institutions, political parties, interest groups and public debate. Female emancipation was therefore defined in terms of access to the public sphere, and especially the acquisition of political rights already enjoyed by men. One of the central themes of the 'second-wave' of feminism, however, has been that it sought to challenge and overthrow traditional thinking about politics, both about the nature of politics and where it takes place. Radical feminists in particular objected to the idea that politics is rooted in the public/private divide. In the first place, they argued that associating politics only with activities that take place in the public sphere effectively excludes women from political life. This is because, albeit to varying degrees, all contemporary and historical societies are characterized by a sexual division of labour in which the public sphere,

encompassing politics (as conventionally understood), work, art and literature, has been the preserve of men, while women have been predominantly confined to a 'private' existence, centred on the family and domestic responsibilities. Moreover, if politics focuses only on public activities and institutions, the sexual division of labour between 'public man' and 'private woman' appears, somehow, to be a natural fact of life, rather than a key mechanism through which the system of male power is established and preserved.

Nevertheless, the most influential feature of the radical feminist critique of conventional view of politics is that it emphasizes that politics takes place not only in the public sphere but also, and more significantly, in the private sphere. This idea was advanced through the slogan: 'the personal is the political'. By redefining politics in terms of power, control and domination, radical feminists portrayed family and domestic life as the crucial political arena because the dominance of the husband-father over both his wife and children conditions girls and boys to accept quite different social roles and to have quite different life expectations. The patriarchal structure of family life thus reproduces male domination in society at large, generation by generation. If, from this perspective, women are going to challenge patriarchal oppression, they must start with 'the personal', instead of primarily addressing problems such as the under-representation of women in senior positions in public life, they should focus on their underlying cause: the contrasting stereotypes of 'masculinity' and 'femininity' that are nurtured within the family and which accustom men to domination and encourage women to accept subordination.

establishment of a classless communist society. This, in turn, will eventually lead to the 'withering away' of the state, also bringing politics in the conventional sense to an end.

STUDYING POLITICS

Approaches to the study of politics

Disagreement about the nature of political activity is matched by controversy about the nature of politics as an academic discipline. One of the most ancient spheres of intellectual enquiry, politics was originally seen as an arm of philosophy, history or law. Its central purpose was to uncover the principles on which human society should be based. From the late nineteenth century onwards, however, this philosophical emphasis was gradually displaced by an attempt to turn politics into a scientific discipline. The high point of this development was reached in the 1950s and 1960s with an open rejection of the earlier tradition as meaningless metaphysics. Since then, however, enthusiasm for a strict science of politics has waned, and there has been a renewed recognition of the enduring importance of political values and normative theories. If the 'traditional' search for universal values acceptable to everyone has largely been abandoned, so has been the insistence that science alone provides a means of disclosing truth. The resulting discipline is more fertile and more exciting, precisely because it embraces a range of theoretical approaches and a variety of schools of analysis.

The philosophical tradition

The origins of political analysis date back to Ancient Greece and a tradition usually referred to as 'political philosophy'. This involved a preoccupation with essentially ethical, prescriptive or **normative** questions, reflecting a concern with what 'should', 'ought' or 'must' be brought about, rather than with what 'is'. Plato and Aristotle are usually identified as the founding fathers of this tradition. Their ideas resurfaced in the writings of medieval theorists such as Augustine (354–430) and Aquinas (1225–74). The central theme of Plato's work, for instance, was an attempt to describe the nature of the ideal society, which in his view took the form of a benign dictatorship dominated by a class of philosopher kings.

Such writings have formed the basis of what is called the 'traditional' approach to politics. This involves the analytical study of ideas and doctrines that have been central to political thought. Most commonly, it has taken the form of a history of political thought that focuses on a collection of 'major' thinkers (that spans, for instance, Plato to Marx) and a canon of 'classic' texts. This approach has the character of literary analysis: it is interested primarily in examining what major thinkers said, how they developed or justified their views, and the intellectual context within which they worked. Although such analysis may be carried out critically and scrupulously, it cannot be **objective** in any scientific sense, as it deals with normative questions such as 'Why should I obey the state?', 'How should rewards be distributed?' and 'What should the limits of individual freedom be?'

CONCEPT

Science

Science is a field of study that aims to develop reliable explanations of phenomena through repeatable experiments, observation and deduction. The 'scientific method', by which hypotheses are verified (proved true) by testing them against the available evidence, is therefore seen as a means of disclosing value-free and objective truth. Karl Popper (1902–94), however, suggested that science can only falsify hypotheses, since 'facts' may always be disproved by later experiments.

● **Normative**: The prescription of values and standards of conduct; what 'should be' rather than what 'is'.

● **Objective**: External to the observer, demonstrable; untainted by feelings, values or bias.

Plato (427–347 BCE)

Greek philosopher. Plato was born of an aristocratic family. He became a follower of Socrates, who is the principal figure in his ethical and philosophical dialogues. After Socrates' death in 399 BCE, Plato founded his own academy in order to train the new Athenian ruling class. Plato taught that the material world consists of imperfect copies of abstract and eternal 'ideas'. His political philosophy, expounded in *The Republic* and *The Laws*, is an attempt to describe the ideal state in terms of a theory of justice. Both works are decidedly authoritarian and pay no attention to individual liberty, believing that power should be vested in the hands of an educated elite, the philosopher kings. He was therefore a firm critic of democracy. Plato's work has exerted wide influence on Christianity and on European culture in general.

The empirical tradition

Although it was less prominent than normative theorizing, a descriptive or **empirical** tradition can be traced back to the earliest days of political thought. It can be seen in Aristotle's attempt to classify constitutions (see pp. 267–8), in Machiavelli's realistic account of statecraft, and in Montesquieu's (see p. 312) sociological theory of government and law. In many ways, such writings constitute the basis of what is now called 'comparative government', and they gave rise to an essentially institutional approach to the discipline. In the USA, and the UK in particular, this developed into the dominant tradition of analysis. The empirical approach to political analysis is characterized by the attempt to offer a dispassionate and impartial account of political reality. The approach is 'descriptive', in that it seeks to analyse and explain, whereas the normative approach is 'prescriptive', in the sense that it makes judgements and offers recommendations.

Descriptive political analysis acquired its philosophical underpinning from the doctrine of empiricism, which spread from the seventeenth century onwards through the work of theorists such as John Locke (see p. 31) and David Hume (1711–76). The doctrine of empiricism advanced the belief that experience is the only basis of knowledge and that, therefore, all hypotheses and theories should be tested by a process of observation. By the nineteenth century, such ideas had developed into what became known as 'positivism', an intellectual movement particularly associated with the writings of Auguste Comte (1798–1857). This doctrine proclaimed that the social sciences, and, for that matter, all forms of philosophical enquiry, should adhere strictly to the methods of the natural sciences. Once science was perceived to be the only reliable means of disclosing truth, the pressure to develop a science of politics became irresistible.

Behaviouralism

Since the mid-nineteenth century, mainstream political analysis has been dominated by the 'scientific' tradition, reflecting the growing impact of **positivism**. In the 1870s, 'political science' courses were introduced in the universities of

● **Empirical**: Based on observation and experiment; empirical knowledge is derived from sense data and experience.

● **Positivism**: The theory that social, and indeed all forms of, enquiry should adhere strictly to the methods of the natural sciences.

Oxford, Paris and Columbia, and by 1906 the *American Political Science Review* was being published. However, enthusiasm for a science of politics peaked in the 1950s and 1960s with the emergence, most strongly in the USA, of a form of political analysis that drew heavily on **behaviouralism**. For the first time, this gave politics reliably scientific credentials, because it provided what had previously been lacking: objective and quantifiable data against which hypotheses could be tested. Political analysts such as David Easton (1979, 1981) proclaimed that politics could adopt the methodology of the natural sciences, and this gave rise to a proliferation of studies in areas best suited to the use of quantitative research methods, such as voting behaviour, the behaviour of legislators, and the behaviour of municipal politicians and lobbyists. Attempts were also made to apply behaviouralism to IR, in the hope of developing objective 'laws' of international relations.

Behaviouralism, however, came under growing pressure from the 1960s onwards. In the first place, it was claimed that behaviouralism had significantly constrained the scope of political analysis, preventing it from going beyond what was directly observable. Although behavioural analysis undoubtedly produced, and continues to produce, invaluable insights in fields such as voting studies, a narrow obsession with quantifiable data threatens to reduce the discipline of politics to little else. More worryingly, it inclined a generation of political scientists to turn their backs on the entire tradition of normative political thought. Concepts such as 'liberty', 'equality', 'justice' and 'rights' were sometimes discarded as being meaningless because they were not empirically verifiable entities. Dissatisfaction with behaviouralism grew as interest in normative questions revived in the 1970s, as reflected in the writings of theorists such as John Rawls (see p. 45) and Robert Nozick (see p. 68).

Moreover, the scientific credentials of behaviouralism started to be called into question. The basis of the assertion that behaviouralism is objective and reliable is the claim that it is 'value-free': that is, that it is not contaminated by ethical or normative beliefs. However, if the focus of analysis is observable behaviour, it is difficult to do much more than describe the existing political arrangements, which implicitly means that the status quo is legitimized. This conservative value **bias** was demonstrated by the fact that 'democracy' was, in effect, redefined in terms of observable behaviour. Thus, instead of meaning 'popular self-government' (literally, government by the people), democracy came to stand for a struggle between competing elites to win power through the mechanism of popular election. In other words, democracy came to mean what goes on in the so-called democratic political systems of the developed West.

Rational-choice theory

Amongst recent theoretical approaches to politics is what is called 'formal political theory', variously known as 'rational-choice theory', 'public-choice theory' (see p. 252) and 'political economy' (see p. 129). This approach to analysis draws heavily on the example of economic theory in building up models based on procedural rules, usually about the rationally self-interested behaviour of the individuals involved. Most firmly established in the USA, and associated in particular with the so-called Virginia School, formal political theory provides at

● **Behaviouralism**: The belief that social theories should be constructed only on the basis of observable behaviour, providing quantifiable data for research.

● **Bias**: Sympathies or prejudices that (often unconsciously) affect human judgement; bias implies distortion (see 'political bias', p. 183).

least a useful analytical device, which may provide insights into the actions of voters, lobbyists, bureaucrats and politicians, as well as into the behaviour of states within the international system. This approach has had its broadest impact on political analysis in the form of what is called 'institutional public-choice theory'. The use of such techniques by writers such as Anthony Downs (1957), Mancur Olson (1968) and William Niskanen (1971), in fields such as party competition, interest-group behaviour and the policy influence of bureaucrats, is discussed in later chapters. The approach has also been applied in the form of game theory, which has been developed more from the field of mathematics than from economics. It entails the use of first principles to analyse puzzles about individual behaviour. The best-known example in game theory is the 'prisoners' dilemma' (see Figure 1.5). Game theory has been used by IR theorists to explain why states find it difficult, for instance, to prevent the overfishing of the seas, or the scale of arms to undesirable regimes.

By no means, however, has the rational-choice approach to political analysis been universally accepted. While its supporters claim that it introduces greater rigour into the discussion of political phenomena, critics have questioned its basic assumptions. It may, for instance, overestimate human rationality in that it ignores the fact that people seldom possess a clear set of preferred goals and rarely make decisions in the light of full and accurate knowledge. Furthermore, in proceeding from an abstract model of the individual, rational-choice theory pays insufficient attention to social and historical factors, failing to recognize, amongst other things, that human self-interestedness may be socially conditioned, and not merely innate.

New institutionalism

Until the 1950s, the study of politics had largely involved the study of **institutions**. This 'traditional' or 'old' institutionalism focused on the rules, procedures and formal organization of government, and employed methods akin to those used in the study of law and history. The advent of the 'behavioural revolution', combined with growing concerns about its unreflective and essentially descriptive methods (which sometimes threatened to reduce politics to a collection of organizational rules and structures), led to institutionalism being marginalized during the 1960s and 1970s. However, interest in it was revived from the 1980s onwards by the emergence of what was called 'new institutionalism'. While remaining faithful to the core institutionalist belief that 'institutions matter', in the sense that political structures are thought to shape political behaviour, new institutionalism has revised our understanding of what constitutes an 'institution' in a number of respects.

Political institutions are no longer equated with political organizations; they are thought of not as 'things' but as sets of 'rules', which guide or constrain the behaviour of individual actors. These rules, moreover, are as likely to be informal as formal, policy-making processes sometimes being shaped more by unwritten conventions or understandings than by formal arrangements. Apart from anything else, this can help to explain why institutions are often difficult to reform, transform or replace. Finally, rather than viewing institutions as independent entities, in which case they exist almost outside of time and space, new institutionalists emphasize that institutions are 'embedded' in a particular

● **Institution**: A well-established body with a formal role and status; more broadly, a set of rules that ensure regular and predictable behaviour, the 'rules of the game'.

CONCEPT

Constructivism

Constructivism (or social constructivism) is an approach to analysis that is based on the belief that there is no objective social or political reality independent of our understanding of it. Constructivists do not therefore regard the social world as something 'out there', in the sense of an external world of concrete objects; instead, it exists only 'inside', as a kind of inter-subjective awareness. In the final analysis, people, whether acting as individuals or as social groups, 'construct' the world according to those constructions. People's beliefs and assumptions become particularly significant when they are widely shared and create a sense of identity and distinctive interests.

● **Post-positivism:** An approach to knowledge that questions the idea of an 'objective' reality, emphasizing instead the extent to which people conceive, or 'construct', the world in which they live.

normative and historical context. Thus, just as actors within an institutional setting are socialized to accept key rules and procedures, the institution itself operates within a larger and more fundamental body of assumptions and practices. Nevertheless, despite these shifts, institutionalism has continued to attract criticism. For example, it is sometimes accused of subscribing to a structuralist logic in which, to a greater or lesser extent, political actors are viewed as 'prisoners' of the institutional contexts in which they operate.

Critical approaches

Since the 1980s, the range of critical approaches to politics has expanded considerably. Until that point, Marxism had constituted the principal alternative to mainstream political science. Indeed, Karl Marx can be seen as the first theorist to have attempted to describe politics in scientific terms. Using his so-called 'materialist conception of history' (see pp. 40–1), Marx strove to uncover the driving force of historical development. This enabled him to make predictions about the future based on 'laws' that had the same status in terms of proof as laws in the natural sciences. However, modern political analysis has become both richer and more diverse as a result of the emergence of new critical perspectives, notable examples including feminism (see pp. 49–50), critical theory, green politics (see pp. 50–1), constructivism, post-structuralism and postcolonialism (see p. 52). What do these new critical voices have in common, and in what sense are they 'critical'? In view of their diverse philosophical underpinnings and contrasting political viewpoints, it is tempting to argue that the only thing that unites them is a shared antipathy towards mainstream thinking.

Nevertheless, they exemplify two broad, and sometimes linked, characteristics. The first is that they are 'critical' in that, in their different ways, they seek to contest the political status quo, by (usually) aligning themselves with the interests of marginalized or oppressed groups. Each of them, thus, seeks to uncover inequalities and asymmetries that mainstream approaches intend to ignore. Feminism, for example, has drawn attention to systematic and pervasive structures of gender inequality that characterize politics in all its forms and at every level. Critical theory, which is rooted in the neo-Marxism (see p. 64) of the Frankfurt School, has extended the notion of critique to all social practices, drawing on a wide range of influences, including Freud and Weber (see p. 82). Green politics, or ecologism (see p. 51), has challenged the anthropocentric (human-centred) emphasis of established political and social theory, and championed holistic approaches to political and social understanding. Postcolonialism emphasizes the cultural dimension of colonial rule, showing how western cultural and political hegemony (see p. 174) over the rest of the world has been preserved despite the achievement of formal political independence across almost the entire developing world.

The second characteristic of critical approaches to politics is that, albeit in different ways and to different degrees, they have tried to go beyond the positivism of mainstream political science, emphasizing instead the role of consciousness in shaping social conduct and, therefore, the political world. These so-called **post-positivist** approaches (sometimes called 'interpretivism' or 'anti-foundationalism') are therefore 'critical', in that they not only take issue with the conclusions of mainstream approaches, but also subject these

Focus on . . .
The prisoners' dilemma

Two prisoners, held in separate cells, are faced with the choice of 'squealing' or 'not squealing' on one another. If only one of them confesses, but provides evidence to convict the other, he will be released without charge, while his partner will take the whole blame and be jailed for ten years. If both prisoners confess, they will each be jailed for six years. If both refuse to confess, they will only be convicted of a minor crime, and they will each receive a one-year sentence. Figure 1.3 shows the options available to the prisoners and their consequences in terms of jail sentences.

In view of the dilemma confronting them it is likely that both prisoners will confess, fearing that if they do not the other will 'squeal' and they will receive the

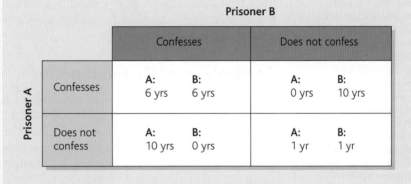

Figure 1.3   Options in the prisoners' dilemma

maximum sentence. Ironically, the game shows that rational behaviour can result in the least favourable outcome (in which the prisoners jointly serve a total of 12 years in jail). In effect, they are punished for their failure to cooperate or trust one another. However, if the game is repeated several times, it is possible that the prisoners will learn that self-interest is advanced by cooperation, which will encourage both to refuse to confess.

approaches themselves to critical scrutiny, exposing biases that operate within them and examining their implications. This can be seen, in particular, in relation to constructivism and post-structuralism. Constructivism has had a significantly greater impact on IR than it has had on political science, with many now treating constructivism as a mainstream international relations theory. However, constructivism is not so much a substantive theory as an analytical tool. In arguing that people, in effect, 'construct' the world in which they live, suggesting that the world operates through a kind of 'inter-subjective' awareness, constructivists have thrown mainstream political analysis's claim to objectivity into question. For example, as subjective entities, political actors have no fixed or objective interests or identities; rather, these are fashioned (and can be re-fashioned) through the traditions, values and sentiments that prevail at any time.

Post-structuralism emerged alongside postmodernism (see p. 18), the two terms sometimes being used interchangeably. Post-structuralism emphasizes that all ideas and concepts are expressed in language which itself is enmeshed in complex relations of power. Influenced particularly by the writings of the French philosopher and radical intellectual Michel Foucault (1926–84), post-

Postmodernism

Postmodernism is a term that was first used to describe experimental movements in western arts, architecture and cultural development in general. As a tool of social and political analysis, postmodernism highlights the shift away from societies structured by industrialization and class solidarity to increasingly fragmented and pluralistic 'information' societies. In these, individuals are transformed from producers to consumers, and individualism replaces class, religious and ethnic loyalties. Postmodernists argue that there is no such thing as certainty; the idea of absolute and universal truth must be discarded as an arrogant pretence.

● **Discourse**: Human interaction, especially communication; discourse may disclose or illustrate power relations.

● **Deconstruction**: A close reading of philosophical or other texts with an eye to their various blind spots and/or contradictions.

structuralists have drawn attention to the link between power and systems of thought using the idea of **discourse**, or 'discourses of power'. In crude terms, this implies that knowledge is power. However, in the absence of a universal frame of reference or overarching perspective, there exists only a series of competing perspectives, each of which represents a particular discourse of power. Although post-structuralism and postmodernism reject the idea of absolute and universal truth (foundationalism), post-structuralists argue that it is possible to expose hidden meanings in particular concepts, theories and interpretations through a process of **deconstruction**.

Concepts, models and theories

Concepts, models and theories are the tools of political analysis. However, as with most things in politics, the analytical tools must be used with care. First, let us consider concepts. A concept is a general idea about something, usually expressed in a single word or a short phrase. A concept is more than a proper noun or the name of a thing. There is, for example, a difference between talking about a cat (a particular and unique cat) and having a concept of a 'cat' (the idea of a cat). The concept of a cat is not a 'thing' but an 'idea', an idea composed of the various attributes that give a cat its distinctive character: 'a furry mammal', 'small', 'domesticated', 'catches rats and mice', and so on. The concept of 'equality' is thus a principle or ideal. This is different from using the term to say that a runner has 'equalled' a world record, or that an inheritance is to be shared 'equally' between two brothers. In the same way, the concept of 'presidency' refers not to any specific president but, rather, to a set of ideas about the organization of executive power.

What, then, is the value of concepts? Concepts are the tools with which we think, criticize, argue, explain and analyse. Merely perceiving the external world does not in itself give us knowledge about it. In order to make sense of the world, we must, in a sense, impose meaning on it, and this we do through the construction of concepts. Quite simply, to treat a cat as a cat, we must first have a concept of what it is. Concepts also help us to classify objects by recognizing that they have similar forms or similar properties. A cat, for instance, is a member of the class of 'cats'. Concepts are therefore 'general': they can relate to a number of objects, indeed to any object that complies with the characteristics of the general idea itself. It is no exaggeration to say that our knowledge of the political world is built up through developing and refining concepts that help us make sense of that world. Concepts, in that sense, are the building blocks of human knowledge.

Nevertheless, concepts can also be slippery customers. In the first place, the political reality we seek to understand is constantly shifting and is highly complex. There is always the danger that concepts such as 'democracy', 'human rights' and 'capitalism' will be more rounded and coherent than the unshapely realities they seek to describe. Max Weber tried to overcome this problem by recognizing particular concepts as 'ideal types'. This view implies that the concepts we use are constructed by singling out certain basic or central features of the phenomenon in question, which means that other features are downgraded or ignored altogether. The concept of 'revolution' can be regarded as an ideal type in this sense, in that it draws attention to a process of fundamental,

Debating...
Should students of politics seek to be objective and politically neutral?

Many believe that a strict distinction should be drawn between studying politics and practising politics, between having an academic interest in the subject and being politically engaged or committed. But does this distinction stand up to examination? Should we (teachers as well as students) approach the study of politics in a neutral manner, adopting a stance of 'scientific' objectivity? Or should we accept that, in politics, interest and commitment are inevitably linked, and even that political conviction may drive political understanding?

YES

Desire to explain. The motives for studying politics and practising politics are – or should be – different. Students of politics should seek, above all, to understand and explain the (all too often complex and baffling) political world. As they want to 'make sense' of things, any personal preferences they may hold must be treated as of strictly secondary importance. In contrast, practitioners of politics (politicians, activists and the like) are principally concerned with reshaping the political world in line with their own convictions or preferences. Political convictions thus blind people to 'inconvenient' truths, allowing political analysis to service the needs of political advocacy.

Objective knowledge. There is an approach to the acquisition of knowledge that has unrivalled authority in the form of scientific method, and this should be applied to all areas of learning, politics (or 'political science') included. Using observation, measurement and experimentation, scientific method allows hypotheses to be verified or falsified by comparing them with what we know about the 'real world'. Systematic enquiry, guided by such scientific principles, is the only reliable means of producing and accumulating knowledge. This knowledge is 'objective' because it is generated through a value-free approach that is concerned with empirical questions and does not seek to make normative judgements.

Free-floating intellectuals. Education and intellectual enquiry are themselves a training-ground in dispassionate scholarship, allowing students and teachers to distance themselves, over time, from the allegiances and biases that derive from social and family backgrounds. The German sociologist Karl Mannheim (1893–1947) thus argued that objectivity is strictly the preserve of the 'socially unattached intelligentsia', a class of intellectuals who alone can engage in disciplined and dispassionate enquiry. As free-floating intellectuals, they can stand back from the world they seek to understand, and thereby see it more clearly.

NO

Myth of neutrality. Whereas natural scientists may be able to approach their studies from an objective and impartial standpoint, this is impossible in politics. However politics is defined, it addresses questions about the structure and functioning of the society in which we live and have grown up. Family background, social experience, economic position, political sympathies and so on therefore build into each and every one of us preconceptions about the political world we are seeking to study. Indeed, perhaps the greatest threat to reliable knowledge comes not from bias as such, but from the failure to acknowledge bias, reflected in bogus claims to political neutrality.

Emancipatory knowledge. Very few people are drawn to the study of politics through a disinterested quest for knowledge alone. Instead, they seek knowledge for a purpose, and that purpose invariably has a normative component. As Marx famously put it, 'The philosophers have only interpreted the world, in various ways; the point is to change it'. Such an approach is most clearly embraced by modern critical theorists, who adopt an explicit commitment to emancipatory politics. The purpose of critical theory is to uncover structures of oppression and injustice in domestic and global politics in order to advance the cause of individual and collective freedom.

Competing realities. Post-positivist theorists question the very idea of scientific objectivity, arguing that there is more than one way in which the world can be understood. There is thus no single, overarching truth about the 'real world' out there, separate from the beliefs, ideas and assumptions of the observer. If the subject (the student of politics) cannot in any reliable way be distinguished from the object (the political world), then dispassionate scholarship must be treated as, at best, an unachievable ideal, social and political analysis being an inevitably value-laden activity.

CONCEPT

Ideal type

An ideal type (sometimes 'pure type') is a mental construct in which an attempt is made to draw out meaning from an otherwise almost infinitely complex reality through the presentation of a logical extreme. Ideal types were first used in economics, for instance, in the notion of perfect competition. Championed in the social sciences by Max Weber, ideal types are explanatory tools, not approximations of reality; they neither 'exhaust reality' nor offer an ethical ideal. Weberian examples include types of authority (see p. 4) and bureaucracy (see p. 361).

and usually violent, political change. It thus helps us make sense of, say, the 1789 French Revolution and the Eastern European revolutions of 1989–91 by highlighting important parallels between them. The concept must nevertheless be used with care because it can also conceal vital differences, and thereby distort understanding – in this case, for example, about the ideological and social character of revolution. Sartori (1970) highlighted similar tendencies by drawing attention to the phenomena of conceptual 'travelling' (the application of concepts to new cases) and conceptual 'stretching' (the distortion that occurs when these concepts do not fit the new cases). For these reason, it is better to think of concepts or ideal types not as being 'true' or 'false', but as being more or less 'useful'.

A further problem is that political concepts are often the subject of deep ideological controversy. Politics is, in part, a struggle over the legitimate meaning of terms and concepts. Enemies may argue, fight and even go to war, all claiming to be 'defending freedom', 'upholding democracy' or 'having justice on their side'. The problem is that words such as 'freedom', 'democracy' and 'justice' have different meanings to different people. How can we establish what is 'true' democracy, 'true' freedom or 'true' justice? The simple answer is that we cannot. Just as with the attempt to define 'politics', we have to accept that there are competing versions of many political concepts. Such concepts are best regarded as 'essentially contested' concepts (Gallie, 1955/56), in that controversy about them runs so deep that no neutral or settled definition can ever be developed. In effect, a single term can represent a number of rival concepts, none of which can be accepted as its 'true' meaning. For example, it is equally legitimate to define politics as what concerns the state, as the conduct of public life, as debate and conciliation, and as the distribution of power and resources.

Models and theories are broader than concepts; they comprise a range of ideas rather than a single idea. A **model** is usually thought of as a representation of something, usually on a smaller scale, as in the case of a doll's house or a toy aeroplane. In this sense, the purpose of the model is to resemble the original object as faithfully as possible. However, conceptual models need not in any way resemble an object. It would be absurd, for instance, to insist that a computer model of the economy should bear a physical resemblance to the economy itself. Rather, conceptual models are analytical tools; their value is that they are devices through which meaning can be imposed on what would otherwise be a bewildering and disorganized collection of facts. The simple point is that facts do not speak for themselves: they must be interpreted, and they must be organized. Models assist in the accomplishment of this task because they include a network of relationships that highlight the meaning and significance of relevant empirical data. The best way of understanding this is through an example. One of the most influential models in political analysis is the model of the political system developed by David Easton (1979, 1981). This can be represented diagrammatically (see Figure 1.4).

This ambitious model sets out to explain the entire political process, as well as the function of major political actors, through the application of what is called systems analysis. A system is an organized or complex whole, a set of interrelated and interdependent parts that form a collective entity. In the case of the political system, a linkage exists between what Easton calls 'inputs' and 'outputs'. Inputs

● **Model**: A theoretical representation of empirical data that aims to advance understanding by highlighting significant relationships and interactions.

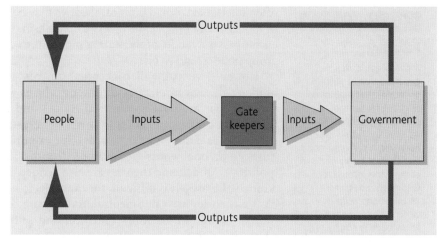

Figure 1.4 The political system

into the political system consist of demands and supports from the general public. Demands can range from pressure for higher living standards, improved employment prospects, and more generous welfare payments to greater protection for minority and individual rights. Supports, on the other hand, are ways in which the public contributes to the political system by paying taxes, offering compliance, and being willing to participate in public life. Outputs consist of the decisions and actions of government, including the making of policy, the passing of laws, the imposition of taxes, and the allocation of public funds. Clearly, these outputs generate 'feedback' which, in turn, shapes further demands and supports. The key insight offered by Easton's model is that the political system tends towards long-term equilibrium or political stability, as its survival depends on outputs being brought into line with inputs.

However, it is vital to remember that conceptual models are at best simplifications of the reality they seek to explain. They are merely devices for drawing out understanding; they are not reliable knowledge. In the case of Easton's model, for example, political parties and interest groups are portrayed as 'gate-keepers', the central function of which is to regulate the flow of inputs into the political system. Although this may be one of their significant functions, parties and interest groups also manage public perceptions, and thereby help to shape the nature of public demands. In short, these are more interesting and more complex institutions in reality than the systems model suggests. In the same way, Easton's model is more effective in explaining how and why political systems respond to popular pressures than it is in explaining why they employ repression and coercion, as, to some degree, all do.

The terms '**theory**' and 'model' are often used interchangeably in politics. Theories and models are both conceptual constructs used as tools of political analysis. However, strictly speaking, a theory is a proposition. It offers a systematic explanation of a body of empirical data. In contrast, a model is merely an explanatory device; it is more like a hypothesis that has yet to be tested. In that sense, in politics, while theories can be said to be more or less 'true', models can only be said to be more or less 'useful'. Clearly, however, theories and models are

● **Theory**: A systematic explanation of empirical data, usually (unlike a hypothesis) presented as reliable knowledge.

Paradigm

A paradigm is, in a general sense, a pattern or model that highlights relevant features of a particular phenomenon. As used by Kuhn (1962), however, it refers to an intellectual framework comprising interrelated values, theories and assumptions, within which the search for knowledge is conducted. 'Normal' science is therefore conducted within the established paradigm, while 'revolutionary' science, attempts to replace an old paradigm with a new one. The radical implication of this theory is that 'truth' and 'falsehood' are only provisional judgements.

often interlinked: broad political theories may be explained in terms of a series of models. For example, the theory of pluralism (discussed in Chapters 4 and 5) encompasses a model of the state, a model of electoral competition, a model of group politics, and so on.

However, virtually all conceptual devices, theories and models contain hidden values or implicit assumptions. This is why it is difficult to construct theories that are purely empirical; values and normative beliefs invariably intrude. In the case of concepts, this is demonstrated by people's tendency to use terms as either 'hurrah! words' (for example 'democracy', 'freedom' and 'justice') or 'boo! words' (for example, 'conflict', 'anarchy', 'ideology', and even 'politics'). Models and theories are also 'loaded' in the sense that they contain a range of biases. It is difficult, for example, to accept the claim that rational-choice theories are value-neutral. As they are based on the assumption that human beings are basically egoistical and self-regarding, it is perhaps not surprising that they have often pointed to policy conclusions that are politically conservative. In the same way, class theories of politics, advanced by Marxists, are based on broader theories about history and society and, indeed, they ultimately rest on the validity of an entire social philosophy.

There is therefore a sense in which analytical devices, such as models and microtheories, are constructed on the basis of broader macrotheories. These major theoretical tools of political analysis are those that address the issues of power and the role of the state: pluralism (see p. 100), elitism (see p. 102), class analysis and so on. These theories are examined in Chapters 4 and 5. At a still deeper level, however, many of these macrotheories reflect the assumptions and beliefs of one or other of the major ideological traditions. These traditions operate in a similar way to the 'paradigms' to which Thomas Kuhn refers in *The Structure of Scientific Revolutions* (1962). A paradigm is a related set of principles, doctrines and theories that helps to structure the process of intellectual enquiry. In effect, a paradigm constitutes the framework within which the search for knowledge is conducted. In economics, this can be seen in the replacement of Keynesianism by monetarism (and perhaps the subsequent shift back to neo-Keynesianism); in transport policy it is shown in the rise of green ideas.

According to Kuhn, the natural sciences are dominated at any time by a single paradigm; science develops through a series of 'revolutions' in which an old paradigm is replaced by a new one. Political and social enquiry is, however, different, in that it is a battleground of contending and competing paradigms. These paradigms take the form of broad social philosophies, usually called 'political ideologies': liberalism, conservatism, socialism, fascism, feminism and so on. Each presents its own account of social existence; each offers a particular view of the world. To portray these ideologies as theoretical paradigms is not, of course, to say that most, if not all, political analysis is narrowly ideological, in the sense that it advances the interests of a particular group or class. Rather, it merely acknowledges that political analysis is usually carried out on the basis of a particular ideological tradition. Much of academic political science, for example, has been constructed according to liberal–rationalist assumptions, and thus bears the imprint of its liberal heritage.

The various levels of conceptual analysis are shown diagrammatically in Figure 1.5.

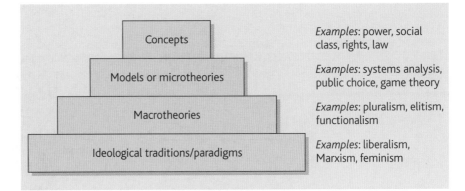

Figure 1.5   Levels of conceptual analysis

POLITICS IN A GLOBAL AGE

Beyond the domestic/international divide?

As an academic discipline, politics has conventionally focused on the state and particularly on its governmental apparatus: the institutional framework of the state, where power lies within it, how decisions are made, and so on. This state-based paradigm is one in which politics has a distinct spatial or territorial character. In short, borders and boundaries matter. This especially applies in the case of distinction between *domestic* politics, which is concerned with the state's role in maintaining order and carrying out regulation within its own borders, and *international* politics, which is concerned with relations between or among states. In that sense, sovereignty (see p. 58), the supreme or unquestionable authority of the state, is a 'hard shell' that divides the 'inside' of politics from the 'outside'. This domestic/international, or 'inside/outside', divide also separates what have been conventionally been seen as two quite different spheres of political interaction (see Figure 1.6). Whereas politics 'inside' has an orderly or regulated character, stemming from the ability of the state within the domestic sphere to impose rule from above, politics in the 'outside' has an anarchic character, derived from the fact that there is no authority in the international sphere higher than the sovereign state. The spatial division that the state-based paradigm has inculcated is, furthermore, reflected in a traditional sub-disciplinary division of labour between 'political science' and 'international relations', or IR. While political science has tended to view states as macro-level actors within the political world, IR has typically treated states as micro-level actors within the larger international arena.

The state-based paradigm of politics has nevertheless come under pressure as a result of recent trends and developments, not least those associated with globalization (see p. 142). In particular, there has been a substantial growth in cross-border, or **transnational**, flows and transactions – movements of people, goods, money, information and ideas. As state borders have become increasingly 'porous', the conventional domestic/international, or 'inside/outside', divide has become more difficult to sustain. This can be illustrated both by the substantially greater vulnerability of domestic economies to events that take place elsewhere

● **Transnational:**
Configuration, which may apply to events, people, groups or organizations, that takes little or no account of national governments or state borders.

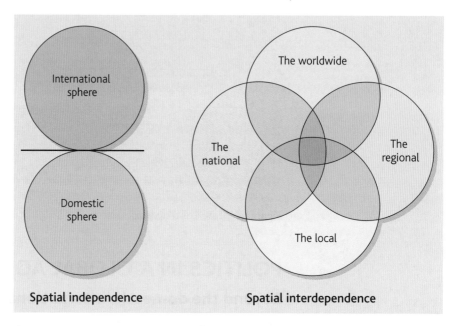

Figure 1.6   Contrasting models of spatial politics

in the world, as demonstrated by the wide-ranging impact of the 2007–09 global financial crisis, and by the wider use of digital technologies that enable people to communicate with each other through means such as mobile phones and the internet that national governments find very difficult to control. The increase in the scale, scope and, sometimes, nature of spatial interdependence has encouraged some to speculate that the disciplinary divide between political science and international relations should be dissolved (Hay, 2010). If political activity can no longer be seen to take place within discrete domestic and international spheres, politics is perhaps best understood in terms of overlaps and interrelationships between and amongst a number of spheres – the global, the regional, the national and the local (see Figure 1.6). Nevertheless, it would be a mistake to portray such an approach to politics as entirely novel, as the domestic/international divide has usually been treated more as a way of prioritizing a particular sphere and set of interactions, rather than as a rigid doctrine. For instance, liberal IR theorists have long argued that the constitutional structure of the state influences its external behaviour, while political scientists studying the causes of revolution have always accepted that war and invasion may sometimes be decisive factors in their outbreak.

Where does this leave us as far as political analysis is concerned? One of the implications of accepting that politics takes place not only in global, regional, national and local spheres, but also, crucially, through relationships between these various spheres, is that it so expands the parameters and complexity of politics that it becomes difficult, and maybe impossible, to make sense of it as a whole. This would require, for example, that we study topics such as elections, political parties, constitutions, assemblies and other aspects of national government alongside topics such as war and peace, nuclear proliferation, terrorism, poverty and development, international organizations and so forth. Moreover,

Focus on...
Politics and IR: two disciplines or one?

Are political science and international relations (IR) two separate disciplines, or should they be thought of as sub-fields, or different levels of analysis, within the same broad discipline: politics or political analysis? In most contexts, political science and IR emerged independently from one another. Political science was established as an academic discipline from the mid-nineteenth century onwards in the USA and across Europe, while IR developed in the aftermath of WWI, and was largely shaped by the desire to uncover the conditions for enduring peace (a concern about the policy relevance of its work that has never applied in the same way to political science). Politics and IR constitute separate fields of knowledge, in the sense that the former addresses 'domestic' issues and developments (concerned with what goes on *within* the state), while the latter addresses 'international' issues and developments (concerned with what occurs *between* states). Politics and IR have therefore developed their own analytical tools and theoretical perspectives, helping each to enjoy the same degree of disciplinary authenticity as, say, economics or sociology.

However, the disciplinary divide between politics and IR may always have been arbitrary. In this view, politics and IR can be seen not as discrete but as overlapping disciplines: they ask very similar questions, albeit about different (if always related) levels of political interaction. Both politics and IR are primarily concerned with questions about power (its distribution, exercise, consequences and so forth), and both place a strong emphasis on the nature, role and activities of the state, even if political science views the state as a macro-level actor, while IR views it as a micro-level actor. Questions about the balance between conflict and cooperation in social relations are also central to both disciplines. The idea of a disciplinary divide has become particularly problematic due to the advent of an increasingly interdependent world, in which 'the domestic' and 'the international' affect one another to a greater degree than ever before. Globalization, climate change, multi-level governance, security and crime are only some of the issues that confound the traditional domestic/international divide, and perhaps suggest that rigid disciplinary or sub-disciplinary fault lines should be dispensed with (Hay, 2002).

although the domestic/international divide has undoubtedly been compromised by globalizing trends, it is difficult to argue that it has been rendered entirely meaningless. Only so-called 'hyperglobalizers', who subscribe to the fanciful idea that politics – and, for that matter, everything else – has been caught up in a swirl of interconnectedness that effectively absorbs all of its parts into an indivisible, global whole, fail to acknowledge that states, though often transformed, continue to be the most significant actors in both the domestic and the international spheres. Sovereignty may no longer be a 'hard shell' that separates politics 'inside' from politics 'outside', but it remains at least a 'soft shell'. Although this book adopts a holistic approach, which accepts the implications of spatial interdependence and, particularly, that what goes on *within* states and what goes on *between* states impact on each other to a greater degree than ever before, it considers the interactions of politics from a primarily domestic perspective. In contrast, its companion volume, *Global Politics* (2011), examines the interactions of politics from a primarily international or global perspective, and so gives particular attention to ideas, issues and theories that have conventionally been studied within the field of international relations.

SUMMARY

● Politics is the activity through which people make, preserve and amend the general rules under which they live. As such, it is an essentially social activity, inextricably linked, on the one hand, to the existence of diversity and conflict, and, on the other, to a willingness to cooperate and act collectively. Politics is better seen as a search for conflict resolution than as its achievement, as not all conflicts are, or can be, resolved.

● Politics has been understood differently by different thinkers and within different traditions. Politics has been viewed as the art of government or as 'what concerns the state'; as the conduct and management of public affairs; as the resolution of conflict through debate and compromise; and as the production, distribution and use of resources in the course of social existence.

● There is considerable debate about the realm of 'the political'. Conventionally, politics has narrowly been seen as embracing institutions and actors operating in a 'public' sphere concerned with the collective organization of social existence. However, when politics is understood in terms of power-structured relationships, it may be seen to operate in the 'private' sphere as well.

● A variety of approaches has been adopted in the study of politics as an academic discipline. These include political philosophy, or the analysis of normative theory, and an empirical tradition particularly concerned with the study of institutions and structures, as well as behavioural analysis, rational-choice theory, so-called 'new' institutionalism and a variety of critical approaches.

● Concepts, models and theories are the tools of political analysis, providing the building blocks of knowledge. However, they are only analytical devices. Although they help to advance understanding, they are more rounded and coherent than the unshapely and complex realities they seek to describe. Ultimately, all political and social enquiry is conducted within a particular intellectual framework or ideological paradigm.

● A distinction has traditionally been drawn between the domestic and international realms of politics, reflecting differences between what happens within the state and what occurs in relations between states. This domestic/international divide has helped to sustain a disciplinary distinction between political science and international relations. However, globalization and the advent of an interdependent world has cast significant doubt upon the viability of these distinctions.

Questions for discussion

● If politics is essentially social, why is not all social activity political?

● Should politics be thought of as an arena or a process?

● Why has power so often been thought of as the defining feature of politics?

● On what grounds can politics be defended?

● Is politics inevitable? Could politics ever be brought to an end?

● How do mainstream and critical approaches to the study of politics differ?

● Why has the idea of a science of politics been so attractive?

● Is it possible to study politics objectively and without bias?

● Is the distinction between the domestic and international realms of politics any longer sustainable?

Further reading

Hay, C., (ed.), *New Directions in Political Science: Responding to the Challenge of an Independent World* (2010). A series of astute reflections on the nature, extent and implication of global interdependence for politics and a variety of political issues.

Leftwich, A. (ed.), *What is Politics? The Activity and Its Study* (2004). A very useful collection of essays examining different concepts of politics as well as contrasting views of the discipline.

Marsh, D. and G. Stoker (eds), *Theory and Methods in Political Science*, 3rd edn (2010). An accessible, yet comprehensive and sophisticated, exploration of the nature and scope of the discipline of political science.

Savigny, H. and L. Marsden, *Doing Political Science and International Relations: Theories in Action* (2011). An introduction to political science that uses case studies to examine a wide range of theories and approaches.

CHAPTER 2

Political Ideas and Ideologies

'The philosophers have only interpreted the world in various ways: the point is to change it.'

KARL MARX, *Theses on Feuerbach* (1845)

PREVIEW

All people are political thinkers. Whether they know it or not, people use political ideas and concepts whenever they express their opinions or speak their mind. Everyday language is littered with terms such as freedom, fairness, equality, justice and rights. In the same way, words such as conservative, liberal, fascist, socialist or feminist are regularly employed by people either to describe their own views, or those of others. However, even though such terms are familiar, even commonplace, they are seldom used with any precision or a clear grasp of their meaning. What, for instance, is 'equality'? What does it mean to say that all people are equal? Are people born equal, should they be treated by society as if they are equal? Should people have equal rights, equal opportunities, equal political influence, equal wages? Similarly, words such as communist or fascist are commonly misused. What does it mean to call someone a 'fascist'? What values or beliefs do fascists hold, and why do they hold them? How do communist views differ from those of, say, liberals, conservatives or socialists? This chapter examines political ideas from the perspective of the key ideological traditions. It focuses, in particular, on the 'classical' ideologies (liberalism, conservatism and socialism), but it also considers a range of other ideological traditions, which have arisen either out of, or in opposition to, the classical ones. Each ideological tradition constitutes a distinctive intellectual framework or paradigm, and so offers a particular 'lens' on political world. However, before examining the various ideological traditions, it is necessary to consider the nature of political ideology itself.

KEY ISSUES

- What is political ideology?
- Is politics intrinsically linked to ideology? Can ideology come to an end?
- What are the key ideas and theories of the major ideological traditions?
- What internal tensions do each of the major ideologies encompass?
- How has ideological thought changed over time?
- How can the rise and fall of ideologies be explained?

CONCEPT

Ideology

From a social-scientific viewpoint, an ideology is a more or less coherent set of ideas that provides a basis for organized political action, whether this is intended to preserve, modify or overthrow the existing system of power relationships. All ideologies therefore (1) offer an account of the existing order, usually in the form of a 'world-view', (2) provide a model of a desired future, a vision of the Good Society, and (3) outline how political change can and should be brought about. Ideologies are not, however, hermetically sealed systems of thought; rather, they are fluid sets of ideas that overlap with one another at a number of points.

WHAT IS POLITICAL IDEOLOGY?

Ideology is one of the most controversial concepts encountered in political analysis. Although the term now tends to be used in a neutral sense, to refer to a developed social philosophy or world-view, it has in the past had heavily negative or pejorative connotations. During its sometimes tortuous career, the concept of ideology has commonly been used as a political weapon to condemn or criticize rival creeds or doctrines.

The term 'ideology' was coined in 1796 by the French philosopher Destutt de Tracy (1754–1836). He used it to refer to a new 'science of ideas' (literally, an idea-ology) that set out to uncover the origins of conscious thought and ideas. De Tracy's hope was that ideology would eventually enjoy the same status as established sciences such as zoology and biology. However, a more enduring meaning was assigned to the term in the nineteenth century in the writings of Karl Marx (see p. 41). For Marx, ideology amounted to the ideas of the 'ruling class', ideas that therefore uphold the class system and perpetuate exploitation. In their early work *The German Ideology*, Marx and Engels wrote the following:

> The ideas of the ruling class are in every epoch the ruling ideas, i.e. the class which is the ruling material force in society, is at the same time the ruling intellectual force. The class which has the means of mental production at its disposal, has control at the same time over the means of mental production. (Marx and Engels, [1846] 1970:64)

The defining feature of ideology in the Marxist sense is that it is false: it mystifies and confuses subordinate classes by concealing from them the contradictions on which all class societies are based. As far as capitalism is concerned, the ideology of the property-owning bourgeoisie (bourgeois ideology) fosters delusion or 'false consciousness' amongst the exploited proletariat, preventing them from recognizing the fact of their own exploitation. Nevertheless, Marx did not believe that all political views had an ideological character. He held that his own work, which attempted to uncover the process of class exploitation and oppression, was scientific. In his view, a clear distinction could be drawn between science and ideology, between truth and falsehood. This distinction tended, however, to be blurred in the writings of later Marxists such as Lenin (see p. 99) and Gramsci (see p. 175). These referred not only to 'bourgeois ideology', but also to 'socialist ideology' or 'proletarian ideology', terms that Marx would have considered absurd.

Alternative uses of the term have also been developed by liberals and conservatives. The emergence of totalitarian dictatorships in the interwar period encouraged writers such as Karl Popper (1902–94), J. L. Talmon and Hannah Arendt (see p. 7) to view ideology as an instrument of social control to ensure compliance and subordination. Relying heavily on the examples of fascism and communism, this Cold War liberal use of the term treated ideology as a 'closed' system of thought, which, by claiming a monopoly of truth, refuses to tolerate opposing ideas and rival beliefs. In contrast, liberalism, based as it is on a fundamental commitment to individual freedom, and doctrines such as conservatism and democratic socialism that broadly subscribe to liberal principles are clearly not ideologies. These doctrines are 'open' in the sense that they permit, and even insist on, free debate, opposition and criticism.

Debating...
Can politics exist without ideology?

The term 'ideology' has traditionally carried pejorative implications, often expressed through predictions of its imminent (and usually welcome) demise. Nevertheless, despite its varied obituaries, political ideology has stubbornly refused to die: while particular ideologies may rise or fall, ideological forms of politics seem to be an enduring feature of world history. Is politics intrinsically linked to ideology? Or may politics finally be able to emerge from the shadow cast by ideological belief?

YES

Overcoming falsehood and delusion. Most critiques of ideology associate it with falsehood and manipulation, implying that reason and critical understanding can, and will, emancipate us from ideological politics. In this view, ideologies are, in effect, political religions, sets of values, theories and doctrines that demand faith and commitment from 'believers', who are then unable to think outside or beyond their chosen world-view. If ideologies are intellectual prisons, the solution is to see the world 'as it is', something that can be achieved through the application of value-free scientific method. The purpose of political science is thus to disengage politics from ideology.

Rise of technocratic politics. Political ideology arose in the form of contrasting attempts to shape emergent industrial society. The left/right divide (see p. 225) and the struggle between socialism and capitalism has always been at the heart of ideological debate. However, the collapse of communism and the near worldwide acceptance of market capitalism means that this rivalry has become irrelevant to modern politics. Politics has therefore come to revolve not around ideological questions to do with ownership and the distribution of wealth, but around 'smaller' questions to do with the effective management of the capitalist system. Ideological politics has given way to technocratic politics.

Rise of consumerist politics. Ideology has little place in modern democratic systems due to the logic of electoral competition. Elections force political parties to behave like businesses in the marketplace, formulating 'products' (policies) in the hope of attracting the largest number of 'consumers' (voters). Parties thus increasingly respond to consumer/voter demands, rather than trying to reshape these demands in the light of a pre-existing ideological vision. Whether parties have historically been left-wing, right-wing or centrist in orientation, they recognise the electoral value of 'travelling light' in ideological terms. Electoral politics therefore contributes to a process of party de-ideologization.

NO

Ideology as an intellectual framework. Political ideology will always survive because it provides politicians, parties and other political actors with an intellectual framework which helps them to make sense of the world in which they live. Ideologies are not systematic delusions but, rather, rival visions of the political world, each illuminating particular aspects of a complex and multifaceted reality. Ideologies are therefore neither, in a simplistic sense, true nor false. Perhaps the most dangerous delusion is the notion of a clear distinction between science and ideology. Science itself is constructed on the basis of paradigms that are destined to be displaced over time (Kuhn, 1962).

Ideological renewal. The secret of ideology's survival and continued relevance is its flexibility, the fact that ideological traditions go through a seemingly endless process of redefinition and renewal. As old ideologies fade, new ones emerge, helping to preserve the relevance of political ideology. The world of ideologies does not stand still, but changes in response to changing social and historical circumstances. The declining relevance of the left/right divide has not led to the 'end of ideology' or the 'end of history'; it has merely opened up new ideological spaces that have been filled by the likes of feminism, green politics, multiculturalism and cosmopolitanism.

The 'vision thing'. As the principal source of meaning and idealism in politics, ideology touches those aspects of politics that no other political form can reach. Ideology gives people a reason to believe in something larger than themselves, because people's personal narratives only make sense when they are situated within a broader historical narrative. A post-ideological age would therefore be an age without hope, without vision. If politicians cannot cloak their pursuit of power in ideological purpose, they risk being seen simply as power-seeking pragmatists, and their policy programmes will appear to lack coherence and direction.

30

A distinctively conservative use of the term 'ideology' has been developed by thinkers such as Michael Oakeshott (see p. 177). This view reflects a characteristically conservative scepticism about the value of **rationalism**, born out of the belief that the world is largely beyond the capacity of the human mind to fathom. As Oakeshott put it, in political activity 'men sail a boundless and bottomless sea'. From this perspective, ideologies are seen as abstract 'systems of thought'; that is, as sets of ideas that distort political reality because they claim to explain what is, frankly, incomprehensible. This is why conservatives have traditionally dismissed the notion that they subscribe to an ideology, preferring instead to describe conservatism as a disposition, or an 'attitude of mind', and placing their faith in **pragmatism**, tradition (see p. 82) and history.

The drawback of each of these usages, however, is that, as they are negative or pejorative, they restrict the application of the term. Certain political doctrines, in other words, are excluded from the category of 'ideologies'. Marx, for instance, insisted that his ideas were scientific, not ideological, liberals have denied that liberalism should be viewed as an ideology, and conservatives have traditionally claimed to embrace a pragmatic rather than ideological style of politics. Moreover, each of these definitions is loaded with the values and orientation of a particular political doctrine. An inclusive definition of 'ideology' (one that applies to all political traditions) must therefore be neutral: it must reject the notion that ideologies are 'good' or 'bad', true or false, or liberating or oppressive. This is the virtue of the modern, social-scientific meaning of the term, which treats ideology as an action-orientated belief system, an interrelated set of ideas that in some way guides or inspires political action.

However, much of the debate about ideology since the mid-twentieth century has focused on predictions of its demise, or at least of its fading relevance. This came to be known as the 'end of ideology' debate. It was initiated in the 1950s, stimulated by the collapse of fascism at the end of World War II and the decline of communism in the developed West. In *The End of Ideology* (1960), the US sociologist Daniel Bell (1919–2011) declared that the stock of political ideas had been exhausted. In his view, ethical and ideological questions had become irrelevant because in most western societies parties competed for power simply by promising higher levels of economic growth and material affluence. This debate was revived in the aftermath of the collapse of communism by 'end of history' theorists, such as Fukuyama (see p. 271), who suggested that a single ideology, liberal democracy, had triumphed over all its rivals, and that this triumph was final (see p. 44). At the heart of such debates lies questions about the relationship between politics and ideology, and specifically about whether politics can exist without ideology (see p. 29).

● **Rationalism**: The belief that the world can be understood and explained through the exercise of human reason, based on assumptions about its rational structure.

● **Pragmatism**: A theory or practice that places primary emphasis on practical circumstances and goals; pragmatism implies a distrust of abstract ideas.

CLASSICAL IDEOLOGICAL TRADITIONS

Political ideology arose out of the transition from feudalism to industrial capitalism. In simple terms, the earliest, or 'classical' ideologies – liberalism, conservatism and socialism – developed as contrasting attempts to shape emerging industrial society. This meant that the central theme in ideological debate and argument during this period and beyond was the battle between two rival economic philosophies: capitalism (see p. 131) and socialism. Political ideology

John Locke (1632–1704)

English philosopher and politician. Locke studied medicine at Oxford University before becoming secretary to Anthony Ashley Cooper, First Earl of Shaftsbury, in 1661. His political views were developed against the backdrop of the English Revolution, and are often seen as providing a justification for the 'Glorious Revolution' of 1688, which ended absolutist rule and established a constitutional monarchy in Britain. Locke was a key thinker of early liberalism, placing particular emphasis on 'natural' or God-given rights, identified as the rights to life, liberty and property. An exponent of representative government and toleration, Locke's views had a considerable impact on the American Revolution. His most important political works are *A Letter Concerning Toleration* (1689) and *Two Treatises of Government* ([1690] 1965).

thus had a strong economic focus. The battle lines between capitalism and socialism were significantly sharpened by the 1917 Russian Revolution, which created the world's first socialist state. Indeed, throughout what is sometimes called the 'short' twentieth century (from the outbreak of World War I to the fall of communism, 1989–91), and particularly during the Cold War period (1945–90), international politics was structured along ideological lines, as the capitalist West confronted the communist East. Although ideological debate has became richer and certainly progressively more diverse since the 1960s, not least as a result of the rise of so-called 'new' ideologies such as feminism and green politics, the classical ideologies have retain their central importance. In large part, this has been because of their capacity to reinvent themselves. In the process of doing so, the dividing lines between them have often been blurred.

Liberalism

Any account of political ideologies must start with liberalism. This is because liberalism is, in effect, the ideology of the industrialized West, and is sometimes portrayed as a **meta-ideology** that is capable of embracing a broad range of rival values and beliefs. Although liberalism did not emerge as a developed political creed until the early nineteenth century, distinctively liberal theories and principles had gradually been developed during the previous 300 years. Early liberalism certainly reflected the aspirations of a rising industrial middle class, and liberalism and capitalism have been closely linked (some have argued intrinsically linked) ever since. In its earliest form, liberalism was a political doctrine. As relected in the ideas of thinkers such as John Locke, it attacked absolutism (see p. 268) and feudal privilege, instead advocating constitutional and, later, representative government. By the early nineteenth century, a distinctively liberal economic creed had developed that extolled the virtues of *laissez-faire* (see p. 132) and condemned all forms of government intervention. This became the centrepiece of classical, or nineteenth-century, liberalism. From the late nineteenth century onwards, however, a form of social liberalism emerged that looked more favourably on welfare reform and economic intervention. Such an emphasis became the characteristic theme of modern, or twentieth-century, liberalism.

● **Meta-ideology**: A higher or second-order ideology that lays down the grounds on which ideological debate can take place.

Liberalism: key ideas

◆ **Individualism:** Individualism (see p. 158) is the core principle of liberal ideology. It reflects a belief in the supreme importance of the human individual as opposed to any social group or collective body. Human beings are seen, first and foremost, as individuals. This implies both that they are of equal moral worth and that they possess separate and unique identities. The liberal goal is therefore to construct a society within which individuals can flourish and develop, each pursuing 'the good' as he or she defines it, to the best of his or her abilities. This has contributed to the view that liberalism is morally neutral, in the sense that it lays down a set of rules that allow individuals to make their own moral decisions.

◆ **Freedom:** Individual freedom (see p. 339), or liberty (the two terms are interchangeable), is the core value of liberalism; it is given priority over, say, equality, justice or authority. This arises naturally from a belief in the individual and the desire to ensure that each person is able to act as he or she pleases or chooses. Nevertheless, liberals advocate 'freedom under the law', as they recognize that one person's liberty may be a threat to the liberty of others; liberty may become licence. They therefore endorse the ideal that individuals should enjoy the maximum possible liberty consistent with a like liberty for all.

◆ **Reason:** Liberals believe that the world has a rational structure, and that this can be uncovered through the exercise of human reason and by critical enquiry. This inclines them to place their faith in the ability of individuals to make wise judgements on their own behalf, being, in most cases, the best judges of their own interests. It also encourages liberals to believe in **progress** and the capacity of human beings to resolve their differences through debate and argument, rather than bloodshed and war.

◆ **Equality:** Individualism implies a belief in foundational equality: that is, the belief that individuals are 'born equal', at least in terms of moral worth. This is reflected in a liberal commitment to equal rights and entitlements, notably in the form of legal equality ('equality before the law') and political equality ('one person, one vote; one vote, one value'). However, as individuals do not possess the same levels of talent or willingness to work, liberals do not endorse social equality or an equality of outcome. Rather, they favour equality of opportunity (a 'level playing field') that gives all individuals an equal chance to realize their unequal potential. Liberals therefore support the principle of **meritocracy**, with merit reflecting, crudely, talent plus hard work.

◆ **Toleration:** Liberals believe that toleration (that is, forbearance: the willingness of people to allow others to think, speak and act in ways of which they disapprove) is both a guarantee of individual liberty and a means of social enrichment. They believe that pluralism (see p. 100), in the form of moral, cultural and political diversity, is positively healthy: it promotes debate and intellectual progress by ensuring that all beliefs are tested in a free market of ideas. Liberals, moreover, tend to believe that there is a balance or natural harmony between rival views and interests, and thus usually discount the idea of irreconcilable conflict.

◆ **Consent:** In the liberal view, authority and social relationships should always be based on consent or willing agreement. Government must therefore be based on the 'consent of the governed'. This is a doctrine that encourages liberals to favour representation (see p. 197) and democracy, notably in the form of liberal democracy (see p. 270). Similarly, social bodies and associations are formed through contracts willingly entered into by individuals intent on pursuing their own self-interest. In this sense, authority arises 'from below' and is always grounded in legitimacy (see p. 81).

◆ **Constitutionalism:** Although liberals see government as a vital guarantee of order and stability in society, they are constantly aware of the danger that government may become a tyranny against the individual ('power tends to corrupt' (Lord Acton)). They therefore believe in limited government. This goal can be attained through the fragmentation of government power, by the creation of checks and balances amongst the various institutions of government, and by the establishment of a codified or 'written' constitution embodying a bill of rights that defines the relationship between the state and the individual.

Classical liberalism

The central theme of classical liberalism is a commitment to an extreme form of individualism. Human beings are seen as egoistical, self-seeking and largely self-reliant creatures. In what C. B. Macpherson (1962) termed 'possessive individualism', they are taken to be the proprietors of their own persons and capacities, owing nothing to society or to other individuals. This **atomist** view of society is underpinned by a belief in 'negative' liberty, meaning non-interference, or the absence of external constraints on the individual. This implies a deeply unsympathetic attitude towards the state and all forms of government intervention.

In Tom Paine's (see p. 199) words, the state is a 'necessary evil'. It is 'necessary' in that, at the very least, it establishes order and security, and ensures that contracts are enforced. However, it is 'evil' in that it imposes a collective will on society, thus limiting the freedom and responsibilities of the individual. The classical liberal ideal is therefore the establishment of a minimal or 'nightwatchman' state, with a role that is limited to the protection of citizens from the encroachments of fellow citizens. In the form of **economic liberalism**, this position is underpinned by a deep faith in the mechanisms of the free market and the belief that the economy works best when left alone by government. *Laissez-faire* capitalism is thus seen as guaranteeing prosperity, upholding individual liberty, and, as this allows individuals to rise and fall according to merit, ensuring social justice.

Modern liberalism

Modern liberalism is characterized by a more sympathetic attitude towards state intervention. Indeed, in the USA, the term 'liberal' is invariably taken to imply support for **'big' government** rather than 'minimal' government. This shift was born out of the recognition that industrial capitalism had merely generated new forms of injustice and left the mass of the population subject to the vagaries of the market. Influenced by the work of J. S. Mill (see p. 198), the so-called 'New Liberals' (figures such as T. H. Green (1836–82), L. T. Hobhouse (1864–1929) and J. A. Hobson (1858–1940)) championed a broader, 'positive' view of freedom. From this perspective, freedom does not just mean being left alone, which might imply nothing more than the freedom to starve. Rather, it is linked to personal development and the flourishing of the individual; that is, the ability of the individual to gain fulfilment and achieve self-realization.

This view provided the basis for social or welfare liberalism. This is characterized by the recognition that state intervention, particularly in the form of social welfare, can enlarge liberty by safeguarding individuals from the social evils that blight individual existence. These evils were identified in the UK by the 1942 Beveridge Report as the 'five giants': want, ignorance, idleness, squalor and disease. In the same way, modern liberals abandoned their belief in *laissez-faire* capitalism, largely as a result of J. M. Keynes' (see p. 137) insight that growth and prosperity could be maintained only through a system of managed or regulated capitalism, with key economic responsibilities being placed in the hands of the state. Nevertheless, modern liberals' support for collective provision and government intervention has always been conditional. Their concern has been with the plight of the weak and vulnerable, those who are literally not able to help themselves. Their goal is to raise individuals to the point where they are able, once

● **Progress**: Moving forwards; the belief that history is characterized by human advancement based on the accumulation of knowledge and wisdom.

● **Meritocracy**: Rule by the talented; the principle that rewards and positions should be distributed on the basis of ability.

● **Atomism**: The belief that society is made up of a collection of largely self-sufficient individuals who owe little or nothing to one another.

● **Economic liberalism**: A belief in the market as a self-regulating mechanism tending naturally to deliver general prosperity and opportunities for all.

● **Big government**: Interventionist government, usually understood to imply economic management and social regulation.

again, to take responsibility for their own circumstances and make their own moral choices. The most influential modern attempt to reconcile the principles of liberalism with the politics of welfare and **redistribution** was undertaken by John Rawls (see p. 45). (The liberal approach to international politics is examined in Chapter 18.)

Conservatism

Conservative ideas and doctrines first emerged in the late eighteenth century and early nineteenth century. They arose as a reaction against the growing pace of economic and political change, which was in many ways symbolized by the French Revolution. In this sense, conservatism harked back to the **ancien régime**. In trying to resist the pressures unleashed by the growth of liberalism, socialism and nationalism, conservatism stood in defence of an increasingly embattled traditional social order. However, from the outset, divisions in conservative thought were apparent. In continental Europe, a form of conservatism emerged that was characterized by the work of thinkers such as Joseph de Maistre (1753–1821). This conservatism was starkly autocratic and reactionary, rejecting out of hand any idea of reform. A more cautious, more flexible and, ultimately, more successful form of conservatism nevertheless developed in the UK and the USA, characterized by Edmund Burke's belief in 'change in order to conserve'. This stance enabled conservatives in the nineteenth century to embrace the cause of social reform under the paternalistic banner of 'One Nation'. The high point of this tradition in the UK came in the 1950s as the Conservative Party came to accept the postwar settlement and espouse its own version of Keynesian social democracy. However, such ideas increasingly came under pressure from the 1970s onwards as a result of the emergence of the New Right. The New Right's radically antistatist and antipaternalist brand of conservatism draws heavily on classical liberal themes and values.

Paternalistic conservatism

The **paternalistic** strand in conservative thought is entirely consistent with principles such as organicism, hierarchy and duty, and it can therefore be seen as an outgrowth of traditional conservatism. Often traced back to the early writings of Benjamin Disraeli (1804–81), paternalism draws on a combination of prudence and principle. In warning of the danger of the UK being divided into 'two nations: the Rich and the Poor', Disraeli articulated a widespread fear of social revolution. This warning amounted to an appeal to the self-interest of the privileged, who needed to recognize that 'reform from above' was preferable to 'revolution from below'. This message was underpinned by an appeal to the principles of duty and social obligation rooted in neofeudal ideas such as **noblesse oblige**. In effect, in this view, duty is the price of privilege; the powerful and propertied inherit a responsibility to look after the less well-off in the broader interests of social cohesion and unity. The resulting One-Nation principle, the cornerstone of what since the early nineteenth century has been termed a **Tory** position, reflects not so much the ideal of social equality as a cohesive and stable hierarchy that arises organically.

● **Redistribution**: A narrowing of material inequalities brought about through a combination of progressive taxation and welfare provision.

● **Ancien régime**: (French) Literally, 'old order'; usually linked with the absolutist structures that predated the French Revolution.

● **Paternalism**: An attitude or policy that demonstrates care or concern for those unable to help themselves, as in the (supposed) relationship between a father and a child.

● **Noblesse oblige**: (French) Literally, the 'obligations of the nobility'; in general terms, the responsibility to guide or protect those less fortunate or less privileged.

● **Toryism**: An ideological stance within conservatism characterized by a belief in hierarchy, an emphasis on tradition, and support for duty and organicism.

● **Natural aristocracy**: The idea that talent and leadership are innate or inbred qualities that cannot be acquired through effort or self-advancement.

Conservatism: key ideas

◆ **Tradition:** The central theme of conservative thought, 'the desire to conserve', is closely linked to the perceived virtues of tradition, respect for established customs, and institutions that have endured through time. In this view, tradition reflects the accumulated wisdom of the past, and institutions and practices that have been 'tested by time', and it should be preserved for the benefit of the living and for generations yet to come. Tradition also has the virtue of promoting a sense of social and historical belonging.

◆ **Pragmatism:** Conservatives have traditionally emphasized the limitations of human rationality, which arise from the infinite complexity of the world in which we live. Abstract principles and systems of thought are therefore distrusted, and instead faith is placed in experience, history and, above all, pragmatism: the belief that action should be shaped by practical circumstances and practical goals, that is, by 'what works'. Conservatives have thus preferred to describe their own beliefs as an 'attitude of mind' or an 'approach to life', rather than as an ideology, although they reject the idea that this amounts to unprincipled opportunism.

◆ **Human imperfection:** The conservative view of human nature is broadly pessimistic. In this view, human beings are limited, dependent, and security-seeking creatures, drawn to the familiar and the tried and tested, and needing to live in stable and orderly communities. In addition, individuals are morally corrupt: they are tainted by selfishness, greed and the thirst for power. The roots of crime and disorder therefore reside within the human individual rather than in society. The maintenance of order (see p. 400) therefore requires a strong state, the enforcement of strict laws, and stiff penalties.

◆ **Organicism:** Instead of seeing society as an artefact that is a product of human ingenuity, conservatives have traditionally viewed society as an organic whole, or living entity. Society is thus structured by natural necessity, with its various institutions, or the 'fabric of society' (families, local communities, the nation and so on), contributing to the health and stability of society. The whole is more than a collection of its individual parts. Shared (often 'traditional') values and a common culture are also seen as being vital to the maintenance of the community and social cohesion.

◆ **Hierarchy:** In the conservative view, gradations of social position and status are natural and inevitable in an organic society. These reflect the differing roles and responsibilities of, for example, employers and workers, teachers and pupils, and parents and children. Nevertheless, in this view, hierarchy and inequality do not give rise to conflict, because society is bound together by mutual obligations and reciprocal duties. Indeed, as a person's 'station in life' is determined largely by luck and the accident of birth, the prosperous and privileged acquire a particular responsibility of care for the less fortunate.

◆ **Authority:** Conservatives hold that, to some degree, authority is always exercised 'from above', providing leadership (see p. 300), guidance and support for those who lack the knowledge, experience or education to act wisely in their own interests (an example being the authority of parents over children). Although the idea of a **natural aristocracy** was once influential, authority and leadership are now more commonly seen as resulting from experience and training. The virtue of authority is that it is a source of social cohesion, giving people a clear sense of who they are and what is expected of them. Freedom must therefore coexist with responsibility; it therefore consists largely of a willing acceptance of obligations and duties.

◆ **Property:** Conservatives see property ownership as being vital because it gives people security and a measure of independence from government, and it encourages them to respect the law and the property of others. Property is also an exteriorization of people's personalities, in that they 'see' themselves in what they own: their houses, their cars, and so on. However, property ownership involves duties as well as rights. In this view, we are, in a sense, merely custodians of property that has either been inherited from past generations ('the family silver'), or may be of value to future ones.

Edmund Burke (1729–97)

Dublin-born UK statesman and political theorist who is often seen as the father of the Anglo-American conservative tradition. Burke's enduring reputation is based on a series of works, notably *Reflections on the Revolution in France* ([1790] 1968), that were critical of the French Revolution. Though sympathetic to the American Revolution, Burke was deeply critical of the attempt to recast French politics in accordance with abstract principles such as liberty, equality and fraternity, arguing that wisdom resided largely in experience, tradition and history. Nevertheless, he held that the French monarchy was, in part, responsible for its own fate since it had obstinately refused to 'change in order to conserve'. Burke had a gloomy view of government, recognizing that it could prevent evil but rarely promote good. He supported free market economics on the grounds that it reflects 'natural law'.

The One-Nation tradition embodies not only a disposition towards social reform, but also an essentially pragmatic attitude towards economic policy. This is clearly seen in the 'middle way' approach adopted in the 1950s by UK Conservatives. This approach eschewed the two ideological models of economic organization: *laissez-faire* capitalism on the one hand, and state socialism and central planning on the other. The former was rejected on the grounds that it results in a free for all, which makes social cohesion impossible, and penalizes the weak and vulnerable. The latter was dismissed because it produces a state monolith and crushes all forms of independence and enterprise. The solution therefore lies in a blend of market competition and government regulation – 'private enterprise without selfishness' (H. Macmillan).

Very similar conclusions were drawn after 1945 by continental European conservatives, who embraced the principles of **Christian democracy**, most rigorously developed in the 'social market' philosophy (see p. 133) of the German Christian Democrats (CDU). This philosophy embraces a market strategy, insofar as it highlights the virtues of private enterprise and competition; but it is social, in that it believes that the prosperity so gained should be employed for the broader benefit of society. Such a position draws from Catholic social theory, which advances an organic view of society that stresses social harmony. Christian democracy thus highlights the importance of intermediate institutions, such as churches, unions and business groups, bound together by the notion of 'social partnership'. The paternalistic strand of modern conservatism thought is often linked to the idea of 'compassionate conservatism'.

The New Right

The New Right represents a departure in conservative thought that amounted to a kind of counter-revolution against both the post-1945 drift towards state intervention and the spread of liberal or progressive social values. New Right ideas can be traced back to the 1970s and the conjunction between the apparent failure of Keynesian social democracy, signalled by the end of the postwar boom, and growing concern about social breakdown and the decline of authority. Such

● **Christian democracy**: An ideological tendency within European conservatism, characterized by commitment to social market principles and qualified interventionism.

Friedrich von Hayek (1899–1992)

Austrian economist and political philosopher. An academic who taught at the London School of Economics and the Universities of Chicago, Freiburg and Salzburg, Hayek was awarded the Nobel Prize for Economics in 1974. As an exponent of the so-called 'Austrian School', he was a firm believer in individualism and market order, and an implacable critic of socialism. *The Road to Serfdom* (1948) was a pioneering work that attacked economic interventionism. In later works such as *The Constitution of Liberty* (1960) and *Law, Legislation and Liberty* (1979) Hayek developed themes in political philosophy. Hayek's writings fused liberal and conservative elements, and had a considerable impact on the emergent New Right.

ideas had their greatest impact in the UK and the USA, where they were articulated in the 1980s in the form of Thatcherism and Reaganism, respectively. They have also had a wider, even worldwide, influence in bringing about a general shift from state- to market-orientated forms of organization. However, the New Right does not so much constitute a coherent and systematic philosophy as attempt to marry two distinct traditions, usually termed 'neoliberalism' and 'neoconservatism'. Although there is political and ideological tension between these two, they can be combined in support of the goal of a strong but minimal state: in Andrew Gamble's (1981) words, 'the free economy and the strong state'.

Neoliberalism

Neoliberalism (see p. 144) is an updated version of classical political economy that was developed in the writings of free-market economists such as Friedrich Hayek and Milton Friedman (see p. 138), and philosophers such as Robert Nozick (see p. 68). The central pillars of neoliberalism are the market and the individual. The principal neoliberal goal is to 'roll back the frontiers of the state', in the belief that unregulated market capitalism will deliver efficiency, growth and widespread prosperity. In this view, the 'dead hand' of the state saps initiative and discourages enterprise; government, however well-intentioned, invariably has a damaging effect on human affairs. This is reflected in the liberal New Right's concern with the politics of ownership, and its preference for private enterprise over state enterprise or nationalization: in short, 'private, good; public, bad'. Such ideas are associated with a form of rugged individualism, expressed in Margaret Thatcher's famous assertion that 'there is no such thing as society, only individuals and their families'. The '**nanny state**' is seen to breed a culture of dependence and to undermine freedom, which is understood as freedom of choice in the marketplace. Instead, faith is placed in self-help, individual responsibility and entrepreneurialism. Such ideas are widely seen to be advanced through the process of globalization (see p. 142), viewed by some as neoliberal globalization.

● **Nanny state:** A state with extensive social responsibilities; the term implies that welfare programmes are unwarranted and demeaning to the individual.

Neoconservatism

Neoconservatism reasserts nineteenth-century conservative social principles. The conservative New Right wishes, above all, to restore authority and return to traditional values, notably those linked to the family, religion and the nation. Authority is seen as guaranteeing social stability, on the basis that it generates discipline and respect, while shared values and a common culture are believed to generate social cohesion and make civilized existence possible. The enemies of neoconservatism are therefore **permissiveness**, the cult of the self and 'doing one's own thing', thought of as the values of the 1960s. Indeed, many of those who style themselves neoconservatives in the USA are former liberals who grew disillusioned with the progressive reforms of the Kennedy–Johnson era. Another aspect of neoconservatism is the tendency to view the emergence of multicultural and multireligious societies with concern, on the basis that they are conflict-ridden and inherently unstable. This position also tends to be linked to an insular form of nationalism that is sceptical about both multiculturalism (see p. 167) and the growing influence of supranational bodies such as the UN and the EU. Neoconservatism also developed into a distinctive approach to foreign policy, particularly in the USA under George Bush Jr, linked to attempts to consolidate US global domination, in part through militarily imposed 'regime change'.

Socialism

Although socialist ideas can be traced back to the Levellers and Diggers of the seventeenth century, or to Thomas More's *Utopia* ([1516] 1965), or even Plato's *Republic*, socialism did not take shape as a political creed until the early nineteenth century. It developed as a reaction against the emergence of industrial capitalism. Socialism first articulated the interests of artisans and craftsmen threatened by the spread of factory production, but it was soon being linked to the growing industrial working class, the 'factory fodder' of early industrialization. In its earliest forms, socialism tended to have a fundamentalist (see p. 53), utopian and revolutionary character. Its goal was to abolish a capitalist economy based on market exchange, and replace it with a qualitatively different socialist society, usually to be constructed on the principle of common ownership. The most influential representative of this brand of socialism was Karl Marx, whose ideas provided the foundations for twentieth-century communism (see p. 275).

From the late nineteenth century onwards, however, a reformist socialist tradition emerged that reflected the gradual integration of the working classes into capitalist society through an improvement in working conditions and wages, and the growth of trade unions and socialist political parties. This brand of socialism proclaimed the possibility of a peaceful, gradual and legal transition to socialism, brought about through the adoption of the 'parliamentary road'. Reformist socialism drew on two sources. The first was a humanist tradition of ethical socialism, linked to thinkers such as Robert Owen (1771–1858), Charles Fourier (1772–1837) and William Morris (1834–96). The second was a form of **revisionist** Marxism developed primarily by Eduard Bernstein (see p. 43).

During much of the twentieth century, the socialist movement was thus divided into two rival camps. Revolutionary socialists, following the example of Lenin and the Bolsheviks, called themselves 'communists', while reformist socialists, who practised a form of constitutional politics, embraced what increasingly came to be called 'social democracy'. This rivalry focused not only on the most appropriate means of achieving socialism, but also on the nature of the socialist

● **Permissiveness**: The willingness to allow people to make their own moral choices; permissiveness suggests that there are no authoritative values.

● **Revisionism**: The modification of original or established beliefs; revisionism can imply the abandonment of principle or a loss of conviction.

Socialism: key ideas

◆ **Community:** The core of socialism is the vision of human beings as social creatures linked by the existence of a common humanity. As the poet John Donne put it, 'no man is an Island entire of itself; every man is a piece of the Continent, a part of the main'. This refers to the importance of community, and it highlights the degree to which individual identity is fashioned by social interaction and membership of social groups and collective bodies. Socialists are inclined to emphasize nurture over nature, and to explain individual behaviour mainly in terms of social factors, rather than innate qualities.

◆ **Fraternity:** As human beings share a common humanity, they are bound together by a sense of comradeship or fraternity (literally meaning 'brotherhood', but broadened in this context to embrace all humans). This encourages socialists to prefer cooperation to competition, and to favour collectivism over individualism (see p. 158). In this view, cooperation enables people to harness their collective energies and strengthens the bonds of community, while competition pits individuals against each other, breeding resentment, conflict and hostility.

◆ **Social equality:** Equality (see p. 454) is the central value of socialism. Socialism is sometimes portrayed as a form of egalitarianism, the belief in the primacy of equality over other values. In particular, socialists emphasize the importance of social equality, an equality of outcome as opposed to equality of opportunity. They believe that a measure of social equality is the essential guarantee of social stability and cohesion, encouraging individuals to identify with their fellow human beings. It also provides the basis for the exercise of legal and political rights. However, socialists disagree about the extent to which social equality can and should be brought about. While Marxists have believed in absolute social equality, brought about by the collectivization of production wealth, social democrats have favoured merely narrowing material inequalities, often being more concerned with equalizing opportunities than outcomes.

◆ **Need:** Sympathy for equality also reflects the socialist belief that material benefits should be distributed on the basis of need, rather than simply on the basis of merit or work. The classic formulation of this principle is found in Marx's communist principle of distribution: 'from each according to his ability, to each according to his need'. This reflects the belief that the satisfaction of basic needs (hunger, thirst, shelter, health, personal security and so on) is a prerequisite for a worthwhile human existence and participation in social life. Clearly, however, distribution according to need requires people to be motivated by moral incentives, rather than just material ones.

◆ **Social class:** Socialism has often been associated with a form of class politics. First, socialists have tended to analyse society in terms of the distribution of income or wealth, and they have thus seen social class (see p. 153) as a significant (usually the most significant) social cleavage. Second, socialism has traditionally been associated with the interests of an oppressed and exploited working class (however defined), and it has traditionally regarded the working class as an agent of social change, even social revolution (see p. 85). Nevertheless, class divisions are remediable: the socialist goal is either the eradication of economic and social inequalities, or their substantial reduction.

◆ **Common ownership:** The relationship between socialism and common ownership has been deeply controversial. Some see it as the *end* of socialism itself, and others see it instead simply as a *means* of generating broader equality. The socialist case for common ownership (in the form of either Soviet-style state collectivization, or selective nationalization (a 'mixed economy')) is that it is a means of harnessing material resources to the common good, with private property being seen to promote selfishness, acquisitiveness and social division. Modern socialism, however, has moved away from this narrow concern with the politics of ownership.

goal itself. Social democrats turned their backs on fundamentalist principles such as common ownership and planning, and recast socialism in terms of welfare, redistribution and economic management. Both forms of socialism, however, experienced crises in the late twentieth century that encouraged some to proclaim the 'death of socialism' and the emergence of a postsocialist society. The most dramatic event in this process was the collapse of communism brought about by the Eastern European revolutions of 1989–91, but there was also a continued retreat of social democracy from traditional principles, making it, some would argue, indistinguishable from modern liberalism.

Marxism

As a theoretical system, Marxism has constituted the principal alternative to the liberal rationalism that has dominated western culture and intellectual enquiry in the modern period. As a political force, in the form of the international communist movement, Marxism has also been seen as the major enemy of western capitalism, at least in the period 1917–91. This highlights a central difficulty in dealing with Marxism: the difference between Marxism as a social philosophy derived from the classic writings of Karl Marx and Friedrich Engels (1820–95), and the phenomenon of twentieth-century communism, which in many ways departed from and revised classical principles. Thus, the collapse of communism at the end of the twentieth century need not betoken the death of Marxism as a political ideology; indeed, it may give Marxism, now divorced from the vestiges of **Leninism** and **Stalinism**, a fresh lease of life.

Marx's ideas and theories reached a wider audience after his death, largely through the writings of his lifelong collaborator Engels, the German socialist leader Karl Kautsky (1854–1938) and the Russian theoretician Georgi Plekhanov (1856–1918). A form of orthodox Marxism, usually termed '**dialectical materialism**' (a term coined by Plekhanov, not Marx), came into existence that was later used as the basis for Soviet communism. This 'vulgar' Marxism undoubtedly placed a heavier stress on mechanistic theories and historical determinism than did Marx's own writings.

Classical Marxism

The core of classical Marxism – the Marxism of Marx – is a philosophy of history that Engels described as the 'materialist conception of history', or **historical materialism**. This highlights the importance of economic life and the conditions under which people produce and reproduce their means of subsistence. Marx held that the economic 'base', consisting essentially of the 'mode of production', or economic system, conditions or determines the ideological and political 'superstructure'. Following Hegel (see p. 59), Marx believed that the driving force of historical change was the dialectic, a process of interaction between competing forces that results in a higher stage of development. In its materialist version, this model implies that historical change is a consequence of internal contradictions within a 'mode of production', reflected in class conflict. Like all earlier class societies, capitalism is therefore doomed to collapse; in this case, as a result of conflict between the bourgeoisie or capitalist class, the owners of productive wealth, and the proletariat, who are, in effect, 'wage slaves'. This conflict is irreconcilable, because the proletariat is necessarily and systematically exploited

● **Leninism**: Lenin's theoretical contributions to Marxism, notably his belief in the need for a 'vanguard' party to raise the proletariat to class consciousness.

● **Stalinism**: The structures of Stalin's USSR, especially a centrally placed economy linked to systematic and brutal political oppression.

● **Dialectical materialism**: The crude and deterministic form of Marxism that dominated intellectual life in orthodox communist states.

● **Historical materialism**: The Marxist theory that holds that economic conditions ultimately structure law, politics, culture and other aspects of social existence.

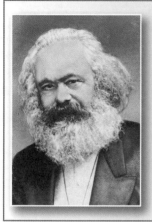

Karl Marx (1818–83)

German philosopher, economist and political thinker, usually portrayed as the father of twentieth-century communism. After a brief career as a university teacher, Marx took up journalism and became increasingly involved with the socialist movement. He settled in London after being expelled from Prussia, and worked for the rest of his life as an active revolutionary and writer, supported by his friend and lifelong collaborator Friedrich Engels. In 1864, Marx helped to found the First International, which collapsed in 1871 because of growing antagonism between Marx's supporters and anarchists led by Bakunin. Marx's classic work was the three-volume *Capital* ([1867, 1885, 1894] 1970). His best-known and most accessible work is the *Communist Manifesto* ([1848] 1967).

under capitalism, the bourgeoisie living by extracting 'surplus value' from its labour.

According to Marx, the inevitable proletarian revolution will occur once a series of deepening crises have brought the proletariat to full class consciousness. This would allow the working masses to recognize the fact of their own exploitation and so become a revolutionary force. The proletarian revolution would usher in a transitionary 'socialist' period of development, characterized by the '**dictatorship of the proletariat**'. However, as class antagonisms fade and a fully communist society comes into existence, this proletarian state will 'wither away', meaning that a communist society will be both classlessness and statelessness. As a system of 'commodity production' gives rise to one based on 'production for use' and geared to the satisfaction of genuine human needs, 'the free development of each would become the precondition for the free development of all' (Marx).

Orthodox communism

Marxism in practice is inextricably linked to the experience of Soviet communism (see p. 275), and especially to the contribution of the first two Soviet leaders, V. I. Lenin and Joseph Stalin (1879–1953). Indeed, twentieth-century communism is best understood as a form of Marxism–Leninism: that is, as orthodox Marxism modified by a set of Leninist theories and doctrines. Lenin's central contribution to Marxism was his theory of the revolutionary or vanguard party. This reflected Lenin's fear that the proletariat, deluded by bourgeois ideas and beliefs, would not realize its revolutionary potential because it could not develop beyond 'trade-union consciousness': a desire to improve working and living conditions rather than to overthrow capitalism. A revolutionary party, armed with Marxism, was therefore needed to serve as the 'vanguard of the working class'. In due course, this 'vanguard' or 'Leninist' party, composed of professional and dedicated revolutionaries, became the model for communist parties across the globe.

The USSR was, however, more profoundly affected by Stalin's 'second revolution' in the 1930s than it had been by the 1917 Bolshevik Revolution. In reshaping Soviet society, Stalin created a model of orthodox communism that was followed in the post-1945 period by states such as China, North Korea and Cuba, and throughout Eastern Europe. What may be called 'economic Stalinism' was

● **Dictatorship of the proletariat**: A temporary proletarian state, established to prevent counter-revolution and oversee the transition from capitalism to communism.

Herbert Marcuse (1898–1979)

German political philosopher and social theorist, and co-founder of the Frankfurt School. A refugee from Hitler's Germany, Marcuse lived in the USA from 1934. He developed a form of neo-Marxism that drew heavily on Hegel and Freud. Marcuse came to prominence in the 1960s as a leading thinker of the New Left and a 'guru' of the student movement. He portrayed advanced industrial society as an all-encompassing system of repression that subdued argument and debate, and absorbed opposition. His hopes rested not on the proletariat, but on marginalized groups such as students, ethnic minorities, women and workers in the developing world. His most important works include *Reason and Revolution* (1941), *Eros and Civilization* (1958) and *One-Dimensional Man* (1964).

initiated with the launch in 1928 of the first Five Year Plan, which brought about the swift and total eradication of private enterprise. This was followed in 1929 by the collectivization of agriculture. All resources were brought under the control of the state, and a system of central planning dominated by the State Planning Committee (*Gosplan*) was established. Stalin's political changes were no less dramatic. During the 1930s, Stalin transformed the USSR into a personal dictatorship through a series of purges that eradicated all vestiges of opposition and debate from the Communist Party, the state bureaucracy and the military. In effect, Stalin turned the USSR into a totalitarian dictatorship, operating through systematic intimidation, repression and terror.

Although the more brutal features of orthodox communism did not survive Stalin's death in 1953, the core principles of the Leninist party (hierarchical organization and discipline) and of economic Stalinism (state collectivization and central planning) stubbornly resisted pressure for reform. This was highlighted by Gorbachev's *perestroika* reform process (1985–91), which merely succeeded in exposing the failings of the planning system, and in releasing long-suppressed political forces. These eventually consigned Soviet communism to what Trotsky (see p. 369) had, in very different circumstances, called 'the dustbin of history'. However, political Stalinism survives in China, despite the embrace of market reforms, and North Korea remains a thoroughgoing orthodox communist regime. The collapse of communism during the 1989–91 period is widely seen as the most significant ideological event of the modern period (see p. 44).

Neo-Marxism

A more complex and subtle form of Marxism developed in western Europe. By contrast with the mechanistic and avowedly scientific notions of Soviet Marxism, western Marxism or neo-Marxism (see p. 64) tended to be influenced by Hegelian ideas and by the stress on 'Man the creator' found in Marx's early writings. In other words, human beings were seen as makers of history, and not simply as puppets controlled by impersonal material forces. By insisting that there was an interplay between economics and politics, between the material

● *Perestroika*: (Russian) Literally, 'restructuring'; a slogan that refers to the attempt to liberalize and democratize the Soviet system within a communist framework.

Eduard Bernstein (1850–1932)

German socialist politician and theorist. An early member of the German SPD, Bernstein became one of the leading advocates of revisionism, the attempt to revise and modernize orthodox Marxism. Influenced by British Fabianism and the philosophy of Kant (see p. 410), Bernstein developed a largely empirical critique that emphasized the absence of class war, and proclaimed the possibility of a peaceful transition to socialism. This is described in *Evolutionary Socialism* ([1898] 1962). He left the SPD over his opposition to World War I, although he subsequently returned and served as the secretary of state for the economy and finance in the Ebert government (1918–19). Bernstein is often seen as one of the founding figures of modern social democracy.

circumstances of life and the capacity of human beings to shape their own destinies, neo-Marxists were able to break free from the rigid 'base–superstructure' straitjacket. This indicated an unwillingness to treat the class struggle as the beginning and end of social analysis.

The Hungarian Marxist Georg Lukács (1885–1971) was one of the first to present Marxism as a humanistic philosophy. He emphasized the process of 'reification', through which capitalism dehumanizes workers by reducing them to passive objects or marketable commodities. In his *Prison Notebooks*, written in 1929–35, Antonio Gramsci emphasized the degree to which capitalism was maintained not merely by economic domination, but also by political and cultural factors. He called this ideological 'hegemony' (see p. 174). A more overtly Hegelian brand of Marxism was developed by the so-called 'Frankfurt School', the leading members of which were Theodor Adorno (1903–69), Max Horkheimer (1895–1973) and Herbert Marcuse (see p. 42). Frankfurt theorists developed what was called 'critical theory', a blend of Marxist political economy, Hegelian philosophy and Freudian psychology, which had a considerable impact on the New Left in the 1960s. A later generation of Frankfurt members included Jürgen Habermas (see p. 84).

While early critical theorists were primarily concerned with the analysis of discrete societies, later theorists have tended to give greater attention to uncovering inequalities and asymmetries in world affairs. This has been evident in an emphasis on the hegemonic power of the USA (Cox, 1987) and the analysis of capitalism as a 'world-system' (Wallerstein, 1984).

Social democracy

• **Fundamentalist socialism**: A form of socialism that seeks to abolish capitalism and replace it with a qualitatively different kind of society.

Social democracy lacks the theoretical coherence of, say, classical liberalism or **fundamentalist socialism**. Whereas the former is ideologically committed to the market, and the latter champions the cause of common ownership, social democracy stands for a balance between the market and the state, a balance between the individual and the community. At the heart of social democracy there is a compromise between, on the one hand, an acceptance of capitalism as

Fall of communism: the triumph of liberal democracy?

Events: The collapse of communism was precipitated by a series of revolutions that took place during the momentous year of 1989. The first popular challenge to a communist regime in 1989 was the Tiananmen Square protests in Beijing, China, which began in April, but were suppressed by a military crackdown on 4 June. Events in Eastern Europe nevertheless gathered momentum the following day, as Solidarity, the newly-legalized independent trade union movement, swept the board in parliamentary elections, leading, by September, to the formation of the first non-communist government in the Eastern bloc. In October, the Hungarian parliament adopted legislation providing for multiparty elections and, eventually, the establishment of a second non-communist government. Pressure for political change built up in East Germany, the USSR's firmest Eastern bloc ally, as thousands of East Germans escaped to West Germany, via Hungary, and a growing wave of demonstrations eventually culminated on the night of 9/10 November in the fall of the Berlin Wall, the chief symbol of the Cold War and of Europe's East–West divide. Whereas peaceful protest led to the collapse of communist rule in Czechoslovakia (the 'velvet revolution') in December, and in Bulgaria in February 1990, the process was more violent in Romania, where the communist leader Ceauşescu and his wife Elena were summarily executed on Christmas Day 1989. The period of revolutionary upheaval eventually culminated in December 1991 with the official dissolution of the USSR, the world's first communist state, following a succession of nationalist uprisings across the multinational Soviet state.

Significance: The ideological significance of the fall of communism has been profound and far-reaching, and, in some senses, it remains a continuing process. The dominant early interpretation of the collapse of communism was advanced by so-called 'end of history' theorists such as Fukuyama (see p. 271). In this view, the collapse of ortho-dox communist regimes across Eastern Europe and beyond indicated the death of Marxism as an ideology of world-historical importance, revealing western-style, and more specifically US-style, liberal democracy as the determinant end-point of human history. The events of 1989–91 there-fore merely illustrate the irresistible fact that human soci-eties are destined to converge around an essentially liberal model of economic and social development, as only western liberalism can offer the benefits of social mobility and material security, on the one hand, and the opportunity for personal self-development without the interference of the state, on the other hand. Such an analysis suggests not only that communism is a spent ideological force, but also that socialism in its wider forms has been seriously compromised by the dramatic failure of the world's only significant non-capitalist economic systems. Social-democratic parties have, as a result, gone through a process of de-radicalization, encouraging some to proclaim that socialism, as a distinctive ideology, is dead.

However, there are reasons for thinking that the 'end of history' thesis was at best premature and at worst wholly misconceived. In the first place, the period since 1989–91 has certainly not witnessed worldwide ideological conver-gence around the principles of liberal democracy. Indeed, in the non-western world, liberalism has sometimes been contested more ferociously than ever before, not least by the forces of ethnic nationalism and religious fundamental-ism, especially in the Muslim world. In China, and across much of East and Southeast Asia, Confucian and other indigenous ideas have gained renewed political currency, gaining strength in large part from the desire to resist the spread of atomistic and rights-orientated liberal thinking. Similarly, in its western heartland, liberalism's ascendancy has been challenged by an array of ideological forces, ranging from green politics and certain strains within femi-nism to communitarianism, multiculturalism and postmod-ernism. Finally, despite its undoubted resilience, it is difficult to see how liberal capitalism will ever achieve a universal appeal, given its inherent tendency towards social inequal-ity and instability.

John Rawls (1921–2002)

US academic and political philosopher. His major work, *A Theory of Justice* (1970), is regarded as the most important work of political philosophy written in English since World War II. It has influenced modern liberals and social democrats alike. Rawls proposed a theory of 'justice as fairness' that is based on the belief that social inequality can be justified only if it is of benefit to the least advantaged. This presumption in favour of equality is rooted in Rawls' belief that most people, deprived of knowledge about their own talents and abilities, would choose to live in an egalitarian society, rather than an inegalitarian one. As, for most people, the fear of being poor outweighs the desire to be rich, redistribution and welfare can be defended on grounds of fairness. Rawls' other works include *Political Liberalism* (1993) and *The Laws of People* (1999).

the only reliable mechanism for generating wealth and, on the other, a desire to distribute wealth in accordance with moral, rather than market, principles. For socialists, this conversion to the market was a difficult, and at times painful, process that was dictated more by practical circumstances and electoral advantage than by ideological conviction.

The chief characteristic of modern social democratic thought is a concern for the underdog in society, the weak and vulnerable. There is a sense, however, in which social democracy cannot simply be confined to the socialist tradition. It may draw on a socialist belief in compassion and a common humanity, a liberal commitment to positive freedom and equal opportunities, or, for that matter, a conservative sense of paternal duty and care. Whatever its source, it has usually been articulated on the basis of principles such as welfarism, redistribution and social justice. In the form of Keynesian social democracy, which was widely accepted in the early period after World War II, it was associated with a clear desire to 'humanize' capitalism through state intervention. It was believed that Keynesian economic policies would secure full employment, a mixed economy would help government to regulate economic activity, and comprehensive welfare provision funded via progressive taxation would narrow the gap between rich and poor.

Since the 1980s, a further process of revisionism has taken place within social democracy. This occurred for a variety of reasons. In the first place, changes in the class structure, and particularly the growth of professional and clerical occupations, meant that social-democratic policies orientated around the interests of the traditional working class were no longer electorally viable. Second, globalization appeared to render all specifically national forms of economic management, such as Keynesianism, redundant. Third, nationalized industries and economic planning proved to be inefficient, at least in developed states. Fourth, the collapse of communism undermined the intellectual and ideological credibility not just of state collectivization, but of all 'top-down' socialist models. In this context, it became increasingly fashionable for politicians and political parties to rethink or revise 'traditional' social democracy.

CONCEPT

Third way

The term the third way encapsulates the idea of an alternative to both capitalism and socialism. Initially used by fascists, the term is now firmly linked to 'new' or modernized social democracy. In this context the third way is an alternative to old-style social democracy and neoliberalism. The former is rejected because it is wedded to statist structures that are inappropriate to the modern knowledge-based and market-orientated economy. The latter is rejected because it generates a free-for-all that undermines the moral foundations of society.

'New' social democracy

'New' social democracy (sometimes called 'neo-revisionism' or the 'third way') is a term that refers to a variety of attempts by social-democratic parties, in countries ranging from Germany, Italy and the Netherlands to the UK and New Zealand, to reconcile old-style social democracy with, at least, the electorally-attractive aspects of neoliberalism. Although 'new' social democracy is imprecise and subject to a number of interpretations, certain characteristic themes can nevertheless be identified. The first of these is the belief that socialism, at least in the form of 'top-down' state intervention, is dead: there is no alternative to what Clause 4 of the UK Labour Party's constitution, rewritten in 1995, refers to as 'a dynamic market economy'. With this goes a general acceptance of globalization and the belief that capitalism has mutated into a 'knowledge economy', which places a premium on information technology, individual skills, and both labour and business flexibility. In this light, the state came to be seen not as a vehicle for wholesale social restructuring, but as a means of promoting international competitiveness; particularly by building up education and skills.

A further feature of 'new' social-democratic politics is that it has broken with socialist egalitarianism (which is seen as a form of 'levelling') and embraced, instead, the liberal ideas of equality of opportunity and meritocracy. Neorevisionist politicians typically endorse welfare reform. They reject both the neoliberal emphasis on 'standing on your own two feet' and the 'traditional' social-democratic commitment to 'cradle to grave' welfare in favour of an essentially modern liberal belief in 'helping people to help themselves', or, as the former US president Bill Clinton put it, giving people 'a hand up, not a hand out'. This has led to support for what has been called a 'workfare state', in which government provision in terms of benefits or education is conditional on individuals seeking work and becoming self-reliant. Critics of 'new' social democracy, on the other hand, argue either that it is contradictory, in that it simultaneously endorses the dynamism of the market and warns against its tendency to social disintegration, or that, far from being a centre-left project, it amounts to a shift to the right.

OTHER IDEOLOGICAL TRADITIONS

Liberalism, conservatism and socialism by no means exhaust the field of ideological politics. Other ideological traditions have nevertheless tended to develop either out of, or in opposition to, these core ideologies. Where they have drawn, to a significant extent, on liberal, conservative and/or socialist thinking, these other ideologies have a 'cross-cutting' character, in that they incorporate elements from 'bigger' ideological traditions. This applies, albeit in different ways, to anarchism, feminism, green politics and cosmopolitanism, as well as to nationalism and multiculturalism; ideological traditions that are examined, respectively, in Chapters 5 and 7. Where other ideological traditions have emerged largely in opposition to liberalism, conservatism and socialism, they have been marked by an attempt to challenge and overturn core features of the western political tradition itself. This applies in the case of

Adolf Hitler (1889–1945)

German Nazi dictator. Hitler was the son of an Austrian customs official. He joined the German Worker's Party (later the Nationalsozialistische Deutsche Arbeiterpartei (NSDAP), or Nazi Party) in 1919, becoming its leader in 1921. He was appointed Chancellor of Germany in 1933, and declared himself *Führer* (Leader) the following year, by which time he had established a one-party dictatorship. The central feature of Hitler's world-view, outlined in *Mein Kampf* ([1925] 1969), was his attempt to fuse expansionist German nationalism and virulent anti-Semitism into a theory of history in which there was an endless battle between the Germans and the Jews, who represented, respectively, the forces of good and evil. Hitler's policies contributed decisively to both the outbreak of World War II and the Holocaust.

fascism and certain trends in non-western ideological thought, notably political Islam.

Fascism

Whereas liberalism, conservatism and socialism are nineteenth-century ideologies, fascism is a child of the twentieth century. Some would say that it is specifically an interwar phenomenon. Although fascist beliefs can be traced back to the late nineteenth century, they were fused together and shaped by World War I and its aftermath and, in particular, by the potent mixture of war and revolution that characterized the period. The two principal manifestations of fascism were Mussolini's Fascist dictatorship in Italy in 1922–43, and Hitler's Nazi dictatorship in Germany in 1933–45. Forms of neofascism and neo-Nazism have also resurfaced in recent decades, taking advantage of the combination of economic crisis and political instability that often followed the collapse of communism or, more widely, of increased anxieties over immigration and multiculturalism (see p. 167).

In many respects, fascism constituted a revolt against the ideas and values that had dominated western political thought since the French Revolution: in the words of the Italian Fascist slogan, '1789 is dead'. Values such as rationalism, progress, freedom and equality were thus overturned in the name of struggle, leadership, power, heroism and war. In this sense, fascism has an 'anticharacter'. It is defined largely by what it opposes: it is a form of anticapitalism, antiliberalism, anti-individualism, anticommunism, and so on. A core theme that, nevertheless, runs throughout fascism is the image of an organically unified national community. This is reflected in a belief in 'strength through unity'. The individual, in a literal sense, is nothing; individual identity must be absorbed entirely into that of the community or social group. The fascist ideal is that of the 'new man', a hero, motivated by duty, honour and self-sacrifice, prepared to dedicate his life to the glory of his nation or race, and to give unquestioning obedience to a supreme leader.

Not all fascists, however, think alike. Italian Fascism was essentially an extreme form of statism (see p. 71) that was based on unquestioning respect and absolute loyalty towards a 'totalitarian' state. As the Fascist philosopher Gentile (1875–1944) put it, 'everything for the state; nothing against the state; nothing outside the state'. German National Socialism (or Nazism), on the other hand, was constructed largely on the basis of racialism (see p. 120). Its two core theories were Aryanism (the belief that the German people constitute a 'master race' and are destined for world domination), and a virulent form of anti-Semitism (see p. 121) that portrayed the Jews as inherently evil, and aimed at their eradication. This latter belief found expression in the 'Final Solution'.

Anarchism

Anarchism is unusual amongst political ideologies in that no anarchist party has ever succeeded in winning power, at least at national level. Nevertheless, anarchist movements were powerful in, for example, Spain, France, Russia and Mexico through to the early twentieth century, and anarchist ideas continue to fertilize political debate by challenging the conventional belief that law, government and the state are either wholesome or indispensable. Anarchist thinking has also been influential within the modern anti-capitalist, or anti-globalization, movement. The central theme within anarchism is the belief that political authority in all its forms, and especially in the form of the state, is both evil and unnecessary (anarchy literally means 'without rule'). Nevertheless, the anarchist preference for a stateless society in which free individuals manage their own affairs through voluntary agreement and cooperation has been developed on the basis of two rival traditions: liberal individualism, and socialist communitarianism. Anarchism can thus be thought of as a point of intersection between liberalism and socialism: a form of both 'ultraliberalism' and 'ultrasocialism'.

The liberal case against the state is based on individualism, and the desire to maximize liberty and choice. Unlike liberals, individualist anarchists such as William Godwin (1756–1836) believed that free and rational human beings would be able to manage their affairs peacefully and spontaneously, government being merely a form of unwanted coercion. Modern individualists have usually looked to the market to explain how society would be regulated in the absence of state authority, developing a form of **anarcho-capitalism**, an extreme version of free-market economics. The more widely-recognized anarchist tradition, however, draws on socialist ideas such as community, cooperation, equality and common ownership. Collectivist anarchists (sometimes called social anarchists) stress the capacity for social solidarity that arises from our sociable, gregarious and essentially cooperative natures. On this basis, the French anarchist Pierre-Joseph Proudhon (see p. 381), for instance, developed what he called '**mutualism**'. Other anarchists, such as the Russian Peter Kropotkin (1842–1921), advanced a form of **anarcho-communism**, the central principles of which were common ownership, decentralization and workers' self-management. Modern thinkers influenced by anarchism include Noam Chomsky (see p. 181) and the US libertarian and social ecologist Murray Bookchin (1921–2006).

● **Anarcho-capitalism**: An ararchist tradition which holds that unregulated market competition can and should be applied to all social arrangements, making the state unnecessary.

● **Mutualism**: A system of fair and quitable exchange, in which individuals or groups trade goods and services with one another without profiteering or exploitation.

● **Anarcho-communism**: An anarchist tradition which takes common ownership to be the sole reliable basis for social solidarity, thereby linking statelessness to classlessness.

Feminism

Although feminist aspirations have been expressed in societies dating back to Ancient China, they were not underpinned by a developed political theory until the publication of Mary Wollstonecraft's (see p. 50) *A Vindication of the Rights of Women* ([1792] 1985). Indeed, it was not until the emergence of the women's suffrage movement in the 1840s and 1850s that feminist ideas reached a wider audience, in the form of so-called 'first-wave feminism'. The achievement of female suffrage in most western countries in the early twentieth century deprived the women's movement of its central goal and organizing principle. 'Second-wave feminism', however, emerged in the 1960s. This expressed the more radical, and sometimes revolutionary, demands of the growing Women's Liberation Movement (WLM). Feminist theories and doctrines are diverse, but their unifying feature is a common desire to enhance, through whatever means, the social role of women. The underlying themes of feminism are therefore, first, that society is characterized by sexual or gender inequality and, second, that this structure of male power can, and should be, overturned.

Feminist thinking has traditionally been analysed in terms of a division between liberal, socialist and radical schools of thought. **Liberal feminists**, such as Wollstonecraft and Betty Friedan (see p. 263), have tended to understand female subordination in terms of the unequal distribution of rights and opportunities in society. This 'equal-rights feminism' is essentially reformist. It is concerned more with the reform of the 'public' sphere; that is, with enhancing the legal and political status of women, and improving their educational and career prospects, than with reordering 'private' or domestic life. In contrast, **socialist feminists** typically highlight the links between female subordination and the capitalist mode of production, drawing attention to the economic significance of women being confined to a family or domestic life where they, for example, relieve male workers of the burden of domestic labour, rear and help to educate the next generation of capitalist workers, and act as a reserve army of labour.

However, the distinctive flavour of second-wave feminism results mainly from the emergence of a feminist critique that is not rooted in conventional political doctrines; namely, **radical feminism**. Radical feminists believe that gender divisions are the most fundamental and politically significant cleavages in society. In their view, all societies, historical and contemporary, are characterized by patriarchy (see p. 65), the institution whereby, as Kate Millett (1969) put it, 'that half of the population which is female is controlled by that half which is male'. Radical feminists therefore proclaim the need for a sexual revolution, a revolution that will, in particular, restructure personal, domestic and family life. The characteristic slogan of radical feminism is thus 'the personal is the political'. Only in its extreme form, however, does radical feminism portray men as 'the enemy', and proclaim the need for women to withdraw from male society, a stance sometimes expressed in the form of political lesbianism. However, since the 1970s feminism has, in many ways, moved beyond the threefold division into liberal, socialist and radical traditions. Although 'new feminism' or 'third-wave feminism' are disparate, they tend to be characterized by doubts about the conventional goal of gender equality, placing an emphasis

● **Liberal feminism**: A feminist tradition whose core goal is equal access for women and men to the public realm, based on a belief of genderless personhood.

● **Socialist feminism**: A feminist tradition that seeks to restructure economic life to achieve gender equality, based in links between patriarchy and capitalism.

● **Radical feminism**: A feminist tradition that aims to overthrow patriarchy through a radical transformation of all spheres of life, but especially 'the personal'.

Mary Wollstonecraft (1759–97)

UK social theorist and feminist. Deeply influenced by the democratic radicalism of Rousseau, Wollstonecraft developed the first systematic feminist critique some 50 years before the emergence of the female-suffrage movement. Her most important work, *A Vindication of the Rights of Women* ([1792] 1985), was influenced by Lockean liberalism, and it stressed the equal rights of women, especially the right to education, on the basis of the notion of 'personhood'. However, the work developed a more complex analysis of womanhood itself that is relevant to the concerns of contemporary feminism. Wollstonecraft was married to the anarchist William Godwin, and she was the mother of Mary Shelley, the author of *Frankenstein*.

instead on differences, both between women and men and between women themselves.

Green politics

Although green politics, or ecologism (see p. 51), is usually seen as a new ideology that is linked to the emergence of the environmental movement since the late twentieth century, its roots can be traced back to the nineteenth-century revolt against industrialization. Green politics therefore reflects concern about the damage done to the natural world by the increasing pace of economic development (exacerbated since the second half of the twentieth century by the advent of nuclear technology, acid rain, ozone depletion, global warming and so on), and anxiety about the declining quality of human existence and, ultimately, the survival of the human species. Such concerns are sometimes expressed through the vehicle of conventional ideologies. For instance, ecosocialism explains environmental destruction in terms of capitalism's rapacious desire for profit. Ecoconservatism links the cause of conservation to the desire to preserve traditional values and established institutions. And ecofeminism locates the origins of the ecological crisis in the system of male power, reflecting the fact that men are less sensitive than women to natural processes and the natural world.

However, what gives green politics its radical edge is the fact that it offers an alternative to the **anthropocentric**, or human-centred, stance adopted by all other ideologies; it does not see the natural world simply as a resource available to satisfy human needs. By highlighting the importance of ecology, green politics develops an ecocentric world-view that portrays the human species as merely part of nature. One of the most influential theories in this field is the Gaia hypothesis, advanced by James Lovelock (1979, 2006). This portrays the planet Earth as a living organism that is primarily concerned with its own survival. Others have expressed sympathy for such radical **holism** by drawing on the ideas of Eastern religions that emphasize the oneness of life, such as Taoism and Zen Buddhism (Capra, 1983). 'Shallow' or humanist ecologists, such as those in some environmental pressure groups, believe that an appeal to self-interest and common sense will persuade humankind to adopt ecologically sound policies and lifestyles, usually in line with the principle of sustainable development (see

● **Anthropocentrism:** The belief that human needs and interests are of overriding moral and philosophical importance; the opposite of ecocentrism.

● **Holism:** The belief that the whole is more imortant than its parts, implying that understanding is gained only by studying relationships among its parts.

CONCEPT

Ecologism

Ecology (a term first used by Ernst Haeckel in 1873) is the study of the relationship between living organisms and their environment. It thus draws attention to the network of relationships that sustain all forms of life. Ecologism is a political doctrine or ideology that is constructed on the basis of ecological assumptions, notably about the essential link between humankind and the natural world: humans are part of nature, not its 'masters'. Ecologism is sometimes distinguished from environmentalism, in that the former implies the adoption of a biocentric perspective, while the latter is concerned with protecting nature, ultimately for human benefit.

Figure 2.1   As ecologists argue, human-centredness poses a threat to both nature and, ultimately, human survival (Ferrybridge, UK).

p. 140). 'Deep' ecologists, on the other hand, insist that nothing short of a fundamental reordering of political priorities, and a willingness to place the interests of the ecosystem before those of any individual species, will ultimately secure planetary and human survival. Members of both groups can be found in the 'anti-party' green parties that have sprung up in Germany, Austria and elsewhere in Europe since the 1970s.

Cosmopolitanism

Although cosmopolitan ideas can be traced back to the Cynics of Ancient Greece and the Stoics of Ancient Rome, cosmopolitanism has only been treated as an ideological tradition in its own right since the 1990s. This occurred as the moral, political and cultural implications of growing global interconnectedness became increasingly apparent. In that sense, cosmopolitanism can be viewed as the ideological expression of globalization (although the relationship between the two is complex, cosmopolitans often calling for radical changes in the currently dominant forms of globalization). In a literal sense, cosmopolitanism means a belief in a *cosmopolis* or 'world state'. However, such 'political' cosmopolitanism, which is reflected in the quest to establish global political institutions, has limited relevance to modern cosmopolitan thinking, due to its association with the unfashionable idea of **world government**. Modern cosmopolitanism therefore tends to have a moral or cultural character.

'Moral' cosmopolitanism, the notion that underpins much anti-globalization activism, is the belief that the world constitutes a single moral community. This implies that people have obligations (potentially) towards all other people in the world, regardless of nationality, religion, ethnicity and so forth. Such ethical thinking is based on the core idea that the individual, rather than any political community, is the principal focus of moral concern. Most commonly, this is asserted through the doctrine of human rights (see p. 342). Nevertheless, moral cosmopolitanism has taken contrasting liberal and socialist forms.

● **World government**: The idea of all of humankind united under one common political authority, whether a unitary world state with supranational authority or a federal body that shares sovereignty with nation-states.

CONCEPT

Postcolonialism

Postcolonialism is a trend in literary, cultural and political studies that seeks to expose and overturn the cultural and psychological dimensions of colonial rule. As such, it recognizes that 'inner' subjugation can persist long after the political structures of colonialism have been removed. A major thrust of postcolonialism has been to establish the legitimacy of non-western, and sometimes anti-western, political ideas and traditions. Postcolonialism has nevertheless taken a variety of forms. These range from Gandhi's attempt to fuse Indian nationalism with ideas rooted in Hinduism to forms of religious fundamentalism.

Liberal cosmopolitanism has been expressed in two ways. The first is the attempt to universalize civic and political rights, especially classic 'liberal' rights such as the right to life, liberty and property, freedom of expression and freedom from arbitrary arrest. This form of cosmopolitanism has been associated with, amongst other things, support for humanitarian intervention (see p. 424) and attempts to strengthen the framework of international law, notably through international courts and tribunals. The second form of liberal cosmopolitanism derives from economic liberalism, and places particular stress on attempts to universalize market society, seen as a means of widening individual freedom and promoting material advancement. In marked contrast, socialist cosmopolitanism is rooted in the Marxist belief that proletarian class solidarity has a transnational character, graphically expressed in the famous final words of the *Communist Manifesto*: 'Working men of all countries, unite!' Modern versions of such thinking are, nevertheless, more likely to be based on the idea of economic and social rights, than on Marxist analysis. The key theme in this form of cosmopolitanism is the quest for global social justice, implying both a substantial redistribution of wealth from the global North to the global South and a radical reform of the system of global economic governance (discussed in Chapter 19).

Such thinking is often associated with 'cultural' cosmopolitanism, which highlights the extent to which people's values and lifestyles have been reconfigured as a result of intensified global interconnectedness. In this sense, political community is in the process of being redefined as people come to think of themselves as 'global citizens', rather than merely citizens of a particular state. The supposed evidence for this is the shift from nationalism to multiculturalism, or, at least, a form of multiculturalism that emphasizes hybridity and cultural mixing, or 'mongrelization' (Waldron, 1995). However, although cosmopolitanism has had a growing impact on ethical thinking, it has had only a limited impact in terms of cultural restructuring. Nationalism may be under growing pressure from forces both within and without, but (as discussed in Chapter 5) the nation remains the pre-eminent basis for political community, with no international body, including the European Union, coming close to rivalling its ability to foster affection and civic allegiance.

Non-western ideological trends

In origin, political ideology was a distinctively western construct. The major ideological traditions developed as contrasting attempts to shape emergent industrial society, their ideas and theories being indelibly shaped by historical experience in Europe and North America. Moreover, in the case of liberalism and socialism in particular, political ideology drew from an Enlightenment tradition that emphasized the ideas of reason and progress, and helped to shape wider intellectual and cultural developments in the West. As political ideology spread, it therefore exported to the rest of the world an essentially western model of modernity, or, more accurately, competing western models of modernity. Ideological trends such as 'Arab nationalism', 'African socialism' or 'Chinese communism' therefore amounted to attempts to apply western ideas in non-western contexts, although, at times, western doctrines were also entangled with indigenous values and ideas. As Julius Nyerere, president of Tanzania, 1964-85,

CONCEPT

Fundamentalism

Fundamentalism refers to a style of thought in which certain principles are recognized as essential 'truths' which have unchallengeable and overriding authority. Substantive fundamentalisms have little or nothing in common, except that their supporters tend to evince an earnestness or fervour born out of doctrinal certainty. Although it is usually associated with religion and the literal truth of sacred texts, fundamentalism can also be found in political creeds. The term is controversial because it is often used pejoratively, to imply inflexibility, dogmatism and authoritarianism.

pointed out, 'We, in Africa, have no more real need to be "converted" to socialism, than we have of being "taught" democracy'. He therefore described his own views as 'tribal socialism'.

Postcolonialism

Nevertheless, more explicit attempts to give political ideology a non-western identity emerged out of trends associated with postcolonialism (see p. 52). The characteristic feature of postcolonialism is that it sought to give the non-western world a distinctive political voice separate from, in particular, the universalist pretensions of liberalism and socialism. An early but influential attempt to do this was undertaken at the Bandung Conference of 1955, when 29 mostly newly-independent African and Asian countries, including Egypt, Ghana, India and Indonesia, initiated what later became known as the **Non-Aligned Movement**. They saw themselves as an independent power bloc, offering a 'Third World' perspective on global political, economic and cultural priorities. This 'third-worldism' defined itself in contradistinction to both western and Soviet models of development.

However, postcolonial ideological trends have been highly disparate. They have been reflected in Gandhi's (see p. 54) political philosophy, which was based on a religious ethic of non-violence and self-sacrifice that was ultimately rooted in Hinduism. In this view, violence, 'the doctrine of the sword', was a western imposition on India. In contrast, the Martinique-born French revolutionary theorist Franz Fanon (1926–61) highlighted the extent to which colonial rule operates at a psycho-political level through the asymmetrical relationship between 'whites' and 'blacks', and that this could only be destroyed through the purifying force of 'absolute violence' (Fanon, 1968).

Religious fundamentalism

Postcolonialism has, nevertheless, been expressed most forcibly through the upsurge, especially since the late 1970s, in religious fundamentalism and, most importantly, Islamic fundamentalism, or political Islam. The idea that an intense and militant faith that Islamic beliefs constitute the overriding principles of social life and politics first emerged in the writings of thinkers such as Sayyid Qutb (1906–66) and through the activities of the Muslim Brotherhood. Their goal was the establishment of an Islamic state based on the principles of *shari'a* law. Political Islam was brought to prominence by the Iranian revolution of 1979, which led to the founding of the world's first Islamic state, under Ayatollah Khomeini (see p. 164). It subsequently spread throughout the Middle East, across North Africa, and into parts of Asia. Although the Shi'a fundamentalism of Iran has generated the fiercest commitment and devotion, Islamism (see p. 165) in general has been a vehicle for expressing anti-westernism, reflecting both antipathy towards the neo-colonial policies of western powers and anxiety about the 'imposition' of permissive and materialist values. This was clearly reflected in the Taliban regime of Afghanistan (1997–2001), and also in the growth of **jihadist** groups such as al-Qaeda, for whom the spiritual quest became synonymous with militant politics, armed struggle and possibly martyrdom.

● **Non-Aligned Movement:** An organization of countries, founded in Belgrade in 1961, that sought to avoid formal political and economic affiliation with either the capitalist West or the communist East.

● *Jihad*: (Arabic) Conventionally translated as 'holy war' but, more correctly, as 'holy struggle' or 'effort'; intense and all-consuming devotion to Islamic goals.

Mohandas Karamchand Gandhi (1869–1948)

An Indian spiritual and political leader (called *Mahatma*, 'Great Soul'), Gandhi trained as a lawyer in the UK and worked in South Africa, where he organized protests against discrimination. After returning to India in 1915, he became the leader of the nationalist movement, campaigning tirelessly for independence, finally achieved in 1947. Gandhi's ethic of non-violent resistance, *satyagraha*, reinforced by his ascetic lifestyle, gave the movement for Indian independence enormous moral authority. Derived from Hinduism, Gandhi's political philosophy was based on the assumption that the universe is regulated by the primacy of truth, or *satya*, and that humankind is 'ultimately one'. Gandhi was assassinated in 1948 by a fanatical Hindu, becoming a victim of the ferocious Hindu-Muslim violence which followed independence.

Asian values

Other non-western ideological trends have had no connection with fundamentalist religion, however. During the 1980s and 1990s, for example, the idea of so-called **'Asian values'** gained growing currency, fuelled by the emergence of Japan as an economic superpower and the success of the 'tiger' economies of Hong Kong, South Korea, Thailand and Singapore. While not rejecting the idea of universal human rights, Asian values drew attention to supposed differences between western and Asian value systems, highlighting the extent to which human rights had traditionally been constructed on the basis of culturally-biased western assumptions. Asian values had sought to rectify this by offering a vision of social harmony and cooperation grounded in loyalty, duty and respect for authority. Although their influence declined markedly following the 1997–98 Asian financial crisis, they have resurfaced through their association with Confucianism (see p. 278), bolstered by the rise of China.

Beyond dualism

An alternative non-western ideological trend has contrasted the non-dualistic emphasis found in some non-western philosophical traditions with the resolute **dualism** of conventional western philosophy. Aristotle's (see p. 6) insistence that everything has a distinctive essence that it cannot lack, expressed through the idea that 'everything must either be or not be', can thus be contrasted with the Buddhist philosopher Nagarjuna's (*ca.* 150–250 CE) doctrine of *sunyata* or 'emptiness'. According to this, all concepts and objects lack 'own-being', highlighting intrinsic interdependence. Such thinking, often influenced by Buddhism or Taoism, was also been expressed by Kyoto School philosophers in Japan such as Nishada Kitaro (1870–1945), who asserted that the world is characterized by the 'absolute unity of opposites'. If western 'either/or' thinking is set aside in favour of a world-view that stresses integration and oneness, all other forms of dualism – mind/body, good/evil, subject/object, humankind/nature and so on – begin to collapse. Non-dualistic thinking has had its greatest ideological impact in relation to green politics, where it provides the philosophical foundation for many forms of deep ecology.

● **Asian values**: Values that supposedly reflect the history, culture and religious backgrounds of Asian societies; examples include social harmony, respect for authority and a belief in the family.

● **Dualism**: The belief that reality consists of two basic principles, often taken to be mind and matter but it may extend to other dualities.

SUMMARY

● Ideology is a controversial political term that has often carried pejorative implications. In the social-scientific sense, a political ideology is a more or less coherent set of ideas that provides a basis for organized political action. Its central features are an account of existing power relationships, a model of a desired future, and an outline of how political change can and should be brought about.

● Ideologies link political theory with political practice. On one level, ideologies resemble political philosophies, in that they constitute a collection of values, theories and doctrines; that is, a distinctive world-view. On another level, however, they take the form of broad political movements, and are articulated through the activities of political leaders, parties and groups.

● Every ideology can be associated with a characteristic set of principles and ideas. Although these ideas 'hang together', in the sense that they interlock in distinctive ways, they are systematic or coherent only in a relative sense. All ideologies thus embody a range of rival traditions and internal tensions. Conflict within ideologies is thus sometimes more passionate than that between ideologies.

● Ideologies are by no means hermetically sealed and unchanging systems of thought. They overlap with one another at a number of points, and they sometimes have shared concerns and a common vocabulary. They are also always subject to political or intellectual renewal, both because they interact with, and influence the development of, other ideologies, and because they change over time as they are applied to changing historical circumstances.

● The significance of particular ideologies rises and falls in relation to the ideology's relevance to political, social and economic circumstances, and its capacity for theoretical innovation. Development during the twentieth century and beyond have forced major ideologies such as liberalism, conservatism and socialism to re-examine their traditional principles. Since around the 1960s, the ideological landscape has been transformed by the emergence of so-called 'new' ideologies, such as feminism, green politics and cosmopolitanism, and by a growing recognition of the ideological significance of a range of non-western ideas and theories.

Questions for discussion

● Why has the concept of ideology so often carried negative associations?

● Is it any longer possible to distinguish between liberalism and socialism?

● To what extent do New Right ideas conflict with those of traditional conservatism?

● Is 'new' social democracy a meaningful and coherent ideological stance?

● Has Marxism a future?

● What circumstances are most conducive to the rise of fascism?

● Do anarchists demand the impossible?

● Why have feminism, green politics and comopolitanism grown in significance?

● To what extent do non-western ideological trends challenge western ideologies?

Further reading

Freedman, M., *Ideology: A Very Short Introduction* (2003). A brief (as promised) but authoritative guide to the nature of ideology and its place in the modern world.

Heywood, A., *Political Ideologies: An Introduction* (5th edn) (2012). An accessible, up-to-date and comprehensive guide to the major ideological traditions.

Good introductions to particular ideologies include the following: Arblaster (1984) on liberalism, O'Sullivan (1976) on conservatism, Wright (1987) on socialism, Giddens (2001) on the 'third way', Marshall (1991) on anarchism, Laqueur (1979) on fascism, Bryson (2003) on feminism, Dobson (1990) on green politics, Appiah (2007) on cosmopolitanism, and Marty and Appleby (1993) on religious fundamentalism.

CHAPTER 3

Politics and the State

'The purpose of the State is always the same: to limit the individual, to tame him, to subordinate him, to subjugate him.'

MAX STIRNER, *The Ego and His Own* (1845)

PREVIEW   The shadow of the state falls on almost every human activity. From education to economic management, from social welfare to sanitation, and from domestic order to external defence, the state shapes and controls; where it does not shape or control it regulates, supervises, authorizes or proscribes. Even those aspects of life usually thought of as personal or private (marriage, divorce, abortion, religious worship and so on) are ultimately subject to the authority of the state. It is not surprising, therefore, that politics is often understood as the study of the state, the analysis of its institutional organizations, the evaluation of its impact on society and so on. Ideological debate and party politics, certainly, tend to revolve around the issue of the proper function or role of the state: what should be done by the state and what should be left to private individuals and associations? The nature of state power has thus become one of the central concerns of political analysis. This chapter examines the feature that are usually associated with the state, from both a domestic and an international perspective. It considers the issue of the nature of state power, and, in the process, touches on some of the deepest and most abiding divisions in political theory. This leads to a discussion of the contrasting roles and responsibilities of the state and the different forms that states have assumed. Finally, it looks whether, in the light of globalization and other developments, the state is losing its central importance in politics.

KEY ISSUES

- What is the state, and why does it play such a crucial role in politics?
- How has state power been analysed and explained?
- Is the state a force for good or a force for evil?
- What roles have been assigned to the state? How have responsibilities been apportioned between the state and civil society?
- To what extent does politics now operate outside or beyond the state?

POLITICS AND THE STATE

The state is a political

CONCEPT

The state

The state is a political association that establishes sovereign jurisdiction within defined territorial borders, and exercises authority through a set of permanent institutions. These institutions are those that are recognizably 'public', in that they are responsible for the collective organization of communal life, and are funded at the public's expense. The state thus embraces the various institutions of government, but it also extends to the courts, nationalized industries, social security system, and so forth; it can be identified with the entire 'body politic'.

● **Idealism**: A view of politics that emphasizes the importance of morality and ideals; philosophical idealism implies that ideas are more 'real' than the material world.

● **Civil society**: A private sphere of autonomous groups and associations, independent from state or public authority (see p. 6).

DEFINING THE STATE

The term 'state' has been used to refer to a bewildering range of things: a collection of institutions, a territorial unit, a philosophical idea, an instrument of coercion or oppression, and so on. This confusion stems, in part, from the fact that the state has been understood in four quite different ways; from an **idealist** perspective, a functionalist perspective, an organizational perspective and an international perspective. The *idealist* approach to the state is most clearly reflected in the writings of G. W. F. Hegel (see p. 59). Hegel identified three 'moments' of social existence: the family, civil society and the state. Within the family, he argued, a 'particular altruism' operates that encourages people to set aside their own interests for the good of their children or elderly relatives. In contrast, civil society was seen as a sphere of 'universal egoism' in which individuals place their own interests before those of others. Hegel conceived of the state as an ethical community underpinned by mutual sympathy – 'universal altruism'. The drawback of idealism, however, is that it fosters an uncritical reverence for the state and, by defining the state in ethical terms, fails to distinguish clearly between institutions that are part of the state and those that are outside the state.

Functionalist approaches to the state focus on the role or purpose of state institutions. The central function of the state is invariably seen as the maintenance of social order (see p. 400), the state being defined as that set of institutions that uphold order and deliver social stability. Such an approach has, for example, been adopted by neo-Marxists (see p. 64), who have been inclined to see the state as a mechanism through which class conflict is ameliorated to ensure the long-term survival of the capitalist system. The weakness of the functionalist view of the state, however, is that it tends to associate *any* institution that maintains order (such as the family, mass media, trade unions and the church) with the state itself. This is why, unless there is a statement to the contrary, an organizational approach to the definition of the state is adopted throughout this book

The *organizational* view defines the state as the apparatus of government in its broadest sense; that is, as that set of institutions that are recognizably 'public', in that they are responsible for the collective organization of social existence and are funded at the public's expense. The virtue of this definition is that it distinguishes clearly between the state and **civil society** (see p. 6). The state comprises the various institutions of government: the bureaucracy (see p. 361), the military, the police, the courts, the social security system and so on; it can be identified with the entire 'body politic'. The organizational approach allows us to talk about 'rolling forward' or 'rolling back' the state, in the sense of expanding or contracting the responsibilities of the state, and enlarging or diminishing its institutional machinery.

In this light, it is possible to identify five key features of the state:

● The state is *sovereign*. It exercises absolute and unrestricted power, in that it stands above all other associations and groups in society. Thomas Hobbes (see p. 61) conveyed the idea of sovereignty (see p. 58) by portraying the state as a 'leviathan', a gigantic monster, usually represented as a sea creature.
● State institutions are recognizably '*public*', in contrast to the 'private' institutions of civil society. Public bodies are responsible for making and

CONCEPT

Sovereignty

Sovereignty, in its simplest sense, is the principle of absolute and unlimited power. However, sovereignty can be understood in different ways. *Legal* sovereignty refers to supreme legal authority, defined in terms of the 'right' to command compliance, while *political* sovereignty refers to absolute political power, defined in terms of the 'ability' to command compliance. *Internal* sovereignty is the notion of supreme power/authority within the state (e.g. parliamentary sovereignty: see p. 336). *External* sovereignty relates to a state's place in the international order and its capacity to act as an independent and autonomous entity.

enforcing collective decisions, while private bodies, such as families, private businesses and trade unions, exist to satisfy individual interests.

- The state is an exercise in *legitimation*. The decisions of the state are usually (although not necessarily) accepted as binding on the members of society because, it is claimed, they are made in the public interest, or for common good; the state supposedly reflects the permanent interests of society.
- The state is an instrument of *domination*. State authority is backed up by coercion; the state must have the capacity to ensure that its laws are obeyed and that transgressors are punished. For Max Weber (see p. 82), the state was defined by its monopoly of the means of 'legitimate violence'.
- The state is a *territorial* association. The jurisdiction of the state is geographically defined, and it encompasses all those who live within the state's borders, whether they are citizens or non-citizens. On the international stage, the state is therefore regarded (at least, in theory) as an autonomous entity.

The *international* approach to the state views it primarily as an actor on the world stage; indeed, as the basic 'unit' of international politics. This highlights the dualistic structure of the state; the fact that it has two faces, one looking outwards and the other looking inwards. Whereas the previous definitions are concerned with the state's inward-looking face, its relations with the individuals and groups that live within its borders, and its ability to maintain domestic order, the international view deals with the state's outward-looking face, its relations with other states and, therefore, its ability to provide protection against external attack. The classic definition of the state in international law is found in the Montevideo Convention on the Rights and Duties of the State (1933). According to Article 1 of the Montevideo Convention, the state has four features:

- a defined territory
- a permanent population
- an effective government
- the capacity to enter into relations with other states.

This approach to the state brings it very close to the notion of a 'country'. The main difference between how the state is understood by political philosophers and sociologists, and how it is understood by IR scholars is that while the former treat civil society as *separate from* the state, the latter treat civil society as *part of* the state, in that it encompasses not only an effective government, but also a permanent population. For some, the international approach views the state essentially as a legal person, in which case statehood depends on formal recognition by other states or international bodies. In this view, the United Nations (UN) is widely accepted as the body that, by granting full membership, determines when a new state has come into existence. Nevertheless, while, from this perspective, states may be legally equal, they are in political terms very different. Although their rights and responsibilities as laid out in international law may be identical, their political weight in world affairs varies dramatically. Some states are classified as '**great powers**', or even 'superpowers' (see p. 422), whereas others are 'middle' or 'small' powers and, in cases such as the small highland countries of the Caribbean and the Pacific, they may be regarded as 'micro-states'.

- **Great power**: A state deemed to rank amongst the most powerful in a hierarchical state system, reflecting its influence over minor states.

Georg Wilhelm Friedrich Hegel (1770–1831)

German philosopher. Hegel was the founder of modern idealism and developed the notion that consciousness and material objects are, in fact, unified. In *Phenomenology of Spirit* (1807), he sought to develop a rational system that would substitute for traditional Christianity by interpreting the entire process of human history, and indeed the universe itself, in terms of the progress of absolute Mind towards self-realization. In his view, history is, in essence, a march of the human spirit towards a determinate endpoint. His major political work, *Philosophy of Right* (1821), portrays the state as an ethical ideal and the highest expression of human freedom. Hegel's work had a considerable impact on Marx and other so-called 'young Hegelians'. It also shaped the ideas of liberals such as T. H. Green (1836–82), and influenced fascist thought.

Regardless of the different ways in which the state has been understood, there is general agreement about when and where it emerged. The state is a historical institution: it emerged in sixteenth- and seventeenth-century Europe as a system of centralized rule that succeeded in subordinating all other institutions and groups, including (and especially) the Church, bringing an end to the competing and overlapping authority systems that had characterized Medieval Europe. By establishing the principle of territorial sovereignty, the Peace of Westphalia (1648), concluded at the end of the Thirty Years' War, is often taken to have formalized the modern notion of statehood, by establishing the state as the principal actor in domestic and international affairs. There is less agreement, however, about why the state came into existence. According to Charles Tilly (1990), for instance, the central factor that explains the development of the modern state was its ability to fight wars. In this view, the transformation in the scale and nature of military encounters that was brought about from the sixteenth century onwards (through, for instance, the introduction of gun powder, the use of organized infantry and artillery, and the advent of standing armies) not only greatly increased the coercive power that rulers could wield, but also forced states to extend their control over their populations by developing more extensive systems of taxation and administration. As Tilly (1975) thus put it, 'War made the state, and the state made war'. Marxists, in contrast, have explained the emergence of the state largely in economic terms, the state's origins being traced back to the transition from feudalism to capitalism, with the state essentially being a tool used by the emerging bourgeois class (Engels, [1884] 1972). Michael Mann (1993), for his part, offered an account of the emergence of the state that stresses the state's capacity to combine ideological, economic, military and political forms of power (sometimes called the 'IEMP model').

The state nevertheless continued to evolve in the light of changing circumstances. Having developed into the **nation-state** during the nineteenth century, and then going through a process of gradual democratization, the state acquired wider economic and social responsibilities during the twentieth century, and especially in the post-1945 period, only for these, in many cases, to be 'rolled back' from the 1980s and 1990s. The European state model, furthermore, spread

● **Nation-state**: A sovereign political association within which citizenship and nationality overlap; one nation within a single state (see p. 124).

to other lands and other continents. This occurred as the process of decolonization accelerated in the decades following World War II, independence implying the achievement of sovereign statehood. One result of this process was a rapid growth in UN membership. From its original 51 member states in 1945, the UN grew to 127 members by 1970, and reached 193 members by 2011 (with the recognition of South Sudan). The state has therefore become the universal form of political organization around the world. However, in order to assess the significance of the state, and explore its vital relationship to politics, two key issues have to be addressed. These deal with the nature of state power and with the roles and responsibilities the state has assumed and should assume.

DEBATING THE STATE

Rival theories of the state

What is the nature of state power, and whose interests does the state represent? From this perspective, the state is an 'essentially contested' concept. There are various rival theories of the state, each of which offers a different account of its origins, development and impact on society. Indeed, controversy about the nature of state power has increasingly dominated modern political analysis and goes to the heart of ideological and theoretical disagreements in the discipline. These relate to questions about whether, for example, the state is autonomous and independent of society, or whether it is essentially a product of society, a reflection of the broader distribution of power or resources. Moreover, does the state serve the common or collective good, or is it biased in favour of privileged groups or a dominant class? Similarly, is the state a positive or constructive force, with responsibilities that should be enlarged, or is it a negative or destructive entity that must be constrained or, perhaps, smashed altogether? Four contrasting theories of the state can be identified as follows:

- the pluralist state
- the capitalist state
- the leviathan state
- the patriarchal state.

The pluralist state

The **pluralist** theory of the state has a very clear liberal lineage. It stems from the belief that the state acts as an 'umpire' or 'referee' in society. This view has also dominated mainstream political analysis, accounting for a tendency, at least within Anglo-American thought, to discount the state and state organizations and focus instead on 'government'. Indeed, it is not uncommon in this tradition for 'the state' to be dismissed as an abstraction, with institutions such as the courts, the civil service and the military being seen as independent actors in their own right, rather than as elements of a broader state machine. Nevertheless, this approach is possible only because it is based on underlying, and often unacknowledged, assumptions about state neutrality. The state can be ignored only because it is seen as an impartial arbiter or referee that can be bent to the will of the government of the day.

● **Pluralism**: A belief in, or commitment to diversity or multiplicity; or the belief that power in modern societies is widely and evenly distributed (see p. 100).

Thomas Hobbes (1588–1679)

English political philosopher. Hobbes was the son of a minor clergyman who subsequently abandoned his family. He became tutor to the exiled Prince of Wales Charles Stewart, and lived under the patronage of the Cavendish family. Writing at a time of uncertainty and civil strife, precipitated by the English Revolution, Hobbes developed the first comprehensive theory of nature and human behaviour since Aristotle (see p. 6). His classic work, *Leviathan* (1651), discussed the grounds of political obligation and undoubtedly reflected the impact of the Civil War. It provided a defence for absolutist government but, by appealing to reasoned argument in the form of the social contract, also disappointed advocates of **divine right**.

● **Divine right**: The doctrine that earthly rulers are chosen by God and thus wield unchallengeable authority; a defence for monarchical absolutism.

● **Political obligation**: The duty of the citizen towards the state; the basis of the state's right to rule.

● **State of nature**: A society devoid of political authority and of formal (legal) checks on the individual; usually employed as a theoretical device.

● **Anarchy**: Literally, 'without rule'; anarchy is often used pejoratively to suggest instability, or even chaos.

The origins of this view of the state can be traced back to the social-contract theories (see p. 62) of thinkers such as Thomas Hobbes and John Locke (see p. 31). The principal concern of such thinkers was to examine the grounds of **political obligation**, the grounds on which the individual is obliged to obey and respect the state. They argued that the state had arisen out of a voluntary agreement, or social contract, made by individuals who recognized that only the establishment of a sovereign power could safeguard them from the insecurity, disorder and brutality of the **state of nature**. Without a state, individuals abuse, exploit and enslave one another; with a state, order and civilized existence are guaranteed and liberty is protected. As Locke put it, 'where there is no law there is no freedom'.

In liberal theory, the state is thus seen as a neutral arbiter amongst the competing groups and individuals in society; it is an 'umpire' or 'referee' that is capable of protecting each citizen from the encroachments of fellow citizens. The neutrality of the state reflects the fact that the state acts in the interests of *all* citizens, and therefore represents the common good or public interest. In Hobbes' view, stability and order could be secured only through the establishment of an absolute and unlimited state, with power that could be neither challenged, nor questioned. In other words, he held that citizens are confronted by a stark choice between absolutism (see p. 268) and **anarchy**. Locke, on the other hand, developed a more typically liberal defence of the limited state. In his view, the purpose of the state is very specific: it is restricted to the defence of a set of 'natural' or God-given individual rights; namely, 'life, liberty and property'. This establishes a clear distinction between the responsibilities of the state (essentially, the maintenance of domestic order and the protection of property) and the responsibilities of individual citizens (usually seen as the realm of civil society). Moreover, since the state may threaten natural rights as easily as it may uphold them, citizens must enjoy some form of protection against the state, which Locke believed could be delivered only through the mechanisms of constitutional and representative government.

These ideas were developed in the twentieth century into the pluralist theory of the state. As a theory of society, pluralism asserts that, within liberal democracies, power is widely and evenly dispersed. As a theory of the state, pluralism holds that the state is neutral, insofar as it is susceptible to the influence of

Focus on . . .

Social-contract theory

A social contract is a voluntary agreement made amongst individuals through which an organized society, or state, is brought into existence. Used as a theoretical device by thinkers such as Hobbes, Locke and Rousseau (see p. 97), the social contract has been revived by modern theorists such as John Rawls (see p. 45). The social contract is seldom regarded as a historical act. Rather, it is used as a means of demonstrating the value of government and the grounds of political obligation; social-contract theorists wish individuals to act as if they had concluded the contract themselves. In its classic form, social-contract theory has three elements:

- The image of a hypothetical stateless society (a 'state of nature') is established. Unconstrained freedom means that life is 'solitary, poor, nasty, brutish and short' (Hobbes).
- Individuals therefore seek to escape from the state of nature by entering into a social contract, recognizing that only a sovereign power can secure order and stability.
- The social contract obliges citizens to respect and obey the state, ultimately in gratitude for the stability and security that only a system of political rule can deliver.

various groups and interests, and all social classes. The state is not biased in favour of any particular interest or group, and it does not have an interest of its own that is separate from those of society. As Schwarzmantel (1994) put it, the state is 'the servant of society and not its master'. The state can thus be portrayed as a 'pincushion' that passively absorbs pressures and forces exerted upon it. Two key assumptions underlie this view. The first is that the state is effectively subordinate to government. Non-elected state bodies (the civil service, the judiciary, the police, the military and so on) are strictly impartial and are subject to the authority of their political masters. The state apparatus is therefore thought to conform to the principles of public service and political accountability. The second assumption is that the democratic process is meaningful and effective. In other words, party competition and interest-group activity ensure that the government of the day remains sensitive and responsive to public opinion. Ultimately, therefore, the state is only a weather vane that is blown in whichever direction the public-at-large dictates.

Modern pluralists, however, have often adopted a more critical view of the state, termed the neopluralist (see p. 63) theory of the state. Theorists such as Robert Dahl (see p. 250), Charles Lindblom and J. K. Galbraith (see p. 155) have come to accept that modern industrialized states are both more complex and less responsive to popular pressures than classical pluralism suggested. Neopluralists, for instance, have acknowledged that business enjoys a 'privileged position' in relation to government that other groups clearly cannot rival. In *Politics and Markets* (1980), Lindblom pointed out that, as the major investor and largest employer in society, business is bound to exercise considerable sway over any government, whatever its ideological leanings or manifesto commitments. Moreover, neopluralists have accepted that the state can, and does, forge its own sectional interests. In this way, a state elite, composed of senior civil servants,

Neopluralism

Neopluralism is a style of social theorizing that remains faithful to pluralist values while recognizing the need to revise or update classical pluralism in the light of, for example, elite, Marxist and New Right theories. Although neopluralism embraces a broad range of perspectives and positions, certain central themes can be identified. First, it takes account of modernizing trends, such as the emergence of postindustrial society. Second, while capitalism is preferred to socialism, free-market economic doctrines are usually regarded as obsolete. Third, western democracies are seen as 'deformed polyarchies', in which major corporations exert disproportionate influence.

● **Bourgeoisie**: A Marxist term, denoting the ruling class of a capitalist society, the owners of productive wealth.

judges, police chiefs, military leaders and so on, may be seen to pursue either the bureaucratic interests of their sector of the state, or the interests of client groups. Indeed, if the state is regarded as a political actor in its own right, it can be viewed as a powerful (perhaps the most powerful) interest group in society. This line of argument encouraged Eric Nordlinger (1981) to develop a state-centred model of liberal democracy, based on 'the autonomy of the democratic state'.

The capitalist state

The Marxist notion of a capitalist state offers a clear alternative to the pluralist image of the state as a neutral arbiter or umpire. Marxists have typically argued that the state cannot be understood separately from the economic structure of society. This view has usually been understood in terms of the classic formulation that the state is nothing but an instrument of class oppression: the state emerges out of, and in a sense reflects, the class system. Nevertheless, a rich debate has taken place within Marxist theory in recent years that has moved the Marxist theory of the state a long way from this classic formulation. In many ways, the scope to revise Marxist attitudes towards the state stems from ambiguities that can be found in Marx's (see p. 41) own writings.

Marx did not develop a systematic or coherent theory of the state. In a general sense, he believed that the state is part of a 'superstructure' that is determined or conditioned by the economic 'base', which can be seen as the real foundation of social life. However, the precise relationship between the base and the superstructure, and in this case that between the state and the capitalist mode of production, is unclear. Two theories of the state can be identified in Marx's writings. The first is expressed in his often-quoted dictum from *The Communist Manifesto* ([1848] 1967): 'The executive of the modern state is but a committee for managing the common affairs of the whole bourgeoisie'. From this perspective, the state is clearly dependent on society and entirely dependent on its economically dominant class, which in capitalism is the **bourgeoisie**. Lenin (see p. 99) thus described the state starkly as 'an instrument for the oppression of the exploited class'.

A second, more complex and subtle, theory of the state can nevertheless be found in Marx's analysis of the revolutionary events in France between 1848 and 1851, *The Eighteenth Brumaire of Louis Bonaparte* ([1852] 1963). Marx suggested that the state could enjoy what has come to be seen as 'relative autonomy' from the class system, the Napoleonic state being capable of imposing its will upon society, acting as an 'appalling parasitic body'. If the state did articulate the interests of any class, it was not those of the bourgeoisie, but those of the most populous class in French society, the smallholding peasantry. Although Marx did not develop this view in detail, it is clear that, from this perspective, the autonomy of the state is only *relative*, in that the state appears to mediate between conflicting classes, and so maintains the class system itself in existence.

Both these theories differ markedly from the liberal and, later, pluralist models of state power. In particular, they emphasize that the state cannot be understood except in a context of unequal class power, and that the state arises out of, and reflects, capitalist society, by acting either as an instrument of oppression wielded by the dominant class, or, more subtly, as a mechanism through which class antagonisms are ameliorated. Nevertheless, Marx's attitude towards

CONCEPT

Neo-Marxism

Neo-Marxism (sometimes termed 'modern' or 'western' Marxism) refers to attempts to revise or recast the classical ideas of Marx while remaining faithful to certain Marxist principles or aspects of Marxist methodology. Neo-Marxists typically refuse to accept that Marxism enjoys a monopoly of the truth, and have thus looked to Hegelian philosophy, anarchism, liberalism, feminism, and even rational-choice theory. Although still concerned about social injustice, neo-Marxists reject the primacy of economics over other factors and, with it, the notion that history has a predictable character.

the state was not entirely negative. He argued that the state could be used constructively during the transition from capitalism to communism in the form of the 'revolutionary dictatorship of the **proletariat**'. The overthrow of capitalism would see the destruction of the bourgeois state and the creation of an alternative, proletarian one.

In describing the state as a proletarian 'dictatorship', Marx utilized the first theory of the state, seeing the state as an instrument through which the economically dominant class (by then, the proletariat) could repress and subdue other classes. All states, from this perspective, are class dictatorships. The 'dictatorship of the proletariat' was seen as a means of safeguarding the gains of the revolution by preventing counter-revolution mounted by the dispossessed bourgeoisie. Nevertheless, Marx did not see the state as a necessary or enduring social formation. He predicted that, as class antagonisms faded, the state would 'wither away', meaning that a fully communist society would also be stateless. Since the state emerged out of the class system, once the class system had been abolished, the state, quite simply, loses its reason for existence.

Marx's ambivalent heritage has provided modern Marxists, or neo-Marxists, with considerable scope to further the analysis of state power. This was also encouraged by the writings of Antonio Gramsci (see p. 175), who emphasized the degree to which the domination of the ruling class is achieved by ideological manipulation, rather than just open coercion. In this view, bourgeois domination is maintained largely through 'hegemony' (see p. 174): that is, intellectual leadership or cultural control, with the state playing an important role in the process.

Since the 1960s, Marxist theorizing about the state has been dominated by rival instrumentalist and structuralist views of the state. In *The State in Capitalist Society* ([1969] 2009), Miliband portrayed the state as an agent or *instrument* of the ruling class, stressing the extent to which the state elite is disproportionately drawn from the ranks of the privileged and propertied. The bias of the state in favour of capitalism is therefore derived from the overlap of social backgrounds between, on the one hand, civil servants and other public officials, and, on the other, bankers, business leaders and captains of industry. Nicos Poulantzas, in *Political Power and Social Classes* (1968), dismissed this sociological approach, and emphasized instead the degree to which the *structure* of economic and social power exerts a constraint on state autonomy. This view suggests that the state cannot but act to perpetuate the social system in which it operates. In the case of the capitalist state, its role is to serve the long-term interests of capitalism, even though these actions may be resisted by sections of the capitalist class itself. Neo-Marxists have increasingly seen the state as the terrain on which the struggle amongst interests, groups and classes is conducted. Rather than being an 'instrument' wielded by a dominant group or ruling class, the state is thus a dynamic entity that reflects the balance of power within society at any given time, and the ongoing struggle for hegemony.

The leviathan state

The image of the state as a 'leviathan' (in effect, a self-serving monster intent on expansion and aggrandizement) is one associated in modern politics with the New Right. Such a view is rooted in early or classical liberalism and, in particular,

● **Proletariat**: A Marxist term, denoting a class that subsists through the sale of its labour power; strictly speaking, the proletariat is not equivalent to the working class.

Patriarchy

Patriarchy literally means 'rule by the father', the domination of the husband–father within the family, and the subordination of his wife and his children. However, the term is usually used in the more general sense of 'rule by men', drawing attention to the totality of oppression and exploitation to which women are subject. Patriarchy thus implies that the system of male power in society at large both reflects and stems from the dominance of the father in the family. Patriarchy is a key concept in radical feminist analysis, in that it emphasizes that gender inequality is systematic, institutionalized and pervasive.

a commitment to a radical form of individualism (see p. 158). The New Right, or at least its neoliberal wing, is distinguished by a strong antipathy towards state intervention in economic and social life, born out of the belief that the state is a parasitic growth that threatens both individual liberty and economic security. In this view, the state, instead of being, as pluralists suggest, an impartial umpire or arbiter, is an overbearing 'nanny', desperate to interfere or meddle in every aspect of human existence. The central feature of this view is that the state pursues interests that are separate from those of society (setting it apart from Marxism), and that those interests demand an unrelenting growth in the role or responsibilities of the state itself. New Right thinkers therefore argue that the twentieth-century tendency towards state intervention reflected not popular pressure for economic and social security, or the need to stabilize capitalism by ameliorating class tensions but, rather, the internal dynamics of the state.

New Right theorists explain the expansionist dynamics of state power by reference to both demand-side and supply-side pressures. Demand-side pressures are those that emanate from society itself, usually through the mechanism of electoral democracy. As discussed in Chapter 4 in connection with democracy, the New Right argue that electoral competition encourages politicians to 'outbid' one another by making promises of increased spending and more generous government programmes, regardless of the long-term damage that such policies inflict on the economy in the form of increased taxes, higher inflation and the 'crowding out' of investment. Supply-side pressures, on the other hand, are those that are internal to the state. These can therefore be explained in terms of the institutions and personnel of the state apparatus. In its most influential form, this argument is known as the 'government oversupply thesis'.

The oversupply thesis has usually been associated with public-choice theorists (see p. 252), who examine how public decisions are made on the assumption that the individuals involved act in a rationally self-interested fashion. Niskanen (1971), for example, argued that, as budgetary control in legislatures such as the US Congress is typically weak, the task of budget-making is shaped largely by the interests of government agencies and senior bureaucrats. Insofar as this implies that government is dominated by the state (the state elite being able to shape the thinking of elected politicians), there are parallels between the public-choice model and the Marxist view discussed above. Where these two views diverge, however, is in relation to the interests that the state apparatus serves. While Marxists argue that the state reflects broader class and other social interests, the New Right portrays the state as an independent or autonomous entity that pursues its own interests. In this view, bureaucratic self-interest invariably supports 'big' government and state intervention, because this leads to an enlargement of the bureaucracy itself, which helps to ensure job security, improve pay, open up promotion prospects and enhance the status of public officials. This image of self-seeking bureaucrats is plainly at odds with the pluralist notion of a state machine imbued with an ethic of public service and firmly subject to political control.

The patriarchal state

Modern thinking about the state must, finally, take account of the implications of feminist theory. However, this is not to say that there is a systematic feminist theory of the state. As emphasized in Chapter 2, feminist theory encompasses a range of traditions and perspectives, and has thus generated a range of very different attitudes towards state power. Moreover, feminists have usually not regarded the nature of state power as a central political issue, preferring instead to concentrate on the deeper structure of male power centred on institutions such as the family and the economic system. Some feminists, indeed, may question conventional definitions of the state, arguing, for instance, that the idea that the state exercises a monopoly of legitimate violence is compromised by the routine use of violence and intimidation in family and domestic life. Nevertheless, sometimes implicitly and sometimes explicitly, feminists have helped to enrich the state debate by developing novel and challenging perspectives on state power.

Liberal feminists, who believe that sexual or gender (see p. 163) equality can be brought about through incremental reform, have tended to accept an essentially pluralist view of the state. They recognize that, if women are denied legal and political equality, and especially the right to vote, the state is biased in favour of men. However, their faith in the state's basic neutrality is reflected in the belief that any such bias can, and will, be overcome by a process of reform. In this sense, liberal feminists believe that all groups (including women) have potentially equal access to state power, and that this can be used impartially to promote justice and the common good. Liberal feminists have therefore usually viewed the state in positive terms, seeing state intervention as a means of redressing gender inequality and enhancing the role of women. This can be seen in campaigns for equal-pay legislation, the legalization of abortion, the provision of child-care facilities, the extension of welfare benefits, and so on.

Nevertheless, a more critical and negative view of the state has been developed by radical feminists, who argue that state power reflects a deeper structure of oppression in the form of patriarchy. There are a number of similarities between Marxist and radical feminist views of state power. Both groups, for example, deny that the state is an autonomous entity bent on the pursuit of its own interests. Instead, the state is understood, and its biases are explained, by reference to a 'deep structure' of power in society at large. Whereas Marxists place the state in an economic context, radical feminists place it in a context of gender inequality, and insist that it is essentially an institution of male power. In common with Marxism, distinctive instrumentalist and structuralistversions of this feminist position have been developed. The *instrumentalist* argument views the state as little more than an agent or 'tool' used by men to defend their own interests and uphold the structures of patriarchy. This line of argument draws on the core feminist belief that patriarchy is rooted in the division of society into distinct 'public' and 'private' spheres of life, men dominating the former while women are confined to the later. Quite simply, in this view, the state is run *by* men, and *for* men.

Whereas instrumentalist arguments focus on the personnel of the state, and particularly the state elite, *structuralist* arguments tend to emphasize the degree to which state institutions are embedded in a wider patriarchal system. Modern radical feminists have paid particular attention to the emergence of the welfare state, seeing it as the expression of a new kind of patriarchal power. Welfare may uphold patriarchy by bringing about a transition from private dependence (in which women as 'home makers' are dependent on men as 'breadwinners') to a system of public dependence in which women are increasingly controlled by the institutions of the extended state. For instance, women have become increasingly dependent on the state as clients or customers of state services (such as child-care institutions, nursery education and social work) and as employees, particularly in the so-called 'caring' professions (such as nursing, social work and education).

The role of the state

Contrasting interpretations of state power have clear implications for the desirable role or responsibilities of the state. What should states do? What functions or responsibilities should the state fulfil, and which ones should be left in the hands of private individuals? In many respects, these are the questions around which electoral politics and party competition revolve. With the exception of anarchists, who dismiss the state as fundamentally evil and unnecessary, all political thinkers have regarded the state as, in some sense, worthwhile. Even revolutionary socialists, inspired by the Leninist slogan 'smash the state', have accepted the need for a temporary proletarian state to preside over the transition from capitalism to communism, in the form of the 'dictatorship of the proletariat'. Nevertheless, there is profound disagreement about the exact role the state should play, and therefore about the proper balance between the state and civil society. Among the different state forms that have developed are the following:

- minimal states
- developmental states
- social-democratic states
- collectivized states
- totalitarian states
- religious states

Minimal states

The minimal state is the ideal of classical liberals, whose aim is to ensure that individuals enjoy the widest possible realm of freedom. This view is rooted in social-contract theory, but it nevertheless advances an essentially 'negative' view of the state. From this perspective, the value of the state is that it has the capacity to constrain human behaviour and thus to prevent individuals encroaching on the **rights** and liberties of others. The state is merely a protective body, its core function being to provide a framework of peace and social order within which citizens can conduct their lives as they think best. In Locke's famous simile, the state acts as a nightwatchman, whose services are called upon only when orderly existence is threatened. This nevertheless leaves the 'minimal' or 'nightwatchman' state with three core functions. First and foremost, the state exists to maintain domestic order. Second, it ensures that contracts or voluntary agreements made between private citizens are enforced, and third it provides protection against external attack. The institutional apparatus of a minimal state is thus limited to a police force, a court system and a military of some kind. Economic, social, cultural, moral and other responsibilities belong to the individual, and are therefore firmly part of civil society.

● **Rights**: Legal or moral entitlements to act or be treated in a particular way; civil rights differ from human rights.

Robert Nozick (1938–2002)

US academic and political philosopher. Nozick's major work, *Anarchy, State and Utopia* (1974), had a profound influence on New Right theories and beliefs. He developed a form of libertarianism that was close to Locke's and clearly influenced by nineteenth-century US individualists such as Spooner (1808–87) and Tucker (1854–1939). He argued that property rights should be strictly upheld, provided that wealth has been justly acquired in the first place, or has been justly transferred from one person to another. This position means support for minimal government and minimal taxation, and undermines the case for welfare and redistribution. Nozick's rights-based theory of justice was developed in response to the ideas of John Rawls (see p. 45). In later life, Nozick modified his extreme libertarianism.

The cause of the minimal state has been taken up in modern political debate by the New Right. Drawing on early liberal ideas, and particularly on free-market or classical economic theories, the New Right has proclaimed the need to 'roll back the frontiers of the state'. In the writings of Robert Nozick, this amounts to a restatement of Lockean liberalism based on a defence of individual rights, especially property rights. In the case of free-market economists such as Friedrich von Hayek (see p. 37) and Milton Friedman (see p. 138), state intervention is seen as a 'dead hand' that reduces competition, efficiency and productivity. From the New Right perspective, the state's economic role should be confined to two functions: the maintenance of a stable means of exchange or 'sound money' (low or zero inflation), and the promotion of competition through controls on monopoly power, price fixing and so on.

Developmental states

The best historical examples of minimal states were those in countries such as the UK and the USA during the period of early industrialization in the nineteenth century. As a general rule, however, the later a country industrializes, the more extensive will be its state's economic role. In Japan and Germany, for instance, the state assumed a more active 'developmental' role from the outset. A developmental state is one that intervenes in economic life with the specific purpose of promoting industrial growth and economic development. This does not amount to an attempt to replace the market with a 'socialist' system of planning and control but, rather, to an attempt to construct a partnership between the state and major economic interests, often underpinned by conservative and nationalist priorities.

The classic example of a developmental state is Japan. During the Meiji Period (1868–1912), the Japanese state forged a close relationship with the *zaibutsu*, the great family-run business empires that dominated the Japanese economy up until World War II. Since 1945, the developmental role of the Japanese state has been assumed by the Japanese Ministry of International Trade and Industry (MITI), which, together with the Bank of Japan, helps to shape private investment decisions and steer the Japanese economy towards international competitiveness (see

p. 372). A similar model of developmental intervention has existed in France, where governments of both left and right have tended to recognize the need for economic planning, and the state bureaucracy has seen itself as the custodian of the national interest. In countries such as Austria and, to some extent, Germany, economic development has been achieved through the construction of a 'partnership state', in which an emphasis is placed on the maintenance of a close relationship between the state and major economic interests, notably big business and organized labour. More recently, economic globalization (see p. 142) has fostered the emergence of '**competition states**', examples of which are found amongst the **tiger economies** of East Asia. Competition states are distinguished by their recognition of the need to strengthen education and training as the principal guaranteeing economic success in a context of intensifying transnational competition.

Social-democratic states

Whereas developmental states practise interventionism in order to stimulate economic progress, social-democratic states intervene with a view to bringing about broader social restructuring, usually in accordance with principles such as fairness, equality (see p. 454) and **social justice**. In countries such as Austria and Sweden, state intervention has been guided by both developmental and social-democratic priorities. Nevertheless, developmentalism and social democracy do not always go hand-in-hand. As Marquand (1988) pointed out, although the UK state was significantly extended in the period immediately after World War II along social-democratic lines, it failed to evolve into a developmental state. The key to understanding the social-democratic state is that there is a shift from a 'negative' view of the state, which sees it as little more than a necessary evil, to a 'positive' view of the state, in which it is seen as a means of enlarging liberty and promoting justice. The social-democratic state is thus the ideal of both modern liberals and democratic socialists.

Rather than merely laying down the conditions of orderly existence, the social-democratic state is an active participant; in particular, helping to rectify the imbalances and injustices of a market economy. It therefore tends to focus less upon the generation of wealth and more upon what is seen as the equitable or just distribution of wealth. In practice, this boils down to an attempt to eradicate poverty and reduce social inequality. The twin features of a social-democratic state are therefore Keynesianism and social welfare. The aim of Keynesian economic policies is to 'manage' or 'regulate' capitalism with a view to promoting growth and maintaining full employment. Although this may entail an element of planning, the classic Keynesian strategy involves 'demand management' through adjustments in fiscal policy; that is, in the levels of public spending and taxation. The adoption of welfare policies has led to the emergence of so-called '**welfare states**', whose responsibilities have extended to the promotion of social well-being amongst their citizens. In this sense, the social-democratic state is an 'enabling state', dedicated to the principle of individual empowerment.

Collectivized states

While developmental and social-democratic states intervene in economic life with a view to guiding or supporting a largely private economy, collectivized

● **Competition state**: A state which pursues strategies to ensure long-term competitiveness in a globalized economy.

● **Tiger economies**: Fast-growing and export-orientated economies modelled on Japan: for example, South Korea, Taiwan and Singapore.

● **Social justice**: A morally justifiable distribution of material rewards; social justice is often seen to imply a bias in favour of equality.

● **Welfare state**: A state that takes primary responsibility for the social welfare of its citizens, discharged through a range of social security, health, education and other services (albeit different in different societies).

Debating...
Is the state a force for good?

Political and ideological debate so often revolves around the issue of the state and, in particular, the proper balance between the state and civil society. At one extreme, anarchists claim that states and, for that matter, all systems of rule are illegitimate. Other views range from a grudging acceptance of the state as a necessary evil to a positive endorsement of the state as a force for good. Does the state have a positive or negative impact on our lives? Should it be celebrated or feared?

YES	NO

Key to civilized existence. The most basic argument in favour of the state is that it is a vital guarantee of order and social stability. A state is absolutely necessary because only a sovereign body that enjoys a monopoly of the means of coercion is able to prevent (regrettable, but inevitable) conflict and competition from spilling over into barbarism and chaos. Life in the absence of a state would be, as Hobbes famously put it, 'solitary, poor, nasty, brutish and short'. This is a lesson that is underlined by the sad misfortunes suffered by so-called 'failed' states (see p. 76), where civil war and warlordism take hold in the absence of a credible system of law and order.

Foundation of public life. The state differs from other bodies and institutions in that it is the only one that represents the common or collective interests, rather than the selfish or particular ones. The state speaks for the whole of society, not just its parts. As such, the state makes possible a 'public' realm of existence, which allows people to be involved in something larger than themselves, discharging responsibilities towards fellow citizens and, where appropriate, participating in making collective decisions. In a tradition that dates back to Aristotle and Hegel, the state can therefore be seen to be morally superior to civil society.

Agent of social justice. The state is a key agent of modernization and delivers a range of economic and social benefits. Even supporters of free-market economics acknowledge this in accepting that the economy can only function in a context of civic order that can only be established by the state. Beyond this, the state can counter the inherent instability of a market economy by intervening to ensure sustainable growth and full employment, and it can protect people from poverty and other forms of social disadvantage by delivering publicly-funded welfare services that no amount of private philanthropy can rival in terms of reach and quality.

Cause of disorder. As anarchists argue, the state is the cause of the problem of order, not its solution. The state breeds conflict and unrest because, by robbing people of their moral autonomy and forcing them to obey rules they have not made themselves, it 'infantalizes' them and blocks their moral development. This leaves them under the sway of base instincts and allows selfishness, greed and aggression to spread. As moral development flourishes in conditions of freedom and equality, reducing the authority of the state or, preferably, removing it altogether, will allow order to arise 'from below', naturally and spontaneously.

Enemy of freedom. The state is, at best, a necessary evil. Even when its benefits in terms of upholding order are accepted, the state should be confined to a strictly minimal role. This is because, as state authority is sovereign, compulsory and coercive, the 'public' sphere is, by its nature, a realm of oppression. While anarchists therefore argue that all states are illegitimate, others suggest that this only applies when the state goes beyond its essential role of laying down the conditions for orderly existence. Freedom is enlarged to the extent that the 'public' sphere contracts, civil society being morally superior to the state.

Recipe for poverty. The economy works best when it is left alone by the state. Market economies are self-regulating mechanisms; they tend towards long-term equilibrium, as the forces of demand and supply come into line with one another. The state, in contrast, is a brute machine: however well-meaning state intervention in economic and social life may be, it inevitably upsets the natural balance of the market and so imperils growth and prosperity. This was a lesson most graphically illustrated by the fate of orthodox communist systems, but it has also been underlined by the poor economic performance of over-regulated capitalist systems.

CONCEPT

Statism

Statism (or, in French, *étatisme*) is the belief that state intervention is the most appropriate means of resolving political problems, or bringing about economic and social development. This view is underpinned by a deep, and perhaps unquestioning, faith in the state as a mechanism through which collective action can be organized and common goals can be achieved. The state is thus seen as an ethical ideal (Hegel), or as serving the 'general will' or public interest. Statism is most clearly reflected in government policies that regulate and control economic life, possibly extending to Soviet-style state collectivization.

● **Collectivization:** The abolition of private property in favour of a system of common or public ownership.

● **Totalitarianism:** An all-encompassing system of political rule, involving pervasive ideological manipulation and open brutality (see p. 269).

states bring the entirety of economic life under state control. The best examples of such states were in orthodox communist countries such as the USSR and throughout Eastern Europe. These sought to abolish private enterprise altogether, and set up centrally planned economies administered by a network of economic ministries and planning committees. So-called 'command economies' were therefore established that were organized through a system of 'directive' planning that was ultimately controlled by the highest organs of the communist party. The justification for state **collectivization** stems from a fundamental socialist preference for common ownership over private property. However, the use of the state to attain this goal suggests a more positive attitude to state power than that outlined in the classical writings of Marx and Engels (1820–95).

Marx and Engels by no means ruled out nationalization; Engels, in particular, recognized that, during the 'dictatorship of the proletariat', state control would be extended to include factories, the banks, transportation and so on. Nevertheless, they envisaged that the proletarian state would be strictly temporary, and that it would 'wither away' as class antagonisms abated. In contrast, the collectivized state in the USSR became permanent, and increasingly powerful and bureaucratic. Under Stalin, socialism was effectively equated with statism, the advance of socialism being reflected in the widening responsibilities and powers of the state apparatus. Indeed, after Khrushchev announced in 1962 that the dictatorship of the proletariat had ended, the state was formally identified with the interests of 'the whole Soviet peoples'.

Totalitarian states

The most extreme and extensive form of interventionism is found in totalitarian states. The essence of **totalitarianism** is the construction of an all-embracing state, the influence of which penetrates every aspect of human existence. The state brings not only the economy, but also education, culture, religion, family life and so on under direct state control. The best examples of totalitarian states are Hitler's Germany and Stalin's USSR, although modern regimes such as Saddam Hussein's Iraq arguably have similar characteristics. The central pillars of such regimes are a comprehensive process of surveillance and terroristic policing, and a pervasive system of ideological manipulation and control. In this sense, totalitarian states effectively extinguish civil society and abolish the 'private' sphere of life altogether. This is a goal that only fascists, who wish to dissolve individual identity within the social whole, are prepared openly to endorse. It is sometimes argued that Mussolini's notion of a totalitarian state was derived from Hegel's belief in the state as an 'ethical community' reflecting the altruism and mutual sympathy of its members. From this perspective, the advance of human civilization can clearly be linked to the aggrandisement of the state and the widening of its responsibilities.

Religious states

On the face of it, a religious state is a contradiction in terms. The modern state emerged largely through the triumph of civil authority over religious authority, religion increasingly being confined to the private sphere, through a separation between church and state. The advance of state sovereignty thus usually went hand in hand with the forward march of secularization. In the USA, the secular nature of the state was enshrined in the First Amendment of the constitution, which guarantees that freedom of worship shall not be abridged, while in France the separation of church and state has been maintained through a strict emphasis on the principle of *laïcité*. In countries such as Norway, Denmark and the UK, 'established' or **state religions** have developed, although the privileges these religions enjoy stop well short of theocratic rule, and their political influence has generally been restricted by a high level of social secularization.

Nevertheless, the period since the 1980s has witnessed the rise of the religious state, driven by the tendency within religious fundamentalism (see p. 53) to reject the public/private divide and to view religion as the basis of politics. Far from regarding political realm as inherently corrupt, fundamentalist movements have typically looked to seize control of the state and to use it as an instrument of moral and spiritual regeneration. This was evident, for instance, in the process of 'Islamization' introduced in Pakistan under General Zia-ul-Haq after 1978, the establishment of an 'Islamic state' in Iran as a result of the 1979 revolution, and, despite its formal commitment to secularism, the close links between the Sri Lankan state and Sinhala Buddhism, particularly during the years of violent struggle against Tamil separatism. Although, strictly speaking, religious states are founded on the basis of religious principles, and, in the Iranian model, contain explicitly theocratic features, in other cases religiously-orientated governments operate in a context of constitutional secularism. This applies in the case of the AKP in Turkey (see p. 280) and, since 2012, the Muslim Brotherhood in Egypt.

ECLIPSE OF THE STATE?

Since the late 1980s, debate about the state has been overshadowed by assertions about it 'retreat' or 'decline'. The once-mighty leviathan – widely seen to be co-extensive with politics itself – had seemingly been humbled, state authority having been undermined by the growing importance of, amongst other things, the global economy, the market, major corporations, non-state actors and international organisations. The clamour for 'state-centric' approaches to domestic and international politics to be rethought, or abandoned altogether, therefore grew. However, a simple choice between 'state-centrism' and 'retreat-ism' is, at best, misleading. For instance, although states and markets are commonly portrayed as rival forces, they also interlock and complement one another. Apart from anything else, markets cannot function without a system of property rights that only the state can establish and protect. Moreover, although states may have lost authority in certain respects; in others, they may have become stronger.

Decline and fall of the state

Globalization and state transformation

The rise of globalization has stimulated a major debate about the power and significance of the state in a globalized world. Three contrasting positions can be identified. In the first place, some theorists have boldly proclaimed the emergence of 'post-sovereign governance' (Scholte, 2005), suggesting that the rise of

● *Laïcité*: (French) The principle of the absence of religious involvement in government affairs, and of government involvement in religious affairs.

● **State religion**: A religious body that is officially endorsed by the state, giving it special privileges, but (usually) not formal political authority.

globalization is inevitably marked by the decline of the state as a meaningful actor. Power shifts away from the state and towards global marketplaces and transnational corporations (TNCs) (see p. 149) in particular. In the most extreme version of this argument, advanced by so-called 'hyperglobalists', the state is seen to be so 'hollowed out' as to have become, in effect, redundant. Others, nevertheless, deny that globalization has altered the core feature of world politics, which is that, as in earlier eras, sovereign states are the primary determinants of what happens within their borders, and remain the principal actors on the world stage. In this view, globalization and the state are not separate or, still less, opposing forces; rather, and to a surprising degree, globalization has been created by states and thus exists to serve their interests. Between these two views, however, there is a third position, which acknowledges that globalization has brought about qualitative changes in the role and significance of the state, and in the nature of sovereignty, but emphasizes that these have transformed the state, rather than simply reduced or increased its power.

Developments such as the rise of international migration and the spread of cultural globalization have tended to make state borders increasingly 'permeable'. However, most of the discussion about the changing nature and power of the state has concerned the impact of economic globalization (discussed in more detail in Chapter 6). The central feature of economic globalization is the rise of '**supraterritoriality**', the process through which economic activity increasingly takes place within a 'borderless world' (Ohmae, 1989). This is particularly clear in relation to financial markets that have become genuinely globalized, in that capital flows around the world seemingly instantaneously; meaning, for example, that no state can be insulated from the impact of financial crises in other parts of the world. If borders have become permeable and old geographical certainties have been shaken, state sovereignty, at least in its traditional sense, cannot survive. This is the sense in which governance (see p. 74) in the twenty-first century has assumed a genuinely postsovereign character. It is difficult, in particular, to see how **economic sovereignty** can be reconciled with a globalized economy. Sovereign control over economic life was only possible in a world of discrete national economies; to the extent that these have been, or are being, incorporated into a single globalized economy, economic sovereignty becomes meaningless. However, the rhetoric of a 'borderless' global economy can be taken too far. For example, there has been, if anything, a growing recognition that market-based economies can only operate successfully within a context of legal and social order that only the state can guarantee (Fukuyama, 2005).

Increased global competition has also generated pressure to develop more efficient and responsive means of developing public policy and delivering public services. For many, this reflected a shift from government to 'governance'. As societies became more complex and fluid, new methods of governing have had to be devised that relied less on hierarchical state institutions and more on networks and the market, thus blurring the distinction between the state and society. The 'governance turn' in politics has been characterized by what has been called the 'reinvention' of government, reflected, in particular, in a move away from direct service provision by the state to the adoption of an 'enabling' or 'regulating' role. Such developments have led, some argue, to the transformation of the state itself, reflecting the rise of what has variously been called the 'competition' state, the 'market' state or the 'postmodern' state. Philip Bobbitt (2002)

● **Supraterritoriality**: The reconfiguration of geography that has occurred through the declining importance of state borders, geographical distance and territorial location.

● **Economic sovereignty**: The absolute authority of the state over national economic life, involving independent control of fiscal and monetary policies, and control over trade and capital flows.

CONCEPT

Governance

Governance is a broader term than government (see p. 266). Although lacking a settled or agreed definition, it refers, in its widest sense, to the various ways through which social life is coordinated. Government can therefore be seen as one of the institutions involved in governance; it is possible to have 'governance without government' (Rhodes, 1996). The wider use of the term reflects a blurring of the state/society distinction, resulting from changes such as the development of new forms of public management and the growth of public–private partnerships. (See multilevel governance p. 380).

● **Market state**: A state that aims to enlarge citizens' rights and opportunities, rather than assume control over economic and social life.

● **Political globalization**: The growing importance of international bodies and organizations, and of transnation political forces generally.

went as far as to argue that the transition from the nation-state to what he termed the '**market state**' heralded a profound shift in world politics, in that it marked the end of the 'long war' between liberalism, fascism and communism to define the constitutional form of the nation-state. The core feature of the market state is a shift away from 'top-down' economic management, based on the existence of discrete national economies, to an acceptance of the market as the only reliable principle of economic organization. Instead of trying to 'tame' capitalism, market states 'go with the flow'. Whereas states were previously judged on their effectiveness in promoting growth and prosperity, alleviating poverty and narrowing social inequality, market states base their legitimacy on their capacity to maximize the opportunities available to citizens, and their ability to ensure effective and unimpeded market competition. The speed with which this has happened varies in different parts of the world, as states embrace the market-state model with greater or less enthusiasm, and try to adapt it to their political cultures and economic needs.

Non-state actors and international bodies

A further manifestation of the decline of the state is evident in the rise of non-state or transnational actors and the growing importance of international organizations. This reflects the fact that, increasingly, major aspects of politics no longer take place merely in or through the state but, rather, outside or beyond the state. Amongst non-state actors, TNCs are often regarded as the most significant, their number having risen from 7,000 in 1970 to 38,000 in 2009. TNCs often dwarf states in terms of their economic size. Based on the (rather crude) comparison between corporate sales and countries' GDP, 51 of the world's 100 largest economies are corporations; only 49 of them are countries. General Motors is broadly equivalent, in this sense, to Denmark; Wal-Mart is roughly the same size as Poland; and Exxon Mobil has the same economic weight as South Africa. However, economic size does not necessarily translate into political power or influence. States, after all, can do things that TNCs can only dream about, such as make laws and raise armies. Non-governmental organizations (NGOs) (see p. 248) have also steadily grown in number and influence, particularly since the 1990s. Estimates of the total number of international NGOs usually exceed 30,000, with over 1,000 groups enjoying formal consultative status by the UN. Their expertise, moral authority and high public profiles enable NGOs such as Greenpeace, Amnesty International and Care International to exert a level of influence within international organizations that may at times rival, or even surpass, that of national governments. NGOs are therefore the key agents of what is increasingly called 'global civil society' (see p. 106). Other non-state actors range from the women's movement and the anti-capitalist movement to terrorist networks, such as al-Qaeda, guerrilla armies and transnational criminal organizations. As such groups have a 'trans-border' character, they are often able to operate in ways that elude the jurisdiction of any state.

The growth of politics beyond the state has also been apparent in the trend towards **political globalization**. However, its impact has been complex and, in some ways, contradictory. On the one hand, international bodies such as the UN, the European Union (EU) and the World Trade Organization (WTO) have undermined the capacity of states to operate as self-governing political units. As the range and importance of decisions that are made at intergovernmental or supranational level has increased, states have been forced to exert influence in and through regional or global bodies, or to operate within frameworks established by them. In the case of the EU, a growing range of decisions (for example, on monetary policy, agriculture and fisheries policy, defence and foreign affairs) are made by EU institutions, rather than member states. This has led to the phenomenon of multilevel governance, as discussed in Chapter 17. The WTO, for its part, acts as the judge and jury of global trade disputes and serves as a forum for negotiating trade deals between and amongst its members. On the other hand, political globalization opens up opportunities for the state as well as diminishes them. This occurs through the 'pooling' of sovereignty. For example, the EU Council of Ministers, the most powerful policy-making body in the EU, is very much a creature of its member states and provides a forum that allows national politicians to make decisions on a supranational level. By 'pooling' sovereignty, member states of the EU arguably gain access to a larger and more meaningful form of sovereignty. The 'pooled' sovereignty of the EU may be greater than the combined national sovereignties of its various member states.

Failed states and state-building

In the developing world, debate about the decline of the state has sometimes been displaced by concern about weak, failing or collapsed states. Cooper (2004) portrayed what he called the 'pre-modern' world as a world of postcolonial chaos, in which such state structures as exist are unable to establish (in Weber's words) a legitimate monopoly of the use of force, thus leading to endemic **warlordism**, widespread criminality and social dislocation. Such conditions do not apply consistently across the developing world, however. In cases such as India, South Korea and Taiwan, developing world states have been highly successful in pursuing strategies of economic modernization and social development. Others, nevertheless, have been distinguished by their weakness, sometimes being portrayed as 'quasi-states' or 'failed states' (see p. 76). Most of the weakest states in the world are concentrated in sub-Saharan Africa, classic examples being Somalia, Sierra Leone, Liberia and the Democratic Republic of the Congo. These states fail the most basic test of state power: they are unable to maintain domestic order and personal security, meaning that civil strife and even civil war become almost routine.

The failure of such states stems primarily from the experience of colonialism (see p. 122), which, when it ended (mainly in the post-1945 period), bequeathed formal political independence to societies that lacked an appropriate level of political, economic, social and educational development to function effectively as separate entities. As the borders of such states typically represented the extent of colonial ambition, rather than the existence of a culturally cohesive population, postcolonial states also often encompass deep ethnic, religious and tribal divisions. Although some explain the increase in state failure since the 1990s primarily in terms of domestic factors (such as a disposition towards authoritarian rule, backward institutions and parochial value systems which block the transition from pre-industrial, agrarian societies to modern industrial ones), external factors have also played a major role. This has applied not least through the tendency of globalization to re-orientate developing world economies

• **Warlordism:** A condition in which locally-based militarized bands vie for power in the absence of a sovereign state.

CONCEPT

Failed state

A failed state is a state that is unable to perform its key role of ensuring domestic order by monopolizing the use of force within its territory. Examples of failed states in recent years include Cambodia, Haiti, Rwanda, Liberia and Somalia. Failed states are no longer able to operate as viable political units, in that they lack a credible system of law and order. They are no longer able to operate as viable economic units, in that they are incapable of providing for their citizens and have no functioning infrastructure. Although relatively few states collapse altogether, a much larger number barely function and are dangerously close to collapse.

around the dictates of global markets, rather than domestic needs, and to widen inequality.

State failure is not just a domestic problem, however. Failed states often have a wider impact through, for example, precipitating refugee crises, providing a refuge for drug dealers, arms smugglers and terrorist organizations, generating regional instability, and, sometimes, provoking external intervention to provide humanitarian relief and/or to keep the peace. In this light, there has been a growing emphasis on **state-building**, typically associated with the larger process of peace-building and attempts to address deep-rooted, structural causes of violence in post-conflict situations. The provision of humanitarian relief and the task of conflict resolution become almost insuperably difficult in the absence of a functioning system of law and order. The wider acceptance of humanitarian intervention (see p. 424) since the early 1990s has meant that ordered rule is often provided, initially at least, by external powers. However this does not constitute a long-term solution. As examples such as Somalia, Iraq and Afghanistan demonstrate, externally-imposed order is only sustainable for a limited period of time, both because the economic and human cost to the intervening powers may be unsustainable in the long run, and because, sooner or later, the presence of foreign troops and police provokes resentment and hostility. Foreign intervention has therefore come, over time, to focus increasingly on the construction of effective indigenous leadership and building legitimate national institutions, such as an army, a police force, a judiciary, a central bank, a tax collection agency and functioning education, transport, energy and healthcare systems. As examples such as Liberia demonstrate, state-building is often a profoundly difficult task (see p. 77).

Return of the state?

Discussion about the state in the early twenty-first century has been dominated by talk of retreat, decline, or even collapse. The reality is more complex, however. For instance, although globalization may make state borders more 'porous', globalization has not been imposed on unwilling states; rather, it is a process that has been devised by states in pursuit of what they identify as their national interests. Similarly, international organizations typically act as forums through which states can act in concert over matters of mutual interest, rather than as bodies intent on usurping state power. Moreover, a number of developments in recent years have helped to strengthen the state and underline its essential importance. What explains the return of the state? In the first place, the state's unique capacity to maintain domestic order and protect its citizens from external attack has been strongly underlined by new security challenges that have emerged in the twenty-first century; notably, those linked to transnational terrorism (as discussed in Chapter 18). This underlines what Bobbitt (2002) viewed as a basic truth: 'The State exists to master violence'; it is therefore essentially a 'warmaking institution'. The decline in military expenditure that occurred at the end of the Cold War, the so-called 'peace dividend', started to be reversed in the late 1990s, with global military expenditure rising steeply after the September 11 terrorist attacks and the launch of the 'war on terror'. Furthermore, counter-terrorism strategies have often meant that states have imposed tighter border controls and assumed wider powers of surveillance, control and sometimes detention, even becoming 'national security states'.

● **State-building** The construction of a functioning state through the establishment of legitimate institutions for the formulation and implementation of policy across key areas of government.

POLITICS IN ACTION . . .

Liberia: a failed state rebuilt?

Events: During the 1990s, Liberia was often cited as a classic example of a failed state. Its ethnic and religious mixes, widespread poverty, endemic corruption, collapse of institutions and infrastructure, and tendency towards warlordism and violence imperilled the security and welfare of its citizens and affected other states, notably neighbouring Sierra Leone. Liberia, Africa's oldest republic, had collapsed into civil war in the late 1980s when Charles Taylor's National Patriotic Front of Liberia (NPFL) rebels overran much of the countryside, seizing the capital, Monrovia, in 1990. Around 250,000 people were killed and many thousands more fled the country as fighting intensified between rebel splinter groups, the Liberian army and West African peacekeepers. The 14-year civil war ended in 2003 when, under mounting international pressure and hemmed in by rebels, Taylor stepped down and went into exile in Nigeria (he was later found guilty of war crimes by an international tribunal in The Hague, linked to atrocities carried out in Sierra Leone). A transitional government steered the country towards elections in 2005, which brought the Harvard-educated economist Elaine Johnson-Sirleaf to power, becoming Africa's first female head of state. Sirleaf was re-elected in an uncontested run-off presidential election in November 2011.

Significance: Successful state-building has to overcome at least three challenges. First, new institutions and structures have to be constructed in a context of often deep political and ethnic tension, economic and social dislocation, and endemic poverty. In Liberia, the process of reconstructing the economic and social infrastructure was accelerated once Sirleaf and her Unity Party (UP) assumed power in 2005. Central Monrovia was transformed with improved roads and shining new buildings; investment in education and health saw the building of hundreds of new schools and health facilities, some of them free and affordable; and, alongside the elected presidency and legislature, progress was made in establishing an independent judiciary, and a disciplined police and military. Other important institutions have included Liberia's Truth and Reconciliation Commission, modelled on the experience of South Africa, and the National Election Commission (NEC), which presided over its first elections in 2011. Nevertheless, many development goals have yet to be achieved, despite considerable sums of money having been provided by international donors. For example, most people in Monrovia still do not have elec-

tricity or running water, and unemployment remains extremely high, with young people being most affected.

Second, the indigenous leadership and new institutions need to enjoy a significant measure of legitimacy. This is why state-building is invariably linked to the promotion of 'good governance', with the eradication of corruption being a key goal. Before contesting the presidency, Sirleaf had resigned her post as head of the Governance Reform Commission, criticizing the transitional government's inability to fight corruption. However, her opponents claim that her administration is guilty of some of the crimes it associates with previous governments. In 2009, the Truth and Reconciliation Commission implicated Sirleaf in the civil war and recommended that she be banned from public office for 30 years. The 2011 elections were also highly divisive. Sirleaf's main opponent, Winston Tubman, boycotted the run-off election, claiming that the NEC was biased in favour of the president and had manipulated vote-counting in her favour.

Third, successful state-building often requires external support, although this may become more of a hindrance than a help. State-building 'from above', associated with military intervention, as in Afghanistan and Iraq, clearly has its drawbacks, not least because indigenous leaders and new institutions are in danger of being seen to serve external interests rather than domestic ones. In the case of Liberia, the support of the Economic Community of West African States (ECOWAS) and the presence of a 15,000-strong UN peacekeeping force certainly aided economic development and helped to keep civil strife under control. Nevertheless, Liberia's peace may be fragile, and this may be tested either when the UN peacekeeping forces withdraw, or when President Sirleaf leaves office.

Second, although the days of command-and-control economic management may be over, the state has sometimes reasserted itself as an agent of modernization. Competition states have done this by improving education and training in order to boost productivity and provide support for key export industries. States such as China and Russia each modernized their economies by making significant concessions to the market, but an important element of state control has been retained or re-imposed (these developments are examined in more detail in Chapter 6 in relation to 'state capitalism'). On a wider level, the state's vital role in economic affairs was underlined by the 2007–09 global financial crisis. Although the G20 may have provided states with a forum to develop a coordinated global response, the massive packages of fiscal and other interventions that were agreed were, and could only have been, implemented by states. Indeed, one of the lessons of the 2007–09 crash, and of subsequent financial and fiscal crises, may be that the idea that the global economy works best when left alone by the state (acting alone, or through international organizations) has been exposed as a myth.

SUMMARY

● The state is a political association that exercises sovereign jurisdiction within defined territorial borders. As a system of centralized rule that emerged in Europe between the seventeenth and nineteenth centuries, and succeeded in subordinating all other institutions and groups, the state came to dominate political life in all its forms. The spread of the European model of the state to other lands and continents has seen the state become the universal form of political organization around the world

● There are a number of rival theories of the state. Pluralists hold that the state is a neutral body that arbitrates between the competing interests of society. Marxists argue that the state maintains the class system by either oppressing subordinate classes or ameliorating class conflict. The New Right portrays the state as a self-serving monster that is intent on expansion and aggrandizement. Radical feminists point to patriarchal biases within the state that support a system of male power.

● Those who support the state see it either as a means of defending the individual from the encroachments of fellow citizens, or as a mechanism through which collective action can be organized. Critics, however, tend to suggest that the state reflects either the interests of dominant social groups, or interests that are separate from, and antithetical to, society.

● States have fulfilled very different roles. Minimal states merely lay down the conditions for orderly existence. Developmental states attempt to promote growth and economic development. Social-democratic states aim to rectify the imbalances and injustices of a market economy. Collectivized states exert control over the entirety of economic life. Totalitarian states bring about all-encompassing politicization and, in effect, extinguish civil society. Religious states are used as instruments of moral and spiritual renewal.

● Modern debate about the state is dominated by talk of retreat, decline and even collapse. The decline of the state is often explained in terms of the impact of globalization, the rise of non-state actors and the growing importance of international organizations. Most dramatically, some postcolonial states have collapsed, or barely function as states, having a negligible capacity to maintain order. However, the retreat of the state may have been exaggerated and, in relation to security and economic development in particular, the state may be reviving in importance.

Questions for discussion

● How should the state be defined?

● Would life in a stateless society really be 'nasty, brutish and short'?

● Why has politics traditionally been associated with the affairs of the state?

● Can the state be viewed as a neutral body in relation to competing social interests?

● Does the nature and background of the state elite inevitably breed bias?

● What is the proper relationship between the state and civil society?

● Does globalization mean that the state has become irrelevant?

● Have nation-states been transformed into market states?

● To what extent can state capacity be 're-built'?

Further reading

Hay, C., M. Lister and D. Marsh, *The State: Theories and Issues* (2006). An accessible, comprehensive and contemporary introduction to the theoretical perspectives on the state and to key issues and controversies.

Jessop, B., *State Theory: Putting Capitalist States in Their Place* (1990). A demanding but worthwhile collection of essays through which Jessop develops his own approach to state theory.

Pierre, J. and B. Guy Peters, *Governance, Politics and the State* (2000). A useful discussion of the phenomenon of governance, and of its implications for the role and nature of the state.

Sørensen, G., *The Transformation of the State: Beyond the Myth of Retreat* (2004). A systematic analysis of the contemporary state that assesses the nature and extent of its transformation in a global era.

CHAPTER 4

Democracy and Legitimacy

'Democracy is the worst form of government except all the other forms that have been tried from time to time.'

WINSTON CHURCHILL, Speech, UK House of Commons (11 November, 1947)

PREVIEW Although states may enjoy a monopoly of coercive power, they seldom remain in existence through the exercise of force alone. As Jean-Jacques Rousseau put it, 'The strongest is never strong enough unless he turns might into right and obedience into duty'. This is why all systems of rule seek legitimacy or 'rightfulness', allowing them to demand compliance from their citizens or subjects. Legitimacy is thus the key to political stability; it is nothing less than the source of a regime's survival and success. In modern politics, debates about legitimacy are dominated by the issue of democracy, so much so that 'democratic legitimacy' is sometimes viewed as the only meaningful form of legitimacy. However, the link between legitimacy and democracy is both a relatively new idea and one that is culturally specific. Until well into the nineteenth century, the term 'democracy' continued to have pejorative implications, suggesting a form of 'mob rule'; and, in parts of the developing world, democracy promotion continues to be associated with 'westernization'. Nevertheless, there is a sense in which we are all now democrats. Liberals, conservatives, socialists, communists, anarchists and even fascists are eager to proclaim the virtues of democracy and to demonstrate their own democratic credentials. Indeed, as the major ideological systems have faltered or collapsed since the late twentieth century, the flame of democracy has appeared to burn yet more strongly. As the attractions of socialism have faded, and the merits of capitalism have been called into question, democracy has emerged as perhaps the only stable and enduring principle in the postmodern political landscape.

KEY ISSUES
- How do states maintain legitimacy?
- Are modern societies facing a crisis of legitimation?
- Why is political legitimacy so often linked to the claim to be democratic?
- What are the core features of democratic rule?
- What models of democratic rule have been advanced?
- How do democratic systems operate in practice?

CONCEPT

Legitimacy

Legitimacy (from the Latin *legitimare*, meaning 'to declare lawful') broadly means 'rightfulness'. Legitimacy therefore confers on an order or command an authoritative or binding character, thus transforming power (see p. 5) into authority (see p. 4). Political philosophers treat legitimacy as a moral or rational principle; that is, as the grounds on which governments may demand obedience from citizens. The *claim* to legitimacy is thus more important than the *fact* of obedience. Political scientists, however, usually see legitimacy in sociological terms; that is, as a willingness to comply with a system of rule regardless of how this is achieved.

LEGITIMACY AND POLITICAL STABILITY

The issue of legitimacy, the rightfulness of a regime or system of rule, is linked to the oldest and one of the most fundamental of political debates, the problem of political obligation. Why should citizens feel obliged to acknowledge the authority of government? Do they have a duty to respect the state and obey its laws? In modern political debate, however, legitimacy is usually understood less in terms of moral obligations, and more in terms of political behaviour and beliefs. In other words, it addresses not the question of why people *should* obey the state, in an abstract sense, but the question of why they *do* obey a particular state or system of rule. What are the conditions or processes that encourage them to see authority as rightful, and therefore underpin the stability of a regime? This reflects a shift from philosophy to sociology, but it also highlights the contested nature of the concept of legitimacy.

Legitimizing power

The classic contribution to the understanding of legitimacy as a sociological phenomenon was provided by Max Weber (see p. 82). Weber was concerned to categorize particular 'systems of domination', and to identify in each case the basis on which legitimacy was established. He did this by constructing three ideal types (see p. 20), or conceptual models, which he hoped would help to make sense of the highly complex nature of political rule. These ideal types amount to three kinds of authority:

- traditional authority
- charismatic authority
- legal–rational authority.

Each of these is characterized by a particular source of political legitimacy and, thus, different reasons that people may have for obeying a regime. In the process, Weber sought to understand the transformation of society itself, contrasting the systems of domination found in relatively simple traditional societies with those typically found in industrial and highly bureaucratic ones.

Weber's first type of political legitimacy is based on long-established customs and traditions (see p. 82). In effect, *traditional* authority is regarded as legitimate because it has 'always existed': it has been sanctified by history because earlier generations have accepted it. Typically, it operates according to a body of concrete rules: that is, fixed and unquestioned customs that do not need to be justified because they reflect the way things have always been. The most obvious examples of traditional authority are found amongst tribes or small groups in the form of patriarchalism (the domination of the father within the family, or the 'master' over his servants) and gerontocracy (the rule of the aged, normally reflected in the authority of village 'elders'). Traditional authority is closely linked to hereditary systems of power and privilege, as reflected, for example, in the survival of dynastic rule in Saudi Arabia, Kuwait and Morocco. Although it is of marginal significance in advanced industrial societies, the survival of monarchy (see p. 292), albeit in a constitutional form, in the UK, Belgium, the Netherlands

Max Weber (1864–1920)

German political economist and sociologist. Following a breakdown in 1898, Weber withdrew from academic teaching, but he continued to write and research until the end of his life. He was one of the founders of modern sociology, and he championed a scientific and value-free approach to scholarship. He also highlighted the importance to social action of meaning and consciousness. Weber's interests ranged from social stratification, law, power and organization to religion. He is best known for the thesis that the Protestant ethic encourages the development of capitalism, and for his analysis of bureaucracy. Weber's most influential works include *The Protestant Ethic and the Spirit of Capitalism* (1902), *The Sociology of Religion* (1920) and *Economy and Society* (1922).

CONCEPT

Tradition

Tradition may refer to anything that is handed down or transmitted from the past to the present (long-standing customs and practices, institutions, social or political systems, values and beliefs, and so on). Tradition thus denotes continuity with the past. This continuity is usually understood to link the generations, although the line between the traditional and the merely fashionable is often indistinct. 'Traditional' societies are often contrasted with 'modern' ones, the former being structured on the basis of status (see p. 152) and by supposedly organic hierarchies, and the latter on the basis of contractual agreement and by democratic processes.

and Spain, for example, helps to shape political culture by keeping alive values such as deference, respect and duty.

Weber's second form of legitimate domination is *charismatic* authority. This form of authority is based on the power of an individual's personality; that is, on his or her 'charisma' (see p. 83). Owing nothing to a person's status, social position or office, charismatic authority operates entirely through the capacity of a leader to make a direct and personal appeal to followers as a kind of hero or saint. Although modern political leaders such as de Gaulle, Kennedy and Thatcher undoubtedly extended their authority through their personal qualities and capacity to inspire loyalty, this did not amount to charismatic legitimacy, because their authority was essentially based on the formal powers of the offices they held. Napoleon, Mussolini, Hitler (see p. 47), Ayatollah Khomeini (see p. 167), Fidel Castro and Colonel Gaddafi are more appropriate examples.

However, charismatic authority is not simply a gift or a natural propensity; systems of personal rule are invariably underpinned by 'cults of personality' (see p. 302), the undoubted purpose of which is to 'manufacture' charisma. Nevertheless, when legitimacy is constructed largely, or entirely, through the power of a leader's personality, there are usually two consequences. The first is that, as charismatic authority is not based on formal rules or procedures, it often has no limits. The leader is a Messiah, who is infallible and unquestionable; the masses become followers or disciples, who are required only to submit and obey. Second, so closely is authority linked to a specific individual, that it is difficult for a system of personal rule to outlive its founding figure. This certainly applied in the case of the regimes of Napoleon, Mussolini and Hitler.

Weber's third type of political legitimacy, *legal–rational* authority, links authority to a clearly and legally defined set of rules. In Weber's view, legal–rational authority is the typical form of authority operating in most modern states. The power of a president, prime minister or government official is determined in the final analysis by formal, constitutional rules, which constrain or limit what an office holder is able to do. The advantage of this form of authority over both traditional and charismatic authority is that, as it is attached to an office rather than a person, it is far less likely to be abused or to give rise to injustice. Legal–rational authority therefore maintains limited government and, in

CONCEPT

Charisma

Charisma was originally a theological term meaning the 'gift of grace'. This was supposedly the source of the power that Jesus exerted over his disciples. As a sociopolitical phenomenon, charisma refers to charm or personal power: the capacity to establish leadership (see p. 300) through psychological control over others. Charismatic authority therefore includes the ability to inspire loyalty, emotional dependence and even devotion. Although it is usually seen as a 'natural' capacity, all political leaders cultivate their charismatic qualities through propaganda, practised oratory and honed presentational skills.

addition, promotes efficiency through a rational division of labour. However, Weber also recognised a darker side to this type of political legitimacy. The price of greater efficiency would, he feared, be a more depersonalized and inhuman social environment typified by the relentless spread of bureaucratic (see p. 361) forms of organization.

Although Weber's classification of types of legitimacy is still seen as relevant, it also has its limitations. One of these is that, in focusing on the legitimacy of a political regime or system of rule, it tells us little about the circumstances in which political authority is challenged as a result of unpopular policies, or a discredited leader or government. More significantly, as Beetham (1991) pointed out, to see legitimacy, as Weber did, as nothing more than a 'belief in legitimacy' is to ignore how it is brought about. This may leave the determination of legitimacy largely in the hands of the powerful, who may be able to 'manufacture' rightfulness through public-relations campaigns and the like.

Beetham suggested that power can only be said to be legitimate if three conditions are fulfilled. First, power must be exercised according to established rules, whether these are embodied in formal legal codes or in informal conventions. Second, these rules must be justified in terms of the shared beliefs of the government and the governed. Third, legitimacy must be demonstrated by an expression of consent on the part of the governed. This highlights two key features of the legitimation process. The first is the existence of elections and party competition, a system through which popular consent can be exercised (as discussed below in connection with democratic legitimacy). The second is the existence of constitutional rules that broadly reflect how people feel they should be governed (which are examined in Chapter 15).

Legitimation crises and revolutions

An alternative to the Weberian approach to legitimacy has been developed by neo-Marxist (see p. 64) theorists. While orthodox Marxists were inclined to dismiss legitimacy as bogus, seeing it as nothing more than a bourgeois myth, modern Marxists, following Gramsci (see p. 175), have acknowledged that capitalism is in part upheld by its ability to secure political support. Neo-Marxists such as Jürgen Habermas (see p. 84) and Claus Offe (1984) have therefore focused attention not merely on the class system, but also on the machinery through which legitimacy is maintained (the democratic process, party competition, welfare and social reform, and so on). Nevertheless, they have also highlighted what they see as the inherent difficulty of legitimizing a political system that is based on unequal class power. In *Legitimation Crisis* (1973), Habermas identified a series of 'crisis tendencies' within capitalist societies that make it difficult for them to maintain political stability through consent alone. At the heart of this tension, he argued, lie contradictions and conflicts between the logic of capitalist accumulation, on the one hand, and the popular pressures that democratic politics unleashes, on the other.

From this perspective, capitalist economies are seen to be bent on remorseless expansion, dictated by the pursuit of profit. However, the extension of political and social rights in an attempt to build legitimacy within such systems has stimulated countervailing pressures. In particular, the democratic process has led to escalating demands for social welfare, as well as for increased popular

Jürgen Habermas (born 1929)

German philosopher and social theorist. After growing up during the Nazi period, Habermas was politicized by the Nuremburg trials and the growing awareness after the war of the concentration and death camps. Drawn to study with Adorno (1903–69) and Horkheimer (1895–1973), he became the leading exponent of the 'second generation' of the Frankfurt School of critical theory. Habermas work ranges over epistemology, the dynamics of advanced capitalism, the nature of rationality, and the relationship between social science and philosophy. During the 1970s, he developed critical theory into what became a theory of 'communicative action'. Habermas' main works include *Towards a Rational Society* (1970), *Theory and Practice* (1974) and *The Theory of Communicative Competence* (1984, 1988).

participation and social equality. The resulting expansion of the state's responsibilities into economic and social life, and the inexorable rise of taxation and public spending, nevertheless constrain capitalist accumulation by restricting profit levels and discouraging enterprise. In Habermas' view, capitalist democracies cannot permanently satisfy both popular demands for social security and welfare rights, and the requirements of a market economy based on private profit. Forced either to resist popular pressures or to risk economic collapse, such societies would find it increasingly difficult, and eventually impossible, to maintain legitimacy. (The implications for political stability of economic and financial crises are discussed in Chapter 6.)

A very similar problem has been identified since the 1970s in the form of what is called government 'overload'. Writers such as Anthony King (1975) and Richard Rose (1980) argued that governments were finding it increasingly difficult to govern because they were subject to over-demand. This had come about both because politicians and political parties were encouraged to outbid one another in the attempt to get into power, and because pressure groups were able to besiege government with unrelenting and incompatible demands. Government's capacity to deliver was further undermined by a general drift towards corporatism (see p. 251) that created growing interdependence between government agencies and organized groups. However, whereas neo-Marxists believed that the 'crisis tendencies' identified in the 1970s were beyond the capacity of capitalist democracies to control, overload theorists tended to call for a significant shift of political and ideological priorities in the form of the abandonment of a 'big' government approach.

In many ways, the rise of the New Right since the 1980s can be seen as a response to this legitimation, or overload, crisis. Influenced by concerns about a growing **fiscal crisis of the welfare state**, the New Right attempted to challenge and displace the theories and values that had previously legitimized the progressive expansion of the state's responsibilities. In this sense, the New Right amounted to a 'hegemonic project' that tried to establish a rival set of pro-individual and pro-market values and theories. This constituted a public philosophy that extolled rugged individualism, and denigrated the 'nanny state'. The success of this project is demonstrated by the fact that socialist parties in states as differ-

● **Fiscal crisis of the welfare state**: The crisis in state finances that occurs when expanding social expenditure coincides with recession and declining tax revenues.

Focus on . . .
Why do revolutions occur?

Why do regimes collapse? Should revolutions be understood primarily in political terms, or are they more a reflection of deeper economic or social developments? Contrasting theories of revolution have been advanced by Marxists and non-Marxists. In Marxist theory, revolution emerges out of contradictions that exist at a socio-economic level. Marx (see p. 41) believed that revolution marks the point at which the class struggle develops into open conflict, leading one class to overthrow and displace another. Just as the French Revolution was interpreted as a 'bourgeois' revolution, the Russian Revolution was later seen as a 'proletarian' revolution that set in motion a process that would culminate in the establishment of socialism and, eventually, full communism. However, revolutions have not come about as Marx forecast. Not only have they tended to occur in relatively backward societies, not (as he predicted) in the advanced capitalist countries, but Marxist revolutions were often *coup d'états* rather than popular revolutions.

A variety of non-Marxist theories of revolution have been advanced. Systems theorists have argued that revolution results from 'disequilibrium' in the political system, brought about by economic, social, cultural or international changes to which the system itself is incapable of responding – the 'outputs' of government become structurally out of line with the 'inputs'. The idea of a 'revolution of rising expectations' suggests that revolutions occur when a period of economic and social development is abruptly reversed, creating a widening gap between popular expectations and the capabilities of government. The classic statement of this theory is found in Ted Gurr's *Why Men Rebel* (1970), which links rebellion to 'relative deprivation'.

The social-structural theory of revolution implies that regimes usually succumb to revolution when, through international weakness and/or domestic ineffectiveness, they lose their ability, or the political will, to maintain control through the exercise of coercive power. Theda Skocpol (1979) explained the outbreak of the French, Russian and Chinese revolutions in these terms, but they could equally be applied to the swift and largely bloodless collapse of the Eastern European communist regimes in the autumn and winter of 1989 (see p. 44).

● **Revolution**: A popular uprising, involving extra-legal mass action, which brings about fundamental change (a change in the political system itself) as opposed to merely a change of policy or governing elite.

● **Reform**: Change brought about within a system, usually by peaceful and incremental measures; reform implies improvement.

ent as the UK, France, Spain, Australia and New Zealand have accommodated themselves to broadly similar goals and values. As this happened, a political culture that once emphasized social justice, welfare rights and public responsibilities gave way to one in which choice, enterprise, competition and individual responsibility are given prominence.

However, legitimation crises may have more dramatic consequences. When faltering support for a regime can no longer be managed by adjustments in public policy or a change in leadership, legitimacy may collapse altogether, leading either to a resort to repression, or to **revolution**. While evolutionary change is usually thought of as **reform**, revolution involves root-and-branch change. Revolutions recast the political order entirely, typically bringing about an abrupt and often violent break with the past. Although there is considerable debate about the causes of revolution, there is little doubt that revolution has played a crucial role in shaping the modern world. The American Revolution (1776) led to the creation of a constitutional republic independent from Britain and gave practical expression to the principle of representation. The French Revolution (1789) set out to destroy the old order under the banner of 'liberty, equality and fraternity', advancing democratic ideals and sparking an 'age of revolution' in early nineteenth-century Europe. The Russian Revolution (1917), the first 'communist' revolution, provided a model for subsequent twentieth-century revolutions, including the Chinese Revolution (1949), the Cuban Revolution (1959), the Vietnamese Revolution (1975) and the Nicaraguan Revolution (1979). The Eastern European Revolutions (1989-91) and the rebellions of the Arab Spring (2011) (see p. 88) nevertheless re-established the link between revolution and the pursuit of political democracy.

Democratic legitimacy

Modern discussions about legitimacy are dominated by its relationship to democracy, so much so that democratic legitimacy is now widely accepted as the only meaningful form of legitimacy. The claim that a political organization is legitimate is therefore intrinsically linked to its claim to be democratic. The next main section examines competing models of democratic rule and debates how democracy operates in practice, but this section considers the nature of the link between democracy and legitimacy. Democracy can be seen to promote legitimacy in at least three ways. In the first place, it does so through **consent**. Although citizens do not explicitly give their consent to be governed, thereby investing political authority with a formal 'right to rule', they do so implicitly each time they participate in the political process. In this respect, democracy underpins legitimacy by expanding the opportunities for political participation, most importantly though the act of voting, but also through activities such as joining a political party or interest group or by engaging in protests or demonstrations. Political participation, in this sense, binds government and the people, encouraging the latter to view the rules of the political game as rightful and so to accept that they have an obligation to respect and obey those in authority.

Second, the essence of democratic governance is a process of compromise, conciliation and negotiation, through which rival interests and groups find a way of living together in relative peace, rather than resorting to force and the use of naked power. The mechanisms through which this non-violent conflict resolution takes place, notably elections, assembly debates, party competition and so forth, thus tend to enjoy broad popular support as they ensure that power is widely dispersed, each group having a political voice of some kind or other. Third, democracy operates as a feedback system that tends towards long-term political stability, as it brings the 'outputs' of government into line with the 'inputs' or pressures placed upon it. As democracy provides a mechanism through which governments can be removed and public policy changed, it tends to keep 'disequilibrium' in the political system to a minimum, enabling legitimation crises to be managed effectively and substantially undermining the potential for civil strife, rebellion or revolution.

Nevertheless, the notion of an intrinsic link between legitimacy and democracy has also been questioned. Some, for example, argue that the high levels of political stability and low incidence of civic strife and popular rebellion in democratic societies can be explained more persuasively by factors other than democracy. These include the fact that, having in the main advanced capitalist economies, democratic societies tend to enjoy widespread prosperity and are effective in 'delivering the goods'. Democratic legitimacy

● **Consent**: Assent or permission; in politics, usually an agreement to be governed or ruled.

CONCEPT

Trust

Trust means faith, a reliance on, or confidence in, the honesty, worth and reliability of another person. It is therefore based on expectations of others' future actions. Political trust consists in the level of confidence people have in one another in discharging their civic responsibilities and, crucially, the confidence citizens have that politicians generally, and leaders in particular, will keep their promises and carry out their public duties honestly and fairly. In liberal theory, trust arises through voluntary contracts that we uphold through mutual self-interest. In communitarian theory, trust is grounded in a sense of social duty and a common morality.

may therefore be less significant than 'capitalist legitimacy'. A further factor is that democratic societies tend to be liberal as well as democratic, liberal democracy (see p. 270) being the dominant form of democracy worldwide. Liberal societies offer wide opportunities for personal freedom, self-expression and social mobility, and these may be as important, or perhaps more important, in maintaining legitimacy than the opportunities that democracy offers for political participation.

Even if democracy is accepted as the principal mechanism through which legitimacy is promoted, there are reasons for thinking that its effectiveness in this respect may be faltering. In particular, mature democratic societies appear to be afflicted by growing political disenchantment or disaffection. This has been most evident in declining electoral turnouts and in the falling membership of mainstream political parties. For some, this 'democratic malaise' is a product of the tendency within democratic systems for politicians to seek power by promising more than they can deliver, thereby creating an expectations gap. As this gap widens, trust in politicians declines and healthy scepticism about the political process threatens to turn into corrosive cynicism. The issue of political disenchantment is examined in greater detail in Chapter 20.

Non-democratic legitimacy?

If democracy is taken to be the only genuine basis for legitimacy, this implies that non-democratic regimes are, by their nature, illegitimate. Nevertheless, some authoritarian regimes survive for many decades with relatively little evidence of mass political disaffection, still less concerted opposition. Clearly, this can very largely be explained through the use of coercion and repression, fear rather than consent being the principal means through which citizens are encouraged to obey the state. However, non-democratic regimes rarely seek to consolidate their hold on power through coercion alone. They typically adopt a two-pronged approach in which political control is exercised alongside claims to legitimacy. But, in the absence of democracy, what means of legitimation are available to such regimes?

Three key forms of non-democratic legitimation have been used. First, elections, albeit one-party, sometimes non-competitive or 'rigged' elections, have been used to give a regime a democratic façade, helping both to create the impression of popular support and to draw people into a ritualized acceptance of the regime. This legitimation device was used in Nazi Germany and Fascist Italy, and has also been used African one-party states and communist regimes. Second, non-democratic regimes have sought performance legitimation based on their ability to deliver, amongst other things, rising living standards, public order, improved education and health care, and so forth. Communist regimes thus emphasize the delivery of a package of socio-economic benefits to their citizens, a strategy that continues to be practised by China through its ability to generate high levels of economic growth.

Third, ideological legitimation has been used, either in an attempt to uphold the leader's, military's or party's right to rule, or to establish broader goals and principles that invest the larger regime with a sense of rightfulness. Examples of the former include Gamal Abdel Nasser's portrayal of the Egyptian military as the 'vanguard of the revolution' after its 1952 *coup*, and Colonel Gaddafi's proclama-

POLITICS IN ACTION . . .

The Arab Spring: democracy comes to the Arab world?

Events: The 'Arab Spring' (also known as the 'Arab revolutions' or the 'Arabic rebellions') was a revolutionary wave of demonstrations and protests that swept through North Africa and parts of the Middle East during 2011, toppling four dictators. The process was initiated by Tunisia's 'Jasmine' revolution, in which a growing wave of anti-government rallies in early January turned into a nationwide revolt due to incidents of police repression. On 14 January, President Ben Ali fled the country, bringing an end to his 23-year rule. Inspired by events in Tunisia, Egyptian demonstrators took to the streets on January 25, calling for the removal of President Hosni Mubarak; Tahrir Square, in Cairo, becoming the centre of protests. Under growing pressure from the Egyptian military and after 18 days of protests, Mubarak resigned on 11 February. In Libya, the 42-year rule of President Muammar Gaddafi was brought to an end by an eight-month civil war, in which rebel forces were supported by NATO aerial attacks, thanks to a no-fly zone imposed by the UN Security Council. Gaddafi's death on October 22 signalled the final collapse of his regime. Other significant popular uprisings in the Arab world occurred in Yemen (where President Saleh was forced from power in November 2011), in Syria (against President Assad) and in Bahrain.

Significance: There are significant debates about both the causes and consequences of the Arab Spring. Why did the uprisings occur? Clearly, as with the 1989 East European Revolutions, demonstrators were inspired, inflamed or emboldened by developments elsewhere, creating a chain reaction of protest, in this case often facilitated by the internet and social networking sites such as Facebook. The underlying factors were nevertheless common to much of the Arab world: poor living standards, widening inequality, rampant unemployment (particularly affecting the young), police violence and a lack of human rights. Ethnic and religious tensions were also significant in countries such as Syria, Libya and Bahrain. Nevertheless, such circumstances did not always translate into successful revolutions, or even, as in cases such as Sudan and Saudi Arabia, popular uprisings. Where these revolutions succeeded, three factors were significant. A broad section of the population, spanning ethnic and religious groups, and socio-economic classes, were mobilized; the loyalty of key elites, and especially in the military, started to fracture; and international powers either refused to defend embattled governments or gave moral and, in the case of Libya, military support to opponents of the regime.

What kind of political change will the Arab Spring bring about? Three possibilities offer themselves. The first is a transition to democratic rule, giving the lie to the view that, being mired in 'backward' cultural and religious beliefs, the Arab world is not ready for democracy. Certainly, the key demands of protestors were for the introduction of western-style democratic reforms, notably free and competitive elections, the rule of law and protections for civil liberties. Moreover, where regimes collapsed, this was invariably accompanied by the promise to hold free elections, as duly occurred during 2011 in Tunisia in October and in Egypt in November–December. The second possibility is that the hope for a smooth transition to stable democracy will be disappointed as some kind of recast authoritarianism emerges once the post-revolutionary honeymoon period ends. This scenario is supported by the crucial role still played by the military, especially in Egypt, and by the likelihood that, as divisions start to surface within the former-opposition, a perhaps lengthy period of political instability and policy reversals may develop. The third possibility is that, although the revolutions were strongest in the relatively secular Arab republics of North Africa, the long-term beneficiaries of the Arab Spring will be Islamist radicals, who initially appeared to play a marginal role. Not only are Islamist groups, such as the Muslim Brotherhood, generally better organized than their rivals, but post-revolutionary chaos and uncertainty offer fertile ground for advancing the politics of religious regeneration.

tion of a 'Green revolution' after seizing power in Libya in 1969. Examples of the latter include the emphasis on Marxism-Leninism in communist states and the use of Wahhabism to support monarchical rule in Saudi Arabia. However, when such strategies fail, all semblance of legitimation evaporates and non-democratic regimes are forced either to resort to progressively more draconian means of survival, or else they collapse in the face of popular uprisings. This can be seen in the case of the so-called 'Arab Spring' of 2011 (see p. 88).

DEMOCRACY

Understanding democracy

Debates about democracy extend well beyond its relationship to legitimacy. These stem, most basically, from confusion over the nature of democracy. The origins of the term 'democracy' can be traced back to Ancient Greece. Like other words ending in 'cracy' (for example, autocracy, aristocracy and bureaucracy), democracy is derived from the Greek word *kratos*, meaning power, or rule. Democracy thus means 'rule by the *demos*' (the *demos* referring to 'the people', although the Greeks originally used this to mean 'the poor' or 'the many'). However, the simple notion of 'rule by the people' does not get us very far. The problem with democracy has been its very popularity, a popularity that has threatened the term's undoing as a meaningful political concept. In being almost universally regarded as a 'good thing', democracy has come to be used as little more than a 'hurrah! word', implying approval of a particular set of ideas or system of rule. In Bernard Crick's (1993) words, 'democracy is perhaps the most promiscuous word in the world of public affairs'. A term that can mean anything to anyone is in danger of meaning nothing at all. Amongst the meanings that have been attached to the word 'democracy' are the following:

- a system of rule by the poor and disadvantaged
- a form of government in which the people rule themselves directly and continuously, without the need for professional politicians or public officials
- a society based on equal opportunity and individual merit, rather than hierarchy and privilege
- a system of welfare and redistribution aimed at narrowing social inequalities
- a system of decision-making based on the principle of majority rule
- a system of rule that secures the rights and interests of minorities by placing checks upon the power of the majority
- a means of filling public offices through a competitive struggle for the popular vote
- a system of government that serves the interests of the people regardless of their participation in political life.

Perhaps a more helpful starting point from which to consider the nature of democracy is Abraham Lincoln's Gettysburg Address (1863). Lincoln extolled the virtues of what he called 'government of the people, by the people, and for

CONCEPT

Political equality

Political equality means, broadly, an equal distribution of political power and influence. Political equality can thus be thought of as the core principle of democracy, in that it ensures that, however 'the people' is defined, each individual member carries the same weight: all voices are equally loud. This can be understood in two ways. In liberal-democratic theory, political equality implies an equal distribution of political rights: the right to vote, the right to stand for election and so on. In contrast, socialists, amongst others, link political influence to factors such as the control of economic resources and access to the means of mass communication.

● **Majority rule**: The rule that the will of the majority, or numerically strongest, overrides the will of the minority, implying that the latter should accept the views of the former.

● **Cosmopolitan democracy**: A form of democracy that operates at supranational levels of governance and is based on the idea of transnational or global citizenship.

the people'. What this makes clear is that democracy links government to the people, but that this link can be forged in a number of ways: government *of*, *by* and *for* the people. This section explores the implications of these links by considering three questions. Who are the people? In what sense should the people rule? And how far should popular rule extend?

Who are the people?

One of the core features of democracy is the principle of political equality, the notion that political power should be distributed as widely and as evenly as possible. However, within what body or group should this power be distributed? In short, who constitutes 'the people'? On the face of it, the answer is simple: 'the *demos*', or 'the people', surely refers to *all* the people; that is, the entire population of the country. In practice, however, every democratic system has restricted political participation, sometimes severely.

As noted, early Greek writers usually used *demos* to refer to 'the many': that is, the disadvantaged and usually propertyless masses. Democracy therefore implied not political equality, but a bias towards the poor. In Greek city-states, political participation was restricted to a tiny proportion of the population, male citizens over the age of 20, thereby excluding all women, slaves and foreigners. Strict restrictions on voting also existed in most western states until well into the twentieth century, usually in the form of a property qualification or the exclusion of women. Universal suffrage was not established in the UK until 1928, when women gained full voting rights. In the USA, it was not achieved until the early 1960s, when African-American people in many Southern states were able to vote for the first time, and in Switzerland universal suffrage was established in 1971 when women were eventually enfranchised. Nevertheless, an important restriction continues to be practised in all democratic systems in the form of the exclusion of children from political participation, although the age of majority ranges from 21 down to as low as 15 (as in Iranian presidential elections up to 2007). Technical restrictions are also often placed on, for example, the certifiably insane and imprisoned criminals.

Although 'the people' is now accepted as meaning virtually all adult citizens, the term can be construed in a number of different ways. The people, for instance, can be viewed as a single, cohesive body, bound together by a common or collective interest: in this sense, the people are one and indivisible. Such a view tends to generate a model of democracy that, like Rousseau's (see p. 97) theory, examined in the next main section, focuses upon the 'general will' or collective will, rather than the 'private will' of each individual. Alternatively, as division and disagreement exist within all communities, 'the people' may in practice be taken to mean 'the majority'. In this case, democracy comes to mean the strict application of the principle of **majority rule**. This can, nevertheless, mean that democracy degenerates into the 'tyranny of the majority'. Finally, there is the issue of the body of people within which democratic politics should operate. Where should be the location or 'site' of democracy? Although, thanks to the potency of political nationalism, the definition 'the people' is usually understood in national terms, the ideas of local democracy and, in the light of globalization (see p. 142), **cosmopolitan democracy** (discussed in the final section of the chapter) have also been advanced.

How should the people rule?

Most conceptions of democracy are based on the principle of 'government *by* the people'. This implies that, in effect, people govern themselves – that they participate in making the crucial decisions that structure their lives and determine the fate of their society. This participation can take a number of forms, however. In the case of direct democracy, popular participation entails direct and continuous involvement in decision-making, through devices such as referendums (see p. 201), mass meetings, or even interactive television. The alternative and more common form of democratic participation is the act of voting, which is the central feature of what is usually called 'representative democracy'. When citizens vote, they do not so much make the decisions that structure their own lives as choose who will make those decisions on their behalf. What gives voting its democratic character, however, is that, provided that the election is competitive, it empowers the public to 'kick the rascals out', and it thus makes politicians publicly accountable.

There are also models of democracy that are built on the principle of 'government *for* the people', and that allow little scope for public participation of any kind, direct or indirect. The most grotesque example of this was found in the so-called '**totalitarian democracies**' that developed under fascist dictators such as Mussolini and Hitler. The democratic credentials of such regimes were based on the claim that the 'leader', and the leader alone, articulated the genuine interests of the people, thus implying that a 'true' democracy can be equated with an absolute dictatorship. In such cases, popular rule meant nothing more than ritualized submission to the will of an all-powerful leader, orchestrated through rallies, marches and demonstrations. This was sometimes portrayed as plebiscitary democracy. Although totalitarian democracies have proved to be a travesty of the conventional notion of democratic rule, they demonstrate the tension that can exist between 'government *by* the people' (or popular participation), and 'government *for* the people' (rule in the public interest). Advocates of representative democracy, for example, have wished to confine popular participation in politics to the act of voting, precisely because they fear that the general public lack the wisdom, education and experience to rule wisely on their own behalf.

How far should popular rule extend?

Now that we have decided who 'the people' are, and how they should rule, it is necessary to consider how far their rule should extend. What is the proper realm of democracy? What issues is it right for the people to decide, and what should be left to individual citizens? In many respects, such questions reopen the debate about the proper relationship between the public realm and the private realm that was discussed in Chapter 1. Models of democracy that have been constructed on the basis of liberal individualism have usually proposed that democracy be restricted to political life, with politics being narrowly defined. From this perspective, the purpose of democracy is to establish, through some process of popular participation, a framework of laws within which individuals can conduct their own affairs and pursue their private interests. Democratic solutions, then, are appropriate only for matters that specifically relate to the

● **Totalitarian democracy**: An absolute dictatorship that masquerades as a democracy, typically based on the leader's claim to a monopoly of ideological wisdom.

Focus on . . .
Direct democracy or representative democracy?

Direct democracy (sometimes 'classical', 'participatory', or 'radical' democracy) is based on the direct, unmediated and continuous participation of citizens in the tasks of government. Direct democracy thus obliterates the distinction between government and the governed, and between the state and civil society; it is a system of popular self-government. It was achieved in ancient Athens through a form of government by mass meeting; its most common modern manifestation is the use of the referendum (see p. 201). The merits of direct democracy include the following:

- It heightens the control that citizens can exercise over their own destinies, as it is the only pure form of democracy.
- It creates a better-informed and more politically sophisticated citizenry, and thus it has educational benefits.
- It enables the public to express their own views and interests without having to rely on self-serving politicians.
- It ensures that rule is legitimate, in the sense that people are more likely to accept decisions that they have made themselves.

Representative democracy is a limited and indirect form of democracy. It is limited in that popular participation in government is infrequent and brief, being restricted to the act of voting every few years. It is indirect in that the public do not exercise power themselves; they merely select those who will rule on their behalf. This form of rule is democratic only insofar as representation (see p. 197) establishes a reliable and effective link between the government and the governed. This is sometimes expressed in the notion of an electoral mandate (see p. 200). The strengths of representative democracy include the following:

- It offers a practicable form of democracy (direct popular participation is achievable only in small communities).
- It relieves ordinary citizens of the burden of decision-making, thus making possible a division of labour in politics.
- It allows government to be placed in the hands of those with better education, expert knowledge and greater experience.
- It maintains stability by distancing ordinary citizens from politics, thereby encouraging them to accept compromise.

- **Radical democracy**: A form of democracy that favours decentralization and participation, the widest possible dispersal of political power.

- **Economic democracy**: A broad term that covers attempts to apply democratic principles to the workplace, ranging from profit-sharing and the use of workers' councils to full workers' self-management.

community; used in other circumstances, democracy amounts to an infringement of liberty. Not uncommonly, this fear of democracy is most acute in the case of direct or participatory democracy.

However, an alternative view of democracy is often developed by, for example, socialists and radical democrats. In **radical democracy**, democracy is seen not as a means of laying down a framework within which individuals can go about their own business but, rather, as a general principle that is applicable to all areas of social existence. People are seen as having a basic right to participate in the making of *any* decisions that affect their lives, with democracy simply being the collective process through which this is done. This position is evident in socialist demands for the collectivization of wealth and the introduction of workers' self-management, both of which are seen as ways of democratizing economic life. Instead of endorsing mere political democracy, socialists have therefore called for 'social democracy' or '**economic democracy**'. Feminists, similarly, have demanded the democratization of family life, understood as the right of all to

CONCEPT

Plebiscitary democracy

Plebiscitary democracy is a form of democratic rule that operates through an unmediated link between the rulers and the ruled, established by plebiscites (or referendums). These allow the public to express their views on political issues directly. However, this type of democracy is often criticized because of the scope it offers for demagoguery (rule by political leaders who manipulate the masses through oratory, and appeal to their prejudices and passions). This type of democracy may amount to little more than a system of mass acclamation that gives dictatorship a populist (see p. 307) gloss.

participate in the making of decisions in the domestic or private sphere. From this perspective, democracy is regarded as a friend of liberty, not as its enemy. Only when such principles are ignored can oppression and exploitation flourish.

Models of democracy

All too frequently, democracy is treated as a single, unambiguous phenomenon. It is often assumed that what passes for democracy in most western societies (a system of regular and competitive elections based on a universal franchise) is the only, or the only legitimate, form of democracy. Sometimes this notion of democracy is qualified by the addition of the term 'liberal', turning it into liberal democracy. In reality, however, there are a number of rival theories or models of democracy, each offering its own version of popular rule. This highlights not merely the variety of democratic forms and mechanisms, but also, more fundamentally, the very different grounds on which democratic rule can be justified. Even liberal democracy is a misleading term, as competing liberal views of democratic organization can be identified. Four contrasting models of democracy can be identified as follows:

- classical democracy
- protective democracy
- developmental democracy
- people's democracy.

Classical democracy

The classical model of democracy is based on the *polis*, or city-state, of Ancient Greece, and particularly on the system of rule that developed in the largest and most powerful Greek city-state, Athens. The form of direct democracy that operated in Athens during the fourth and fifth centuries BCE is often portrayed as the only pure or ideal system of popular participation. Nevertheless, although the model had considerable impact on later thinkers such as Rousseau and Marx (see p. 41), Athenian democracy (see p. 95) developed a very particular kind of direct popular rule, one that has only a very limited application in the modern world. Athenian democracy amounted to a form of government by mass meeting.

What made Athenian democracy so remarkable was the level of political activity of its citizens. Not only did they participate in regular meetings of the Assembly, but they were also, in large numbers, prepared to shoulder the responsibility of public office and decision-making. The most influential contemporaneous critic of this form of democracy was the philosopher Plato (see p. 13). Plato attacked the principle of political equality on the grounds that the mass of the people possess neither the wisdom nor the experience to rule wisely on their own behalf. His solution, advanced in *The Republic*, was that government be placed in the hands of a class of philosopher kings, Guardians, whose rule would amount to a kind of enlightened dictatorship. On a practical level, however, the principal drawback of Athenian democracy was that it could operate only by excluding the mass of the population from political activity. Participation was restricted to Athenian-born males who were over 20 years of age. Slaves (the majority of the population), women and foreigners had no political rights

Debating . . .
Is democracy always the best form of government?

In modern politics, democracy has come to be so widely accepted that it appears to be almost politically incorrect to question it. The 'right' solution to a political problem is thus the democratic solution; that is, one made either by the people themselves or, more commonly, by politicians who are accountable to the people. But why is democracy so widely revered? And are there circumstances in which democratic rule is inappropriate or undesirable?

YES

The highest form of politics. The unique strength of democracy is that it is able to address the central challenge of politics – the existence of rival views and interests within the same society – while containing the tendency towards bloodshed and violence. In short, democratic societies are stable and peaceful. This occurs because democracy relies on open debate, persuasion and compromise. People with rival views or competing interests are encouraged to find a way of living together in relative harmony because each has a political voice. Democracy is therefore a kind of political safety valve, democratic participation preventing the build up of anger and frustration and, thereby, containing political extremism.

Democracy as a universal value. It is now widely argued that democracy is a human right: a fundamental and absolute right that belongs to all people, regardless of nationality, religion, gender and other differences. Rights of political participation and access to power, especially the right to vote, are universally applicable because they stem from the basic entitlement to shape the decisions that affect one's own life – the right to self-rule. Indeed, an equal access to power and the right to political participation could be viewed not simply as virtues in their own right, but as preconditions for the maintenance of all other rights and freedoms.

Keeping tyranny at bay. All systems of rule are apt to become tyrannies against the people, reflecting the fact that those in power (and, for that matter, all people) are inclined to place self-interest before the interests of others. Governments and leaders therefore need to be checked or constrained, and there is no more effective constraint on power than democracy. This is because democratic rule operates through a mechanism of accountability, which ultimately allows the public to 'kick the rascals out'. Democratic societies are therefore not only the most stable societies in the world, but also the societies in which citizens enjoy the widest realm of freedom.

NO

The disharmony of democracy. Far from being a guarantee of stability, democracy is biased in favour of conflict and disharmony. This is because democracy sets up an ongoing electoral battle between opponents who are encouraged to condemn one another, exaggerating their faults and denying their achievements. Democratic politics is often, as a result, noisy and unedifying. While the disharmony of democracy is unlikely to threaten structural breakdown in mature and relatively prosperous societies, democracy in the developing world may make things worse rather than better (Hawksley, 2009). 'Democratization' may therefore deepen tribal, regional or ethnic tensions, and strengthen the tendency towards charismatic leadership, thereby breeding authoritarianism.

Democracy as westernization. Rather than being universally applicable, democracy is based on values and assumptions that betray the cultural biases of its western heartland. Democracy is rooted in ideas such as individualism, notably through the principle of equal citizenship and 'one person, one vote', and notions of pluralism and competition that are intrinsically liberal in character. The dominant form of democracy is therefore western-style democracy, and its spread, sometimes imposed and always encouraged, to the non-western world can therefore be viewed as a form of cultural imperialism.

Good government not popular government. Democratic solutions to problems are often neither wise nor sensible. The problem with democracy is that the dictates of wisdom and experience tend to be ignored because the views of the well-educated minority are swamped by those of the less well-educated majority. Being committed to the principle of political equality, democracy cannot cope with the fact that the majority is not always right. This is a particular concern for economic policy, where options, such as raising taxes or cutting government spending, which may best promote long-term economic development, may be ruled out simply because they are unpopular.

CONCEPT

Athenian democracy

Athenian democracy is characterized by the high level of citizen involvement in the affairs of the city-state. Major decisions were made by the Assembly, or *Ecclesia*, to which all citizens belonged. When full-time public officials were needed, they were chosen on a basis of lot or rota to ensure that they constituted a microcosm of the larger citizenry. A Council, consisting of 500 citizens, acted as the executive or steering committee of the Assembly, and a 50-strong Committee, in turn, made proposals to the Council. The President of the Committee held office for only a single day, and no Athenian could hold this honour more than once in his lifetime.

● **Natural rights**: God-given rights that are fundamental to human beings and are therefore inalienable (they cannot be taken away).

whatsoever. Indeed, Athenian citizens were able to devote so much of their lives to politics only because slavery relieved them of the need to engage in arduous labour, and the confinement of women to the private realm freed men from domestic responsibilities. Nevertheless, the classical model of direct and continuous popular participation in political life has been kept alive in, for instance, the township meetings of New England in the USA, the communal assemblies that operate in the smaller Swiss cantons and in the wider use of referendums.

Protective democracy

When democratic ideas were revived in the seventeenth and eighteenth centuries, they appeared in a form that was very different from the classical democracy of Ancient Greece. In particular, democracy was seen less as a mechanism through which the public could participate in political life, and more as a device through which citizens could protect themselves from the encroachments of government, hence 'protective democracy'. This view appealed particularly to early liberal thinkers whose concern was, above all, to create the widest realm of individual liberty. The desire to protect the individual from over-mighty government was expressed in perhaps the earliest of all democratic sentiments, Aristotle's response to Plato: 'who will guard the Guardians?'.

This same concern with unchecked power was taken up in the seventeenth century by John Locke (see p. 31), who argued that the right to vote was based on the existence of **natural rights** and, in particular, on the right to property. If government, through taxation, possessed the power to expropriate property, citizens were entitled to protect themselves by controlling the composition of the tax-setting body: the legislature. In other words, democracy came to mean a system of 'government by consent' operating through a representative assembly. However, Locke himself was not a democrat by modern standards, as he believed that only property owners should vote, on the basis that only they had natural rights that could be infringed by government. The more radical notion of universal suffrage was advanced from the late eighteenth century onwards by utilitarian theorists such as Jeremy Bentham and James Mill (1773–1836). The utilitarian (see p. 353) case for democracy is also based on the need to protect or advance individual interests. Bentham came to believe that, since all individuals seek pleasure and the avoidance of pain, a universal franchise (conceived in his day as manhood suffrage) was the only way of promoting 'the greatest happiness for the greatest number'.

However, to justify democracy on protective grounds is to provide only a qualified endorsement of democratic rule. In short, protective democracy is but a limited and indirect form of democracy. In practice, the consent of the governed is exercised through voting in regular and competitive elections. This thereby ensures the accountability of those who govern. Political equality is thus understood in strictly technical terms to mean equal voting rights. Moreover, this is, above all, a system of constitutional democracy that operates within a set of formal or informal rules that check the exercise of government power. If the right to vote is a means of defending individual liberty, liberty must also be guaranteed by a strictly enforced separation of powers via the creation of a separate executive, legislature and judiciary, and by the maintenance of basic rights and freedoms, such as freedom of expression, freedom of movement, and freedom

Jeremy Bentham (1748–1832)

UK philosopher, legal reformer and founder of utilitarianism. Bentham developed a moral and philosophical system that was based on the idea that human beings are rationally self-interested creatures or utility maximizers, which he believed provided a scientific basis for legal and political reforms. Using the 'greatest happiness' principle, his followers, the Philosophic Radicals, were responsible for many of the reforms in social administration, law, government and economics in the UK in the nineteenth century. A supporter of *laissez-faire* economics, in later life Bentham also became a firm advocate of political democracy. His utilitarian creed was developed in *Fragments on Government* ([1776] 1948), and more fully in *Principles of Morals and Legislation* (1789).

from arbitrary arrest. Ultimately, protective democracy aims to give citizens the widest possible scope to live their lives as they choose. It is therefore compatible with *laissez-faire* capitalism (see p. 132) and the belief that individuals should be entirely responsible for their economic and social circumstances. Protective democracy has therefore particularly appealed to classical liberals and, in modern politics, to supporters of the New Right.

Developmental democracy

Although early democratic theory focused on the need to protect individual rights and interests, it soon developed an alternative focus: a concern with the development of the human individual and the community. This gave rise to quite new models of democratic rule that can broadly be referred to as systems of developmental democracy. The most novel, and radical, such model was developed by Jean-Jacques Rousseau. In many respects, Rousseau's ideas mark a departure from the dominant, liberal conception of democracy, and they came to have an impact on the Marxist and anarchist traditions as well as, later, on the New Left. For Rousseau, democracy was ultimately a means through which human beings could achieve freedom (see p. 339) or autonomy, in the sense of 'obedience to a law one prescribes to oneself'. In other words, citizens are 'free' only when they participate directly and continuously in shaping the life of their community. This is an idea that moves well beyond the conventional notion of electoral democracy and offers support for the more radical ideal of direct democracy. Indeed, Rousseau was a strenuous critic of the practice of elections used in England, arguing in *The Social Contract* ([1762] 1913) as follows:

> The English people believes itself to be free, it is gravely mistaken; it is only free when it elects its member of parliament; as soon as they are elected, the people are enslaved; it is nothing. In the brief moment of its freedom, the English people makes such use of its freedom that it deserves to lose it.

● **General will**: The genuine interests of a collective body, equivalent to the common good; the will of all, provided each person acts selflessly.

However, what gives Rousseau's model its novel character is his insistence that freedom ultimately means obedience to the **general will**. Rousseau believed the

Jean-Jacques Rousseau (1712–78)

Geneva-born French moral and political philosopher, perhaps the principal intellectual influence upon the French Revolution. Rousseau was entirely self-taught. He moved to Paris in 1742, and became an intimate of leading members of the French Enlightenment, especially Diderot. His writings, ranging over education, the arts, science, literature and philosophy, reflect a deep belief in the goodness of 'natural man' and the corruption of 'social man'. Rousseau's political teaching, summarized in *Émile* (1762) and developed in *The Social Contract* ([1762] 1913), advocates a radical form of democracy that has influenced liberal, socialist, anarchist and, some would argue, fascist thought. His autobiography, *Confessions* (1770), examines his life with remarkable candour and demonstrates a willingness to expose weaknesses.

general will to be the 'true' will of each citizen, in contrast to his or her 'private' or selfish will. By obeying the general will, citizens are therefore doing nothing more than obeying their own 'true' natures, the general will being what individuals would will if they were to act selflessly. In Rousseau's view, such a system of radical developmental democracy required not merely political equality, but a relatively high level of economic equality. Although not a supporter of common ownership, Rousseau nevertheless proposed that 'no citizen shall be rich enough to buy another and none so poor as to be forced to sell himself' ([1762] 1913).

Rousseau's theories have helped to shape the modern idea of participatory democracy taken up by New Left thinkers in the 1960s and 1970s. This extols the virtues of a 'participatory society', a society in which each and every citizen is able to achieve self-development by participating in the decisions that shape his or her life. This goal can be achieved only through the promotion of openness, **accountability** and decentralization within all the key institutions of society: within the family, the workplace and the local community just as much as within 'political' institutions such as parties, interest groups and legislative bodies. At the heart of this model is the notion of 'grass-roots democracy'; that is, the belief that political power should be exercised at the lowest possible level. Nevertheless, Rousseau's own theories have been criticized for distinguishing between citizens' 'true' wills and their 'felt' or subjective wills. The danger of this is that, if the general will cannot be established by simply asking citizens what they want (because they may be blinded by selfishness), there is scope for the general will to be defined from above, perhaps by a dictator claiming to act in the 'true' interests of society. Rousseau is therefore sometimes seen as the architect of so-called 'totalitarian democracy' (Talmon, 1952).

However, a more modest form of developmental democracy has also been advanced that is compatible with the liberal model of representative government. This view of developmental democracy is rooted in the writings of John Stuart Mill (see p. 198). For Mill, the central virtue of democracy was that it promotes the 'highest and harmonious' development of individual capacities. By participating in political life, citizens enhance their understanding, strengthen their sensibilities and achieve a higher level of personal development. In short, democracy is essentially an educational experience. As a result, Mill proposed the

● **Accountability**:
Answerability; a duty to explain one's conduct and be open to criticism by others.

CONCEPT

Parliamentary democracy

Parliamentary democracy is a form of democratic rule that operates through a popularly elected deliberative assembly, which mediates between government and the people. Democracy, in this sense, means responsible and representative government. Parliamentary democracy thus balances popular participation against elite rule: government is accountable not directly to the public but to the public's elected representatives. The alleged strength of such a system is that representatives are, by virtue of their education and experience, better able than citizens themselves to define their best interests.

broadening of popular participation, arguing that the franchise should be extended to all but those who are illiterate. In the process, he suggested (radically, for his time) that suffrage should also be extended to women. In addition, he advocated strong and independent local authorities in the belief that this would broaden the opportunities available for holding public office.

On the other hand, Mill, in common with all liberals, was also aware of the dangers of democracy. Indeed, Mill's views are out of step with mainstream liberal thought in that he rejected the idea of formal political equality. Following Plato, Mill did not believe that all political opinions are of equal value. Consequently, he proposed a system of plural voting: unskilled workers would have a single vote, skilled workers two votes, and graduates and members of the learned professions five or six votes. However, his principal reservation about democracy was derived from the more typical liberal fear of what Alexis de Tocqueville (see p. 245) famously described as 'the tyranny of the majority'. In other words, democracy always contains the threat that individual liberty and minority rights may be crushed in the name of the people. Mill's particular concern was that democracy would undermine debate, criticism and intellectual life in general by encouraging people to accept the will of the majority, thereby promoting uniformity and dull conformism. Quite simply, the majority is not always right; wisdom cannot be determined by the simple device of a show of hands. Mill's ideas therefore support the idea of **deliberative democracy** or parliamentary democracy.

People's democracy

The term 'people's democracy' is derived from the orthodox communist regimes that sprang up on the Soviet model in the aftermath of World War II. It is here used, however, to refer broadly to the various democratic models that the Marxist tradition has generated. Although they differ, these models offer a clear contrast to the more familiar liberal democratic ones. Marxists have tended to be dismissive of liberal or parliamentary democracy, seeing it as a form of 'bourgeois' or 'capitalist' democracy. Nevertheless, Marxists were drawn to the concept or ideal of democracy because of its clear egalitarian implications. The term was used, in particular, to designate the goal of social equality brought about through the common ownership of wealth ('social democracy' in its original sense), in contrast to 'political' democracy, which establishes only a facade of equality.

Marx believed that the overthrow of capitalism would be a trigger that would allow genuine democracy to flourish. In his view, a fully communist society would come into existence only after a transitionary period characterized by 'the revolutionary dictatorship of the proletariat'. In effect, a system of 'bourgeois' democracy would be replaced by a very different system of 'proletarian' democracy. Although Marx refused to describe in detail how this transitionary society would be organized, its broad shape can be discerned from his admiration for the Paris Commune of 1871, which was a short-lived experiment in what approximated to direct democracy.

The form of democracy that was developed in twentieth-century communist states, however, owed more to the ideas of V. I. Lenin (see p. 99) than it did to those of Marx. Although Lenin's 1917 slogan 'All power to the Soviets' (the workers' and soldiers' and sailors' councils) had kept alive the notion of

● **Deliberative democracy**: A form of democracy that emphasizes the need for discourse and debate to help to define the public interest.

Vladimir Ilyich Lenin (1870–1924)

Russian Marxist theorist and active revolutionary. As leader of the Bolsheviks, Lenin masterminded the 1917 Russian Bolshevik Revolution, and became the first leader of the USSR. His contributions to Marxism were his theory of the revolutionary (or vanguard) party, outlined in *What is to be Done?* ([1902] 1968); his analysis of colonialism as an economic phenomenon, described in *Imperialism, the Highest Stage of Capitalism* ([1916] 1970); and his firm commitment to the 'insurrectionary road to socialism', developed in *State and Revolution* (1917). Lenin's reputation is inevitably tied up with the subsequent course of Soviet history; he is seen by some as the father of Stalinist oppression, but by others as a critic of bureaucracy and a defender of debate and argument.

commune democracy, in reality power in Soviet Russia quickly fell into the hands of the Bolshevik party (soon renamed the 'Communist Party'). In Lenin's view, this party was nothing less than 'the vanguard of the working class'. Armed with Marxism, the party claimed that it was able to perceive the genuine interests of the proletariat and thus guide it to the realization of its revolutionary potential. This theory became the cornerstone of '**Leninist democracy**', and it was accepted by all other orthodox communist regimes as one of the core features of Marxism–Leninism. However, the weakness of this model is that Lenin failed to build into it any mechanism for checking the power of the Communist Party (and, particularly, its leaders), and for ensuring that it remained sensitive and accountable to the proletarian class. To rephrase Aristotle, 'who will guard the Communist Party?'

Democracy in practice: rival views

Although there continues to be controversy about which is the most desirable form of democracy, much of contemporary debate revolves around how democracy works in practice and what 'democratization' (see p. 272) implies. This reflects the fact that there is broad, even worldwide, acceptance of a particular model of democracy, generally termed liberal democracy. Despite the existence of competing tendencies within this broad category, certain central features are clear:

- Liberal democracy is an indirect and representative form of democracy, in that political office is gained through success in regular elections that are conducted on the basis of formal political equality.
- It is based on competition and electoral choice. These are achieved through political pluralism, tolerance of a wide range of contending beliefs, and the existence of conflicting social philosophies and rival political movements and parties.
- It is characterized by a clear distinction between the state and civil society. This is maintained through the existence of autonomous groups and interests, and the market or capitalist organization of economic life.

● **Leninist democracy**: A form of democracy in which the communist party, organized on the basis of 'democratic centralism', articulates the interest of the proletariat.

Pluralism

In its broad sense, pluralism is a belief in, or a commitment to, diversity or multiplicity (the existence of many things). As a descriptive term, pluralism may be used to denote the existence of party competition (political pluralism), a multiplicity of moral values (ethical pluralism), or a variety of cultural norms (cultural pluralism). As a normative term, it suggests that diversity is healthy and desirable, usually because it safeguards individual liberty and promotes debate, argument and understanding. More narrowly, pluralism is a theory of the distribution of political power. It holds that power is widely and evenly dispersed in society.

● **Madisonian democracy**: A form of democracy that incorporates constitutional protections for minorities that enable them to resist majority rule.

● It provides protection for minorites and individuals, particularly through the allocation of basic rights that safeguard them from the will of the majority.

Nevertheless, there is a considerable amount of disagreement about the meaning and significance of liberal democracy. Does it, for instance, ensure a genuine and healthy dispersal of political power? Do democratic processes genuinely promote long-term benefits, or are they self-defeating? Can political equality coexist with economic inequality? In short, this form of democracy is interpreted in different ways by different theorists. The most important of these interpretations are advanced by:

● pluralism
● elitism
● corporatism
● the New Right
● Marxism.

Pluralist view

Pluralist ideas can be traced back to early liberal political philosophy, and notably to the ideas of Locke and Montesquieu (see p. 312). Their first systematic development, however, is found in the contributions of James Madison (see p. 319) to *The Federalist Papers* (Hamilton *et al.*, [1787–89] 1961). In considering the transformation of America from a loose confederation of states into the federal USA, Madison's particular fear was the 'problem of factions'. In common with most liberals, Madison argued that unchecked democratic rule might simply lead to majoritarianism, to the crushing of individual rights and to the expropriation of property in the name of the people. What made Madison's work notable, however, was his stress upon the multiplicity of interests and groups in society, and his insistence that, unless each such group possessed a political voice, stability and order would be impossible. He therefore proposed a system of divided government based on the separation of powers (see p. 313), bicameralism and federalism (see p. 382), that offered a variety of access points to competing groups and interests. The resulting system of rule by multiple minorities is often referred to as '**Madisonian democracy**'. Insofar as it recognizes both the existence of diversity or multiplicity in society, and the fact that such multiplicity is desirable, Madison's model is the first developed statement of pluralist principles.

The most influential modern exponent of pluralist theory is Robert Dahl (see p. 250). As described in *Who Governs? Democracy and Power in an American City* (1961), Dahl carried out an empirical study of the distribution of power in New Haven, Connecticut, USA. He concluded that, although the politically privileged and economically powerful exerted greater power than ordinary citizens, no ruling or permanent elite was able to dominate the political process. His conclusion was that 'New Haven is an example of a democratic system, warts and all'. Dahl recognized that modern democratic systems differ markedly from the classical democracies of Ancient Greece. With Charles Lindblom, he coined the term 'polyarchy' (see p. 273) to mean rule by the many, as distinct from rule by all citizens. The key feature of such a system of pluralist democracy (see p. 101) is that

CONCEPT

Pluralist democracy

The term pluralist democracy is sometimes used interchangeably with liberal democracy. More specifically, it refers to a form of democracy that operates through the capacity of organized groups and interests to articulate popular demands and ensure responsive government. The conditions for a healthy pluralist democracy include: (1) a wide dispersal of political power amongst competing groups, specifically the absence of elite groups; (2) a high degree of internal responsiveness, group leaders being accountable to members; and (3) a neutral governmental machine that is sufficiently fragmented to offer groups a number of points of access.

competition between parties at election time, and the ability of interest or pressure groups to articulate their views freely, establishes a reliable link between the government and the governed, and creates a channel of communication between the two. While this may fall a long way short of the ideal of popular self-government, its supporters nevertheless argue that it ensures a sufficient level of accountability and popular responsiveness for it to be regarded as democratic.

However, the relationship between pluralism and democracy may not be a secure one. For instance, one of the purposes of the Madisonian system was, arguably, to constrain democracy in the hope of safeguarding property. In other words, the system of rule by multiple minorities may simply have been a device to prevent the majority (the propertyless masses) from exercising political power. A further problem is the danger of what has been called 'pluralist stagnation'. This occurs as organized groups and economic interests become so powerful that they create a log jam, resulting in the problem of government 'overload'. In such circumstances, a pluralist system may simply become ungovernable. Finally, there is the problem identified by Dahl in later works, such as *A Preface to Economic Democracy* (1985); notably, that the unequal ownership of economic resources tends to concentrate political power in the hands of the few, and deprive the many of it. This line of argument runs parallel to the conventional Marxist critique of pluralist democracy, and has given rise to neopluralism (see p. 63).

Elitist view

Elitism (see p. 102) developed as a critique of egalitarian ideas such as democracy and socialism. It draws attention to the fact of elite rule, either as an inevitable and desirable feature of social existence, or as a remediable and regrettable one. Classical elitists, such as Vilfredo Pareto (1848–1923), Gaetano Mosca (1857–1941) and Robert Michels (1876–1936), tended to take the former position. For them, democracy was no more than a foolish delusion, because political power is always exercised by a privileged minority: an elite. For example, in *The Ruling Class* ([1896] 1939), Mosca proclaimed that, in all societies, 'two classes of people appear – a class that rules and a class that is ruled'. In his view, the resources or attributes that are necessary for rule are always unequally distributed, and, further, a cohesive minority will always be able to manipulate and control the masses, even in a parliamentary democracy. Pareto suggested that the qualities needed to rule conforms to one of two psychological types: 'foxes' (who rule by cunning and are able to manipulate the consent of the masses), and 'lions' (whose domination is typically achieved through coercion and violence). Michels developed an alternative line of argument based on the tendency within all organizations, however democratic they might appear, for power to be concentrated in the hands of a small group of dominant figures who can organize and make decisions. He termed this 'the iron law of oligarchy' (see p. 232).

Whereas classical elitists strove to prove that democracy was always a myth, modern elitist theorists have tended to highlight how far particular political systems fall short of the democratic ideal. An example of this can be found in C. Wright Mills' influential account of the power structure in the USA. In contrast to the pluralist notion of a wide and broadly democratic dispersal of power, Mills, in *The Power Elite* (1956), offered a portrait of a USA dominated by a nexus of leading groups. In his view, this 'power elite' comprised a triumvirate of

CONCEPT

Elitism

Elite originally meant, and can still mean, 'the highest', 'the best', or 'the excellent'. Used in an empirical sense, it refers to a minority in whose hands power, wealth or privilege is concentrated. Elitism is a belief in, or practice of, rule by an elite or minority. *Normative* elitism suggests that political power should be vested in the hands of a wise or enlightened minority. *Classical* elitism claimed to be empirical (although normative beliefs often intruded), and saw elite rule as an unchangeable fact of social existence. *Modern* elitism is also empirical, but it is more critical and discriminating about the causes of elite rule.

big business (particularly defence-related industries), the US military and political cliques surrounding the President. Drawing on a combination of economic power, bureaucratic control and access to the highest levels of the executive branch of government, the power elite is able to shape key 'history-making' decisions, especially in the fields of defence and foreign policy, as well as strategic economic policy. The power-elite model suggests that liberal democracy in the USA is largely a sham. Elitists have, moreover, argued that empirical studies have supported pluralist conclusions only because Dahl and others have ignored the importance of non-decision-making as a manifestation of power (see p. 9).

Certain elite theorists have nevertheless argued that a measure of democratic accountability is consistent with elite rule. Whereas the power-elite model portrays the elite as a cohesive body, bound together by common or overlapping interests, competitive elitism (sometimes called 'democratic elitism') highlights the significance of elite rivalry (see Figure 4.1). In other words, the elite, consisting of the leading figures from a number of competing groups and interests, is fractured. This view is often associated with Joseph Schumpeter's (see p. 141) 'realistic' model of democracy outlined in *Capitalism, Socialism and Democracy* (1942):

> The democratic method is that institutional arrangement for arriving at political decisions in which individuals acquire the power to decide by means of a competitive struggle for the people's vote.

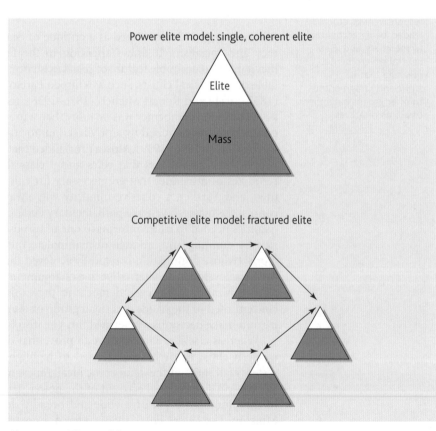

Figure 4.1   Elite models

The electorate can decide which elite rules, but cannot change the fact that power is always exercised by an elite. This model of competitive elitism was developed by Anthony Downs (1957) into the 'economic theory of democracy'. In effect, electoral competition creates a political market in which politicians act as entrepreneurs bent upon achieving government power, and individual voters behave like consumers, voting for the party with the policies that most closely reflect their own preferences. Downs argued that a system of open and competitive elections guarantees democratic rule because it places government in the hands of the party whose philosophy, values and policies correspond most closely to the preferences of the largest group of voters. As Schumpeter put it, 'democracy is the rule of the politician'. As a model of democratic politics, competitive elitism at least has the virtue that it corresponds closely to the workings of the liberal-democratic political system. Indeed, it emerged more as an attempt to *describe* how the democratic process works than through a desire to *prescribe* certain values and principles – political equality, popular participation, freedom or whatever.

Corporatist view

The origins of corporatism (see p. 251) date back to the attempt in Fascist Italy to construct a so-called 'corporate state' by integrating both managers and workers into the processes of government. Corporatist theorists, however, have drawn attention to parallel developments in the world's major industrialized states. In the form of **neocorporatism**, or liberal corporatism, this gave rise to the spectre of 'tripartite government', in which government is conducted through organizations that allow state officials, employers' groups and unions to deal directly with one another. To a large extent, this tendency to integrate economic interests into government (which was common in the post-1945 period, and particularly prominent in, for example, Sweden, Norway, the Netherlands and Austria) was a consequence of the drift towards economic management and intervention. As government sought to manage economic life and deliver an increasingly broad range of public services, it recognized the need for institutional arrangements designed to secure the cooperation and support of major economic interests. Where attempts have been made to shift economic policy away from state intervention and towards the free market (as in the UK since 1979), the impact of corporatism has markedly diminished.

The significance of corporatism in terms of democratic processes is clearly considerable. There are those who, like the British guild socialists, argue that corporatism makes possible a form of functional representation, in that individuals' views and interests are articulated more by the groups to which they belong than through the mechanism of competitive elections. What is called 'corporate pluralism' thus portrays tripartism as a mechanism through which the major groups and interests in society compete to shape government policy. Some commentators, however, see corporatism as a threat to democracy. In the first place, corporatism only advantages groups that are accorded privileged access to government. 'Insider' groups therefore possess a political voice, while 'outsider' groups are denied one. Second, corporatism can work to the benefit of the state, rather than major economic interests, in that the **peak associations** that the government chooses to deal with can be used to exert discipline over their

● **Neocorporatism**: A tendency found in western polyarchies for organized interests to be granted privileged and institutionalized access to policy formulation.

● **Peak association**: A group recognized by government as representing the general or collective interests of businesses or workers.

members and to filter out radical demands. Finally, corporatism threatens to subvert the processes of electoral or parliamentary democracy. Policy is made through negotiations between government officials and leaders of powerful economic interests, rather than through the deliberations of a representative assembly. Interest-group leaders may thus exert considerable political power, even though they are in no way publicly accountable and their influence is not subject to public scrutiny.

New Right view

The emergence of the New Right from the 1970s onwards has generated a very particular critique of democratic politics. This has focused on the danger of what has been called 'democratic overload': the paralysis of a political system that is subject to unrestrained group and electoral pressures. One aspect of this critique has highlighted the unsavoury face of corporatism. New Right theorists are keen advocates of the free market, believing that economies work best when left alone by government. The danger of corporatism from this perspective is that it empowers sectional groups and economic interests, enabling them to make demands on government for increased pay, public investment, subsidies, state protection and so on. In effect, corporatism allows well-placed interest groups to dominate and dictate to government. The result of this, according to the New Right, is an irresistible drift towards state intervention and economic stagnation (Olson, 1982).

Government 'overload' can also be seen to be a consequence of the electoral process. This was what Brittan (1977) referred to as 'the economic consequences of democracy'. In this view, electoral politics amounts to a self-defeating process in which politicians are encouraged to compete for power by offering increasingly unrealistic promises to the electorate. Both voters and politicians are held to blame here. Voters are attracted by promises of higher public spending because they calculate that the cost (an increased tax burden) will be spread over the entire population. Politicians, consumed by the desire to win power, attempt to outbid one another by making ever more generous spending pledges to the electorate. According to Brittan, the economic consequences of unrestrained democracy are high levels of inflation fuelled by public borrowing, and a tax burden that destroys enterprise and undermines growth. As characterized by Marquand (1988), the New Right view is that 'democracy is to adults what chocolate is to children: endlessly tempting; harmless in small doses; sickening in excess'. New Right theorists therefore tend to see democracy in strictly protective terms, regarding it essentially as a defence against arbitrary government, rather than a means of bringing about social transformation.

Marxist view

As pointed out in relation to people's democracy, the Marxist view of democratic politics is rooted in class analysis. In this view, political power cannot be understood narrowly in terms of electoral rights, or in terms of the ability of groups to articulate their interests by lobbying and campaigning. Rather, at a deeper level, political power reflects the distribution of economic power and, in particular, the unequal ownership of productive wealth. The Marxist critique of liberal democracy thus focuses upon the inherent tension between democracy and capitalism; that is, between the political equality that liberal democracy proclaims and the social inequality that a capitalist economy inevitably generates. Liberal democracies are thus seen as 'capitalist' or 'bourgeois' democracies that are manipulated and controlled by the entrenched power of a **ruling class**.

Marxism thus offers a distinctive critique of pluralist democracy. Power cannot be widely and evenly dispersed in society as long as class power is unequally distributed. Indeed, in many respects, the Marxist view parallels the elitist critique of pluralism. Both views suggest that power is ultimately concentrated in the hands of the few, the main difference being whether the few is conceived of as a 'power elite' or as a 'ruling class'. However, significant differences can also be identified. For instance, whereas elitists suggest that power derive from a variety of sources (education, social status, bureaucratic position, political connections, wealth and so on), Marxists emphasize the decisive importance of economic factors; notably, the ownership and control of the means of production. Modern Marxists, however, have been less willing to dismiss electoral democracy as nothing more than a sham. **Eurocommunists**, for example, abandoned the idea of revolution, embracing instead the notion of a peaceful, legal and democratic 'road to socialism'.

Towards cosmopolitan democracy?

The idea of cosmopolitan democracy has received growing attention due to the advance of globalization and the evident 'hollowing out' of domestic democratic processes focused on the nation-state. If global interconnectedness means that policy-making authority has shifted from national governments to international organizations, surely democracy should be recast in line with this? However, what would cosmopolitan democracy look like, and how would it operate? Two basic models have been advanced. The first would involve the construction of a world parliament, a body whose role would be to introduce greater scrutiny and openness to the process of global decision-making by calling to account established international organizations, such as the United Nations, the World Trade Organization, the International Monetary Fund and so forth. Very few advocates of such an idea contemplate the creation of a fully-fledged world government or global state; most, instead, favour a multilevel system of post-sovereign governance in which no body or level is able to exercise final authority. Held (1995) proposed a package of measures, including the establishment of a 'global parliament', reformed and more accountable international organizations, and the 'permanent shift of a growing proportion of a nation state's coercive capacity to regional and global institutions'. Monbiot (2004), for his part, backed the creation of a popularly elected world parliament, composed of 600 representatives, each with a constituency of about 10 million people, many of which would straddle national borders.

The alternative model of cosmopolitan democracy is less ambitious and formalized, relying less on the construction of new bodies and more on the reform of existing international organizations, often linked to the strengthening of global civil society (see p. 106). This model places its faith in non-governmental organizations (NGOs) (see p. 248) to reconfigure global power by offering an alternative to top-down corporate globalization. This idea of 'globalization from

● **Ruling class**: A Marxist term, denoting a class that dominates other classes and society at large by virtue of its ownership of productive wealth.

● **Eurocommunism**: A form of deradicalized communism that attempted to blend Marxism with liberal-democratic principles.

CONCEPT

Global civil society

Global civil society refers to a realm in which transnational non-governmental groups and associations interact. These groups are typically voluntary and non-profitmaking, setting them apart from TNCs (see p. 149). However, the term 'global civil society' is complex and contested. In its 'activist' version, transnational social movements are the key agents of global civil society, giving it an 'outsider' orientation, and a strong focus on cosmopolitan ideals. In its 'policy' version, NGOs are the key agents of global civil society, giving it an 'insider' orientation and meaning that it overlaps with global governance (see p. 432).

below' amounts to a bottom-up democratic vision of a civilizing world order. Such an approach would be effective to the extent that NGOs and transnational social movements could introduce an element of public scrutiny and accountability to the working of international bodies, conferences, summits and the like, meaning that global civil society functions as a channel of communications between the individual and global institutions.

However, the prospects for cosmopolitan democracy are far from rosy. In the first place, states, and especially major states, are likely to block any trend towards global democracy, or ensure that any 'alternative' bodies that may be created will lack credibility and remain peripheral to global decision-making. In a wider sense, the egalitarian thrust implicit in the idea of cosmopolitan democracy is simply out of step with the deep economic, political and military disparities of the existing global system. Aside from the obstacles confronting the transition to cosmopolitan democracy, critics have argued that the project itself may be profoundly misconceived. In the first place, however structured and composed, any global institution that is tasked with ensuring public accountability is doomed to failure. The inevitable 'gap' between popularly-elected global political institutions and ordinary citizens around the world would mean that any claim that these institutions are democratic would be mere pretence. Democracy, in this light, is perhaps only meaningful if it is local or national, and all international organizations, whether these are regional or global, are destined to suffer from a debilitating 'democratic deficit'. Second, the democratic credentials of NGOs and, for that matter, social movements may be entirely bogus. Large memberships, committed activists and the ability to mobilize popular protests and demonstrations undoubtedly give social movements and NGOs political influence, but they do not invest them with democratic authority. Quite simply, there is no way of testing the weight of their views against those of the population at large.

SUMMARY

● Legitimacy maintains political stability because it establishes a regime's right to rule, and so underpins the regime's authority over its people. Legitimacy may be based on traditional, charismatic or legal–rational authority. Nevertheless, structural imbalances in modern society may make it increasingly difficult to maintain legitimacy. Legitimation crises may arise from the conflict between the pressure for social and economic interventionism generated by democracy on the one hand, and the pressure generated by market economy on the other.

● Democratic legitimacy is now widely accepted as the only meaningful form of legitimacy. However, it has been suggested that economic and other factors may be more effective than democracy in maintaining legitimacy, that evidence of growing political disengagement in mature democracies indicates that democracy's capacity to deliver legitimacy is declining, and that non-democratic regimes may enjoy at least a measure of legitimacy.

● There are a number of rival models of democracy, each offering its own version of popular rule. Classical democracy, which is based on the political system of Ancient Athens, is defended on the grounds that it alone guarantees government by the people. Protective democracy gives citizens the greatest scope to live their lives as they choose. Developmental democracy has the virtue that, in extending participation, it widens liberty and fosters personal growth. People's democracy aims to achieve economic emancipation, rather than merely the extension of political rights.

● There is considerable controversy about how liberal-democratic systems work in practice. Pluralists praise the system's capacity to guarantee popular responsiveness and public accountability. Elitists highlight the tendency for political power to be concentrated in the hands of a privileged minority. Corporatists draw attention to the incorporation of groups into government. The New Right focuses on the dangers of 'democratic overload'. And Marxists point to tensions between democracy and capitalism.

● Growing global interdependence has stimulated interest in whether democracy can, and should, operate at a global or cosmopolitan level, either through the construction of some kind of world parliament, or through a global civil society. However, major obstacles stand in the way of cosmopolitan democracy, with many rejecting the idea as unfeasible in principle.

Questions for discussion

● Why does power need legitimation?
● Are capitalist societies inevitably prone to legitimation crises?
● Is democratic legitimacy the only meaningful form of legitimacy?
● Is direct democracy in any way applicable to modern circumstances?
● Have the virtues of democracy been overstated?
● Which model of democracy is the most attractive, and why?
● Do modern forms of representative democracy deserve to be described as democratic?
● What are the major threats to democracy in modern society?
● Is cosmopolitan democracy possible, or desirable?

Further reading

Beetham, D., *The Legitimation of Power* (1991). A clear and authoritative introduction to the idea of legitimacy, which also considers the role of democracy and other factors in legitimizing power.

Dahl, R., *Democracy and its Critics* (1991). A wide-ranging and thorough discussion of the democratic ideal and democratic practices.

Gill, G., *The Dynamics of Democratization: Elite, Civil Society and the Transition Process* (2000). A clear and accessible overview of the scale, scope and character of democratization in the contemporary world.

Held, D., *Models of Democracy* (3rd edn) (2006). A rigorous and stimulating examination of rival models of democracy and the present state of democratic theory.

CHAPTER **5** # Nations and Nationalism

'Nationalism is an infantile disease. It is the measles of mankind.'

ALBERT EINSTEIN, *Letter* (1921)

PREVIEW
For the last 200 years, the nation has been regarded as the most appropriate (and perhaps the only proper) unit of political rule. Indeed, international law is largely based on the assumption that nations, like individuals, have inviolable rights; notably, the right to political independence and self-determination. Nowhere, however, is the importance of the nation more dramatically demonstrated than in the potency of nationalism as a political creed. In many ways, nationalism has dwarfed the more precise and systematic political ideologies examined in Chapter 2. It has contributed to the outbreak of wars and revolutions. It has caused the birth of new states, the disintegration of empires and the redrawing of borders; and it has been used to reshape existing regimes, as well as to bolster them. However, nationalism is a complex and highly diverse political phenomenon. Not only are there distinctive political and cultural forms of nationalism, but the political implications of nationalism have been wide-ranging and sometimes contradictory. This has occurred because nationalism has been linked to very different ideological traditions, ranging from liberalism to fascism. It has therefore been associated, for instance, with both the quest for national independence and projects of imperial expansion. Nevertheless, there are reasons to believe that the age of the nation may be drawing to a close. The nation-state, the goal that generations of nationalists have strived to achieve, is increasingly beset by pressures, both internal and external.

KEY ISSUES
- What is a nation?
- How do cultural nationalism and political nationalism differ?
- How can the emergence and growth of nationalism be explained?
- What political forms has nationalism assumed? What causes has it articulated?
- What are the attractions or strengths of the nation-state?
- Does the nation-state have a future?

WHAT IS A NATION?

Nation

Nations (from the Latin *nasci*, meaning 'to be born') are complex phenomena that are shaped by a collection of factors. *Culturally*, a nation is a group of people bound together by a common language, religion, history and traditions, although nations exhibit various levels of cultural heterogeneity. *Politically*, a nation is a group of people who regard themselves as a natural political community, classically expressed through the quest for sovereign statehood. *Psychologically*, a nation is a group of people distinguished by a shared loyalty or affection in the form of patriotism (see p. 118).

Many of the controversies surrounding the phenomenon of nationalism can be traced back to rival views about what constitutes a nation. So widely accepted is the idea of the nation that its distinctive features are seldom examined or questioned; the nation is simply taken for granted. Nevertheless, confusion abounds. The term 'nation' tends to be used with little precision, and is often used interchangeably with terms such as 'state', 'country', 'ethnic group' and 'race'. The United Nations, for instance, is clearly misnamed, as it is an organization of states, not one of national populations. What, then, are the characteristic features of the nation? What distinguishes a nation from any other social group, or other sources of collective identity?

The difficulty of defining the term 'nation' springs from the fact that all nations comprise a mixture of objective and subjective features, a blend of cultural and political characteristics. In objective terms, nations are cultural entities: groups of people who speak the same language, have the same religion, are bound by a shared past and so on. Such factors undoubtedly shape the politics of nationalism. The nationalism of the Québecois in Canada, for instance, is based largely on language differences between French-speaking Quebec and the predominantly English-speaking rest of Canada (see p. 114). Nationalist tensions in India invariably arise from religious divisions, examples being the struggle of Sikhs in Punjab for a separate homeland (Khalistan), and the campaign by Muslims in Kashmir for the incorporation of Kashmir into Pakistan. Nevertheless, it is impossible to define a nation using objective factors alone. All nations encompass a measure of cultural, ethnic and racial diversity. The Swiss nation has proved to be enduring and viable despite the use of three major languages (French, German and Italian), as well as a variety of local dialects. Divisions between Catholics and Protestants that have given rise to rival nationalisms in Northern Ireland have been largely irrelevant in mainland UK, and of only marginal significance in countries such as Germany.

This emphasizes the fact that, ultimately, nations can only be defined *subjectively* by their members. In the final analysis, the nation is a psycho-political construct. What sets a nation apart from any other group or collectivity is that its members regard themselves as a nation. What does this mean? A nation, in this sense, perceives itself to be a distinctive political community. This is what distinguishes a nation from an ethnic group. An **ethnic group** undoubtedly possesses a communal identity and a sense of cultural pride, but, unlike a nation, it lacks collective political aspirations. These aspirations have traditionally taken the form of the quest for, or the desire to maintain, political independence or statehood. On a more modest level, however, they may consist of a desire to achieve a measure of autonomy, perhaps as part of a federation or confederation of states.

The complexity does not end there, however. Nationalism is a difficult political phenomenon, partly because various nationalist traditions view the concept of a nation in different ways. Two contrasting concepts have been particularly influential. One portrays the nation as primarily a cultural community, and emphasizes the importance of ethnic ties and loyalties. The other sees it essentially as a political community, and highlights the significance of civil bonds and allegiances. These rival views not only offer alternative accounts of the origins of nations, but have also been linked to very different forms of nationalism.

● **Ethnic group**: A group of people who share a common cultural and historical identity, typically linked to a belief in common descent.

Johann Gottfried Herder (1744–1803)

German poet, critic and philosopher, often portrayed as the 'father' of cultural nationalism. A teacher and Lutheran clergyman, Herder travelled throughout Europe before settling in Weimar in 1776, as the clerical head of the Grand Duchy. Although influenced in his early life by thinkers such as Kant (see p. 410), Rousseau (see p. 97) and Montesquieu (see p. 312), he became a leading intellectual opponent of the Enlightenment and a crucial influence on the growth in Germany of the romantic movement. Herder's emphasis on the nation as an organic group characterized by a distinctive language, culture and 'spirit' helped both to found cultural history, and to give rise to a particular form of nationalism that emphasized the intrinsic value of national culture.

Nations as cultural communities

The idea that a nation is essentially an ethnic or cultural entity has been described as the 'primary' concept of the nation (Lafont, 1968). Its roots can be traced back to late eighteenth-century Germany and the writings of figures such as Herder and Fichte (1762–1814). For Herder, the innate character of each national group was ultimately determined by its natural environment, climate and physical geography, which shaped the lifestyle, working habits, attitudes and creative propensities of a people. Above all, he emphasized the importance of language, which he believed was the embodiment of a people's distinctive traditions and historical memories. In his view, each nation thus possesses a *Volksgeist*, which reveals itself in songs, myths and legends, and provides a nation with its source of creativity. Herder's nationalism therefore amounts to a form of culturalism that emphasizes an awareness and appreciation of national traditions and collective memories instead of an overtly political quest for statehood. Such ideas had a profound impact on the awakening of national consciousness in nineteenth-century Germany, reflected in the rediscovery of ancient myths and legends in, for example, the folk tales of the brothers Grimm and the operas of Richard Wagner (1813–83).

The implication of Herder's **culturalism** is that nations are 'natural' or organic entities that can be traced back to ancient times and will, by the same token, continue to exist as long as human society survives. A similar view has been advanced by modern social psychologists, who point to the tendency of people to form groups in order to gain a sense of security, identity and belonging. From this perspective, the division of humankind into nations reflects nothing more than the natural human propensity to draw close to people who share a culture, background and lifestyle that is similar to their own. Such psychological insights, however, do not explain nationalism as a historical phenomenon; that is, as one that arose at a particular time and place, specifically in early nineteenth-century Europe.

In *Nations and Nationalism* (1983), Ernest Gellner emphasized the degree to which nationalism is linked to modernization and, in particular, to the process of industrialization. Gellner stressed that, while premodern or 'agroliterate' soci-

● *Volksgeist*: (German) Literally, the spirit of the people; the organic identity of a people reflected in their culture and, particularly, their language.

● **Culturalism**: The belief that human beings are culturally-defined creatures, culture being the universal basis for personal and social identity.

Cultural nationalism

Cultural nationalism is a form of nationalism that places primary emphasis on the regeneration of the nation as a distinctive civilization, rather than as a discrete political community. Whereas political nationalism is 'rational', and usually principled, cultural nationalism is 'mystical', in that it is based on a romantic belief in the nation as a unique, historical and organic whole, animated by its own 'spirit'. Typically, it is a 'bottom-up' form of nationalism that draws more on 'popular' rituals, traditions and legends than on elite, or 'higher', culture.

eties were structured by a network of feudal bonds and loyalties, emerging industrial societies promoted social mobility, self-striving and competition, and so required a new source of cultural cohesion. This was provided by nationalism. Nationalism therefore developed to meet the needs of particular social conditions and circumstances. On the other hand, Gellner's theory suggests that nationalism is now ineradicable, as a return to premodern loyalties and identities is unthinkable. However, in *The Ethnic Origins of Nations* (1986) Anthony Smith challenged the idea of a link between nationalism and modernization by highlighting the continuity between modern nations and premodern ethnic communities, which he called 'ethnies'. In this view, nations are historically embedded: they are rooted in a common cultural heritage and language that may long predate the achievement of statehood, or even the quest for national independence. Smith nevertheless acknowledged that, although ethnicity is the precursor of nationalism, modern nations came into existence only when established ethnies were linked to the emerging doctrine of political sovereignty (see p. 58). This conjunction occurred in Europe in the late eighteenth century and early nineteenth century, and in Asia and Africa in the twentieth century.

Regardless of the origins of nations, certain forms of nationalism have a distinctively cultural, rather than political, character. Cultural nationalism commonly takes the form of national self-affirmation; it is a means through which a people can acquire a clearer sense of its own identity through the heightening of national pride and self-respect. This is demonstrated by Welsh nationalism, which focuses much more on attempts to preserve the Welsh language and Welsh culture in general than on the search for political independence. Black nationalism in the USA, the West Indies and many parts of Europe also has a strong cultural character. Its emphasis is on the development of a distinctively black consciousness and sense of national pride, which, in the work of Marcus Garvey (see p. 162) and Malcolm X (1925–65), was linked to the rediscovery of Africa as a spiritual and cultural 'homeland'. A similar process can be seen at work in modern Australia and, to some extent, New Zealand. The republican movement in Australia, for example, reflects the desire to redefine the nation as a political and cultural unit separate from the UK. This is a process of self-affirmation that draws heavily on the Anzac myth, the relationship with indigenous peoples, and the rediscovery of a settler folk culture.

The German historian Friedrich Meinecke (1907) went one step further and distinguished between 'cultural nations' and 'political nations'. 'Cultural' nations are characterized by a high level of ethnic homogeneity; in effect, national and ethnic identities overlap. Meinecke identified the Greeks, the Germans, the Russians, the English and the Irish as examples of cultural nations, but the description could equally apply to ethnic groups such as the Kurds, the Tamils and the Chechens. Such nations can be regarded as 'organic', in that they have been fashioned by natural or historical forces, rather than by political ones. The strength of cultural nations is that, bound together by a powerful and historical sense of national unity, they tend to be stable and cohesive. On the other hand, cultural nations tend to view themselves as exclusive groups. Membership of the nation is seen to derive not from a political allegiance, voluntarily undertaken, but from an ethnic identity that has somehow been inherited. Cultural nations thus tend to view themselves as extended kinship groups distinguished by common descent. In this sense, it is not possible to 'become' a German, a Russian

CONCEPT

Race

Race refers to physical or genetic differences amongst humankind that supposedly distinguish one group of people from another on biological grounds such as skin and hair colour, physique, and facial features. A race is thus a group of people who share a common ancestry and 'one blood'. The term is, however, controversial, both scientifically and politically. Scientific evidence suggests that there is no such thing as 'race' in the sense of a species-type difference between peoples. Politically, racial categorization is commonly based on cultural stereotypes, and is simplistic at best and pernicious at worst.

or a Kurd simply by adopting the language and beliefs of the people. Such exclusivity has tended to breed insular and regressive forms of nationalism, and to weaken the distinction between nations and races.

Nations as political communities

The view that nations are essentially political entities emphasizes civic loyalties and political allegiances, rather than cultural identity. The nation is thus a group of people who are bound together primarily by shared citizenship, regardless of their cultural, ethnic and other loyalties. This view of the nation is often traced back to the writings of Jean-Jacques Rousseau (see p. 97), sometimes seen as the 'father' of modern nationalism. Although Rousseau did not specifically address the nation question, or discuss the phenomenon of nationalism, his stress on popular sovereignty, expressed in the idea of the 'general will' (in effect, the common good of society), was the seed from which nationalist doctrines sprang during the French Revolution of 1789. In proclaiming that government should be based on the general will, Rousseau developed a powerful critique of monarchical power and aristocratic privilege. During the French Revolution, this principle of radical democracy was reflected in the assertion that the French people were 'citizens' possessed of inalienable rights and liberties, no longer merely 'subjects' of the crown. Sovereign power thus resided with the 'French nation'. The form of nationalism that emerged from the French Revolution therefore embodied a vision of a people or nation governing itself, and was inextricably linked to the principles of liberty, equality and fraternity.

The idea that nations are political, not ethnic, communities has been supported by a number of theories of nationalism. Eric Hobsbawm (1983), for instance, highlighted the degree to which nations are 'invented traditions'. Rather than accepting that modern nations have developed out of long-established ethnic communities, Hobsbawm argued that a belief in historical continuity and cultural purity was invariably a myth, and, what is more, a myth created by nationalism itself. In this view, nationalism creates nations, not the other way round. A widespread consciousness of nationhood (sometimes called 'popular nationalism') did not, for example, develop until the late nineteenth century, perhaps fashioned by the invention of national anthems and national flags, and the extension of primary education. Certainly, the idea of a 'mother tongue' passed down from generation to generation and embodying a national culture is highly questionable. In reality, languages live and grow as each generation adapts the language to its own distinctive needs and circumstances. Moreover, it can be argued that the notion of a 'national' language is an absurdity, given the fact that, until the nineteenth century, the majority of people had no knowledge of the written form of their language and usually spoke a regional dialect that had little in common with the language of the educated elite.

Benedict Anderson (1983) also portrayed the modern nation as an artefact, in his case as an 'imagined community'. Anderson pointed out that nations exist more as mental images than as genuine communities that require a level of face-to-face interaction to sustain the notion of a common identity. Within nations, individuals only ever meet a tiny proportion of those with whom they supposedly share a national identity. If nations exist, they exist as imagined artifices, constructed for us through education, the mass media and a process of political socialization (see p. 178). Whereas in Rousseau's view a nation is animated by ideas of democracy and political freedom, the notion that nations are 'invented' or 'imagined' communities has more in common with the Marxist belief that nationalism is a species of bourgeois ideology. From the perspective of orthodox Marxism, nationalism is a device through which the ruling class counters the threat of social revolution by ensuring that national loyalty is stronger than class solidarity, thus binding the working class to the existing power structure.

Whether nations spring out of a desire for liberty and democracy, or are merely cunning inventions of political elites or a ruling class, certain nations have an unmistakably political character. Following Meinecke, these nations can be classified as 'political nations'. A 'political' nation is one in which citizenship has greater political significance than ethnic identity; not uncommonly, political nations contain a number of ethnic groups, and so are marked by cultural heterogeneity. The UK, the USA and France have often been seen as classic examples of political nations. The UK is a union of what, in effect, are four 'cultural' nations: the English, the Scottish, the Welsh and the Northern Irish (although the latter may comprise two nations, the Protestant Unionists and the Catholic Republicans). Insofar as there is a distinctively British national identity, this is based on political factors such as a common allegiance to the Crown, respect for the Westminster Parliament, and a belief in the historic rights and liberties of the British people. As a 'land of immigrants', the USA has a distinctively multi-ethnic and multicultural character, which makes it impossible for it to construct a national identity on the basis of shared cultural and historical ties. Instead, a sense of American nationhood has been consciously developed through the educational system, and through the cultivation of respect for a set of common values, notably those outlined in the Declaration of Independence and the US Constitution. Similarly, French national identity is closely linked to the traditions and principles of the 1789 French Revolution.

What such nations have in common is that, in theory, they were founded on a voluntary acceptance of a common set of principles or goals, as opposed to an existing cultural identity. It is sometimes argued that the style of nationalism that develops in such societies is typically tolerant and democratic. If a nation is primarily a political entity, it is an inclusive group, in that membership is not restricted to those who fulfil particular language, religious, ethnic or suchlike criteria. Classic examples are the USA, with its image as a 'melting pot' nation, and the 'new' South Africa, seen as a 'rainbow society'. On the other hand, political nations may at times fail to experience the organic unity and sense of historical rootedness that is found in cultural nations. This may, for instance, account for the relative weakness of specifically British nationalism in the UK, by comparison with Scottish and Welsh nationalism and the insular form of English nationalism that is sometimes called 'little Englander' nationalism.

Developing-world states have encountered particular problems in their struggle to achieve a national identity. Such nations can be described as 'political' in two senses. First, in many cases, they have achieved statehood only after a struggle against colonial rule (see p. 122). In this case, the nation's national identity is deeply influenced by the unifying quest for national liberation and freedom. Developing-world nationalism therefore tends to have a strong anti-

POLITICS IN ACTION ...

Canada: one nation or two?

Events: Canada is a federation comprising ten provinces and three territories, the former enjoying wider political autonomy than the latter. Almost 24 per cent of Canadians are francophones, who speak French as their first language and largely live (85 per cent) in the Atlantic province of Quebec. Since the 1970s, Canadian domestic politics has been dominated by the issue of Quebec's relationship to predominantly anglophone Canada. The paramilitary Quebec Liberation Front, was active during 1963–70; the separatist political party, *Parti Québécois* (PQ), won power in Quebec in 1976; since 1990, PQ has operated on a federal level through the *Bloc Québécois* (BQ). Referendums on independence for Quebec were held in 1980 and 1995, but both failed, the latter by a margin of 1 per cent. Attempts to address the challenge of Quebec nationalism through constitutional reform, notably through the Meech Lake Accord of 1987, also failed. However, the principles of multiculturalism and biculturalism have been enshrined in law through section 27 of the 1982 Canadian Charter of Rights and Freedoms and the 1988 Canadian Multiculturalism Act. In 2006, the Canadian House of Commons passed a motion recognizing that the 'Québécois form a nation within a united Canada'.

Significance: The nationalism of the Québécois in Canada raises important questions about both the nature of nationalism and the circumstances in which it rises or falls. From the mid-nineteenth to the mid-twentieth century, Quebec nationalism was distinctively cultural in orientation, being shaped by conservative clerical allegiances, centred on the Catholic Church, and reflecting the rural and familial values of a historically agricultural territory. However, by the 1960s, this elite version of society was being unsettled by trends such as urbanization, secularization, Americanization, and the spread of liberal and progressive values. In this context, Québécois identity started to be re-articulated, becoming more self-confident and assertive, and expressing itself increasingly through political demands, especially for independence. Political factors also facilitated this process. The introduction, in the early 1960s, of the so-called 'Quiet Revolution' by the province's Liberal government promoted social and cultural modernization and, by increasing the power of the provincial government, sparked the growth of popular demands for secession. Similarly, under the premierships of Pierre Trudeau (1968–79, 1980–84), the Canadian

government attempted to satisfy Quebec nationalism by making concessions in terms of language rights and by adjusting both Canada's and Quebec's constitutional status, which strengthened the tide of nationalism, rather than containing it.

However, despite the transition from cultural concerns to political demands, language remained central to Quebec nationalism, and, in some respects, became more important. This occurred both because of the perception that French was being threatened by the spread of English (and other languages) due to growing immigration (Canada has one of the highest per capita immigration rates in the world), and because language was increasingly equated with identity, and thus became part of a politics of politico-cultural self-assertion. Nevertheless, following the failure of the 1995 referendum, the tide started to turn against secessionist nationalism. In the 2007 provincial election, PQ was defeated by both the Liberals and the conservative *Action démocratique du Québec* (ADQ), marking the first time since 1973 that the party did not form either the government or the official opposition. The reasons for this include a growing recognition of the economic benefit of remaining within the Canadian federation, and the fact that progress in securing Quebec's cultural and language rights has, over time, weakened the sense of threat and injustice that had once helped to fuel secessionist politics. In many respects, multiculturalism (see p. 167), rather than nationalism, has proved to be the solution to the 'Quebec problem', especially as, since the 1990s, Canada has acknowledged the territorial and self-government rights of its so-called 'First Nations'.

colonial character. Second, these nations have often been shaped by territorial boundaries inherited from their former colonial rulers. This has particularly been the case in Africa. African 'nations' often encompass a wide range of ethnic, religious and regional groups that are bound together by little more than a shared colonial past. In contrast to the creation of classic European cultural nations, which sought statehood on the basis of a pre-existing national identity, an attempt has been made in Africa to 'build' nations on the foundations of existing states. However, the resulting mismatch of political and ethnic identities has bred recurrent tensions, as has been seen in Nigeria, Sudan, Rwanda and Burundi, for example. However, such conflicts are by no means simply manifestations of ancient 'tribalism'. To a large extent, they are a consequence of the divide-and-rule policies used in the colonial past.

VARIETIES OF NATIONALISM

Immense controversy surrounds the political character of nationalism. On the one hand, nationalism can appear to be a progressive and liberating force, offering the prospect of national unity or independence. On the other, it can be an irrational and reactionary creed that allows political leaders to conduct policies of military expansion and war in the name of the nation. Indeed, nationalism shows every sign of suffering from the political equivalent of multiple-personality syndrome. At various times, nationalism has been progressive and reactionary, democratic and authoritarian, liberating and oppressive, and left-wing and right-wing. For this reason, it is perhaps better to view nationalism not as a single or coherent political phenomenon, but as a series of 'nationalisms'; that is, as a complex of traditions that share but one characteristic – each, in its own particular way, acknowledges the central political importance of the nation.

This confusion derives, in part, from the controversies examined above as to how the concept of a nation should be understood, and about whether cultural or political criteria are decisive in defining the nation. However, the character of nationalism is also moulded by the circumstances in which nationalist aspirations arise, and by the political causes to which it is attached. Thus, when nationalism is a reaction against the experience of foreign domination or colonial rule, it tends to be a liberating force linked to the goals of liberty, justice and democracy. When nationalism is a product of social dislocation and demographic change, it often has an insular and exclusive character, and can become a vehicle for racism (see p. 120) and **xenophobia**. Finally, nationalism is shaped by the political ideals of those who espouse it. In their different ways, liberals, conservatives, socialists, fascists and even communists have been attracted to nationalism (of the major ideologies, perhaps only anarchism is entirely at odds with nationalism). In this sense, nationalism is a cross-cutting ideology. The principal political manifestations of nationalism are:

- liberal nationalism
- conservative nationalism
- expansionist nationalism
- anticolonial nationalism.

● **Tribalism**: Group behaviour characterized by insularity and exclusivity, typically fuelled by hostility towards rival groups.

● **Xenophobia**: A fear or hatred of foreigners; pathological ethnocentrism.

Giuseppe Mazzini (1805–72)

Italian nationalist and apostle of liberal republicanism. Mazzini was born in Genoa, Italy, and was the son of a doctor. He came into contact with revolutionary politics as a member of the patriotic secret society, the Carbonari. This led to his arrest and exile to France and, after his expulsion from France, to Britain. He returned briefly to Italy during the 1848 Revolutions, helping to liberate Milan and becoming head of the short-lived Roman Republic. A committed republican, Mazzini's influence thereafter faded as other nationalist leaders, including Garibaldi (1807–82), looked to the House of Savoy to bring about Italian unification. Although he never officially returned to Italy, Mazzini's liberal nationalism had a profound influence throughout Europe, and on immigrant groups in the USA.

Liberal nationalism

Liberal nationalism can be seen as the classic form of European liberalism; it dates back to the French Revolution, and embodies many of its values. Indeed, in continental Europe in the mid-nineteenth century, to be a nationalist meant to be a liberal, and vice versa. The 1848 Revolutions, for example, fused the struggle for national independence and unification with the demand for limited and constitutional government. Nowhere was this more evident than in the '*Risorgimento*' (rebirth) nationalism of the Italian nationalist movement, especially as expressed by the 'prophet' of Italian unification, Guiseppe Mazzini. Similar principles were espoused by Simon Bolívar (1783–1830), who led the Latin-American independence movement in the early nineteenth century, and helped to expel the Spanish from Hispanic America. Perhaps the clearest expression of liberal nationalism is found in US President Woodrow Wilson's 'Fourteen Points'. Drawn up in 1918, these were proposed as the basis for the reconstruction of Europe after World War I, and provided a blueprint for the sweeping territorial changes that were implemented by the Treaty of Versailles (1919).

In common with all forms of nationalism, liberal nationalism is based on the fundamental assumption that humankind is naturally divided into a collection of nations, each possessed of a separate identity. Nations are therefore genuine or organic communities, not the artificial creation of political leaders or ruling classes. The characteristic theme of liberal nationalism, however, is that it links the idea of the nation with a belief in popular sovereignty, ultimately derived from Rousseau. This fusion was brought about because the multinational empires against which nineteenth-century European nationalists fought were also autocratic and oppressive. Mazzini, for example, wished not only to unite the Italian states, but also to throw off the influence of autocratic Austria. The central theme of this form of nationalism is therefore a commitment to the principle of **national self-determination**. Its goal is the construction of a nation-state (see p. 124); that is, a state within which the boundaries of government coincide as far as possible with those of nationality. In J. S. Mill's ([1861] 1951) words:

● **National self-determination**: The principle that the nation is a sovereign entity; self-determination implies both national independence and democratic rule.

Internationalism

Internationalism is the theory or practice of politics based on transnational or global cooperation. It is rooted in universalist assumptions about human nature that put it at odds with political nationalism. The major internationalist traditions are drawn from liberalism and socialism. *Liberal internationalism* is based on individualism reflected in the assumption that human rights have a 'higher' status than claims based on national sovereignty. *Socialist internationalism* is grounded in a belief in international class solidarity (proletarian internationalism), underpinned by assumptions about a common humanity. Feminism and green politics have also advanced distinctively internationalist positions.

● **Universalism**: The theory that there is a common core to human identity shared by people everywhere.

● **Human rights**: Rights to which people are entitled by virtue of being human; universal and fundamental rights (see p. 342).

When the sentiment of nationality exists in any force, there is a prima facie case for uniting all members of the nationality under one government, and a government to themselves apart. This is merely saying that the question of government should be decided by the governed.

Liberal nationalism is, above all, a principled form of nationalism. It does not uphold the interests of one nation against other nations. Instead, it proclaims that each and every nation has a right to freedom and self-determination. In this sense, all nations are equal. The ultimate goal of liberal nationalism, then, is the construction of a world of sovereign nation-states. Mazzini thus formed the clandestine organization Young Italy to promote the idea of a united Italy, but he also founded Young Europe in the hope of spreading nationalist ideas throughout the continent. Similarly, at the Paris Peace Conference that drew up the Treaty of Versailles, Woodrow Wilson advanced the principle of self-determination not simply because the break-up of European empires served US national interests, but because he believed that the Poles, the Czechs, the Yugoslavs and the Hungarians all had the same right to political independence that the Americans already enjoyed.

From this perspective, nationalism is not only a means of enlarging political freedom, but also a mechanism for securing a peaceful and stable world order. Wilson, for instance, believed that World War I had been a consequence of an 'old order' that was dominated by autocratic and militaristic empires bent on expansionism and war. In his view, democratic nation-states, however, would be essentially peaceful, because, possessing both cultural and political unity, they lacked the incentive to wage war or subjugate other nations. In this light, nationalism is not seen as a source of distrust, suspicion and rivalry. Rather, it is a force capable of promoting unity within each nation and brotherhood amongst nations on the basis of mutual respect for national rights and characteristics.

There is a sense, nevertheless, in which liberalism looks beyond the nation. This occurs for two reasons. The first is that a commitment to individualism (see p. 158) implies that liberals believe that all human beings (regardless of factors such as race, creed, social background and nationality) are of equal moral worth. Liberalism therefore subscribes to **universalism**, in that it accepts that individuals everywhere have the same status and entitlements. This is commonly expressed nowadays in the notion of **human rights**. In setting the individual above the nation, liberals establish a basis for violating national sovereignty, most clearly through 'humanitarian intervention' (see p. 424) designed to protect the citizens of another country from their own government. The second reason is that liberals fear that a world of sovereign nation-states may degenerate into an international 'state of nature'. Just as unlimited freedom allows individuals to abuse and enslave one another, national sovereignty may be used as a cloak for expansionism and conquest. Freedom must always be subject to the law, and this applies equally to individuals and to nations. Liberals have, as a result, been in the forefront of campaigns to establish a system of international law supervised by supranational bodies such as the League of Nations, the United Nations and the European Union. In this view, nationalism and internationalism are not rival or mutually exclusive principles; rather, from a liberal perspective, the latter compliments the former.

CONCEPT

Patriotism

Patriotism (from the Latin *patria*, meaning 'fatherland') is a sentiment, a psychological attachment to one's nation (a 'love of one's country'). The terms 'nationalism' and 'patriotism' are often confused. Nationalism has a doctrinal character and embodies the belief that the nation is in some way the central principle of political organization. Patriotism provides the affective basis for that belief. Patriotism thus underpins all forms of nationalism; it is difficult to conceive of a national group demanding, say, political independence without possessing at least a measure of patriotic loyalty.

Criticisms of liberal nationalism tend to fall into two categories. In the first category, liberal nationalists are accused of being naive and romantic. They see the progressive and liberating face of nationalism; theirs is a tolerant and rational nationalism. However, they perhaps ignore the darker face of nationalism; that is, the irrational bonds of tribalism that distinguish 'us' from a foreign and threatening 'them'. Liberals see nationalism as a universal principle, but they have less understanding of the emotional power of nationalism, which, in time of war, can persuade people to fight, kill and die for 'their' country, almost regardless of the justice of their nation's cause. Such a stance is expressed in the assertion: 'my country, right or wrong'.

Second, the goal of liberal nationalism (the construction of a world of nation-states) may be fundamentally misguided. The mistake of Wilsonian nationalism, on the basis of which large parts of the map of Europe were redrawn, was that it assumed that nations live in convenient and discrete geographical areas, and that states can be constructed to coincide with these areas. In practice, all so-called 'nation-states' comprise a number of linguistic, religious, ethnic and regional groups, some of which may consider themselves to be 'nations'. This has nowhere been more clearly demonstrated than in the former Yugoslavia, a country viewed by the peacemakers at Versailles as 'the land of the Slavs'. However, in fact, it consisted of a patchwork of ethnic communities, religions, languages and differing histories. Moreover, as the disintegration of Yugoslavia in the early 1990s demonstrated, each of its constituent republics was itself an ethnic patchwork. Indeed, as the Nazis (and, later, the Bosnian Serbs) recognized, the only certain way of achieving a politically unified and culturally homogeneous nation-state is through a programme of **ethnic cleansing**.

Conservative nationalism

Historically, conservative nationalism developed rather later than liberal nationalism. Until the latter half of the nineteenth century, conservative politicians treated nationalism as a subversive, if not revolutionary, creed. As the century progressed, however, the link between conservatism and nationalism became increasingly apparent; for instance, in Disraeli's 'One Nation' ideal, in Bismarck's willingness to recruit German nationalism to the cause of Prussian aggrandisement, and in Tsar Alexander III's endorsement of pan-Slavic nationalism. In modern politics, nationalism has become an article of faith for most, if not all, conservatives. In the UK, this was demonstrated most graphically by Margaret Thatcher's triumphalist reaction to victory in the Falklands War of 1982, and it is evident in the engrained '**Euroscepticism**' of the Conservative right, particularly in relation to its recurrent bogey: a 'federal Europe'. A similar form of nationalism was rekindled in the USA through the adoption of a more assertive foreign policy; by Ronald Reagan in the invasion of Grenada (1983) and the bombing of Libya (1986), and by George W. Bush in the invasion of Afghanistan (2001) and Iraq (2003).

Conservative nationalism is concerned less with the principled nationalism of universal self-determination, and more with the promise of social cohesion and public order embodied in the sentiment of national patriotism. Above all, conservatives see the nation as an organic entity emerging out of a basic desire

● **Ethnic cleansing**: The forcible expulsion or extermination of 'alien' peoples; often used as a euphemism for genocide

● **Euroscepticism**: Opposition to further European integration, usually not extending to the drive to withdraw from the EU (anti-Europeanism).

of humans to gravitate towards those who have the same views, habits, lifestyles and appearance as themselves. In short, human beings seek security and identity through membership of a national community. From this perspective, patriotic loyalty and a consciousness of nationhood is rooted largely in the idea of a shared past, turning nationalism into a defence of values and institutions that have been endorsed by history. Nationalism thus becomes a form of traditionalism. This gives conservative nationalism a distinctively nostalgic and backward-looking character. In the USA, this is accomplished through an emphasis on the Pilgrim Fathers, the War of Independence, the Philadelphia Convention and so on. In the case of British nationalism (or, more accurately, English nationalism), national patriotism draws on symbols closely associated with the institution of monarchy. The UK national anthem is God Save the Queen, and the Royal Family play a prominent role in national celebrations, such as Armistice Day, and on state occasions, such as the opening of Parliament.

Conservative nationalism tends to develop in established nation-states rather than in those that are in the process of nation-building. It is typically inspired by the perception that the nation is somehow under threat, either from within or from without. The traditional 'enemy within' has been class antagonism and the ultimate danger of social revolution. In this respect, conservatives have seen nationalism as the antidote to socialism: when patriotic loyalties are stronger than class solidarity, the working class is, effectively, integrated into the nation. Calls for national unity and the belief that unabashed patriotism is a civic virtue are therefore recurrent themes in conservative thought.

The 'enemies without' that threaten national identity, from a conservative perspective, include immigration and supranationalism. In this view, immigration poses a threat because it tends to weaken an established national culture and ethnic identity, thereby provoking hostility and conflict. This fear was expressed in the UK in the 1960s by Enoch Powell, who warned that further Commonwealth immigration would lead to racial conflict and violence. A similar theme was taken up in 1979 by Margaret Thatcher in her reference to the danger of the UK being 'swamped' by immigrants. Anti-immigration campaigns waged by the British National Party, Le Pen's National Front in France, and far-right groups such as the Freedom Party in Austria and the Danish People's Party also draw their inspiration from conservative nationalism. National identity and, with it, our source of security and belonging, is threatened in the same way by the growth of supranational bodies and by the globalization of culture. Resistance in the UK and in other EU member states to a single European currency reflects not merely concern about the loss of economic sovereignty, but also a belief that a national currency is vital to the maintenance of a distinctive national identity.

Although conservative nationalism has been linked to military adventurism and expansion, its distinctive character is that it is inward-looking and insular. If conservative governments have used foreign policy as a device to stoke up public fervour, this is an act of political opportunism, rather than because conservative nationalism is relentlessly aggressive or inherently militaristic. This leads to the criticism that conservative nationalism is essentially a form of elite manipulation or ruling-class ideology. From this perspective, the 'nation' is invented, and certainly defined, by political leaders and ruling elites with a view to manufacturing consent or engineering political passivity. In crude terms, when in

Racialism, racism

The terms racialism and racism tend to be used interchangeably. Racialism refers to any belief or doctrine that draws political or social conclusions from the idea that humankind is divided into biologically distinct races (a notion that has no, or little, scientific basis). Racialist theories are thus based on that assumption the cultural, intellectual and moral differences amongst humankind derive from supposedly more fundamental genetic differences. In political terms, racialism is manifest in calls for racial segregation (apartheid), and in doctrines of 'blood' superiority and inferiority (Aryanism and anti-Semitism).

● Jingoism: A mood of public enthusiasm and celebration provoked by military expansion or imperial conquest.

trouble, all governments play the 'nationalism card'. A more serious criticism of conservative nationalism, however, is that it promotes intolerance and bigotry. Insular nationalism draws on a narrowly cultural concept of the nation; that is, the belief that a nation is an exclusive ethnic community, broadly similar to an extended family. A very clear line is therefore drawn between those who are members of the nation and those who are alien to it. By insisting on the maintenance of cultural purity and established traditions, conservatives may portray immigrants, or foreigners in general, as a threat, and so promote, or at least legitimize, racialism and xenophobia.

Expansionist nationalism

The third form of nationalism has an aggressive, militaristic and expansionist character. In many ways, this form of nationalism is the antithesis of the principled belief in equal rights and self-determination that is the core of liberal nationalism. The aggressive face of nationalism first appeared in the late nineteenth century as European powers indulged in 'the scramble for Africa' in the name of national glory and their 'place in the sun'. Nineteenth-century European imperialism (see p. 427) differed from the colonial expansion of earlier periods in that it was fuelled by a climate of popular nationalism in which national prestige was linked to the possession of an empire, and each colonial victory was greeted by demonstrations of popular enthusiasm, or **jingoism**. To a large extent, both world wars of the twentieth century resulted from this expansionist form of nationalism. When World War I broke out in August 1914, following a prolonged arms race and a succession of international crises, the prospect of conquest and military glory provoked spontaneous public rejoicing in all the major capitals of Europe. World War II was largely a result of the nationalist-inspired programmes of imperial expansion pursued by Japan, Italy and Germany. The most destructive modern example of this form of nationalism in Europe was the quest by the Bosnian Serbs to construct a 'Greater Serbia' in the aftermath of the break-up of Yugoslavia in the early 1990s.

In its extreme form, such nationalism arises from a sentiment of intense, even hysterical, nationalist enthusiasm, sometimes referred to as 'integral nationalism', a term coined by the French nationalist Charles Maurras (1868–1952), leader of the right-wing Action Française. The centrepiece of Maurras' politics was an assertion of the overriding importance of the nation: the nation is everything and the individual is nothing. The nation thus has an existence and meaning beyond the life of any single individual, and individual existence has meaning only when it is dedicated to the unity and survival of the nation. Such fanatical patriotism has a particularly strong appeal for the alienated, isolated and powerless, for whom nationalism becomes a vehicle through which pride and self-respect can be regained. However, integral nationalism breaks the link previously established between nationalism and democracy. An 'integral' nation is an exclusive ethnic community, bound together by primordial loyalties, rather than voluntary political allegiances. National unity does not demand free debate, and an open and competitive struggle for power; it requires discipline and obedience to a single, supreme leader. This led Maurras to portray democracy as a source of weakness and corruption, and to call instead for the re-establishment of monarchical absolutism.

CONCEPT

Anti-Semitism

'Semites' are by tradition the descendants of Shem, son of Noah. They include most of the peoples of the Middle East. Anti-Semitism is prejudice or hatred specifically towards Jews. In its earliest form, *religious* anti-Semitism reflected the hostility of the Christians towards the Jews, based on their alleged complicity in the murder of Jesus and their refusal to acknowledge him as the son of God. *Economic* anti-Semitism developed from the Middle Ages onwards, and expressed distaste for Jews in their capacity as moneylenders and traders. *Racial* anti-Semitism developed from the late nineteeth century onwards, and condemned the Jewish peoples as fundamentally evil and destructive.

● **Pan-nationalism**: A style of nationalism dedicated to unifying a disparate people through either expansionism or political solidarity ('pan' means all or every).

This militant and intense form of nationalism is invariably associated with chauvinistic beliefs and doctrines. Derived from the name of Nicolas Chauvin, a French soldier noted for his fanatical devotion to Napoleon and the cause of France, chauvinism is an irrational belief in the superiority or dominance of one's own group or people. National chauvinism therefore rejects the idea that all nations are equal in favour of the belief that nations have particular characteristics and qualities, and so have very different destinies. Some nations are suited to rule; others are suited to be ruled. Typically, this form of nationalism is articulated through doctrines of ethnic or racial superiority, thereby fusing nationalism and racialism. The chauvinist's own nation is seen to be unique and special, in some way a 'chosen people'. For early German nationalists such as Fichte and Jahn (1783–1830), only the Germans were a true *Volk* (an organic people). They alone had maintained blood purity and avoided the contamination of their language. For Maurras, France was an unequalled marvel, a repository of all Christian and classical virtues.

No less important in this type of nationalism, however, is the image of another nation or race as a threat or enemy. In the face of the enemy, the nation draws together and gains an intensified sense of its own identity and importance, achieving a kind of 'negative integration'. Chauvinistic nationalism therefore establishes a clear distinction between 'them' and 'us'. There has to be a 'them' to deride or hate in order for a sense of 'us' to be forged. The world is thus divided, usually by means of racial categories, into an 'in group' and an 'out group'. The 'out group' acts as a scapegoat for all the misfortunes and frustrations suffered by the 'in group'. This was most graphically demonstrated by the virulent anti-Semitism that was the basis of German Nazism. Hitler's *Mein Kampf* ([1925] 1969) portrayed history as a Manichean struggle between the Aryans and the Jews, respectively representing the forces of light and darkness, or good and evil.

A recurrent theme of expansionist nationalism is the idea of national rebirth or regeneration. This form of nationalism commonly draws on myths of past greatness or national glory. Mussolini and the Italian Fascists looked back to the days of Imperial Rome. In portraying their regime as the 'Third Reich', the German Nazis harked back both to Bismarck's 'Second Reich' and Charlemagne's Holy Roman Empire, the 'First Reich'. Such myths plainly give expansionist nationalism a backward-looking character, but they also look to the future, in that they mark out the nation's destiny. If nationalism is a vehicle for re-establishing greatness and regaining national glory, it invariably has a militaristic and expansionist character. In short, war is the testing ground of the nation. At the heart of integral nationalism there often lies an imperial project: a quest for expansion or a search for colonies. This can be seen in forms of **pan-nationalism**. However, Nazi Germany is, again, the best-known example. Hitler's writings mapped out a three-stage programme of expansion. First, the Nazis sought to establish a 'Greater Germany' by bringing ethnic Germans in Austria, Czechoslovakia and Poland within an expanded Reich. Second, they intended to achieve *Lebensraum* (living space) by establishing a German-dominated empire stretching into Russia. Third, Hitler dreamed of ultimate Aryan world domination.

Anticolonial and postcolonial nationalism

The developing world has spawned various forms of nationalism, all of which have in some way drawn inspiration from the struggle against colonial rule. The irony of this form of nationalism is that it has turned doctrines and principles first developed through the process of 'nation-building' in Europe against the European powers themselves. Colonialism, in other words, succeeded in turning nationalism into a political creed of global significance. In Africa and Asia, it helped to forge a sense of nationhood shaped by the desire for 'national liberation'. Indeed, during the twentieth century, the political geography of much of the world was transformed by anticolonialism. Independence movements that sprang up in the interwar period gained new impetus after the conclusion of World War II. The overstretched empires of Britain, France, the Netherlands and Portugal crumbled in the face of rising nationalism.

India had been promised independence during World War II, which was eventually granted in 1947. China achieved genuine unity and independence only after the 1949 communist revolution, having fought an eight-year war against the occupying Japanese. A republic of Indonesia was proclaimed in 1949 after a three-year war against the Netherlands. A military uprising forced the French to withdraw from Vietnam in 1954, even though final liberation, with the unification of North and South Vietnam, was not achieved until 1975, after 14 further years of war against the USA. Nationalist struggles in Southeast Asia inspired similar movements in Africa, with liberation movements emerging under leaders such as Nkrumah in Ghana, Dr Azikiwe in Nigeria, Julius Nyerere in Tanganyika (later Tanzania), and Hastings Banda in Nyasaland (later Malawi). The pace of decolonization in Africa accelerated from the late 1950s onwards. Nigeria gained independence from the UK in 1960 and, after a prolonged war fought against the French, Algeria gained independence in 1962. Kenya became independent in 1963, as did Tanzania and Malawi the next year. Africa's last remaining colony, South-West Africa, finally became independent Namibia in 1990.

Early forms of anticolonialism drew heavily on 'classical' European nationalism and were inspired by the idea of national self-determination. However, emergent African and Asian nations were in a very different position from the newly-created European states of the nineteenth century. For African and Asian nations, the quest for political independence was inextricably linked to a desire for social development and for an end to their subordination to the industrialized states of Europe and the USA. The goal of 'national liberation' therefore had an economic as well as a political dimension. This helps to explain why anticolonial movements typically looked not to liberalism but to socialism, and particularly to Marxism–Leninism, as a vehicle for expressing their nationalist ambitions. On the surface, nationalism and socialism appear to be incompatible political creeds. Socialists have traditionally preached internationalism, since they regard humanity as a single entity, and argue that the division of humankind into separate nations breeds only suspicion and hostility. Marxists, in particular, have stressed that the bonds of class solidarity are stronger and more genuine than the ties of nationality, or, as Marx put it in the *Communist Manifesto* ([1848] 1967): 'Working men have no country'.

The appeal of socialism to the developing world was based on the fact that the values of community and cooperation that socialism embodies are deeply

CONCEPT

Colonialism

Colonialism is the theory or practice of establishing control over a foreign territory and turning it into a 'colony'. Colonialism is thus a particular form of imperialism (see p. 427). Colonialism is usually distinguished by settlement and by economic domination. As typically practised in Africa and Southeast Asia, colonial government was exercised by a settler community from a 'mother country'. In contrast, *neocolonialism* is essentially an economic phenomenon based on the export of capital from an advanced country to a less developed one (for example, so-called US 'dollar imperialism' in Latin America).

established in the cultures of traditional, pre-industrial societies. In this sense, nationalism and socialism are linked, insofar as both emphasize social solidarity and collective action. By this standard, nationalism may simply be a weaker form of socialism, the former applying the 'social' principle to the nation, the latter extending it to cover the whole of humanity. More specifically, socialism, and especially Marxism, provide an analysis of inequality and exploitation through which the colonial experience could be understood and colonial rule challenged. In the same way as the oppressed and exploited proletariat saw that they could achieve liberation through the revolutionary overthrow of capitalism, developing-world nationalists saw 'armed struggle' as a means of achieving both political and economic emancipation, thus fusing the goals of political independence and social revolution. In countries such as China, North Korea, Vietnam and Cambodia, anticolonial movements openly embraced Marxism–Leninism. On achieving power, they moved to seize foreign assets and nationalize economic resources, creating Soviet-style planned economies. African and Middle Eastern states developed a less ideological form of nationalistic socialism, which was practised, for example, in Algeria, Libya, Zambia, Iraq and South Yemen. The 'socialism' proclaimed in these countries usually took the form of an appeal to a unifying national cause or interest, typically championed by a powerful 'charismatic' leader.

However, nationalists in the developing world have not always been content to express their nationalism in a language of socialism or Marxism borrowed from the West. Especially since the 1970s, Marxism–Leninism has often been displaced by forms of religious fundamentalism (see p. 53) and, particularly, Islamic fundamentalism. This has given the developing world a specifically non-western – indeed an anti-western, voice. In theory at least, Islam attempts to foster a transnational political identity that unites all those who acknowledge the 'way of Islam' and the teachings of the Prophet Muhammad within an 'Islamic nation'. However, the Iranian revolution of 1979, which brought Ayatollah Khomeini (1900–89) to power, demonstrated the potency of Islamic fundamentalism as a creed of national and spiritual renewal. The establishment of an 'Islamic republic' was designed to purge Iran of the corrupting influence of western materialism in general, and of the 'Great Satan' (the USA) in particular, through a return to the traditional values and principles embodied in the Shari'a, or divine Islamic law. By no means, however, does Islamic nationalism have a unified character. In Sudan and Pakistan, for example, Islamification has essentially been used as a tool of statecraft to consolidate the power of ruling elites.

A FUTURE FOR THE NATION-STATE?

Since the final decades of the twentieth century, it has become fashionable to declare that the age of nationalism is over. This has not been because nationalism had been superseded by 'higher' cosmopolitan allegiances, but because its task had been completed: the world had become a world of nation-states. In effect, the nation had been accepted as the sole legitimate unit of political rule. Certainly, since 1789, the world had been fundamentally remodelled on nationalist lines. In 1910, only 15 of the 193 states recognized in 2011 as full members

Nation-state

The nation-state is a
form of political
organization and a
political ideal. In the first
case, it is an autonomous
political community
bound together by the
overlapping bonds of
citizenship and
nationality. In the latter,
it is a principle, or ideal
type (see p. 20), reflected
in Mazzini's goal: 'every
nation a state, only one
state for the entire
nation'. As such, the
nation-state principle
embodies the belief that
nations are 'natural'
political communities. For
liberals and most
socialists, the nation-
state is largely fashioned
out of civic loyalties and
allegiances. For
conservatives and
integral nationalists, it is
based on ethnic or
organic unity.

of the United Nations existed. Well into the twentieth century, most of the peoples of the world were still colonial subjects of one of the European empires. Only 3 of the current 72 states in the Middle East and Africa existed before 1910, and no fewer than 108 states have come into being since 1959. These changes have been fuelled largely by the quest for national independence, with these new states invariably assuming the mantle of the nation-state.

History undoubtedly seems to be on the side of the nation-state. The three major geopolitical upheavals of the twentieth century (World War I, World War II and the collapse of communism in Eastern Europe) each gave considerable impetus to the concept of the nation as a principle of political organization. Since 1991, at least 22 new states have come into existence in Europe alone (15 of them as a result of the disintegration of the USSR), and all of them have claimed to be nation-states. The great strength of the nation-state is that it offers the prospect of both cultural cohesion and political unity. When a people who share a common cultural or ethnic identity gain the right to self-government, community and citizenship coincide. This is why nationalists believe that the forces that have created a world of independent nation-states are natural and irresistible, and that no other social group could constitute a meaningful political community. They believe that the nation-state is ultimately the only viable political unit. This view implies, for instance, that supranational bodies such as the European Union will never be able to rival the capacity of national governments to establish legitimacy and command popular allegiance. Clear limits should therefore be placed on the process of European integration because people with different languages, cultures and histories will never come to think of themselves as members of a united political community.

Nevertheless, just as the principle of the nation-state has achieved its widest support, other, very powerful forces have emerged that threaten to make the nation-state redundant. A combination of internal pressures and external threats has produced what is commonly referred to as a 'crisis of the nation-state'. Internally, nation-states have been subject to centrifugal pressures, generated by an upsurge in ethnic, regional and multicultural politics. This heightened concern with ethnicity and culture may, indeed, reflect the fact that, in a context of economic and cultural globalization (see p. 142), nations are no longer able to provide a meaningful collective identity or sense of social belonging. Given that all nation-states embody a measure of cultural diversity, the politics of ethnic assertiveness cannot but present a challenge to the principle of the nation, leading some to suggest that nationalism is in the process of being replaced by multiculturalism (see p. 167). Unlike nations, ethnic, regional or cultural groups are not viable political entities in their own right, and have thus sometimes looked to forms of federalism (see p. 382) and confederalism to provide an alternative to political nationalism. For example, within the framework provided by the European Union, the Belgian regions of Flanders and Wallonia have achieved such a degree of self-government that Belgium remains a nation-state only in a strictly formal sense. The nature of such centrifugal forces is discussed more fully in Chapter 17.

External threats to the nation-state have a variety of forms. First, advances in the technology of warfare, and especially the advent of the nuclear age, have brought about demands that world peace be policed by intergovernmental or supranational bodies. This led to the creation of the League of Nations and, later,

Debating...
Are nations 'natural' political communities?

Nationalism is based on two core assumptions: first, that humankind is naturally divided into distinct nations and, second, that the nation is the most appropriate, and perhaps only legitimate, unit of political rule. This is why nationalists have strived, wherever possible, to bring the borders of the state into line with the boundaries of the nation. But is humankind 'naturally' divided into distinct nations? And why should the national communities be accorded this special, indeed unique, political status?

YES

'Natural' communities: For primordialist scholars, national identity is historically embedded: nations are rooted in a common cultural heritage and language that may long predate statehood or the quest for independence (Smith, 1986). In this view, nations evolve organically out of more simple ethnic communities, reflecting the fact that people are inherently group-orientated, drawn naturally towards others who are similar to themselves because they share the same cultural characteristics. Above all, national identity is forged by a combination of a sense of territorial belonging and a shared way of life (usually facilitated by a common language), creating deep emotional attachments that resemble kinship ties.

Vehicle for democracy: The nation acquired a political character only when, thanks to the doctrine of nationalism, it was seen as the ideal unit of self-rule, a notion embodied in the principle of national self-determination. Nationalism and democracy therefore go hand-in-hand. Bound together by ties of national solidarity, people are encouraged to adopt shared civic allegiances and to participate fully in the life of their society. Moreover, democratic nations are inclusive and tolerant, capable of respecting the separate identities of minority groups. Nationality, thus, does not suppress other sources of personal identity, such as ethnicity and religion.

Benefits of national partiality: Nationalism inevitably implies partiality, the inclination to favour the needs and interests of one's 'own' people over those of other peoples. This, as communitarian theorists argue, reflects the fact that morality begins at home. From this perspective, morality only makes sense when it is locally-based, grounded in the communities to which we belong, and which have shaped our lives and values. National partiality is thus an extension of the near universal inclination to accord moral priority to those we know best, especially our families and close friends. There is no reason, moreover, why national partiality should preclude a moral concern for 'strangers'.

NO

'Invented' communities: Rather than being natural or organic entities, nations are, to a greater or lesser extent, political constructs. Nations are certainly 'imagined communities', in the sense that people only ever meet a tiny proportion of those with whom they supposedly share a national identity (Anderson, 1983). Marxists and others go further and argued that ruling or elite groups have 'invented' nationalism in order to bind the working class, and the disadvantaged generally, to the existing power structure (Hobsbawm, 1983). National anthems, national flags and national myths and legends are thus little more than a form of ideological manipulation.

'Hollowed-out' nations: The nation has had its day as a meaningful political unit and as a basis for democracy and citizenship. Nations were appropriate political communities during an industrial age that was shaped though the development of relatively discrete national economies. However, the growth of an interdependent world, and the transfer of decision-making authority from national governments to intergovernmental or supranational bodies, has seriously weakened the political significance of the nation. Not only have nations been 'hollowed-out' in terms of their political role, but the seemingly remorseless trends towards international migration and cultural diversity has fatally compromised the nation's organic unity (if it ever existed).

Miniaturizing humanity: National identity encourages people to identify with part of humanity, rather than with humanity as a whole. As such, it narrows our moral sensibilities and destroys our sense of a common humanity. Worse, nationalism breeds inevitable division and conflict. If one's own nation is unique or 'special', other nations are inevitably seen as inferior and possibly threatening. Nationalism therefore gives rise to, not a world of independent nation-states, but a world that is scared by militarism, aggression and conquest. For humankind to progress beyond struggle and war, nationalism must be abandoned and treated like the infantile disease it has always been.

the United Nations. Second, economic life has been progressively globalized. Markets are now world markets, businesses have increasingly become transnational corporations (see p. 149), and capital is moved around the globe in the blink of an eye. Is there a future for the nation-state in a world in which no national government can control its economic destiny? Third, the nation-state may be the enemy of the natural environment and a threat to the global ecological balance. Nations are concerned primarily with their own strategic and economic interests, and most pay little attention to the ecological consequences of their actions. The folly of this was demonstrated in the Ukraine in 1986 by the Chernobyl nuclear accident, which released a wave of nuclear radiation across Northern Europe that will cause an estimated 2000 cancer-related deaths over 50 years in Europe.

Finally, distinctive national cultures and traditions, the source of cohesion that distinguishes nation-states from other forms of political organization, have been weakened by the emergence of a transnational, and even global, culture. This has been facilitated by international tourism and the dramatic growth in communications technologies, from satellite television to the 'information superhighway'. When US films and television programmes are watched throughout the world, Indian and Chinese cuisine is as popular in Europe as native dishes, and people can communicate as easily with the other side of the world as with their neighbouring town, is the nation-state any longer a meaningful entity? These and related issues are discussed in greater depth in Chapter 8.

SUMMARY

- Nations are defined by a combination of cultural and political factors. Culturally, they are groups of people who are bound together by a common language, religion, history and traditions. Ultimately, however, nations define themselves through the existence of a shared civic consciousness, classically expressed as the desire to achieve or maintain statehood.

- Distinctive cultural and political forms of nationalism can be identified. Cultural nationalism emphasizes the regeneration of the nation as a distinctive civilization on the basis of a belief in the nation as a unique, historical and organic whole. Political nationalism, on the other hand, recognizes the nation as a discrete political community, and is thus linked with ideas such as sovereignty and self-determination.

- Some political thinkers portray nationalism as a modern phenomenon associated with industrialization and the rise of democracy, while others trace it back to premodern ethnic loyalties and identities. The character of nationalism has varied considerably, and has been influenced by both the historical circumstances in which it has arisen and the political causes to which it has been attached.

- There have been a number of contrasting manifestations of political nationalism. Liberal nationalism is based on a belief in a universal right to self-determination. Conservative nationalism values the capacity of national patriotism to deliver social cohesion and political unity. Expansionist nationalism is a vehicle for aggression and imperial conquest. Anticolonial nationalism is associated with the struggle for national liberation, often fused with the quest for social development.

- The most widely recognized form of political organization worldwide is the nation-state, which is often seen as the sole legitimate unit of political rule. Its strength is that it offers the prospect of both cultural cohesion and political unity, thus allowing those who share a common cultural or ethnic identity to exercise the right to independence and self-government.

- The nation-state now confronts a number of challenges. Nation-states have been subject to centrifugal pressures generated by the growth in ethnic politics. Externally, they have confronted challenges from the growing power of supranational bodies, the advance of economic and cultural globalization, and the need to find international solutions to the environmental crisis.

Questions for discussion

- Where do nations come from? Are they natural or artificial formations?
- Why have national pride and patriotic loyalty been valued?
- Does cultural nationalism merely imprison a nation in its past?
- Why has nationalism proved to be such a potent political force?
- Does nationalism inevitably breed insularity and conflict?
- Can nationalism be viewed as a form of elite manipulation?
- Are nationalism and internationalism compatible?
- Is the nation-state the sole legitimate unit of political rule?
- Is a postnationalist world possible?

Further reading

Brown, D., *Contemporary Nationalism: Civic, Ethnocultural and Multicultural Politics* (2000). A clear and illuminating framework for understanding nationalist politics.

Hearn, J., *Rethinking Nationalism: A Critical Introduction* (2006). A comprehensive account of approaches to understanding nationalism that draws on sociology, politics, anthropology and history, and develops its own critique.

Hobsbawm, E., *Nations and Nationalism Since 1780* (2nd edn) (1993). An analysis of the phenomenon of nationalism from a modern Marxist perspective.

Spencer, P. and H. Wollman (eds), *Nations and Nationalism: A Reader* (2005). A wide-ranging and stimulating collection of mainstream and less mainstream writings on nationalism.

CHAPTER 6

Political Economy and Globalization

'It's the economy, stupid.'

Reminder on the wall of Bill Clinton's office during the 1992
US presidential election campaign

PREVIEW

At almost every level, politics is intertwined with economics. Politics affects economic outcomes in a variety of ways, ranging from the ability of the state ensure a framework of public order in which property rights are protected and contracts are upheld, to the capacity of government to regulate the economy, or even exert direct control over economic life through planning and nationalization. No less important are the ways in which economics affects political outcomes. Political parties, for instance, compete for power by promising to increase economic growth, reduce inflation, tackle poverty and so on. As President Clinton recognized, election results are often determined by the state of the economy: governments win elections when the economy booms, but are likely to be defeated during recessions or slumps. Indeed, orthodox Marxists go further and suggest that politics is merely a part of a 'superstructure' determined or conditioned by the economic 'base', the political process being nothing more than a *reflection* of the class system. Although few people (including Marxists) now hold such a simplistic view, no one would deny that political life is intimately bound up with economic conditions and, most importantly, the nature of the economic system. The advent of globalization nevertheless threatens to overturn all conventional assumptions about the relationship between politics and economics, marking, some argue, the point at which economics finally triumphed over politics. When governments, almost everywhere, seem to be powerless in the face of the pressures exerted by global markets and intensifying international competitiveness, what role is left for politics?

KEY ISSUES

- Why and how are politics and economics inextricably linked?
- What is the relationship between states and markets?
- Is capitalism a single economic form, or are there a variety of capitalisms?
- Are there any viable alternatives to capitalism?
- What is economic globalization? How has it restructured the economy and politics?
- What has been the legacy of the 2007–09 Crash?

CONCEPT

Political economy

Political economy, broadly, is the study of the interaction of politics and economics. As a *topic*, political economy focuses on the relationship between states and markets. Although political economy, in this sense, encompasses a variety of approaches, the term has a long association with Marxism, reflecting the tendency within Marxist analysis to link power to the ownership of wealth. As a *method*, political economy refers to the use of theories and approaches developed within economics to analyse politics, and includes rational-choice, public-choice, social-choice and games theories.

● **Mercantilism**: An economic philosophy that takes the state to be the most significant economic actor, highlighting the extent to which economic relations are determined by political power.

● **Protectionism**: Import restrictions such as quotas and tariffs, designed to protect domestic producers.

● **Beggar-thy-neighbour policies**: Policies pursued at the expense of other states that are believed to be in their own country's short-term best interests.

POLITICAL ECONOMY

Approaches to political economy

The term 'political economy' implies that the disciplinary separation of 'politics' from 'economics' is ultimately unsustainable. Political factors are crucial in determining economic outcomes, and economic factors are crucial in determining political outcomes. In short, there is no escaping political economy. Although this lesson has been underlined by growing contemporary interest in political economy, not least in the emergence of so-called 'new political economy', it is one that has a long and respectable history. From Adam Smith's *Wealth of Nations* ([1776] 1930) and David Ricardo's *Principles of Political Economy and Taxation* (1817) to Karl Marx's *Economic and Philosophical Manuscripts* (1844) and J. S. Mill's *Principles of Political Economy* (1848), what would now be called 'economics' was generally referred to as 'political economy'. However, in what ways are politics and economics intertwined? How are 'the political' and 'the economic' linked? The problem with such questions is that they spawn many and various responses, suggesting that political economy encompasses a variety of perspectives and approaches. For example, political economy may focus primarily on the responsibilities of the state with regard to the economy. In this sense, it considers issues such as the implications of state intervention for growth and prosperity, and the respective strengths of the state and the market as a means of distributing wealth. Alternatively, political economy may focus on the ways in which economic factors affect political decision-making (Lindblom, 1977). In this sense, it is concerned with issues such as the political influence of business groups, and the extent to which global markets serve as a constraint on national governments. At a deeper level, however, political economy encompasses a range of competing traditions. The most important of these are the following:

● state-centric political economy
● classical/neo-classical political economy
● Marxist political economy.

State-centric political economy

State-centric political economy developed out of **mercantilism**, sometimes called 'economic nationalism', which was most influential in Europe from the fifteenth century to the late seventeenth century. In this view, economic markets are not 'natural', but exist within a social context largely shaped by the exercise of state power. The classic mercantilist strategy was to build up a state's wealth, power and prestige by developing a favourable trading balance through producing goods for export while keeping imports low. The chief device for doing this was **protectionism**. Defensive mercantilism was designed to protect 'infant' industries and weaker economies from 'unfair' competition from stronger economies, while aggressive mercantilism aimed to strengthen the national economy in order to provide the basis for expansionism and war. State-centric approaches to political economy declined in significance due to their association with the '**beggar-thy-neighbour**' **policies** of the 1930s, which were held to have deepened, or at least prolonged, the Great Depression. However, they have been revived through the idea of 'state capitalism', discussed later in the chapter.

Adam Smith (1723–90)

Scottish economist and philosopher, usually seen as the founder of the 'Dismal Science'. After holding the chair of logic and then moral philosophy at Glasgow University, Smith became tutor to the Duke of Buccleuch, which enabled him to visit France and Geneva, and to develop his economic theories. *The Theory of Moral Sentiments* (1759) developed a theory of motivation that tried to reconcile human self-interestedness with an unregulated social order. Smith's most famous work, *The Wealth of Nations* ([1776] 1930), was the first systematic attempt to explain the workings of the economy in market terms, emphasizing the importance of the division of labour. Though he is often seen as a free-market theorist, Smith was nevertheless also aware of the limitations of the market.

Classical and neoclassical political economy

Classical political economy derives from the writings of Adam Smith and David Ricardo (1772–1823). It is based squarely on liberal assumptions about human nature; notably, the idea that individuals, as rationally self-interested creatures, or 'utility maximizers', are the key economic actors (utility maximizers act to achieve the greatest pleasure over pain, calculated in terms of material consumption). In line with the deeper liberal belief in balance or harmony amongst competing forces, the key idea of classical political economy is that an unregulated market economy tends towards long-run equilibrium, in that the price mechanism – the 'invisible hand' of the market, as Smith put it – brings supply (what producers are willing and able to produce) and demand (what consumers are willing and able to consume) into line with one another. From the perspective of classical political economy, this implies a policy of *laissez-faire* (see p. 132), in which the state leaves the economy alone and the market is left to manage itself. Economic exchange via the market is therefore a positive-sum game, in that greater efficiency produces economic growth and benefits everyone. Neo-classical political economy developed from the late nineteenth century onwards, drawing classical ideas and assumptions into more developed theories, in particular about the behaviour of firms and the optimal use of scarce resources in conditions of **perfect competition**.

Marxist political economy

Marxist political economy portrays capitalism as a system of class exploitation and treats social classes as the key economic actors. Karl Marx (see p. 41) defined class in terms of economic power; specifically, where people stand in relation to the ownership of productive wealth, or the 'means of production'. He believed that capitalist society was increasingly divided into 'two great classes', the bourgeoisie (the capitalist class, the owners of productive wealth) and the proletariat (non-owners, who subsist through selling their labour power). Crucially, for Marx and later Marxists, the relationship between these classes is one of irreconcilable antagonism, the proletariat being necessarily and systematically exploited

● **Perfect competition:** A hypothetical market structure in which markets are free and open, consumers have perfect knowledge and no producer is large enough to affect the price of goods.

CONCEPT

Capitalism

Capitalism can be viewed as either an economic system or as an ideology. As an *economic system*, capitalism is a system of generalized commodity production. Its key features are: (1) productive wealth is predominantly privately owned; (2) economic life is organized according to market principles, resources being allocated through the price mechanism; (3) wage labour replaces bonded serfdom; and (4) material self-interest and profit maximization provide the motivation for enterprise and hard work. As an *ideology*, capitalism overlaps substantially with classical liberalism, both creeds defending private property, personal self-striving and meritocracy.

● **Surplus value:** A Marxist term denoting the value that is extracted from the labour of the proletariat through the mechanism of capitalist exploitation.

● **Economic system:** A form of organization through which goods and services are produced, distributed and exchanged; seen by Marxists as a 'mode of production'.

by the bourgeoisie, the 'ruling class'. This Marx explained by reference to the idea of **surplus value**. Capitalism's quest for profit can only be satisfied through the extraction of surplus value from its workers, by paying them less than the value their labour generates. Economic exploitation is therefore an essential feature of the capitalist mode of production, and it operates regardless of the meanness or generosity of particular employers. This irreconcilable class conflict invests capitalism with an inherent and, ultimately, fatal instability. As capitalism experiences deepening crises of over-production, the proletariat will eventually be brought to class consciousness and will realize its destiny as the 'gravedigger of capitalism'.

Varieties of capitalism

In its broadest form, political economy examines how different **economic systems** affect institutional and political arrangements and are, in turn, affected by a process of political decision-making. Traditionally, this has involved the analysis of the nature and implication of two rival economic systems: capitalism and socialism. Either economic life was based on private ownership and organized by the market, as in the 'capitalist West', or it was based on state ownership and organized through a system of central planning, as in the 'communist East'. In practice, however, economic systems were always more complex and difficult to categorize than this simplistic 'capitalism versus socialism' model of economic organization implied. Not only did different societies construct their own models of capitalism and socialism depending on their particular economic and political circumstances, and their cultural and historical inheritance, but the notion of a 'pure' capitalist system and a 'pure' socialist one was always an illusion. No capitalist system is entirely free of 'socialist' impurities, such as labour laws and, at least, a safety net level of welfare, and there has never been a socialist system that did not have 'capitalist' impurities, such as a market in labour and some form of 'black' economy. Nevertheless, the abrupt abandonment of central planning following the Eastern European revolutions of 1989–91, and the introduction of market reforms in China (see p. 136) and other surviving communist states, has radically altered the landscape of political economy, appearing to leave capitalism as the only viable basis for economic organization across the world. This, however, has heightened the awareness that capitalism does not constitute just a single economic form but, rather, a variety of economic forms (Brown, 1995; Hall and Soskice, 2001). Three types of capitalist system can be identified in the modern world:

● enterprise capitalism
● social capitalism
● state capitalism.

Enterprise capitalism

Enterprise capitalism (sometimes called the 'American business model') is widely seen, particularly in the Anglo-American world, as 'pure' capitalism; that is, as an ideal towards which other capitalisms are inevitably drawn (Friedman, 1962). It is, nevertheless, apparent that this model has been rejected in most parts of the world

Laissez-faire

Laissez-faire (in French, meaning literally 'leave to do') is the principle of non-intervention of government in economic affairs. It is the heart of the doctrine that the economy works best when left alone by government. The central assumption of *laissez-faire* is that an unregulated market economy tends naturally towards equilibrium. This is usually explained by the theory of 'perfect competition'. From this perspective, government intervention is seen as damaging unless it is restricted to actions that promote market competition, such as checks on monopolies and the maintenance of stable prices.

● **Economic globalization**: The incorporation of national economies into a single 'borderless' global economy, through transnational production and capital flows.

except for the USA (the home of enterprise capitalism) and, despite its early post-1945 flirtation with Keynesian social democracy, the UK. Enterprise capitalism is based on the ideas of classical economists such as Smith and Ricardo updated by modern theorists such as Milton Friedman (see p. 138) and Friedrich von Hayek (see p. 37). Its central feature is faith in the untrammelled workings of market competition, born out of the belief that the market is a self-regulating mechanism (or, as Adam Smith put it, an 'invisible hand'), in line with the principle of *laissez-faire*. This idea is expressed in Adam Smith's famous words: 'it is not from the benevolence of the butcher, the brewer, or the baker, that we expect our dinner, but from their regard to their own interest'. In the USA such free-market principles have helped to keep public ownership to a minimum, and ensure that welfare provision operates as little more than a safety net. US businesses are typically profit-driven, and a premium is placed on high productivity and labour flexibility. Trade unions are usually weak, reflecting the fear that strong labour organizations are an obstacle to profit maximization. The emphasis on growth and enterprise of this form of capitalism stems, in part, from the fact that productive wealth is owned largely by financial institutions, such as insurance companies and pension funds, that demand a high rate of return on their investments.

The undoubted economic power of the USA bears testament to the vigour of enterprise capitalism. Despite clear evidence of relative decline (whereas the USA accounted for half of the world's manufacturing output in 1945, this had fallen to less than one-fifth by 2007), the average productivity of the USA is still higher than Germany's and Japan's. The USA clearly enjoys natural advantages that enable it to benefit from the application of market principles, notably a continent-wide domestic market, a wealth of natural resources, and a ruggedly individualist popular culture, seen as a 'frontier ideology'. However, its success cannot be put down to the market alone. For instance, the USA possesses, in the main, a strong and clear sense of national purpose, and has a network of regulatory bodies that constrain the worst excesses of competitive behaviour. The principles of enterprise capitalism have nevertheless become more prominent since the 1980s, a shift brought about by the adoption by the Regan administration in the USA and the Thatcher government in the UK of neoliberal policies designed to get government 'off the back of business'. The linkage between **economic globalization** and neoliberalism (see p. 144) has also ensured that the tendency towards enterprise capitalism has extended far beyond its Anglo-American heartland, as discussed later in the chapter.

Enterprise capitalism also has serious disadvantages, however. Perhaps the most significant of these is a tendency towards wide material inequalities and social fragmentation. This is demonstrated in the USA by levels of absolute poverty that are not found, for example, in Europe, and in the growth of a poorly educated and welfare-dependent underclass. The tensions that such problems generate may be contained by growth levels that keep alive the prospect of social mobility. In societies such as that in the UK, however, which lack the cultural and economic resources of the USA, enterprise capitalism may generate such deep social tensions as to be unsustainable in the long run. A further problem is that enterprise capitalism's 'turbo' features (supposedly evident in the 1990s) may have less to do with the dynamism of the market or technological innovation than with an unsustainable boom in the housing and financial markets, and the growth of public and private debt. This economic model may therefore be

CONCEPT

CONCEPT

Social market

The idea of a social-market economy emerged in Germany in the 1950s. A social market is an economy that is structured by market principles and largely free from government interference, operating in a society in which cohesion is maintained through a comprehensive welfare system and effective public services. The market is thus not an end in itself so much as a means of generating wealth in order to achieve broader social ends. A stress on partnership, cooperation and subsidiarity distinguishes a social market from a free market.

particularly vulnerable to the vagaries of financial markets and to shifts in consumer or business confidence, as perhaps demonstrated by the 2007–09 global financial crisis (discussed in the final section of the chapter).

Social capitalism

Social capitalism refers to the form of capitalism that has developed in much of central and western Europe. Germany is its natural home, but the principles of social capitalism have been adopted in various forms in Austria, the Benelux countries, Sweden, France and much of Scandinavia. This economic form has drawn more heavily on the flexible and pragmatic ideas of economists such as Friedrich List (1789–1846) than on the strict market principles of classical political economy as formulated by Smith and Ricardo. A leading advocate of the *Zollverein* (the German customs union), List nevertheless emphasized the economic importance of politics and political power, arguing, for instance, that state intervention should be used to protect infant industries from the rigours of foreign competition. The central theme of this model is the idea of a social market; that is, an attempt to marry the disciplines of market competition with the need for social cohesion and solidarity.

In Germany, this system is founded on a link between industrial and financial capital in the form of a close relationship between business corporations and regionally-based banks, which are often also major shareholders in the corporations. This has been the pivot around which Germany's economy has revolved since World War II, and it has orientated the economy towards long-term investment, rather than short-term profitability. Business organization in what has been called Rhine–Alpine capitalism also differs from Anglo-American capitalism, in that it is based on social partnership. Trade unions enjoy representation through works councils, and participate in annual rounds of wage negotiation that are usually industry-wide. This relationship is underpinned by comprehensive and well-funded welfare provisions that provide workers and other vulnerable groups with social guarantees. In this way, a form of 'stakeholder capitalism' has developed that takes into account the interests of workers and those of the wider community. This contrasts with the 'shareholder capitalism' found in the USA and the UK (Hutton, 1995).

The strengths of social capitalism were clearly demonstrated by the 'economic miracle' that transformed war-torn Germany into Europe's leading economic power by the 1960s. High and stable levels of capital investment, together with a strong emphasis on education and training, particularly in vocational and craft skills, enabled Germany to achieve the highest productivity levels in Europe. However, the virtues of the social-market model are by no means universally accepted. One of its drawbacks is that, because it places such a heavy stress on consultation, negotiation and consensus, it tends to encourage inflexibility and make it difficult for businesses to adapt to changing market conditions (for example, economic globalization and intensified competition from Eastern Europe, Latin America and East Asia). Further strain is imposed by the relatively high levels of social expenditure required to maintain high-quality welfare provision. These push up taxes, and so burden both employers and employees. Whereas the supporters of the social market insist that the social and the market are intrinsically linked, its critics argue that social capitalism is nothing more than a contradiction in terms. In their view, the price of financing ever-expanding social programmes is a decline in international competitiveness and a weakening of the wealth-creating base of the economy.

State capitalism

The term 'state capitalism' has been defined in a number of ways. For instance, Trotskyites used it to highlight the tendency of the USSR under Stalin to use its control of productive power to oppress the working class, in a manner similar to capitalist societies. However, in its modern usage, state capitalism is more commonly used to describe capitalist economies in which the state plays a crucial directive role. These are often non-liberal capitalist societies. Hall and Soskice (2001) distinguished between 'liberal market economies', in which firms coordinate their activities on the basis of competitive market arrangements, and 'coordinated market economies', which depend heavily on non-market arrangements. Some aspects of state capitalism could be found in post-1945 Japan. This was the model that the East and Southeast Asian 'tigers' (Hong Kong, South Korea, Taiwan, Singapore and so on) eagerly adopted, and it has influenced emergent Chinese capitalism as well as, in some respects, Russian capitalism.

The distinctive character of state capitalism is its emphasis on cooperative, long-term relationships, for which reason it is sometimes called 'collective capitalism'. This allows the economy to be directed not by an impersonal price mechanism, but through what have been called 'relational markets'. An example of this is the pattern of interlocking share ownership that ensures that there is a close relationship between industry and finance in Japan, enabling Japanese firms to adopt strategies based on long-term investment, rather than on short- or medium-term profit. Firms themselves provide the social core of life in state capitalism. Workers (particularly male workers in large businesses) are 'members' of firms in a way that does not occur in the USA, or even in social market Europe. In return for their loyalty, commitment and hard work, workers have traditionally expected lifetime employment, pensions, social protection and access to leisure and recreational opportunities. Particular stress is placed on teamwork and the building up of a collective identity which has been underpinned by relatively narrow income differentials between managers and workers. The final element in this economic mix is the government. Although East Asian levels of public spending and taxation are relatively low by international standards (often below 30 per cent of GNP) the state has played a vital role in 'guiding' investment, research and trading decisions. The model here was undoubtedly the Ministry of International Trade and Industry (MITI), which oversaw the Japanese 'economic miracle' in the post-1945 period.

Although the Japanese version of state capitalism was highly successful in the early post-1945 period, accounting for Japan's ability to recover from wartime devastation to become the world's second largest economy, Japan's economic slow-down in the 1990s (the 'lost decade' which threatened to become the 'lost decades') and the 1997 Asian financial crisis cast a darker cloud over state capitalism. Its critics highlighted, amongst other things, its inflexibility and unresponsiveness to changing global market conditions, and the tendency for individualism and entre-preneurialism to be stifled by a continuing emphasis on values such as duty and hierarchy. In this context, China has become the standard-bearer for state capital-ism, having consistently achieved growth rates of about 10 per cent since the late

1980s, and having overtaken Japan to become the second largest economy in the world in 2011. China's mixture of burgeoning capitalism and Stalinist political control has been remarkable effective in delivering sustained economic growth, benefiting from a huge supply of cheap labour and massive investment in the economic infrastructure. Whether 'market Stalinism' will continue to remain a viable economic model as the twenty-first century progresses is, nevertheless, debatable (see p. 136).

Russia's conversion to state capitalism occurred in the aftermath of the chaos and dislocation of the 1990s, when 'shock treatment' market reforms were introduced under Boris Yeltsin. From 1999 onwards, Vladimir Putin acted to reassert state power in both political and economic life; in part, in order to wrest power back from the so-called 'oligarchs', newly-rich business magnates who had been criticized for siphoning off wealth out of the country and for contributing to the 1998 Russian financial crisis. A key aspect of Putin's economic strategy has been to exploit Russia's vast energy reserves, both as a motor for economic growth and to give Russia greater leverage over neighbouring states – and, indeed, over much of Europe. The chief weakness of Russian state capitalism, however, is its failure sufficiently to diversify the economy, meaning that Russia's economic prospects are closely linked to the price, in particular, of oil and natural gas as determined by global markets. The major wider weakness of state capitalism is the contradiction between economic liberalism and non-liberal political arrangements, as authoritarianism may either become a fetter on enterprise and innovation, or it may generate resentment and demands for political freedom that make such systems unsustainable. State capitalism will only constitute a viable alternative to western-based capitalist models if it is possible for market economics to prosper in the long-term in the absence of political liberalism.

Managed or unmanaged capitalism?

As this review of the world's capitalisms makes clear, the central issue in economic policy is the proper balance between politics and economics, and thus between the state and the market. Does a capitalist economy work best when it is left alone by government, or can stable growth and general prosperity be achieved only through a system of economic management? In practice, this question boils down to an evaluation of two rival economic strategies: **Keynesianism** and neoliberalism. The centrepiece of Keynes' (see p. 137) challenge to neo-classical political economy, advanced in *The General Theory of Employment, Interest and Money* ([1936] 1965), was the rejection of the idea of a natural economic order based on a self-regulating market. He argued that *laissez-faire* policies that established a strict distinction between government and the economy had merely resulted in instability and unemployment, most clearly demonstrated by the Great Depression of the 1930s.

In Keynes' view, capitalist economies had spiralled downwards into deepening depression during the 1930s because, as unemployment grew, market forces brought about cuts in wages that further reduced the demand for goods and services. Keynes argued against free-market orthodoxy by stating that the level of economic activity is geared to 'aggregate demand'; that is, the total level of demand in the economy, which government has the capacity to manage through its tax and spending policies. When unemployment rises, government should

● **Keynesianism**: A theory (developed by J. M. Keynes) or policy of economic management, associated with regulating aggregate demand to achieve full employment.

POLITICS IN ACTION . . .

Market reform in China: a viable economic model?

Events: When Mao Zedong, the founder of The People's Republic of China in 1949, died in 1976, the goal of transforming China from an agricultural to an industrial economy remained unfulfilled. The process of economic reform in China was initiated in 1978, prompted by the rapid re-emergence of the pragmatic and once disgraced Deng Xiaoping (1904–97). Aiming to achieve 'socialism with Chinese characteristics', Deng's reforms shifted central planning away from a 'top-down' Soviet model towards a system of indirect management through market mechanisms, whilst also fostering greater private ownership, competition and economic openness. Key initiatives included the de-collectivization of agriculture, with People's communes being divided into a collection of private plots; the creation of Special Economic Zones, which provided opportunities both for foreign investment and for entrepreneurs to set up businesses; and, particularly after the relaunching of the reform process in 1992, the privatization of much state-owned industry and the wider use of contracting-out, together with a lifting of price controls and reduced protectionism. As political change in modern China has been much slower than economic change, meaning that the Chinese Communist Party (CCP) still retains overall control of the economy and society, the Chinese system is perhaps best thought of as one of 'market Stalinism'.

Significance: China's economic success since the introduction of market reforms in the late 1970s has been remarkable by any standards. Growth rates of consistently around 10 per cent per year for over 30 years have made the Chinese economy the second largest in the world, after the USA. China is the second largest trading state in the world, the largest exporter and the second largest importer of goods. If current trends persist, China will become the largest economy in the world during the 2020s. China's economic success can be explained in various ways. First, with a population of 1.3 billion, and with a historically unprecedented shift in people from the countryside to fast-expanding towns and cities, China has benefited from a seemingly inexhaustible supply of cheap labour. Second, in common with Japan and the Asian 'tigers' before it, China has adopted an export-led growth strategy founded on the manufacturing industry, making it the 'workshop of the world'. Third, a high savings ratio means that investment in China largely comes from internal sources and means that the Chinese banking system can resist global financial 'contagions'. Fourth, China has engaged selectively with globalization, taking advantage of the expansion of global markets whilst keeping its currency cheap in relation to the US dollar, thereby boosting the competitiveness of Chinese exports. Fifth, the Chinese government invests heavily in infrastructure projects and gears its foreign policy towards the goal of achieving resource security; in particular, by guaranteeing supplies of oil, iron ore, copper, aluminium and other industrial minerals.

Nevertheless, critics have argued that China's 'market Stalinism' is ultimately flawed. Key sources of vulnerability include the fact that since the mid-2000s, there have been signs of wage inflation in China. This suggests that cheap labour may not be in inexhaustible supply and puts at risk China's ability to undercut the rest of the world in manufacturing goods. A further vulnerability is the fact that Chinese goods are generally less technologically sophisticated, and lack the brand profile of US and Japanese goods, in particular. Significant concerns have been raised over China's heavy dependency on export markets and its need to boost domestic consumption levels. Although progress in these respects would help to protect China from global economic recessions, it may further boost inflationary pressures and reduce China's current strongly positive trade balances. However, the most serious challenge facing the Chinese economic model is what some argue is a fundamental contradiction between the nature of its economic system and its political system. This contradiction spells a level of political instability which can only damage economic performance and, perhaps, lead to the collapse of the market Stalinist system itself.

John Maynard Keynes (1883–1946)

UK economist. Keynes' reputation was established by his critique of the Treaty of Versailles, outlined in *The Economic Consequences of the Peace* (1919). His major work, *The General Theory of Employment, Interest and Money* ([1936] 1965), departed significantly from neoclassical economic theories, and went a long way towards establishing the discipline now known as 'macroeconomics'. By challenging *laissez-faire* principles, he provided the theoretical basis for the policy of demand management, which was widely adopted by western governments in the early post-World War II period. Keynesian theories have had a profound effect on both modern liberalism and social democracy.

'reflate' the economy either by increasing public spending or by cutting taxes. The resulting budget deficit, Keynes suggested, would be sustainable because the growth thus brought about would boost tax revenues and reduce the need for government borrowing. Moreover, any such stimulus to the economy would be magnified by the **multiplier effect**.

The advent of Keynesian demand management in the early post-World War II period revolutionized economic policy and appeared to provide governments with a reliable means of delivering sustained growth and ever-widening prosperity. For many, Keynesianism was the key to the 'long boom' of the 1950s and 1960s, the most sustained period of economic growth the world has ever seen. The intellectual credibility of Keynesianism, however, was damaged by the emergence in the 1970s of '**stagflation**', a condition that Keynes' theories had not anticipated and could not explain. Politically, Keynesian ideas were undermined by their association with the 'tax and spend' policies that, free-market economists claimed, had sapped enterprise and initiative, and undermined growth by creating permanently high inflation (a general increase in the price level). In such circumstances, pre-Keynesian free-market ideas gained a new lease of life, particularly on the political right.

The rise of neoliberalism, particularly influenced by the work of economists such as Friedrich von Hayek and Milton Friedman, signalled a shift in economic priorities away from government intervention and towards the free market. In a move pioneered by 'Reaganism' in the USA and 'Thatcherism' in the UK, attempts were made to 'roll back' the frontiers of the state in order to release what was thought of as the natural dynamism of the market. Neoliberalism therefore amounts to a form of **market fundamentalism**. The key virtue of the market, as articulated by Hayek, was that it operates as a vast nervous system that is capable of regulating the economy because it can convey an almost infinite number of messages simultaneously via the price mechanism. Influenced by monetarism, neoliberals sought to replace the Keynesian emphasis on achieving full employment with a focus instead on ensuring 'sound money', by achieving low or even zero inflation. The implication of monetarism is that Keynesian policies designed to boost output and reduce unemployment merely fuel inflation by encouraging governments to borrow, and so 'print money'. The alternative is to shift attention away from demand-side policies that encourage

● **Multiplier effect**: The mechanism through which a change in aggregate demand has an increased effect on national income as it circulates through the economy.

● **Stagflation**: A combination of economic stagnation, reflected in high or rising unemployment, and an increase in inflation.

● **Market fundamentalism**: An absolute faith in the market, reflected in the belief that the market mechanism offers solutions to all economic and social problems.

Milton Friedman (1912–2006)

US academic and economist. Professor of Economics at the University of Chicago from 1948 and founder of the so-called 'Chicago School', Friedman also worked as a *Newsweek* columnist and a US presidential advisor. He was awarded the Nobel prize for economics in 1976. A leading exponent of monetarism and free-market economics, Friedman was a powerful critic of Keynesian theory and 'tax and spend' government policies, helping to shift economic priorities during the 1970s and 1980s in the USA, and the UK in particular. His major works, *Capitalism and Freedom* (1962) and, with his wife Rose, *Free to Choose* (1980), have had a considerable impact on the economic thinking of the New Right.

consumers to consume, and towards supply-side policies that encourage producers to produce. For neoliberals, this invariably means deregulation and tax cuts.

To a large extent, however, modern economics has moved beyond the simplistic nostrums of Keynesianism and neoliberalism, and developed more sophisticated economic strategies, even a 'new' political economy. Neoliberalism, at the very least, succeeded in convincing Keynesians of the importance of inflation and of the significance of the economy's supply side. 'Crude' Keynesianism has been superseded as a result of economic globalization, 1950s-style and 1960s-style economic management having been based on the existence of discrete national economies. On the other hand, the idea of an unregulated market economy has also been difficult to sustain, particularly in the light of the tendency for this type of economy to bring about low investment, short-termism, and social fragmentation or breakdown. As Francis Fukuyama (1996) pointed out, wealth creation of any kind depends on **social capital** in the form of trust, and not just on impersonal market forces. However, renewed tensions between Keynesianism and neoliberalism have surfaced as a result of the 2007–09 global financial crisis and disagreements over how to revive the post-Crash global economy (examined later in the chapter).

Alternatives to capitalism

The belief that capitalism is the sole reliable means of generating wealth is relatively recent (only having been widely held since the collapse of communism through the revolutions of 1989–91) and it may prove to be a temporary one, especially in the light of turmoil in the global capitalist economy since the late 2000s. What are, or have been, the major alternatives to the capitalist mode of production? How else may economic life be organized? The main alternatives to capitalism are the following:

- state socialism
- market socialism
- green economics.

● **Social capital**: Cultural and moral resources that help to promote social cohesion, political stability and prosperity (see p. 175).

State socialism

Throughout much of the twentieth century, there was no doubt that there was a viable economic alternative to capitalism in the form of **state socialism** or communism (see p. 275) . Following the Bolshevik Revolution of 1917, the USSR became the first society to adopt an explicitly socialist model of economic organization. This model was not fully developed until Stalin's so-called 'second revolution' in the 1930s, significant aspects of market organization having continued under Lenin's New Economic Policy (NEP) in the 1920s. The model that was later exported to Eastern Europe and which dominated orthodox communism in the period after World War II can therefore be dubbed 'economic Stalinism'. This system was based on state collectivization, which brought all economic resources under the control of the party–state apparatus. In the USSR, a system of 'directive planning' placed overall control of economic policy in the hands of the highest organs of the Communist Party, which supervised the drawing up of output targets (in the form of Five Year Plans) by a network of planning agencies and committees.

The spectacular collapse of the state socialist model in Eastern Europe and the USSR in the revolutions of 1989–91 has been widely used to demonstrate the inherent flaws of central planning, and has gone a long way towards discrediting the very idea of planning. However, this is to ignore the undoubted achievements of Soviet-style planning. For example, the central-planning system was remarkably successful in building up 'heavy' industries, and provided the USSR, by 1941, with a sufficiently strong industrial base to enable it to withstand the Nazi invasion. Moreover, although planning failed dismally in its attempt to produce western-style consumer goods, it nevertheless helped the USSR and much of Eastern Europe to eradicate homelessness, unemployment and absolute poverty, problems that continue to blight the inner cities in some advanced capitalist countries. Despite chronic economic backwardness, Cuba, for instance, achieved a literacy rate of over 98 per cent and a system of primary health care that compares favourably with those in many western countries.

However, the drawbacks of central planning are difficult to disguise. Perhaps the most fundamental of these is its inherent inefficiency, which results from the fact that, however competent and committed the planners may be, they are confronted by a range and complexity of information that is simply beyond their capacity to handle (Hayek, 1948). It is estimated, for example, that planners in even a relatively small central-planning system are confronted by a range of options that exceed the number of atoms in the universe. A further explanation of the poor economic performance of the communist system is that the social safeguards built into central planning, together with its relatively egalitarian system of distribution, did little to encourage enterprise or promote efficiency. Quite simply, although all Soviet workers had a job, it was more difficult to ensure that they actually worked. Finally, central planning was associated with the emergence of new social divisions based on political or bureaucratic position. In Milovan Djilas' (1957) phrase, a 'new class' of party–state bureaucrats emerged who enjoyed a status and privileges equivalent to those of the capitalist class in western societies.

● **State socialism**: A form of socialism in which the state controls and directs economic life – in theory, in the interests of the people.

CONCEPT

Sustainable development

Sustainable development refers to 'development that meets the needs of the present without compromising the ability of future generations to meet their own needs' (Brundtland Report (1987)). However, there are contrasting models of sustainable development. So-called 'weak sustainability' takes economic growth to be desirable but simply insists that growth levels must be limited to ensure that environmental costs do not threaten the prosperity of future generations. Strong sustainability rejects the pro-growth implications of weak sustainability, and focuses on the need to preserve 'natural capital'.

● **Market socialism**: An economy in which self-managing enterprises operate within a context of market competition, supposedly delivering efficiency without exploitation.

● **Industrialism**: An economic theory or system based on large-scale factory production and the relentless accumulation of capital.

Market socialism

As an alternative to the heavily centralized Soviet economic model, attempts were made to reconcile the principles of socialism with the dynamics of market competition. Such a model was introduced in Yugoslavia following the split between President Tito of Yugoslavia and Stalin in 1949, and it was also taken up in Hungary after the USSR suppressed the political uprising of 1956. Similar ideas were applied in the USSR during Mikhail Gorbachev's *perestroika* programme of 'economic restructuring' in 1985–90. *Perestroika* developed as a rolling programme that initially permitted the development of cooperatives and single-proprietor businesses to supplement the central-planning system, but eventually allowed Soviet enterprises to disengage themselves from the planning system altogether, and become self-financing and self-managing. Other models of **market socialism** can be found in Lenin's NEP (1921–28) and, arguably, modern-day China.

The attraction of market socialism is that it appears to compensate for many of the most serious defects of central planning. Not only does a market environment provide a guarantee of consumer responsiveness and efficiency, but the dangers of bureaucratic power are also kept at bay. However, this is not to say that a socialist market is entirely unplanned and unregulated. Indeed, most attempts to propose a 'feasible' or 'viable' form of socialism (Nove, 1983; Breitenbach *et al.*, 1990) acknowledge the continuing need for a framework of planning, albeit one that uses collaborative and interactive procedures. At the same time, although self-management encourages cooperation and ensures a high level of material equality, it cannot be denied that the market imposes harsh disciplines. Failed businesses collapse and unprofitable industries decline, but this, in the long run, is the price that has to be paid for a vibrant and prosperous economy.

Neither the Yugoslav nor Hungarian economies, however, despite their early promise, proved to be more successful or enduring than the Soviet central-planning system. One of the chief weaknesses of market socialism is that self-management conflicts with market disciplines, as it dictates that enterprises respond, first and foremost, to the interests of their workforces. Free-market economists have therefore usually argued that only hierarchically organized private businesses can achieve optimal efficiency, because only they are capable of responding consistently to the dictates of the market, in that they place profit maximization above all other considerations.

Green economics

While interest in socialist alternatives to capitalism has declined (temporarily or otherwise), greater interest has focused on ecological, or green, alternatives. From the green perspective, capitalism and socialism are merely different manifestations of the same 'super-ideology' of **industrialism**. In other words, they are seen, essentially, as alternative ways of exploiting nature in order to satisfy the material interests of humankind. Green theorists argue not only that this obsession with economic growth has led to the despoiling of the natural environment, but also that it has, by damaging the fragile ecosystem on which all life depends, threatened the survival of the human species itself. The green alternative is to

E. F. Schumacher (1911–77)

German-born UK economist and environmental theorist. 'Fritz' Schumacher moved to the UK in 1930 as an Oxford Rhodes scholar. He went on to gain practical experience in business, farming and journalism before re-entering academic life. He was an economic advisor to the British Control Commission in Germany (1946–50) and the UK National Coal Board (1950–70). His seminal *Small is Beautiful: A Study of Economics as if People Mattered* (1973) championed the cause of human-scale production, and advanced a 'Buddhist' economic philosophy (economics 'as if people mattered') that stresses the importance of morality and 'right livelihood'. Schumacher founded the Intermediate Technology Development Group to help spread his ideas.

recast economic priorities on the basis of **sustainability**. Although **ecosocialists** have held capitalism's relentless pursuit of profit to be responsible for environmental destruction, the record of state socialist regimes in achieving sustainable development (see p. 140) is hardly inspiring. The principle of sustainability perhaps suggests that questions about the ownership and organization of wealth are secondary to the more fundamental issue of the relationship between humankind and the natural world. In order to abandon the view that nature is essentially a resource available to satisfy human needs, it is necessary for an entirely different value system to be constructed, placing ecology before economics and morality before materialism. Such ideas were developed by E. F. Schumacher (1973) into the notion of 'Buddhist economics'. In the light of the challenge of climate change, other green thinkers have championed the idea of a carbon-neutral economy.

GLOBALIZATION

Understanding globalization

● **Sustainability**: The capacity of a system to maintain its health and continue in existence.

● **Ecosocialism**: A tradition within green politics that views capitalism as the prime cause of environment degradation, combining 'red' and 'green' themes.

● **Supraterritoriality**: A condition in which social life transcends territory through the growth of 'transborder' and 'transglobal' communication and interactions.

Globalization is a slippery and elusive concept. Despite intensifying interest in the phenomenon of globalization since the 1980s, the term is still used to refer, variously, to a process, a policy, a marketing strategy, a predicament, or even an ideology. The problem with globalization is that it is not so much an 'it' as a 'them': it is not a single process but a complex of processes, sometimes overlapping and interlocking processes but also, at times, contradictory and oppositional ones. It is difficult therefore to reduce globalization to a single theme. Perhaps the best attempt to do this was in Kenichi Ohmae's (1989) idea of a 'borderless world'. This not only refers to the tendency of traditional political borders, based on national and state boundaries, to become permeable; it also implies that divisions between people previously separated by time and space have become less significant and are sometimes entirely irrelevant. Scholte (2005) therefore argued that globalization is linked to the growth of '**supraterritorial**' relations between people. For instance, huge flows of electronic money

Globalization

Globalization is the emergence of a complex web of inter-connectedness that means that our lives are increasingly shaped by events that occur, and decisions that are made, at a great distance from us. The central feature of globalization is therefore that geographical distance and territorial boundaries, such as those between nation-states, are of declining relevance. By no means, however, does globalization imply that 'the local' and 'the national' are subordinate to 'the global'. Rather, it highlights the deepening, as well as the broadening, of the political process, in the sense that local, national and global events constantly interact.

now surge around the world at the flick of a computer switch, ensuring that currency and other financial markets react almost immediately to economic events anywhere in the world. Similarly, cable and satellite technology allow telephone messages and television programmes to be transmitted around the world almost instantaneously.

The interconnectedness that globalization has spawned is multidimensional (see Figure 6.1). The popular image of globalization is that it is a top-down process, the establishment of a single global system that imprints itself on all parts of the world. In this view, globalization is linked to **homogenization** as cultural, social, economic and political diversity are destroyed in a world in which we all watch the same television programmes, buy the same commodities, eat the same food, support the same sports stars and follow the antics of the same celebrities. Nevertheless, globalization often goes hand-in-hand with localization, regionalization and multiculturalism (see p. 167). This occurs for a variety of reasons. In the first place, the declining capacity of the nation-state to organize economic and political life in a meaningful way allows power to be sucked downwards, as well as squeezed upwards. Thus, as allegiances based on the nation and political nationalism fade, they are often replaced by ones linked to local community or region, or religious and ethnic identity. Religious fundamentalism (see p. 53) can, for instance, be seen as a response to globalization. Second, the fear or threat of homogenization, especially when it is perceived as a form of imperialism, provokes cultural and political resistance. This can lead to a resurgence of interest in declining languages and minority cultures, as well as to a backlash against globalization, most obviously through the emergence of new 'anti-capitalist' and anti-free-trade social movements. Third, rather than simply bringing about a global monoculture, globalization has in some ways fashioned more complex patterns of social and cultural diversity in developing and developed states alike. In developing states, western consumer goods and images have been absorbed into more traditional cultural practices through a process of **indigenization**. Developed states, also, have not escaped the wider impact of cultural exchange, being, in return for Coca-Cola, McDonald's and

● **Homogenization**: The tendency for all parts or elements (in this case, countries) to become similar or identical

● **Indigenization**: The process through which alien goods and practices are absorbed by being adapted to local needs and circumstances.

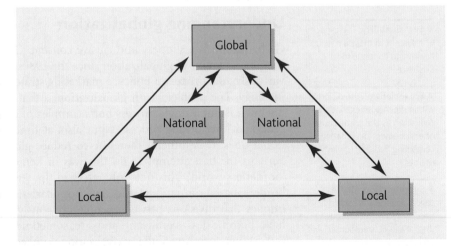

Figure 6.1   Systemic interdependencies

MTV, increasingly influenced by non-western religions; medicines and therapeutic practices; and art, music and literature.

Distinctive forms of globalization can also be identified. The most significant of these are:

- economic globalization
- cultural globalization
- political globalization.

Economic globalization

Economic globalization is reflected in the idea that no national economy is now an island: all economies have, to a greater or lesser extent, been absorbed into an interlocking global economy. The OECD (1995) thus defined globalization as 'a shift from a world of distinct national economies to a global economy in which production is internationalized and financial capital flows freely and instantly between countries'. The collapse of communism gave powerful impetus to economic globalization, in that it paved the way for the absorption into the global capitalist system of the last significant block of states that had remained outside it. Economic globalization, for that matter, also helped to precipitate the collapse of communism, in that lower trade barriers, an end to exchange controls and freer movement of investment capital from the 1980s onwards had helped to widen the economic gap between the capitalist West and an economically stagnant communist East. One of the key implications of economic globalization is the reduced capacity of national governments to manage their economies and, in particular, to resist their restructuring along free-market lines.

Cultural globalization

Cultural globalization is the process whereby information, commodities and images that have been produced in one part of the world enter into a global flow that tends to 'flatten out' cultural differences between nations, regions and individuals. This has sometimes been portrayed as a process of **McDonaldization**. Driven, in part, by the growth of transnational companies and the emergence of global commodities, cultural globalization is also fuelled by the so-called 'information revolution', the spread of satellite communication, telecommunications networks, information technology and the internet, and global media corporations. However, as pointed out earlier, culture both serves and constrains the forces of globalization. In addition to the ubiquity of Hollywood movies, Nike running shoes and Starbucks coffee houses, selling goods across the world requires a sensitivity to indigenous cultures and social practices.

● **McDonaldization:** The process whereby global commodities and commercial and marketing practices associated with the fast-food industry have come to dominate progressively more economic sectors.

Political globalization

Political globalization is evident in the growing importance of international organizations. These are organizations that are transnational in that they exercise jurisdiction not within a single state, but within an international area comprising several states. Most such organizations have emerged in the post-1945 period: examples include the United Nations, NATO, the European Economic

CONCEPT

Neoliberalism

Neoliberalism (sometimes called 'neoclassical liberalism') is an updated version of classical liberalism and, particularly, classical political economy. Its central theme is the idea that the economy works best when left alone by government, reflecting a belief in free-market economics and atomistic individualism. While unregulated market capitalism delivers efficiency, growth and widespread prosperity, the 'dead hand' of the state saps initiative and discourages enterprise. Key neoliberal policies include privatization, low public spending, deregulation, tax cuts and reduced welfare provision.

Community and its various successors, the EC and the EU, the World Bank, the International Monetary Fund (IMF), the Organization for Economic Cooperation and Development (OECD) and the World Trade Organization (WTO). When they conform to the principles of intergovernmentalism (see p. 395), international organizations provide a mechanism that enables states, at least in theory, to take concerted action without sacrificing national sovereignty (see p. 58). Supranational bodies, on the other hand, are able to impose their will on nation-states. The inter-state emphasis of political globalization sets it apart from the rival conceptions of economic and cultural globalization, which highlight the role of non-state and market-based actors. Moreover, insofar as it reflects an idealist commitment to internationalism and some form of world government, political globalization lags markedly behind economic and cultural globalization. Whereas a global state remains a very distant prospect, global civil society, based on the activities of transnational corporations (TNCs) (see p. 149), non-governmental organizations (NGOs) (see p. 248) and international pressure groups, has become very much a reality.

Rise of neoliberal globalization

There is nothing new about the broad process of economic globalization. The development of transborder and transnational economic structures has been a central feature of imperialism (see p. 427), and, arguably, the high point of economic globalization came in the late nineteenth century with the scramble of European states for colonies in Africa and Asia. Nevertheless, modern and past forms of globalization differ in important ways. Earlier forms of globalization, sometimes seen as 'proto-globalization', usually established transnational economic organizations on the back of expansionist political projects. Regardless of their spread and success, empires never succeeded in obliterating boundaries and borders; they merely readjusted them to the benefit of politically dominant powers, often establishing new boundaries between the 'civilized' world and the 'barbarian' one. In the case of the contemporary phenomenon of globalization, in contrast, the web of economic interconnectedness and interdependence has extended so far that it is possible, for the first time, to conceive of the world economy as a single global entity. This is the sense in which economic life has become 'borderless'.

A further difference is that globalization in the modern period has gone hand-in-hand with the advance of neoliberalism, so much so that the two forces are commonly thought of as parts of the same larger phenomenon: neoliberal globalization. Why are economic globalization and neoliberalism so closely linked? This can be seen to have happened for several reasons. In particular, intensified international competition encouraged governments to deregulate their economies and reduce tax levels in the hope of attracting 'inward' investment and preventing TNCs from relocating elsewhere. Strong downward pressure was exerted on public spending, and particularly welfare budgets, by the fact that, in a context of heightened global competition, the control of inflation has displaced the maintenance of full employment as the principle goal of economic policy. Such pressures, together with the revived growth and productivity rates of the US economy and the relatively sluggish performance of other models of national capitalism, in Japan and Germany in particular, meant that by the late

The Washington consensus

The term the Washington consensus was coined by John Williamson (1990, 1993) to describe the policies that the international institutions based in Washington, the IMF, the World Bank and US Treasury Department had come to favour for the reconstruction of economies in the developing world. Based on the 'orthodox' model of development as growth and drawing on the ideas of neoliberalism, the essence of the Washington consensus can be summed up as 'stabilize, privatize and liberalize'.

• **Financialization**: The reconstruction of the finances of businesses, public bodies and individual citizens to allow them to borrow money and so raise their spending.

1990s neoliberalism appeared to stand unchallenged as the dominant ideology of the 'new' world economy. Only a few states, such as China, were able to deal with neoliberal globalization on their own terms, limiting their exposure to competition by, for instance, holding down their exchange rate.

The remaking of the world economy on neoliberal lines was also stimulated by the conversion, during the 1990s, of the institutions of global economic governance, especially the World Bank and the International Monetary Fund (IMF), to the ideas of what during the 1990s came to be called the 'Washington consensus'. This led developing states and, after the collapse of communism, 'transition' states, to pursue policies such as free trade, the liberalization of capital markets, flexible exchange rates, balanced budgets and so on. The advance of neoliberal globalization coincided not only with three decades of growth in the USA and its renewed economic ascendancy in the 1990s, but also three decades of growth in the world economy. This encouraged supporters of neoliberalism to argue that its growth model had clearly demonstrated its superiority over the Keynesian orthodoxy of old, which had, anyway, been in decline since the USA withdrew from the Bretton Woods system of fixed exchange rates in 1971. At the core of the neoliberal growth model are financial markets and the process of '**financialization**'. This was made possible by a massive expansion of the financial sector of the economy, explaining the growing importance of Wall Street, the City of London, Frankfurt, Singapore and elsewhere. In the process, capitalism was turned into 'turbo-capitalism', benefiting from greatly expanded monetary flows that were seeking an outlet in increased investment and higher consumption. Although this process involved a considerable growth of public and often private debt, this was thought to be sustainable due to the underlying growth that the debt fuelled. Other key features of the neoliberal growth model included strong faith in open markets and trade liberalization, encouraged after 1995 by the creation of the (WTO), and a shift in many developed economies from manufacturing to services, the former increasingly being 'exported' to the developing world where labour and other costs are cheaper.

Neoliberal globalization, nevertheless, has its critics. They have, for example, argued that, in rolling back welfare provision and promoting an ethic of material self-interest ('greed is good'), neoliberalism struggles to maintain popular legitimacy as an economic doctrine because of its association with widening inequality and social breakdown. This led to a modification, although not a rejection, of the 'neoliberal revolution' in counties, such as New Zealand, Canada and the UK during the 1990s, and even to a reappraisal of neoliberal priorities in the USA under President Obama from 2009 onwards. In the case of Russia, the growth of unemployment and inflation, and the deep insecurities unleashed by the 'shock therapy' application of neoliberal principles in the 1990s, created a backlash against market reform and led to strengthened support for nationalist and authoritarian movements. At a deeper level, Robert Cox (1987) argued that what he called 'hyper-liberal globalizing capitalism' is rooted in major contradictions and struggles, meaning that its dominance is destined to be challenged and, eventually, overthrown. These contradictions include the 'democratic deficit' that is generated by the 'internationalization of the state' (the tendency of the state to respond to the dictates of the global economy, rather than public opinion), the growing pressure to protect the environment from the ravages caused by relentless economic growth, and the surrender of state authority to corporate financial and economic interests. A still darker interpretation of neoliberalism has been developed by Naomi Klein (2008). In highlighting the rise of 'disaster capitalism', she drew attention to the extent to which the advance of neoliberalism has been implicated with 'shocks', states of emergency and crises of one kind or another, thus suggesting that the USA's foreign policy adventurism, from the CIA's role in the overthrow of Salvador Allende in Chile in 1973 to the 'war on terror' (see p. 401) has been linked to the spread of neoliberalism. For many, the underlying weaknesses of neoliberal globalization were exposed most effectively by the 2007–09 global financial crisis.

The 2007–09 Crash and its legacy

The most iconic moment in the 2007–09 global financial crisis came on 15 September 2008 when the 158-year old US investment bank, Lehman Brothers, filed for bankruptcy. This occurred amid turmoil in US financial markets. Amongst other things, the two government-sponsored mortgage corporations, Fannie Mae and Freddie Mac, had to be bailed out by the Federal authorities; the insurance giant AIG was only saved by a $58 billion government rescue package; and Wachovia, the fourth largest US bank, was bought by Citigroup absorbing $42 billion of bad debt. Banking crises erupted elsewhere and stock markets went into freefall worldwide, massively reducing share values and betokening the onset of a global recession. However briefly, global capitalism appeared to teeter on the brink of the abyss, threatening to tip over into systemic failure.

Debates about the implications of the 2007–09 Crash are closely linked to disagreements about its underlying causes. Was the crisis rooted in the US banking system, in Anglo-American enterprise capitalism, or in the nature of the capitalist system itself? At one level, the crisis was linked to inappropriate lending strategies adopted by US banks and mortgage institutions, the so-called 'sub-prime' mortgage market. These high-risk loans to applicants with poor or non-existent credit histories were unlikely to be repaid and, when the scale of 'toxic debt' became apparent, shock waves ran through the US financial system and beyond. At a deeper level, however, the 'sub-prime' problem in the USA was merely a symptom of the defects and vulnerabilities of the neoliberal capitalism that had taken root in the USA and the UK in particular, based on free markets and an inflated and under-regulated financial system. In this view, the Crash highlighted the flaws of market fundamentalism, providing a dramatic reminder of the need for financial (and possibly wider) regulation. At a deeper level still, the crisis has been interpreted as exposing serious imperfections not only in a particular form of capitalism, but in the capitalist system itself. In this light, capitalism, in both its global and national forms, can be viewed as inherently unstable and crisis-prone (see p. 147).

The 2007–09 Crash was the first genuinely global crisis in the world economy since the 'stagflation' crisis of the 1970s, and it gave rise to the most severe falls in global production levels since the Great Depression of the 1930s. As most major economies returned to growth in 2009, it appeared that the massive efforts quickly initiated by national governments and coordinated by the G20 (which displaced the G8 as the principal forum for managing international economic policy) had been successful. These had seen the recapitalizing of banks, substan-

Debating . . .
Is global capitalism inherently unstable and crisis-prone?

Whereas ideological debate once centred on the battle between capitalism and socialism, it now, particularly in a post-Crash period, focuses on the benefits and drawbacks of the global capitalist system. Are risk, uncertainty and a tendency towards crisis inevitable features of global capitalism? Or is instability merely a symptom of the remarkable dynamism of capitalism, a dynamism that is ultimately capable of delivering global prosperity.

YES

Crises of over-production: The earliest and most damning critique of capitalism was advanced by Karl Marx (see p. 41). Marx drew attention to capitalism's tendency towards cyclical crises of over-production. Booms and slumps were inevitable because of the tendency of businesses to over-expand output (over-production) during times of growth but to over-contract output (under-production) during times of recession. For Marx, these crises would become progressively deeper, eventually leading to systemic collapse. This analysis applies equally to domestic and global capitalism.

Creative destruction: For Joseph Schumpeter (1942), capitalism's inherent instability stems from spurts of innovation that destroy established enterprises and yield new ones. The notion of 'creative destruction' captures both the idea that it is entrepreneurs who shape economies, generating growth and, through success or failure, setting business cycles in motion, and the idea that innovation is the main driver of wealth. Schumpeter (see p. 202) was pessimistic about the long-term prospects of capitalism, arguing that the human and social costs of periodic slumps, and the stifling of dynamism, creativity and individualism through the growth of elitism and state intervention would ultimately lead to capitalism's demise.

Casino capitalism: Modern global capitalism's heightened susceptibility towards crisis can be explained in terms of the emergence of a globalized financial system that leaves states vulnerable and exposed to the vagaries of global markets. In what Susan Strange (1986) dubbed 'casino capitalism', massive amounts of 'mad money' surge around the world creating the phenomenon of financial contagion, which occurs as panic spreads well beyond the scope of an initial problem. Such instabilities are accentuated by the fact that most modern financial growth has occurred in the form of purely money-dealing currency and security exchanges, such as so-called 'hedge funds' and 'derivatives'. Globalized financial flows thus create booms and slumps that may have little to do with the performance of 'real' economies.

NO

Dynamism within equilibrium: No supporter of capitalism would argue that a susceptibility to booms and slumps can ever be completely eradicated from the capitalist system. To deny this would be to misunderstand the essentially dynamic nature of capitalism, the fact that market economies exist always in conditions of flux. This flux, nevertheless, is much more creative than destructive: businesses and industries fail, but only to be replaced by ones that are more successful. Eradicate risk and uncertainty from a market economy and you rob it of its potential for growth. The point is that the tendency towards flux and dynamism within capitalism is neither random nor unstructured. At the heart of the capitalist system is a bias in favour of balance or equilibrium, brought about as the market draws resources towards their optimal use in terms of profitability, thus leading to greater efficiency and, over time, wider prosperity. Boom-and-bust cycles should therefore be seen as part of a process of long-term economic development.

Regulated globalization: In an alternative defence of global capitalism, the tendency towards instability and crisis in the world economy can be substantially contained (but never eradicated) by regulation. This was borne out by the 'long boom' of the post-World War II period, when Keynesian strategies dominated national economic policy-making and were embodied in the Bretton Woods system, constructed in 1944. The misfortune of early global capitalism was that it became entangled with a neoliberal philosophy that encouraged an undue faith in free markets, and that it flourished before the institutions of global economic governance had the capacity to exercise effective regulation. The result was a succession of financial crises that led up to and continued beyond the Crash of 2007–09. Global capitalism can, nevertheless, be protected from itself. For example, greater stability could be injected into the global financial system if (as Keynes, in fact, had originally proposed) the IMF became a global bank, acting as the lender of last resort.

tial cuts in interest rates (monetary stimulus) and a boost to domestic demand by allowing spending to exceed taxation (fiscal stimulus). Above all, international action prevented a recurrence of the most serious mistake made in the aftermath of the 1929 Wall Street Crash: a resort to protectionism, which helped to ensure that a financial crisis turned into a deep and prolonged economic crisis. However, renewed and severe economic problems emerged from late 2010 onwards, not least in the form of **sovereign debt crises** in a number of 'euro-zone' economies (see p. 396). This suggested that the legacy of the Crash may be more serious and far-reaching than at first thought. The consequences of the Crash continued to unfold, but their most significant include:

- widespread and unsustainable debt in many developed economies
- the paradoxes and pitfalls of deficit reduction
- the possible end of neoliberal globalization
- a major redistribution of power in the global economy.

Of all the structural problems that have been exposed by the Crash, chronic public and private indebtedness in many developed economies is the most serious. This has occurred for at least three reasons. First, a combination of the failure of productivity growth to produce increases in 'real' wages (which, in the USA, has continued for almost 30 years) and rising inequality meant that many developed economies had lost their 'demand engines'. In this context, growth could only be injected into the economy through ever-higher levels of borrowing (in the form of mortgages, bank loans, the use of credit cards and hire purchase, and so on), which governments either condoned or actively encouraged. This has been called 'privatized Keynesianism' (Crouch, 2009), reflecting the extent to which private debt had displaced public debt as the key motor of growth. Second, governments allowed sovereign debt to rise, both because they assumed that growth would continue, so keeping tax revenues healthy, and because of the political benefits sustaining or boosting public spending without commensurate tax increases. Third, the global economic downturn that occurred, particularly in the developed world, in the wake of the Crash substantially reduced tax revenues, often throwing public finances into chaos with a resulting explosion of borrowing.

However, the (obvious) solution to high or growing levels of public borrowing may be worse than the disease, or, at least, it may make the disease worse not better. If chronic indebtedness is the problem, the solution would appear to be debt reduction, brought about by 'fiscal retrenchment' (reducing public spending or increasing tax levels). This, nevertheless, brings with it major economic and political difficulties. The economic problem of deficit reduction is that what might make good sense for a single economy trying to get its finances in order, spells catastrophe if adopted by a large number of economies at the same time. As suggested by the '**paradox of thrift**', popularized by Keynes, the net result of everyone saving money (in this case, governments cutting spending levels or raising taxes) is that everyone suffers as insufficient demand in the economy leads to economic stagnation and soaring unemployment. The political challenges of debt reduction include that it promotes an 'age of austerity' in which populations have to be reconciled to steady-state, or even falling, living standards and political stability can no longer be underpinned by the prospect of ever-rising prosperity (these problems are examined in greater detail in Chapter 20).

● **Sovereign debt crisis**: A structural imbalance in state finances that occurs when public spending so exceeds tax revenues that levels of borrowing become unsustainable, threatening a default on interest repayments.

● **The paradox of thrift**: The paradox that increased saving by individual households may lead to a reduced overall saving because of its negative impact on consumption and growth.

CONCEPT

Transnational corporations

A transnational corporation (TNC) is a company that controls economic activity in two or more countries. The term transnational corporation is now generally preferred to multinational corporation (MNC) because it captures the extent to which corporate strategies and processes transcend national borders, rather than merely crossing them. Integration across economic sectors and the growth of intra-firm trade has allowed TNCs to become economies in their own right, benefiting from geographical flexibility, advantages in product innovation and the ability to pursue global marketing strategies.

One of the most widely anticipated consequences of the Crash was that it would lead to a re-evaluation, and possibly a rejection, of the neoliberal model of globalization. This was because the Crash originated, and was initially most severe, in those economies that had embraced neoliberalism with the greatest enthusiasm (the USA and the UK), and because a major factor in explaining the crisis was an over-reliance on an, arguably, inherently unstable financial sector. Moreover, history seems to suggest that major crises lead to transformations in the management of the world economy (Casey, 2011). The Great Depression of the 1930s led, via Roosevelt's New Deal in the USA, to a shift in the post-1945 world in favour of Keynesianism, while the 'stagflation' crisis of the 1970s contributed to the abandonment of Keynesianism and the rise of neoliberalism. Nevertheless, there has, to date, been relatively little evidence of a shift of similar proportions in response to the 2017–09 Crash. For example, progress on the construction of a 'new Bretton Woods', widely muted in the immediate aftermath of September 2008, which would re-orientate the institutions of global economic governance away from neoliberalism, has been slow. The reasons for this may include the fact that political choice is constrained by the structural power of the interests most closely linked to neoliberal globalization – (TNCs), major banks, global markets and so forth – but it also reflects the intellectual and ideological failure of the political left, be it in the form of left-wing or centre-left political parties, or the anti-globalization movement, to develop an alternative model of globalization that is both economically and politically viable. Nevertheless, it is worth noting that the full ideological significance of the Great Depression only became apparent after almost a decade of mass unemployment and an intervening world war.

Finally, the 2007–09 Crash may come to be seen as a pivotal moment in the transfer of power in the global economy from the West to the East in general, and from the USA to China in particular. Much of the growth in the world economy in the two decades preceding the Crash had, anyway, been generated by the economic emergence of China, India, Brazil and other developing-world economies; in part, because their ability to produce cheap manufactured goods concealed the structural defects from which many developed economies were suffering. In addition, China and many emerging economies weathered the storms of 2007–09 far better than did developed economies; China, for instance, experienced only a mild dip in its growth rate during this period. Emerging economies also entered the post-Crash period with the advantage that they usually had significant trade surpluses and were often major creditor countries, having bought much of the debt of the developing world. However, such shifts in the balance of economic power occurs within the context of a world that is more interdependent than ever before. Just as economic recovery in the USA is important to China because China holds much of the USA's sovereign debt, so the developing world needs recovery in the developed world to provide a market for its manufacturing goods. Perhaps the key lesson of the Crash, then, is that it reminds us that, in a globalized world, no economy is an island.

SUMMARY

- Political economy, in its broadest sense, refers to the interplay between politics and economics. As a topic, political economy encompasses a range of thinking about the relationship between states and markets. As a method, it stands for the use of approaches developed within economics to analyse politics. Distinctive state-centric, classical/neoclassical and Marxist approaches to political economy can be identified.

- Capitalism is a system of generalized commodity production in which wealth is owned privately and economic life is organized according to market principles. Enterprise capitalism, social capitalism and state capitalism nevertheless differ in relation to the balance within them between the market and the state.

- State socialism, or communism, was the major twentieth-century alternative to capitalism, but it ultimately failed to rival capitalism in terms of producing modern consumer goods and delivering widespread prosperity, so leading to experiments in market socialism. Green economics calls for the economy to be restructured around the principles of ecological balance and sustainability.

- Globalization is a complex web of interconnectedness that means that our lives are increasingly shaped by decisions and actions taken at a distance from ourselves. Economic globalization reflects the increase in transnational flows of capital and goods, destroying the idea of economic sovereignty. Cultural globalization is a homogenizing force, whereas political globalization is linked to the growing importance of international organizations.

- Economic globalization has gone hand-in-hand with neoliberalism, so much so that they are often considered to be a single phenomenon, neoliberal globalization. Debate has raged over the implications of the Crash of 2007–09 for neoliberal globalization, but other key consequences of the Crash include massive indebtedness in many developed economies and a major shift in the global balance of economic power.

Questions for discussion

- Does politics shape economics, or does economics shape politics?

- What type of capitalist system will prove to be the most viable in the twenty-first century?

- Are free-market economies inherently unstable and prone to inequality?

- Are socialist economic models any longer of relevance?

- What would be the features of an ecologically sustainable economy?

- Is globalization a myth or a reality?

- Does a globalized economy mean opportunity for all, or greater insecurity and deeper inequality?

- To what extent did the crash of 2007–09 mark a turning point in the development of the global economy?

- Does neoliberal globalization have a future?

Further reading

Albritton, R., B. Jessop and R. Westra (eds), *Political Economy and Global Capitalism* (2010). A useful collection that offers a critical perspective on political economy in an age of global capitalism.

Hall, P. and D. Soskice (eds), *Varieties of Capitalism: The Institutional Foundations of Comparative Advantage* (2001). A stimulating examination of differences among national economies and of the impact of economic globalization.

Scholte, A., *Globalization: A Critical Introduction* (2nd edn) (2005). An excellent and accessibly written account of the nature of globalization, and debate about its implications.

Stilwell, F., *Political Economy: The Context of Economic Ideas* (3rd edn) (2011). A comprehensive and insightful overview of political economy that investigates the main traditions of economic thought.

CHAPTER 7

Politics, Society and Identity

Society is inside man and man is inside society.'
ARTHUR MILLER, *The Shadow of the Gods* (1958)

PREVIEW To suggest, as textbooks tend to do, that politics takes place in a social context fails to convey just how intimately politics and social life are related. Politics, by its very nature, is a social activity, and it is viewed by some as nothing more than the process through which the conflicts of society are articulated and, perhaps, resolved. In this sense, society is no mere 'context', but the very stuff and substance of politics itself. Although later chapters examine the interaction between society and politics in relation to particular channels of communication, such as the media, elections, political parties, interest groups and so on, this chapter focuses on the broader political implications of how society is structured and how it has changed and continues to change. For example, the transition from agrarian societies to industrial societies and then to so-called post-industrial society has profoundly altered levels of social connectedness and given rise to new political battle lines. Not only has post-industrialism been associated with the declining significance of social class, but technological change, particularly in the fields of information and communication, has altered the breadth and depth of connections between people, as well as the nature of these connections. These and related factors have been linked to the strengthening of individualism, with major political consequences. Modern thinking about the relationship between politics and society is, nevertheless, increasingly focused on the question of identity, many claim, giving rise to a new politics of group self-assertion, or identity politics. This trend has helped, amongst other things, to highlight the political significance of race and ethnicity, gender, religion and culture.

KEY ISSUES
- What have been the political implications of the emergence of post-industrial societies?
- Is the 'information society' a myth or a reality?
- How has the growth of individualism affected community and social cohesion?
- Why has the politics of identity become so prominent in recent years?
- How have race and ethnicity, gender, religion and culture provided the basis for identity politics?
- Is identity politics a liberating force or a political dead-end?

CONCEPT

Status

Status is a person's position within a hierarchical order. It is characterized by the person's role, rights and duties in relation to the other members of that order. As status is a compound of factors such as honour, prestige, standing and power, it is more difficult to determine than an essentially economic category such as class. Also, because it is a measure of whether someone is 'higher' or 'lower' on a social scale, it is more subjective. Although status hierarchies have faded in significance in modern societies, they continue to operate in relation to factors such as family background, gender, and race and ethnicity.

POLITICS AND SOCIETY

What do we mean by 'society'? In its most general sense, a society is a collection of people who occupy the same territorial area. However, not every group of people constitutes a society. Societies are characterized by regular patterns of social interaction. This suggests the existence of some kind of social *structure*; that is, a usually stable set of interrelationships amongst a number of elements. Moreover, 'social' relationships involve a sense of connectedness, in the form of mutual awareness and, at least, a measure of cooperation. For instance, strictly speaking, warring tribes do not constitute a 'society', even though they may live in close proximity to one another and interact regularly. Societies are also usually characterized by social *divisions*, in which groups and individuals occupy very different positions, reflecting an unequal distribution of status, wealth and/or power within the society. The nature of these divisions or cleavages, and the political significance of particular divisions (class, race, gender, age, religion and so on), of course, differ from society to society.

In all cases, though, society can be seen to shape politics in a number of important ways:

- The distribution of wealth and other resources in society conditions the nature of state power (as discussed in Chapter 3).
- Social divisions and conflicts help to bring about political change in the form of legitimation crises (as discussed in Chapter 4).
- Society influences public opinion and the political culture (as discussed in Chapter 8).
- The social structure shapes political behaviour; that is, who votes, how they vote, who joins parties and so on (as discussed in Chapters 9–11).

The nature of society, however, is one of the most contentious areas of political and ideological debate, being no less controversial, in fact, than the attempt to define the content of human nature. For example, whereas Marxists and others hold that society is characterized by irreconcilable conflict, liberals tend to emphasize that harmony exists amongst competing interests and groups. Similarly, while liberals are inclined to view society as an artefact fashioned by individuals to satisfy their various needs, conservatives have traditionally portrayed it as organic, ultimately shaped by the forces of natural necessity. Nevertheless, the nature of society, and therefore of social connectedness, have changed significantly over time. Modern society appears to be characterized by a 'hollowing out' of social connectedness, a transition from the 'thick' connectedness of close social bonds and fixed allegiances to the 'thin' connectedness of more fluid, individualized social arrangements. These changes have been linked to developments such as the advent of 'post-industrialism' and the fading significance of social class (see p. 153), the emergence of so-called 'information societies', and the growth of individualism (see p. 158).

From industrialism to post-industrialism

Industrialization has been the most powerful factor shaping the structure and character of modern societies. It has, for instance, contributed to a dramatic

CONCEPT

Social class

A class is, broadly, a group of people who share a similar social and economic position. For Marxists, class is linked to economic power, which is defined by the individual's relationship to the means of production. From this perspective, the key class division is between the owners of productive wealth (the bourgeoisie) and those who live off the sale of their labour power (the proletariat). Non-Marxist definitions of class are usually based on income and status differences between occupational groups. Distinctions are thus made between 'middle' class (or non-manual) workers and 'working' class (or manual) workers.

● **Gemeinschaft**: (German) Community; social ties typically found in traditional societies and characterized by natural affection and mutual respect.

● **Gesellschaft**: (German) Association; the loose, artificial and contractual bonds typically found in urban and industrial societies.

● **Class consciousness**: A Marxist term denoting a subjective awareness of a class's objective situation and interests; the opposite of 'false consciousness'.

● **Post-industrial society**: A society based on service industries, rather than on manufacturing industries, and accompanied by a significant growth in the white-collar workforce.

increase in geographical mobility through the process of urbanization (by the early 2000s, most of the world's then 6.3 billion people had come to live in towns and cities, rather than in rural areas). In the process, the nature of social connectedness underwent significant changes. One of the most influential attempts to convey this transition was undertaken by the German sociologist Ferdinand Tönnies (1855–1936). Tönnies distinguished between **Gemeinschaft** and **Gesellschaft**. The advance of industrialization also changed the structure of society, with economically-based class divisions displacing the fixed social hierarchies of more traditional societies, which were usually based on status and linked to land ownership. Social class thus emerged as the central organizing principle of society.

However, any analysis of the relationship between class and politics is bedevilled by problems, not least about how social class should be defined and the role that social classes play. The leading protagonists of class politics have come from the Marxist tradition. Marxists regard class as the most fundamental, and politically the most significant, social division. As Marx (see p. 41) put it at the beginning of the *Communist Manifesto* ([1848] 1967), 'the history of all hitherto existing societies is the history of class struggle'. From the Marxist perspective, capitalist societies are dominated by a 'ruling class' of property owners (the bourgeoisie) who oppress and exploit a class of wage slaves (the proletariat). This gives rise to a two-class model of industrial capitalism that emphasizes irreconcilable conflict and progressive polarization, with social classes being the key actors on the political stage. Marx predicted that, as capitalist development would be characterized by deepening crises, the proletariat would eventually achieve **class consciousness** and fulfil its destiny as the 'gravedigger' of capitalism. The proletariat would thus be transformed from a 'class in-itself' (an economically defined category) and become a 'class for-itself' (a revolutionary force).

Decline of class politics

The Marxist two-class model has, however, been discredited by the failure of Marx's predictions to materialize, and by declining evidence of class struggle, at least in advanced capitalist societies. Even by the end of the nineteenth century, it was clear that the class structure of industrial societies was becoming increasingly complex, and that it varies from system to system, as well as over time. Max Weber (see p. 82) was one of the first to take stock of this shift, developing a theory of stratification that acknowledged economic or class differences, but also took account of the importance of political parties and social status. In drawing attention to status as a 'social estimation of honour' expressed in the lifestyle of a group, Weber helped to prepare the ground for the modern notion of occupational class, widely used by social and political scientists. For some, however, the late twentieth century was characterized by the final eclipse of class politics. By the 1960s, neo-Marxists such as Herbert Marcuse (see p. 42) were lamenting the deradicalization of the urban proletariat, and looked instead to the revolutionary potential of students, women, ethnic minorities and the developing world. The traditional link between socialism and the working class was formally abandoned in works such as André Gorz's *Farewell to the Working Class* (1982).

Most commentators agree that, behind the declining political significance of class, lies the emergence of so-called '**post-industrial societies**'. One of the

Fordism, post-Fordism

Fordism refers to the large-scale mass-production methods pioneered by Henry Ford in Detroit in the USA. These used mechanization and highly-regimented production-line labour processes to produce standardized, relatively cheap products. Fordist societies were structured largely by solidaristic class loyalties. Post-Fordism emerged as the result of the introduction of more flexible microelectronics-based machinery that gave individual workers greater autonomy and made possible innovations such as subcontracting and batch production. Post-Fordism has been linked to decentralization in the workplace and a greater emphasis on choice and individuality.

● **Atomism**: The tendency for society to be made up of a collection of self-interested and largely self-sufficient individuals, operating as separate atoms.

● **Underclass**: A poorly defined and politically controversial term that refers, broadly, to people who suffer from multiple deprivation (unemployment or low pay, poor housing, inadequate education and so on)

● **Internet**: A global 'network of networks' that connects computers around the world; 'virtual' space in which users can access and disseminate online information.

key features of such societies has been the process of de-industrialization, reflected in the decline of labour-intensive 'heavy' industries such as coal, steel and shipbuilding. These tended to be characterized by a solidaristic culture rooted in clear political loyalties and, usually, strong union organization. In contrast, the expanding service sectors of economies foster more individualistic and instrumentalist attitudes. Post-industrial societies are therefore distinguished by growing **atomism** and the weakening of social connectedness. The term 'post-industrialism' was popularized by Daniel Bell in *The Coming of Post-industrial Society* (1973). For Bell, post-industrial societies were characterized, amongst other things, by the transition from a labour theory of value to a knowledge theory of value, as implied by the idea of an 'information society' (see p. 156), discussed below. Piore and Sabel (1984) interpreted the transition as part of a shift from a Fordist to a post-Fordist era. In this light, the eclipse of the system of mass production and mass consumption, the chief features of Fordism, has produced more pluralized and fluid class formations.

The shrinkage of the traditional working class has led to the development of so-called 'two-thirds, one-third' societies, in which the two-thirds are relatively prosperous, a product of a marked tendency towards social levelling associated with mass education, rising affluence and consumerism (Hutton, 1995). One of the most influential attempts to discuss the political implications of this development is found in J. K. Galbraith's *The Culture of Contentment* (1992). Galbraith (see p. 155) pointed to the emergence in modern societies, at least amongst the politically active, of a 'contented majority' whose material affluence and economic security encourages them to be politically conservative. This contented majority, for instance, has provided an electoral base for the anti-welfarist and tax-cutting policies that have become fashionable since the 1970s. Debate about the plight of the one-third and about the nature of social inequality in modern societies has increasingly focused not so much on social class, but more on what has been called the '**underclass**'. The underclass suffers less from poverty as it has been traditionally understood (deprivation of material necessities) and more from social exclusion, reflected in cultural, educational and social impediments to meaningful participation in the economy and society. However, attitudes towards social differentiation and debates about the appropriate response to the growth of an underclass are rooted in deeper disagreements about the causes and political implications of social inequality (see p. 156).

New technology and the 'information society'

One of the features most commonly associated with post-industrialism is the increased importance that is placed on knowledge and information generally, on intellectual capital (ideas), rather than material capital (things). This is often seen as a consequence of what has been called the 'third' modern information revolution, which has witnessed the advent of so-called 'new' media; notably, mobile phones, cable and satellite television, cheaper and more powerful computers, and, most importantly, the **internet**. (The first revolution involved the development of the telegraph, telephone and radio, while the second centred on television, early-generation computers and satellites). The third information

John Kenneth Galbraith (1908–2006)

Canadian economist and social theorist. Following wartime service as the Director of the US Strategic Bombing Survey, Galbraith became a professor of economics at Harvard University and served as the US Ambassador to India, 1961–63. Galbraith was closely identified with the Democratic Party, and was perhaps the leading modern exponent of Keynesian economics (and certainly its most innovative advocate). He became one of the USA's most eminent social commentators. In *The Affluent Society* (1958), Galbraith highlighted the contrast between private affluence and public squalor, arguing that economic resources are often used in the wasteful gratification of trivial wants. *The New Industrial State* (1967) advanced a critique of corporate power in the USA. His other major works include *The Culture of Contentment* (1992).

revolution has concerned the technologies of **connectivity**, and have been particularly significant. The extraordinary explosion that has occurred in the quantity of information and communication exchanges, made possible by digital technologies, has marked, some argue, the birth of the 'information age' (in place of the industrial age). Society has been transformed into an 'information society' and the economy has become a '**knowledge economy**', even a 'weightless' economy.

The emergence of new media has helped to alter both the scope and the nature of social connectedness. As far as the scope of social connectedness is concerned, new media have given huge impetus to the process of globalization. Indeed, so-called 'hyperglobalist' theorists subscribe to a kind of technological determinism in arguing that accelerated globalization became inevitable once new information and communication technologies (ICT) became widely available (Ohmae, 1989). While the industrial age (and the first two communications revolutions) created new mechanisms for communicating at a national, rather than a local level (via national newspapers, telephone systems, radio and television services, and so on), the technologies of the information age are, by their nature, transnational: mobile phones, satellite television and the internet (usually) operate regardless of borders. This, in turn, has facilitated the growth of transborder groups, bodies and institutions, ranging from non-governmental organizations (NGOs) (see p. 248), protest movements and transnational corporations (TNCs) (see p. 149) to international criminal organizations and global terrorist groups such as al-Qaeda. Not only do states struggle to control and constrain groups and organizations that have transborder structures, but they also have a greatly reduced capacity to control what their citizens see, hear and know. For instance, although states such as China, Burma and Iran have, at various times, tried to restrict transborder communications via mobile phones and the internet, the pace of technological change is very likely to weaken such controls in the longer term. The former US Presisent Bill Clinton likened China's attempts to control the internet to trying to nail Jell-O to the wall.

Not only do information societies connect more people to more other people – and, increasingly, to people who live in other societies – but the nature

● **Connectivity**: A computer buzzword that refers to the links between one device (usually a computer) and others, affecting the speed, ease and extent of information exchanges.

● **Knowledge economy**: An economy in which knowledge is the key source of competitiveness and productivity, especially through the application of information and communications technology.

Debating...
Does social equality matter?

The issue of social equality lies at the heart of ideological debate and argument. While left-wingers tend to support equality, seeing it as the key to social justice, right-wingers typically accepted inequality as inevitable if not desirable. How does material inequality, particularly income inequality, affect politics and society? Do governments have a moral obligation to promote social equality, and, if so, on what grounds?

YES

Inequality and social dysfunction. Socialists have long argued that social inequality breeds resentment, hostility and strife, even, in the case of Marxists, associating class inequality with inevitable social revolution. Such concerns have also been borne out by empirical studies that link inequality to a range of negative personal and social outcomes. Comparative studies of 'high' inequality countries, such as the USA, the UK and Portugal, and 'low' inequality countries, such as Japan and the Scandinavian states, suggests that inequality leads to shorter, unhealthier and unhappier lives, reflected in increased rates of, for instance, teenage pregnancies, violence, obesity, imprisonment and addiction (Wilkinson and Pickett, 2010).

Justice as equality. The moral case in favour of equality includes that poverty and social disadvantage impair people's opportunities and life chances. As social differentiation more often results from unequal treatment by society than from unequal natural endowment, justice dictates that social rewards should generally be distributed more equally, and that this should be done through policies of welfare and redistribution. According to John Rawls (see p. 45), if people were unaware of their personal attributes and qualities, most would favour equality over inequality, as their fear of being destitute would outweigh their desire for great wealth.

Social citizenship. Social equality (or, more accurately, reduced social inequality) is a necessary condition for healthy democracy and meaningful citizenship. Citizens have to enjoy freedom from poverty, ignorance and despair if they are to participate fully in the affairs of their community, an idea embodied in the concept of social citizenship. Groups such as women, ethnic minorities, the poor and the unemployed, commonly regard themselves as 'second class citizens' if social disadvantage prevents their full civic and political participation (see p. 444). Social inequality thus correlates with low voter turnout and fuels dissent and civil unrest.

NO

Inequality and economic growth. Liberal political economists link social equality to economic stagnation. This occurs because social 'levelling' serves to cap aspirations and remove the incentive for enterprise and hard work. The sterility and inertia of communist states was thus in large part a consequence of high levels of job security and low income differentials. In contrast, the USA, the world's leading economy, demonstrates how inequality promotes economic vigour, as the rich can always get richer and the poor can always become more poor. Indeed, by strengthening incentives, inequality may actually benefit the poor, whose living standards may be higher in relatively unequal societies than they are in relatively equal societies.

Justice as inequality. Inequality is justifiable quite simply because people are different: they have different aspirations, talents, dispositions and so forth. To treat them as equals must therefore result in injustice. As Aristotle (see p. 6) put it, injustice arises not only when equals are treated unequally, but also when unequals are treated equally. Justice may require equality of opportunity, giving each person the same starting point in life, but certainly not equality of outcome. In line with the principle of meritocracy, the talented and hardworking should rise, while the lazy and feckless should fall. Pursuing equality thus involves penalizing talent.

Politics of envy. The socialist principle of equality is based on social envy, the desire to have what others possess. Instead of encouraging the less well-off to focus on improving their own living standards, it encourages them to resent the wealthy, seeing them, somehow, as the architects of their misfortune. As the politics of envy grows, individual freedom is diminished, both through the emergence of an extensive system of manipulation and 'social engineering', and by the fact that redistribution, in effect, legalizes theft (as government transfers wealth from one group of people to another without their consent).

CONCEPT

Information society

An information society is a society in which the creation, distribution and manipulation of information are core economic and cultural activities, underpinned, in particular, by the wider use of computerized processes and the internet. Information and knowledge are thus seen to have replaced physical capital as the principal source of wealth. In an 'information age', or 'cyber age', the principal responsibility of government is to improve education and training, both to strengthen international competitiveness and to widen opportunities for the individual.

of those connections has also changed. One of the most influential attempts to explain this was advanced in Manuel Castells' (1996) notion of the 'network society'. Whereas the dominant mode of social organization in industrial societies had been hierarchies, more complex and pluralized information societies operate either on the basis of markets (reflecting the wider role of market economics, as well as the impact of economic globalization, as discussed in Chapter 6), or on the basis of looser and more diffuse **networks**. According to Castells, businesses increasingly function as 'network corporations'. Many TNCs, for instance, are organized as networks of franchises and subsidiaries. Similar trends can be witnessed in social and political life. For example, hierarchical bodies such as trade unions and pressure groups have increasingly lost influence through the emergence of network-based social movements (see p. 260), such as the anti-globalization movement and the environmental movement.

Nevertheless, opinions are divided over the implications of the wider use of new communications technologies for politics and society. Dating back to Ivan Illich's pioneering *Tools for Conviviality* (1973), the potential for computer-based technologies to give individual citizens independent access to specialized knowledge, allowing them to escape from dependency on technocratic elites, has been lauded. In this light, new media are a source of citizen empowerment and (potentially) a significant constraint on government power. Critics, in contrast, point out that the internet does not discriminate between good ideas and bad ones. It provides a platform for the dissemination not only of socially-worthwhile and politically-neutral views, but also of political extremism, racial and religious bigotry, and pornography of various kinds. A further danger has been the growth of a 'cult of information', whereby the accumulation of data and information becomes an end in itself, impairing the ability of people to distinguish between information, on the one hand, and knowledge, experience and wisdom, on the other (Roszak, 1994). Such a criticism is linked to allegations that 'surfing' the internet actually impairs people's ability to think and learn by encouraging them to skim and jump from one piece of information to the next, ruining their ability to concentrate. New media may therefore be making people stupid, rather than better-informed (Carr, 2008, 2010). The impact of new media on democracy and governance is examined in greater detail in Chapter 8.

No such thing as society?

Although the advent of post-industrialism and the spread of IT-based, network relationships have encouraged the 'thinning' of social connectedness, at the heart of this trend lies a deeper process: the rise of individualism. In many parts of the world, the notion of 'the individual' is now so familiar that its political and social significance, as well as its relatively recent origins, are often overlooked. In traditional societies, there was typically little idea of individuals having their own interests, or possessing personal and unique identities. Rather, people were seen as members of the social groups to which they belonged: their family, village, tribe, local community and so on. Their lives and identities were largely determined by the character of these groups in a process that had changed little from one generation to the next. The rise of individualism is widely seen as a conse-

● **Network**: A means of co-ordinating social life through loose and informal relationships between people or organizations, usually for the purpose of knowledge dissemination or exchange.

CONCEPT

Individualism

Individualism is the belief in the supreme importance of the individual over any social group or collective body. As such, individualism has two key implications. First, each individual has a separate, indeed unique, identity, reflecting his or her 'inner' or personal qualities. This is evident in the idea of individuality, and is linked to the notion of people as self-interested, and largely self-reliant, creatures. Second, all individuals share the same moral status as 'persons', irrespective of factors such as race, religion, nationality, sex and social position. This is reflected in the idea of rights, and especially in the doctrine of human rights (see p. 342).

● **Economic individualism**: The belief that individuals are entitled to autonomy in matters of economic decision-making; economic individualism is lo0sely linked to property rights.

● **Community**: A principle or sentiment based on the collective identity of a social group; bonds of comradeship, loyalty and duty.

● **Anomie**: A weakening of values and normative rules, associated with feelings of isolation, loneliness and meaninglessness.

quence of the establishment of industrial capitalism as the dominant mode of social organization, first in western societies and, thanks to globalization, beyond. Industrial capitalism meant that people were confronted by a broader range of choices and social possibilities. They were encouraged, perhaps for the first time, to think for themselves, and to think of themselves in personal terms. A peasant, for example, whose family may always have lived and worked on the same piece of land, became a 'free man' and acquired some ability to choose who to work for, or maybe the opportunity to leave the land altogether and look for work in the growing towns or cities. As individuals, people were more likely to be self-seeking, acting in accordance with their own (usually material) interests, and they were encouraged to be self-sufficient, in the sense of taking responsibility for their economic and social circumstances. This gave rise to the doctrine of **economic individualism**.

A child of industrial capitalism, individualism has been further strengthened by the growth, especially since the 1960s, of the consumer society and, later, by the general shift in favour of neoliberal economics, as examined in Chapter 6, Whereas earlier versions of industrial capitalism had linked people's status in society to their productive roles (most clearly demonstrated by the importance traditionally placed on social class, a consumer society, or consumer capitalism), encouraged people to define themselves increasingly in terms of what they own and how much they own. While an emphasis on production tends to foster social solidarity, in that it highlights what people have in common with other people, consumerism encourages people to think and act more in individual terms, focusing on personal gratification, even seeing consumption as a form of self-expression. Daniel Bell (1976) interpreted this as evidence of a cultural contradiction that lies at the heart of the capitalist system, arguing that the ethic of acquisitiveness and immediate gratification (which encourages consumers to consume) was winning out over the ethic of asceticism and delayed gratification (which encourages workers to work). The growing prominence of neoliberalism (see p. 144) from the 1980s onwards, especially in countries that had embraced free-market thinking with the greatest enthusiasm, such as the USA and the UK, further strengthened individualism. This occurred both through the tendency to extol the virtues of entrepreneurialism and individual self-striving, creating, critics argued, a philosophy of 'greed is good', and through the rolling back of welfare, based on the desire for people to 'stand on their own two feet'. Margaret Thatcher's famous assertion, that 'There is no such thing as society . . . only individual men and women and their families', is often seen to encapsulate the thrust of neoliberal individualism.

However, there is deep disagreement over the implications of the spread of individualism. For many, the spread of individualism has profoundly weakened **community** and our sense of social belonging. For instance, academic sociology largely arose in the nineteenth century as an attempt to explore the (usually negative) social implications of the spread of industrialization and urbanization, both of which had encouraged increasing individualism and competition. The French sociologist Émile Durkheim (1858–1917) thus emphasized the degree to which the weakening of social codes and norms had resulted in the spread of '**anomie**'. For Durkheim (1897), this had led to an increase in the number of suicides in industrial societies. Similar misgivings about the rise of individualism have been expressed by modern communitarian thinkers, who have linked the

CONCEPT

Consumerism

Consumerism is a psychic and social phenomenon whereby personal happiness is equated with the acquisition and consumption of material possessions. Its growth has been shaped by the development of new advertising and marketing techniques that took advantage of the emergence of the mass media and the spread of mass affluence. Rising consumerism has important socio-economic and cultural implications. Whereas 'productionist' societies emphasize the values of discipline, duty and hard work (the Protestant work ethic, for example), consumer societies emphasize materialism, hedonism and immediate, rather than delayed, gratification.

● **Social reflexivity**: The tendency of individuals and other social actors to reflect, more or less continuously, on the conditions of their own actions, implying higher levels of self-awareness, self-knowledge and contemplation.

growth of egoism and atomism to a weakening of social duty and moral responsibility. Communitarian theorists, such as Michael Sandel (1982) and Alisdair MacIntyre (1981), have thus argued that, in conceiving the individual as logically prior to and 'outside' the community, liberal individualism has legitimized selfishness and greed, and downgraded the importance of the public good. Robert Putnam (2000) and others have associated such trends with a decline of social capital (see p. 175) across many modern societies, as discussed at greater length in Chapter 8.

On the other hand, liberal theorists, in particular, have viewed rising individualism as a mark of social progress. In this view, the forward march of individualism has been associated with the spread of progressive, even 'enlightened', social values; notably, toleration and equality of opportunity. If human beings are thought of, first and foremost, as individuals, they must be entitled to the same rights and the same respect, meaning that all forms of disadvantage or discrimination, based on factors such as gender (see p. 163), race (see p. 112), colour, creed, religion or social background, are viewed as morally questionable, if not indefensible. All modern societies have, to a greater or lesser extent, been affected by the spread of such ideas, not least through the changing gender roles and family structures that have resulted from the spread of feminism. The link between individualism and the expansion of choice and opportunity has also been highlighted by the spread in modern societies of **social reflexivity** (Giddens, 1994). This has occurred for a variety of reasons, including the development of mass education; much wider access to information through radio, television, the internet and so on; and intensified cultural flows within and between societies. However, social reflexivity brings both benefits and dangers. On the one hand, it has greatly widened the sphere of personal freedom, the ability of people to define who they are and how they wish to live, a tendency reflected in the increasing domination of politics by so-called 'lifestyle' issues. On the other hand, its growth has coincided with a strengthening of consumerism and materialist ethics.

Nevertheless, it is important not to overstate the advance of individualism or, for that matter, the erosion of community. Individualism has been embraced most eagerly in the English-speaking world, where it has been most culturally palatable, given the impact of Protestant religious ideas about personal salvation and the moral benefits of individual self-striving. In contrast, Catholic societies in Europe and elsewhere have been more successful in resisting individualism and in maintaining the ethics of social responsibility, reflected in a stronger desire to uphold welfare provision as both an expression of social responsibility and a means of upholding social cohesion. However, the best examples of successful anti-individualist societies can be found in Asia, especially in Japan, China and Asian 'tiger' states such as Taiwan, South Korea and Singapore. This has led to a debate about the viability of a set of so-called 'Asian values', and especially those associated with Confucianism (see p. 278), as an alternative to the individualism of western, liberal societies. In addition, the image of modern societies being increasingly dominated by 'thin' forms of social connectedness is undermined by evidence of the resurgence of 'thick' social connectedness in many societies; notably, through the rise of identity politics and the growing importance of ethnicity, gender (see p. 160), culture and religion in many parts of the world.

Ethnicity

Ethnicity is the sentiment of loyalty towards a distinctive population, cultural group or territorial area. The term is complex because it has both racial and cultural overtones. The members of ethnic groups are often seen, correctly or incorrectly, to have descended from common ancestors, and the groups are thus thought of as extended kinship groups, united by blood. More commonly, ethnicity is understood as a form of cultural identity, albeit one that operates at a deep and emotional level. An 'ethnic' culture encompasses values, traditions and practices but, crucially, it also gives a people a common identity and sense of distinctiveness, usually by focusing on their origins.

● **Identity politics**: A style of politics that seeks to counter group marginalization by embracing a positive and assertive sense of collective identity.

● **Eurocentrism**: A culturally biased approach to understanding that treats European, and generally western, ideas, values and assumptions as 'natural'.

● **Race**: A group of people who share a common ancestry and 'one blood': 'racial' differences linked to skin and hair colour and facial features have no scientific basis (see p. 112).

IDENTITY POLITICS

Rise of identity politics

One of the prominent features of modern politics has been a growing recognition of the significance of cultural differences within society, often portrayed as '**identity politics**', or the 'politics of difference'. Identity politics is an orientation towards social or political theorizing, rather than a coherent body of ideas with a settled political character. It seeks to challenge and overthrow oppression by reshaping a group's identity through what amounts to a process of politico-cultural self-assertion. This reflects two core beliefs. The first is that group marginalization operates through stereotypes and values developed by dominant groups that structure how marginalized groups see themselves and are seen by others. These typically inculcate a sense of inferiority, even shame. The second belief is that subordination can be challenged by reshaping identity to give the group concerned a sense of pride and self-respect (for instance, 'black is beautiful' or 'gay pride'). In seeking to reclaim a 'pure' or 'authentic' sense of identity, identity politics expresses defiance against marginalization and disadvantage, and serves as a source of liberation. This is what gives identity politics its typically combative character and imbues it with psycho-emotional force.

The foundations for identity politics were laid by the postcolonial theories that emerged from the collapse of the European empires in the early post-1945 period. The significance of postcolonialism (see p. 52) was that it sought to challenge and overturn the cultural dimension of imperial rule by establishing the legitimacy of non-western – and sometimes anti-western – political ideas and traditions. For example, Franz Fanon (1926–61) developed a theory of imperialism (see p. 427) that gave particular emphasis to the psychological dimension of colonial subjugation. For Fanon (1968), decolonization was not merely a political process, but one through which a new 'species' of man is created. He argued that only the cathartic experience of violence is powerful enough to bring about this psycho-political regeneration. Edward Said (see p. 161) developed a critique of **Eurocentrism** through his notion of 'orientalism' (Said, 1978). Orientalism highlights the extent to which western cultural and political hegemony over the rest of the world, but over the Orient in particular, had been maintained through elaborate stereotypical fictions that belittled and demeaned non-western people and culture. Examples of this would include notions such as the 'mysterious East', 'inscrutable Chinese' and 'lustful Turks'. However, manifestations of identity politics are varied and diverse. This is because identity can be shaped around many principles. The most important of these are:

● race and ethnicity
● gender
● religion
● culture.

Race and ethnicity

Racial and ethnic divisions are a significant feature of many modern societies. There is nothing new, however, in the link between **race** and politics. The first

Edward Said (1935–2003)

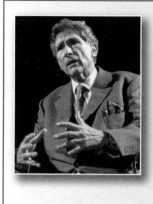

A Jerusalem-born US academic and literary critic, Said was a leading literary critic, a prominent advocate of the Palestinian cause and a founding figure of postcolonial theory. From the 1970s onwards, he developed a humanist critique of the western Enlightenment that uncovered its links to colonialism and highlighted 'narratives of oppression', cultural and ideological biases that disempowered colonized peoples by representing them as the non-western 'other'. He is best known for the notion of 'orientalism', which operated through a 'subtle and persistent Eurocentric prejudice against Arabo-Islamic peoples and culture'. His key texts include *Orientalism* (1978) and *Culture and Imperialism* (1993).

explicitly racialist (see p. 120) political theories were developed in the nineteenth century against the background of European imperialism. Works such as Gobineau's *Essay on the Inequality of Human Races* (Gobineau, [1855] 1970) and H. S. Chamberlain's *The Foundations of the Nineteenth Century* ([1899] 1913) attempted to provide a pseudoscientific justification for the dominance of the 'white' races of Europe and North America over the 'black', 'brown' and 'yellow' peoples of Africa and Asia. Anti-Semitic (see p. 121) political parties and movements emerged in countries such as Germany, Austria and Russia in the late nineteenth century. The most grotesque twentieth-century manifestation of such racialism was found in German Nazism, which, through the so-called 'Final Solution', attempted to carry out the extermination of European Jewry. Apartheid (Afrikaans for 'apartness') in South Africa consisted of the strict segregation of whites and non-whites between the election of the Nationalist Party in 1948 and the establishment of a non-racial democracy under the leadership of the African National Congress (ANC) in 1994. Elsewhere, racialism has been kept alive through campaigns against immigration, organized, for example, by the British National Party (BNP) and Le Pen's *Front National* (FN) in France.

Very different forms of racial or ethnic politics have, nevertheless, developed out of the struggle against colonialism (see p. 122) in particular, and as a result of racial discrimination and disadvantage in general. Indeed, in seeking to challenge economic and social marginalization, black nationalism in the USA and elsewhere constituted the prototype for identity politics, especially through its emphasis on '**consciousness raising**'. The origins of the black consciousness movement date back to the early twentieth century and the emergence of a 'back to Africa' movement, inspired by activists such as Marcus Garvey (see p. 162). Black politics, however, gained greater prominence in the 1960s with an upsurge in both the reformist and revolutionary wings of the movement. In its reformist guise, the movement took the form of a struggle for civil rights that reached national prominence in the USA under the leadership of Martin Luther King (1929–68) and the National Association for the Advancement of Coloured People (NAACP). The strategy of protest and non-violent civil disobedience was, nevertheless, rejected by the emerging Black Power movement, which supported black separatism and, under the leadership of the Black Panther Party, founded

● **Consciousness raising**: Strategies to remodel social identity and challenge cultural inferiority by an emphasis on pride, self-worth and self-assertion.

Marcus Garvey (1887–1940)

Jamaican political thinker and activist, and an early advocate of black nationalism. Garvey was the founder in 1914 of the Universal Negro Improvement Association (UNIA). He left Jamaica for New York in 1916, where his message of black pride and economic self-sufficiency gained him a growing following, particularly in ghettos such as Harlem. Although his black business enterprises failed, and his call for a return to Africa was largely ignored, Garvey's emphasis on establishing black pride and his vision of Africa as a 'homeland' provided the basis for the later Black Power movement. Rastafarianism is also based largely on his ideas. Garvey was imprisoned for mail fraud in 1923, and was later deported, eventually dying in obscurity in London.

in 1966, promoted the use of physical force and armed confrontation. Of more enduring significance in US politics, however, have been the Black Muslims, who advocate a separate creed based on the idea that black Americans are descended from an ancient Muslim tribe. Founded in 1930, the Black Muslims were led for over 40 years by Elijah Muhammad (1897–1975), and they counted amongst their most prominent activists in the 1960s the militant black leader Malcolm X (1925–65). Renamed the Nation of Islam, the movement continues to exert influence in the USA under the leadership of Louis Farrakhan. Other manifestations of ethnic consciousness include the secessionist nationalist movements that sprang up in many parts of western Europe and North America in the 1960s and early 1970s. This was most evident in Quebec in Canada, Scotland and Wales in the UK, Catalonia and the Basque area in Spain, Corsica in France, and Flanders in Belgium.

The rise of ethnic consciousness has by no means occurred only in the West. Although ethnic rivalry (often portrayed as 'tribalism') is sometimes seen as an endemic feature of African and Asian politics, it is better understood as a phenomenon linked to colonialism (see p. 122). However, the divide-and-rule policies of the colonial period often bequeathed to many newly-independent 'nations' a legacy of bitterness and resentment. In many cases, this was subsequently exacerbated by the attempt of majority ethnic groups to consolidate their dominance under the guise of 'nation-building'. Such tensions, for instance, resulted in the Biafran war in Nigeria in the 1960s, a long-running civil war in Southern Sudan, and a resort to terrorism by the predominantly Christian Tamils in Sri Lanka. The worst recent example of ethnic bloodshed, however, occurred in Rwanda in 1994, where an estimated 800,000 Tutsis and moderate Hutus were slaughtered in an uprising by militant Hutus. The spectre of ethnic rivalry and regional conflict has also been created by the collapse of communism in Eastern Europe. In the former USSR, Czechoslovakia and Yugoslavia, for example, this led to state collapse and the creation of a series of new states. Nevertheless, these newly-created states have themselves been subject to deep ethnic rivalries and tensions. This has been demonstrated by the rebellion of the Chechens in Russia, and the fragmentation of the former Yugoslav republic of Bosnia into 'ethnically pure' Muslim, Serb and Croat areas.

CONCEPT

Gender

Gender refers to social and cultural distinctions between males and females, (as opposed to 'sex' which highlights biological, and therefore ineradicable, differences between men and women). Gender is therefore a social construct, usually based on stereotypes of 'feminine' and 'masculine' behaviour. Feminists typically emphasize the distinction in order to demonstrate that physical or biological differences (sexual differences) need not mean that women and men must have different social roles and positions (gender differences). In short, gender equality is based on the belief that sexual differences have no social or political significance.

● **First-wave feminism**: The early form of feminism, dating from the mid-nineteenth century to the 1960s, which sought to achieve gender equality in the areas of legal and political rights, particularly suffrage rights.

● **Second-wave feminism**: The form of feminism that emerged in the 1960s and 1970s, and was characterized by a more radical concern with 'women's liberation', including, and perhaps especially, in the private sphere.

Gender politics

An awareness of the political significance of gender dates back to the emergence of so-called '**first-wave feminism**', which emerged in the nineteenth century and was shaped, above all, by the campaign for female suffrage: the right to vote. Its core belief was that women should enjoy the same legal and political rights as men, with a particular emphasis being placed on female suffrage on the grounds that if women could vote, all other forms of other sexual discrimination or prejudice would quickly disappear. This essentially liberal form of feminism was nevertheless 'difference-blind', in that its goal was the achievement of genderless 'personhood', allowing women and men to transcend 'difference'. However, the emergence of **second-wave feminism** in the 1960s and 1970s served to recast feminism as a form of identity politics. Radical feminists, such as Kate Millett (1970) and Mary Daly (1978), argued that gender divisions are the deepest and most politically significant of all social cleavages. All contemporary and historical societies are therefore seen to be characterized by patriarchy (see p. 65); that is, the dominance of men and the subordination of women, usually rooted in the rule of the husband-father within the family. From this perspective, nothing short of a 'sexual revolution' that would fundamentally transform cultural and personal relationships, as well as economic and political structures, could bring an end to gender inequality.

The emphasis within feminism on identity and difference increased with the emergence of strains within radical feminism that emphasized the fundamental and unalterable differences between women and men. An example of this was the 'pro-woman' position, which has been particularly strong in France and the USA. This position extols the positive virtues of fertility and motherhood, and rejects the idea that women should try to be 'more like men'. Instead, they should recognize and embrace their sisterhood, the bonds that link them to all other women. The pro-woman position therefore accepts that women's attitudes and values are different from men's, but implies that, in certain respects, women are superior, possessing qualities of creativity, sensitivity and caring which men can never fully appreciate or develop. The acknowledgement of deep, and possibly ineradicable, differences between women and men also led some feminists to argue that the roots of patriarchy lie within the male sex itself. In this view, 'all men' are physically and psychologically disposed to oppress 'all women'; in other words, 'men are the enemy'. In *Against Our Will* (1975), Susan Brownmiller therefore argued that men dominate women through a process of physical and sexual abuse. Men have created an 'ideology of rape', which amounts to a 'conscious process of intimidation by which all men keep all women in a state of fear'. Such a line of argument leads in the direction of feminist separatism, whereby women retreat from corrupt and corrupting male society. For some radical feminists, this had important implications for women's personal and sexual conduct. Only women who remain celibate or choose lesbianism can regard themselves as 'woman-identified women'. In the slogan attributed to Ti-Grace Atkinson: 'feminism is the theory; lesbianism is the practice' (Charvet, 1982).

Since the 1990s, a younger generation of feminist theorists have sought to articulate a feminist 'third wave', distinct from the campaigns and demands of the women's movement of the 1960s and 1970s. This has usually involved a more radical engagement with the politics of difference, especially going beyond those

Ayatollah Khomeini (1900–89)

Iranian cleric and political leader. Khomeini was one of the foremost scholars in the major theological centre of Qom until he was expelled from Iran in 1964. His return from exile in 1979 sparked the 'Islamic Revolution', leaving the Ayatollah (literally, 'gift of Allah') as the supreme leader of the world's first Islamic state until his death. Breaking decisively with the Shi'a tradition that the clergy remain outside politics, Khomeini's world-view was rooted in a clear division between the oppressed (understood largely as the poor and excluded of the developing world) and the oppressors (seen as the twin Satans: the USA and the USSR, capitalism and communism). Islam thus became a theo-political project aimed at regenerating the Islamic world by ridding it of occupation and corruption from outside.

strands within radical feminism that had emphasized that women are different from men, to a concern with differences between women. In so doing, third-wave feminists have tried to rectify an over-emphasis within earlier forms of feminism on the aspirations and experiences of middle-class, white women in developed societies, meaning that the contemporary women's movement is characterized by diversity, **hybridity**, and even contradiction. This has allowed the voices of, amongst others, low-income women, women in the developing world and 'women of colour' to be heard more effectively. Black feminism has been particularly effective in this respect, challenging the tendency within conventional forms of feminism to ignore racial differences and suggesting that women endure a common oppression by virtue of their sex. Especially strong in the USA, black feminism portrays sexism and racism as linked systems of oppression, and highlights the particular and complex range of gender, racial and economic disadvantages that confront women of colour.

Religion and politics

● **Hybridity**: A condition of social and cultural mixing; the term derives from cross-breeding between genetically dissimilar plants or animals.

● **Secularism**: The belief that religion should not intrude into secular (worldly) affairs, usually reflected in the desire to separate church from state.

● **Secularization thesis**: The theory that modernization is invariably accompanied by the victory of reason over religion and the displacement of spiritual values by secular ones.

The impact of religion on political life had been progressively restricted by the spread of liberal culture and ideas, a process that has been particularly prominent in the industrialized West. Nevertheless, liberal **secularism** is by no means an anti-religious tendency. Rather, it is concerned to establish a 'proper' sphere and role for religion. Emphasizing the importance of the public/private divide, it has sought to confine religion to a private arena, leaving public life to be organized on a strictly secular basis. However, the emergence of new, and often more assertive, forms of religiosity, the increasing impact of religious movements and, most importantly, a closer relationship between religion and politics, especially since the 1970s, has confounded the so-called '**secularization thesis**'. This was dramatically demonstrated by the 1979 'Islamic Revolution' in Iran, which brought the Ayatollah Khomeini to power as the leader of the world's first Islamic state. Nevertheless, it soon became clear that this was not an exclusively Islamic development, as 'fundamentalist' movements emerged within Christianity, particularly in the form of the so-called 'new Christian Right' in the USA, and within Hinduism and Sikhism in India. Other manifestations of this

Islamism

Islamism (also called 'political Islam' or 'radical Islam') is a politico-religious ideology, as opposed to a simple belief in Islam. Although Islamist ideology has no single creed or political manifestation, certain common beliefs can be identified, as follows.
(1) Society should be reconstructed in line with the ideals of Islam.
(2) The modern secular state should be replaced by an 'Islamic state'.
(3) The West and western values are viewed as corrupt and corrupting, justifying, for some, the notion of a *jihad* against them. However, distinct Sunni and Shi'a versions of Islamism have been developed, the former linked to Wahhabism, the latter to Iran's 'Islamic Revolution'.

● **Moral relativism:** A condition in which there is deep and widespread disagreement over moral issues (see p. 453).

● **Theocracy:** Literally, rule by God; the principle that religious authority should prevail over political authority, usually through the domination of church over state.

● **Shari'a** (Arabic): Literally, the 'way' or 'path'; divine Islamic law, based on principles expressed in the Koran.

● **Clash of civilizations thesis:** The idea that twenty-first century conflict will be primarily cultural in character, rather than ideological, political or economic (Huntington, 1996).

include the spread of US-style Pentecostalism in Latin America, Africa and East Asia; the growth in China of Falun Gong, a spiritual movement that has been taken by the authorities to express anti-communism and is reportedly supported by 70 million people; the regeneration of Orthodox Christianity in post-communist Russia; the emergence of the Aum Shinrikyo Doomsday cult in Japan; and growing interest across western societies in myriad forms of Eastern mysticism, and spiritual and therapeutic systems (yoga, meditation, Pilates, Shiatsu and so forth).

Although religious revivalism can be seen as a consequence of the larger upsurge in identity politics, religion has proved to be a particularly potent means of regenerating personal and social identity in modern circumstances. As modern societies are increasingly atomistic, diffuse and pluralized, there is, arguably, a greater thirst for the sense of meaning, purpose and certainty that religious consciousness appears to offer. This applies because religion provides believers with a world-view and moral vision that has higher, or indeed supreme, authority, as it stems from a supposedly divine source. Religion thus defines the very grounds of people's being; it gives them an ultimate frame of reference, as well as a moral orientation in a world increasingly marked by **moral relativism**. In addition, religion generates a powerful sense of social solidarity, connecting people to one another at a 'thick' or deep level, as opposed to the 'thin' connectedness that is conventional in modern societies.

The link between religion and politics has been clearest in relation to Islam, where it has been reflected in an upsurge in Islamic fundamentalism, often termed 'Islamism'. Fundamentalism in Islam does not imply a belief in the literal truth of the Koran, for this is accepted by all Muslims and, in that sense, all Muslims are fundamentalists. Instead, it means an intense and militant faith in Islamic beliefs as the overriding principles of social life and politics, as well as of personal morality. Islamic fundamentalists wish to establish the primacy of religion over politics. In practice, this means the founding of an 'Islamic state', a **theocracy**, ruled by spiritual rather than temporal authority, and applying the **Shari'a**. The Shari'a lays down a code for legal and religious behaviour, including a system of punishment for most crimes, as well as rules of personal conduct for both men and women. However, Islam should be distinguished from Islamism. Islamism refers either to a political creed based on Islamic ideas and principles, or to the political movement that has been inspired by that creed. It has had three core aims. First, it promotes pan-Islamic unity, distinguishing Islamism from traditional political nationalism. Second, it seeks the purification of the Islamic world through the overthrow of 'apostate' leaders of Muslim states (secularized or pro-western leaders). Third, it calls for the removal of western, and especially US, influence from the Muslim world, and possibly a wider politico-cultural struggle against the West itself. The rise of Islamism has sometimes been interpreted as evidence of an emerging '**clash of civilizations**' between Islam and the West, a notion that has profound implications for both global politics and for western societies which have significant Muslim communities (see p. 168).

Cultural diversity

One of the most powerful factors underpinning the global significance of identity politics has been the growth of international migration, particularly since

CONCEPT

Transnational community

A transnational community is a community whose cultural identity, political allegiances and psychological orientations cut across or transcend national borders. Transnational communities can therefore be thought of as 'deterritorialized nations' or 'global tribes'. The strength of transnational allegiances depends on factors such as the circumstances of migration and the length of stay in the new country. Nevertheless, transnational communities typically have multiple attachments, as allegiances to a country of origin do not preclude the formation of attachments to a country of settlement.

● **Diaspora**: Literally, dispersion (from the Hebrew); implies displacement or dispersal by force, but is also used to refer to the communities that have arisen as a result of such dispersal.

● **Affirmative action**: Reverse or 'positive' discrimination which accords preferential treatment to groups on the basis of their past disadvantage.

● **Assimilation**: The process through which immigrant communities lose their cultural distinctiveness by adjusting to the values, allegiances and lifestyles of the 'host' society.

the 1950s. This has given an increasing number of societies a distinctively multicultural character, with examples of still highly homogenous countries, such as Japan, becoming rarer. Ethnic minority communities developed in many European countries as a result of the end of empire and of deliberate attempts by governments to recruit workers from abroad to help in the process of postwar reconstruction. Since the 1980s, however, there has been a significant intensification of cross-border migration across the globe, creating what some have seen as a 'hyper-mobile planet'. This has happened for two main reasons. First, there have been a growing number of refugees (reaching a peak of about 18 million in 1993), which resulted from war, ethnic conflict and political upheaval in areas ranging from Algeria, Rwanda and Uganda to Iraq and Afghanistan. Second, economic globalization (see p. 142) has intensified pressures for international migration, both because people have been 'pushed' to migrate through the disruption that has been caused to many developing economies by the pressures generated by global markets and because they have been 'pulled' to migrate by the growth of a stratum of low-paid, low-skilled and low-state jobs in developed societies that indigenous populations are increasingly unwilling to fill. This has led to a position in which, for instance, roughly one-third of the total population of the Gulf states, and two-thirds of their working populations, are (predominantly female) non-nationals, largely from South and Southeast Asia. Such trends have significantly strained national identity in many countries and contributed to the development of so-called 'transnational communities', sometimes call **diasporic** communities.

As a growing number of countries have come to accept as an irreversible fact that their populations have a multi-ethnic, multireligious or multicultural character, various attempts have been made to reconcile cultural diversity and identity-related difference with civic and political cohesion. However, how is political stability to be maintained in societies in which the monocultural bonds of political nationalism have been fatally undermined? Some, indeed, view this as the central political challenge of the twenty-first century. Attempts to balance diversity against cohesion are usually dubbed 'multiculturalism' (see p. 167). Multiculturalism is a broad and often ill-defined term, which may simply stress cultural differentiation that is based on race, ethnicity or language. However, multiculturalism not only recognizes the fact of cultural diversity; it also holds that such differences should be respected and publicly affirmed.

Although the USA, as an immigrant society, has long been a multicultural society, the cause of multiculturalism in this sense was not taken up until the rise of the black consciousness movement and the advent of '**affirmative action**'. Australia has been officially committed to multiculturalism since the early 1970s, in recognition of its increasing 'Asianization' through an acceptance of the rights of its aboriginal peoples. In New Zealand, multiculturalism is linked to a recognition of the role of Maori culture in forging a distinctive national identity. In Canada, the country that has demonstrated the greatest official commitment to multiculturalism, it is associated with attempts to achieve reconciliation between French-speaking Quebec and the English-speaking majority population (see p. 114), and an acknowledgement of the rights of the indigenous Inuit peoples. In the UK, multiculturalism recognizes the existence of significant black and Asian communities, and abandons the demand that they **assimilate** into white society. In Germany, this applies to Turkish groups.

CONCEPT

Multiculturalism

Multiculturalism is used as both a descriptive and a normative term. As a descriptive term, it refers to cultural diversity arising from the existence within a society of two or more groups whose beliefs and practices generate a distinctive sense of collective identity. As a normative term, multiculturalism implies a positive endorsement of communal diversity, based on either the right of cultural groups to respect and recognition, or the alleged benefits to the larger society of moral and cultural diversity. Multiculturalism, in this sense, acknowledges the importance of beliefs, values and ways of life in establishing a sense of self-worth for individuals and groups alike.

The central theme within all forms of multiculturalism is that individual identity is culturally embedded, in the sense that people largely derive their understanding of the world and their framework of moral beliefs from the culture in which they live and develop. Distinctive cultures therefore deserve to be protected or strengthened, particularly when they belong to minority or vulnerable groups. This leads to the idea of minority or multicultural rights, sometimes seen as 'special' rights. Will Kymlicka (1995) identified three kinds of minority rights: self-government rights, polyethnic rights and representation rights. Self-government rights belong, Kymlicka argued, to what he called 'national minorities', peoples who are territorially concentrated, possess a shared language and are characterized by a 'meaningful way of life across the full range of human activities'. Examples would include the Native Americans, the Inuits in Canada, the Maoris in New Zealand and the Aborigines in Australia. In these cases, he argued, the right to self-government should involve the devolution of political power, usually through federalism (see p. 382), although it may extend to the right of secession and, therefore, to sovereign independence. Polyethnic rights are rights that help ethnic groups and religious minorities, that have developed through immigration to express and maintain their cultural distinctiveness. They would, for instance, provide the basis for legal exemptions, such as the exemption of Jews and Muslims from animal slaughtering laws, the exemption of Sikh men from wearing motorcycle helmets, and the exemption of Muslim girls from school dress codes. Special representation rights attempt to redress the under-representation of minority or disadvantaged groups in education, and in senior positions in political and public life. Such rights, which in the USA take the form of affirmative action, imply the practice of reverse or 'positive' discrimination, which attempts to compensate for past discrimination or continuing cultural subordination. Their justification is not only that they ensure full and equal participation, but also that they are the only means of guaranteeing that public policy reflects the interests of all groups and peoples, and not merely those of traditionally dominant groups.

However, there is neither a settled view of how multicultural societies should operate, nor of how far multiculturalism should go in positively endorsing communal diversity. There are three main models of multiculturalism:

- Liberal multiculturalism
- Pluralist multiculturalism
- Cosmopolitan multiculturalism.

Liberal multiculturalism is rooted in a commitment to freedom and toleration: the ability to choose one's own moral beliefs, cultural practices and way of life, regardless of whether these are disapproved of by others. However, the liberal model of multiculturalism only provides a qualified endorsement of communal diversity, highlighting the dangers that may also be implicit in identity politics. In particular, liberals are only prepared to tolerate views, values and social practices that are themselves tolerant; that is, to those that are compatible with personal freedom and autonomy. Liberal multiculturalists may therefore be unwilling to endorse practices such as female circumcision, forced (and possibly arranged) marriages and female dress codes, however much the groups concerned may believe that these are crucial to the maintenance of their cultural identity.

POLITICS IN ACTION . . .

Muslims in the West: an internal clash of civilizations?

Events: In 2011, estimates of the number of Muslims living in the European Union ranged from 15 to 20 million. In the early post-1945 period, immigration mainly came from former colonies. The majority of France's Muslim population (about 6 million – the largest in Europe) thus have a heritage in Algeria, Morocco and Tunisia, while most of the UK's Muslims (almost 2 million) came originally from Pakistan. Later Muslim immigration has often been linked to war and civil strife in countries such as Bosnia, Iraq, Afghanistan and Somalia. Nevertheless, in recent years several incidents have raised issues about the relationship between western European states in particular and, at least, elements in their Muslim populations, including the following:

- the 1989 'Rushdie affair', in which Muslim protesters in several countries denounced Salman Rushdie's *The Satanic Verses* as blasphemous and Ayatollah Khomeini issued a *fatwa* condemning the author to death
- the 2004 murder of Theo van Gogh, a Dutch film director who had collaborated on a film criticizing the treatment of women in Muslim countries
- the 2004 Madrid train bombings, carried out by an 'al-Qaeda-inspired' group
- the 2005 'Danish cartoons affair', in which the publication of 12 cartoons of the Prophet Mohammad by the newspaper *Jyllands-Posten* provoked protests across the Muslim world
- the 2005 London bombings, carried out by so-called 'home-grown' Islamist terrorists.

Significance: The existence of significant Muslim populations in the West has been seen by some as a threat to social cohesion and possibly national security (Caldwell, 2009). Such a view is in line with Huntington's (1996) 'clash of civilizations' thesis, which suggests that Islamic values and beliefs are fundamentally incompatible with those of the liberal-democratic West. Clashes over issues such as whether protecting 'sacred' beliefs justifies the curtailment of free speech and press freedom thus highlight a more profound divide over whether the public realm should be strictly secular, or shaped by Islamic ideas and values. As, in this view, Islam is anti-liberal and anti-pluralist, the politics of cultural recognition threatens to entrench Muslim separatism and sow the seeds of civic conflict. The most appropriate response to Muslim communities in the West is therefore to reject multi-

culturalism and insist on a strategy of integration. Such a stance has been adopted most clearly in France, where, in 2004, a law was passed forbidding the wearing of any 'ostentatious' religious articles, including Islamic headscarves, in state-funded schools, with a ban on the wearing of face-covering headgear, including *niqads* and other veils, in public places coming into force in 2011.

Others, however, view multiculturalism as the most appropriate response to what has been called the 'Muslim question' (Modood, 2007; Parekh, 2008). From this perspective, the image of Muslims in the West as an 'enemy within' is based on a serious misrepresentation of Islam and of the views of Muslim populations. Surveys, for instance, consistently show that Muslims in the Europe are predominantly satisfied with the secular nature of western society and hold political views little different from other cultural groups. Moreover, when Muslim identity politics has become entangled with extremism, even violence, this is better explained by social or political factors than by cultural incompatibility. Muslim communities in Europe, for example, tend to be socially marginalized, facing higher unemployment and poverty rates, and having lower educational achievement than the general population. Moreover, international developments since 9/11 have seen a range of western states participating in wars against and occupations of Muslim countries. In this light, the politics of cultural recognition is likely to weaken the trend towards extremism and violence, by giving Muslim populations a clearer stake in society, while a strategy of 'enforced' integration threatens to be counter-productive, being perceived as evidence of 'Islamophobia' and helping to deepen alienation and resentment.

Isaiah Berlin (1909–97)

UK historian of ideas and philosopher. Berlin was born in Riga, Latvia, and came to Britain in 1921. He developed a form of liberal pluralism that was grounded in a life-long commitment to empiricism and influenced by the ideas of counter-Enlightenment thinkers, including Vico (1668–1744), Herder (see p. 110) and Alexander Herzen (1812–70). Basic to Berlin's philosophical stance was a belief in moral pluralism, the idea that conflicts of values are intrinsic to human life. His best-known political writing is *Four Essays on Liberty* (1958), in which he extolled the virtues of 'negative' freedom over 'positive' freedom. Berlin's writings constitute a defence of western liberalism against totalitarianism.

Pluralist multiculturalism provides firmer foundations for a theory of cultural diversity because it is based on the idea of **value pluralism**. Developed in particular in the writings of Isaiah Berlin, this holds that people are bound to disagree about the ultimate ends of life. As values conflict, the human predicament is inevitably characterized by moral conflict. In this view, liberal or western beliefs, such as support for personal freedom, democracy and secularization, have no greater moral authority than rival beliefs. This form of multiculturalism also focuses more explicitly on unequal power relations in society, particularly the extent to which the dominant culture in western societies reflects the values and interests of the majority group and so subordinates minority communities. Cultural recognition therefore counters oppression and serves to expose the corrupt and corrupting nature of western culture, values and lifestyles, believed to be tainted by the inheritance of colonialism and racialism, or by materialism and 'godless' permissiveness. Such thinking has been especially controversial in relation to Muslim minorities in western societies (see p. 168).

Cosmopolitan multiculturalism endorses cultural diversity and identity politics, but, in contrast to both liberal and pluralist views, sees them more as transitional states in a larger reconstruction of political sensibilities and priorities. This form of multiculturalism celebrates diversity on the grounds of what each culture can learn from other cultures, and because of the prospects for personal self-development offered by a world of wider cultural opportunities and lifestyle choices. Its acceptance of multiple identities and hybridity lead to a kind of pick-and-mix multiculturalism, which portrays society as a 'melting pot', as opposed to a 'cultural mosaic' of separate ethnic or religious groups.

● **Value pluralism:** The theory that there is no single, overriding conception of the 'good life' but, rather, a number of competing and equally legitimate conceptions.

SUMMARY

● Societies are characterized by regular patterns of social interaction. However, the 'thick' social connectedness of close bonds and fixed allegiances is giving way to the 'thin' connectedness of more fluid, individualized social arrangements. This reflects, in large part, the transition from industrial to so-called post-industrial society, and, particularly, the declining importance of social class.

● Post-industrialism is characterized, amongst other things, by an increasing emphasis on knowledge and information generally, with the advent of the internet and the wider use of computer-based technologies having given rise to the 'information society'. Not only do information societies connect more people to more other people, but the nature of those connections has also changed, especially through the development of looser and more diffuse networks.

● At the heart of the trend towards the 'thinning' of social connectedness is the rise of individualism. Individualism was a child of industrial capitalism, but it has been boosted by a growing ethic of materialism and consumerism, given greater prominence, from the 1980s onwards, by the wider influence of neoliberal or free-market thinking. However, the spread of individualism may weaken community and people's sense of social belonging, a trend that may be particularly evident in the English-speaking world.

● The rise of identity politics has been evident in the growing recognition of cultural and other forms of difference, especially providing a vehicle through which groups can challenge marginalization by adopting a more positive and assertive sense of identity. Nevertheless, identity politics does not have a settled political character and it has been shaped around many principles, the most important of which are race and ethnicity, gender, religion and culture.

● Attempts to regenerate personal and social identity have given rise to new, and sometimes more radical, forms of politics. These include forms of ethnic assertiveness, often associated with black nationalism; second-wave feminism and a stronger emphasis on issues of gender equality and gender difference; religious revivalism, commonly expressed through fundamentalist movements, especially in Islam; and multiculturalism and the 'celebration' of cultural diversity.

Questions for discussion

● Why has social connectedness become 'thinner'?

● Has class conflict in modern society been resolved or merely suppressed?

● Has the network society substituted 'virtual' communities for real communities, and with what consequences?

● Is individualism the enemy of social solidarity and cohesion?

● Does consumerism liberate people or enslave them?

● What are the main factors explaining the growth of identity politics?

● Is identity politics a liberating or oppressive force?

● To what extent has the recognition of ethnic and gender divisions produced meaningful political change?

● Do modern societies need to be protected from cultural diversity?

Further reading

Bauman, Z. *Liquid Modernity* (2000). An examination of the changing nature of human connectedness in the light of the emergence of 'liquid' or 'light' modernity.

Beck, U. and E. Beck-Gernsheim, *Individualization: Institutionalized Individualism and its Social and Political Consequences* (2001). A critical examination of the process of individualization that examines both its causes and its wide-ranging consequences.

Kumar, K. *From Post-Industrial to Post-Modern Society: New Theories of the Contemporary World* (2004). A lucid and insightful study of the idea of the information society and theories of post-Fordism and post-modernity.

Parekh, B. *A New Politics of Identity: Political Principles of an Interdependent World* (2008). A wide-ranging analysis of the impact of global interconnectedness on ethnic, religious, national and other identities.

CHAPTER **8** # Political Culture and the Media

'Mankind, in general, judge more by their eyes than their hands;
for all can see the appearance, but few can touch the reality.'

NICCOLÒ MACHIAVELLI, *The Prince* (1532)

PREVIEW   Much of politics takes place in our heads; that is, it is shaped by our ideas, values
and assumptions about how society should be organized, and our expectations,
hopes and fears about government. Ultimately, what we believe about the society
in which we live may be more important than the reality of its power structure, and
the actual distribution of resources and opportunities within it. Perception may not
only be more important than reality; in practical terms, perception may *be* reality.
This highlights the vital role played by what is called 'political culture'. People's
beliefs, symbols and values structure both their attitude to the political process and,
crucially, their view of the regime in which they live. However, there is significant
disagreement about the nature and role of the political culture, not least over
whether it sustains democracy or is aligned with the interests of dominant groups.
Others have highlighted concerns about the political culture's (apparently)
declining capacity to foster civic engagement and a sense of social belonging. The
issue of the political culture also draws attention to the extent to which the politics
of modern societies is conducted through the media – newspapers, television, the
internet, mobile phones and so on. The media constitute much more than a
channel of communications; they are part of the political process itself, affecting,
and not merely reflecting, the distribution of power in society at large. Long-
standing debate about the media's relationship with democracy and styles of
governance have been given a fresh twist by the advent of electronic-based 'new'
media, while media influence generally has been associated with a growing
emphasis in politics on 'news managment' and so-called 'spin'.

KEY ISSUES   ● How do individuals and groups acquire their political attitudes and
values?

● Do democratic regimes depend on the existence of a distinctive 'civic
culture'?

● Are modern societies characterized by free competition between values
and ideas, or by a 'dominant' culture?

● To what extent do the media shape political attitudes?

● How do the media affect the distribution of political power?

● Is the politics of 'spin' inevitable in the media age?

CONCEPT

Political culture

Culture, in its broadest sense, is the way of life of a people. Sociologists and anthropologists tend to distinguish between 'culture' and 'nature', the former encompassing that which is passed on from one generation to the next by learning, rather than through biological inheritance. Political scientists, however, use the term in a narrower sense to refer to a people's psychological orientation, political culture being the 'pattern of orientations' to political objects such as parties, government, the constitution, expressed in beliefs, symbols and values. Political culture differs from public opinion in that it is fashioned out of long-term values rather than simply people's reactions to specific policies and problems.

POLITICAL CULTURE

Political thinkers through the ages have acknowledged the importance of attitudes, values and beliefs. However, these past thinkers did not see them as part of a 'political culture'. Burke (see p. 36), for instance, wrote about custom and tradition, Marx (see p. 41) about ideology, and Herder (see p. 110) about national spirit. All of them, nevertheless, agreed about the vital role that values and beliefs play in promoting the stability and survival of a regime. Interest amongst political scientists in the idea of political culture emerged in the 1950s and 1960s as new techniques of behavioural analysis displaced more traditional, institutional approaches to the subject. The classic work in this respect was Almond and Verba's *The Civic Culture* (1963), which used opinion surveys to analyse political attitudes and democracy in five countries: the USA, the UK, West Germany, Italy and Mexico. This work was stimulated, in part, by a desire to explain the collapse of representative government in interwar Italy, Germany and elsewhere, and the failure of democracy in many newly-independent developing states after 1945. Although interest in political culture faded in the 1970s and 1980s, the debate has been revitalized since the 1990s as a result of efforts in Eastern Europe to construct democracy out of the ashes of communism, and growing anxiety in mature democracies, such as the USA, about the apparent decline of social capital (see p. 175) and civic engagement. However, there is also debate about whether or not political culture is shaped by the ideas and interests of elite groups. This, in turn, is linked to rival views of the mass media (see p. 179) and the extent to which government can now manipulate political communication, considered later in the chapter.

Civic culture or ideological hegemony?

Debate about the nature of political culture has often focused on the idea of **civic culture**, usually associated with the writings of Almond and Verba (1963, 1980). Almond and Verba set out to identify the political culture that most effectively upheld democratic politics. They identified three general types of political culture:

- A *participant* political culture. This is one in which citizens pay close attention to politics, and regard popular participation as both desirable and effective.
- A *subject* political culture. This is characterized by more passivity amongst citizens, and the recognition that they have only a very limited capacity to influence government.
- A *parochial* political culture. This is marked by the absence of a sense of citizenship, with people identifying with their locality, rather than the nation, and having neither the desire nor the ability to participate in politics.

● **Civic culture**: A set of specific attitudes which are crucial to the success of modern democracies.

Although Almond and Verba accepted that a participant culture came closest to the democratic ideal, they argued that the 'civic culture' is a blend of all three, in that it reconciles the participation of citizens in the political process with the vital necessity for government to govern. Democratic stability, in their view, is underpinned by a political culture that is characterized by a blend of activity and passivity on the part of citizens, and a balance between obligation and perform-ance on the part of government.

In their initial study (1963), Almond and Verba concluded that the UK came closest to the civic culture, exhibiting both participant and subject features. In other words, while the British thought that they could influence government, they were also willing to obey authority. The USA also scored highly, its relative weakness being that, as participant attitudes predominated over subject ones, Americans were not particularly law-abiding. The difficulty of building or rebuilding a civic culture was underlined by the examples of both West Germany and Italy. By the early 1960s, neither country appeared to have a strong par-ticipant culture; while the subject culture was dominant in Germany, parochial attitudes remained firmly entrenched in Italy. Almond and Verba's later study (1980) highlighted a number of shifts, notably declining national pride and confidence in the UK and the USA, which contrasted with a rise in civic propen-sities in Germany.

The civic-culture approach to the study of political attitudes and values has, however, been widely criticized. In the first place, its model of the psychological dispositions that make for a stable democracy is highly questionable. In particu-lar, the emphasis on passivity and the recognition that deference to authority is healthy has been criticized by those who argue that political participation (see p. 444) is the very stuff of democratic government. Almond and Verba suggested a 'sleeping dogs' theory of democratic culture that implies that low participation indicates broad satisfaction with government, which politicians, in turn, will be anxious to maintain. On the other hand, when less than half the adult popula-tion bothers to vote, as regularly occurs in the USA, this could simply reflect widespread alienation and ingrained disadvantage. (The link between declining participation rates and the health of the political system is discussed in greater detail in Chpater 20.)

Second, the civic-culture thesis rests on the unproven assumption that polit-ical attitudes and values shape behaviour, and not the other way round. In short, a civic culture may be more a consequence of democracy than its cause. If this is the case, political culture may provide an index of the health of democracy, but it cannot be seen as a means of promoting stable democratic rule. Finally, Almond and Verba's approach tends to treat political culture as homogeneous; that is, as little more than a cipher for national culture or national character. In so doing, it pays little attention to political subcultures and tends to disguise fragmentation and social conflict. In contrast, radical approaches to political culture tend to highlight the significance of social divisions, such as those based on class, race and gender (see Chapter 7).

A very different view of the role and nature of political culture has been developed within the Marxist tradition. Although Marx portrayed capitalism as a system of class exploitation and oppression operating through the ownership of the means of production, he also acknowledged the power of ideas, values and beliefs. As Marx and Engels put it in *The German Ideology* ([1846]1970), 'the ideas of the ruling class are in every epoch the ruling ideas, i.e. the class which is the ruling *material* force of society, is at the same time the ruling *intellectual* force'. In Marx's view, ideas and culture are part of a 'superstructure' that is conditioned or determined by the economic 'base', the mode of production.

CONCEPT

Hegemony

Hegemony (from the Greek *hegemonia*, meaning 'leader') is, in its simplest sense, the ascendancy or domination of one element of a system over others. In Marxist theory, the term is used in a more specific sense. In the writings of Gramsci (see p. 175), hegemony refers to the ability of a dominant class to exercise power by winning the consent of those it subjugates, as an alternative to the use of coercion. As a non-coercive form of class rule, hegemony typically operates through the dissemination of bourgeois values and beliefs throughout society.

These ideas have provided Marxism with two theories of culture. The first suggests that culture is essentially class-specific: as members of a class share the same experiences and have a common economic position and interests, they are likely to have broadly similar ideas, values and beliefs. In Marx's words, 'it is not the consciousness of men that determines their existence, but their social existence that determines their consciousness'. Proletarian culture and ideas can therefore be expected to differ markedly from bourgeois ones. The second theory of culture emphasizes the degree to which the ideas of the ruling class (what Marx referred to as 'ideology') pervade society and become the 'ruling ideas' of the age. In this view, political culture, or even civic culture, is thus nothing more than **bourgeois ideology**. What is important about this view is that it sees culture, values and beliefs as a form of power. From the Marxist perspective, the function of ideology is to reconcile subordinate classes to their exploitation and oppression by propagating myths, delusions and falsehoods (in Engels' words, 'false consciousness'). Later Marxists have understood this process in terms of bourgeois 'hegemony'.

Modern Marxists have been quick to acknowledge that, in no sense, do the 'ruling ideas' of the bourgeoisie monopolize intellectual and cultural life in a capitalist society, excluding all rival views. Rather, they accept that cultural, ideological and political competition does exist, but stress that this competition is unequal. Quite simply, ideas and values that uphold the capitalist order have an overwhelming advantage over ideas and values that question or challenge it. Such ideological hegemony may, in fact, be successful precisely because it operates behind the illusion of free speech, open competition and political pluralism – what Herbert Marcuse (see p. 42) termed 'repressive tolerance'.

The most influential twentieth-century exponent of this view was Antonio Gramsci (see p. 175). Gramsci drew attention to the degree to which the class system is upheld not simply by unequal economic and political power, but also by bourgeois hegemony. This consists of the spiritual and cultural supremacy of the ruling class, brought about through the spread of bourgeois values and beliefs via 'civil society'; the mass media, the churches, youth movements, trade unions and so forth. What makes this process so insidious is that it extends beyond formal learning and education into the very common sense of the age. The significance of Gramsci's analysis is that, in order for socialism to be achieved, a 'battle of ideas' has to be waged through which proletarian principles, values and theories displace, or at least challenge, bourgeois ideas.

The Marxist view of culture as ideological power rests on the distinction between subjective or *felt* interests (what people think they want) and objective or *real* interests (what people would want if they could make independent and informed choices). This draws attention to what Stephen Lukes (2004) called a 'radical view of power' (see p. 9): '*A* exercises power over *B* when *A* affects *B* in a manner contrary to *B*'s interests'. Such a view of political culture has, however, attracted considerable criticism. Some have argued that it is unwarrantedly patronizing to suggest that the values and beliefs of ordinary people have been foisted upon them by manipulation and indoctrination. The acceptance of capitalist values and beliefs by the working classes may, for instance, merely reflect their perception that capitalism works.

The dominant-ideology model of political culture may also overstate the degree of homogeneity in the values and beliefs of modern societies. While a

● **Bourgeois ideology**: A Marxist term, denoting ideas and theories that serve the interests of the bourgeoisie by disguising the contradictions of capitalist society.

Antonio Gramsci (1891–1937)

Italian Marxist and social theorist. The son of a minor public official. Gramsci joined the Socialist Party in 1913, and in 1921 became the General Secretary of the newly-formed Italian Communist Party. Although an elected member of parliament, he was imprisoned by Mussolini in 1926. He remained in prison until his death. His *Prison Notebooks* (Gramsci, 1971), written in 1929–35, tried to counterbalance the emphasis within orthodox Marxism on 'scientific' determinism by stressing the importance of the political and intellectual struggle. Although proponents of Eurocommunism have claimed him as an influence, he remained throughout his life a Leninist and a revolutionary.

CONCEPT

Social capital

The concept of social capital was developed in the 1970s to highlight the social and cultural factors that underpin wealth creation. The term has since been used to refer to social connectedness, as represented by networks, norms and trust that promote civic engagement. In common with economic assets, social capital can decline or rise, usually through education and a stress on active citizenship. The alleged decline in social capital in modern society has been linked, variously, to the 'parenting deficit', the rise of individualism and the increase in social and geographical mobility.

'ruling' ideology may provide a dominant class with self-belief and a sense of purpose, it is less clear, as Abercrombie *et al.*, (1980) argued, that subordinate classes have been successfully integrated into this value system. Finally, the Marxist view, which purports to establish a link between unequal class power and cultural and ideological bias, may do nothing more than describe a tendency found in all societies for powerful groups to propagate self-serving ideas. Whether this constitutes a dominant value *system*, in which a coherent and consistent message is disseminated through the media, schools, the churches and so on, is rather more questionable.

Decline of social capital?

The process of political and economic reconstruction in former communist states has stimulated renewed interest in the issue of political culture since the 1990s. This is because pervasive state control over a number of generations had evidently destroyed or suppressed the social connections and sense of civic responsibility that usually sustain democratic politics. In other words, there was a perceived need to rebuild civil society (see p. 6), in the sense of a realm of autonomous groups and associations, including businesses, interest groups, clubs and so on. Indeed, such ideas can be traced back to Alexis de Tocqueville (see p. 245), who, in the nineteenth century, had explained the USA's egalitarian institutions and democratic practices by reference to the American's propensity for participation and civic association. No sooner had this revived concern with political culture arisen in relation to postcommunist states than it was being applied to perceived problems in mature democracies.

Robert Putnam (see p. 176), for example, argued that variations in the quality of local government in different regions of Italy were determined by the presence, or absence, of traditions of civic engagement, reflected in differing levels of voter turnout, newspaper readership, and membership of choral societies and football clubs. In *Bowling Alone* (2000), Putnam drew attention to the USA's declining 'social capital', and argued that other industrialized countries are likely to follow US trends. He highlighted the emergence of a 'post-civic' generation. This was demonstrated by a 25–50 per cent drop in the number of voluntary

Robert D. Putnam (born 1941)

US political scientist and social commentator. Putnam's work has revived interest in civil society and focused attention on the importance of 'social capital': the social networks in a society that build trust and cooperation and develop 'the "I" into the "we"'. His most influential work, *Bowling Alone: The Collapse and Revival of American Community* (2000), used the image of a man bowling alone, rather than in a team, to illustrate the decline of community activity and political engagement in the USA. Amongst the causes of this decline, Putnam identifies the growing influence of television, two-career families and longer commutes. His other works include *Making Democracy Work: Civic Traditions in Italy* (1993).

CONCEPT

Communitarianism

Communitarianism is the belief that the self or person is constituted through the community, in the sense that individuals are shaped by the communities to which they belong and thus owe them a debt of respect and consideration. *Left-wing* communitarians hold that community demands unrestricted freedom and social equality. *Centrist* communitarians hold that community is grounded in reciprocal rights and responsibilities. *Right-wing* communitarians hold that community requires respect for authority and established values.

clubs and associations since 1965, and by sharp declines in attendance at public, town and school meetings, as well as in the membership of, and work done for, political parties. Putnam's view, which is influenced by communitarianism, explains declining social capital in a variety of ways. These include the spread of suburbanization and, therefore, of longer journeys to work; the rise of two-career families and their impact on the quantity and quality of parenting; and the tendency of television to privatize leisure time, misshape social perceptions and reduce achievement levels in children. From an alternative social-democratic perspective, however, the decline of civic engagement is explained by the triumph of consumer capitalism and the spread of materialist and individualist values.

Conservative thinkers have long supported their own view of social capital in the form of tradition (see p. 82) and, in particular, 'traditional values'. These are values and beliefs that have supposedly been passed down from earlier generations and so constitute a kind of cultural bedrock. Conservative politicians regularly call for such values to be 'strengthened' or 'defended', believing that they are the key to social cohesion and political stability. In the UK in the 1980s, for example, Margaret Thatcher called for the resurrection of what she called 'Victorian values', while John Major's ill-starred 'Back to Basics' initiative attempted much the same in the 1990s. In the USA, Ronald Reagan embraced the notion of the 'frontier ideology', harking back to the conquest of the American West and the virtues of self-reliance, hard work and adventurousness that he believed it exemplified. Not uncommonly, such values are linked to the family, the church and the nation; that is, to long-established institutions that supposedly embody the virtues of continuity and endurance.

In his essay 'Rationalism in Politics', Michael Oakeshott (1962) developed a further defence of continuity and tradition. Oakeshott (see p. 177) argued that traditional values and established customs should be upheld and respected on account of their familiarity, which engenders a sense of reassurance, stability and security. This suggests that there is a general human disposition to favour tradition over innovation, the established over the new. To be a conservative, Oakeshott suggested, is 'to prefer the familiar to the unknown, to prefer the tried to the untried, fact to mystery, the actual to the possible, the

Michael Oakeshott (1901–90)

UK political philosopher. Oakeshott was a professor of political science at the London School of Economics from 1951 until his retirement in 1968. His collection of essays *Rationalism in Politics and Other Essays* (1962) and his more systematic work of political philosophy *On Human Conduct* (1975) are often seen as major contributions to conservative traditionalism. By highlighting the importance of civil association and insisting on the limited province of politics, he also developed themes closely associated with liberal thought. Though often seen as an advocate of a non-ideological style of politics, in line with the ideas of Edmund Burke (see p. 36), Oakeshott influenced many of the thinkers of the New Right.

see p. 36

CONCEPT

Postmaterialism

Postmaterialism is a theory that explains the nature of political concerns and values in terms of levels of economic development. It is loosely based on Abraham Maslow's (1908–70) 'hierarchy of needs', which places esteem and self-actualization above material or economic needs. Postmaterialism assumes that conditions of material scarcity breed egoistical and acquisitive values, meaning that politics is dominated by economic issues. However, in conditions of widespread prosperity, individuals express more interest in 'postmaterial' or 'quality of life' issues, typically concerned with morality, political justice and personal fulfilment.

limited to the unbound, the near to the distant, the sufficient to the super abundant, the convenient to the perfect, present laughter to utopian bliss' (Oakeshott, 1962).

The defence of traditional values and established beliefs has been one of the central themes of neoconservatism, advanced in the USA by social theorists such as Daniel Bell (1976) and Irving Kristol (1983), who have warned against the destruction of spiritual values brought about both by market pressures and by the spread of permissiveness. The problem with this position, however, is that it assumes there is an authoritative moral system upon which order and stability can be based. The simple fact is that, in modern multicultural and multireligious societies, it is doubtful whether any set of values can be regarded as authoritative. To define certain values as 'traditional', 'established' or 'majority' values may simply be an attempt to impose a particular moral system on the rest of society. Indeed, empirical evidence appears to support the view that political culture is becoming increasingly fragmented, and that modern societies are characterized by growing moral and cultural diversity.

An alternative view of the social capital debate suggests not that there has been a decline of civic engagement or social connectedness, but that the forms these have taken have changed. According to Inglehart (1977, 1990), such shifts are linked to the spread of affluence and to the growth, particularly amongst young people, of 'postmaterial' values. As new generations have grown up since the 1960s accustomed, in advanced industrial countries at least, to economic security and material well-being, 'traditional' ideas about subjects such as sex, marriage and personal conduct have been displaced by more 'liberal' or 'permissive' attitudes. At the same time, traditional political attitudes and allegiances have been weakened and sometimes replaced by growing interest in issues such as feminism, nuclear disarmament, animal rights and environmental protection. Thus party membership and electoral turnout may have declined but there has been a growth of interest in single-issue protest politics and campaigning groups. Post-Fordist (see p. 154) theorists argue that such cultural changes are irresistible, because they are linked to a wholesale shift in economic and political organization that is bringing about a decline in deference and a rise of individualism (see p. 158).

see p. 154 ... see p. 158

THE MEDIA AND POLITICAL COMMUNICATION

Political socialization

Political socialization is the process through which individuals acquire political beliefs and values, and by which these are transmitted from one generation to the next. Families and schools are usually viewed as 'primary' agents of political socialization, while the workplace, peer groups and the media are viewed as 'secondary' agents of political socialization. Interest in political socialization peaked during the so-called 'behavioural revolution', as external stimuli were seen to explain (and possibly determine) political attutudes or behaviour.

Any examination of the factors that influence people's psychological orientation to politics, whether their long-term beliefs and values (political culture) or their short-term reaction to particular policies or problems (public opinion), must, in modern circumstances, take account of the crucial role played by the media. The mass media have been recognized as politically significant since the advent of mass literacy and the popular press in the late nineteenth century. However, it is widely accepted that, through a combination of social and technological changes, the media have become increasingly powerful political actors and, in some respects, more deeply enmeshed in the political process. Three developments are particularly noteworthy. First, the impact of the so-called 'primary' agents of political socialization, such as the family and social class, has declined. Whereas once people acquired, in late childhood and adolescence in particular, a framework of political sympathies and leanings that adult experience tended to modify or deepen, but seldom radically transformed, this has been weakened in modern society by greater social and geographical mobility, and by the spread of individualist and consumerist values. This, in turn, widens the scope for the media's political influence, as they are the principal mechanism through which information about issues and policies, and therefore political choices, is presented to the public.

Second, the development of a mass television audience from the 1950s onwards, and more recently the proliferation of channels and media output associated with the **'new' media**, has massively increased the media's penetration of people's everyday lives. This means that the public now relies on the media more heavily than ever before. For instance, television is a much more important source of news and current-affairs information than political meetings; many more people watch televised sport than participate in it; and even shopping is increasingly being carried out through shopping channels and the internet. Particular interest has focused on the burgeoning political significance of the internet, with, by 2011, two billion people worldwide having access to it. Although the highest internet penetration is in North America (78 per cent), Oceania/Australia (60 per cent) and Europe (58 per cent), the highest usage growth is in Africa, the Middle East and Latin America.

Third, the media have become more powerful economic actors. Not only are major media corporations major global players, but also a series of mergers has tended to incorporate the formerly discrete domains of publishing, television, film, music, computers and telecommunications into a single massive 'infotainment' industry (Scammel, 2000). Media businesses such as Microsoft, Time Warner Inc, Disney and News Corporation have accumulated so much economic and market power that no government can afford to ignore them.

● **'New' media**: A generic term for the many different forms of electronic communication made possible through digital or computer technology.

Theories of the mass media

Few commentators doubt the media's ability to shape political attitudes and values or, at least, to structure political and electoral choice by influencing public perceptions about the nature and importance of issues and problems, thereby.

However, there is considerable debate about the political significance of this influence. A series of rival theories offer contrasting views of the media's political impact. The most important of these are the following:

- the pluralist model
- the dominant-ideology model
- the elite-values model
- the market model.

Pluralist model

Pluralism (see p. 100) highlights diversity and multiplicity generally. The pluralist model of the mass media portrays the media as an ideological marketplace in which a wide range of political views are debated and discussed. While not rejecting the idea that the media can affect political views and sympathies, this nevertheless suggests that their impact is essentially neutral, in that they tend to reflect the balance of forces within society at large.

The pluralist view, nevertheless, portrays the media in strongly positive terms. In ensuring an 'informed citizenry', the mass media both enhance the quality of democracy and guarantee that government power is checked. This 'watchdog' role was classically demonstrated in the 1974 *Washington Post* investigation into the Watergate scandal, which led to the resignation of Richard Nixon as US president. Some, moreover, argue that the advent of the new media, and particularly the internet, has strengthened pluralism and political competition by giving protest groups, including 'anti-capitalist' activists, a relatively cheap and highly effective means of disseminating information and organizing campaigns, as discussed later in the chapter. However, the pluralist model suffers from significant deficiencies. For example, weak and unorganized groups are excluded from access to mainstream publishing and broadcasting, meaning that the media's ideological marketplace tends to be relatively narrow and generally pro-establishment in character. In addition, private ownership and formal independence from government may not be sufficient to guarantee the media's oppositional character in the light of the increasingly symbiotic relationship between government and journalists and broadcasters.

Dominant-ideology model

The dominant-ideology model portrays the mass media as a politically conservative force that is aligned to the interests of economic and social elites, and serves to promote compliance or political passivity amongst the masses. In its Marxist version, rooted in the larger Marxist critique of political culture (discussed earlier in the chapter) and particularly the ideas of Gramsci, it suggests that the media propagate bourgeois ideas and maintain capitalist hegemony, acting in the interests of major corporations and media moguls. Ownership, in other words, ultimately determines the political and other views that the mass media disseminate, and ownership is increasingly concentrated in the hands of a small number of global media conglomerates. The six largest are Time Warner Inc, News Corporation, Viacom, Disney, CBS and Bertelsmann.

CONCEPT

Mass media

The media comprise those societal institutions that are concerned with the production and distribution of all forms of knowledge, information and entertainment. The 'mass' media channel communication towards a large and undifferentiated audience using relatively advanced technology. The clearest examples are the 'broadcast' media (television and radio) and the 'print' media (newspapers and magazines). The 'new' media (cable and satellite telecommunications, the Internet and so on) has, subverted the notion of mass media by dramatically increasing audience fragmentation.

From this perspective, the media play an important role in promoting globalization (see p. 142), in that their tendency to spread ideas, images and values that are compatible with western consumerism (see p. 159) helps to open up new markets and extend business penetration worldwide.

One of the most influential and sophisticated versions of the dominant-ideology model was developed by Noam Chomsky (see p. 181) and Ed Herman in *Manufacturing Consent* (2006), in the form of the 'propaganda model'. They identified five 'filters' through which news and political coverage are distorted by the structures of the media itself. These filters are as follows:

- the business interests of owner companies
- a sensitivity to the views and concerns of advertisers and sponsors
- the sourcing of news and information from 'agents of power', such as governments and business-backed think-tanks
- 'flak' or pressure applied to journalists, including threats of legal action
- an unquestioning belief in the benefits of market competition and consumer capitalism.

Chomsky's analysis emphasizes the degree to which the mass media can subvert democracy, helping, for example, to mobilize popular support in the USA for imperialist foreign policy goals. The dominant-ideology model is, nevertheless, also subject to criticism. Objections to it include that it underestimates the extent to which the press and broadcasters, particularly public service broadcasters, pay attention to progressive social, racial and development issues. Moreover, the assumption that media output shapes political attitudes is determinist and neglects the role played by people's own values in filtering, and possibly resisting, media messages.

Elite-values model

The elite-values model shifts attention away from the ownership of media corporations to the mechanism through which media output is controlled. This view suggests that editors, journalists and broadcasters enjoy significant professional independence, and that even the most interventionist of media moguls are able only to set a broad political agenda, but not to control day-to-day editorial decision-making. The media's political bias (see p. 183) therefore reflects the values of groups that are disproportionally represented amongst its senior professionals. However, there are a number of versions of this model, depending on the characteristics that are considered to be politically significant.

One version of the elite-valuies model holds that the anti-socialist and politically conservative views of most mainstream newspapers, magazines and television stations derive from the fact that their senior professionals are well-paid and generally from middle-class backgrounds. A quite different version is sometimes advanced by conservatives, who believe that the media reflect the views of university-educated, liberal intellectuals, whose values and concerns are quite different from those of the mass of the population. In its feminist version, this model highlights the predominance of males amongst senior journalists and broadcasters, implying that this both explains the inadequate attention given to

Noam Chomsky (born 1928)

US linguistic theorist and radical intellectual. Chomsky first achieved distinction as a scholar in the field of linguistic studies. His *Syntactic Structures* (1957) revolutionized the discipline with the theory of 'transformational grammar', which proposed that humans have an innate capacity to acquire language. Radicalized during the Vietnam War, Chomsky subsequently became the leading radical critic of US foreign policy, developing his views in an extensive range of works including *American Power and the New Mandarins* (1969), *New Military Humanism* (1999) and *Hegemony and Survival* (2004). In works such as (with Edward Herman) *Manufacturing Consent* ([1988] 2006), he developed a radical critique of the mass media and examined how popular support for imperialist aggression is mobilized.

women's views and issues by the mass media, and accounts for the confrontational style of interviewing and political discussion sometimes adopted by broadcasters and journalists. Although the elite-values model helps to explain why the range of political views expressed by the mass media is often more restricted than pluralists suggest, it also has its limitations. Chief amongst these is that it fails to take full enough account of the pressures that bear upon senior media professionals; these, for example, include the views and interests of owners and commercial considerations; notably, 'ratings' figures.

Market model

The market model of the mass media differs from the other models, in that it dispenses with the idea of media bias: it holds that newspapers and television *reflect*, rather than shape, the views of the general public. This occurs because, regardless of the personal views of media owners and senior professionals, private media outlets are, first and foremost, businesses concerned with profit maximization and thus with extending market share. The media therefore give people 'what they want', and cannot afford to alienate existing or potential viewers or readers by presenting political viewpoints with which they may disagree. Such considerations may be less pressing in relation to public service broadcasters, such as the BBC, which are more insulated from commercial and advertiser pressures but, even here, the tyranny of 'ratings' is increasingly evident.

Nevertheless, although this model dispenses with the idea that at least the privately-owned mass media should be seen as part of the political process, it helps to explain some significant trends in political life. One of these may be growing popular disenchantment with politics resulting from the trivialization of political coverage. Fearful of losing 'market share', television companies in particular have reduced their coverage of serious political debate, and thus abandoned their responsibility for educating and informing citizens, in favour of 'infotainment'.

Media, democracy and governance

Custodians of democracy?

The impact that the media have on democracy is one of the most widely-debated aspects of the relationship between the media and politics. For many, the existence of a **free press** is one of the key features of democratic governance. However, how do the media act as custodians of democracy? And why have some questioned the media's democratic credentials, even arguing that they may undermine it? The media has traditionally been said to promote democracy in two key ways: by fostering public debate and political engagement, and by acting as a 'public watchdog' to check abuses of power. (The specific impact of the new media on democracy and politics more generally is considered later in the chapter.)

The capacity to provide a civic forum in which meaningful and serious political debate can take place is often viewed as the key democratic role of the media. The virtue of this is that better-informed citizens with more independent and considered views will be more politically engaged. The media are therefore agents of political education. Indeed, the media may have largely replaced formal representative institutions, such as assemblies, parliaments and local councils, as arenas for the dialogue, debate and deliberation that are the very stuff of democratic politics. This has happened because the media are, arguably, better-suited to this role than are traditional representative bodies. In addition to offering the public perhaps its only meaningful opportunity to watch politicians in action (through, for example, interviews with politicians and televised assembly debates), the media provide a forum for the expression of a much wider range of viewpoints and opinions than is possible within representative institutions composed only of elected politicians. Thus, academics and scientists, business leaders and trade union bosses, and representatives of interest groups and lobbyists of all kinds are able to express views and engage in public debate through the mechanism of media. Not only do the media substantially widen the range of views and opinions expressed in political debate, but they also present debate and discussion in a way that is lively and engaging for the general public, devoid of the formality, even stuffiness, that characterizes the exchanges that take place in assemblies and council chambers around the world.

The 'watchdog' role of the media is, in a sense, a subset of the political debate argument. The role of the media, from this perspective, is to ensure that public accountability takes place, by scrutinizing the activities of government and exposing abuses of power. Once again, in carrying out this role the media is supplementing and, to some extent, replacing the work of formal representative institutions. Media professionals such as researchers, journalists and television presenters are particularly suited to this role because they are 'outside' politics and have no interest other than to expose incompetence, corruption or simply muddled thinking whenever and wherever it can be found. By contrast, if public accountability is left solely in the hands of professional politicians, it may be constrained by the fact that those who attempt to expose ineptitude or wrong-doing wish themselves, at some stage, to hold government power. This may not only taint their motives, but it may also discourage them from criticizing processes and practices that they may wish to take advantage of in the future.

● **Free press**: Newspapers (and, by extension, other media outlets) that are free from censorship and political interference by government and, usually, are privately owned.

CONCEPT

Political bias

Political bias refers to political views that systematically favour the values or interests of one group over another as opposed to 'balanced' or 'objective' beliefs. Bias, however, may take various forms (McQuail, 1992). *Partisan* bias is explicit and deliberately promoted (newspaper editorials). *Propaganda* bias is deliberate but unacknowledged ('lazy' students or 'militant' Muslims). *Unwitting* bias occurs through the use of seemingly professional considerations (the 'newsworthiness' of a story). *Ideological* bias operates on the basis of assumptions and value judgements that are embedded in a particular belief system (wealth is gained through talent and hard work).

However, the media can only perform this role effectively if they are properly independent, and not dominated by government. Democratic governance therefore requires either that the publicly financed media are accountable to an independent commission, or that there is an appropriate level of competition from 'free' or privately financed media. The example of WikiLeaks nevertheless highlight how controversial the media's 'watchdog' role can be in practice (see p. 184).

However, reservations have also been expressed about the capacity of the media to promote effective democratic governance. The first of these, as advanced by dominant-ideology and elite-values theorists, is that, far from providing citizens with a wide and balanced range of political views, the content of the media is tainted by clear political biases. Whether political bias stems from the opinions and values of editors, journalists and broadcasters, or from a more general alignment between the interests of the media and those of economic and social elites, it is difficult to see how the media's duty to provide objective information and remain faithful to public-service principles can be discharged reliably and consistently in practice. Particular emphasis has, in this respect, been placed on the implications of media ownership, and the fact that the views and interests of major corporations or powerful media moguls cannot but, at some level, influence media output. Insofar as the mass media affects the political agenda, this agenda is likely to be politically conservative and, at least, compatible with the interests of dominant groups in society.

Second, as the mass media is not subject to public accountability, it is the classic example of 'power without responsibility' (Curran and Seaton, 2009). However well-informed, knowledgeable and stimulating the views of journalists and broadcasters may be, and however eager they may be to portray themselves as the 'voice of the people', media professionals – unlike elected politicians – 'represent' no one other than themselves, and have no meaningful basis for claiming to articulate public opinion. Third, there are reasons for doubting the independence of the media from government. As discussed in the final section of this chapter, all too often a symbiotic relationship develops between media professionals and the political elite which constrains both the mass media's political views and its capacity to act as an effective 'watchdog'.

The media and governance

Apart from its impact (for good or ill) on democracy, the prominence of the mass media in an 'information age' has affected the processes of governance (see p. 74) in a variety of ways. The most significant of these include the transformation of political leadership and, with it, a reapportionment of government power; changes to the political culture that, some have warned, are leading to a growing disenchantment with politics and making societies more difficult to govern; and alterations to the behaviour of governments and the nature of policy-making.

The chief way in which the media has transformed political leadership is through growing interest in the personal lives and private conduct of senior political figures, at the expense of serious and 'sober' policy and ideological debate. This, in part, stems from the media's, and particularly television's, obsession with image rather than issues, and with personality rather than policies. In the UK and other parliamentary systems, it is evident in a tendency towards the

POLITICS IN ACTION . . .

WikiLeaks: speaking truth to power?

Events: WikiLeaks was launched in 2006 as a project of the Sunshine Press. Since January 2007, its key spokesperson has been Julian Assange, an Australian internet activist, often described as the 'founder of WikiLeaks'. The main purpose of Wikileaks is to publish and comment on leaked documents alleging government and corporate misconduct, with documents and other materials being submitted anonymously through an electronic 'drop box'. Either directly, or through collaboration with other media (including, at times, *The Guardian*, the *New York Times* and *Der Spiegel*), WikiLeaks has published a massive quantity of documents on issues ranging from war, killing, torture and detention to the suppression of free speech and free press, and ecology and climate change. Many of the most high profile leaks have shed light on US military, security and intelligence activities. These have included almost 400,00 previously secret US military field reports about the Iraq War; secret US files on the war in Afghanistan which reveal civilian killings, 'friendly fire' deaths and the activities of special forces; more than 250,000 US state department cables, sent from, or to, US embassies around the world (so-called 'CableGate'); and US military files containing secret assessments of the 779 detainees held at the Guantánamo Bay detention centre.

Significance: Making use of the new internet culture and modern technology, WikiLeaks has been responsible for the biggest leak of secret information in history. However, assessments of the implications and value of its work have varied starkly. Supporters have used two key arguments to uphold media freedom. The first is that transparency is the only effective means of preventing, or at least reducing, conspiracy, corruption, exploitation and oppression. Quite simply, those in power, whether in government, the military, the security forces or in the world of business and finance will be less likely to abuse their positions and engage in unethical activities if they know that their actions are likely to be publicly exposed. Open governance thus promotes good governance. Second, media freedom underpins democracy, in that it allows citizens to make up their own minds, having access to information from all sources and not merely 'official' sources. There is therefore a clear public interest defence for 'whistleblowing', or 'principled leaking'. This was accepted by the 1971 'Pentagon Papers' case, in which the US Supreme Court upheld the right of the *New York Times*

to publish classified documents about the conduct of the Vietnam War, leaked by Daniel Ellsberg, on the grounds that 'only a free and unconstrained press can effectively expose deception in government'.

WikiLeak's activities have also attracted criticism, however. These have included that WikiLeaks has been over-concerned with generating publicity for itself and with promoting funding (especially in the light of restrictions imposed by the financial industry on online payments to WikiLeaks). However, the most serious criticisms have alleged that WikiLeaks has allowed information to get into the public domain that could both threaten national security and leave intelligence operatives working in foreign countries, together with those who assist them, vulnerable to identification and reprisals. This has been claimed, in particular, in relation to CableGate, where the alleged source of the leaked embassy cables, Private Bradley Manning, a US army intelligence analyst, was accused in a pre-trial military court hearing in December 2011 of 'aiding the enemy'. The release of the CableGate documents stimulated a wave of criticism not only from governments around the world, but also from human rights groups and former sympathizers and partners, including *The Guardian*. Some have accused Wikileaks of going beyond a traditional liberal defence of openness and transparent government in supporting 'free information fundamentalism', a stance that has deeply libertarian, if not anarchist, implications. For example, the private rituals of the Masons, Mormons and other groups were published even though this did not serve a clear political purpose.

'presidentialization', or 'Americanization', of politics (as discussed in Chapter 13). Such trends reflect not so much conscious bias on the part of the media, as an attempt to 'sell' politics to a mass audience that is deemed to be little interested in issues and policies. This also accounts for the tendency to treat elections as 'horse races', the public's attention being focused less on policy significance of the outcome and more on who is going to win. These two tendencies invariably coincide, turning elections into 'beauty contests' between leading politicians, each of whom serves as the 'brand image' of their party. Leaders are therefore judged largely on the basis of their 'televisual' skills (relaxed manner, sense of humour, ability to demonstrate the 'popular touch' and so on), rather than their mastery of political issues and capacity for serious political debate. However, has exposing leading politicians to the unrelenting glare of media attention merely given them celebrity status, or has media attention affected the location of power within the governmental system?

There can be little doubt that the advent of the 'media age' has changed the behaviour of political leaders, as well as affected the career prospects of individual politicians. For example, presentational factors, such as personal appearance, hairstyle, dress sense and so on, have become more important in determining political preferment or advancement. However, such developments have not merely changed the 'face' of modern politics; they have reordered power relationships both within the political executive and between the executive and the assembly. The growth of '**celebrity politics**' gives presidents, prime ministers and other party leaders the ability to make personalized appeals to the voters, creating the phenomenon of **spatial leadership**. This allows leaders to appeal 'over the heads' of their senior colleagues, parties and government institutions, directly to the public. Furthermore, the messages they give, and the policy and ideological stances they adopt, are increasingly determined by leading politicians personally, supported, it appears, by an ever-expanding band of public relations consultants, 'spin doctors', media managers, pollsters and publicity directors. One of the consequences of this is that junior politicians may have an additional reason for deferring to their leaders: their fear of damaging their leader's image and reputation. If the leader is damaged, especially by splits and internal criticism, all members of his or her party or government suffer. Political power thus comes to be structured on the basis of the publicity and media attention received by individual politicians. The greater the media attention, the greater the political leverage. However, media attention is far from an unqualified benefit for political leaders. Although their triumphs and successes can be publicly trumpeted, their flaws, failings and transgressions can also be ruthlessly exposed. Indeed, the ultimate vulnerability of contemporary political leaders may well be that negative media coverage may turn them into 'electoral liabilities', encouraging their parties and colleagues to remove them in order to 'save the party', or their own political careers.

The second way in which the media has affected governance is through its impact on the political culture. The media is sometimes charged with having created a climate of corrosive cynicism amongst the public, leading to growing popular disenchantment with politics generally, and a lack of trust in governments and politicians of all complexions (Lloyd, 2004). This may, in turn, be linked to trends that have afflicted mature democracies in particular, such as declining voter turnout and falling party membership. The UK is often seen as

● **Presidentialization**: A growing emphasis on personal leadership, in line with the role and powers of an executive president.

● **Celebrity politics**: Either or both the cultivation of 'celebrityhood' by elected politicians, or interventions by stars of popular culture into the political domain.

● **Spatial leadership**: The tendency of political leaders to distance themselves from their parties and governments by presenting themselves as 'outsiders', or developing their own political stance or ideological position.

CONCEPT

E-democracy

E-democracy (sometimes called 'digital democracy' or 'cyberdemocracy') refers to the use of computer-based technologies to enhance citizens' engagement in democratic processes. This nevertheless, may happen in different ways. (1) In the *representative* model, e-democracy seeks to strengthen the operation of established democratic mechanisms (e-voting and e-petitions,). (2) In the *deliberative* model, e-democracy aims to open up new opportunities for direct popular participation (electronic direct democracy). (3) In the *activist* model, e-democracy attempts to strengthen political and social movements and bolster citizen power generally ('virtual' communities and ICT-based protests).

the most advanced example of such a media-driven 'culture of contempt', but similar tendencies are evident elsewhere; notably, in the USA, Australia and Canada. Why has this happened? A critical stance towards politicians in general and governments in particular is, of course, vital to the maintenance of democratic governance. However, the distinction between legitimate criticism and systematic and relentless negativity may, in practice, be difficult to uphold. This occurs, in part, because increasingly intense commercial pressures have forced the media to make their coverage of politics 'sexy' and attention-grabbing. The media, after all, is a business, and this places inevitable pressure on the coverage of news and current affairs. Facts are absorbed progressively more quickly into a swirl of comment and interpretation, blurring, seemingly altogether, the distinction between what happens and what it means. Similarly, routine political debate and policy analysis receive less and less attention, as the media focus instead on – or 'hype' – scandals of various kinds and allegations of incompetence, policy failure or simple inertia. Leading politicians have, as a result, come to live in a kind of ongoing reality-television programme, the sole purpose of which appears to be to embarrass and denigrate them at every possible turn. The public, for their part, tend to view politicians as untrustworthy and deceitful, according them the same level of respect they would accord any other reality-television programme participant (The implications of such developments are examined further in Chapter 20.)

The final way in which the media has influenced governance is through its impact on the policy-making process. This has happened in at least two ways. The first is that, just like everyone else in society, government is bombarded by a much greater quantity of information arriving almost immediately. Knowing too much can sometimes be as dangerous as knowing too little. An example of this can be found in the USA's inability to predict and prevent the September 11 terrorist attacks in 2001. The problem the USA faced was not that it lacked information about al-Qaeda, its plans and movements, but that the sheer quantity of national-security intelligence available made effective analysis almost impossible. Moreover, as news and information spreads around the globe at a faster pace, governments are forced to react to events more quickly, and often before they have been fully discussed and digested. An age of '24/7 news' inevitably becomes one of '24/7 government'. Politicians are encouraged, even forced, to take a stance on issues simply to avoid being criticized for inertia or inactivity, leaving little time for the analysis of policy options and their implications. Second, greater reliance on the media means that it is often the media, and not government, that sets the political agenda and dictates the direction of policy-making. For example, the fact that television pictures of the Asian tsunami in December 2004 were broadcast almost immediately across the globe, creating an outpouring of public sympathy for its victims and leading to unprecedented levels of private charitable donations, forced governments around the world, within days, to make substantial increases in the scale of their of aid and support.

New media and the rise of e-politics

The revolution in communication technologies, brought about since the 1990s especially by the spread of satellite and cable television, mobile phones, the internet and digital technology generally, has transformed the media and society, helping to create what has been called an 'information society' or a 'network society' (as discussed in Chapter 7). This is also a process that has occurred with remarkable rapidity. For instance, internet penetration worldwide went from about 1 in 17 of the world's population in 2000, to almost 1 in 3 by 2012, and Twitter, Facebook, YouTube, Wikipedia and Google, unknown only a few years ago, have become part of many people's everyday lives. But how, and to what extent, has new media affected politics? The most common claim is that new media are a progressive force, helping to improve the quality of political life, in particular by contributing to a general transfer power from governments and political elites to the public at large. This is often summed up in the idea of 'e-democracy'. However, e-democracy is a vague and contested term which covers a diverse range of activities, some of which may be 'top-down' (initiated by government or other public bodies) while others are 'bottom-up' (initiated by citizens and activists), with a further distinction being made between those that involve a one-way flow of information from government to citizens and those involving a two-way process of interaction. Examples of e-democracy include the following:

- online voting (e-voting) in elections or referendums
- online petitions (e-petitions) organized by governments or other bodies
- the use of ICT to publicize, organize, lobby or fundraise (e-campaigning)
- accessing political information, news and comments via websites, blogs (web-logs) and so on
- the use of interactive television or social networking sites, or **social media**, to allow citizens to engage in political debate and, possibly, policy-making
- the use of mobile phones and social media to organize popular protests and demonstrations.

New media can be seen to have changed, or be changing, politics in at least three key ways. In the first place, electronic mechanisms have altered the conduct of elections. This is particularly apparent in the case of election campaigns, which increasingly revolve around internet-based activities. Websites, emails and podcasts provide political candidates and parties with a fast and cheap means of getting their message across to a (potentially) large audience, in the process allowing them also to recruit campaign volunteers and raise campaign funds. E-campaigning has the advantage that it is particularly effective in reaching younger people, who are often the most difficult section of the population to engage through conventional strategies. Although the internet has been used in campaigning since the mid-1990s, particularly in the USA, it became particularly prominent during Barack Obama's 2008 presidential campaign. Obama's team used forums and social media such as Facebook and MySpace to build relationships particularly with supporters and would-be supporters aged 18–29, also encouraging the spread of wider networks of support via the website MyBarackObama.com. Sympathizers were also sent regular updates on events and policy positions via emails and text messages. Nevertheless, new technologies were certainly not the be-all and end-all of the Obama campaign, which also relied heavily, and spent most of its money, on more traditional strategies such as television advertising and poster campaigns.

A further way in which digital innovations have affected elections is through growing experiments in electronic voting, sometimes portrayed as 'push-button

● **Social media**: Forms of elecronic communication that facilitate social interaction and the formation of online communities through the exchange of user-generated content.

democracy'. E-voting has been particularly important in countries such as India, where it has proved to be the only practicable solution to the problem of tallying some 400 million votes without substantial delays occurring in announcing election results. The first experiments in India in the use of electronic voting machines located at polling stations started in 1982, with e-voting subsequently being adopted, first, for state elections and, later, for national elections. Similar electronic mechanisms have been used in countries ranging from France, Germany and Finland to Romania and the Philippines. However, although trials have taken place in the use of 'remote' e-voting, through use of the internet (sometimes called 'i-voting'), its wider adoption has been hampered because fears about the greater likelihood of electoral fraud have yet to be allayed.

Second, new media offer citizens wider and easier access to political information and political comment. This has occurred in a number of ways. For example, governments in all parts of the world have, albeit at different speeds, recognized the advantage of making government information available online, and, in a growing number of cases, of allowing citizens to access government services through websites, so-called 'e-government'. The most significant new sources of information are, nevertheless, non-governmental in character. The proliferation of websites developed, variously, by professional groups, businesses, lobbying bodies and think-tanks means that, for the first time, citizens and citizen groups are privy to a quantity and quality of information that may rival that of government. This has generally empowered non-state actors at the expense of national governments and traditional political elites. Non-governmental organizations (see p. 248) and interest groups (see p. 247) have thus become more effective in challenging the positions and actions of government and, sometimes, even displaced government as an authoritative source of views and information about specialist subjects ranging from the environment and global poverty to public health and civil liberties. A further development has been the impact of new media on journalism. This has occurred in two ways. In the first, the rise of the blog has greatly expanded the contours of political commentary, as the growing 'blogosphere' allows writers, academics, politicians and others to share their observations and opinions about political matter with whoever may be interested in accessing them. In the second, there has been a growth of 'user-generated content', stemming from the increased willingness of private citizens, often in newsworthy or politically-charged situations, to share their thoughts, experiences and, frequently, pictures with other via social media.

Third, new media have supported the development of political and social movements, and increased their effectiveness, thus giving rise to a new style of activist politics, sometimes called the 'new politics', and contributing, some argue, to a general shift of power from governments to citizens. The key advantage of new media, from this perspective, is not just that they open up new opportunities for political participation, but also that these forms of participation are, by their nature, decentralized and non-hierarchic. Armed with mobile phones and through the use of the internet, anti-globalization or 'anti-capitalist' protesters have been able to mount demonstrations, and engage in agitation and direct action, a trend that first became apparent during the so-called 'Battle of Seattle' in 1999, when some 50,000 activists forced the cancellation of the opening ceremony of a World Trade Organization meeting. Social media such as Twitter and Facebook were, similarly, instrumental in facilitating the spread of pro-democracy protests during the 2011 Tunisian revolution, at the beginning of the Arab Spring (see p. 88). Their capacity to promote self-management and grass-roots organization has made new media particularly attractive for modern anarchist and libertarian groups, sometimes dubbed 'new' anarchists. Old-style anarchist collectives have therefore given way to online anarchist (or anarchist-style) networks such as Anonymous, which, since 2008, has engaged in campaigns and protests, usually associated with internet freedom or exposing corporate malpractice, and sometimes associated with what has been called 'hacktivism'.

New media have, nevertheless, also attracted criticism. These have, for instance, linked the trend towards e-democracy with the growth of a privatized and consumerist form of citizenship. How meaningful is democratic participation if it lacks a genuinely public dimension and fails to engender meaningful debate and discussion. Perhaps an underlying problem with the debate over the impact of new media is the tendency to believe that political problems (such as low voter turnout rates or declining party membership), can be solved by 'technical fixes'. Similarly, it is perhaps a mistake to suggest that technology, in itself, has a particular political character, whether positive or negative; rather, technology may be either liberating or oppressive, depending on who is using it and the uses to which it is put. It is worth remembering, for instance, that the same technologies that helped in the spread and coordination of pro-democracy demonstrations during the Tunisian revolution were the same technologies that, only six months later, were also used to organize looting during riots in London and other English cities.

Media globalization

An aspect of the media's influence that has attracted growing political attention is its role in strengthening globalization. Radio and television started this process, as it became increasingly difficult to insulate the populations of one country from news, information and images broadcast from other countries. An example of this was the extent to which the communist regimes of Eastern Europe were destabilized by the growing penetration of pro-western, and therefore pro-capitalist, radio and television broadcasts from Western Europe and the USA, contributing to the revolutions of 1989–91. New media, and especially satellite television, mobile phones and the internet, have dramatically intensified this process, both because of their dramatic spread and because of their inherently transnational characters. China and Singapore are amongst the few countries still trying to censor the internet, with such attempts likely to become less and less successful over time. Insofar as the media facilitates, or even fuels, globalization, it has contributed to a far-reaching range of political developments, including the growth of a globalized capitalist economy, the declining (or, at least, changing) role of the state, and the emergence of what some see as a homogenized global culture.

The role of the media in promoting **cultural globalization** has been an area of particular controversy. The power of the media, allied to the growth of transnational corporations (see p. 149) and trends such as mass tourism, is often held to be responsible for the development of a single global system that imprints itself on all parts of the world; this results, in effect, in a global mono-

● **Hacktivism:** The use of computers and computer networks to achieve political ends by methods including 'denial-of-service' attacks on targeted websites.

● **Cultural globalization:** The process whereby information, commodities and images produced in one part of the world enter into a global flow that tends to 'flatten out' cultural differences between nations and regions.

Debating...
Does the wider use of new media enrich politics?

It is generally accepted that new digital or computer technologies are having a profound impact on society and politics, but it is less clear what that impact is. Is ICT a motor for decentralization and democracy, or may new technologies debase politics and threaten freedom?

YES

Modernizing politics. Technological development reflects an ongoing desire to use science and innovation to make human existence more convenient and comfortable, and this applies in politics as well as other spheres of life. E-voting and 'virtual' referendums thus enable citizens to express their views easily and conveniently, possibly without having to leave home. Falling electoral turnouts may therefore simply be a consequence of the failure of the democratic process to keep up-to-date with how citizens in an 'information society' wish to participate in politics.

Knowledge is power. New technologies massively enlarge citizens' access to information, making possible, for the first time, a truly free exchange of ideas and views. The internet already makes available to private citizens specialist information that was only available to governments. Accessing information through Wikipedia and the myriad other online sources is not only almost instantaneous, but it also exposes the public to a rich diversity of views, including radical and dissident ones.

Citizen empowerment. The great advantage of new tech-nologies is that they make possible a two-way transmis-sion of views, thereby promoting active and engaged citizenship. Instead of participating in politics simply through the act of voting every few years, citizens can express views and opinions on an almost continuous basis, through, for instance, online consultations on draft legislation and online petitions. More radically, new media may foster direct popular participation, making a reality of Athenian-style democracy, for so long dismissed as impracticable, or relevant only to township meetings.

Decentralized activism. The broadest claim made for new media is that, in contributing to a wholesale shift in power from political elites to the public at large, it is bringing about a process of radical democratization. This occurs because new technologies are implicitly egalitarian (being relatively cheap, easily accessible and simple to use), and also facilitate decentralized and spontaneous social action. As modern protest movements clearly demonstrate, the use of mobile phones and social media in particular helps to make leadership and formal organi-zation unnecessary, even irrelevant.

NO

Technological 'Big Brother'. Technology has always been developed to serve the interests of elite or powerful groups, and ICT is no exception. Contrary to the popular image that they are tools of liberation, mobile phones and the internet actually provide the police, security forces, tax officials and so on with access to a massive amount of information about the movements, views and activities of private citizens. As such, new media provide a highly effective means of controlling dissident behav-iour and containing political opposition.

Dangers of information anarchy. Many of the new polit-ical spaces opened up by new media have been polluted by both the nature of the views they feature and the style of expression they tend to encourage. The internet provides a platform for religious fundamentalists, racists, ethnic nationalists and other extremists, who would otherwise struggle to attract public attention. Similarly, the blogosphere tends to be dominated by shrill, uncivil and opinionated views, fashioned, seemingly, by the desire to create notoriety.

New inequalities. The claim that new technologies are implicitly egalitarian is bogus. Most obviously, a 'digital divide' has opened up based on the fact that access to new communication technologies is not universal. The 'infor-mation rich' have come to dominate the 'information poor'. In the feminist version of this argument, computers and technology generally have been seen to benefit men, since they reflect essentially male interests and patterns of thought. New media also provide private business with new opportunities to advertise, generate profits and improve their public image.

Impoverished, debased democracy. E-democracy, or 'virtual' democracy, threatens to turn the democratic process into a series of push-button referendums while citizens sit alone in their own living rooms. This further erodes the 'public' dimension of political participation, reducing democratic citizenship to a set of consumer choices, somewhat akin to voting in the television show *Big Brother*. By weakening face-to-face human interac-tion, the danger is that people will be consumed by their own opinions, and become indifferent to those of others.

Propaganda

Propaganda is information (or disinformation) disseminated in a deliberate attempt to shape opinions and, possibly, stimulate political action. Propaganda is a pejorative term, implying both untruth or distortion, and a (usually crude) desire to manipulate and control public opinion. Propaganda differs from political bias, in that it is systematic and deliberate, whereas the latter may be partial and unintentional. A distinction is sometimes drawn between 'black' propaganda (blatant lies), 'grey' propaganda (distortions and half truths) and 'white' propaganda (the truth).

culture. The most prominent feature of this process has been the worldwide advance of consumerism and of the materialistic values and appetites that underpin burgeoning global capitalism. Benjamin Barber (1995) dubbed this emerging world 'McWorld', to capture the idea that mass communications and modern commerce, tied together by technology, has created a world in which people everywhere are mesmerized by 'fast music, fast computers, fast food – with MTV, McIntosh and McDonald's pressing nations into one commercially homogeneous theme park'. In this view of cultural globalization, the rich diversity of global cultures, religions, traditions and lifestyles is being subverted by a process of 'westernization' or 'Americanization', made possible by what has been called 'media imperialism'. The western – or, more specifically, American – character of cultural globalization stems not only from the fact that the West is the home of consumer capitalism, but also from the tendency of global media content to derive disproportionately from the West, and particularly from the USA. This is reflected in the rise of English as the global language, and in the global dominance of Hollywood films and US-produced television programmes.

However, this image of cultural homogenization fuelled by the global mass media fails to capture what is, in practice, a complex and often contradictory process. Alongside the media's tendency to 'flatten out' cultural differences, there are also strong tendencies towards diversity and pluralization. This has occurred in a number of ways and for a variety of reasons. In the first place, as Barber (1995) argued, the rise of McWorld has been symbiotically linked to the emergence of countervailing forces, the most notable of which is militant Islam, or what Barber called '*Jihad*'. The second development is that new media have substantially reduced the cost of mass communication, as well as widened access to it. An example of this is the success of the Qatar-based television station Al Jazeera, launched in 1996, in providing a forum for the expression of non-western views and opinions across the Arab world and beyond, offering a rival to, for instance, CNN, Voice of America and the BBC. Third, cultural exchange facilitated through the media is by no means a 'top-down' or one-way process; instead, all societies, including the economically and politically powerful, have become more varied and diverse as a result of the emergence of a globalized cultural marketplace. In return for Coca-Cola, McDonald's and MTV, developed states have increasingly been 'penetrated' by Bollywood films, Chinese martial arts epics, 'world music', and non-western religions and therapeutic practices.

Political communication

Propaganda machines

The notion that government and the media are always opposing forces, the latter exposing the failings and flaws of the former (either for the public's benefit or for commercial advantage), is highly misleading. Instead, the media have often been controlled, directly or indirectly, by government and used as a form of propaganda machine. The classic example of a propaganda machine was that constructed under Joseph Goebbels in Nazi Germany. The Nazis set out to 'coordinate' German society through an elaborate process of ideological indoctrination. For example, youth organizations were set up in the form of the Hitler Youth and the League of German Maidens; the school curriculum was entirely revised and all teachers coerced to join the Nazi Teachers' League; and the German Labour Front replaced free trade unions, providing workers with recreational facilities through the 'Strength through Joy' organization. As chief propagandist of the Nazi Party, in 1933 Goebbels created a new department, the Reich Ministry of Information and Propaganda, which inundated Germany with an unending flood of propaganda. Little in the field of mass communication and entertainment escaped the **censorship** of Goebbels' ministry. It supervised all the writing, music, theatre, dance, painting, sculpture, film and radio. Goebbels placed particular stress on radio broadcasting and encouraged the manufacture of a cheap 'people's' radio set, which resulted in huge and ever-growing audiences for his propaganda through the radio. He began the world's first regular television service in 1935, which, although restricted to closed-circuit showing in Berlin, kept going until near the end of World War II.

Media propaganda was also a significant feature of communist regimes. The Soviet Union, for example, not only operated a system of strict censorship over the mass media, but also fostered a journalistic culture (the 'internal censor') that demanded total support of the ideology and policies of the Communist Party, or CPSU. Both the print and broadcast media were used as propaganda tools by the Soviet authorities, with media content unwaveringly mirroring the policies of the state at each stage in the history of the Soviet Union (Oates, 2005). However, the introduction of '*glasnost*' by Mikhail Gorbachev when he became CPSU General Secretary in 1985 initiated changes in the Soviet media that were to have far-reaching, and ultimately unstoppable, political implications. The high point of the media's influence came in August 1991, when journalists and broadcasters defied the *coup* that had toppled Gorbachev and was intended to reinstate authoritarian rule. In so doing, they contributed both to the collapse of the *coup* and, later in the year, to the downfall of the Soviet regime itself. Russia's record of media freedom in the postcommunist era has nevertheless been patchy. Despite the formal abolition of censorship in 1990 and the inclusion of freedom from censorship in the 1993 Russian Constitution (Article 29), the Russian media, and television in particular, continue to be dominated by state interests. Television channels such as Channel 1, NTV and RTR have been criticized during election campaigns of systematic bias towards Vladimir Putin and the government-backed United Russia party, and Russia remains one of the most dangerous places in the world to be a journalist (Shiraev, 2010).

Criticisms of the use of the media as a propaganda machine are not restricted to totalitarian regimes and new democracies, however. For instance, controversy was sparked in Italy by Silvio Berlusconi's periods as prime minister in 1994–05, 2001–06 and 2008–11. Berlusconi, who is Italy's richest person, owns Mediaset, which controls three of Italy's six privately-owned television channels. In 1993 he founded the Forza Italia political movement, in part to further his own political ambitions. The success of Forza Italia was certainly linked to widespread disenchantment with Italy's sclerotic party system, but the movement undoubtedly also benefited from the consistently positive coverage it received in the Berlusconi-owned media. During his period in power, however, Berlusconi was frequently criticized for trying to extend his media control beyond the Mediaset channels, bringing pressure to bear also on the publicly-owned RAI television channels. This, his critics alleged, gave Berlusconi control of almost all television sources of information in Italy, ensuring favourable coverage for Berlusconi

● **Censorship**: A policy or act of control over what can be said, written, published or performed in order to suppress what is considered morally or politically unacceptable.

● *Glasnost*: (Russian) Literally, 'openness' or 'transparency'; the liberalization of controls over political expression and the media.

personally and for the centre-right views of Forza Italia. Although the Italian example is unusual because of Berlusconi's joint role as media mogul and political leader, attempts by democratic politicians to exert influence over the media are by no means uncommon. Indeed, they have become routine in an emerging age of '**spin**' and news management.

Politics of spin

In addition to political biases that operate in and through the mass media, growing concern has been expressed about the closer relationship in modern politics between government and the media, and about how each uses the other for its own purposes. This has led to a transformation in the style and substance of political communication in democratic regimes, affecting both public opinion and, more widely, the political culture. Governments of whatever complexion have always had an unreliable relationship with truth. Politicians are concerned primarily with winning and retaining power, and are thus ever sensitive to the need to maintain public support. The desire to accentuate the positive and conceal the negative is therefore irresistible. In a liberal-democratic context, in which the existence of free media rules out 'official' propaganda and crude ideological manipulation, governments have come to shape the news agenda by new techniques for the control and dissemination of information, often described as 'news management' or 'political marketing'. The favourable presentation of information and policies, or what has come to be called 'spin', has thus become a major preoccupation of modern governments.

The art of 'spin', practised by so-called 'spin-doctors', has many facets. These include the following:

- the careful 'vetting' of information and arguments before release to the media
- the control of sources of information to ensure that only an official 'line' is presented
- the use of unattributable briefings or 'leaks'
- the feeding of stories only to sympathetic media sources
- the release of information close to media deadlines to prevent checking or the identification of counter-arguments
- the release of 'bad' news at times when other, more important events dominate the news agenda.

News management of this kind is most advanced in the USA, where it has become common for election strategists and campaign managers to take up senior White House posts, if their candidate wins the presidency. The Clinton administration was widely seen to have taken 'spin' and the skills of policy presentation to new and more sophisticated levels. The Blair government in the UK also devoted particular attention to the 'packaging' of politics, leading some to criticize it for being concerned more with style than with substance. Amongst the developments that occurred under Blair were the centralizing of government communications under the control of the prime minister's press office; a 'carrot and stick' approach to journalists, who were rewarded with information for sympathetic coverage but penalized for criticism; and the politicization of

● **Spin**: The presentation of information so as to elicit a desired response, or being 'economical with the truth'.

departmental information offices through the imposition of control from Downing Street. Blair also employed a former senior editor of a tabloid newspaper (Alistair Campbell) as his director of communications, 1997–2003, as did David Cameron, 2007–10, (Andy Coulson).

It would be a mistake, however, to assume that the media have been reluctant or passive players in the development of news management. The media need government as much as government needs the media. Government has always been an important source of news and information, but its role has become even more vital as the expansion in media outlets – television channels, websites, magazines and newspapers – has created greater pressure for the acquisition of 'newsworthy' stories. In some cases, publishers, editors and journalists conspire with 'spin-doctors' to manage the news for mutual benefit. This was alleged in the UK in relation to the Blair government and the Murdoch press, as, for instance, the government's unwillingness to press ahead with privacy legislation coincided with the (temporary) conversion of, first, the *Sun*, the UK's largest selling tabloid, and then *The Times* into Labour-supporting newspapers.

In addition to undermining the rigour and independence of political reporting, the advent of media-orientated government has a range of other implications. Some, for example, argue that it strengthens democracy by allowing government to deal with the public more directly and to respond more effectively to popular views and concerns. Others, however, see it as a threat to the democratic process, in that it widens the scope for manipulation and dishonesty, and weakens the role of representative institutions such as assemblies or parliaments. Moreover, it may engender apathy and undermine interest in conventional forms of political activity; in particular, voting and party membership. This occurs because 'spin', style and presentation themselves become the focus of media attention, strengthening the image of government as a vast publicity machine that is disengaged from the lives and concerns of ordinary people.

SUMMARY

- There are rival theories of the media's political impact. Pluralists portray the media as an ideological market-place that enhances debate and electoral choice. However, others highlight systematic media bias, stemming either from links between the media and economic and social elites, or from the personal views of the editor, broadcasters and journalists. The market model suggests that the media output simply reflects the views of the general public.

- The media play a key democratic role in four senses. They promote political education by providing a public forum for meaningful and serious debate; act as a public watchdog, exposing abuses of power; tend, through the 'new' media in particular, to widen access to information and facilitate political activism; and serve as a mechanism through which democracy takes place. Concerns have, nevertheless, been raised about the political views of the media, their lack of democratic accountability and their over-close links to government.

- The mass media has affected governance in various ways. These include that they have transformed political leadership and, in the process, reapportioned government power. They have also changed the political culture and, some have warned, contributed to declining respect for politicians and politics in general. Finally, the growing influence of the media is evident in a policy-making process that has to react more rapidly and make sense of a vast amount of information.

- The use of new media has been defended on the grounds that it facilitates political participation, widens citizen's access to information, and stimulates new forms of decentralized political activism. Critics, nevertheless, warn against the growth of a consumerist form of citizenship and doubt the value of 'technological fixes'.

- The role of the media in promoting globalization has provoked particular controversy. Some have warned against 'media imperialism', drawing attention to the media's role in spreading a global culture of consumerism and in strengthening 'westernization or 'Americanization'. However, cultural exchange facilitated by the mass media is by no means always a 'top-down' or one-way process.

- Governments have sometimes used the media as a propaganda machine. This involves direct control over all kinds of media output to ensure that only 'official' views and ideas are distributed. Classic examples of this can be found in Nazi Germany and in communist regimes, but there has been a growing tendency for democratic regimes to engage in news management and the politics of 'spin', providing evidence of a symbiotic relationship that tends to develop between government and the media.

Questions for discussion

- Is civic culture a cause or a consequence of effective democratic rule?
- Do the mass media reflect public opinion or shape it?
- Is a free media vital for democratic rule?
- How has the media changed the nature of political leadership? Are leaders stronger or weaker as a result?
- What is new about the 'new' media?
- Is the media an agent of cultural homogenization?
- Do all governments use propaganda, or only some?
- Are modern governments more concerned with political marketing than with political performance?

Further reading

Almond, G. A. and S. Verba (eds), *The Civic Culture Revisited* (1989). An updated version of the authors' classic 1963 analysis of the conditions required for democratic stability.

Jenkins, H. and D. Thorburn (eds), *Democracy and New Media* (2004). A wide-ranging collection of essays that discuss, from a variety of perspectives, the relationship between democracy and cyberspace.

Putnam, R. *Bowling Alone: The Collapse and Revival of American Community* (2000). A highly influential anaysis of the decline of civic engagement and social participation in the USA.

Street, J., *Mass Media, Politics and Democracy*, 2nd edn (2011). A readable and wide-ranging overview of all aspects of the relationship between the media and politics.

CHAPTER 9

Representation, Elections and Voting

'If voting changed anything they'd abolish it.'

Anarchist slogan

PREVIEW   Elections are often thought of as the heart of the political process. Perhaps no questions in politics are as crucial as 'Do we elect the politicians who rule over us?', and 'Under what rules are these elections held?' Elections are seen as nothing less than democracy in practice. They are a means through which the people can control their government, ultimately by 'kicking the rascals out'. Central to this notion is the principle of representation. Put simply, representation portrays politicians as servants of the people, and invests them with a responsibility to act for or on behalf of those who elect them. When democracy, in the classical sense of direct and continuous popular participation, is regarded as hopelessly impractical, representation may be the closest we can come to achieving government by the people. There is, nevertheless, considerable disagreement about what representation means and how it can be achieved in practice. Although it is widely accepted that elections play a pivotal role in the process of representative democracy, electoral systems are many and various and debate has long raged over which system is the 'best'. Not only do different systems have different strengths or advantages, but there is no consensus over the criteria that should be used for assessing them. Finally, elections need voters, but there is little agreement about why voters vote as they do, and especially about the extent to which their behaviour is rationally-based, as opposed to being influenced by underlying psychological, social or ideological forces.

KEY ISSUES

- What is representation? How can one person 'represent' another?
- How can representation be achieved in practice?
- What do elections do? What are their functions?
- How do electoral systems differ? What are their strengths and weaknesses?
- What do election results mean?
- Why do people vote as they do? How can voting behaviour be explained?

CONCEPT

Representation

Representation is, broadly, a relationship through which an individual or group stands for, or acts on behalf of, a larger body of people. Representation differs from democracy in that, while the former acknowledges a distinction between government and the governed, the latter, at least in its classical form, aspires to abolish this distinction and establish popular *self*-government. Representative democracy (see p. 92) may nevertheless constitute a limited and indirect form of democratic rule, provided that the representation links government and the governed in such a way that the people's views are articulated, or their interests secured.

REPRESENTATION

The issue of representation has generated deep and recurrent political controversy. Even the absolute monarchs of old were expected to rule by seeking the advice of the 'estates of the realm' (the major landed interests, the clergy, and so on). In this sense, the English Civil War of the seventeenth century, fought between King and Parliament, broke out as a result of an attempt to deny representation to key groups and interests. Similarly, debate about the spread of democracy in the nineteenth and twentieth centuries centred largely on the question of who should be represented. Should representation be restricted to those who have the competence, education and, perhaps, leisure to act wisely and think seriously about politics (variously seen as men, the propertied, or particular racial or ethnic groups), or should representation be extended to all adult citizens?

Such questions have now largely been resolved through the widespread acceptance of the principle of political equality (see p. 90), at least in the formal sense of universal suffrage and 'one person, one vote'. Plural voting, for example, was abolished in the UK in 1949, women were enfranchised in one canton in Switzerland in 1971, and racial criteria for voting were swept away in South Africa in 1994. However, this approach to representation is simplistic, in that it equates representation with elections and voting, politicians being seen as 'representatives' merely because they have been elected. This ignores more difficult questions about how one person can be said to represent another, and what it is that he or she represents. Is it the views of the represented, their best interests, the groups from which they come, or what?

Theories of representation

There is no single, agreed theory of representation. Rather, there are a number of competing theories, each of which is based on particular ideological and political assumptions. For example, does representative government imply that government 'knows better' than the people, that government has somehow 'been instructed' by the people what to do and how to behave; or that the government 'looks like' the people, in that it broadly reflects their characteristics or features? Such questions are not of academic interest alone. Particular models of representation dictate very different behaviour on the part of representatives. For instance, should elected politicians be bound by policies and positions outlined during an election and endorsed by the voters, or is it their job to lead public opinion and thereby help to define the public interest? Moreover, it is not uncommon for more than one principle of representation to operate within the same political system, suggesting, perhaps, that no single model is sufficient in itself to secure representative government.

Four principal models of representation have been advanced:

- trusteeship
- delegation
- the mandate
- resemblance.

John Stuart Mill (1806–73)

UK philosopher, economist and politician. Mill was subject to an intense and austere regime of education by his father, the utilitarian theorist James Mill (1773–1836). This resulted in a mental collapse at the age of 20, after which he developed a more human philosophy influenced by Coleridge and the German Idealists. His major writings, including *On Liberty* (1859), *Considerations on Representative Government* (1861) and *The Subjection of Women* (1869), had a powerful influence on the development of liberal thought. In many ways, Mill's work straddles the divide between classical and modern liberalism. His distrust of state intervention was firmly rooted in nineteenth-century principles, but his emphasis on the quality of individual life (reflected in a commitment to 'individuality') looked forward to later developments.

Trustee model

A **trustee** is a person who acts on behalf of others, using his or her superior knowledge, better education or greater experience. The classic expression of representation as trusteeship is found in Edmund Burke's (see p. 36) speech to the electors of Bristol in 1774:

> You choose a member indeed; but when you have chosen him he is not member of Bristol, but he is a member of parliament . . . Your representative owes you, not his industry only, but his judgement; and he betrays, instead of serving you, if he sacrifices it to your opinion (Burke, 1975).

For Burke, the essence of representation was to serve one's constituents by the exercise of 'mature judgement' and 'enlightened conscience'. In short, representation is a moral duty: those with the good fortune to possess education and understanding should act in the interests of those who are less fortunate. This view had strongly elitist implications, since it stresses that, once elected, representatives should think for themselves and exercise independent judgement on the grounds that the mass of people do not know their own best interests. A similar view was advanced by John Stuart Mill in the form of the liberal theory of representation. This was based on the assumption that, although all individuals have a right to be represented, not all political opinions are of equal value. Mill therefore proposed a system of plural voting in which four or five votes would be allocated to holders of learned diplomas or degrees, two or three to skilled or managerial workers, and a single vote to ordinary workers. He also argued that rational voters would support politicians who could act wisely on their behalf, rather than those who merely reflected the voters' own views. Trustee representation thus portrays professional politicians as representatives, insofar as they are members of an educated elite. It is based on the belief that knowledge and understanding are unequally distributed in society, in the sense that not all citizens know what is best for them.

● **Trustee**: A person who is vested with formal (and usually legal) responsibilities for another's property or affairs.

This Burkean notion of representation has also attracted severe criticism, however. For instance, it appears to have clearly antidemocratic implications. If

Thomas Paine (1737–1809)

UK-born writer and revolutionary. Paine was brought up in a Quaker family and spent his early years as an undistinguished artisan. He went to America in 1774 and fought for the colonists in the War of Independence. He returned to England in 1789, but, after being indicted for treason, fled to France as a supporter of the republican cause, where he narrowly escaped the guillotine during the Terror. Paine's radicalism fused a commitment to political liberty with a deep faith in popular sovereignty, providing inspiration for both liberal republicanism and socialist egalitarianism. He was an important figure in revolutionary politics in the USA, the UK and France. His most important writings include *Common Sense* ([1776] 1987), *The Rights of Man* (1791/92) and *The Age of Reason* (1794).

politicians should think for themselves because the public is ignorant, poorly educated or deluded, then surely it is a mistake to allow the public to elect their representatives in the first place. Second, the link between representation and education is questionable. Whereas education may certainly be of value in aiding the understanding of intricate political and economic problems, it is far less clear that it helps politicians to make correct moral judgements about the interests of others. There is little evidence, for example, to support Burke's and Mill's belief that education breeds **altruism** and gives people a broader sense of social responsibility. Finally, there is the fear traditionally expressed by radical democrats such as Thomas Paine that, if politicians are allowed to exercise their own judgement, they will simply use that latitude to pursue their own selfish interests. In this way, representation could simply become a substitute for democracy. In his pamphlet *Common Sense* ([1776] 1987), Paine came close to the rival ideal of delegate representation in insisting that 'the elected should never form to themselves an interest separate from the electors'.

Delegate model

A **delegate** is a person who acts as a conduit conveying the views of others, while having little or no capacity to exercise his or her own judgement or preferences. Examples include sales representatives and ambassadors, neither of whom are, strictly speaking, authorized to think for themselves. Similarly, a trade-union official who attends a conference with instructions on how to vote and what to say is acting as a delegate, not as a Burkean representative. Those who favour this model of representation as delegation usually support mechanisms that ensure that politicians are bound as closely as possible to the views of the represented. These include what Paine referred to as 'frequent interchange' between representatives and their constituents in the form of regular elections and short terms in office. In addition, radical democrats have advocated the use of **initiatives** and the right of **recall** as means of giving the public more control over politicians. Although delegation stops short of direct democracy, its supporters nevertheless usually favour the use of referendums (see p. 201) to supplement the representative process.

● **Altruism**: A concern for the welfare of others, based on either enlightened self-interest, or a recognition of a common humanity.

● **Delegate**: A person who is chosen to act for another on the basis of clear guidance and instruction; delegates do not think for themselves.

● **Initiative**: A type of referendum through which the public is able to raise legislative proposals.

● **Recall**: A process whereby the electorate can call unsatisfactory public officials to account and ultimately remove them.

CONCEPT

Mandate

A mandate is an instruction or command from a higher body that demands compliance. The idea of a *policy* mandate arises from the claim on behalf of a winning party in an election that its manifesto promises have been endorsed, giving it authority to translate these into a programme of government. The doctrine of the mandate thus implies that the party in power can only act within the mandate it has received. The more flexible notion of a *governing* mandate, or, for an individual leader, a *personal* mandate, has sometimes been advanced, but it is difficult to see how this in any way restricts politicians once they are in power.

● **Popular sovereignty**: The principle that there is no higher authority than the will of the people (the basis of the classical concept of democracy).

● **Manifesto**: A document outlining (in more or less detail) the policies or programme a party proposes to pursue if elected to power.

The virtue of what has been called 'delegated representation' is that it provides broader opportunities for popular participation and serves to check the self-serving inclinations of professional politicians. It thus comes as close as is possible in representative government to realizing the ideal of **popular sovereignty**. Its disadvantages are, nevertheless, also clear. In the first place, in ensuring that representatives are bound to the interests of their constituents, it tends to breed narrowness and foster conflict. This is precisely what Burke feared would occur if members of the legislature acted as ambassadors who took instructions from their constituents, rather than as representatives of the nation. As he put it, 'Parliament is a deliberative assembly of one nation, with one interest, that of the whole'. A second drawback is that, because professional politicians are not trusted to exercise their own judgement, delegation limits the scope for leadership (see p. 300) and statesmanship. Politicians are forced to reflect the views of their constituents or even pander to them, and are thus not able to mobilize the people by providing vision and inspiration.

Mandate model

Both the trustee model and the delegate model were developed before the emergence of modern political parties, and therefore view representatives as essentially independent actors. However, individual candidates are now rarely elected mainly on the basis of their personal qualities and talents; more commonly, they are seen, to a greater or lesser extent, as foot soldiers for a party, and are supported because of its public image or programme of policies. New theories of representation have therefore emerged. The most influential of these is the so-called 'doctrine of the mandate'. This is based on the idea that, in winning an election, a party gains a popular mandate that authorizes it to carry out whatever policies or programmes it outlined during the election campaign. As it is the party, rather than individual politicians, that is the agent of representation, the mandate model provides a clear justification for party unity and party discipline. In effect, politicians serve their constituents not by thinking for themselves or acting as a channel to convey their views, but by remaining loyal to their party and its policies.

The strength of the mandate doctrine is that it takes account of the undoubted practical importance of party labels and party policies. Moreover, it provides a means of imposing some kind of meaning on election results, as well as a way of keeping politicians to their word. Nevertheless, the doctrine has also stimulated fierce criticism. First, it is based on a highly questionable model of voting behaviour, insofar as it suggests that voters select parties on the grounds of policies and issues. Voters are not always the rational and well-informed creatures that this model suggests. They can be influenced by a range of 'irrational' factors, such as the personalities of leaders, the images of parties, habitual allegiances and social conditioning.

Second, even if voters are influenced by policies, it is likely that they will be attracted by certain **manifesto** commitments, but be less interested in, or perhaps opposed to, others. A vote for a party cannot therefore be taken to be an endorsement of its entire manifesto or, indeed, of any single election promise. Third, the doctrine imposes a straitjacket. It limits government policies to those positions and proposals that the party took up during the election, and leaves no

Focus on . . .
Referendums: for or against?

A referendum is a vote in which the electorate can express a view on a particular issue of public policy. It differs from an election in that the latter is essentially a means of filling a public office and does not provide a direct or reliable method of influencing the content of policy. The referendum is therefore a device of direct democracy (see p. 92). It is typically used not to replace representative institutions, but to supplement them. Referendums may be either advisory or binding; they may also raise issues for discussion (initiatives), or be used to decide policy questions (propositions or plebiscites).

Amongst the advantages of referendums are the following:

- They check the power of elected governments, ensuring that they stay in line with public opinion.
- They promote political participation, thus helping to create a more educated and better-informed electorate.

- They strengthen legitimacy by providing the public with a way of expressing their views about specific issues.
- They provide a means either of settling major constitutional questions, or of gauging public opinion on issues not raised in elections because major parties agree on them.

The disadvantages of referendums include the following:

- They leave political decisions in the hands of those who have the least education and experience, and are most susceptible to media and other influences.
- They provide, at best, only a snapshot of public opinion at one point in time.
- They allow politicians to manipulate the political agenda and absolve themselves of responsibility for making difficult decisions.
- They tend to simplify and distort political issues, reducing them to questions that have a yes/no answer.

scope to adjust policies in the light of changing circumstances. What guidance do mandates offer in the event of, say, international or economic crises? Finally (as discussed in the next main section of this chapter), the doctrine of the mandate can be applied only in the case of majoritarian electoral systems, and its use even there may appear absurd if the winning party fails to gain 50 per cent of the popular vote.

Resemblance model

● **Microcosm**: Literally, a little world; a miniature version of a larger body, but exact in its features and proportions.

● **Descriptive representation**: A model of representation that takes account of politicians' social and other characteristics, usually based on the idea that they should be a 'representative sample' of the larger society.

The final theory of representation is based less on the manner in which representatives are selected than on whether they typify or resemble the group they claim to represent. This notion is embodied in the idea of a 'representative cross-section', as used by market researchers and opinion pollsters. By this standard, a representative government would constitute a **microcosm** of the larger society, containing members drawn from all groups and sections in society (in terms of social class, gender, age and so on), and in numbers that are proportional to the size of the groups in society at large. The idea of **descriptive representation**, or as it has been called 'microcosmic representation', has traditionally been endorsed by socialist, feminist and other radical thinkers. They argue that the 'under-representation' of groups such as the working class, women and racial

Joseph Schumpeter (1883–1950)

Moravian-born US economist and sociologist. Following an early academic career and a brief spell as Minister of Finance in post-First-World-War Austria, Schumpeter became professor of economics at Harvard University in 1932. His economic thought, developed in *Theory of Economic Development* (1912) and *Business Cycles* (1939), centred on the long-term dynamics of the capitalist system and in particular the role of 'risk-loving' entrepreneurs. In *Capitalism, Socialism and Democracy* (1942), Schumpeter drew on economic, sociological and political theories to advance the famous contention that western capitalism was, impelled by its very success, evolving into a form of socialism.

minorities at senior levels in key institutions ensures that their interests are marginalized, or ignored altogether.

The resemblance model suggests that only people who come from a particular group, and have shared the experiences of that group, can fully identify with its interests. This is the difference between 'putting oneself in the shoes of another' and having direct and personal experience of what other people go through. A 'new man' or a 'pro-feminist' male may, for instance, sympathize with women's interests and support the principle of gender equality, but will never take women's problems as seriously as women do themselves, because they are not his problems. On the other hand, the idea that representatives should resemble the represented undoubtedly causes a number of difficulties.

One of these is that this model portrays representation in exclusive or narrow terms, believing that only a woman can represent women, only a black person can represent other black people, only a member of the working class can represent the working classes and so on. If all representatives simply advanced the interests of the groups from which they come, the result would be social division and conflict, with no one being able to defend the common good or advance a broader public interest. Moreover, a government that is a microcosm of society would reflect that society's weaknesses as well as its strengths. What would be the advantage, for example, of government resembling society if the majority of the population are apathetic, ill-informed and poorly educated? Finally, the microcosmic ideal can be achieved only by imposing powerful constraints on electoral choice and individual freedom. In the name of representation, political parties may be forced to select quotas of female and minority candidates, constituencies may be set aside for candidates from particular backgrounds, or, more dramatically, the electorate might have to be classified on the basis of class, gender, race and so on, and only be allowed to vote for candidates from their own group.

ELECTIONS

Although controversy continues to rage about the nature of representation, there is one point of universal agreement: the representative process is intrinsically linked to elections and voting. Elections may not, in themselves, be a sufficient condition for political representation but, in modern circumstances, there is little doubt that they are a necessary condition. Indeed, some thinkers have gone further and portrayed elections as the very heart of democracy. This was the view developed by Joseph Schumpeter (see p. 202) in *Capitalism, Socialism and Democracy* (1942), which portrayed democracy as an 'institutional arrangement', as a means of filling public office by a competitive struggle for the people's vote. As he put it, 'democracy means only that the people have the opportunity of accepting or refusing the men [*sic*] who are to rule them'. In interpreting democracy as nothing more than a political method, Schumpeter, in effect, identified it with elections, and specifically with competitive elections. While few modern democratic theorists are prepared to reduce democracy simply to competitive elections, most nevertheless follow Schumpeter in understanding democratic government in terms of the rules and mechanisms that guide the conduct of elections. This focuses attention on the very different forms that elections can take.

First, which offices or posts are subject to the elective principle? Although elections are widely used to fill those public offices whose holders have policy-making responsibilities (the legislature and executive, in particular), key political institutions are sometimes treated as exceptions. This applies, for instance, to the second chambers of legislature in states such as the UK and Canada, and where constitutional monarchs still serve as heads of state. Second, who is entitled to vote, how widely is the franchise drawn? As pointed out, restrictions on the right to vote based on factors such as property ownership, education, gender and racial origin have been abandoned in most countries. Nevertheless, there may be informal restrictions, as in the practice in most US states of leaving electoral registration entirely in the hands of the citizen, with the result that non-registration and non-voting are widespread. On the other hand, in Australia, Belgium and Italy, for instance, voting is compulsory (see p. 204).

Third, how are votes cast? Although public voting was the norm in the USSR until 1989, and it is still widely practised in small organizations in the form of a show of hands, modern political elections are generally held on the basis of a secret ballot (sometimes called an 'Australian ballot', as it was first used in South Australia in 1856). The secret ballot is usually seen as the guarantee of a 'fair' election, in that it keeps the dangers of corruption and intimidation at bay. Nevertheless, electoral fairness cannot simply be reduced to the issue of how people vote. It is also affected by the voters' access to reliable and balanced information, the range of choice they are offered, the circumstances under which campaigning is carried out, and, finally, how scrupulously the vote is counted.

Fourth, are elections competitive or non-competitive? This is usually seen as the most crucial of distinctions, as, until the 1990s, only about half of the countries that used elections offered their electorates a genuine choice of both candidates and parties. Single-candidate elections, for example, were the rule in orthodox communist states. This meant that public office was effectively filled through a nomination process dominated by the communist party. Electoral competition is a highly complex and often controversial issue. It concerns not merely the right of people to stand for election and the ability of political parties to nominate candidates and campaign legally, but also broader factors that affect party performance, such as their sources of funding and their access to the media. From this point of view, the nature of the party system may be as crucial

Debating...
Should voting be compulsory?

In 2005, some 33 countries operated a system of compulsory voting for some or all elected bodies, although only in a minority of cases was this enforced through the threat of punishment (usually by a small fine, or community service). However, while some argue that compulsory voting strengthens democracy, even seeing it as a civic duty, others point out that 'non-voting' is a basic civil right, whose infringement may make a mockery of the democratic process.

YES	NO

YES

Increased participation. The almost certain consequence of introducing compulsory voting would be that turnout rates will increase. Voter turnout in Australia has thus been consistently around 94–96 per cent since the introduction of nationwide compulsory voting in 1924, having previously been as low as 47 per cent. Compulsory voting would, at a stroke, resolve the 'participation crises' that afflict so many mature democracies, in the process counteracting longer-term trends against voting in modern, individualized and consumerist societies.

Greater legitimacy. Governments formed on the basis of compulsory voting would be much more likely to rest on a popular majority (a majority of those eligible to vote), not just an electoral majority (a majority of those who actually vote). Declining turnout in the UK's non-compulsory system meant that, in 2005, the Labour Party was able to gain a comfortable parliamentary majority with the support of just 22 per cent of the electorate. Compulsory voting would therefore strengthen democratic legitimacy and ensure that governments do not neglect sections of society that are less active politically.

Civic duty. Citizenship is based on reciprocal rights and responsibilities. The right to vote therefore involves a duty to exercise that right, and legal compulsion simply ensures that that duty is fulfilled (treating it like paying taxes, jury service and (possibly) military conscription). Moreover, enforcing the responsibility to vote has educational benefits, in that it will stimulate political activism and create a better informed citizenry.

Countering social disadvantage. Voluntary voting effectively disadvantages the most vulnerable elements in society, the poor and less-educated – those who are, as research consistently shows, least likely to vote. Non-compulsion therefore means that the interests of the educated, articulate and better-off prevail over those of other groups. Genuine political equality requires not only that all *can* vote, but that all *do* vote. Only then can political equality serve the interests of social equality.

NO

Abuse of freedom. Compulsion, even in the name of democracy, remains compulsion: a violation of individual freedom. The right *not* to vote may, in some senses, be as important as the right to choose for whom to vote. Non-voting may thus be a conscientious act, a product of rational and considered reflection, an attempt to draw attention to, amongst other things, the lack of choice among mainstream political parties or, perhaps, to express a principled rejection of the political system itself.

Cosmetic democracy. Compulsory voting addresses the symptoms of the problem but not the cause. Making voting compulsory would undoubtedly increase the electoral turnout, but it would not address the deeper problems that account for a growing decline in civic engagement. Higher turnout levels brought about through compulsion may therefore simply mask deeper problems, making it less likely, rather than more likely, that issues such as the decline in trust in politicians, and a lack of effective responsiveness and accountability, will be properly addressed.

Worthless votes. Generally, those who do not vote have the least interest in and understanding of politics. Forcing would-be non-voters to vote would therefore simply increase the number of random and unthinking votes that are cast. This may particularly be the case when some voters, because they only turn up through a fear of punishment, may feel resentful and aggrieved. This is an especially worrying prospect as such 'worthless' votes may, ultimately, determine the outcome of an election.

Distorted political focus. A final problem with compulsory voting is that it may distort the strategies adopted by political parties. Instead of focusing on the interests of the mass of the electorate, parties may be encouraged to frame policies designed to attract more volatile 'marginal' voters (that is, would-be non-voters), thereby leading to a decline in coherence and an increase in polarization.

to the maintenance of genuine competition as are rules about who can stand and who can vote. Finally, how is the election conducted? As will be discussed later, there is a bewildering variety of electoral systems, each of which has its own particular political and constitutional implications.

Functions of elections

Because of the different kinds of elections, and the variety of electoral systems, generalization about the roles or functions of elections is always difficult. Nevertheless, the advance of democratization (see p. 272) in the 1980s and 1990s, stimulated in part by the collapse of communism, has usually been associated with the adoption of liberal-democratic electoral systems, characterized by universal suffrage, the secret ballot and electoral competition. The significance of such systems is, however, more difficult to determine. As Harrop and Miller (1987) explained, there are two contrasting views of the function of competitive elections.

The conventional view is that elections are a mechanism through which politicians can be called to account and forced to introduce policies that somehow reflect public opinion. This emphasizes the bottom-up functions of elections: political recruitment, representation, making government, influencing policy and so on. On the other hand, a radical view of elections, developed by theorists such as Ginsberg (1982), portrays them as a means through which governments and political elites can exercise control over their populations, making them more quiescent, malleable and, ultimately, governable. This view emphasizes top-down functions: building legitimacy, shaping public opinion and strengthening elites. In reality, however, elections have no single character; they are neither simply mechanisms of public accountability, nor a means of ensuring political control. Like all channels of political communication, elections are a 'two-way street' that provides the government and the people, the elite and the masses, with the opportunity to influence one another. The central functions of elections include the following:

- **Recruiting politicians**: In democratic states, elections are the principal source of political recruitment, taking account also of the processes through which parties nominate candidates. Politicians thus tend to possess talents and skills that are related to electioneering, such as charisma (see p. 83), oratorical skills and good looks, not necessarily those that suit them to carrying out constituency duties, serving on committees, running government departments and so on. Elections are typically not used to fill posts that require specialist knowledge or experience, such as those in the civil service or judiciary.
- **Making governments**: Elections make governments directly only in states such as the USA, France and Venezuela, in which the political executive is directly elected. In the more common parliamentary systems, elections influence the formation of governments, most strongly when the electoral system tends to give a single party a clear parliamentary majority. The use of proportional representation (see p. 207) may mean that governments are formed through post-election deals, and that governments can be made and unmade without the need for an election.

- **Providing representation**: When they are fair and competitive, elections are a means through which demands are channelled from the public to the government. Short of the use of initiatives and the recall, however, the electorate has no effective means of ensuring that mandates are carried out, apart from its capacity to inflict punishment at the next election. Moreover, nowhere do elected governments constitute a microcosm of the larger society.
- **Influencing policy**: Elections certainly deter governments from pursuing radical and deeply unpopular policies; however, only in exceptional cases, when a single issue dominates the election campaign, can they be said to influence policy directly. It can also be argued that the range of policy options outlined in elections is typically so narrow that the result can be of only marginal policy significance. Others suggest that government policy is, in any case, shaped more by practical dictates, such as the state of the economy, than it is by electoral considerations.
- **Educating voters**: The process of campaigning provides the electorate with an abundance of information, about parties, candidates, policies, the current government's record, the political system and so on. However, this leads to education only if the information that is provided, and the way it is provided, engages public interest and stimulates debate, as opposed to apathy and alienation. As candidates and parties seek to persuade, rather than to educate, they also have a strong incentive to provide incomplete and distorted information.
- **Building legitimacy**: One reason why even authoritarian regimes bother to hold elections, even if they are non-competitive, is that elections help to foster legitimacy (see p. 81) by providing justification for a system of rule. This happens because the ritual involved in campaigning somehow confers on an election a ceremonial status and importance. Most importantly, by encouraging citizens to participate in politics, even in the limited form of voting, elections mobilize active consent.
- **Strengthening elites**: Elections can also be a vehicle through which elites can manipulate and control the masses. This possibility encouraged Proudhon (see p. 381) to warn that 'universal suffrage is counter-revolution'. Political discontent and opposition can be neutralized by elections that channel them in a constitutional direction, and allow governments to come and go while the regime itself survives. Elections are particularly effective in this respect because, at the same time, they give citizens the impression that they are exercising power over the government.

Electoral systems: debates and controversies

An electoral system is a set of rules that governs the conduct of elections. Not only do these rules vary across the world; they are also, in many countries, the subject of fierce political debate and argument. These rules vary in a number of ways:

- Voters may be asked to choose between candidates or between parties.
- Voters may either select a single candidate, or vote preferentially, ranking the candidates they wish to support in order.

CONCEPT

Proportional representation

Proportional representation is the principle that parties should be represented in an assembly or parliament in direct proportion to their overall electoral strength, their percentage of seats equalling their percentage of votes. The term is generally used to refer not to a single method of election but to a variety of electoral mechanisms, those able to secure proportional outcomes, or at least a high and reliable degree of proportionality. The best known PR systems are the party-list system, the single-transferable-vote system and the additional member system.

- The electorate may or may not be grouped into electoral units or constituencies.
- Constituencies may return a single member or a number of members.
- The level of support needed to elect a candidate varies from a **plurality** to an overall or 'absolute' majority, or a quota of some kind.

For general purposes, however, the systems available can be divided into two broad categories on the basis of how they convert votes into seats. On the one hand, there are majoritarian systems, in which larger parties typically win a higher proportion of seats than the proportion of votes they gain in the election. This increases the chances of a single party gaining a parliamentary majority and being able to govern on its own. In the UK, for example, single-party government prevailed between 1945 and 2010 despite the fact that no party achieved an electoral majority during this period. On the other hand, there are proportional systems, which guarantee an equal (or, at least, more equal) relationship between the seats won by a party and the votes gained in the election. In a pure system of proportional representation (PR), a party that gains 45 per cent of the votes would win exactly 45 per cent of the seats. PR systems therefore make single-party majority rule less likely, and are commonly associated with multiparty systems and coalition government. The electoral systems described in the following Focus boxes range from the most majoritarian type of system to the purest type of proportional system.

Although in some countries the electoral system provokes little debate or interest, in others it is an issue of pressing political and constitutional significance. France, for instance, has changed its electoral system so many times that any statement about it runs the risk of being out of date. The second ballot (see p. 209) was abandoned for parliamentary elections in 1985, when France switched to a regional-list system (see p. 213), but it was reintroduced for the 1993 election. In the UK, although the majoritarian single-member plurality (SMP) system (see p. 208) continues to be used for general elections, since 1999 a number of more proportional systems have been introduced for elections to the devolved bodies in Scotland, Wales and Northern Ireland, the Greater London Authority and the European Parliament. The confusing thing about the electoral reform debate is that the shifts that have occurred reflect no consistent pattern. In 1993, while New Zealand adopted proportional representation in place of the SMP system (see p. 214), Italy moved in the opposite direction, replacing the party list with the less proportional additional member system (see p. 211), before, in 2005, returning to the list system.

Electoral systems attract attention, in part, because they have a crucial impact on party performance and, particularly, on their prospects of winning (or, at least, sharing) power. It would be foolish, then, to deny that attitudes towards the electoral system are shaped largely by party advantage. President Mitterrand's twists and turns in France in the 1980s and 1990s were dictated mainly by his desire to strengthen Socialist representation in the National Assembly. Similarly, the UK Labour Party's interest in electoral reform since the 1980s has waxed and waned according to whether it appeared that the party could win under SMP rules. The party's conversion to PR for devolved bodies and its commitment in 1997 to holding a referendum on electoral reform for the House of Commons were, in part, a consequence of spending 18 years in opposition. It is notable that Labour's

- **Plurality**: The largest number out of a collection of numbers, not necessarily an absolute majority (50 per cent or more of all the numbers combined).

Focus on . . .

Electoral systems: single-member plurality (SMP) system ('first past the post')

Used: The UK (House of Commons), the USA, Canada and India, for example. **Type**: Majoritarian.

Features:
- The country is divided into single-member constituencies, usually of equal size.
- Voters select a single candidate, usually marking his or her name with a cross on the ballot paper.
- The winning candidate needs only to achieve a plurality of votes (the 'first past the post' rule).

Advantages:
- The system establishes a clear link between representatives and constituents, ensuring that constituency duties are carried out.
- It offers the electorate a clear choice of potential parties of government.
- It allows governments to be formed that have a clear mandate from the electorate, albeit often on the basis of plurality support amongst the electorate.
- It keeps extremism at bay by making it more difficult for small radical parties to gain seats and credibility.
- It makes for strong and effective government in that a single party usually has majority control of the assembly.

- It produces stable government, in that single-party governments rarely collapse as a result of disunity and internal friction.

Disadvantages:
- The system 'wastes' many (perhaps most) votes, those cast for losing candidates and those cast for winning ones over the plurality mark.
- It distorts electoral preferences by 'under-representing' small parties and ones with geographically evenly distributed support (the 'third-party effect').
- It offers only limited choice because of its duopolistic (two-major-parties) tendencies.
- It undermines the legitimacy of government, in that governments often enjoy only minority support, producing a system of plurality rule.
- It creates instability because a change in government can lead to a radical shift of policies and direction.
- It leads to unaccountable government in that the legislature is usually subordinate to the executive, because the majority of its members are supporters of the governing party.
- It discourages the selection of a socially broad spread of candidates in favour of those who are attractive to a large body of voters.

landslide victories in 1997 and 2001 coincided with declining interest in the party in changing Westminster elections. However, other less cynical and more substantial considerations need to be taken into account. The problem, though, is that there is no such thing as a 'best electoral system'.

The electoral reform debate is, at heart, a debate about the desirable nature of government and the principles that underpin 'good' government. Is representative government, for instance, more important than effective government? Is a bias in favour of compromise and consensus preferable to one that favours conviction and principle? These are normative questions that do not permit objective answers. Moreover, in view of the complex role they play, elections can be judged according to a diverse range of criteria, which not uncommonly contradict one another. Electoral systems therefore merit only a qualified

Focus on . . .

Electoral systems: second ballot system

Used: Traditionally in France, but it is used for presidential elections in countries such as Austria, Chile and Russia. **Type**: Majoritarian.

Features:

- There are single-candidate constituencies and single-choice voting, as in the single-member plurality (SMP) system.
- To win on the first ballot, a candidate needs an overall majority of the votes cast.
- If no candidate gains a first-ballot majority, a second, run-off ballot is held between the leading two candidates.

Advantages:

- The system broadens electoral choice: voters can vote with their hearts for their preferred candidate

in the first ballot, and with their heads for the least-bad candidate in the second.

- As candidates can win only with majority support, they are encouraged to make their appeal as broad as possible.
- Strong and stable government is possible, as with SMP systems.

Disadvantages:

- As the system is little more proportional than the SMP system, it distorts preferences and is unfair to 'third' parties.
- Run-off candidates are encouraged to abandon their principles in search of short-term popularity, or as a result of deals with defeated candidates.
- The holding of a second ballot may strain the electorate's patience and interest in politics.

endorsement, reflecting a balance of advantages over disadvantages and their strength relative to other systems. These criteria fall into two general categories: those related to the quality of representation, and those linked to the effectiveness of government.

Majoritarian systems are usually thought to be at their weakest when they are evaluated in terms of their representative functions. To a greater or lesser extent, each majoritarian system distorts popular preferences, in the sense that party representation is not commensurate with electoral strength. This is most glaringly apparent in their 'unfairness' to small parties and parties with evenly distributed geographical support, and their 'over-fairness' in relation to large parties and those with geographically concentrated support. For example, in 2010 in the UK, the Conservative Party gained 47 per cent of the parliamentary seats with 36 per cent of the vote, the Labour Party won 40 per cent of the seats with 29 per cent of the vote, and the Liberal Democrats gained merely 9 per cent representation with 23 per cent of the vote. Such biases are impossible to justify in representative terms, especially since the unfortunate 'third' parties are often centrist parties, and not the extremist parties of popular image.

Two-party systems and single-party government are thus 'manufactured' by the majoritarian bias of the electoral system, and do not reflect the distribution of popular preferences. Moreover, the fact that parties can come to power with barely two-fifths of the popular vote (in 2005 in the UK, for example, the Labour Party gained a House of Commons majority with 35.3 per cent of the vote) strains the legitimacy of the entire political system, and creates circumstances in which radical,

Focus on . . .

Electoral systems: alternative vote (AV) system; supplementary vote (SV)

Used: Australia (House of Representatives (AV)), and the UK (London mayor (SV)). **Type:** Majoritarian.

Features:

- There are single-member constituencies.
- There is preferential voting. In AV, voters rank the candidates in order of preference: 1 for their first preference, 2 for their second preference and so on. In SV, there is only a single 'supplementary' vote.
- Winning candidates must gain 50 per cent of all the votes cast.
- Votes are counted according to the first preferences. If no candidate reaches 50 per cent, the bottom candidate is eliminated and his or her votes are redistributed according to the second (or subsequent) preferences. This continues until one candidate has a majority. In SV, all candidates drop out except the top two.

Advantages:

- Fewer votes are 'wasted' than in the SMP system.
- Unlike the second-ballot system, the outcome cannot be influenced by deals made between candidates.
- Although winning candidates must secure at least 50 per cent support, single-party majority government is not ruled out.

Disadvantages:

- The system is not much more proportional than the SMP system, and so is still biased in favour of large parties.
- The outcome may be determined by the preferences of those who support small, possibly extremist, parties.
- Winning candidates may enjoy little first-preference support, and have only the virtue of being the least unpopular candidate available.

ideologically-driven parties can remain in power for prolonged periods under little pressure to broaden their appeal. The Conservatives in the UK were thus able to implement a programme of market-orientated reforms in the 1980s and 1990s while never gaining more than 43 per cent of support in general elections. When the majority of voters oppose the party in power, it is difficult to claim that that party has a popular mandate for anything.

Looked at in this light, proportional electoral systems seem to be manifestly more representative. Nevertheless, it may be naive simply to equate electoral fairness with **proportionality**. For instance, much of the criticism of PR systems stems from the fact that they make coalition government (see p. 239) much more likely. Although it can be argued that, unlike single-party governments, coalitions enjoy the support of at least 50 per cent of the electors, their policies are typically thrashed out in post-election deals, and thus are not endorsed by any set of electors. An additional danger is that parties within a coalition government may not exert influence in line with their electoral strength. The classic example of this is when small centre parties (such as the Free Democrats in Germany) can dictate to larger parties (for example, the CDU or the SPD in Germany) by threatening to switch their support to another party. Then, in effect, 'the tail wags the dog'.

The defence of majoritarian systems is more commonly based on government functions, and specifically on the capacity of such systems to deliver stable

● **Proportionality:** The degree to which the allocation of seats amongst parties reflects the distribution of the popular vote.

Focus on . . .

Electoral systems: mixed-member proportional (MMP) system; additional member system (AMS)

Used: Germany, Italy, New Zealand and the UK (Scottish Parliament and Welsh Assembly).
Type: Proportional.

Features:

- A proportion of seats (50 per cent in Germany, but more in Italy, Scotland and Wales, for instance) are filled by the SMP system using single-member constituencies.
- The remaining seats are filled using the party-list system (see p. 213).
- Electors cast two votes: one for a candidate in the constituency election, and the other for a party.

Advantages:

- The hybrid nature of this system balances the need for constituency representation against the need for electoral fairness. The party-list process ensures that the whole assembly is proportionally representative.
- Although the system is broadly proportional in terms of its outcome, it keeps alive the possibility of single-party government.

- It allows electors to choose a constituency representative from one party and yet support another party to form a government.
- It takes account of the fact that representing constituents and holding ministerial office are very different jobs that require very different talents and experience.

Disadvantages:

- The retention of single-member constituencies prevents the achievement of high levels of proportionality.
- The system creates two classes of representative, one burdened by insecurity and constituency duties, the other having higher status and the prospect of holding ministerial office.
- Constituency representation suffers because of the size of constituencies (generally, twice as large as in SMP systems).
- Parties become more centralized and powerful under this system, as they decide not only who has the security of being on the list and who has to fight constituencies, but also where on the list candidates are placed.

and effective rule. In other words, a lack of proportionality may simply be the price that is paid for strong government. In these systems, the bias in favour of single-party rule means that the electorate can usually choose between two parties, each of which has the capacity to deliver on its election promises by translating its manifesto commitments into a programme of government. Supported by a cohesive majority in the assembly, such governments are usually able to survive for a full term in office. In contrast, coalition governments are weak and unstable, in the sense that they are endlessly engaged in a process of reconciling opposing views, and are always liable to collapse as a result of internal splits and divisions. The classic example here is post-1945 Italy which, up to 2012, had had no fewer than 63 governments.

Supporters of PR argue, on the other hand, that having a strong government, in the sense of a government that is able to push through policies, is by no means an unqualified virtue, tending as it does to restrict scrutiny and parliamentary accountability. Instead, they suggest that 'strong' government should be understood

Focus on . . .

Electoral systems: single-transferable-vote (STV) system

Used: The Republic of Ireland and the UK (Northern Ireland Assembly). **Type**: Proportional.

Features:

- There are multimember constituencies, each of which usually returns between three and eight members.
- Parties may put forward as many candidates as there are seats to fill.
- Electors vote preferentially, as in the alternative vote system.
- Candidates are elected, if they achieve a quota. This is the minimum number of votes needed to elect the stipulated number of candidates, calculated according to the Droop formula:

$$\text{quota } 5 \ \frac{\text{total number of votes cast}}{(\text{number of seats to be filled} + 1)} + 1$$

For example, if 100,000 votes are cast in a constituency that elects four members, the quota is 100,000/(4 + 1) + 1 = 20,001.

- The votes are counted according to first preferences. If not all the seats are filled, the bottom candidate is eliminated. His or her votes are redistributed according to second preferences and so on, until all the seats have been filled.

Advantages:

- The system is capable of achieving highly proportional outcomes.
- Competition amongst candidates from the same party means that they can be judged on their records and on where they stand on issues that cut across party lines.
- The availability of several members means that constituents can choose to whom to take their grievances.

Disadvantages:

- The degree of proportionality achieved varies, largely on the basis of the party system.
- Strong and stable single-party government is unlikely.
- Intra-party competition may be divisive, and may allow members to evade their constituency responsibilities.

in terms of popular support, and the willingness of citizens to obey and respect the government. Broadly-based coalitions may possess these qualities in greater abundance than do single-party governments. By the same token, 'stable' government could mean a consistent development of government policies over a number of governments, rather than a government with the ability to survive for a single electoral term. This is more likely to be achieved by coalition governments (in which one or more parties may remain in power over a number of governments, albeit reshuffled) than by single-party governments, in which more sweeping changes in personnel and priorities are unavoidable when power changes hands.

The electoral reform debate, however, constantly risks overestimating the importance of electoral systems. In practice, elections are only one amongst a variety of factors that shape the political process, and may not be the most crucial. Indeed, the impact of particular electoral systems is conditioned largely by other circumstances; namely, the political culture, the nature of the party system, and the economic and social context within which politics is conducted. Generalizations about the nature of coalition government are always highly

Focus on . . .
Electoral systems: party-list system

Used: Israel, and in countries throughout Europe, including Belgium, Luxembourg and Switzerland, and the European Parliament. **Type**: Proportional.

Features:
- Either the entire country is treated as a single constituency, or, in the case of regional party lists, there are a number of large multimember constituencies.
- Parties compile lists of candidates to place before the electorate, in descending order of preference.
- Electors vote for parties, not for candidates.
- Parties are allocated seats in direct proportion to the votes they gain in the election. They fill these seats from their party list.
- A 'threshold' may be imposed (5 per cent in Germany) to exclude small, possibly extremist, parties from representation.

Advantages:
- This is the only potentially pure system of proportional representation, and is therefore fair to all parties.
- The system promotes unity by encouraging electors to identify with their nation or region, rather than with a constituency.
- The system makes it easier for women and minority candidates to be elected, provided, of course, they feature on the party list.
- The representation of a large number of small parties ensures that there is an emphasis upon negotiation, bargaining and consensus.

Disadvantages:
- The existence of many small parties can lead to weak and unstable government.
- The link between representatives and constituencies is entirely broken.
- Unpopular candidates who are well-placed on a party list cannot be removed from office.
- Parties become heavily centralized, because leaders draw up party lists, and junior members have an incentive to be loyal in the hope of moving up the list.

suspect, for instance. Whereas coalitions in Italy have typically been weak and short-lived, in Germany they have usually produced stable and effective government. Similarly, although majoritarian systems can produce significant shifts in policy as one government follows another, broad policy consensuses are also not uncommon. In the 1950s and 1960s, despite an alternation in power between the Conservative and the Labour parties, UK government policy displayed a remarkable consistency of policy direction, rooted in a cross-party commitment to Keynesian social democracy. Furthermore, it is far from clear what damage electoral systems can cause. Despite Italy's famed political instability, often blamed on its now-abandoned party-list electoral system, in the post-World War II period the north of the country at least experienced steady economic growth, making Italy, by the 1990s, the third most prosperous state in the EU.

What do elections mean?

The importance of elections cannot be doubted. At the very least, they provide the public with its clearest formal opportunity to influence the political process, and also help, directly or indirectly, to determine who will hold government

POLITICS IN ACTION . . .

Electoral reform in New Zealand: politics renewed?

Events: In a non-binding referendum in New Zealand in 1992, 85 per cent of electors voted to change the established single-member plurality (SMP) electoral system, (popularly known as 'first past the post') with 71 per cent of voters backing the mixed-member proportional (MMP) system as their preferred alternative. In a binding second referendum the following year, MMP gained the support of 54 per cent in a straight contest against SMP. The first election using MMP was held in 1996, and it has been used in each of the subsequent elections. The issue of electoral reform had gained growing prominence in New Zealand after two successive elections (in 1978 and 1981) had been won by the 'wrong' party (the National Party won parliamentary majorities even though the Labour Party gained more votes). Other factors included growing discontent with the electoral system amongst Labour supporters, due to the National Party being in power for all but six years during 1949–84, and the belief that proportional representation would boost Maori representation.

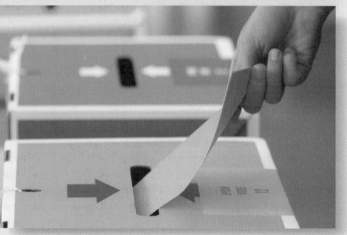

Significance: Has electoral reform in New Zealand been a success? As ever with electoral reform, the debate turns on how 'success' is defined. Supporters of electoral reform have argued that MMP in New Zealand has brought about greater responsiveness and accountability. The clearest evidence of this has been a significant widening of the representation of parties, both in the House of Representatives and in government. The Labour-National two-party system has undoubtedly been broken, giving way to a multiparty system. The average number of parties represented in the House under MMP has increased from 2.4 during the period 1946–93 to 7. Most tellingly, since reform, neither National nor Labour has been able to govern alone on the basis of a parliamentary majority. The succession of coalition governments that has resulted from reform has shifted the focus of New Zealand politics away from simple rivalry between National and Labour towards a more complex process of consensus-building, as both major parties look to forge alliances with smaller parties. After the 2011 election, for instance, National formed a coalition government through an agreement with ACT, United Future and the Maori Party. Moreover, since 1996, New Zealand governments have been minority governments for all but two years, a situation that allows parties outside of government, such as the Green Party, to exert a measure of policy influence.

However, criticisms of MMP continue to be voiced in New Zealand, not least by the National Party, which remains committed to a return to SMP. Critics claim that the two-vote system causes voter confusion and leads to the 'contamination effect', whereby views about constituency candidates affect the distribution of party-list votes. It is also far from clear that the introduction of MMP has had a beneficial impact on voter turnout, the second election under MMP, in 1999, having recorded the lowest turnout of any twentieth-century New Zealand election. Two, deeper concerns about MMP continue to be voiced, however. First, MMP has been portrayed as the enemy of strong government, in that, being divided, coalition governments are often unable to deliver decisive leader-ship. Second, misgivings have been expressed about the power of so-called 'pivotal parties', small parties whose policy influence greatly exceeds their electoral strength because they are able to do deals with both major parties. Concerns such as these encouraged National to call a further electoral reform referendum which coincided with the 2011 general election and offered voters a straight choice between MMP and a return to SMP. However, the resulting 58 per cent in favour of keeping MMP (a 4 per cent increase on the vote in 1993) indicated broad satis-faction with the new system and suggests that it is unlikely to be abandoned in the near future.

CONCEPT

Public interest

The public interest consists of the general or collective interests of a community; that is, that which is good for society as a whole. Two contrasting notions of the public interest can be identified. Strong versions distinguish clearly between the interests of the public as a collective body and the selfish or personal interests of each individual. In the view of Rousseau and many socialists, the interests of the public are 'higher' than, or morally superior to, those of the individual. Weak versions recognize only private interests, and therefore see the public interest as nothing more than the sum of private interests.

power. From this perspective, elections are about results – in other words, who wins and who loses. This view is encouraged by media coverage, which, with the aid of opinion polls, increasingly turns elections into horseraces. Nevertheless, politicians are not backward in claiming that elections have a broader and more profound meaning. Elections are, in this sense, seen as nothing less than a visible manifestation of the public interest; in short, 'the public has spoken'. Political commentators also express their opinions, proclaiming, for instance, that elections reflect a 'shift in the popular mood'. The problem, however, is that all such claims and interpretations have a strongly arbitrary character; any attempt to invest an election with 'meaning' is fraught with dangers. The people may have spoken, but it is frustratingly difficult to know what they have said.

Many of these problems stem from the difficult notion of the 'public interest'. If such a thing as a 'public' interest exists, it surely reflects the common or collective interests of all citizens. This is precisely what Rousseau (see p. 97) implied in the idea of the 'general will', which he understood to mean the will of all citizens, provided each of them acts selflessly. The difficulty with this view is obvious. Quite simply, individuals do not, in practice, act selflessly in accordance with a general or collective will; there is no such thing as an indivisible public interest. All generalizations about 'the public' or 'the electorate' must therefore be treated with grave suspicion. There is no electorate as such, only a collection of electors who each possess particular interests, sympathies, allegiances and so on. At best, election results reflect the preferences of a majority, or perhaps a plurality, of voters. However, even then there are perhaps insuperable problems in deciding what these votes 'mean'.

The difficulty in interpreting election results lies in the perhaps impossible task of knowing why voters vote as they do. As is made clear in the next section, generations of political scientists have grappled with the question of electoral behaviour, but have failed to develop a universally accepted theory of voting. Voting, on the surface a very simple act, is shaped by a complex of factors, conscious and unconscious, rational and irrational, selfish and selfless. All theories are therefore partial and must be qualified by a range of other considerations. This can be seen in relation to the so-called 'economic theory of democracy', advanced by Anthony Downs (1957). This theory suggests that the act of voting reflects an expression of self-interest on the part of voters, who select parties in much the same way as consumers select goods or services for purchase. On this basis, the winning party in an election can reasonably claim that its policies most closely correspond to the interests of the largest group of voters.

On the other hand, it can be argued that, rather than 'buying' policies, voters are typically poorly-informed about political issues and are influenced by a range of 'irrational' factors such as habit, social conditioning, the image of the parties and the personalities of their leaders. Moreover, the ability of parties to attract votes may have less to do with the 'goods' they put up for purchase than with the way those goods are 'sold' through advertising, political campaigning, propaganda and so on. To the extent that this is true, election results may reflect not so much the interests of the mass of voters, as the resources and finances available to the competing parties.

A further – and, some would argue, more intractable – problem is that no elective mechanism may be able reliably to give expression to the multifarious preferences of voters. This is a problem that the US economist Kenneth Arrow described in terms of his 'impossibility theorem'. In *Social Choice and Individual Values* (1951) Arrow drew attention to the problem of 'transitivity' that occurs when voters are allowed to express a range of preferences for candidates or policy options, rather than merely cast a single vote. The drawback of casting but a single vote is not only that it is a crude all-or-nothing device, but also that no single candidate or option may gain majority support. For instance, candidate *A* may gain 40 per cent of the vote, candidate *B* 34 per cent, and candidate *C* 26 per cent. The situation could, nevertheless, become more confused if second preferences were taken into account.

Let us assume, for the sake of argument, that the second preferences of all candidate *A*'s supporters go to candidate *C*, the second preferences of candidate *B* favour candidate *A*, and the second preferences of candidate *C* go to candidate *B*. This creates a situation in which each candidate can claim to be preferred by a majority of voters. The first and second preferences for candidate *A* add up to 74 per cent (40 per cent plus *B*'s 34 per cent). Candidate *B* can claim 60 per cent support (34 per cent plus *C*'s 26 per cent), and candidate *C* can claim 66 per cent support (26 per cent plus *A*'s 40 per cent). This problem of 'cyclical majorities' draws attention to the fact that it may not be possible to establish a reliable link between individual preferences and collective choices. In other words, election results cannot speak for themselves, and politicians and political commentators who claim to find meaning in them are, to some extent, acting arbitrarily. Nevertheless, the latitude that this allows politicians is not unlimited, because they know that they will be called to account at the next election. In this light, perhaps the most significant function of elections is to set limits to arbitrary government by ensuring that politicians who claim to speak for the public must ultimately be judged by the public.

VOTING BEHAVIOUR

The growth of academic interest in voting behaviour coincided with the rise of behavioural political science. As the most widespread and quantifiable form of political behaviour, voting quickly became the focus for new techniques of sample surveying and statistical analysis. *The American Voter* (Campbell *et al.*, 1960), the product of painstaking research by the University of Michigan, became the leading work in the field and stimulated a wealth of similar studies, such as Butler and Stokes' *Political Change in Britain* (1969). At the high point of the behavioural revolution, it was thought that voting held the key to disclosing all the mysteries of the political system, perhaps allowing for laws of mass political psychology to be developed. Even though these lofty hopes have not been fulfilled, psephology (the scientific study of voting behaviour) still commands a central position in political analysis. This is because voting provides one of the richest sources of information about the interaction between individuals, society and politics. By investigating the mysteries of voting behaviour, we are thus able to learn important lessons about the nature of the political system, and gain insight into the process of social and political change.

Voting behaviour is clearly shaped by short-term and long-term influences. Short-term influences are specific to a particular election and do not allow conclusions to be drawn about voting patterns in general. The chief short-term influence is the state of the economy, which reflects the fact that there is usually a link

CONCEPT

Partisan dealignment

Partisan dealignment is a decline in the extent to which people align themselves with a party by identifying with it. This implies that the 'normal' support of parties falls, and a growing number of electors become 'floating' or 'swing' voters. As party loyalties weaken, electoral behaviour becomes more volatile, leading to greater uncertainty and, perhaps, the rise of new parties, or the decline of old ones. The principal reasons for partisan dealignment are the expansion of education, increased social mobility, and growing reliance on television as a source of political information.

between a government's popularity and economic variables such as unemployment, inflation and disposable income. Optimism about one's own material circumstances (the so-called 'feel-good' factor) appears to be particularly crucial here. Indeed, it is often alleged that governments attempt to create pre-election booms in the hope of improving their chances of gaining re-election. The chances that political and business cycles can be brought into conjunction are clearly strengthened by flexible-term elections that allow the government to choose when to 'go to the country'.

Another short-term influence on voting is the personality and public standing of party leaders. This is particularly important, because media exposure portrays leaders as the brand image of their party. This means that a party may try to rekindle popular support by replacing a leader who is perceived to be an electoral liability. Another factor is the style and effectiveness of the parties' electoral campaigning. The length of the campaign can vary from about three weeks for flexible-term elections to up to two years in the case of fixed-term elections, such as those for the US president. Opinion polls are usually thought to be significant in this respect, either giving a candidate's or party's campaign momentum, or instilling disillusionment, or even complacency, amongst voters.

A final short-term influence, the mass media (see p. 179), may also be of long-term significance if biased or partisan coverage reflects structural, and therefore continuing, factors such as press ownership. However, the pattern of media coverage may change from election to election. For instance, under Tony Blair's leadership, the UK Labour Party made concerted attempts to court the Murdoch press in particular, helping to explain the party's longest period in power, between 1997 and 2010. All such considerations, nevertheless, operate within a context of psychological, sociological, economic and ideological influences on voting. These are best examined in relation to rival models of voting. The most significant of these are the following:

- the party-identification model
- the sociological model
- the rational-choice model
- the dominant-ideology model.

Theories of voting

Party-identification model

The earliest theory of voting behaviour, the party-identification model, is based on the sense of psychological attachment that people have to parties. Electors are seen as people who identify with a party, in the sense of being long-term supporters who regard the party as 'their' party. Voting is therefore a manifestation of partisanship, not a product of calculation influenced by factors such as policies, personalities, campaigning and media coverage. This model places heavy stress on early political socialization (see p. 178), seeing the family as the principal means through which political loyalties are forged. These are then, in most cases, reinforced by group membership and later social experiences.

In this model, attitudes towards policies and leaders, as well as perceptions about group and personal interests, tend to be developed on the basis of party

CONCEPT

Class dealignment

Class dealignment is the weakening of the relationship between social class and party support. Social class may nevertheless remain a significant (even the most significant) factor influencing electoral choice. The impact of dealignment has been to undermine traditional class-based parties (notably, working class parties of the left), often bringing about a realignment of the party system. Explanations of class dealignment usually focus on changes in the social structure that have weakened the solidaristic character of class identity, such as post-industrialism.

identification. Events are thus interpreted to fit with pre-existing loyalties and attachments. This partisan alignment tends to create stability and continuity, especially in terms of habitual patterns of voting behaviour, often sustained over a lifetime. From this point of view, it should be possible to calculate the 'normal' vote of a party by reference to partisanship levels. Deviations from this 'normal' level presumably reflect the impact of short-term factors. One of the weaknesses of this model is the growing evidence from a number of countries of partisan dealignment (see p. 217). This indicates a general fall in party identification and a decline in habitual voting patterns. In the USA, partisan dealignment is reflected in a decline in the number of registered Democrats and Republicans, and a rise in the number of Independents (up from 6 per cent in 1952 to 36 per cent in 2009). In the UK, it is demonstrated by a decline in the strength of allegiance to the Conservative Party and the Labour Party, 'very strong' identification with either party having fallen from 43 per cent in 1966 to 9 per cent in 2005.

Sociological model

The sociological model links voting behaviour to group membership, suggesting that electors tend to adopt a voting pattern that reflects the economic and social position of the group to which they belong. Rather than developing a psychological attachment to a party on the basis of family influence, this model highlights the importance of a social alignment, reflecting the various divisions and tensions within society. The most significant of these divisions are class, gender, ethnicity, religion and region. Although the impact of socialization is not irrelevant to this model, social-base explanations allow for rationality insofar as group interests may help to shape party allegiances. For many analysts, the sociological model is best understood as an 'interest plus socialization' approach to voting (Denver, 2012). This has perhaps been clearest in relation to social class (see p. 153).

Not uncommonly, party systems have been seen to reflect the class system, with the middle classes providing the electoral base for right-wing parties, and the working classes providing the electoral base for left-wing parties. The Labour–Conservative two-party system in the UK was traditionally understood in precisely this light. Peter Pulzer (1967) was able to declare, famously, 'class is the basis of British party politics; all else is embellishment and detail'. The sociological model, however, has been attacked on the grounds that, in focusing on social groups, it ignores the individual and the role of personal self-interest. Moreover, there is growing empirical evidence that the link between sociological factors and party support has weakened in modern societies. In particular, attention has been paid to the phenomenon of class dealignment. Evidence of class dealignment can be found in most western societies. For example, absolute class voting (the proportion of voters who support their 'natural' class party) fell in the UK from 66 per cent in 1966 to 47 per cent in 1983. In 1997, the Labour Party, for the first time, received more votes from non-manual workers than from manual workers.

Rational-choice model

Rational-choice models of voting shift attention onto the individual, and away from socialization and the behaviour of social groups. In this view, voting is seen as a rational act, in the sense that individual electors are believed to decide their party preference on the basis of personal self-interest. Rather than being habitual, a manifestation of broader attachments and allegiances, voting is seen as essentially instrumental; that is, as a means to an end. Rational-choice models differ in that some, following the example of V. O. Key (1966), see voting as a retrospective comment on the party in power and how its performance has influenced citizen's choice. Others, such as Himmelveit *et al.*, (1985), portray voters as active, in the sense that they behave like consumers expressing a choice amongst the available policy options.

The latter view stresses the importance of what is called '**issue voting**', and suggests that parties can significantly influence their electoral performance by revising and reshaping their policies. It is generally accepted that this has been one of the consequences of partisan and class dealignment. This has also been encouraged by the pluralism and individualism that postmodernism (see p. 18) has fostered. The weakness of rational-choice theories is that they abstract the individual voter from his or her social and cultural context. In other words, to some extent, the ability to evaluate issues and calculate self-interest (the essence of instrumental voting) is structured by broader party attachments and group loyalties.

Dominant-ideology model

Radical theories of voting tend to highlight the degree to which individual choices are shaped by a process of ideological manipulation and control. In some respects, such theories resemble the sociological model, in that voting is seen to reflect a person's position in a social hierarchy. Where these theories differ from the sociological model, however, is in emphasizing that how groups and individuals interpret their position depends on how it has been presented to them through education, by the government and, above all, by the mass media. (The influence of the media on political debate and party competition is examined in greater detail in Chapter 8.)

In contrast to the earlier view that the media merely reinforce pre-existing preferences, this suggests that the media are able to distort the flow of political communications, both by setting the agenda for debate and by structuring preferences and sympathies. The consequence of this is that, if voters' attitudes conform to the tenets of a dominant ideology, parties will not be able to afford to develop policies that fall outside that ideology. In this way, far from challenging the existing distribution of power and resources in society, the electoral process tends to uphold it. The weakness of the dominant-ideology model is that, by overstating the process of social conditioning, it takes individual calculation and personal autonomy out of the picture altogether.

● **Issue voting**: Voting behaviour that is shaped by party policies and (usually) a calculation of personal self-interest.

SUMMARY

● Representation is a relationship in which an individual or group stands for, or acts on behalf of, a larger body of people. This may be achieved through the exercise of wisdom by an educated elite, through guidance or instructions given to a delegate, through the winning of a popular mandate, or through representatives being drawn from the groups they represent.

● In modern politics, representation is invariably linked with elections. Elections may not be a sufficient condition for political representation, but are certainly a necessary condition. For elections to serve representative purposes, however, they must be competitive, free and fair, and conducted on the basis of universal adult suffrage.

● Elections have a variety of functions. On the one hand, they have 'bottom-up' functions, such as political recruitment, representation, making government and influencing policy. On the other hand, radical theorists emphasize their 'top-down' functions, which include that they build legitimacy, shape public opinion and help to strengthen elites.

● Electoral systems are often classified as either majoritarian systems or proportional systems. In majoritarian systems, large parties typically win a higher proportion of seats than votes, thereby increasing the chances of single-party government. In proportional systems, there is an equal (or at least, more equal) relationship between the percentages of seats and votes won, increasing the likelihood of coalition government.

● Majoritarian systems are usually defended on the grounds that they offer the electorate a clear choice of potential governments, invest winning parties with a policy mandate, and help to promote strong and stable government. In contrast, proportional systems are defended on the grounds that they usually give government a broader electoral base, promote consensus and cooperation amongst a number of parties, and establish a healthy balance between the executive and the assembly.

● The meaning of elections is closely linked to the factors that shape voting behaviour. Amongst the various theories of voting are models that highlight the importance of party identification and habitual attachments, those that emphasize the importance of group membership and social alignment, those that are based on rational choice and calculations of self-interest, and those that suggest that individual choices are shaped by ideological manipulation and control.

Questions for discussion

● Is representation merely a substitute for democracy?

● What conditions best promote representative government?

● Are elections more significant in calling politicians to account, or in ensuring the survival of a regime?

● Is there inevitably a trade-off between electoral fairness and strong and stable government?

● Should electoral systems seek to deliver proportionality?

● Is there a 'best' electoral system?

● How successful are elections in defining the public interest?

● To what extent is voting behaviour a rational and issue-based activity?

Further reading

Birch, A. H., *The Concepts and Theories of Democracy* (3rd edn) (2007). A clear and thorough discussion of the concept of representation and the theory of representative democracy.

Farrell, D., *Electoral Systems: A Comparative Introduction* (2nd edn) (2011). A clear introduction to the six principal types of election system currently used.

Gallagher, M. and P. Mitchell (eds), *The Politics of Electoral Systems* (2008). An analysis of the operation of electoral systems in 22 states that highlights the complex relationship between electoral systems and the larger political process.

LeDuc, L., R. Niemi and P. Norris (eds), *Comparing Democracies 3: Elections and Voting in the 21st Century* (2010). A wide-ranging collection of essays that examine the nature and health of electoral democracy and the significance of electoral systems.

CHAPTER 10

Parties and Party Systems

'In politics, shared hatreds are almost always the basis of friendships.'

ALEXIS DE TOCQUEVILLE, *Democracy in America* (1835)

PREVIEW   So fundamental are political parties to the operation of modern politics that their role and significance are often taken for granted. It is forgotten, for instance, that parties are a relatively recent invention. As political machines organized to win elections and wield government power, parties came into existence only in the early nineteenth century. Now, however, they are virtually ubiquitous. The only parts of the world in which they do not exist are those where they are suppressed by dictatorship or military rule. Quite simply, the political party has become the major organizing principle of modern politics. Political parties are the vital link between the state and civil society, between the institutions of government and the groups and interests that operate within society. However, parties are by no means all alike. Not only do they differ in terms of matters such as organizational structure and ideological orientation, but they also carry out different roles within the larger political system. Political parties have thus been both lauded as the great tools of democracy and criticized as a source of tyranny and repression. Their impact, moreover, is crucially influenced by what is known as the party system, the network of relationships between and among parties, structured in particular by the number of parties in existence. One-party systems operate very differently from competitive party systems, but there are also important contrasts between two-party and multiparty systems. Nevertheless, parties and party systems have increasingly come under attack. They have been blamed for failing to articulate the new and more diverse aspirations that have emerged in modern societies, and for failing to solve, or perhaps even to address, many of their most troubling problems.

KEY ISSUES
- What is a political party? How can parties be classified?
- What are the key functions of political parties?
- How are parties organized, and where is power located within them?
- What kinds of party system are there?
- How does the party system shape the broader political process?
- Are parties in decline, and is this decline terminal?

CONCEPT

Political party

A political party is a group of people that is organized for the purpose of winning government power, by electoral or other means. Parties typically exhibit the following characteristics (1) They aim to exercise government power by winning political office (small parties may nevertheless use elections more to gain a platform than to win power). (2) They are organized bodies with a formal 'card carrying' membership. (3) They typically adopt a broad issue focus, addressing each of the major areas of government policy (small parties, however, may have a single-issue focus). (4) To varying degrees, they are united by shared political preferences and a general ideological identity.

PARTY POLITICS

Political parties are found in the vast majority of countries and in most political systems. Parties may be authoritarian or democratic; they may seek power through elections or through revolution; and they may espouse ideologies of the left, right or centre, or, indeed, disavow political ideas altogether. However, parties of some kind exist from Brazil to Burundi and from Norway to New Zealand. The development of political parties and the acquisition of a party system came to be recognized as a mark of political modernization. By the late 1950s, some 80 per cent of the world's states were ruled by political parties. During the 1960s and early 1970s, however, a decline set in with the spread of military rule in the developing world. Political parties were accused of being divisive, and of failing to solve overriding problems of poverty, and ethnic and tribal rivalry. They also proved to be inconvenient for economic and military elites. The upsurge of democratization (see p. 272) since the 1980s has, nevertheless, led to a renewed flourishing of parties. In Asia, Africa and Latin America, the relaxation or collapse of military rule was invariably accompanied by the re-emergence of parties. In former communist states, one-party rule was replaced by the establishment of competitive party systems.

It would be a mistake, however, to assume that parties have always been with us. Political parties are part of the structures of mass politics, ushered in by the advent of representative government and the progressive extension of the franchise during the nineteenth century. Until then, what were called 'factions' (see p. 223) or 'parties' were little more than groups of like-minded politicians, usually formed around a key leader or family. So-called 'court' parties, for instance, often developed within autocratic monarchies as a result of the struggle for influence amongst notables and advisers. Thus, when Edmund Burke (see p. 36) in the late eighteenth century described a party as 'a body of men united . . . upon some particular principle upon which they all agree', he was thinking about fluid and informal groupings such as the Whigs and the Tories, and not about the organized and increasingly disciplined machines into which they were to develop.

Parties of the modern kind first emerged in the USA. Despite the abhorrence of parties felt by the 'founding fathers' who created the US constitution, the Federalist Party (later the Whigs and, from 1860, the Republican Party) appeared as a mass-based party during the US presidential election of 1800. Many conservative and liberal parties started life as legislative factions. Only later, forced to appeal to an ever-widening electorate, did they develop an extraparliamentary machinery of constituency branches, local agents and so on. In contrast, socialist parties and parties representing religious, ethnic and language groups were invariably born as social movements, or interest groups, operating outside government. Subsequently, they developed into fully-fledged parliamentary parties in the hope of winning formal representation and shaping public policy. By the beginning of the twentieth century, parties and party systems had, in effect, become the political manifestation of the social and other cleavages that animated society at large. However, the resulting party forms varied considerably.

Types of party

A variety of classifications have been used for political parties. The most important of these are the following:

CONCEPT

Faction, factionalism

A faction is a section or group within a larger formation, usually a political party. Its aims and organizational status must therefore be compatible with those of its host party; otherwise the group is a 'party within a party'. A distinction is sometimes drawn between 'factions' and 'tendencies', the latter being looser and more informal groups, distinguished only by a common policy or ideological disposition. Factionalism refers either to the proliferation of factions, or to the bitterness of factional rivalry. The term faction is often used pejoratively; the term factionalism is always pejorative, implying debilitating infighting.

- cadre and mass parties
- representative and integrative parties
- constitutional and revolutionary parties
- left-wing and right-wing parties.

The most common distinction is that between cadre parties and mass parties. The term *cadre* party originally meant a 'party of notables', dominated by an informal group of leaders who saw little point in building up a mass organization. Such parties invariably developed out of parliamentary factions or cliques at a time when the franchise was limited. However, the term 'cadre' is now more commonly used (as in communist parties) to denote trained and professional party members who are expected to exhibit a high level of political commitment and doctrinal discipline. In this sense, the Communist Party of the Soviet Union (CPSU), the Nazi Party in Germany, and the Fascist Party in Italy were cadre parties, as are the Chinese Communist Party (CCP) and, in certain respects, the Indian Congress Party in the modern period. The distinguishing feature of cadre parties is their reliance on a politically active elite (usually subject to quasi-military discipline) that is capable of offering ideological leadership to the masses. Although strict political criteria are laid down for party membership, careerism and simple convenience are often powerful motives for joining such parties, as both the CPSU and the Nazis found out.

A *mass* party, on the other hand, places a heavy emphasis on broadening membership and constructing a wide electoral base. Although the extension of the franchise forced liberal and conservative parties to seek a mass appeal, the earliest examples of mass parties were European socialist parties, such as the German Social Democratic Party (SPD) and the UK Labour Party, which constructed organizations specifically designed to mobilize working-class support. The key feature of such parties is that they place heavier stress on recruitment and organization than on ideology and political conviction. Although such parties often have formally democratic organizations, except for a minority of activists, membership usually entails little in the way of participation and only general agreement about principles and goals.

Most modern parties fall into the category of what Otto Kirchheimer (1966) termed 'catch-all parties'. These are parties that drastically reduce their ideological baggage in order to appeal to the largest possible number of voters. Kirchheimer particularly had in mind the Christian Democratic Union (CDU) in Germany, but the best examples of catch-all parties are found in the USA in the form of the Republicans and the Democrats. Modern de-ideologized socialist parties such as the German Social Democrats and the Labour Party in the UK also fit this description. These parties differ from the classic model of a mass party in that they emphasize leadership and unity, and downgrade the role of individual party members in trying to build up broad coalitions of support, rather than relying on a particular social class or sectional group.

The second party distinction, advanced by Sigmund Neumann (1956), is that between so-called parties of representation and parties of integration. Representative parties see their primary function as being the securing of votes in elections. They thus attempt to reflect, rather than shape, public opinion. In this respect, representative parties adopt a catch-all strategy and therefore place pragmatism before principle and market research before popular mobilization.

The prevalence of such parties in modern politics gave considerable force to arguments based on **rational choice** models of political behaviour, such as those of Joseph Schumpeter (see p. 202) and Anthony Downs (1957), which portray politicians as power-seeking creatures who are willing to adopt whatever policies are likely to bring them electoral success.

Integrative parties, in contrast, adopt proactive, rather than reactive, political strategies; they wish to mobilize, educate and inspire the masses, rather than merely respond to their concerns. Although Neumann saw the typical mobilizing party as an ideologically disciplined cadre party, mass parties may also exhibit mobilizing tendencies. For example, until they became discouraged by electoral failure, socialist parties set out to 'win over' the electorate to a belief in the benefits of public ownership, full employment, redistribution, social welfare and so on. This approach was also, rather ironically, adopted by the UK Conservatives under Margaret Thatcher in the 1980s. Abandoning the party's traditional distaste for ideology (see p. 28) and abstract principle, Thatcher embraced 'conviction politics' in pursuing a mobilizing strategy based on firm support for cutting taxes, encouraging enterprise, promoting individual responsibility, tackling trade union power and so forth.

The third type of classification distinguishes between constitutional parties and revolutionary parties. *Constitutional* parties acknowledge the rights and entitlements of other parties and, thus, operate within a framework of rules and constraints. In particular, they acknowledge that there is a division between the party and the state, between the party in power (the government of the day) and state institutions (the bureaucracy, judiciary, police and so on) that enjoy formal independence and political neutrality. Above all, constitutional parties acknowledge and respect the rules of electoral competition. They recognize that they can be voted out of power as easily as they can be voted in. Mainstream parties in liberal democracies all have such a constitutional character.

Revolutionary parties, on the other hand, are antisystem or anticonstitutional parties, either of the left or of the right. Such parties aim to seize power and overthrow the existing constitutional structure using tactics that range from outright insurrection and popular revolution to the quasi-legalism practised by the Nazis and the Fascists. In some cases, revolutionary parties are formally banned by being classified as 'extremist' or 'anti-democratic', as has been the case in post-World War II Germany. When such parties win power, however, they invariably become 'ruling' or regime parties, suppressing rival parties and establishing a permanent relationship with the state machinery. In one-party systems, whether established under the banner of communism, fascism, nationalism or whatever, the distinction between the party and the state is so weakened that the 'ruling' party, in effect, substitutes itself for the government, creating a fused 'party–state' apparatus. It was common in the USSR, for instance, for the General Secretary of the CPSU to act as the chief executive or head of government without bothering to assume a formal state post.

The final way of distinguishing between parties is on the basis of ideological orientation, specifically between those parties labelled left-wing and those labelled right-wing (see p. 225). Left-wing parties (progressive, socialist and communist parties) are characterized by a commitment to change, in the form of either social reform or wholesale economic transformation. These have traditionally drawn their support from the ranks of the poor and disadvantaged

● **Rational choice**: An approach to politics based on the assumption that individuals are rationally self-interested actors; an 'economic' theory of politics (see p. 14–15).

Focus on . . .
The left/right divide

The left–right political spectrum is a shorthand method of describing political ideas and beliefs, summarizing the ideological positions of politicians, parties and movements. Its origins date back to the French Revolution and the positions that groups adopted at the first meeting of the French Estates-General in 1789. The terms 'left' and 'right' do not have exact meanings, however. In a narrow sense, the *linear* political spectrum (see Figure 10.1) summarizes different attitudes to the economy and the role of the state: left-wing views support intervention and collectivism, right-wing views favour the market and individualism. This supposedly reflects deeper ideological or value differences, as listed below:

An alternative, *horseshoe-shaped* political spectrum (see Figure 10.2) was devised in the post-World War II period to highlight the totalitarian and monistic (anti-pluralist) tendencies of both fascism and communism, by contrast with the alleged tolerance and openness of mainstream creeds. Those, like Hans Eysenck (1964), who have developed a two-dimensional political spectrum (see Figure 10.3) have tried to compensate for the crudeness and inconsistencies of the conventional left–right spectrum by adding a vertical authoritarian–libertarian one. This enables positions on economic organization to be disentangled from those related to civil liberty.

Left			**Right**
	Liberty	Authority	
	Equality	Hierarchy	
	Fraternity	Order	
	Rights	Duties	
	Progress	Tradition	
	Reform	Reaction	
	Internationalism	Nationalism	

(in urban societies, the working classes). Right-wing parties (conservative and fascist parties, in particular) generally uphold the existing social order and are, in that sense, a force for continuity. Their supporters usually include business interests and the materially-contented middle classes. However, this notion of a neat left–right party divide is, at best, simplistic and, at worst, deeply misleading. Not only are both the left and the right often divided along reformist/revolutionary and constitutional/insurrectionary lines, but also all parties, especially constitutional ones, tend to be 'broad churches', in the sense that they encompass their own left and right wings. Moreover, electoral competition has the effect of blurring ideological identities, once-cherished principles commonly being discarded in the search for votes. The definitions of left and right have also changed over time, and often differ from one political system to the next. Finally, the shift away from old class polarities and the emergence of new political issues such as the environment, animal rights and feminism has perhaps rendered the conventional ideas of left and right redundant (Giddens, 1994).

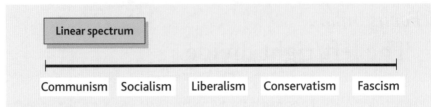

Figure 10.1   Linear political spectrum

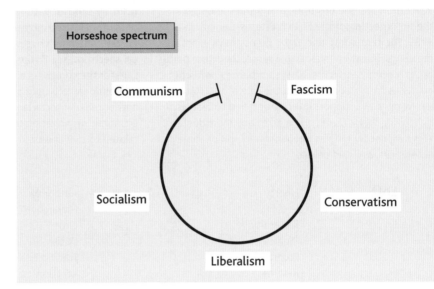

Figure 10.2   Horseshoe political spectrum

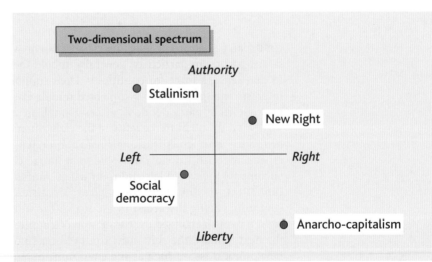

Figure 10.3   Two-dimensional political spectrum

Thomas Jefferson (1743–1826)

US political philosopher and statesman. A wealthy Virginian planter who was Governor of Virginia 1779–81, Jefferson served as the first US Secretary of State, 1789–94. He was the third president of the USA, 1801–09. Jefferson was the principal author of the Declaration of Independence, and wrote a vast number of addresses and letters. He developed a democratic form of agrarianism that sought to blend a belief in rule by a natural aristocracy with a commitment to limited government and *laissez-faire*, sometimes called Jeffersonianism. He also demonstrated sympathy for social reform, favouring the extension of public education, the abolition of slavery and greater economic equality.

Functions of parties

Although political parties are defined by a central function (the filling of political office and the wielding of government power), their impact on the political system is substantially broader and more complex. It goes without saying that there are dangers in generalizing about the functions of parties. Constitutional parties operating in a context of electoral competition tend to be portrayed as bastions of democracy; indeed, the existence of such parties is often seen as the litmus test of a healthy democratic system. On the other hand, regime parties that enjoy a monopoly of political power are more commonly portrayed as instruments of manipulation and political control. Moreover, controversy continues to surround the wider impact of political parties. For instance, Thomas Jefferson and the other 'founding fathers' of the US constitution – and, in the modern period, supporters of so-called '**anti-party parties**' – have portrayed parties in deeply negative terms, seeing them as a source of discord and political regimentation (see p. 230). A number of general functions of parties can nevertheless be identified. The main functions are as follows:

- representation
- elite formation and recruitment
- goal formulation
- interest articulation and aggregation
- socialization and mobilization
- organization of government.

Representation

Representation (see p. 197) is often seen as the primary function of parties. It refers to the capacity of parties to respond to and articulate the views of both the members and the voters. In the language of systems theory, political parties are major 'inputting' devices that ensure that government heeds the needs and wishes of the larger society. Clearly, this is a function that is best carried out, some would say only carried out, in an open and competitive system that forces parties to respond to popular preferences. Rational-choice theorists, following

● **Anti-party party**: Parties that set out to subvert traditional party politics by rejecting parliamentary compromise and emphasizing popular mobilization.

Anthony Downs (1957), explain this process by suggesting that the political market parallels the economic market, in that politicians act essentially as entrepreneurs seeking votes, meaning that parties behave very much like businesses. Power thus ultimately resides with the consumers, the voters. This 'economic model' can, however, be criticized on the grounds that parties seek to 'shape' or mobilize public opinion, as well as respond to it; that the image of voters as well-informed, rational and issue-orientated consumers is questionable; and that the range of consumer (or electoral) choice is often narrow.

Elite formation and recruitment

Parties of all kinds are responsible for providing states with their political leaders. Exceptions to this include parties that are, effectively, the creation of powerful politicians and are used as political vehicles to mobilize support for them, such as Silvio Berlusconi's Forza Italia, established in 1993 but rebranded as the People of Freedom party in 2009, and Vladimir Putin's United Russia party, founded in 2001. Much more commonly, however, politicians achieve office by virtue of their party post: contestants in a presidential election are usually party leaders, while in parliamentary systems the leader of the largest party in the assembly normally becomes prime minister. Cabinet and other ministerial posts are usually filled by senior party figures, though exceptions are found in presidential systems such as the USA's, which allow non-party ministers to be appointed.

In most cases, parties therefore provide a training ground for politicians, equipping them with skills, knowledge and experience; and offering them some form of career structure, albeit one that depends on the fortunes of the party. On the other hand, the stranglehold that parties exert over government offices can be criticized for ensuring that political leaders are drawn from a relatively small pool of talent: the senior figures in a handful of major parties. In the USA, however, this stranglehold has been weakened by the widespread use of primary elections, which reduce the control that a party has over the process of candidate selection and nomination.

Goal formulation

Political parties have traditionally been one of the means through which societies set collective goals and, in some cases, ensure that they are carried out. Parties play this role because, in the process of seeking power, they formulate programmes of government (through conferences, conventions, election manifestos and so on) with a view to attracting popular support. Not only does this mean that parties are a major source of policy initiation, it also encourages them to formulate coherent sets of policy options that give the electorate a choice amongst realistic and achievable goals.

This function is most clearly carried out by parties in parliamentary systems that are able to claim a mandate (see p. 200) to implement their policies, if they are elected to power. However, it can also occur in presidential systems with usually non-programmic parties, as in the case of the Republicans' 'Contract with America' in the US congressional elections of 1994. Nevertheless, the tendency towards de-ideologized catch-all parties, and the fact that electoral campaigns increasingly stress personality and image over policies and issues, has generally reduced the impact that parties have on policy formulation. Party programmes, moreover, are almost certain to be modified by pressure from the civil service and interest groups, as well as in the light of domestic and international circumstances. Policy implementation, on the other hand, is usually carried out by bureaucracies rather than parties, except in one-party systems such as those in orthodox communist states, where the 'ruling' party supervises the state apparatus at every level.

Interest articulation and aggregation

In the process of developing collective goals, parties also help to articulate and aggregate the various interests found in society. Parties, indeed, often develop as vehicles through which business, labour, religious, ethnic or other groups advance or defend their various interests. The UK Labour Party, for instance, was created by the trade union movement with the aim of achieving working-class political representation. Other parties have, effectively, recruited interests and groups in order to broaden their electoral base, as the US parties did in the late nineteenth and early twentieth centuries with immigrant groups.

The fact that national parties invariably articulate the demands of a multitude of groups forces them to aggregate these interests by drawing them together into a coherent whole, balancing competing interests against each other. Constitutional parties are clearly forced to do this by the pressures of electoral competition, but even monopolistic parties articulate and aggregate interests through their close relationship with the state and the economy, especially in centrally planned systems. However, not even in competitive party systems are all interests articulated, those of the poor being most vulnerable to exclusion.

Socialization and mobilization

Through internal debate and discussion, as well as campaigning and electoral competition, parties are important agents of political education and socialization. The issues that parties choose to focus on help to set the political agenda, and the values and attitudes that they articulate become part of the larger political culture (see p. 172). In the case of monopolistic parties, the propagation of an 'official' ideology (be it Marxism–Leninism, National Socialism, or simply the ideas of a charismatic leader) is consciously acknowledged to be a central, if not its supreme, function.

Mainstream parties in competitive systems play no less significant a role in encouraging groups to play by the rules of the democratic game, thus mobilizing support for the regime itself. For example, the emergence of socialist parties in the late nineteenth and early twentieth centuries was an important means of integrating the working class into industrial society. Nevertheless, the capacity of parties to mobilize and socialize has been brought into doubt by evidence in many countries of partisan dealignment (see p. 217) and growing disenchantment with conventional pro-system parties. The problem that parties have is that, to some extent, they themselves are socialized (some would say corrupted) by the experience of government, making them, it appears, less effective in engaging partisan sympathies and attracting emotional attachments. (These issues are discussed more fully in Chapter 20.)

Debating...
Do parties breed discord and constrain political debate?

So common are parties in modern politics that it is often forgotten how controversial they were when they first emerged. Although some welcomed them as the agents of a new age of mass politics, others warned that they would deepen conflict and subvert the politics of individual consciousness. The trend towards falling party membership and declining party identification in the modern period has served to revive such criticisms.

YES

Sacrificing personal conscience. By their nature, parties are collective entities, groups of people who agree a common platform, and advance shared views and opinions. Without unity and cohesion, parties have very little reason to exist. And yet this unity comes at the price of personal conscience, as it is inconceivable that any member would genuinely support all of a party's policies in all circumstances. Over matter small and sometimes large, parties therefore come to 'think for' their members, whether this comes about through party discipline and the fear of punishment (including expulsion from the party) or, more insidiously, through an emotional or ideological attachment to the party and its goals.

Disharmony and adversarialism. Party politics is based on partisanship, adherence and, maybe, even devotion to a particular cause or group. This inevitably breeds a tribal mentality in which the flaws and failings of other parties are exaggerated, while those of one's own party are consistently denied. Parties thus promote a one-sided view of politics in which political issues and debates are constantly distorted by considerations of party advantage. This tendency towards mindless adversarialism – disagreement for the sake of disagreement – is hardly a sound basis for advancing the public good.

Domination by the cunning and ambitious. Parties serve to concentrate political power rather than disperse it. In the 'iron law of oligarchy' (see p. 232), this tendency is explained in terms of organization. However, elite rule also reflects the fact that, within parties, 'foot soldiers' are required to do little other than obey and follow, encouraged by the knowledge that loyalty and discipline will be rewarded, while dissent and, in particular, criticism of the leadership will be punished. Those who climb the 'greasy pole' and gain advancement within the party are therefore likely, in George Washington's words, to be 'cunning, ambitious and unprincipled men'. Political parties are, in this sense, a particular example of the corruption of power (as discussed in Chapter 20).

NO

Forums of debate. The image of parties as austere, monolithic bodies, in which free debate is sacrificed in the cause of party unity, is accurate only in the context of authoritarianism. In other circumstances, parties are vibrant and multifarious; indeed, the existence of rival factions and tendencies ensures unending debate about policy issues and strategic concerns. Rather than requiring members to sacrifice personal conscience, parties provide their members with an education in politics, helping them to strengthen their knowledge and skills and making them more engaged citizens. Party membership is therefore an important vehicle for the aspect of personal self-development.

Engaging the people. Parties provide a channel of communication through which political leaders both mobilize citizens and respond to their needs and concerns. This applies most clearly when the electoral process forces parties to compete for the popular vote in order to win or retain government power, but it can also occur (albeit to a limited extent) in authoritarian systems, through attempts by 'ruling' parties to maintain legitimacy. The need to engage with the ideas and interests of the people generates pressure within parties to permit, even encourage, internal debate and argument among their members, rather than uncritical obedience.

Cross-party interaction. Bipartisanship is more common than is often supposed. For instance, the use of proportional electoral systems typically creates a bias in favour of consensus-building and alliances amongst parties based on the fact that no single party is likely to have parliamentary strength to rule on its own. The resulting coalition governments are held together by the fact that conflicts between the parties involved are resolved through a process of ongoing cross-party dialogue. A similar dynamic can develop in presidential systems due to the phenomenon of cohabitation, whereby the executive is in the hands of one party while the assembly is dominated by another party.

CONCEPT

Party democracy

Party democracy is a form of popular rule that operates through the agency of a party. There are two models of party democracy. In the first (intraparty democracy), parties are democratic agents, in that power within them is widely and evenly dispersed. This implies, for instance, that there should be broad participation in the election of leaders and selection of candidates. In the second model, democracy dictates that policy-making power should be concentrated in the hands of party members who are elected and, therefore, publicly accountable. In this view, the first model may lead to the tyranny of non-elected constituency activists.

Organization of government

It is often argued that complex modern societies would be ungovernable in the absence of political parties. In the first place, parties help with the formation of governments, in parliamentary systems, to the extent that it is possible to talk of 'party government' (see p. 236). Parties also give governments a degree of stability and coherence, especially if the members of the government are drawn from a single party and are, therefore, united by common sympathies and attachments. Even governments that are formed from a coalition of parties are more likely to foster unity and agreement than those that consist of separate individuals each with his or her own priorities.

Parties, furthermore, facilitate cooperation between the two major branches of government: the assembly and the executive. In parliamentary systems, this is effectively guaranteed by the fact the government is usually formed from the party or parties that have majority control of the assembly. However, even in presidential systems the chief executive can wield some influence, if not control, through an appeal to party unity. Finally, parties provide, in competitive systems at least, a vital source of opposition and criticism, both inside and outside government. As well as broadening political debate and educating the electorate, this helps to ensure that government policy is more thoroughly scrutinized and, therefore, more likely to be workable.

Party organization: where does power lie?

Because of the crucial role that political parties play, considerable attention has been focused on where power lies within parties. The organization and structure of parties thus provides vital clues about the distribution of power within society as a whole. Can parties function as democratic bodies that broaden participation and access to power? Or do they simply entrench the dominance of leaders and elites?

One of the earliest attempts to investigate internal party democracy was undertaken in Mosei Ostrogorski's *Democracy and the Organization of Political Parties* (1902), which argued that the representation of individual interests had lost out to the growing influence of the party machine and control exerted by a caucus of senior party figures. This view was more memorably expressed by Robert Michels in *Political Parties* ([1911] 1962) in the form of the 'iron law of oligarchy' (see p. 232), or, as Michels put it, 'he who says organization says oligarchy'. Michels (1876–1936), a prominent elite theorist, wished to analyse the power structure of the German SPD; he argued that, despite the party's formally democratic organization, power was concentrated in the hands of a small group of party leaders.

For Michels, the 'law' explained the inevitable failure of democratic socialism and, indeed, exploded the myth of political democracy. Critics, however, point out that Michels' observations are generalizations made on the basis of a single political party at a particular moment in time, and also rest on questionable psychological theories. In practice, party elites have often proved to be more faction-ridden, and mass memberships less deferential and quiescent, than Michels suggested.

Attempts have been made to strengthen the democratic and participatory features of parties through reform. One of the clearest examples of this occurred

Focus on . . .

The iron law of oligarchy

Oligarchy is government or domination by the few. The 'iron law of oligarchy', formulated by Robert Michels ([1911] 1962), suggests that there is an inevitable tendency for political organizations, and by implication all organizations, to be oligarchic. Participatory or democratic structures cannot check oligarchic tendencies; they can only disguise them.

Michels advanced a number of arguments in support of his law:

- Elite groups result from the need for specialization. Elite members have greater expertise and better organizational skills than those possessed by ordinary members.
- Leaders form cohesive groups because they recognize that this improves their chances of remaining in power.
- Rank-and-file members of an organization tend to be apathetic and are, therefore, generally disposed to accept subordination and venerate leaders.

in the USA in the 1970s and 1980s. US parties differ in many respects from their European counterparts. Being loose coalitions of sometimes conflicting interests held together by little more than the need to contest presidential elections, they are highly decentralized and generally non-programmic. Traditionally, state-based or city-based party bosses (a legacy of the **machine politics** of the early twentieth century) acted as power brokers and exercised a decisive influence at nominating conventions. Following protests and clashes at the 1968 Democratic national convention in Chicago, however, a reform movement sprang up aimed at weakening the power of local party leaders and strengthening the role of rank-and-file members.

This was accomplished largely through the wider use of nominating primaries and **caucuses**. These, first with the Democrats and later with the Republicans, attracted a growing number of issue and candidate activists into party politics, leading to the nomination of more ideological candidates such as George McGovern for the Democrats in 1972 and Ronald Reagan for the Republicans in 1980. Such tendencies have, nevertheless, generated concern, particularly amongst Democrats, who feared that more open and participatory structures could simply result in the nomination of unelectable 'outsider' candidates. Both the main US parties have responded to this by modernizing and strengthening their committee structures, especially at national, congressional and senatorial levels. Although this has been portrayed as a process of 'party renewal', it is evidence of the parties' desire to provide better electoral support for individual candidates, rather than of the emergence of European-style, party-focused elections.

The existence of factions and tendencies is as important as formal organization in determining the location of power within a party. While all parties, even those with an apparently monolithic character, embrace some measure of political and ideological rivalry, the degree to which this rivalry is reflected in conflict between organized and coherent groups is crucial in determining the degree of authority of party leaders. In some cases, factions can break away from parties in the manner that European communist parties often emerged out of socialist

- **Machine politics:** A style of politics in which party 'bosses' control a mass organization through patronage and the distribution of favours.

- **Caucus:** A meeting of party members held to nominate election candidates, or to discuss legislative proposals in advance of formal proceedings.

parties in the years following the 1917 Russian Revolution. Factionalism is often linked to the weight that parties place on political ideas and ideological direction. Whereas pragmatic right-wing parties usually merely have to balance or conciliate rival tendencies, more ideological parties of the left often have to deal with open disagreement and institutionalized rivalry. Together with their inclination to endorse internal democracy, this has generally made socialist parties more difficult to lead than liberal or conservative parties.

Perhaps a more significant consideration, however, is the extent to which parties have a secure hold on power. Factionalism is, in a sense, a luxury that only long-time parties of government can afford. This is why monopolistic communist parties were able to keep factionalism at bay only by exercising ruthless discipline enforced through the strictures of **democratic centralism**. It also explains the deeply factional nature of 'dominant' parties such as the Liberal Democratic Party (LDP) in Japan and the Italian Christian Democratic Party (DC). The UK Conservative Party is an example of a party with an ethos that once stressed, above all, deference and loyalty. However, the Party became increasingly factionalized in the 1980s and 1990s through a combination of its more ideological character and its prolonged electoral success after 1979. Bottom-up pressures thus gave the Conservative Party a more democratic character than its formal leader-dominated structure suggested was possible. The most conspicuous casualty of this process was Margaret Thatcher, who was forced to stand down as party leader in 1990 despite having won three successive general elections. Albeit to different degrees, all subsequent Conservative leaders have experienced difficulties in confronting factional resistance inside and outside of Parliament.

PARTY SYSTEMS

Political parties are important not only because of the range of functions they carry out (representation, elite recruitment, aggregation of interests and so on), but also because the complex interrelationships between and among parties are crucial in structuring the way political systems work in practice. This network of relationships is called a **party system**. The most familiar way of distinguishing between different types of party system is by reference to the number of parties competing for power. On this basis, Duverger (1954) distinguished between 'one-party', 'two-party' and 'multiparty' systems. Although such a typology is commonly used, party systems cannot simply be reduced to a 'numbers game'.

As important as the number of parties competing for power is their relative size, as reflected in their electoral and legislative strength. As Sartori (1976) pointed out, what is vital is to establish the 'relevance' of parties in relation to the formation of governments and, in particular, whether their size gives them the prospect of winning, or at least sharing, government power. This approach is often reflected in the distinction made between 'major', or government-orientated, parties and more peripheral, 'minor' ones (although neither category can be defined with mathematical accuracy). A third consideration is how these 'relevant' parties relate to one another. Is the party system characterized by cooperation and consensus, or by conflict and polarization? This is closely linked to the ideological complexion of the party system, and the traditions and history of the parties that compose it.

● **Democratic centralism**: The Leninist principle of party organization, based on a supposed balance between freedom of discussion and strict unity of action.

● **Party system**: A relatively stable network of relationships between parties that is structured by their number, size and ideological orientation.

The mere presence of parties does not, however, guarantee the existence of a party system. The pattern of relationships amongst parties constitutes a system only if it is characterized by stability and a degree of orderliness. Where neither stability nor order exists, a party system may be in the process of emerging, or a transition from one type of party system to another may be occurring. For instance, this can be said of early postcommunist Russia. The collapse of communist rule in 1991 and the initial banning of the CPSU was always going to make the emergence of a competitive party system a difficult, perhaps tortuous, business. Russia's problem was a proliferation of parties and political groupings, none of which came close to establishing a mass membership or a nationwide organization. No fewer than 43 parties contested the 1995 parliamentary elections, with the largest of these, the Russian Communist Party, gaining just 22 per cent of the vote. The subsequent introduction of measures such as electoral **thresholds** and registration on the basis of petitions greatly reduced the number of parties, meaning, for instance, that just seven parties contested the 2011 Russian Duma elections. However, some have argued that, in an age of partisan dealignment and volatile voting patterns, party systems are generally losing their 'systematic' character, making it more difficult to distinguish one system from another. Moreover, where subnational bodies exert significant influence, different party systems may operate at different levels within the political system.

The major party systems found in modern politics are, nevertheless, as follows:

- one-party systems
- two-party systems
- dominant-party systems
- multiparty systems.

One-party systems

Strictly speaking, the term one-party system is contradictory since 'system' implies interaction amongst a number of entities. The term is, nevertheless, helpful in distinguishing between political systems in which a single party enjoys a monopoly of power through the exclusion of all other parties (by political or constitutional means) and those systems characterized by a competitive struggle amongst a number of parties. Because monopolistic parties effectively function as permanent governments, with no mechanism (short of a *coup* or revolution) through which they can be removed from power, they invariably develop an entrenched relationship with the state machine. This allows such states to be classified as 'one-party states', their machinery being seen as a fused 'party–state' apparatus. Two rather different types of one-party system can be identified, however.

The first type has been found in state socialist regimes where 'ruling' communist parties have directed and controlled virtually all the institutions and aspects of society. Such parties are subject to strict ideological discipline, traditionally linked tenets of Marxism–Leninism, and they have highly-structured internal organizations in line with the principles of democratic centralism. These are cadre parties, in the sense that membership is restricted on political and ideological grounds. Almost 6 per cent of the Chinese population are members of the

● **Threshold:** A minimum level of electoral support needed for a party to be eligible to win seats.

Chinese Communist Party (CCP), and around 9 per cent of the Soviet population belonged to the CPSU. In this type of party, the party core consists of well-paid full-time officials, the *apparatchiki*, who run the party *apparat*, or apparatus, and exercise supervision over both the state machine and social institutions.

A central device through which communist parties control the state, economy and society, and ensure the subordination of 'lower' organs to 'higher' ones, is the *nomenklatura* system. This is a system of vetted appointments in which, effectively, all senior posts are filled by party-approved candidates. The justification for both the party's monopoly of power, and its supervision of state and social institutions, lies in the Leninist claim that the party acts as the 'vanguard of the proletariat' in providing the working masses with the ideological leadership and guidance needed to ensure that they fulfil their revolutionary destiny. **Vanguardism** has, however, been criticized for being deeply elitist and providing the seed from which Stalinism later grew. Trotsky (1937), on the other hand, offered an alternative interpretation by suggesting that, far from the 'ruling' party dominating Soviet development, its formal monopoly of power merely concealed the burgeoning influence of the state bureaucracy.

The second type of one-party system is associated with anticolonial nationalism and state consolidation in the developing world. In Ghana, Tanzania and Zimbabwe, for example, the 'ruling' party developed out of an independence movement that proclaimed the overriding need for nation-building and economic development. In Zimbabwe, one-party rule developed only in 1986 (six years after independence) through the merger of the two major parties, ZANU and ZAPU, both former guerrilla groups. In other cases, such parties have developed as little more than vehicles through which a national leader has tried to consolidate power, as with General Ershad's People's Party in Bangladesh in the 1980s and President Mobutu's Popular Movement of the Revolution in Zaire, 1965–97.

One-party systems in Africa and Asia have usually been built around the dominant role of a charismatic leader and drawn whatever ideological identity they have possessed from the views of that leader. Kwame Nkrumah, the leader of the Convention People's Party (CPP) in Ghana until his overthrow in 1966, is often seen as the model such leader, but other examples have been Julius Nyerere in Tanzania and Robert Mugabe in Zimbabwe. Not uncommonly, these parties are weakly organized (very different from the tight discipline found in communist one-party states), and they play, at best, only a peripheral role in the process of policy-making. Their monopolistic position, nevertheless, helps to entrench authoritarianism (see p. 277) and to keep alive the danger of corruption.

Two-party systems

A two-party system is duopolistic in that it is dominated by two 'major' parties that have a roughly equal prospect of winning government power. In its classical form, a two-party system can be identified by three criteria:

- Although a number of 'minor' parties may exist, only two parties enjoy sufficient electoral and legislative strength to have a realistic prospect of winning government power.

● **Vanguardism**: The Leninist belief in the need for a party to lead and guide the proletariat towards the fulfilment of its revolutionary destiny.

- The larger party is able to rule alone (usually on the basis of a legislative majority); the other provides the opposition.
- Power alternates between these parties; both are 'electable', the opposition serving as a 'government in the wings'.

The UK and the USA are the most frequently cited examples of states with two-party systems, though others have included Canada, Australia and, until the introduction of electoral reform in 1993, New Zealand. Archetypal examples of two-party politics are, nevertheless, rare. The UK, for instance, often portrayed as the model two-party system, has conformed to its three defining criteria only for particular (and, some would argue, untypical) periods of its history. Even the apparent Labour–Conservative two-partyism of the early post-World War II period (power alternating four times between 1945 and 1970) was punctuated by 13 years of continuous Conservative rule (1951–64), a period during which time Labour's electability was called into question. Moreover, despite persistent major party domination of the House of Commons in the UK, it is more doubtful that a two-party system has existed 'in the country' since 1974. This is suggested by the decline of combined Labour–Conservative support (down from over 95 per cent in the early 1950s to consistently below 75 per cent since 1974).

Even the seemingly incontrovertible two-partyism of the USA – which, for instance, sees the Republicans and Democrats usually holding between them all the seats in the House of Representatives and the Senate – can be questioned. On the one hand, the presidential system allows one party to capture the White House (the presidency) while the other controls one or both houses of Congress, as, for instance, occurred between 1984 and 2000, meaning that it may not be possible to identify a clear government–opposition divide. On the other hand, 'third' party candidates are sometimes of significance. Ross Perot's 16 per cent of the vote in the 1992 presidential election not only highlighted the decline of the Republican and Democratic parties, but also, arguably, proved decisive in securing victory for Bill Clinton.

Two-party politics was once portrayed as the surest way of reconciling responsiveness with order, representative government with effective government. Its key advantage is that it makes possible a system of party government, supposedly characterized by stability, choice and accountability. The two major parties are able to offer the electorate a straightforward choice between rival programmes and alternative governments. Voters can support a party knowing that, if it wins the election, it will have the capacity to carry out its manifesto promises without having to negotiate or compromise with coalition partners. This is sometimes seen as one of the attractions of majoritarian electoral systems that exaggerate support for large parties. Two-party systems have also been praised for delivering strong but accountable government based on relentless competition between the governing and opposition parties. Although government can govern, it can never relax or become complacent because it is constantly confronted by an opposition that acts as a government in waiting. Two-partyism, moreover, creates a bias in favour of moderation, as the two contenders for power have to battle for 'floating' votes in the centre ground. This was, for example, reflected in the so-called 'social-democratic consensus' that prevailed in the UK from the 1950s to the 1970s.

However, two-party politics and party government have not been so well regarded since the 1970s. Instead of guaranteeing moderation, two-party

---

CONCEPT

Party government

Party government is a system through which single parties are able to form governments and carry through policy programmes. Its key features are as follows. (1) Major parties possess a clear programmic character and thus offer the electorate a meaningful choice between potential governments. (2) The governing party enjoys sufficient ideological and organizational unity to deliver on its manifesto commitments. (3) Responsibility is maintained by the government's accountability to the electorate through its mandate, and by the existence of a credible opposition that acts as a balancing force.

systems such as the UK's have displayed a periodic tendency towards adversary politics (see p. 324). This is reflected in ideological polarization and an emphasis on conflict and argument, rather than consensus and compromise. In the UK in the early 1980s, this was best demonstrated by the movement to the right by a 'Thatcherized' Conservative Party and the movement to the left by a radicalized Labour Party, although a new, post-Thatcherite consensus soon emerged. Adversarial two-partyism has often been explained by reference to the class nature of party support (party conflict being seen, ultimately, as a reflection of the class struggle), or as a consequence of party democratization and the influence of ideologically committed grass-roots activists.

A further problem with the two-party system is that two evenly-matched parties are encouraged to compete for votes by outdoing each other's electoral promises, perhaps causing spiralling public spending and fuelling inflation. This amounts to irresponsible party government, in that parties come to power on the basis of election manifestos that they have no capacity to fulfil. A final weakness of two-party systems is the obvious restrictions they impose in terms of electoral and ideological choice. While a choice between just two programmes of government was perhaps sufficient in an era of partisan alignment and class solidarity, it has become quite inadequate in a period of greater individualism (see p. 158) and social diversity.

Dominant-party systems

Dominant-party systems should not be confused with one-party systems, although they may at times exhibit similar characteristics. A dominant-party system is competitive in the sense that a number of parties compete for power in regular and popular elections, but is dominated by a single major party that consequently enjoys prolonged periods in power. This apparently neat definition, however, runs into problems, notably, in relation to determining how 'prolonged' a governing period must be for a party to be considered 'dominant'. Japan is usually cited as the classic example of a dominant-party system. Until its defeat in 2009, the Liberal Democratic Party (LDP) had been in power almost continuously for 54 years, only having been in opposition for a brief 11-month period between 1993 and 1994. LDP dominance had been underpinned by the Japanese 'economic miracle'. It also reflected the powerful appeal of the party's neo-Confucian principles of duty and obligation in the still-traditional Japanese countryside, and the strong links that the party had forged with business elites. However, economic stagnation and internal divisions have meant that the LDP has lost members and supporters to a number of newly-formed, smaller parties, its decline being underlined in 2009 when the Democratic Party of Japan became the first opposition party since 1945 to win a parliamentary majority.

The Congress Party in India enjoyed an unbroken spell of 30 years in power commencing with the achievement of independence in 1947. Until 1989 it had endured only three years in opposition, following Indira Gandhi's 1975–77 state of emergency. The African National Congress (ANC) has similarly been the dominant party in South Africa since the ending of apartheid in 1993, its position being based on its pre-eminent role in the long struggle against white rule (see p. 238). The best European examples of a dominant-party system are Sweden, where the Social Democratic Labour Party (SAP) held power for 65 of the previous 74 years

POLITICS IN ACTION . . .

The African National Congress: a liberation movement or a 'ruling' party?

Events: In April 1994, South Africa held its first non-racial election. The African National Congress (ANC) won the election, gaining 63 per cent of both votes and seats. The following month, Nelson Mandela was inaugurated as the president of South Africa. The ANC subsequently developed into the ruling party of post-apartheid South Africa. Its majority in the National Assembly increased to 66 per cent in the 1999 election, and again to 70 per cent in the 2004 election, only falling slightly in 2009 to 65 per cent. This has been a remarkable achievement for a political movement that had been banned until 1990, and whose leadership had mostly been either in prison or in exile since the early 1960s.

Significance: What accounts for the ANC's predominant position in South African politics? The key explanation is the leading role the party played in the campaign against extreme Afrikaner nationalism and in helping to promote resistance to the policies of apartheid. In describing itself as a 'liberation movement', rather than a conventional political party, the ANC continues to portray itself as the leader of South Africa's 'national democratic revolution'. This position has been bolstered by two factors. First, the ANC responds to and accommodates a broad diversity of interests and voices. Of particular significance in this respect have been the 'tripartite' alliance the ANC forged with the Congress of South African Trade Unions (COSATU) and the South African Communist Party (SACP), and the ANC's willingness in 1994 to form not a single-party government but a government of national unity, including the (New) National Party (which had abandoned its support for apartheid) and the Inkatha Freedom Party (historically, the voice of Zulu nationalism). Second, the ANC has placed a heavy stress on national reconciliation, seeking to forge a single South African identity and sense of purpose amongst a diverse and splintered population. Made possible by the ANC's long-standing commitment to non-racialism, this was reflected in the establishment in 1995 of the Truth and Reconciliation Commission, which sought to heal the wounds of the apartheid era by exposing the crimes and injustices committed by all sides of the struggle, rather than by handing down punishments.

However, the ANC faces at least three major challenges. First, the party's ability to define itself in terms of the struggle for liberation is certain to decline over time. Not only is the proportion of the ANC's membership (and, in due course, leadership, which has direct experience of anti-apartheid activism) steadily diminishing; in people's wider perceptions, the ANC is certain to be viewed progressively more as a vehicle for government than as a vehicle for liberation. Second, and in common with other dominant parties, the ANC has been afflicted by factionalism and, at times, tumultuous internal conflicts. The most dramatic of these was between supporters of Thabo Mbeki, who became South Africa's second post-apartheid president, serving from 1999 to 2008, and supporters of Jacob Zuma, who defeated Mbeki in 2007 in the contest for the presidency of the ANC and went on to become the president of South Africa in 2009. Third, even though post-apartheid South Africa has clearly embraced liberal-democratic principles and structures, the ANC's dominance has fostered developments more commonly associated with one-party states. In particular, the ANC's apparent electoral invulnerability has blurred the distinction between the party and the state, creating scope for corruption. The most high profile corruption scandal in post-apartheid South Africa emerged in 2005 and led to the conviction of Jacob Zuma's financial advisor, Schabir Shaik, over his role in a 1999 arms deal. Zuma himself was dismissed as deputy president by President Mbeki and was subsequently charged with corruption, although these developments did nothing to diminish Zuma's power base within the ANC, or to damage his subsequent career.

until its defeat in 2006; and Italy, where the Christian Democratic Party (DC) dominated every one of the country's 52 post-World War II governments until the party's effective collapse amidst mounting allegations of corruption in 1992–94.

The most prominent feature of a dominant-party system is the tendency for the political focus to shift from competition between parties to factional conflict within the dominant party itself. The DC in Italy, for example, functioned as little more than a coalition of privileged groups and interests in Italian society, the party acting as a broker to these various factions. The most powerful of these groups were the Catholic Church (which exercised influence through organizations such as Catholic Action), the farming community and industrial interests. Each of these was able to cultivate voting loyalty and exert influence on DC's members in the Italian parliament.

Factions were also an integral institution in the Japanese political process. Within the LDP, which, until its defeat in 2009, had enjoyed 54 years of virtually unbroken rule, a perennial struggle for power took place, as various subgroups coalesced around rising or powerful individuals. Such factionalism was maintained at the local level by the ability of faction leaders to provide political favours for their followers, and at the parliamentary level through the allocation of senior government and party offices. Although the resulting infighting may have been seen as a means of guaranteeing argument and debate in a system in which small parties were usually marginalized, in Japan factionalism tended to revolve more around personal differences than policy or ideological disagreement. One example of this was the conflict between the Fukuda and Tanaka factions during the 1970s and 1980s, which continued long after the two principals had left the scene.

Whereas other competitive party systems have their supporters, or at least apologists, few are prepared to come to the defence of the dominant-party system. Apart from a tendency towards stability and predictability, dominant-partyism is usually seen as a regrettable and unhealthy phenomenon. In the first place, it tends to erode the important constitutional distinction between the state and the party in power. When governments cease to come and go, an insidious process of politicization takes place through which state officials and institutions adjust to the ideological and political priorities of the dominant party. Second, an extended period in power can engender complacency, arrogance and even corruption in the dominant party. The course of Italian and Japanese politics has, for example, regularly been interrupted by scandals, usually involving allegations of financial corruption. Third, a dominant-party system is characterized by weak and ineffective opposition. Criticism and protest can more easily be ignored if they stem from parties that are no longer regarded as genuine rivals for power. Finally, the existence of a 'permanent' party of government may corrode the democratic spirit by encouraging the electorate to fear change and to stick with the 'natural' party of government.

Multiparty systems

A multiparty system is characterized by competition amongst more than two parties, reducing the chances of single-party government and increasing the likelihood of coalitions. However, it is difficult to define multiparty systems in terms of the number of major parties, as such systems sometimes operate

CONCEPT

Coalition

A coalition is a grouping of rival political actors brought together either through the perception of a common threat, or through a recognition that their goals cannot be achieved by working separately. *Electoral* coalitions are alliances through which parties agree not to compete against one another, with a view to maximizing their representation. *Legislative* coalitions are agreements between two or more parties to support a particular bill or programme. *Governing* coalitions are formal agreements between two or more parties that involve a cross-party distribution of ministerial portfolios. A 'grand coalition' or 'national government' comprises all major parties.

through coalitions including smaller parties that are specifically designed to exclude larger parties from government. This is precisely what happened to the French Communist Party (PCF) in the 1950s, and to the Italian Communist Party (PCI) throughout its existence. If the likelihood of coalition government is the index of multipartyism, this classification contains a number of subcategories.

Germany, for example, tends to have a 'two-and-a-half-party' system, in that the CDU and SDP typically have electoral strengths roughly equivalent to those of the Conservative and Labour parties in the UK. However, they were forced into coalitions with the small Free Democrat Party by the workings of the mixed-member proportional electoral system (see p. 211). Italian multipartyism traditionally involves a larger number of relatively small parties. Thus, even the DC rarely came close to achieving 40 per cent of the vote. Sartori (1976) distinguished between two types of multiparty system, which he termed the 'moderate' and 'polarized' pluralist systems. In this categorization, moderate pluralism exists in countries such as Belgium, the Netherlands and Norway, where ideological differences between major parties are slight, and where there is a general inclination to form coalitions and move towards the middle ground. Polarized pluralism, on the other hand, exists when more marked ideological differences separate major parties, some of which adopt an anti-system stance. The existence of electorally strong communist parties (as in France, Italy and Spain until the 1990s), or of significant fascist movements (such as the Movimento Sociale Italiano (MSI) – reborn in 1995 as the 'post-Fascist' Alleanza Nazionale), provided evidence of polarized pluralism.

The strength of multiparty systems is that they create internal checks and balances within government and exhibit a bias in favour of debate, conciliation and compromise. The process of coalition formation and the dynamics of coalition maintenance ensure a broad responsiveness that cannot but take account of competing views and contending interests. Thus, in Germany, the liberal Free Democrats act as a moderating influence on both the conservative CDU and the socialist SPD. Where SPD–Green coalitions have been formed in the *Länder* (provinces), the Green presence has helped to push environmental issues up the political agenda. Similarly, the multiparty features of the Swedish system, which make coalition government more common than not, have encouraged the SAP to build a broad welfare consensus, and to pursue moderate policies that do not alienate business interests.

The principal criticisms of multiparty systems relate to the pitfalls and difficulties of coalition formation. The post-election negotiations and horsetrading that take place when no single party is strong enough to govern alone can take weeks, or (as in Israel and Italy) sometimes months, to complete. More seriously, coalition governments may be fractured and unstable, paying greater attention to squabbles amongst coalition partners than to the tasks of government. Italy is usually cited as the classic example of this, its post-1945 governments having lasted, on average, only 10 months. It would, nevertheless, be a mistake to suggest that coalitions are always associated with instability, as the record of stable and effective coalition government in Germany and Sweden clearly demonstrates. In some respects, in fact, the Italian experience is peculiar, owing as much to the country's political culture and the ideological complexion of its party system as to the dynamics of multipartyism.

A final problem is that the tendency towards moderation and compromise may mean that multiparty systems are so dominated by the political centre that they are unable to offer clear ideological alternatives. Coalition politics tends, naturally, to be characterized by negotiation and conciliation, a search for common ground, rather than by conviction and the politics of principle. This process can be criticized as being implicitly corrupt, in that parties are encouraged to abandon policies and principles in their quest for power. It can also lead to the over-representation of centrist parties and centrist interests, especially when, as in Germany, a small centre party is the only viable coalition partner for both of the larger conservative and socialist parties. Indeed, this is sometimes seen as one of the drawbacks of proportional representation electoral systems, which, by ensuring that the legislative size of parties reflects their electoral strength, are biased in favour of multiparty politics and coalition government.

DECLINE OF PARTIES?

Modern concerns about parties principally stem from evidence of their decline as agents of representation, and as an effective link between government and the people. Evidence of a 'crisis of party politics' can be found in a decline of both party membership and partisanship, reflected in partisan dealignment. For example, by 2007 fewer than 1 per cent of people across the UK belonged to political parties, down from 7 per cent some 50 years before. Membership of the Labour Party fell from more than 1 million in 1956 to around 166,000 in 2009, while Conservative Party membership fell from an estimated 2.8 million to around 250,000 in the same period. A seemingly inexorable rise in the age of party members is as significant, the average age of Conservative Party members in 1998 having risen to 63. Dramatic electoral swings against governing parties have intensified such concerns. Notable examples of this include the slump of the French Socialists in 1993 from 282 seats to just 70, and the virtual annihilation in the same year of the Canadian Progressive Conservatives, who were swept out of office retaining only two seats. Falling voter turnout also illustrates the declining capacity of parties to mobilize electoral support. For instance, Wattenberg (2000) found that, in 19 liberal democracies, turnout had declined on average by 10 per cent between the 1950s and the 1990s, the trend having been particularly prominent in the USA, Western Europe, Japan and Latin America.

Alongside these changes, there is evidence of what has been called 'antipolitics'; that is, the rise of political movements and organizations the only common feature of which appears to be antipathy towards conventional centres of power and opposition to established parties of government. This has been reflected in the emergence of new political movements, the principle attraction of which is that they are untainted by having held power. Good examples have been the dramatic success of Berlesconi's Forza Italia in 1994, and the emergence in the USA since 2008 of the Tea Party movement. The rise of new social movements (see p. 260), such as the women's movement, peace movement and environmental movement, is also part of the same phenomenon. Even when they articulate their views through party organization, as in the case of green parties, these movements tend to assume the mantle of antiparty parties. (The role of such parties and movements in expressing forms of 'anti-politics' is examined in Chapter 20.)

How can the decline of parties be explained? One of the problems that parties suffer from is their real or perceived oligarchical character. Parties are seen as bureaucratized political machines, whose grass-roots members are either inactive, or engaged in dull and routine tasks (attending meetings, sitting on committees and so on). In contrast, single-issue protest groups have been more successful in attracting membership and support, particularly from amongst the young, partly because they are more loosely organized and locally based, and partly because they place a heavier emphasis on participation and activism. The public image of parties has been further tarnished by their links to government and to professional politicians. As political 'insiders', parties are tainted by the power, ambition and corruption that is often associated with high office. In other words, parties are not seen as being 'of the people'; too often, they appear to be consumed by political infighting and the scramble for power, so becoming divorced from the concerns of ordinary people.

An alternative way of explaining party decline is to see it as a symptom of the fact that complex, modern societies are increasingly difficult to govern. Disillusionment and cynicism grow as parties seek power by proclaiming their capacity to solve problems and improve conditions, but fail to deliver once in government. This reflects the mounting difficulties that confront any party of government in the form of the expanding power of interest groups and an increasingly globalized economy. A final explanation is that parties may be declining because the social identities and traditional loyalties that gave rise to them in the first place have started to fade. This can certainly be seen in the decline of class politics, linked to the phenomenon of post-Fordism (see p. 154). In addition, with the decline of old social, religious and other solidarities, new aspirations and sensibilities have come onto the political agenda; notably, those associated with postmaterialism (see p. 177). Whereas broad, programmic parties once succeeded in articulating the goals of major sections of the electorate, issues such as gender equality, nuclear power, animal rights and pollution may require new and different political formations to articulate them. Single-issue groups and social movements may thus be in the process of replacing parties as the crucial link between government and society.

SUMMARY

● A political party is a group of people organized for the purpose of winning government power, and usually displays some measure of ideological cohesion. The principal classifications of parties have distinguished between cadre and mass or, later, catch-all parties, parties of representation and parties of integration, constitutional or 'mainstream' parties and revolutionary or anti-system ones, and left-wing parties and right-wing parties.

● Parties have a number of functions in the political system. These include their role as a mechanism of representation, the formation of political elites and recruitment into politics, the formulation of social goals and government policy, the articulation and aggregation of interests, the mobilization and socialization of the electorate, and the organization of governmental processes and institutional relationships.

● The organization and structure of parties crucially influence the distribution of power within society at large. Party democracy can be promoted either by a wide dispersal of power within the party, or by the concentration of power in the hands of the party's elected and publicly accountable members. Oligarchic tendencies may be an inevitable consequence of organization, or they may arise from the need for party unity and electoral credibility.

● A party system is a network of relationships through which parties interact and influence the political process. In one-party systems, a 'ruling' party effectively functions as a permanent government. In two-party systems, power alternates between two 'major' parties. In dominant-party systems, a single 'major' party retains power for a prolonged period. In multiparty systems, no party is large enough to rule alone, leading to a system of coalition government.

● Party systems shape the broader political process in various ways. They influence the range and nature of choice available to the electorate, and affect the cohesion and stability of governments. They structure the relationship between the executive and the assembly, establish a bias in favour of either conflict or consensus, and shape the general character of the political culture.

● Evidence of a crisis in party politics can be found in the decline in party membership and partisanship, as well as in the rise of 'antiparty' groups and movements. This can be explained by the perception that parties are tainted by power, ambition and corruption, and that they have suffered as a result of general disillusionment caused by the growing inability of governments to deliver on their promises. They are also seen to have failed to articulate the aspirations and sensibilities associated with postmaterialism, or generated within post-industrial societies.

Questions for discussion

● Are all modern political parties essentially catch-all parties?

● Is it possible to have 'post-ideological' parties?

● Could government function in contemporary circumstances without political parties?

● In what ways, and to what extent, do parties promote democracy?

● Why do political parties so often tend to be leader-dominated?

● By what criteria should party systems be judged?

● How have modern parties adjusted to the decline of class and other loyalties?

● Is the age of party politics over?

Further reading

Dalton, R. and D. Farrell, *Political Parties and Democratic Linkage: How Parties Organize Democracy* (2011). An examination of the link between parties and representative government that focuses on their impact on the electoral process and on government.

Katz, R. and W. Crotty (eds), *Handbook of Party Politics* (2006). A wide-ranging collection of articles that discuss the nature, functions and organization of parties and their relationship to society and the state.

Sartori, G., *Parties and Party Systems: A Framework for Analysis* (2005). A classic, if challenging, analysis of the role of parties and the nature of party systems.

Wolinetz, S. (ed.), *Political Parties* (1997). A comprehensive set of articles that examines all aspects of the workings and significance of political parties.

CHAPTER 11

Groups, Interests and Movements

'Ten persons who speak make more noise than ten thousand who are silent.'

NAPOLEON, *Maxims*

PREVIEW   Patterns of political interaction were transformed in the twentieth century by the growing prominence of organized groups and interests. Indeed, in the 1950s and 1960s, at the high point of enthusiasm about 'group politics', it was widely asserted that business interests, trade unions, farm lobbies and the like had displaced assemblies and parties as the key political actors. The interest group universe was further expanded, particularly from the 1960s onwards, by the growth of single-issue protest groups taking up causes ranging from consumer protection to animal rights and from sexual equality to environmental protection. Such groups were often associated with broader social movements (the women's movement, the civil-rights movement, the green movement and so on) and were characterized by the adoption of new styles of activism and campaigning, sometimes termed 'new politics'. Considerable debate, nevertheless, surrounds the nature and significance of groups, interests and movements, especially in relation to their impact on the democratic process. Groups come in all shapes and sizes, and carry out a wide range of functions, being, for instance, agents of citizen empowerment as well as cogs within the machinery of government. There is particular disagreement about political implications of group politics. While some believe that organized groups serve to distribute political power more widely and evenly in society, others argue that groups empower the already powerful and subvert the public interest. These issues are related to questions about how groups exert influence and the factors that allow them to exert political influence. Finally, so-called 'new' social movements have been both praised for stimulating new forms of decentralized political engagement and criticized for encouraging people to abandon the formal representative process.

KEY ISSUES

- What are interest groups, and what different forms do they take?
- What have been the major theories of group politics?
- Do groups help or hinder democracy and effective government?
- How do interest groups exert influence?
- What determines the success or failure of interest groups?
- Why have new social movements emerged, and what is their broader significance?

Alexis de Tocqueville (1805–59)

French politician, political theorist and historian. Following the July Revolution of 1830 in France, Tocqueville visited the USA, ostensibly to study its penal system. This resulted in his epic two-volume *Democracy in America* (1835/40), which developed an ambivalent critique of US democracy with its equality of opportunity, but warned against the 'tyranny of the majority'. His political career was ended by Louis Napoleon's *coup* in 1849, leaving him free to devote his time to historical work such as *The Old Regime and the French Revolution* ([1856] 1947). A friend and correspondent of J. S. Mill, de Tocqueville's writings reflect a highly ambiguous attitude to the advance of political democracy. His ideas have influenced both liberal and conservative theorists, as well as academic sociologists.

GROUP POLITICS

Interest groups (see p. 247), like political parties (see p. 222), constitute one of the major linkages between government and the governed in modern societies. In some respects, their origins parallel those of parties. They were the children of a new age of representativegovernment and came into existence to articulate the increasingly complex divisions and **cleavages** of an emerging industrial society. While political parties, concerned with winning elections, sought to build coalitions of support and broaden their appeal, interest groups usually staked out a more distinct and clear-cut position, in accordance with the particular aspirations or values of the people they represented.

It is difficult to identify the earliest such group. Some groups predated the age of representative government; for example, the Abolition Society, which was founded in Britain in 1787 to oppose the slave trade. The Anti-Corn Law League, established in 1839, is often seen as the model for later UK groups, in that it was set up with the specific purpose of exerting pressure on government. After visiting the USA in the 1830s, Alexis de Tocqueville reported that what he called **association** had already become a 'powerful instrument of action'. Young Italy, set up in 1831 by the Italian patriot Giuseppe Mazzini (see p. 116), became the model for sister nationalist organizations that later sprang up throughout Europe. Similarly, the Society for Women's Rights, founded in France in 1866, stimulated the formation of a worldwide women's suffrage movement. By the end of the nineteenth century powerful farming and business interests operated in most industrial societies, alongside a growing trade-union movement. However, most of the interest groups currently in existence are of much more recent origin. They are, in the main, a product of the explosion in pressure and protest politics that has occurred since the 1960s. As such they may be part of a broader process that has seen the decline of political parties and a growing emphasis on organized groups and social movements (see p. 260) as agents of mobilization and representation.

● **Cleavage**: A social division that creates a collective identity on both sides of the divide.

● **Association**: A group formed by voluntary action, reflecting a recognition of shared interests or common concerns.

Types of group

The task of defining and classifying groups is fraught with danger, given the imprecise nature of groups and their multiplicity of forms. Are we, for instance, concerned with groups or with **interests**? In other words, do we only recognize groups as associations that have a certain level of cohesion and organization, or merely as collections of people who happen to share the same interest but may lack consciousness of the fact? Similarly, are interest groups only concerned with selfish and material interests, or may they also pursue broader causes or public goals? There is also the difficult issue of the relationship between interest groups and government. Are interest groups always autonomous, exerting influence from outside, or may they operate in and through government, perhaps even being part of the government machine itself?

This confusion is compounded by the lack of agreed terminology amongst political scientists active in this field. For instance, whereas the term 'interest group' is used in the USA and elsewhere to describe all organized groups, it tends to be used in the UK to refer only to those groups that advance or defend the interests of their members. The term 'pressure group' is therefore usually preferred in the UK, 'interest group' tending to be used as a subcategory of the broader classification.

Groups can nevertheless be classified into three types:

- communal groups
- institutional groups
- associational groups.

Communal groups

The chief characteristic of communal groups is that they are embedded in the social fabric, in the sense that membership is based on birth, rather than recruitment. Examples of such groups are families, tribes, castes and ethnic groups. Unlike conventional interest groups, to which members choose to belong, and which possess a formal structure and organization, communal groups are founded on the basis of a shared heritage and traditional bonds and loyalties. Such groups still play a major role in the politics of developing states. In Africa, for instance, ethnic, tribal and kinship ties are often the most important basis of interest articulation. Communal groups also continue to survive and exert influence in advanced industrial states, as the resurgence of ethnic nationalism and the significance of Catholic groups in countries like Italy and Ireland demonstrate.

Institutional groups

● **Interest**: That which benefits an individual or group; interests (unlike wants or preferences) are usually understood to be objective or 'real'.

Institutional groups are groups that are part of the machinery of government and attempt to exert influence in and through that machinery. They differ from interest groups in that they enjoy no measure of autonomy or independence. Bureaucracies and the military are the clearest examples of institutional groups, and, not uncommonly, each of these contains a number of competing interests. In the case of authoritarian or totalitarian states, which typically

CONCEPT

Interest group

An interest group (or pressure group) is an organized association that aims to influence the policies or actions of government. Interest groups differ from political parties in the following way. (1) They seek to exert influence from outside, rather than to win or exercise government power. (2) They typically have a narrow issue focus, in that they are usually concerned with a specific cause or the interests of a particular group. (3) They seldom have the broader programmic or ideological features that are generally associated with political parties. Interest groups are distinguished from social movements by their greater degree of formal organization.

• **Direct action**: Political action taken outside the constitutional and legal framework; direct action may range from passive resistance to terrorism.

suppress autonomous groups and movements, rivalry amongst institutional groups may become the principal form of interest articulation. The highly centralized Stalinist system in the USSR, for instance, was driven largely by entrenched bureaucratic and economic interests, in particular those centred around heavy industry. Similarly, the apparently monolithic character of the Hitler state in Germany (1933–45), concealed a reality of bureaucratic infighting as Nazi leaders built up sprawling empires in an endless struggle for power.

Institutional groups are not only of significance in non-democratic regimes. Some go so far as to argue that the bureaucratic elites and vested interests that develop in the ministries, departments and agencies of democratic systems in effect shape the policy process: they serve to constrain, some would say dictate to, elected politicians and elected governments. Such groups certainly also form alliances with conventional interest groups, as in the case of the celebrated 'military–industrial complex'. The significance of the bureaucracy and the military, and the importance of the interests that operate in and through them, are discussed in Chapters 16 and 18, respectively.

Associational groups

Associational groups are ones that are formed by people who come together to pursue shared, but limited, goals. Groups as associations are characterized by voluntary action and the existence of common interests, aspirations or attitudes. The most obvious examples of associational groups are thus what are usually thought of as interest groups or pressure groups. However, the distinction between these and communal groups may sometimes be blurred. For example, when class loyalties are strong and solidaristic, membership of an associational group such as a trade union may be more an expression of social identity than an instrumental act aimed at furthering a particular goal. Although associational groups are becoming increasingly important in developing states, they are usually seen as a feature of industrial societies. Industrialization both generates social differentiation, in the form of a complex web of competing interests, and, in a capitalist setting at least, encourages the growth of self-seeking and individualized patterns of behaviour in the place of ones shaped by custom and tradition. When their primary function is to deal with government and other public bodies, such groups are usually called interest groups.

Interest groups appear in a variety of shapes and sizes. They are concerned with an enormous array of issues and causes, and use tactics that range from serving on public bodies and helping to administer government programmes to organizing campaigns of civil disobedience (see p. 259) and popular protest. Similarly, they may operate at a local, national, or (as discussed later) international level, or at a combination of these. However, anti-constitutional and paramilitary groups are excluded from this classification. Groups such as the Black Panthers and the Irish Republican Army (IRA) may not be categorized as interest groups because they sought fundamentally to restructure the political system, not merely to influence it, and used the tactics of terrorism (see p. 416) and **direct action** instead of pressure politics. Structure must, however, be imposed on the apparently shapeless interest group universe by the attempt to identify the different types of group. The two most common classifications are:

- sectional and promotional groups
- insider and outsider groups.

CONCEPT

Non-governmental organization

A non-governmental organization (NGO) is a private, non-commercial group or body which seeks to achieve its ends through non-violent means. NGOs are usually active in international politics and may be accorded formal consultation rights by bodies such as the UN or EU. *Operational* NGOs are those whose primary purpose is the design and implementation of projects that are usually either development-related or relief-related. *Advocacy* NGOs exist to promote or defend a particular cause, and are more concerned with expertise and specialist knowledge than with operational capacity.

Sectional groups (sometimes called protective or functional groups) exist to advance or protect the (usually material) interests of their members. Trade unions, business corporations, trade associations and professional bodies are the prime examples of this type of group. Their 'sectional' character is derived from the fact that they represent a section of society: workers, employers, consumers, an ethnic or religious group, and so on. Strictly speaking, however, only groups engaged in the production, distribution and exchange of goods and services can be seen as 'functional' groups. In the USA, sectional groups are often classified as 'private interest groups', to stress that their principal concern is the betterment and well-being of their members, not of society in general.

In contrast, *promotional* groups (sometimes termed cause or attitude groups) are set up to advance shared values, ideals or principles. These causes are many and diverse. They include 'pro-choice' and 'pro-life' lobbies on abortion, campaigns in favour of civil liberties or against sex and violence on television, protests about pollution and animal cruelty or in defence of traditional or religious values. In the USA, promotional groups are dubbed 'public interest groups', to emphasize that they promote collective, rather than selective, benefits. When involved in international politics, these groups are often call non-governmental organizations, or NGOs. Promotional groups are therefore defined by the fact that they aim to help groups other than their own members. Save the Whale, for instance, is an organization for whales, not one of whales. Some organizations, of course, have both sectional and promotional features. The National Association for the Advancement of Coloured People (NAACP) addresses the sectional interests of American black people (by opposing discrimination and promoting employment opportunities), but is also concerned with causes such as social justice and racial harmony.

The alternative system of classification is based on the status that groups have in relation to government and the strategies they adopt in order to exert pressure. *Insider* groups enjoy regular, privileged and usually institutionalized access to government through routine consultation or representation on government bodies. In many cases there is an overlap between sectional and insider classifications. This reflects the ability of key economic interests, such as business groups and trade unions, to exert powerful sanctions if their views are ignored by government. Government may also be inclined to consult groups that possess specialist knowledge and information that assists in the formulation of workable policy. Insider status, however, is not always an advantage, since it is conferred only on groups with objectives that are broadly compatible with those of the government and which have a demonstrable capacity to ensure that their members abide by agreed decisions.

Outsider groups, on the other hand, are either not consulted by government or consulted only irregularly and not usually at a senior level. In many cases outsider status is an indication of weakness, in that, lacking formal access to government, these groups are forced to 'go public' in the hope of exercising indirect influence on the policy process. Ironically, then, there is often an inverse relationship between the public profile of an interest group and the political influence it exerts. Radical protest groups in fields such as environmental protection and animal rights may have little choice about being outsiders. Not only are their goals frequently out of step with the priorities of government, but their members and supporters are often attracted by the fact that such groups are untainted by close links with government. In that sense, groups may choose to remain outsiders, both to preserve their ideological purity and independence, and to protect their decentralized power structures.

Models of group politics

Some commentators believe that the pattern and significance of group politics are derived entirely from factors that are specific to each political system. The role of groups thus reflects a particular political culture (see p. 172), party system, set of institutional arrangements, and so on. This means that general conclusions cannot be drawn about the nature of group politics. On the other hand, the understanding of group politics is often shaped by broader assumptions about both the nature of the political process and the distribution of power in society. These assumptions are closely linked to the rival theories of the state examined in Chapter 3. The most influential of these as models of interest group politics are the following:

- pluralism
- corporatism
- the New Right.

Pluralist model

Pluralist theories offer the most positive image of group politics. They stress the capacity of groups to both defend the individual from government and promote democratic responsiveness. The core theme of pluralism (see p. 100) is that political power is fragmented and widely dispersed. Decisions are made through a complex process of bargaining and interaction that ensures that the views and interests of a large number of groups are taken into account. One of the earliest and most influential attempts to develop a pluralist 'group theory' was undertaken by Arthur Bentley in *The Process of Government* ([1908] 1948). Bentley's emphasis on organized groups as the fundamental building blocks of the political process is neatly summed up in his famous dictum: 'when the groups are adequately stated, everything is stated'. David Truman's *The Governmental Process* (1951) is usually seen to have continued this tradition, even if his conclusions were more narrowly focused on the US political process.

Enthusiasm for groups as agents of interest articulation and aggregation was strengthened by the spread of behaviouralism in the 1950s and early 1960s. Systems analysis, for example, portrayed interest groups as 'gatekeepers' that filtered the multiple demands made of government into manageable sets of claims. At the same time, community power studies carried out by analysts such as Robert Dahl (1961) and Nelson Polsby (1963) claimed to find empirical support for the pluralist assertion that no single local elite is able to dominate community decision-making.

From the pluralist perspective, group politics is the very stuff of the democratic process. Indeed, it became common in the 1960s to argue that a form of

Robert Dahl (born 1915)

US political scientist. Appointed professor of political science at Yale University in 1946, Dahl subsequently became one of the USA's most eminent political analysts. In 1953 (with Charles Lindblom) he coined the term 'polyarchy' (rule by the many) to distinguish modern societies from classical democracy. Dahl's early writings reflect the impact of positivist and behaviouralist doctrines and, in the 1950s and early 1960s, he developed a conventional pluralist position. From the late 1960s, however, together with Lindblom and Galbraith (see p. 155), he developed a radicalized form of liberalism, 'neopluralism', that revealed an increasing concern with the power of major capitalist corporations. His major works include *A Preface to Democratic Theory* (1956), *Who Governs?* (1961) and *Dilemmas of Pluralist Democracy* (1982).

pluralist democracy (see p. 101) had superseded more conventional electoral democracy, in that groups and organized interests had replaced political parties as the principal link between government and the governed. The central assumptions of this theory are that all groups and interests have the potential to organize and gain access to government, that they are internally responsive in the sense that leaders broadly articulate the interests or values of their members, and that their political influence is roughly in line with their size and the intensity of their support. One way in which this was demonstrated was by evidence that political power is fragmented in such a way that no group or interest can achieve dominance for any period of time. As Dahl (1956) put it, 'all the active and legitimate groups in the population can make themselves heard at some crucial stage in the process of decision'. The alternative idea of 'countervailing powers', developed in J. K. Galbraith's (see p. 155) early writings, suggests that a dynamic equilibrium naturally emerges amongst competing groups, as the success of, say, business merely encourages opponents, such as labour or consumers, to organize to counter that success. Group politics is thus characterized by a rough balance of power.

This highly optimistic view of group politics has been heavily criticized by elitists and Marxists. Elitists challenge the empirical claims of pluralism by suggesting that they recognize only one 'face' of power: the ability to influence decision-making (see p. 9). In contrast to the notion that power is widely and evenly distributed, elite theorists draw attention to the existence of a 'power elite', comprising the heads of business corporations, political leaders and military chiefs (Mills, 1956). Marxists, for their part, have traditionally emphasized that political power is closely linked to the ownership of productive wealth, which suggests the existence of a capitalist 'ruling class'. For neo-Marxists such as Ralph Miliband (2009) this is reflected in 'unequal competition' between business and labour groups, the former enjoying a control of economic resources, a public status, and a level of access to government that the latter cannot match. The rise of globalization (see p. 142) has renewed such arguments, leading some to suggest that the increased mobility of capital and a free-trade international system has resulted in the 'corporate takeover' of government (Hertz, 2001). In the face of such criticism, a more critical or qualified form of pluralism, neopluralism (see

p. 63), emerged. This has perhaps been most clearly expressed in Charles Lindblom's *Politics and Markets* (1980), which highlighted the privileged position that business groups enjoy in western polyarchies, while acknowledging that this seriously compromises the claim that such societies are democratic.

Corporatist model

Corporatist models of group politics differ from pluralism in that they attempt to trace the implications of the closer links that have developed in industrialized societies between groups and the state. Corporatism is a social theory that emphasizes the privileged position that certain groups enjoy in relation to government, enabling them to influence the formulation and implementation of public policy. Some commentators regard corporatism as a state-specific phenomenon, shaped by particular historical and political circumstances. They thus associate it with countries such as Austria, Sweden, the Netherlands and, to some extent, Germany and Japan, in which the government has customarily practised a form of economic management.

Others, however, see corporatism as a general phenomenon that stems from tendencies implicit in economic and social development, and thus believe that it is manifest, in some form or other, in all advanced industrial states. Even the USA, usually portrayed as the model of pluralist democracy, has invested its regulatory agencies with quasi-legislative powers, thereby fostering the development of formal bonds between government and major interests. From this perspective, corporatist tendencies may merely reflect the symbiotic relationship that exists between groups and government. Groups seek 'insider' status because it gives them access to policy formulation, which enables them better to defend the interests of their members. Government, on the other hand, needs groups, both as a source of knowledge and information, and because the compliance of major interests is essential if policy is to be workable. In increasingly differentiated and complex industrial societies the need for consultation and bargaining continues to grow, with the result that, perhaps inevitably, institutional mechanisms emerge to facilitate it.

The drift towards corporatism in advanced capitalist states, particularly pronounced in the 1960s and 1970s, provoked deep misgivings about the role and power of interest groups. In the first place, corporatism considerably cut down the number and range of groups that enjoyed access to government. Corporatism invariably privileges economic or functional groups, because it leads to a form of **tripartitism** that binds government to business and organized labour. However, it may leave consumer or promotional groups out in the cold, and institutionalized access is likely to be restricted to so-called 'peak' associations that speak on behalf of a range of organizations and groups. In Austria this role is carried out by the Chamber of Commerce and the Trade Union Federation, in the UK by the Confederation of British Industry (CBI) and the Trades Union Congress (TUC), and in the USA by the National Association of Manufacturers and the American Federation of Labor–Congress of Industrial Organizations (AFL–CIO).

A second problem is that, in contrast to the pluralist model, corporatism portrays interest groups as hierarchically ordered and dominated by leaders who are not directly accountable to members. Indeed, it is sometimes argued that the

---

CONCEPT

Corporatism

Corporatism, in its broadest sense, is a means of incorporating organized interests into the processes of government. There are two faces of corporatism. *Authoritarian* corporatism ('state' corporatism) is an ideology or economic form closely associated with Italian Fascism. It was characterized by the political intimidation of industry and the destruction of independent trade unions. *Liberal* corporatism ('societal' corporatism or 'neocorporatism') refers to the tendency found in mature liberal democracies for organized interests to be granted privileged and institutional access to the process of policy formulation.

● **Tripartitism**: The construction of bodies that represent government, business and the unions, designed to institutionalize group consultation.

Public choice

Public-choice theory is a subfield of rational-choice theory (see pp. 14–15) The 'public' character of public-choice theory stems from its concern with the provision of so-called 'public goods'. These are goods that are delivered by government rather than the market, because (as with clean air) their benefit cannot be withheld from individuals who choose not to contribute to their provision. Public-choice theorists have generally highlighted the failures and defects of government in this respect, focusing on issues such as the policy impact of self-serving bureaucrats, and the consequences of interest-group politics.

price that group leaders pay for privileged access to government is a willingness to deliver the compliance of their members. From this point of view, 'government by consultation' may simply be a sham concealing the fact that corporatism acts as a mechanism of social control. Third, concern has been expressed about the threat that corporatism poses to representative democracy. Whereas pluralism suggests that group politics supplements the representative process, corporatism creates the spectre of decisions being made outside the reach of democratic control and through a process of bargaining in no way subject to public scrutiny. Finally, corporatism has been linked to the problem of government 'overload', in which government may effectively be 'captured' by consulted groups and thus be unable to resist their demands. This critique has been advanced most systematically by the New Right.

New Right model

The antipathy of the New Right towards interest groups is derived, ideologically, from the individualism that lies at the heart of neoliberal economics. Social groups and collective bodies of all kinds are therefore viewed with suspicion. This is clearly reflected in the New Right's preference for a market economy driven by self-reliance and entrepreneuralism. However, the New Right has expressed particular concern about the alleged link between corporatism and escalating public spending and the associated problems of over-government. New Right anticorporatism has been influenced by public-choice theory, notably Mancur Olson's *The Logic of Collective Action: Public Goods and the Theory of Groups* (1974). Olson argued that people join interest groups only to secure 'public goods': that is, goods that are to some extent indivisible in that individuals who do not contribute to their provision cannot be prevented from enjoying them.

A pay increase is thus a public good in that workers who are not union members, or who choose not to strike in furtherance of the pay claim, benefit equally with union members and those who did strike. This creates opportunities for individuals to become 'free riders', reaping benefits without incurring the various costs that group membership may entail. This analysis is significant because it implies that there is no guarantee that the existence of a common interest will lead to the formation of an organization to advance or defend that interest. The pluralist assumption that all groups have some kind of political voice therefore becomes highly questionable. Olson also argued that group politics may often empower small groups at the expense of large ones. A larger membership encourages free riding because individuals may calculate that the group's effectiveness will be little impaired by their failure to participate.

This analysis was further developed in Olson's later work, *The Rise and Decline of Nations* (1984), which advanced a trenchant critique of interest group activity, seeing it as a major determinant of the prosperity or economic failure of particular states. The UK and Australia, for example, were seen as suffering from 'institutional sclerosis'. This occurred as strong networks of interest groups emerged that were typically dominated by coalitions of narrow, sectional interests, including trade unions, business organizations and professional associations. The message that there is an inverse relationship between strong and well-organized interest groups, on the one hand, and economic growth and

Debating...
Do interest groups enhance democracy?

Controversy about interest groups largely centres on their impact on democracy and the distribution of political power. While pluralists view group politics as the very stuff of democracy, elitists and others claim that it weakens or undermines the democratic process. Do interest groups empower citizens and widen access to government, or do they strengthen special interests and narrow the distribution of power?

YES

Dispersing power. Interest groups empower groups of people who would otherwise be marginalized and lack political representation. Organized interests, for instance, give a political voice to minorities that tend to be ignored by political parties, which, because of electoral pressures, are more concerned about the views of numerically-strong groups. Few people, moreover, exist outside the interest group universe. Promotional groups are thus formed to act on behalf of people (such as the poor, the elderly or consumers) who find it difficult, for various reasons, to organize themselves, and the use of 'outsider' tactics enables groups to exert influence even though they may lack wealth and institutional power.

Political education. Groups stimulate debate and discussion, helping to create a better-informed and more educated electorate. Not only do interest groups provide citizens with alternative sources of information, but their specialist knowledge and level of technical expertise may even, at times, rival those of government. This is particularly important when it means that radical or critical views (which are inconvenient to the political establishment) can be expressed. Further, interest groups do not support a single viewpoint but rival viewpoints; the most stimulating political debate often takes place between interest groups rather than between interest groups and government.

Boosting participation. While party membership and voter turnout decline, the number of groups and their membership size has steadily increased, meaning that organized interests have become the principal agents of participation in modern political systems. In particular, there has been an explosion of cause or promotional groups, as well as of NGOs. Not only has single-issue politics proved to be popular, but the grass-roots activism and decentralized organization embraced by many campaigning groups have often proved to be attractive to young people and to those who are disillusioned with conventional politics.

NO

Entrenching political inequality. Interest groups typically empower the already powerful. Interest groups that possess money, expertise, institutional leverage and privileged links to government are substantially more powerful than other groups, helping to create a 'power elite'. At the heart of this elite are major corporations, whose influence, in most cases, greatly exceeds the influence of, say, trade unions, charities or environmental groups. By the same token, there are significant, and sometimes large, sections of society that benefit little from interest group representation. This is usually because they lack resources and are difficult, or impossible, to organize.

Non-legitimate power. Unlike conventional politicians, interest group leaders are not popularly elected. Interest groups are therefore not publicly accountable, meaning that the influence they wield is not democratically legitimate. This problem is compounded by the fact that very few interest groups operate on the basis of internal democracy. Leaders are rarely elected by their members and, when they are (as, sometimes, in the case of trade unions), turnout levels are typically low. Indeed, there has been a growing trend for interest groups to be dominated by a small number of senior professionals.

Subverting representative democracy. Interest groups exert influence in ways that are democratically questionable. Insider groups operate 'behind closed doors', their meetings with ministers and government officials being unseen by the public, the media or democratic representatives. No one knows (apart from occasional leaks) who said what to whom, or who influenced whom, and how. Groups subvert representative democracy by both circumventing assemblies and forging direct links with executives, and exerting control over parties and politicians through the provision of campaign finance. Protest groups also undermine democracy when they achieve their objectives through the use of direct action, operating outside the established legal and constitutional framework.

national prosperity on the other had a powerful impact on New Right policies and priorities. The clearest demonstration of this was the backlash against corporatism from the 1980s onwards, spearheaded in the USA by Reagan and in the UK by Thatcher. In the USA, this took the form of an attempt to deregulate the economy by weakening regulatory agencies; in the UK, it was evident in the marginalization and later abolition of corporatist bodies such as the National Economic Development Council (NEDC or Neddy) and a determined assault on trade union power.

Patterns of group politics

How important are interest groups?

It is widely accepted that interest group activity is closely linked to economic and social development. Whereas agrarian or traditional societies tend to be dominated by a small number of interests, advanced industrial ones are complex and highly differentiated. Interest groups thus come to assume a central importance in mediating between the state and a more fragmented society, especially as the spread of education extends political awareness and organizational skills. However, the roles and significance of organized interests vary from system to system, from state to state, and over time. The principal factors determining group influence are the following:

- the political culture
- the institutional structure
- the nature of the party system
- the nature and style of public policy.

The *political culture* is crucial for two reasons. First, it determines whether interest groups are viewed as legitimate or non-legitimate actors, whether their formation and influence is permitted and encouraged, or otherwise. Second, it affects the willingness of people to form or join organized interests or to engage in group politics. At one extreme, regimes can practise **monism**, suppressing all forms of voluntary associational activity in order to ensure a single, unchallengeable centre of state power. This typically occurs in military regimes and one-party states. Although no contemporary or historical state has succeeded in stamping out all forms of group or factional activity, monistic regimes at least push group activity underground or ensure that it is expressed through the party–state apparatus and is thus entangled with the political and ideological goals of the regime. In the case of China, despite the persistence of formal political monolithicism, market reforms and over three decades of relentless economic growth have led to the emergence of new social actors, such as entrepreneurs and migrant workers, creating a form of state corporatism.

Pluralist regimes, on the other hand, not only permit group politics, but encourage and even, in some cases, require it. Groups may be asked to participate in policy formulation or to be represented on public bodies or quangos (see p. 368). One of the reasons for the generally high level of group activity found in the USA, for instance, is the recognition in US political culture of the right of private groups to be heard. This is enshrined in constitutional guarantees of free

● **Monism**: A belief in only one theory or value; monism is reflected politically in enforced obedience to a unitary power and is, thus, implicitly totalitarian.

speech, freedom of the press, freedom of assembly, and so forth. In Japan, the absence of clear distinctions between the public and private realms has created a political culture in which, in predemocratic and democratic periods alike, a close relationship between government and business has been taken for granted.

In contrast, in some European states, organized interests are regarded with suspicion. This has traditionally been the case in France, where, influenced by Jacobin ideology, groups have been seen to both undermine the 'general will' of the people and challenge the strength and unity of the French state. At its high point in 1975, for instance, only 24 per cent of the French workforce belonged to a union, a figure that had fallen to 8 per cent by 2008. However, French political culture also embodies a tradition of direct action, demonstrated by the use by French farmers of road blocks and even lorry hijacks, and by the rebellion of students and trade unionists during the political troubles of May 1968.

The *institutional structure* of government is clearly significant in terms of interest group activity in that it establishes points of access to the policy process. Unitary and centralized political systems, such as the UK's, tend to narrow the scope of group politics and concentrate it around the executive branch of government. Although this does not condemn groups to a marginal existence, it places heavy emphasis on 'insider' status and broadens the capacity of the government of the day to choose whether or not to respond to group pressure. This was most clearly demonstrated in the UK since the 1980s in the downgrading of corporatist bodies and the marginalization of the trade unions. Interest-group activity in France is similarly focused on direct consultation with the administration, particularly since the strengthening of presidential government and the weakening of the National Assembly in the Fifth Republic.

US government, on the other hand, is fragmented and decentralized. This reflects the impact of bicameralism, the separation of powers, federalism and judicial review. The range of 'access points' that this offers interest groups makes the US system peculiarly vulnerable to group pressures. Groups know, for instance, that battles lost in Congress can be refought in the courts, at the state or local level, and so on. Although this undoubtedly acts as a stimulus to group formation, and enlarges the number of influential groups, it may also be self-defeating, in that the activities of groups can end up cancelling each other out. Organized interests may thus act only as 'veto groups'.

The relationship between political parties and interest groups is always complex. In some senses, they are clearly rivals. While parties seek to aggregate interests and form political programmes typically based on broad ideological goals, interest groups are concerned with a narrower and more specific range of issues and objectives. Nevertheless, interest groups often seek to exert influence in and through parties, in some cases even spawning parties in an attempt to gain direct access to power. Many socialist parties, such as the UK Labour Party, were effectively created by the trade unions, and institutional and financial links, albeit modified, endure to this day.

The pattern of interest group politics is also influenced by the *party system*. Dominant-party systems tend, quite naturally, to narrow the focus of group politics, concentrating it on the governing party. Major industrial and commercial interests in Italy and Japan therefore traditionally tried to exert pressure through 'ruling' parties such as the Christian Democrats and the Liberal-Democratic Party, which, in the process, did much to entrench the factional tendencies within these parties. Multiparty systems, on the other hand, are fertile ground for interest group activity, because they broaden the scope of access. The legislative influence of interest groups is perhaps greatest in party systems like the USA's, in which political parties are weak in terms of both organization and discipline. This was demonstrated in the late 1970s by the capacity of business interests effectively to destroy President Carter's energy programme, despite the existence of Democrat majorities in both the House of Representatives and the Senate.

Finally, the level of group activity fluctuates in relation to shifts in *public policy*, particularly the degree to which the state intervenes in economic and social life. As a general rule, **interventionism** goes hand-in-hand with corporatism, although there is a debate about which is the cause and which is the effect. Do interventionist policies force government into a closer relationship with organized interests in the hope of gaining information, advice and cooperation? Or do groups exploit their access to government to extract subsidies, supports and other benefits for their members? Whatever the answer is, it is clear that, amongst western states, the integration of organized interests, particularly functional interests, into public life has been taken furthest where social-democratic policies have been pursued.

The Swedish system is the classic example of this. Interest groups constitute an integral part of the Swedish political scene at every level. There are close, if not institutional, links between the trade unions and the Social Democratic Labour Party (SAP). The legislative process in the *Riksdag* is geared to wide consultation with affected interests, and state officials recognize 'peak' associations such as the Swedish Trade Union Confederation and the Employers' Confederation as 'social partners'. A similar pattern of corporate representation has developed in the Austrian 'chamber' system, which provides statutory representation for major interests such as commerce, agriculture and labour. In Germany, key economic groups such as the Federation of German Employers' Associations, the Federation of German Industry and the German Trades Union Federation are so closely involved in policy formulation that the system has been described as one of 'polyarchic elitism'.

How do groups exert influence?

Interest groups have at their disposal a broad range of tactics and political strategies. Indeed, it is almost unthinkable that a group should confine itself to a single strategy or try to exert influence through just one channel of influence. The methods that groups use vary according to a number of factors. These include the issue with which the group is concerned and how policy in that area is shaped. For instance, in the UK, since most policies relating to civil liberties and political rights are developed by the Ministry of Justice, a group such as Liberty is compelled to seek 'insider' status, which it does by emphasizing itsspecialist knowledge and political respectability. Similarly, the nature of the group and the resources at its disposal are crucial determinants of its political strategy. These resources include the following:

● **Interventionism**:
Government policies designed to regulate or manage economic life; more broadly, a policy of engagement or involvement.

- public sympathy for the group and its goals
- the size of its membership or activist base
- its financial strength and organizational capabilities

Lobby

The term lobby is derived from the areas in parliaments or assemblies where the public may petition legislators, or politicians meet to discuss political business. In modern usage, the term is both a verb and a noun. The verb 'to lobby' means to make direct representations to a policy-maker, using argument or persuasion. Broadly, 'a lobby' (noun) is equivalent to an interest group, in that both aim to influence public policy, as in the case of the farm lobby, the environmental lobby and the roads lobby. Narrowly, following US practice, a lobbyist is a 'professional persuader': that is, a person hired to represent the arguments of interest group clients.

● **Peak group:** A hierarchically organized group that coordinates the work of a collection of groups in the same area of interest, usually formed to strengthen links to government.

- its ability to use sanctions that in some way inconvenience or disrupt government
- personal or institutional links it may have to political parties or government bodies.

Business groups are more likely than, say, trade unions or consumer groups to employ professional lobbyists or mount expensive public-relations campaigns, because, quite simply, they have the financial capacity to do so. The methods used by interest groups are shaped by the channel of access through which influence is exerted. The principal channels of access available are:

- the bureaucracy
- the assembly
- the courts
- political parties
- the mass media
- international organizations.

In all states, interest group activity tends to centre on the *bureaucracy* as the key institution in the process of policy formulation. Access via this channel is largely confined to major economic and functional groups, such as large corporations, employers' associations, trade unions, farming interests and key professions. In Austria, the Netherlands and the Scandinavian states, for example, corporatist institutions have been developed specifically to facilitate group consultation, usually giving **'peak' groups** representing employers' and employees' interests a measure of formal representation. More commonly, the consultative process is informal yet institutionalized, taking place through meetings and regular contacts that are rarely publicized and are beyond the scope of public scrutiny.

The crucial relationship here is usually that between senior bureaucrats and leading business or industrial interests. The advantages that business groups enjoy in this respect include the key role they play in the economy as producers, investors and employers, the overlap in social background and political outlets between business leaders and ministers and senior officials, and the widely held public belief that business interests coincide with the national interest ('what is good for General Motors is good for America'). This relationship is often consolidated by a 'revolving door' through which bureaucrats, on retirement, move into well-paid jobs in private business. In Japan this practice is so clearly established that it is known as *amakudari*, literally meaning 'descent from heaven'. Two factors that have further strengthened big business' control over ministers and bureaucrats are the greater ease with which corporations can relocate production and investment in a global economy, and the advent of the 'new' public management in which governments become increasingly dependent on the private sector for investment in, and sometimes the delivery of, public services (Monbiot, 2001).

Influence exerted through the *assembly*, often called lobbying, is another important form of interest group activity. One manifestation of this is the growth in the number of professional lobbyists, nearly 15,000 of whom were registered in Washington DC in 2009. The significance of the assembly or legislature in this respect depends on two factors: first, the role it plays in the political system and the degree to which it can shape policy, and second, the strength and discipline of the party system. Interest group activity surrounding the US Congress is usually seen as the most intense in the world. This reflects the strength of Congress in terms of its constitutional independence and powerful committee system, and the fact that its decentralized party system allows individual representatives to be easily recruited by groups and causes. Much of this influence is exerted through financial contributions made to election campaigns by political action committees (PACs). However, since the 1990s and as a result of tighter campaign finance laws, 'hard money' donated by PACs has tended to be displaced by 'soft money' (indirect and unregulated donations).

Policy networks (see p. 358) have also developed through institutionalized contacts between legislators (particularly key figures on legislative committees) and 'affected' groups and interests. In the USA these form two 'legs' (executive agencies being the third leg) of the so-called '**iron triangles**' that dominate much of domestic policy-making. Lobbying activities focused on the assembly are less extensive and less significant in states like Canada and the UK in which party discipline is strong and parliaments are usually subject to executive control. Nevertheless, a US-style lobbying industry developed in the UK in the 1980s, with a trebling of the amount of money spent on professional lobbying, usually by parliamentary consultancies. This was in part a consequence of the dismantling of corporatism in the UK. However, it created growing concern about the spectre of 'MPs for hire' and led to the establishment in 1995 of the Committee on Standards in Public Life.

In systems in which the *courts* are unable to challenge legislation and rarely check executive actions, interest group activity focused on the judiciary is of only limited significance. This applies in states like the UK and New Zealand, despite a general tendency since the 1990s towards judicial activism, which has encouraged civil liberties and environmentalist groups in particular to fight campaigns through the courts. Where codified constitutions invest judges with the formal power of judicial review, however, as in Australia and the USA, the court system attracts far greater attention from interest groups. The classic example of this in the USA was the landmark *Brown v Board of Education* Supreme Court ruling in 1954, which rejected the constitutionality of segregation laws. The NAACP had lobbied the US legal community for several years in an attempt to shift attitudes on issues such as race and segregation, and helped to sponsor the case. Similarly, since the 1980s the energies of the US pro-life (anti-abortion) lobby have been largely directed at the Supreme Court, specifically in an attempt to overturn the 1973 *Roe v Wade* judgment, which established the constitutionality of abortion.

Interest group pressure is often also exerted through *political parties*. In some cases, parties and groups are so closely linked by historical, ideological and even institutional ties that they are best thought of as simply two wings of the same social movement. The UK and Australian Labour parties began in this way, and still function, if to a lesser extent, as part of a broader labour movement. Agrarian parties such as the Centre parties in Sweden and Norway are still part of a broad farmers' movement, and even Christian Democratic parties in central Europe can be seen as part of a broad Catholic movement. In other cases, however, the relationship between parties and groups is more pragmatic and instrumental.

The principal means through which groups influence parties is via campaign finance, and the benefits they hope to achieve are clear: 'he who pays the piper

● **Iron triangle**: A closed, mutually supportive relationship in US politics between an executive agency, a special interest group and a legislative committee or subcommittee.

CONCEPT

Civil disobedience

Civil disobedience is law-breaking that is justified by reference to 'higher' religious, moral or political principles. Civil disobedience is an overt and public act; it aims to break a law in order to 'make a point', not to get away with it. Indeed, its moral force is based largely on the willing acceptance of the penalties that follow from law-breaking. This both emphasizes the conscientious or principled nature of the act and provides evidence of the depth of feeling or commitment that lies behind it. The moral character of civil disobedience is normally demonstrated by the strict avoidance of violence.

plays the tune'. Throughout the world, conservative or right-wing parties and candidates are funded largely by business contributions, while support for socialist or left-wing ones traditionally came mainly from organized labour. Spending levels are higher in the USA, where President Obama and his Republican challenger Mitt Romney together spent almost six billion dollars during the 2012 presidential election campaign, mainly donated by business or corporate interests. However, groups may also have good reasons for avoiding too close an association with parties. For one thing, if 'their' party is in opposition, the government of the day may be less sympathetic to their interests; for another, open partisanship may restrict their ability to recruit members from amongst supporters of other parties. As a result, groups such as Shelter and the Child Poverty Action Group in the UK have assiduously guarded their non-partisan status. There are, in addition, examples of political parties that have sought to 'divorce' themselves from interest groups. In the 1990s, the UK Labour Party thus reduced the influence of affiliated trade unions at every level in the party in an attempt to destroy the image that the Labour Party is merely a puppet of the union movement. However, as this was being achieved, the party was also engaged in a 'charm offensive' to attract business backers, the success of which helped to consolidate its shift to the ideological middle ground.

Very different methods are employed by groups that seek to influence government indirectly via the *mass media* (see p. 179) and public opinion campaigns. Tactics here range from petitions, protests and demonstrations to civil disobedience and even the tactical use of violence. Interest groups use such methods for one of two reasons. They may either reflect the group's outsider status and its inability to gain direct access to policy-makers, or they may follow from the nature of the group's activist base or the character of its ideological goals. The traditional practitioners of this form of politics were trade unions, which utilized their 'industrial muscle' in the form of strikes, pickets and marches.

However, the spectacular rise of promotional and cause groups since the 1960s has seen the emergence of new styles of activist politics practised by peace campaigners, environmental lobbyists, animal rights groups, anti-roads protesters, and so on. A common aim of these groups is to attract media attention and stimulate public awareness and sympathy. Greenpeace and Friends of the Earth, for example, have been particularly imaginative in devising protests against nuclear testing, air and water pollution, deforestation, and the use of non-renewable energy sources. The nature and significance of such activities in relation to new social movements are examined in the next main section of the chapter.

Finally, since the closing decades of the twentieth century, interest group activity has increasingly adjusted to the impact of globalization and the strengthening of *international organizations*. Amongst the groups best suited to take advantage of such shifts are charities and environmental campaigners that already possess transnational structures and an international membership. Since its creation in 1961, Amnesty International has developed into a global organization with 52 sections worldwide and a presence in about 100 more countries, and over 3 million members and supporters. Many NGOs enjoy formal representation on international bodies or at international conferences; some 2,400 representatives of NGOs were, for instance, present at the 1992 Rio 'Earth Summit'. The better-funded NGOs now have permanent offices in New York and Brussels, which monitor the work of the UN and EU respectively, and conduct regular lobbying campaigns.

CONCEPT

Social movement

A social movement is a particular form of collective behaviour in which the motive to act springs largely from the attitudes and aspirations of members, typically acting within a loose organizational framework. Being part of a social movement requires a level of commitment and political activism, rather than formal or card-carrying membership: above all, movements move. A movement is different from spontaneous mass action (such as an uprising or rebellion), in that it implies a level of intended and planned action in pursuit of a recognized social goal.

Sectional interest groups in EU member states have adjusted to the fact that, in a number of policy areas, key decisions are increasingly made by EU institutions rather than national ones. This particularly applies in relation to agriculture, trade agreements, competition policy and social and workers' rights. The most financially powerful and best-organized groups operating at the EU level are undoubtedly business interests. Their influence is exerted in various ways: through direct lobbying by large corporations, national trade bodies and peak groups, and through the activities of a new range of EU peak groups such as the European Round Table of Industrialists and the Union of Industrial and Employers' Confederations of Europe (UNICE). The style of lobbying that has developed in the EU focuses primarily on the Commission in Brussels, and, unlike the aggressive lobbying found in the USA and some other domestic contexts, tends to depend on building up long-term relationships based on trust (see p. 87) and reciprocity.

SOCIAL MOVEMENTS

Interest in social movements has been revived by the emergence of so-called 'new' social movements since the 1960s: the women's movement, the environmental or green movement, the peace movement, and so on. However, social movements can be traced back to the early nineteenth century. The earliest were the labour movement, which campaigned for improved conditions for the growing working class, various national movements, usually struggling for independence from multinational European empires, and, in central Europe in particular, a Catholic movement that fought for emancipation through the granting of legal and political rights to Catholics. In the twentieth century it was also common for fascist and right-wing authoritarian groups to be seen as movements rather than as conventional political parties.

New social movements

What is 'new' about the social movements that emerged in the final decades of the twentieth century? In the first place, whereas their more traditional counterparts were movements of the oppressed or disadvantaged, contemporary social movements have more commonly attracted the young, the better-educated and the relatively affluent. This is linked to the second difference: new movements typically have a postmaterial (see p. 177) orientation, being more concerned with 'quality of life' issues than with social advancement. Although the women's movement, for example, addresses material concerns such as equal pay and equal opportunities, it draws from a broader set of values associated with gender equality and opposition to patriarchy. Third, while traditional movements had little in common and seldom worked in tandem, new social movements subscribe to a common, if not always clearly defined, ideology.

In broad terms, their ideological stance is linked to New Left (see p. 261) ideas and values. Such a stance challenges prevailing social goals and political styles, and embraces libertarian aspirations such as personal fulfilment and self-expression. It is therefore not surprising that there is a significant membership overlap, as well as mutual sympathy, amongst the women's, environmental, animal rights, peace, anti-roads, 'anti-capitalist' or anti-globalization and other movements.

Naomi Klein (born 1970)

Canadian journalist, author and anticorporate activist. Klein's *No Logo: Taking Aim at the Brand Bullies* (2000) is a wide-ranging critique of lifestyle branding and labour abuses, and discusses emerging forms of resistance to globalization and corporate domination. It has been described as 'the book that became part of the movement', but has had wider significance in provoking reflection on the nature of consumer capitalism and the tyranny of brand culture. Klein is a frequent and influential media commentator. She lives in Toronto but travels throughout North America, Asia, Latin America and Europe tracking the rise of anticorporate activism and supporting movements campaigning against the negative effects of globalization. Her writings also include *The Shock Doctrine* (2007), which analyses the rise of 'disaster capitalism'.

CONCEPT

New Left

The New Left comprises the thinkers and intellectual movements (prominent in the 1960s and early 1970s) that sought to revitalize socialist thought by developing a radical critique of advanced industrial society. The New Left rejected both 'old' left alternatives: Soviet-style state socialism and de-radicalized western social democracy. Common themes within the New Left include a fundamental rejection of conventional society ('the system') as oppressive, disillusionment with the role of the working class as the revolutionary agent, and a preference for decentralization and participatory democracy.

● **Mass society**: A society characterized by atomism and by cultural and political rootlessness; the concept highlights pessimistic trends in modern societies.

A final difference between traditional and new social movements is that the latter tend to have organizational structures that stress decentralization and participatory decision-making and have also developed new forms of political activism. They thus practise what is sometimes called the 'new politics', which turns away from 'established' parties, interest groups and representative processes towards a more innovative and theatrical form of protest politics. The most dramatic examples of this have been the so-called 'Battle of Seattle' in 1999, in which mass demonstrations against the World Trade Organization degenerated into violent clashes between the police and groups of protesters, and other similar 'anti-capitalist' or anti-globalization protests, for example, in the Occupy movement that sprang up in 2011 (see p. 262). Such demonstrations involve a disparate range of environmental, development, ethnic nationalist, anarchist and revolutionary socialist groups, with the internet and mobile phones providing the principal means of communications. The ideas of the emergent anti-globalization movement have been articulated in the writing of authors such as Noam Chomsky (see p. 181) and Naomi Klein.

The emergence of a new generation of social movements practising new styles of activism has significantly shifted views about the nature and significance of movements themselves. The experience of totalitarianism (see p. 269) in the period between the two world wars encouraged mass society theorists such as Erich Fromm (1900–80) and Hannah Arendt (see p. 7) to see movements in distinctly negative terms. From the **mass society** perspective, social movements reflect a 'flight from freedom' (Fromm, 1941), an attempt by alienated individuals to achieve security and identity through fanatical commitment to a cause and obedience to a (usually fascist) leader. In contrast, new social movements are usually interpreted as rational and instrumental actors, whose use of informal and unconventional means merely reflects the resources available to them (Zald and McCarthy, 1987). The emergence of new social movements is widely seen as evidence of the fact that power in postindustrial societies is increasingly dispersed and fragmented. The class-based politics of old has thus been replaced by a new politics based on what Laclau and Mouffe (2001) called 'democratic pluralism'. Not only do new movements offer new and rival centres of power, but they also diffuse power more effectively by resisting bureaucratization and developing more spontaneous, affective and decentralized forms of organization.

POLITICS IN ACTION . . .

The Occupy movement: a counter-hegemonic force?

Events: On 17 September 2011, about 5,000 people – carrying banners, shouting slogans and banging drums – gathered in New York and started to make their way to Zuccotti Park, located in the Wall Street financial district. There they erected tents, set up kitchens and established peaceful barricades. The Occupy movement was thus born with Occupy Wall Street (OWS), and quickly developed into a truly global wave of protest. On 15 October, tens of thousands of protestors took to the streets in some 82 countries around the world, affecting over 750 towns and cities, many demonstrators following the example of 'the Zuccottis' in setting up semi-permanent protest camps in parks or other prominent public spaces, usually close to financial centres. Although protests in different countries were often shaped by local issues and concerns, the common goals of the Occupy movement were to highlight social and economic inequality, and to condemn as unfair and unstable the dominance of the world economy by big corporations and the global financial system.

Significance: On one level, the Occupy movement is merely a further manifestation of anti-capitalist activism that dates back to the 1999 'Battle of Seattle'. However, the upsurge in Occupy protests was particularly significant in at least two respects. First, and most importantly, it was a response to the global financial crisis of 2007–09 and its aftermath, and thus constituted an attempt to challenge the values and redress the power imbalances that supposedly underpinned the crisis. This was evident in the movement's recurrent focus on the vulnerabilities and injustices that flow from the dominant position that banks and financial institutions have acquired as a result of three decades of neoliberal globalization. Across much of southern Europe and elsewhere, Occupy activism expressed anger at the politics of austerity. In this respect, the Occupy movement expressed anxieties and frustrations that mainstream political parties and conventional interest groups clearly struggled to articulate. Second, the Occupy movement drew inspiration from the Arab Spring (see p. 88), with OWS sometimes being portrayed as the 'Tahir moment' of the Occupy movement (harking back to the waves of demonstrations in Cairo's Tahir Square that helped to bring about the fall of President Mubarak in May 2011). As such, the Occupy protestors were seeking to take advantage of what was seen as a major shift in global politics in favour of 'people power'.

How effective were the Occupy protests? This is a difficult question to answer as new social movements typically seek to raise political consciousness, and to shift values and attitudes, rather than affect specific public policies. In the case of Occupy, it looked to precipitate a 'global spiritual insurrection', a very difficult thing to quantify. The movement also attracted criticism, however. In the first place, it appeared to go little further than previous incarnations of the anti-capitalist movement in developing a systematic and coherent critique of neoliberal globalization, or in outlining a viable alternative. This, in part, reflects the political and ideological diversity within the movement itself. While some Occupy protestors were genuinely 'anti-capitalist', adopting a Marxist-style analysis of capitalism, many within the movement merely wished to remove the 'worst excesses' of capitalism. Second, although radical decentralization and participatory decision-making structures may have been part of Occupy's appeal, especially as far as the young and marginalized are concerned, it is difficult to transform a collection of 'anarchist swarms' into a sustainable mass movement. Finally, Occupy's tactic of establishing protest camps had clear drawbacks, not least because it was highly unlikely that such camps would be allowed to become permanent, meaning that the focus of the protest would be lost. Over time, the Occupy movement has thus become more tactically flexible, placing less emphasis on semi-permanent protest camps, and adopting wider and more innovative forms of protest.

Betty Friedan (1921–2006)

US feminist and political activist, sometimes seen as the 'mother' of women's liberation. Betty Friedan's *The Feminine Mystique* (1963) is often credited with having stimulated the emergence of 'second wave' feminism. In it, she examined 'the problem with no name': the sense of frustration and despair afflicting suburban American women. In 1966, she helped to found the National Organization of Women (NOW), becoming its first president. In *The Second Stage* (1983), Friedan drew attention to the danger that the pursuit of 'personhood' might encourage women to deny the importance of children, the home, and the family. Her later writings include *The Fountain of Age* (1993).

Nevertheless, the impact of social movements is more difficult to assess than that of political parties or interest groups. This is because of the broader nature of their goals, and because, to some extent, they exert influence through less tangible cultural strategies. However, it is clear that in cases like the women's movement and the environmental movement profound political changes have been achieved through shifts in cultural values and moral attitudes brought about over a number of years. For example, the Women's Liberation Movement (WLM) emerged in the 1960s as a collection of groups and organizations mobilized by the emerging ideas of 'second wave' feminism, as expressed in the writings of such as Betty Friedan, Germaine Greer (1970) and Kate Millett (1970). Despite the achievement by the women's movement of advances in specific areas, such as equal pay and the legalization of abortion, perhaps its most significant achievement is an increasing general awareness of gender issues and the eroding of support for patriarchal attitudes and institutions. This is a cultural change that has had a deep, if unquantifiable, impact on public policy at many levels.

The environmental movement has brought about similar politico-cultural shifts. Not only have governments been confronted by interest group campaigns mounted by the likes of Greenpeace, Friends of the Earth and the Worldwide Fund for Nature, but they have also been influenced by broader anxieties about the environment that extend well beyond those expressed by the formal membership of such organizations. Since the 1970s these concerns have also been articulated by green parties. Typically, these parties have embraced the idea of 'new politics', styling themselves as 'anti-system' parties or even 'anti-party' parties, and placing a heavy emphasis on decentralization and popular activism. The impact of the environmental movement has also extended to conventional or 'grey' parties, many of which have responded to new popular sensibilities by trying to establish their green credentials. By contrast, the 'anti-capitalist' movement, or, more accurately, the loose coalition of groups that has been brought together by resistance to globalization and its associated consumerist values and free-trade practices, has as yet been less successful. Although international summit meetings have become much more difficult to arrange, there is little sign of governments or mainstream parties revising their support for free trade (see p. 437) and economic deregulation.

SUMMARY

- An interest or pressure group is an organized association that aims to influence the policies or actions of government. Sectional groups advance or protect the (usually material) interests of their members, while promotional ones are concerned with shared values, ideals or principles. Whereas insider groups enjoy privileged access to policy formulation, outsider groups lack access to government and so are forced to 'go public'.

- Group politics has been understood in a number of ways. Pluralism emphasizes the dispersal of power and the ability of groups to guarantee democratic accountability. Corporatism highlights the privileged position that certain groups enjoy in relation to government. The New Right draws attention to the threat that groups pose in terms of over-government and economic inefficiency.

- Organized groups benefit the political system by strengthening representation, promoting debate and discussion, broadening political participation and acting as a check on government power. They may, nevertheless, pose a threat, in that they entrench political inequality, are socially and politically divisive, exercise non-legitimate and unaccountable power, and make the policy process more closed and secretive.

- Interest groups exert influence through a variety of channels, including the bureaucracy, the assembly, the courts, the mass media, the parties and international bodies. The level of influence that groups have in a particular system, however, relates to how accommodating that system is to group activity in general, and to what access points it offers groups in terms of the distribution of policy-making power.

- Interest groups have at their disposal a wide range of tactics and political strategies. Their resources may include public sympathy for the group and its goals, the size of its membership or activist base, its financial strength and organizational capabilities, its ability to use sanctions against government and its personal or institutional links with political parties or government bodies.

- A social movement is a collective body in which there is a high level of commitment and political activism not necessarily based on a formal organization. New social movements are distinguished by their capacity to attract the young, better-educated and relatively affluent; their generally postmaterial orientation; and their commitment to new forms of political activism, sometimes called the 'new politics'.

Questions for discussion

- Why is it sometimes difficult to distinguish between interest groups and political parties?
- Does group politics allow private interests to prevail over the public good?
- Are organized groups the principal means through which interests are articulated in modern societies?
- Does corporatism work more to the benefit of groups, or more to the benefit of government?
- Do interest groups promote democracy, or undermine it?
- Why are some interest groups more powerful than others?
- In what sense are new social movements 'new'?
- To what extent have new social movements had an impact on public policy?

Further reading

Cigler, C. and B. Loomis (eds), *Interest Group Politics* (2011). A wide-ranging examination of various aspects of group politics that focuses primarily on the USA.

Jordan, G. and W. Maloney, *Democracy and Interest Groups: Enhancing Democracy?* (2007). An analysis of the ways and extent to which interest groups promote democracy, taking account of concerns about growing civic disengagement.

Tarrow, S., *Power in Movement: Social Movements and Contentious Politics* (2011). A useful introduction to the nature and significance of social movements.

Wilson, G., *Interest Groups* (1990). A clear and concise discussion of the role of groups in liberal democracies that remains a useful introduction to the subject.

CHAPTER 12

Governments, Systems and Regimes

'That government is best which governs not at all.'

HENRY DAVID THOREAU, *Civil Disobedience* (1849)

PREVIEW

Classifying the various forms of government has been one of the principal concerns of political analysis through the ages. This process can be traced back to the fourth century BCE, when Aristotle made the first recorded attempt to describe the political regimes then in existence, using terms such as 'democracy', 'oligarchy' and 'tyranny' that are still commonly employed today. From the eighteenth century onwards, governments were increasingly classified as monarchies or republics, or as auto-cratic or constitutional regimes. During the twentieth century, these distinctions were further sharpened. The 'three worlds' classification of political systems, which was particularly fashionable during the Cold War period, created an image of world politics dominated by a struggle between democracy and totalitarianism. However, in the light of modern developments, such as the collapse of communism, the rise of East Asia, and the emergence of political Islam, all such classifications appear outdated. Nevertheless, it is not entirely clear what these shifts mean. Some inter-pret them as an indication that democratization, modelled around the principle and structures of western liberal democracy, is a natural and inevitable process. In this view, liberal democracy constitutes the final form of human government. Others, nevertheless, argue that the modern world is becoming politically more diffuse and fragmented. From this perspective, not only is liberal democracy culturally-bound rather than universally applicable, but alternative regimes including authoritarian systems and forms of illiberal democracy, may prove to be more successful and enduring than expected.

KEY ISSUES

- What is the difference between governments, political systems and regimes?
- What is the purpose of classifying systems of government?
- On what basis have, and should, regimes be classified?
- What are the major regimes of the modern world?
- Has western liberal democracy triumphed worldwide?

CONCEPT

Government

Government in its broadest sense, refers to any mechanism through which ordered rule is maintained, its central features being the ability to make collective decisions and the capacity to enforce them. However, the term is more commonly understood to describe the formal and institutional processes that operate at the national level to maintain public order and facilitate collective action. The core functions of government are, thus, to make law (legislation), implement law (execution) and interpret law (adjudication). In some cases, the political executive (see p. 285) alone is referred to as 'the government'.

● **Political system**: A network of relationships through which government generates 'outputs' (policies) in response to 'inputs' (demands or support) from the general public.

● *Coup d'état*: (French) A sudden and forcible seizure of government power through illegal and unconstitutional action.

● **Government gridlock**: Paralysis resulting from institutional rivalry within government, or the attempt to respond to conflicting public demands.

TRADITIONAL SYSTEMS OF CLASSIFICATION

Before we examine how different systems of rule have been classified, it is necessary for us to reflect on both what is being classified, and why such classifications have been undertaken. First, what is 'government', and how do governments differ from 'political systems' or 'regimes'? 'Government' refers to the institutional processes through which collective and usually binding decisions are made; its various institutions constitute the subject matter of Chapters 12–16 of this book. A **political system** or regime, on the other hand, is a broader term that encompasses not only the mechanisms of government and the institutions of the state, but also the structures and processes through which these interact with the larger society.

A political system is, in effect, a subsystem of the larger social system. It is a 'system', in that there are interrelationships within a complex whole; and 'political', in that these interrelationships relate to the distribution of power, wealth and resources in society. Political regimes can thus be characterized as effectively by the organization of economic life as they are by the governmental processes through which they operate. A regime is therefore a 'system of rule' that endures despite the fact that governments come and go. Whereas governments can be changed by elections, through dynastic succession, as a result of *coups d'état*, and so on, regimes can be changed only by military intervention from without, or by some kind of revolutionary upheaval from within.

Why classify political systems?

The interest in classifying political systems stems from two sources. First, classification is an essential aid to the *understanding* of politics and government. As in most social sciences, understanding in politics is acquired largely through a process of comparison, particularly as experimental methods are generally inapplicable. It is not possible, for instance, to devise experiments to test whether, say, US government would be less susceptible to institutional **government gridlock** if it abandoned the separation of powers (see p. 313), or whether communism (see p. 275) could have survived in the USSR had reforms been instigated a generation earlier. In consequence, we look to comparison to throw into relief what we are studying. Through the highlighting of similarities and differences between what might otherwise be bewildering collections of facts, comparison helps us to distinguish between what is significant and meaningful, and what is not. In this process, we are able both to develop theories, hypotheses and concepts, and, to some extent, to test them. As Alexis de Tocqueville (see p. 245) put it, 'without comparisons to make, the mind does not know how to proceed'. The attempt to classify systems of rule is, therefore, merely a device for making the process of comparison more methodical and systematic.

The second purpose of classification is to facilitate *evaluation*, rather than analysis. Since Aristotle (see p. 6), those who have sought to understand political regimes have often been as keen to 'improve' government as to understand it. In other words, descriptive understanding is closely tied up with normative judgements: questions about what *is* are linked to questions about what *should* be. In

CONCEPT

Utopia, utopianism

A utopia (from the Greek *outopia*, meaning 'nowhere', or *eutopia*, meaning 'good place') is literally an ideal or perfect society. Although utopias of various kinds can be envisaged, most are characterized by the abolition of want, the absence of conflict, and the avoidance of violence and oppression. Utopianism is a style of political theorizing that develops a critique of the existing order by constructing a model of an ideal or perfect alternative. However, the term is often used in a pejorative sense to imply deluded or fanciful thinking, a belief in an impossible goal.

its extreme form, this process may involve a search for an 'ideal' system of rule, or even a utopia, and this can be seen in works such as Plato's (see p. 13) *Republic*, Thomas More's *Utopia* ([1516] 1965), and Peter Kropotkin's *Fields, Factories and Workshops* (1912). In a more modest form, this type of classification allows for qualitative judgements to be made in relation to political structures and governmental forms. Only a comparative approach, for instance, enables us to consider questions such as 'Should the transition to liberal democracy in Russia and other former communist states be welcomed and encouraged?', 'Should India abandon federalism in favour of either a unitary system or regional independence?' and 'Should the UK adopt a "written" constitution?'

All systems of classification have their drawbacks, however. In the first place, as with all analytical devices, there is a danger of simplification. The classification of regimes under the same heading draws attention to the similarities that they share, but there is a risk that the differences that divide them will be ignored or disguised. A related problem is a possible failure to see that a phenomenon may have different meanings in different contexts. For instance, in Japan and throughout East Asia, 'the state' may be different in kind and significance from 'the state' as generally understood in the context of the West (see p. 274). Comparative analysis is therefore hampered by the constant danger of **ethnocentrism**. Second, value biases tend to intrude into the classification process. This can be seen in the tendency to classify communist and fascist regimes as 'totalitarian', implying that western liberal democracies were fighting the *same* enemy in the Cold War as they had done in World War II. Finally, all systems of classification have the drawback that they are necessarily state-bound: they treat individual countries as coherent or independent entities in their own right. Although this approach is by no means invalid, it is now widely viewed as incomplete in the light of the phenomenon of globalization (see p. 142).

Classical typologies

Without doubt, the most influential system of classification was that devised by Aristotle in the fourth century BCE, which was based on his analysis of the 158 Greek city-states then in existence. This system dominated thinking on the subject for roughly the next 2,500 years. Aristotle held that governments could be categorized on the basis of two questions: 'Who rules?', and 'Who benefits from rule?' Government, he believed, could be placed in the hands of a single individual, a small group, or the many. In each case, however, government could be conducted either in the selfish interests of the rulers, or for the benefit of the entire community. He thus identified the six forms of government shown in Figure 12.1.

Aristotle's purpose was to evaluate forms of government on normative grounds in the hope of identifying the 'ideal' constitution. In his view, tyranny, oligarchy and democracy were all debased or perverted forms of rule in which a single person, a small group and the masses, respectively, governed in their own interests and, therefore, at the expense of others. In contrast, monarchy, aristocracy and polity were to be preferred, because in these forms of government the individual, small group and the masses, respectively, governed in the interests of all. Aristotle declared tyranny to be the worst of all possible constitutions, as it reduced citizens to the status of slaves. Monarchy and aristocracy were, on the

● **Ethnocentrism**: The application of values and theories drawn from one's own culture to other groups and peoples; ethnocentrism implies bias or distortion (see p. 355).

CONCEPT

Absolutism

Absolutism is the theory or practice of absolute government, most commonly associated with an absolute monarchy (see p. 292). Government is 'absolute', in the sense that it possesses unfettered power: government cannot be constrained by a body external to itself. The absolutist principle, nevertheless, resides in the claim to an unlimited right to rule (as in divine right), rather than the exercise of unchallengeable power. As it is based on a principled claim, whether religious or rational, absolutism does not invest government with arbitrary power, unlikely dictatorship (see p. 281).

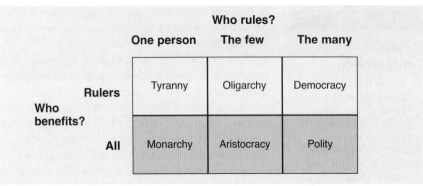

Figure 12.1   Aristotle's six forms of government

other hand, impractical, because they were based on a God-like willingness to place the good of the community before the rulers' own interests. Polity (rule by the many in the interests of all) was accepted as the most practicable of constitutions. Nevertheless, in a tradition that endured through to the twentieth century, Aristotle criticized popular rule on the grounds that the masses would resent the wealth of the few, and too easily fall under the sway of a **demagogue**. He therefore advocated a 'mixed' constitution that combined elements of both democracy and aristocracy, and left the government in the hands of the 'middle classes', those who were neither rich nor poor.

The Aristotelian system was later developed by thinkers such as Thomas Hobbes (see p. 61) and Jean Bodin (1530–96). Their particular concern was with the principle of sovereignty (see p. 58), viewed as the basis for all stable political regimes. Sovereignty was taken to mean the 'most high and perpetual' power, a power that alone could guarantee orderly rule. Bodin's *The Six Bookes of a Commonweale* ([1576] 1962) offered a wider-ranging account of the locus of sovereignty in political regimes, both contemporary and classical. He concluded that absolutism was the most defensible of regimes, as it established a sovereign who makes law but is not bound by those laws. The overriding merit of vesting sovereignty in a single individual was that it would then be indivisible: sovereignty would be expressed in a single voice that could claim final authority. Bodin nevertheless argued that absolute monarchs were constrained by the existence of higher law in the form of the will of God or natural law. On the other hand, in *Leviathan* ([1651] 1968), Hobbes portrayed sovereignty as a monopoly of coercive power, implying that the sovereign was entirely unconstrained.

These ideas were later revised by early liberals such as John Locke (see p. 31) and Montesquieu (see p. 312), who championed the cause of constitutional government. Locke, in *Two Treatises of Government* ([1690] 1965), argued that sovereignty resided with the people, not the monarch, and he advocated a system of limited government to provide protection for natural rights; notably, the rights to life, liberty and property. In his epic *The Spirit of the Laws* ([1748] 1949), Montesquieu attempted to develop a 'scientific' study of human society, designed to uncover the constitutional circumstances that would best protect individual liberty. A severe critic of absolutism and an admirer of the English parliamentary tradition, he proposed a system of checks and balances in the form of a 'separation of powers' between the executive, legislative and judicial

● **Demagogue**: A political leader whose control over the masses is based on the ability to whip up hysterical enthusiasm.

Totalitarianism

Totalitarianism is an all-encompassing system of political rule, typically established by pervasive ideological manipulation and open terror. Totalitarianism differs from autocracy and authoritarianism (see p. 277), in that it seeks to politicize every aspect of social and personal existence, rather than just suppress political opposition. Totalitarian regimes are sometimes identified through a 'six-point syndrome' (Friedrich and Brzezinski, 1963): (1) an official ideology; (2) a one-party state, usually led by an all-powerful leader; (3) a system of terroristic policing; (4) a monopoly of the means of mass communication; (5) a monopoly of the means of armed combat; and (6) state control of all aspects of economic life.

● **Republicanism:** The principle that political authority stems ultimately from the consent of the people; the rejection of monarchical and dynastic principles.

● **Gross domestic product:** The total financial value of final goods and services produced in an economy over one year.

institutions. This principle was incorporated into the US constitution (1787), and it later came to be seen as one of the defining features of liberal democratic government.

The 'classical' classification of regimes, stemming from the writings of Aristotle, was rendered increasingly redundant by the development of modern constitutional systems from the late eighteenth century onwards. In their different ways, the constitutional **republicanism** established in the USA following the American War of Independence of 1775–83, the democratic radicalism unleashed in France by the 1789 French Revolution, and the form of parliamentary government that gradually emerged in the UK created political realities that were substantially more complex than early thinkers had envisaged. Traditional systems of classification were therefore displaced by a growing emphasis on the constitutional and institutional features of political rule. In many ways, this built on Montesquieu's work, in that particular attention was paid to the relationships between the various branches of government. Thus, monarchies were distinguished from republics, parliamentary government (see p. 310) was distinguished from presidential government (see p. 289), and unitary systems were distinguished from federal systems.

The 'three worlds' typology

During the twentieth century, historical developments once again altered the basis of political classification. The appearance in the interwar period of new forms of authoritarianism (see p. 277), particularly in Stalinist Russia, Fascist Italy and Nazi Germany, encouraged the view that the world was divided into two kinds of regime: democratic states and totalitarian states. The stark contrast between democracy and totalitarianism dominated attempts at regime classification through much of the 1950s and 1960s, despite the fact that the fascist and Nazi regimes had collapsed at the end of World War II. Nevertheless, there was a growing awareness that this approach was shaped by the antagonisms of the Cold War, and that it could perhaps be seen as a species of Cold War ideology, and this stimulated the search for a more value-neutral and ideologically impartial system of classification. This led to the growing popularity of the so-called 'three worlds' approach – the belief that the political world could be divided into three distinct blocs:

● a capitalist 'first world'
● a communist 'second world'
● a developing 'third world'.

The three-worlds classification had economic, ideological, political and strategic dimensions. Industrialized western regimes were 'first' in economic terms, in that their populations enjoyed the highest levels of mass affluence. In 1983, these countries generated 63 per cent of the world's **gross domestic product** (GDP) while having only 15 per cent of the world's population (World Bank, 1985). Communist regimes were 'second', insofar as they were largely industrialized and capable of satisfying the population's basic material needs. These countries produced 19 per cent of the world's GDP with 33 per cent of the world's population. The less-developed countries of Africa, Asia and Latin America were

CONCEPT

Liberal democracy

A liberal democracy is a political regime in which a 'liberal' commitment to limited government is blended with a 'democratic' belief in popular rule. Its key features are: (1) the right to rule is gained through success in regular and competitive elections, based on universal adult suffrage; (2) constraints on government imposed by a constitution, institutional checks and balances, and protections for individual and minority rights; and (3) a vigorous civil society including a private enterprise economy, independent trade unions and a free press. The terms liberal democracy and and pluralist democracy (see p. 101) are often used interchangeably.

'third', in the sense that they were economically dependent and often suffered from widespread poverty. They produced 18 per cent of the world's GDP with 52 per cent of the world's population.

The first and second worlds were further divided by fierce ideological rivalry. The first world was wedded to 'capitalist' principles, such as the desirability of private enterprise, material incentives and the free market; the second world was committed to 'communist' values such as social equality, collective endeavour, and the need for centralized planning. Such ideological differences had clear political manifestations. First-world regimes practised liberal-democratic politics based on a competitive struggle for power at election time. Second-world regimes were one-party states, dominated by 'ruling' communist parties. Third-world regimes were typically authoritarian, and governed by traditional monarchs, dictators or, simply, the army. The three-worlds classification was underpinned by a bipolar world order, in which a USA-dominated West confronted a USSR-dominated East. This order was sustained by the emergence of two rival military camps in the form of NATO and the Warsaw Pact. Not infrequently, the 'non-aligned' third world was the battleground on which this geopolitical struggle was conducted, a fact that did much to ensure its continued political and economic subordination.

Since the 1970s, however, this system of classification has been increasingly difficult to sustain. New patterns of economic development have brought material affluence to parts of the third world; notably, the oil-rich states of the Middle East and the newly industrialized states of East Asia, Southeast Asia, and, to some extent, Latin America. In contrast, poverty became, if anything, more deeply entrenched in parts of sub-Saharan Africa which, in the 1990s, in particular, constituted a kind of 'fourth world'. Moreover, the advance of democratization (see p. 272) in Asia, Latin America and Africa, especially during the 1980s and 1990s, has meant that third-world regimes are no longer uniformly authoritarian. Indeed, the phrase 'third world' is widely resented as being demeaning, because it implies entrenched disadvantage. The term 'developing world' is usually seen as preferable.

Without doubt, however, the most catastrophic single blow to the three-worlds model resulted from the eastern European revolutions of 1989–91. These led to the collapse of orthodox communist regimes in the USSR and elsewhere, and unleashed a process of political liberalization and market reform. Indeed, Francis Fukuyama (see p. 271) went so far as to proclaim that this development amounted to the 'end of history' (see p. 44). He meant by this that ideological debate had effectively ended with the worldwide triumph of western liberal democracy. Quite simply, second-world and third-world regimes were collapsing as a result of the recognition that only the capitalist first world offered the prospect of economic prosperity and political stability.

REGIMES OF THE MODERN WORLD

Since the late 1980s, the regime-classification industry has been in a limbo. Older categories, particularly the 'three worlds' division, were certainly redundant, but the political contours of the new world were far from clear. Moreover, the 'end of history' scenario was only fleetingly attractive, having been sustained by the wave

Francis Fukuyama (born 1952)

US social analyst and political commentator. Fukuyama was born in Chicago, USA, the son of a Protestant preacher. He was a member of the Policy Planning Staff of the US State Department before becoming an academic; he is currently at Johns Hopkins University. A staunch Republican, he came to international prominence as a result of his article 'The End of History?' (1989), which he later developed into *The End of History and the Last Man* (1992). These works claimed that the history of ideas had ended with the recognition of liberal democracy as 'the final form of human government'. In *Trust* (1996) and *The Great Disruption* (1999), Fukuyama discussed the relationship between economic development and social cohesion. In *The Origins of Political Order* (2011), he laid down the basis for a theory of political development.

of democratization in the late 1980s and early 2000s, and drawing impetus in particular from the collapse of communism. In some senses, this liberal-democratic triumphalism reflected the persistence of a western-centric viewpoint, and it may, anyway, have been a hangover from the days of the Cold War. The image of a 'world of liberal democracies' suggested the superiority of a specifically western model of development, based perhaps especially on the USA, and it implied that values such as individualism (see p. 158), rights and choice are universally applicable. One result of this was a failure to recognize the significance, for instance, of Islamic and Confucian political forms, which tended to be dismissed as mere aberrations, or simply as evidence of resistance to the otherwise unchallenged advance of liberal democracy.

However, one of the difficulties of establishing a new system of classification is that there is no consensus about the criteria on which such a system should be based. No system of classification relies on a single all-important factor. Nevertheless, particular systems have tended to prioritize different sets of criteria. Among the parameters most commonly used are the following:

- Who rules? Is political participation confined to an elite body or privileged group, or does it encompass the entire population?
- How is compliance achieved? Is government obeyed as a result of the exercise or threat of force, or through bargaining and compromise?
- Is government power centralized or fragmented? What kinds of check and balance operate in the political system?
- How is government power acquired and transferred? Is a regime open and competitive, or is it monolithic?
- What is the balance between the state and the individual? What is the distribution of rights and responsibilities between government and citizens?
- What is the level of material development? How materially affluent is the society, and how equally is wealth distributed?
- How is economic life organized? Is the economy geared to the market or to planning, and what economic role does government play?
- How stable is a regime? Has the regime survived over time, and does it have the capacity to respond to new demands and challenges?

CONCEPT

Democratization

Democratization refers to the process of transition from authoritarianism to liberal democracy. Democratization encompasses three, sometimes overlapping, processes. (1) The break-down of the old regime; this usually involves a loss of legitimacy (see p. 81) and the faltering loyalty of the police and military. (2) 'Democratic transition' witnesses the construction of new liberal-democratic structures and processes. (3) 'Democratic consolidation' sees these new structures and processes becoming so embedded in the minds of elites and the masses that democracy becomes 'the only game in town' (Przeworski, 1991).

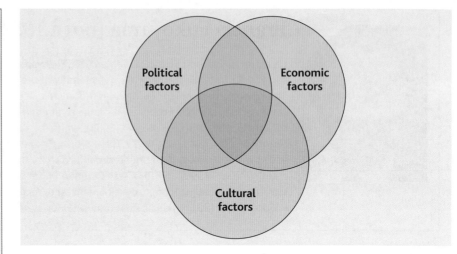

Figure 12.2   Key regime features

A *constitutional–institutional* approach to classification that was influenced by 'classical' typologies was adopted in the nineteenth and early twentieth centuries. This approach highlighted, for instance, differences between codified and uncodified constitutions, parliamentary and presidential systems, and federal and unitary systems. A *structural–functional* approach, however, was developed out of systems theory, which became increasingly prominent in the 1950s and 1960s. This approach was concerned less with institutional arrangements than with how political systems work in practice, and especially with how they translate 'inputs' into 'outputs'. The 'three worlds' approach was *economic–ideological* in orientation, as it paid special attention to a systems level of material development and its broader ideological orientation. The approach adopted here, however, is in some ways different from each of these three. It attempts to take account of three key features of a regime: its political, economic and cultural aspects. The assumption in this approach is that regimes are characterized not so much by particular political, economic or cultural factors as by the way in which these interlock in practice (see Figure 12.2).

The significance of this approach is that it emphasizes the degree to which formal political and economic arrangements may operate differently depending on their cultural context. For instance, multiparty elections and a market economy may have very different implications in western liberal societies than they do in non-western ones. Nevertheless, in view of the profound political upheavals since the late twentieth century, it would be foolish to suggest that any system of classification can be anything but provisional. Indeed, regimes are themselves fluid, and the regime-classification industry is constantly struggling to keep up to date with an ever-changing political reality. Nevertheless, five regime types can be identified in the modern world:

● western polyarchies
● new democracies
● East Asian regimes

- Islamic regimes
- military regimes.

CONCEPT

Polyarchy

Polyarchy (literally, 'rule by many') refers, generally, to the institutions and political processes of modern representative democracy. Polyarchy can be understood as a rough or crude approximation of democracy, in that it operates through institutions that force rulers to take account of the public's wishes. Its central features are (Dahl, 1989): (1) government is based on election; (2) elections are free and fair; (3) practically all adults have the right to vote; (4) the right to run for office is unrestricted; (5) there is free expression and a right to criticize and protest; (6) citizens have access to alternative sources of information; and (7) groups and associations enjoy at least relative independence from government.

● **Liberalization**: The introduction of internal and external checks on government power and/or shifts towards private enterprise and the market.

Western polyarchies

Western polyarchies are broadly equivalent to regimes categorized as 'liberal democracies', or even simply 'democracies'. Their heartlands are therefore North America, western Europe and Australasia. Huntington (see p. 425) argued that such regimes are a product of the first two 'waves' of democratization: the first occurred between 1828 and 1926, and involved countries such as the USA, France and the UK; the second occurred between 1943 and 1962, and involved countries such as West Germany, Italy, Japan and India. Although polyarchies have, in large part, evolved through moves towards democratization and **liberalization**, the term 'polyarchy' is preferable to 'liberal democracy' for two reasons. First, liberal democracy is sometimes treated as a political ideal, and is thus invested with broader normative implications. Second, the use of 'polyarchy' acknowledges that these regimes fall short, in important ways, of the goal of democracy.

The term 'polyarchy' was first used to describe a system of rule by Dahl (p. 250) and Lindblom in *Politics, Economics, and Welfare* (1953), and it was later elaborated in Dahl's *Polyarchy: Participation and Opposition* (1971). In the view of these authors, polyarchical regimes are distinguished by the combination of two general features. In the first place, there is a relatively high tolerance of opposition that is sufficient at least to check the arbitrary inclinations of government. This is guaranteed in practice by a competitive party system, by institutionally guaranteed and protected civil liberties, and by a vigorous and healthy civil society. The second feature of polyarchy is that the opportunities for participating in politics should be sufficiently widespread to guarantee a reliable level of popular responsiveness. The crucial factor here is the existence of regular and competitive elections operating as a device through which the people can control and, if necessary, displace their rulers. In this sense, there is a close resemblance between polyarchy and the form of democratic elitism described by Joseph Schumpeter (see p. 202) in *Capitalism, Socialism and Democracy* (1942). Nevertheless, Lindblom (1977) and Dahl (1985) both acknowledged the impact on polyarchies of the disproportional power of major corporations. For this reason, the notion of 'deformed polyarchy' has sometimes been preferred.

Thus defined, the term 'polyarchy' may be used to describe a large and growing number of regimes throughout the world. All states that hold multi-party elections have polyarchical features. Nevertheless, western polyarchies have a more distinctive and particular character. They are marked not only by representative democracy and a capitalist economic organization, but also by a cultural and ideological orientation that is largely derived from western liberalism. The most crucial aspect of this inheritance is the widespread acceptance of liberal individualism. Individualism, often seen as the most distinctive of western values, stresses the uniqueness of each human individual, and suggests that society should be organized so as to best meet the needs and interests of the individuals who compose it. The political culture of western polyarchies is influenced by liberal individualism in a variety of ways. It generates, for example, a heightened sensitivity to individual rights (perhaps placed above duties), the

The West

The term the West has two overlapping meanings. In a general sense, it refers to the cultural and philosophical inheritance of Europe, as exported through migration or colonialism. The roots of this inheritance lie in Judeo-Christian religion and the learning of 'classical' Greece and Rome, shaped in the modern period by the ideas and values of liberalism. In a narrower sense, fashionable during the Cold War, the West meant the USA-dominated capitalist bloc, as opposed to the USSR-dominated East. Although Eastern Europe no longer belongs to the East in this sense, it has always been unclear whether Russia belongs to the West in the broader sense.

● **Westminster model**: A system of government in which the executive is drawn from, and (in theory) accountable to, the assembly or parliament.

● **Consociational democracy**: A form of democracy that operates through power-sharing and a close association amongst a number of parties or political formations.

● **Exceptionalism**: The features of a political system that are unique or particular to it, and thus restrict the application of broader categories.

general perception that choice and competition (in both political and economic life) are healthy, and a tendency to fear government and regard the state as, at least, a potential threat to liberty.

Western polyarchies are not all alike, however. Some of them are biased in favour of centralization and majority rule, and others tend towards fragmentation and pluralism. Lijphart (1990, 1999) highlighted this fact in distinguishing between 'majority' democracies and 'consensus' democracies. Majority democracies are organized along parliamentary lines according to the so-called '**Westminster model**'. The clearest example of this is the UK system, but the model has also, in certain respects, been adopted by New Zealand, Australia, Canada, Israel and India. Majoritarian tendencies are associated with any, or all, of the following features:

● single-party government
● a fusion of powers between the executive and the assembly
● an assembly that is either unicameral or weakly bicameral
● a two-party system
● a single-member plurality, or first-past-the-post, electoral system (see p. 208)
● unitary and centralized government
● an uncodified constitution and a sovereign assembly.

In contrast, other western polyarchies are characterized by a diffusion of power throughout the governmental and party systems. The US model of pluralist democracy (see p. 101) is based very largely on institutional fragmentation enshrined in the provisions of the constitution itself. Elsewhere, particularly in continental Europe, consensus is underpinned by the party system, and a tendency towards bargaining and power sharing. In states such as Belgium, Austria and Switzerland, a system of **consociational democracy** has developed that is particularly appropriate to societies that are divided by deep religious, ideological, regional, cultural or other differences. Consensual or pluralistic tendencies are often associated with the following features:

● coalition government (see p. 239)
● a separation of powers between the executive and the assembly
● an effective bicameral system
● a multiparty system
● proportional representation (see p. 207)
● federalism (see p. 382) or devolution
● a codified constitution and a bill of rights.

On another level, of course, each polyarchical regime – and, indeed, every regime – is unique, and therefore exceptional. US **exceptionalism**, for instance, is often linked to the absence of a feudal past, and the experience of settlement and frontier expansion. This may explain the USA's deeply individualist political culture, which, uniquely amongst western polyarchies, does not accommodate a socialist party or movement of any note. The USA is also the most overtly religious of western regimes, and it is the only one, for instance, in which Christian fundamentalism has developed into a major political force.

CONCEPT

Communism

Communism, in its simplest sense, is the communal organization of social existence on the basis of the collective ownership of property. For Marxists, communism is a theoretical ideal, characterized by classlessness, rational economic organization and statelessness. 'Orthodox' communism refers to the societies founded in the twentieth century, supposedly on the basis of Marxist principles. In such societies: (1) Marxism-Leninism was used as an 'official' ideology; (2) the communist party had a monopoly of power, based on its 'leading and guiding' role in society; and (3) economic life was collectivized and organized through a system of central planning.

● **Transition countries**: Former Soviet Bloc countries that are in the process of transition from central planning to market capitalism.

● **New democracies**: Regimes in which the process of democratic consolidation is incomplete; democracy is not yet the 'only game in town' (Przeworski, 1991).

India is a still more difficult case. It is certainly not part of the West in cultural, philosophical or religious terms. In contrast to the 'developed' polyarchies of Europe and North America, it also has a largely rural population and a literacy rate of barely 50 per cent. Nevertheless, India has functioned as an effective polyarchy since it became independent in 1947, even surviving Indira Gandhi's 'state of emergency' during 1975–7. Political stability in India was undoubtedly promoted by the cross-caste appeal of the Congress Party and the mystique of the Nehru–Gandhi dynasty. However, the decline of the former and the end of the latter has perhaps transformed modern India into something approaching a consociational democracy. Turkey is another example of a political system that, in some respects, hovers between the East and the West (see p. 280).

New democracies

A third wave of democratization began, according to Huntington (1991), in 1974. It witnessed the overthrow of right-wing dictatorships (see p. 281) in Greece, Portugal and Spain; the retreat of the generals in Latin America; and, most significantly, the fall of communism. Of the 151 countries comprising the world at that time, in 1973 only 45 were electoral democracies. However, by 2003, 63 per cent of states, accounting for about 70 per cent of the world's population, exhibited some of the key features of liberal-democratic governance. Most prominently, this process has been characterized by the adoption of multi-party elections and market-based economic reforms. Nevertheless, many of these states are '**transition countries**', often classified as **new democracies**. The process of democratic transition has been both complex and difficult, highlighting the fact that liberal democracy may not be the 'default position' for human societies (see p. 276). New democracies not only lack developed democratic political cultures, they also have to handle the strains produced by the external forces of globalization, as well as rapid internal change. The most dramatic evidence of their vulnerability is the re-emergence of the armed forces into politics, as occurred, for example, in military *coups* in Pakistan in 1979 and in Thailand in 2006. However, particular problems are faced by postcommunist states in bringing about democratization.

One feature of postcommunist regimes is the need to deal with the politico-cultural consequences of communist rule, especially the ramifications of Stalinist totalitarianism. The ruthless censorship and suppression of opposition that underpinned the communist parties' monopoly of power guaranteed that a civic culture emphasizing participation, bargaining and consensus failed to develop. In Russia, this has produced a weak and fragmented party system that is apparently incapable of articulating or aggregating the major interests of Russian society. As a result, communist parties, or former communist parties, have often continued to provide a point of stability. In Romania and Bulgaria, for example, the institutions of the communist past have survived into the postcommunist era while, in states such as Hungary, Poland and Russia, communist parties – now embracing, if with differing degrees of conviction, the principles of social democracy – have retained a measure of electoral credibility.

A second set of problems stems from the process of economic transition. The 'shock therapy' transition from central planning to *laissez-faire* capitalism, initially advocated by the International Monetary Fund, unleashed deep insecu-

Debating...
Is liberal democracy the 'default position' for human societies?

The seemingly relentless advance of democratization since the early nineteenth century has encouraged some to believe that it is a natural and inevitable process. From this perspective, all systems of rule are destined, sooner or later, to collapse and be remodelled on liberal-democratic lines. Is liberal democracy the only 'normal' political regime?

YES

Mandate of history. Modernization clearly wears a liberal-democratic face. Although the liberal-democratic mix of limited government and popular rule has only been around for about 200 years, it has become the dominant form of government worldwide. Although initially confined to Western Europe and North America, its western 'homeland', liberal democracy demonstrated its universal appeal through its spread to India and Japan after World War II, into Latin America and across Eastern Europe from the 1980s onwards and, more recently, into the Muslim world through the Arab Spring. This, and further waves of democratization, seems set to culminate in the establishment of a world of liberal democracies.

The 'transition paradigm'. Democratization is driven forward through a strong internal dynamic, helping to explain why dictatorship eventually crumbles in the face of advancing liberal democracy. Following an opening phase in which cracks appear in a dictatorial regime that has lost legitimacy, the regime itself collapses and a new, democratic system emerges in its place. Over time, democratic structures gain greater substance, as the new democratic 'rules of the game' come to be accepted by both political elites and the mass of the population. In this view, once competitive elections have been held, even if democratic imperfections persist for some time, a return to dictatorship is unlikely, and may be impossible.

Unrivalled performance. Liberal democracy brings a unique collection of humanitarian, economic and political benefits in its wake. Liberal democracy's humanitarian benefits derive from its capacity to uphold human rights and afford citizens the widest possible sphere of freedom unchecked by the state. Its economic benefits stem from its intrinsic relationship with capitalist economic structures, helping to explain why liberal-democratic regimes are also prosperous and developed. Its political benefits are evident in its tendency towards stability and consensus, open and pluralist politic, ensuring that no significant section of the population is permanently left ignored.

NO

Global context. In the aftermath of World War II, the advance of liberal democracy was underpinned in significant ways by the global hegemony of the USA. This both gave US-style liberal democracy a powerful appeal worldwide and was reflected in the adoption by the USA of a strategy of 'democracy promotion', using diplomatic, economic and, sometimes, military means. However, the shift in global power, from the US-led West to Asia in particular, has not only diminished the USA's willingness and ability to promote democracy elsewhere, but also tarnished the US political and economic model. It is also notable that rising powers such as China and Russia represent very different political models.

Rise of illiberal democracy. Since the late 1990s, the democratization process has slowed down, leading to a 'democratic recession' in the first decade of the twenty-first century (Fukuyama, 2011). Instead of the overthrow of dictatorship and holding of elections leading irresistibly to democratic consolidation, many transition countries have been left, perhaps permanently, in a 'grey area'. These states have become 'managed' or 'illiberal' democracies, in which a form of electoral democracy operates alongside weak checks and balances, and the routine intimidation of oppositional forces. Such arrangements reflect the capacity of political elites to bend democratic politics to their own ends.

Discontents of liberal democracy. It is by no means clear that liberal democracy has performance advantages over other systems of rule. Liberal democracy's difficulties and discontents include: a tendency towards plutocracy, reflecting the fact that capitalism is ultimately incompatible with popular rule; a trend towards atomism and declining civic engagement; and trade-offs between personal freedom and majority opinion that flow from the inherent tension between liberalism and democracy. The rise of state capitalism also challenges the idea that liberal-democratic regimes will always be more prosperous than other regimes, and liberal democracy may be culturally unsuitable for the non-western world.

CONCEPT

Authoritarianism

Authoritarianism is a belief in, or practice of, government 'from above', in which authority is exercised regardless of popular consent. Authoritarianism thus differs from authority, as the latter rests on legitimacy, and so arises 'from below'. Authoritarian regimes emphasize the claims of authority over those of individual liberty. However, authoritarianism is usually distinguished from totalitarianism. Authoritarianism, associated with monarchical absolutism, traditional dictatorships, and most forms of military rule, seeks to exclude the masses from politics rather than abolish civil society.

rity because of the growth of unemployment and inflation, and it significantly increased social inequality. Since the heady days of the early 1990s, the pace of economic liberalization has sometimes been greatly reduced as a consequence of a backlash against market reforms, often expressed in growing support for communist or nationalist parties. A final set of problems result from the weakness of state power, particularly when the state is confronted by centrifugal forces effectively suppressed during the communist era. This has been most clearly demonstrated by the re-emergence of ethnic and nationalist tensions. The collapse of communism in the USSR was accompanied by the break-up of the old Soviet empire and the construction of 15 new independent states, several of which (including Russia) continue to be afflicted by ethnic conflict. Czechoslovakia ceased to exist in 1992 with the creation of the Czech Republic and Slovakia. Ethnic conflict was most dramatic in Yugoslavia, where it precipitated full-scale war between Serbia and Croatia in 1991, and led to civil war in Bosnia in 1992–96.

Important differences between postcommunist states can also be identified. The most crucial of these is that between the more industrially advanced and westernized countries of 'central' Europe, such as the Czech Republic, Hungary and Poland, and the more backward, 'eastern' states such as Romania, Bulgaria and, in certain respects, Russia. In the former group, market reform has proceeded swiftly and relatively smoothly; in the latter, it has either been grudging and incomplete, or it has given rise to deeper political tensions. This was reflected in early membership of the EU for the Czech Republic, Hungary, Poland, Slovakia, Slovenia and the Baltic states (Estonia, Latvia and Lithuania), achieved in 2004. However, Bulgaria and Romania joined the EU in 2007, with other Balkan postcommunist states, including Croatia, Albania, Bosnia-Herzegovina and Serbia, still waiting to join. Another distinction is between the states on which communism was 'imposed' by the Soviet Red Army at the end of World War II and those that were once part of the USSR. Since the late 1990s, the process of democratization in many successor states to the USSR has slowed down and, in some cases, been reversed, leaving them in what Carothers (2004) called a 'grey zone' between dictatorship and liberal democracy. In countries such as Moldova, Kazakhstan, Uzbekistan and Belarus, sometimes dubbed 'Europe's last dictatorship', an official acceptance of democratic legitimacy has been accompanied, albeit in different ways, by the systematic removal of checks on executive power and the erosion of the rule of law. In the case of Russia, the emergence of Putin as the government's leading force has led to a strengthening of executive control over television, the judiciary and the provinces, as well as a more ruthless approach to dealing with potential opponents. However, cracks in what has been portrayed variously as Russia's 'managed democracy' or 'electoral authoritarianism' became apparent after the parliamentary elections of December 2011, both because Putin's United Russia party saw its share of the vote drop to 49 per cent from 64 per cent four years earlier, and because of popular protests against vote rigging that were unprecedented for the Putin era.

East Asian regimes

The rise of East Asia from the final decades of the twentieth century onwards may ultimately prove to be a more important world-historical event than the

Confucianism

Confucianism is a system of ethics formulated by Confucius (551–479 BCE) and his disciples that was primarily outlined in *The Analects*. Confucian thought has concerned itself with the twin themes of human relations and the cultivation of the self. The emphasis on *ren* (humanity or love) has usually been interpreted as implying support for traditional ideas and values; notably, filial piety, respect, loyalty and benevolence. The stress on *junzi* (the virtuous person) suggests a capacity for human development and potential for perfection realized, in particular, through education.

● **Asian values**: Values that supposedly reflect the history, culture and religious backgrounds of Asian societies; examples include social harmony, respect for authority and a belief in the family.

collapse of communism. Certainly, the balance of the world's economy shifted markedly from the West to the East in this period. Since the 1980s, economic growth rates on the western rim of the Pacific Basin have been between two and four times higher than those in the 'developed' economies of Europe and North America. However, the notion that there is a distinctively East Asian political form is a less familiar one. The widespread assumption has been that 'modernization' means 'westernization'. Translated into political terms, this implies that industrial capitalism is always accompanied by liberal democracy. Those who advance this position cite, for example, the success of Japan's 1946 constitution, bequeathed by the departing USA, and the introduction of multiparty elections in countries such as Thailand, South Korea and Taiwan in the 1980s and 1990s. However, this interpretation fails to take account of the degree to which polyarchical institutions operate differently in an Asian context from the way they do in a western one. Most importantly, it ignores the difference between cultures influenced by Confucian ideas and values, and those shaped by liberal individualism. This has led to the idea that there are a specific set of **Asian values** that are distinct from western ones, although this notion has attracted less attention since the Asian financial crisis of 1997/8.

East Asian regimes tend to have similar characteristics. First, they are orientated more around economic goals than around political ones. Their overriding priority is to boost growth and deliver prosperity, rather than to enlarge individual freedom in the western sense of civil liberty. This essentially practical concern is evident in the 'tiger' economies of East and South East Asia (those of South Korea, Taiwan, Hong Kong, Singapore and Malaysia), but it has also been demonstrated in the construction of a thriving market economy in China since the late 1970s, despite the survival there of monopolistic communist rule. Second, there is broad support for 'strong' government. Powerful 'ruling' parties tend to be tolerated, and there is general respect for the state. Although, with low taxes and relatively low public spending (usually below 30 per cent of GDP), there is little room for the western model of the welfare state, there is nevertheless general acceptance that the state as a 'father figure' should guide the decisions of private as well as public bodies, and draw up strategies for national development. This characteristic is accompanied, third, by a general disposition to respect leaders because of the Confucian stress on loyalty, discipline and duty. From a western viewpoint, this invests East Asian regimes with an implicit, and sometimes explicit, authoritarianism. Finally, great emphasis is placed on community and social cohesion, embodied in the central role accorded to the family. The resulting emphasis on what the Japanese call 'group think' tends to restrict the scope for the assimilation of ideas such as individualism and human rights, at least as these are understood in the West.

There is also differentiation between East Asian regimes. The most significant difference is that, although China's acceptance of capitalism has blurred the distinction between it and other East Asian regimes, profound political contrasts survive. China, in political terms at least, and North Korea, in both political and economic terms, are unreconstituted communist regimes, in which a monopolistic communist party still dominates the state machine. China's 'market Stalinism' contrasts sharply with the entrenched and successful electoral democracy of, for instance, Japan. Moreover, East Asian regimes are becoming industrialized and increasingly urbanized, China, despite its dramatic economic growth,

CONCEPT

Theocracy

Theocracy (literally 'rule by God') is the principle that religious authority should prevail over political authority. A theocracy is therefore a regime in which government posts are filled on the basis of the person's position in the religious hierarchy. Theocratic rule is illiberal in two senses. First, it violates the public/private divide, in that it takes religious rules and precepts to be the guiding principles of both personal life and political conduct. Second, it invests political authority with potentially unlimited power, because, as temporal power is derived from spiritual wisdom, it cannot be based on popular consent, or be properly constrained within a constitutional framework.

● **Shari'a**: Islamic law, believed to be based on divine revelation, and derived from the Koran, the Hadith (the teachings of Muhammad), and other sources.

sill has a significant agricultural sector. To some extent, this also explains different modes of economic development. In Japan and 'tiger' economies such as Taiwan and Singapore, growth is now based largely on technological innovation, and an emphasis on education and training, whereas China continues, in certain respects, to rely on her massive rural population to provide cheap and plentiful labour. A final range of differences stems from cultural contrasts between overwhelmingly Chinese states such as Taiwan and China, and Japan and ethnically mixed states such as Singapore and Malaysia. For example, plans to introduce Confucian principles in Singapore schools were dropped for fear of offending the Malay and Indian populations. Similarly, Malaysian development has been based on a deliberate attempt to reduce Chinese influence and emphasize the distinctively Islamic character of Malay culture.

Islamic regimes

The rise of Islam as a political force has had a profound effect on politics in North Africa, the Middle East, and parts of Asia. In some cases, militant Islamic groups have challenged existing regimes, often articulating the interests of an urban poor since the disillusionment in the 1970s with Marxism–Leninism. In other cases, however, regimes have been constructed or reconstructed on Islamic lines. Since its inception in 1932, Saudi Arabia has been an Islamic state. The Iranian revolution of 1979 led to the establishment of an Islamic republic under Ayatollah Khomeini (see p. 164), an example later followed in Pakistan, the Sudan and Afghanistan.

Islam is not, however, and never has been, simply a religion. Rather, it is a complete way of life, defining correct moral, political and economic behaviour for individuals and nations alike. The 'way of Islam' is based on the teachings of the Prophet Muhammad (570–632) as revealed in the Koran, regarded by all Muslims as the revealed word of God, and the Sunna, or 'beaten path', the traditional customs observed by a devout Moslem that are said to be based on the Prophet's own life. Political Islam thus aims at the construction of a theocracy in which political and other affairs are structured according to 'higher' religious principles. Nevertheless, political Islam has assumed clearly contrasting forms, ranging from fundamentalist to pluralist extremes.

The fundamentalist version of Islam is most commonly associated with Iran. The Iranian system of government is a complex mix of theocracy and democracy. The Supreme Leader (currently Ali Khamenei) presides over a system of institutionalized clerical rule that operates through the Islamic Revolutionary Council, a body of 15 senior clerics. Although a popularly elected president and parliament have been established, all legislation is ratified by the Council for the Protection of the Constitution, which ensures conformity to Islamic principles. Shari'a law continues to be strictly enforced throughout Iran as both a legal and a moral code. The forces of revolutionary fundamentalism also asserted themselves through the Taliban regime in Afghanistan, 1997–2001, which was characterized by the imposition of strict theocratic rule and the exclusion of women from education, the economy and public life in general. Fundamentalism (see p. 53) is no less significant in Saudi Arabia, where it has similarly absolutist implications, although the temper of the essentially conservative Sunni regime in Saudi Arabia differs markedly from the revolutionary populism (see p. 307) of Shi'a Iran.

POLITICS IN ACTION . . .

Turkey: between East and West?

Events: Although the republic of Turkey, founded in 1923 by Mustafa Kemal Atatürk (1881–1938), was firmly rooted in secularism, Islamist political parties have been gaining strength since the 1990s. The Welfare Party briefly led a coalition government in 1996, before being broken up by the army and, in the 2002 parliamentary elections, the Justice and Development Party (AKP) won two-thirds of the seats on the basis of 34 per cent of the vote (thanks to the 10 per cent electoral threshold, which excluded all but two parties from representation). In the 2007 election, AKP increased its share of the vote to 47 per cent, which rose again in 2011, this time reaching 50 per cent. Since 2003, AKP's leader Recep Tayyip Erdoğan has been prime minister and, when Abdullah Gül was appointed president in 2007, he became the first openly devout Muslim president in the history of modern Turkey.

Significance: Turkey, a country of 79 million people, lies at the crossroads of Europe and Asia. Its geographical position is, nevertheless, also reflected in its political character, which has been shaped by a shifting combination of polyarchic, military and Islamic features. In line with 'Kemalism' (after Kemal Atatürk), modern Turkey is a constitutional republic committed to the rule of law, popular sovereignty, and a strict separation of politics and religion. In this context, the rise of political Islam during the 1990s and, especially, the rule of the AKP since 2002 have raised major questions about the country's future political direction. Its critics warn that the AKP plans to overturn the secular nature of the Turkish state, possibly establishing an Iranian-style Islamic republic. The ban on the wearing of the Islamic headscarf in Turkish universities (only enforced since the 1980s) was lifted in 2010, and restrictions on the sale of alcohol have been imposed in some parts of Turkey. Turkey has also increasingly looked to build ties with the Arab world and has become increasingly critical of Israel (particularly after Israeli soldiers raided a Turkish-led aid flotilla heading for Gaza in May 2010, causing the deaths of nine Turkish civilians). However, supporters of the AKP argue that it practises a constitutional form of Islamism very different from that found in

Iran, in which moderate conservative politics based on Islamic values are balanced against an acceptance of Turkey's secular democratic framework. Rather than choosing between East and West, the AKP thus tries to establish a Turkish identity that is confident in being part of both. A key aspect of this compromise has been the quest, under the AKP, for membership of the EU, and, related to this, a willingness to introduce reforms in areas such as women's rights, and Kurdish language and cultural rights.

These developments have, nevertheless, had major implications for military-civilian relations in Turkey. The army played a crucial role in the establishment of the Turkish republic, coming to be the custodian of 'Kemalism' and establishing strong links to the bureaucracy, the judiciary and the media. Four times between 1960 and 1997, Turkey's generals have staged military *coups*, the last of which forced from office the country's first Islamist prime minister. While some see the 1 million strong army as the greatest obstacle to Turkey's onward march towards democracy and EU membership, others view it as the vital guarantee of secular and open politics, an obstacle preventing the AKP's moderate Islamism from becoming revolutionary Islamism. Although relations between the AKP government and Turkey's generals remain frayed, a gradual shift in power from the military to civilians, with, for instance, the military becoming more accountable to civilian courts, creates the possibility that the Turkish army may, in future, remain in barracks and out of politics.

CONCEPT

Dictatorship

A dictatorship is, strictly, a form of rule in which absolute power is vested in one individual; in this sense, dictatorship is synonymous with autocracy. Dictators are thus seen as being above the law and as acting beyond constitutional constraints. Early examples of dictators were Sulla, Julius Caesar and Augustus Caesar in Rome, more recent ones are Hitler, Mussolini and Saddam Hussein. More generally, dictatorship is characterized by the arbitrary and unchecked exercise of power, as in 'class dictatorship', 'party dictatorship', 'military dictatorship' and 'personal dictatorship'.

● **Junta**: (Spanish) Literally, 'a council'; a (usually military) clique that seizes power through a revolution or *coup d'état*.

Muslims themselves, however, have often objected to the classification of any Islamic regime as 'fundamentalist', on the grounds that this perpetuates long-established western prejudices against an 'exotic' or 'repressive' East, serving as examples of 'orientalism' (Said, 1978). Evidence that Islam is compatible with a form of political pluralism can be found in Malaysia. Although Islam is the official state religion of Malaysia, with the Paramount Ruler serving as both religious leader and head of state, a form of 'guided' democracy operates as the dominance of the United Malays National Organization (UMNO), operating as a broad coalition, the Barisan Nasional, and within a multiparty framework. The UMNO has, since 1981, pursued a narrowly Islamic and pro-Malay strategy fused with an explicitly Japanese model of economic development. Authoritarian tendencies have, nevertheless, re-emerged since 1988, when the independence of the judiciary effectively collapsed following a wave of political arrests and the imposition of press censorship. Turkey also offers an interesting example of the relationship between Islam and democracy (see p. 280), as does the Arab Spring and developments in countries such as Egypt, Tunisia and Libya.

Military regimes

Whereas most regimes are shaped by a combination of political, economic, cultural and ideological factors, some survive through the exercise, above all, of military power and systematic repression. In this sense, military regimes belong to a broader category of dictatorship. Military dictatorship has been most common in Latin America, the Middle East, Africa and Southeast Asia, but it also emerged in the post-1945 period in Spain, Portugal and Greece. The key feature of a military regime is that the leading posts in the government are filled on the basis of the person's position within the military chain of command. Normal political and constitutional arrangements are usually suspended, and institutions through which opposition can be expressed, such as elected assemblies and a free press, are either weakened or abolished.

Although all forms of military rule are deeply repressive, this classification encompasses a number of regime types. In some military regimes, the armed forces assume direct control of government. The classical form of this is the military junta, most commonly found in Latin America. This operates as a form of collective military government centred on a command council of officers who usually represent the three armed services: the army, navy and air force. *Junta* regimes are often characterized by rivalry between the services and between leading figures, the consequence being that formal positions of power tend to change hands relatively frequently.

The second form of military regime is a military-backed personalized dictatorship. In these cases, a single individual gains pre-eminence within the *junta* or regime, often being bolstered by a cult of personality (see p. 302) designed to manufacture charismatic authority. Examples are Colonel Papadopoulos in Greece in 1974–80, General Pinochet in Chile after the 1973 military *coup*, and General Abacha in Nigeria, 1993–98. In the final form of military regime, the loyalty of the armed forces is the decisive factor that upholds the regime, but the military leaders content themselves with 'pulling the strings' behind the scenes. This, for example, occurred in post-1945 Brazil, as the armed forces generally recognized that the legitimacy of the regime would be strengthened by the maintenance of a distinction between political and military offices and personnel. Such a distinction, however, may fuel an appetite for constitutional and representative politics, and reduce the scope for direct military intervention, thereby, over time, encouraging polyarchical tendencies. However, in what circumstances does the military seize power? Military *coups* appear to be associated with four key sets of circumstances. In the first place, there is a clear link between the incidence of military *coups* and economic underdevelopment. The vast majority of countries that have experienced military government are in the developing world. By the same token, growing prosperity appears to be an antidote to military intervention, as demonstrated by the tendency in Latin America, since the 1970s, for the military to return to the barracks. Second, the military is likely to intervene in politics only when it senses that the legitimacy of the existing institutions and the ruling elite is challenged, and when it calculates that its intervention is going to be successful. The armed forces thus rarely interfere directly in politics when a stable democratic culture has been successfully established. Third, military intervention is associated with the degree to which the values, goals and interests of the armed forces differ from those of the broader regime. In many newly-independent developing states, the military thus took over to 'save the nation', seeing itself as a 'westernizing' or 'modernizing' force confronting a traditionalist, rural, hierarchical and frequently divided political elite. This, for instance, occurred in Nigeria, Indonesia and Pakistan. Finally, the military's decision to seize power may also be affected by international considerations. In some cases, international pressures undoubtedly encourage military action. This was clearly the case with the Pinochet *coup* in Chile. Not only did Pinochet receive covert advice and encouragement from the US Central Intelligence Agency (CIA), but he was also guaranteed US diplomatic support once his new military regime was established.

SUMMARY

- Government is any mechanism through which ordered rule is maintained, its central feature being its ability to make collective decisions and enforce them. A political system, or regime, however, encompasses not only the mechanisms of government and institutions of the state, but also the structures and processes through which these interact with the larger society.

- The classification of political systems serves two purposes. First, it aids understanding by making comparison possible, and helping to highlight similarities and differences between otherwise shapeless collections of facts. Second, it helps us to evaluate the effectiveness or success of different political systems.

- Regimes have been classified on a variety of bases. 'Classical' typologies, stemming from Aristotle, concentrated on constitutional arrangements and institutional structures, while the 'three worlds' approach highlighted material and ideological differences between the systems found in 'first world' capitalist, 'second world' communist and 'third world' developing states.

- The collapse of communism and advance of democratization have made it much more difficult to identify the political contours of the modern world, making conventional systems of classification redundant. It is, nevertheless, still possible to distinguish between regimes on the basis of how their political, economic and cultural characteristics interlock in practice, even though all systems of classification are provisional.

- 'End of history' theorists have proclaimed that history has ended, or is destined to end, with the worldwide triumph of western liberal democracy. Indeed, the most common form of regime in the modern world is now some form of democracy. However, there is evidence that regime types have become both more complex and more diverse. Significant differences can be identified among western polyarchies, new democracies, East Asian regimes, Islamic regimes and military regimes.

- Those who view democratization as an irresistable process usually argue that, once instigated, democratic reform gains an internal momentum, deriving from the ways in which the holding of competitive elections alter public expectations about the political process. Others, however, point out that many transition countries have been left, perhaps permanently in a 'grey area' between democracy and authoritarianism.

Questions for discussion

- Does Aristotle's system of political classification have any relevance to the modern world?
- Is there any longer such a thing as the 'third world'?
- To what extent have postcommunist regimes discarded their communist past?
- Why have liberal-democratic structures proved to be so effective and successful?
- Have some new democracies got stuck in a 'grey zone' between dictatorship and liberal democracy?
- How democratic are western polyarchies?
- Do Confucianism and Islamism constitute viable alternatives to western liberalism as a basis for a modern regime?
- Are military regimes doomed to be short-lived?

Further reading

Brooker, P., *Non-Democratic Regimes; Theory, Government and Politics* (2009). A useful and wide-ranging survey of the different forms of non-democratic regime.

Carothers, T., *Critical Mission: Essays on Democracy Promotion* (2004). A stimulating collection of essays that reflect on strategies for aiding democracy and the nature of the democratic process.

Hague, R. and M. Harrop, *Comparative Government and Politics: An Introduction* (2013). A succinct and stimulating introduction to comparative politics that adopts a genuinely international approach.

Lijphart, A., *Patterns of Democracy: Government Forms and Performance in Thirty-Six Countries* (1999). An updated version of a classic and highly influential attempt to distinguish between forms of democratic rule.

13 # Political Executives and Leadership

'A ruler must learn to be other than good.'

NICCOLÒ MACHIAVELLI, *The Prince* (1532)

PREVIEW　The executive is the irreducible core of government. Political systems can operate without constitutions, assemblies, judiciaries and even parties, but they cannot survive without an executive branch to formulate government policy and ensure that it is implemented. Such is the potential power of executives that much of political development has taken the form of attempts to check or constrain them, either by forcing them to operate within a constitutional framework, or by making them accountable to a popular assembly or democratic electorate. Political executives, and particularly chief executives, are certainly the face of politics with which the general public is most familiar. This is because the executive is the source of political leadership. This role has been greatly enhanced by the widening responsibilities of the state in both the domestic and international realms, and the media's tendency to portray politics in terms of personalities. However, the hopes and expectations focused on executives may also prove to be their undoing. In many political systems, leaders are finding it increasingly difficult to 'deliver the goods'. Debates about the nature, extent and implications of executive power are, nevertheless, linked to the wider issue of political leadership. Widely seen as a vital ingredient of politics, providing it with a necessary sense of purpose and direction, leadership has been interpreted in a variety of ways, ranging from a personal gift to a bureaucratic device. Similarly, leadership can involve a variety of styles, strategies and approaches, affecting not only how effective it is but also the relationship between leadership and democracy.

KEY ISSUES

- What is the executive branch of government? What does it comprise?
- What are the principal functions of political executives?
- How do presidential executives differ from parliamentary executives?
- Where does power lie in political executives?
- How should political leadership be understood and explained?
- Is there a crisis of leadership in modern politics?

Executive

In its broadest sense, the executive is the branch of government that is responsible for the implementation of laws and policies. More commonly, the term is now used in a narrower sense to describe the smaller body of decision-makers who take overall responsibility for the direction and coordination of government policy. This group of senior figures is often called the *political executive* (roughly equivalent to 'the government of the day', or 'the administration'), as opposed to the *official* executive, or bureaucracy (p. 361). For 'core' executive (see p. 299).

● **Parliamentary executive**: An executive, typically composed of a prime minister and cabinet, that is drawn from and accountable to the parliament, and is formed through parliamentary elections.

● **Presidential executive**: An executive that is headed by a separately elected president, who enjoys political and constitutional independence from the parliament.

ROLE OF THE EXECUTIVE

Who's who in the executive?

The executive is, technically, the branch of government that is responsible for the execution or implementation of policy. The division of government into executive, legislative and judicial institutions has been sustained by the doctrine of the separation of powers (see p. 313), and has been the traditional basis on which to analyse government since the time of Montesquieu (see p. 312). From this point of view, three distinct branches of government can be identified:

● Legislatures *make* law; they enact legislation.
● Executives *implement* law; they execute law.
● Judiciaries *interpret* law; they adjudicate on the meaning of law.

In practice, however, the executive's responsibilities tend to be substantially broader, as well as more complex. This complexity also extends to the composition of the executive. Members of executives have been categorized in one of two ways. First, a distinction is often drawn between the 'political' executive and the 'bureaucratic' executive. This highlights the differences between politicians and civil servants, and, more broadly, between politics and administration (see p. 363). Second, various levels of status and responsibility have been identified within executives. Whereas assemblies tend to respect at least the formal equality of their members, executive branches are typically pyramidal, organized according to a clear leadership structure.

The distinction between political and bureaucratic, or official, posts is most clear-cut in the case of **parliamentary executives**, where differences in recruitment, responsibility, status and political orientation can be identified. In parliamentary systems, the political executive comprises elected politicians, ministers drawn from and accountable to the assembly: their job is to make policy, in accordance with the political and ideological priorities of their party, and to oversee its implementation. The official executive comprises appointed and professional civil servants whose job it is to offer advice and administer policy, subject to the requirements of political neutrality (see p. 345) and loyalty to their ministers.

Nevertheless, in parliamentary systems (see p. 310) such as those in Australia, Canada, India and the UK, the political/bureaucratic distinction is blurred by the fact that senior civil servants often make a substantial contribution to policy-making and because use is commonly made of temporary, politically committed advisers. The overlap is usually even greater in **presidential executives**. In the USA, for example, the president is the only elected politician in the executive. Cabinet members are, in effect, appointed officials, and all the senior and many middle-ranking civil servants are politically partisan and temporary. In communist executives, for example in China and the USSR of old, the distinction is rendered virtually redundant by the all-pervasive reach of the 'ruling' communist party. Chinese bureaucrats are thus 'political', in the sense that they are, in all cases, ideologically committed supporters, and usually members, of the Chinese Communist Party.

In comparison with political/bureaucratic distinctions, hierarchical divisions within executive branches are easier to identify. In the first place, executives tend

CONCEPT

Heads of state

The head of state is the personal embodiment of the state's power and authority. As the leading representative of the state, the head of state enjoys the highest status in the land. However, he or she is often a figure of essentially symbolic or formal significance, with real power residing in the hands of the head of government (a post that may or may not be held by the same person). Heads of state exercise a range of ceremonial powers and responsibilities, such as awarding honours, assenting to legislation and treaties, and receiving visiting heads of state. The head of state is usually either a president or monarch (see p. 292).

to be centralized around the leadership (see p. 300) of a single individual. As Montesquieu put it, 'this branch of government, having need of dispatch, is better administered by one than by many'. Two separate posts can, nevertheless, be identified, although they may be held by the same person. On the one hand, there is the head of state, an office of formal authority and largely symbolic importance. On the other, there is the head of government, or the chief executive, a post that carries policy-making and political responsibilities. Whereas executive presidents, as in the USA, Russia and France, 'wear two hats', the posts in parliamentary systems are usually separate. A prime minister serves as the chief executive, and the post of head of state is usually held by a non-partisan figurehead.

Beneath the chief executive, a range of ministers or secretaries have responsibility for developing or implementing policy in specific areas. There is often a hierarchy amongst these departmental bosses, imposed either by the importance of their policy areas (economics and foreign ministers generally hold leading positions), or by their entitlement to sit in the **cabinet** or in senior committees. As discussed further below, cabinets have responsibilities that range from the sharing of policy-making power in a form of collective leadership to the offering of advice and the broader coordination of executive policy. At a lower level are the massed ranks of bureaucrats and administrators (discussed in Chapter 16) who, at least in theory, are concerned less with policy formulation than with policy implementation. Finally, there are enforcement agencies, such as the police force and armed forces, and an array of quasi-governmental bodies, popularly known as 'quangos' (see p. 368). These are part of the executive insofar as they help to put government policy into effect, but they are staffed by personnel who enjoy at least formal independence from the government itself.

Functions of political executives

At its most simple, the task of the political executive is to provide leadership. In this sense, the executive functions as the 'commanding heights' of the state apparatus, the core of the state itself. This role extends over a variety of areas, and this means that the members of the political executive have to carry out several functions, sometimes simultaneously. The most important of the areas are the following:

- ceremonial duties
- control of policy-making
- popular political leadership
- bureaucratic management
- crisis response.

Ceremonial leadership

Heads of state, chief executives and, to a lesser extent, senior ministers or secretaries 'stand for' the state. In giving state authority personal form, they represent the larger society and symbolize, accurately or otherwise, its unity. This role is largely formal and ceremonial, and covers, for example, state occasions, foreign visits, international conferences, and the ratification of treaties and legislation. Non-executive presidents and constitutional monarchs are sometimes charged with these essentially ceremonial responsibilities, allowing other executive

● **Cabinet:** A group of senior ministers that meets formally and regularly, and is chaired by the chief executive; cabinets may make policy or be consultative.

officers to get on with the day-to-day business of government. The role is, nevertheless, of broader significance for two reasons. First, it provides a focus for unity and political loyalty, and so helps to build legitimacy (see p. 81). Second, it allows those at the top of the executive to portray themselves as 'national leaders', which is vital to the maintenance of public support and electoral credibility.

Policy-making leadership

The key function of the political executive is to direct and control the policy process. In short, the executive is expected to 'govern'. This role was substantially expanded during the twentieth century in response to the broadening responsibilities of government. The political executive is looked to, in particular, to develop coherent economic and social programmes that meet the needs of more complex and politically sophisticated societies, and to control the state's various external relationships in an increasingly interdependent world. One important consequence of this has been the growth of the executive's legislative powers, and its encroachment on the traditional responsibilities of the parliament or assembly.

Not only do political executives usually initiate legislative programmes and help, by persuasion or direction, to make the legislative process work, but, in many cases, they also exercise a wide range of law-making powers, using decrees, orders and other instruments. However, it is misleading to imply that the political executive always dominates the policy process. Much policy, for instance, is initiated by political parties and interest groups. Moreover, by virtue of their expertise and specialist knowledge, bureaucrats or civil servants may play a crucial role in policy formulation; at best, leaving the political executive to establish the overall direction of government policy.

Popular leadership

The popularity of the political executive, more than any other part of the political system, is crucial to the character and stability of the regime as a whole. At a policy level, it is the ability of the executive to mobilize support that ensures the compliance and cooperation of the general public. Quite simply, without support from the public, or from key groups in society, policy implementation becomes difficult, perhaps impossible. More importantly, the political executive's popularity is linked to the legitimacy of the broader regime. The unpopularity of a particular government or administration does not, in itself, weaken support for the political system, but it may do so in the absence of a mechanism for removing and replacing that government. This goes some way towards explaining the widespread use of regular and competitive elections. Of course, this is not to say that unpopular and immovable executives always spell systemic breakdown. Such regimes can survive, but only by resorting to authoritarianism (see p. 277), meaning that popular compliance is brought about through repression and ideological manipulation.

Bureaucratic leadership

Its task of overseeing the implementation of policy means that the political executive has major bureaucratic and administrative responsibilities. In this sense, chief executives, ministers and secretaries constitute a 'top management' charged with running the machinery of government. This work is organized largely along departmental lines, senior ministers having responsibility for particular policy areas and for the bureaucrats engaged to administer those areas. At a higher level, there is a need for policy coordination, which is usually accomplished through some kind of cabinet system.

However, doubts have been expressed about the effectiveness of this bureaucratic leadership. First, as political executives are staffed by politicians, they often lack the competence, managerial experience and administrative knowledge to control a sprawling bureaucratic machine effectively. Second, particular government departments can develop their own interests, especially when they forge alliances with powerful client groups. Third, the bureaucracy as a whole can develop interests that are separate from those of the political executive, encouraging it to resist the control of its notional political masters. These issues are examined in greater detail in Chapter 16 in relation to bureaucratic power.

Crisis leadership

A crucial advantage that the political executive has over the assembly is its ability to take swift and decisive action. When crises break out, in either domestic or international politics, it is invariably the executive that responds, by virtue of its hierarchical structure and the scope it provides for personal leadership. It is therefore common for assemblies to grant political executives near-dictatorial powers in times of war, and for executives to seize 'emergency powers' when confronted by domestic crises such as natural disasters, terrorist threats, industrial unrest and civil disorder. Clearly, however, the power to declare 'states of emergency' and to impose effective executive rule is subject to abuse. Not uncommonly, governments have used these powers to weaken or eradicate political opposition under the guise of constitutionalism (see p. 337).

POWER IN THE EXECUTIVE: WHO LEADS?

As already noted, the roles and responsibilities of the political executive have been substantially enhanced by the emergence of democratic politics, growing government intervention, and political and economic globalization (see p. 142). During the twentieth century, political executives acquired ever-wider policy-making and legislative responsibilities, took command of sprawling bureaucratic machines, and increasingly became the focus of popular politics and media attention. These developments have, in turn, profoundly affected the internal organization of the executive branch of government, and the distribution of power within it. By common consent, the main beneficiary of this process has been the chief executive. Heads of government now commonly have institutional responsibilities, a political status, and a public profile that sets them clearly apart from their cabinet or ministerial colleagues. Nevertheless, this image of growing centralization and the rise of personal power conflicts sharply with evidence of leadership failure, and the growing incapacity of chief executives to carry out what people have elected them to do (see p. 305). The complex dynamics of exec-

CONCEPT

Presidential government

A presidential system of government is characterized by a constitutional and political separation of powers between the legislative and executive branches of government. The principal features of a presidential system are: (1) the executive and the legislature are separately elected; (2) there is a formal separation of the personnel between the legislative and the executive branches; (3) the executive cannot be removed by the legislature (except, possibly, through impeachment; (4) the president or executive cannot 'dissolve' the legislature; and (5) executive authority is concentrated in the hands of the president.

● **Presidentialism**: Personalized leadership that is disengaged from parties or other government bodies, in the manner of an executive president.

● **Semi-presidential system**: A system of government in which a separately elected president presides over a government drawn from, and accountable to, the assembly.

utive power can be examined more closely by looking at the roles of presidents, prime ministers and cabinets.

In each of these three cases, however, three dimensions of power must be borne in mind:

● the *formal* dimension of power: the constitutional roles and responsibilities of executive officers and the institutional frameworks in which they operate
● the *informal* dimension of power: the role of personality, political skills and experience, and the impact of factors such as parties and the media
● the *external* dimension of power: the political, economic and diplomatic context of government, and the broader pressures that bear on the executive branch.

Presidents

A president is a formal head of state, a title that is held in other states by a monarch or emperor. An important distinction, however, must be made between constitutional presidents and executive presidents. Constitutional or non-executive presidents, found in India, Israel and Germany, for example, are a feature of parliamentary systems and have responsibilities confined largely to ceremonial duties. In these circumstances, the president is a mere figurehead, and executive power is wielded by a prime minister and/or a cabinet. This section is concerned with executive presidents, who combine the formal responsibilities of a head of state with the political power of a chief executive. Presidencies of this kind constitute the basis of what is called 'presidential government' (see Figure 13.1), as opposed to parliamentary government (see Figure 14.1).

Presidential executives may be either limited or unlimited. Limited presidential executives operate within constraints imposed by a constitution, political democracy, party competition and some form of separation of powers. Above all, the powers of the president are counterbalanced by those of a popularly accountable assembly. The best-known example of limited **presidentialism** is found in the USA, but **semi-presidential systems** like those in France and Finland also conform to this model. In unlimited presidential executives, on the other hand, the president is invested with near-unchecked powers, meaning that these regimes are, effectively, dictatorships (see p. 281). They are commonly found in one-party states that rest heavily on the support of the military. Unlimited executives can be found, for example, in Sudan, Belarus and Kazakhstan.

US-style presidential government has spawned imitations throughout the world, mainly in Latin America and, more recently, in postcommunist states such as Poland, Hungary, the Czech Republic and Russia – although, apart from Russia, most postcommunist presidencies operate within what are effectively parliamentary systems. In investing executive power in a presidency, the architects of the US constitution were aware that they were, in effect, creating an 'elective kingship'. Wishing to avoid the abuse of power they believed had occurred under the British Crown, they established an intricate separation of powers between the legislative, executive and judicial branches. This was more accurately described by Richard Neustadt (1990) as 'separated institutions sharing powers'. Thus, although the president was designated head of state, chief execu-

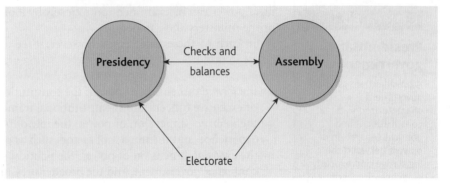

Figure 13.1   Presidential system of government (limited presidentialism)

tive, commander-in-chief of the armed forces and chief diplomat, and was granted wide-ranging powers of **patronage** and the right to veto legislation, Congress was invested with strong counterbalancing powers. In particular, Congress could declare war and override presidential vetoes, and the Senate was empowered to approve appointments and ratify treaties. Indeed, until the early twentieth century the presidency remained a generally secondary institution; such policy leadership as was required was provided by Congress.

The status of the US presidency was then transformed by two key developments. First, a national economy developed that required the government to abandon its traditional *laissez-faire* policies and adopt a more interventionist approach to economic and social life. Second, the USA was forced to drop its policy of isolationism and accept a world role, assuming after World War II a superpower status, in a bipolar, and subsequently unipolar, world system. Since President Franklin Roosevelt's New Deal in the 1930s, US presidents have played the role of chief legislator, and since 1945 have worn the mantle of the leader of the 'free world'. Alarmed by the ease with which President Johnson and President Nixon escalated the Vietnam War without war being formally declared by Congress, Arthur Schlesinger (1974) went so far as to proclaim the emergence of an **'imperial presidency'**.

Presidential power is, nevertheless, often fragile and insubstantial. Neustadt's classic text *Presidential Power* (1990) remains correct: the chief power of the US president is the 'power to persuade'; that is, the ability to bargain, encourage and even cajole, but not dictate. The ability of US presidents to get their way depends on four crucial relationships, specifically those with:

- Congress
- the federal bureaucracy
- the Supreme Court
- the media.

The president's relationship with *Congress* is undoubtedly the most crucial. The success of particular presidents, for instance, is often quantified in terms of their 'success rate' with Congress; that is, the proportion of their legislative

● **Patronage**: The practice of making appointments to office, or, more widely, the granting of favours.

● **Imperial presidency**: A presidency that has broken free from its constitutional bounds and threatens to dominate the other two branches of government.

programme that survives congressional scrutiny. Following the Vietnam War and the Watergate scandal, however, presidents have had to confront more assertive Congresses, intent on reclaiming some of their lost powers. An early example of this was the passage of the War Powers Act 1974, which meant that congressional support was required for the dispatching of US troops abroad. More significantly, the USA's relatively weak party system deprives the president of the major lever of legislative control available to parliamentary executives: an appeal to party unity. This means, as President Jimmy Carter discovered in the 1970s, that presidents can be rebuffed by Congress even when both houses are dominated by their own party.

Presidents may be weaker still when they are confronted by a Congress that is controlled by the opposition party. This was the problem that President Clinton experienced after the election of a Republican Congress in 1994. Barack Obama's influence over Congress was also severely restricted when the Democrats lost 63 seats in, and control of, the House of Representatives in the 2010 mid-term elections. The difficulty confronting the president is that, regardless of party affiliation, both Representatives and Senators are concerned primarily with the 'folks back home'. Indeed, the interest that this forces them to take in domestic affairs has encouraged commentators to speak of the 'two presidencies'. These are the 'domestic' presidency, which is typically characterized by policy failure and gridlock, and from which most presidents retreat; and the 'foreign' presidency, to which they gravitate in the hope of demonstrating their leadership credentials. Even President Clinton, elected to office on a promise to focus 'like a laser beam' on the economy, could not avoid, in Rose's (1987) words, 'going international'. This trend was further strengthened by the so-called 'war on terror' (see p. 401) following the September 11 terrorist attacks on New York and Washington. The ultimate control that Congress exercises over the president resides in the power of **impeachment**, although this has only been used twice (Andrew Johnson in 1868, and Bill Clinton in 1998), and on both occasions the president was aquitted at a trial by the Senate.

In theory, the federal *bureaucracy* exists to serve the president but, in practice, it often acts as an embarrassing constraint. Although presidents make, directly or indirectly, about 4,000 appointments at senior and middle-ranking levels in their administrations, this is a minimal proportion of the total number of professional bureaucrats in the US, who number over 2 million. Moreover, it is widely argued that these bureaucrats frequently respond to interests at odds with the priorities of the administration. As Secretary of the Navy under Woodrow Wilson, F. D. Roosevelt described influencing the Navy Department as like punching a feather mattress: 'you punch and punch but it remains the same'. In his famous comment on his successor, General Eisenhower, President Truman referred to a similar problem:

> He'll sit here and he'll say 'Do this! Do that!' and nothing will happen. Poor Ike – it won't be a bit like the Army.

● **Impeachment**: A formal process for the removal of a public official in the event of personal or professional wrongdoing.

Similar difficulties exist in relation to the *Supreme Court*. Since the 1950s, the Court has played a significant role in US political life, forcing presidents to shape the political agenda, in part, by exercising influence over it. Although presidents appoint justices to the Supreme Court, these appointments may be rejected by

Focus on . . .

The monarchy debate

A monarchy is a system of rule dominated by one person (it literally means 'rule by one person'). In general usage, however, it is the institution through which the post of head of state is filled through inheritance or dynastic succession. In absolute monarchies, the monarch claims, if seldom exercises, a monopoly of political power (examples being Saudi Arabia, Swaziland and the Vatican City). In constitutional monarchies, the monarch fulfils an essentially ceremonial function largely devoid of political significance (for example, in Spain, the Netherlands and the UK).

The advantages of a constitutional monarchy are as follows:

- It provides a solution to the need for a non-partisan head of state who is 'above' party politics.
- The monarch embodies traditional authority, and so serves as a symbol of patriotic loyalty and national unity.
- The monarch constitutes a repository of experience and wisdom, especially in relation to constitutional matters, available to elected governments.

The disadvantages of a constitutional monarchy include the following:

- It violates democratic principles, in that political authority is not based on popular consent and is in no way publicly accountable.
- The monarch symbolizes (and possibly supports) conservative values such as hierarchy, deference and respect for inherited wealth and social position.
- The monarchy binds nations to outmoded ways and symbols of the past, thus impeding progress.

the Senate (as discovered by Nixon twice and Reagan once), and, once they have been appointed, judges cannot be controlled because of their security of tenure. Much of the New Deal programme in the 1930s was blocked by the Supreme Court, until F. D. Roosevelt was able to shift its ideological balance through the 'court revolution' of 1937. Eisenhower, in turn, appointed Earl Warren as Chief Justice, only later discovering his taste for judicial activism and his liberal interpretation of the constitution.

The final key relationship is that between the US president and the *media*. The media are vital to presidents who need to appeal directly to the US public 'over the heads of Congress'. In this respect, presidents such as Ronald Reagan, a former actor and journalist, have been remarkably successful in 'managing' media coverage and ensuring favourable comment. Nevertheless, presidents who live by the media may also die by them. The media are often portrayed as the USA's fourth branch of government, which prizes both its political independence and its reputation for seeking truth. The exposure of the Watergate scandal by *The Washington Post* eventually led to the resignation of President Nixon in 1974, and relentless coverage of the Whitewater affair seriously weakened the Clinton administration in the early 1990s.

The potential within presidential systems for institutional conflict was realized in early postcommunist Russia as the Russian parliament came increasingly under the control of hardliners intent on resisting President Yeltsin's 'shock therapy' reform package. Ultimately, Yeltsin's presidency survived only because of the support of the military in crushing the parliament's rebellion in October

1993, which led to the imposition of presidential rule. The possibility of the emergence in Russia of an unlimited presidential executive was, however, offset by Yeltsin's need to balance the volatile and conflicting pressures within the Russian political system. Russia's tradition of strong executive leadership was nevertheless reasserted after 1999 by President Putin. Putin established a hegemonic presidency based on what he called a 'dictatorship of law'. This system was amended during 2008–12, when Putin served as prime minister under President Medvedev, due to a constitutional restriction on residents serving for three successive terms in office.

A different form of presidential government is found in semi-presidential systems, such as those in France, Austria, Finland and Portugal. These are hybrid systems. They comprise, as in presidential systems, a separately elected president invested with a range of executive powers and, as in parliamentary systems, a government, usually featuring a prime minister and a cabinet, drawn from and accountable to the assembly. In Finland and Austria, for example, such systems operate largely through a division of executive responsibilities, allowing the president to concentrate on foreign affairs and broader constitutional issues, while the prime minister and cabinet take charge of domestic policy.

However, the system constructed in the Fifth French Republic, and completed with the introduction of a separately elected president in 1962, is significantly more complex. On the one hand, in addition to carrying out the roles that the US president plays as head of state, chief executive and dispenser of appointments, French presidents enjoy a fixed five-year term in office, and can also bring the legislature to heel by using their power to dissolve the National Assembly. On the other hand, they are seriously constrained by the need for their governments to maintain parliamentary and public support. Thus, presidents such as de Gaulle (1958–69), Pompidou (1969–74) and Giscard d'Estaing (1974–81) derived their strength largely from the control that Gaullist forces exercised in the National Assembly. However, the right to call a general election does not necessarily guarantee party control of the National Assembly, as the Socialist President Mitterrand discovered in 1986, and again in 1993, when he was forced into **cohabitation** with Gaullist governments. Similarly, despite the fact that he possessed the formal powers of an elected monarch, de Gaulle's presidency ended in resignation in 1969 after the student riots of May 1968 and a financial crisis. The fragility of presidential power was also demonstrated by the pressures on President Chirac, particularly during the period of Jospin's Socialist-led government (1997–2002).

Prime ministers

● **Cohabitation:** An arrangement in a semi-presidential system in which the president works with a government and assembly controlled by a rival party or parties.

Most of the political executives in the modern world can be classified as parliamentary executives. The structure and form of executive power found in parliamentary systems differs significantly from that in presidential ones. Parliamentary executives have three essential features. First, since executive power is derived from the assembly and closely linked to party politics, a separate head of state, in the form of a constitutional monarch or non-executive president, is required to fulfil ceremonial duties and act as a focus of patriotic loyalty. Second, the political executive is drawn from the assembly, which means that the separation of the personnel between the legislature and executive found in presidential systems does not occur in parliamentary systems. Third, the executive is directly responsible to the assembly, or at least to its lower chamber, in the sense that it survives in government only as long as it retains the confidence of the assembly.

The external dynamics of executive power in parliamentary systems thus contrast sharply with those found in presidential ones. In short, parliamentary executives are forced to govern in and through assemblies, while presidential executives tend to rely on a personal mandate and an independent set of constitutional powers. This undoubtedly also affects the internal dynamics of power. In particular, it creates a greater pressure in parliamentary executives for collective decision-making and collaboration, often reflected in the higher status of the cabinet in these systems. However, many commentators have argued that the growth of prime-ministerial power has effectively turned prime ministers into quasi-presidents.

Prime ministers (sometimes seen as chancellors, as in Germany; minister-presidents, as in the Netherlands; or referred to by a local title, such as the Irish Taoiseach) are heads of government whose power is derived from their leadership of the majority party, or coalition (see p. 239) of parties, in the assembly. The range of formal powers with which the office of prime minister is invested are typically modest in comparison with those of executive presidents. The most important of these is the control of patronage – the ability to hire and fire, promote and demote, ministers. In the Netherlands and Australia, for example, even this power is exercised by the assembly or the majority party. As the job of prime minister can have only a loose constitutional description, it is no exaggeration to say that the post is what its holder chooses to make of it or, more accurately, is able to make of it.

In practice, this boils down to two key sets of prime-ministerial relationships. The first set is with the cabinet, individual ministers and government departments; the second is with his or her party and, through it, the assembly and the public. The support of the cabinet is particularly crucial to prime ministers who are designated *primus inter pares* (first among equals), such as those in the UK, India and Australia. This status forces prime ministers to operate through a system of collective cabinet government (see p. 298). Their power is therefore a reflection of the degree to which, by patronage, cabinet management and the control of the machinery of government, they can ensure that ministers serve under them. In contrast, German chancellors are personally empowered by Article 65 of the Basic Law (1949) to decide the general lines of government policy. However, the same article also constrains their power by stipulating that ministers enjoy autonomy in relation to their departments.

There is no doubt that the key to prime-ministerial power and influence lies in his or her position as party leader. Indeed, the modern premiership is largely a product of the emergence of disciplined political parties. Not only is the post of prime minister allocated on the basis of party leadership, it also provides its holder with a means of controlling the assembly and a base from which the image of a national leader can be constructed. The degree of party unity, the parliamentary strength of the prime minister's party (in particular, whether it rules alone or as a member of a coalition), and the authority vested in the assembly (or, at least, its first chamber), are therefore important determinants of prime-ministerial power. For instance, factional rivalry within, and then the decline of, the LDP ensured that the tenure of Japanese prime ministers was short (17 prime ministers came and went between 1974 and 2011) and cabinets were frequently reconstructed. Similarly, Italy's fragmented party system usually forces prime ministers to play the role of a broker within what tend to be fragile coalition governments. German chancellors, for their part, are restricted by the independence of the *Länder*, the power of the second chamber (the *Bundesrat*), and the authority of the Constitutional Court, as well as by the autonomy of the Bundesbank.

There is, nevertheless, agreement that, despite their differing constitutional and political positions, prime-ministerial power has grown in recent years. This results in part from the tendency (of the broadcast media, in particular) to focus on personalities, meaning that prime ministers become a kind of 'brand image' of their parties. The growth of international summitry and foreign visits also provides prime ministers with opportunities to cultivate an image of statesmanship, and gives them scope to portray themselves as national leaders. In some cases, this has led to the allegation that prime ministers have effectively emancipated themselves from cabinet constraints and established a form of prime-ministerial government. For instance, in India an imperial style of premiership developed under Indira Gandhi and her son Rajiv that reached its peak during the state of emergency, 1975–77. This was possible because of the secure majorities that the Congress Party enjoyed in parliament, the ruthless control exerted over the apparatus of central government, and the sway that the Gandhi dynasty continued to exert over important sections of the Indian public.

Allegations of prime-ministerial government have often been made in the UK. The unusual level of power wielded by prime ministers stems from various sources, including the following:

● the level and range of their patronage
● their control of the cabinet system, especially their ability to set up and staff cabinet committees
● their ability to dominate the assembly as leaders of the largest party, especially when that party has majority control of the lower chamber
● their position as head of the civil service, and the control this gives them over the bureaucratic machine
● their direct access to the media, which enables them to make personalized appeals to the voters.

Prime ministers stand at the apex of the administrative and political arms of government, meaning that the cabinet has been turned into a US-style advisory body that no longer exercises policy-making responsibility. The prime-ministerial government thesis appeared to have become a reality in the UK during the 1980s, as Margaret Thatcher effectively recast the nature and authority of the office. In many respects, Tony Blair's premiership after 1997 built on these foundations. What distinguished Thatcher's premiership was the fact that she saw herself as a 'conviction prime minister', her role being to provide ideological leadership and policy coherence, orientated around ideas that came to be called **Thatcherism**. Similarly, Blair strongly associated his leadership of the Labour Party with the advance of the 'modernizing' project; this saw the party rebranded as 'new' Labour and 'third way' ideological priorities displace old-style socialist ones. For Michael Foley (2000), this development exposed the degree to

● **Thatcherism**: The free-market/strong-state ideological stance adopted by Margaret Thatcher; the UK version of the New Right political project.

Focus on . . .
Prime-ministerial government: a virtue or a vice?

Prime-ministerial government has two key features. First, the office of prime minister is the central link between the legislative and executive branches of government, its holder being drawn from and accountable to the assembly, and also serving as chief executive and head of the bureaucracy. Second, prime-ministerial government reflects the centralization of executive power in the hands of the prime minister and the effective subordination of both the cabinet and departmental ministers. In this, it parallels presidentialism.

Prime-ministerial government has been criticized for the following reasons:

- It strengthens centralization by weakening the constraints formerly exerted by the cabinet and government departments.
- It narrows policy debate and weakens scrutiny by excluding criticisms and alternative viewpoints.

However, it can be defended on the following grounds:

- It reflects the personal mandate that prime ministers acquire in general elections.
- It gives government policy clearer direction by checking the centrifugal pressures embodied in departmentalism (see p. 371) and the 'nudge and fudge' of collective decision-making.

which an 'authentically British presidency' had come into existence, highlighting a wider trend in parliamentary systems towards presidentialism.

Although prime ministers who command cohesive parliamentary majorities can wield power that would be the envy of many a president, they are also subject to important constraints. By no means, for instance, do prime ministers have a free hand in terms of hiring and firing. The need to maintain party unity by ensuring that the various factions and ideological wings of the party are represented in the cabinet, and the pressure in countries such as Canada to maintain regional and linguistic representation, act as important checks on prime-ministerial power. The advent of coalition government, as under David Cameron in the UK since 2010, also constrains the prime minister's powers of patronage. Ultimately, prime ministers are only as powerful as their cabinets, parties and broader political circumstances allow them to be. This can be seen in India, where, following the excesses of the emergency in the 1970s, prime ministers such as Desai, Singh and Rao, leading coalition or minority governments, reduced the size of the prime minister's staff, were willing to respect the autonomy of government departments, and interfered less in the affairs of state governments.

It is also interesting that the power wielded by Margaret Thatcher in the UK may have been less a consequence of her indomitable character and ideological resolution than a reflection of the unusually favourable circumstances that confronted her. Chief amongst these were the weak and divided nature of the Labour opposition, the 1982 Falklands War victory, the revival of the world economy in the mid-1980s, and, partly as a result of these, the ability of the Conservatives to win three successive elections under her leadership. However, the fragility of prime-ministerial power was underlined by her removal as leader in 1990.

The UK prime minister: a president in all but name?

Events: In March 2003, the Iraq War started with an invasion launched by the USA and the UK. The UK's involvement in this war was a remarkable example of prime-ministerial power. It showed the then-prime minister, Tony Blair, at his most determined, zealous, even messianic. Blair persisted with his determination to 'stand by the USA', despite mass anti-war demonstrations on the streets of London and other major UK cities, and despite suffering the largest backbench revolt against any government in over a century. What is more, this was a war of choice for Blair. Many in Washington had expected the UK to back away from military action once the Security Council of the United Nations had failed to pass a resolution specifically authorizing the war, and they had planned accordingly. The UK's involvement in the Iraq War was therefore a personal decision on the part of Blair: he did it because he thought it was the right thing to do. But he also did it because he could do it: his position as prime minister allowed him to do it.

Significance: For many, the decision to go to war was a clear reflection of the fact that the UK no longer had a prime minister, but a president. Personal leadership had replaced collective leadership – the prime minister was in charge, not the cabinet or Parliament. In a trend dating back to Harold Wilson in the 1960s and Margaret Thatcher in the 1980s, Blair had been able to emancipate himself from the constraints that typically apply to a parliamentary executive. With two landslide election victories behind him (in 1997 and 2001), Blair had little to fear from a cabinet that was, in the main, unwilling to challenge his authority, or from a Parliament in which Labour's majority was so large that it effectively immunized him from backbench pressure. Although the UK does not have a separately elected executive, a combination of the media's portrayal of politics in terms of personality and image, rather than ideas and policies, and the tendency of parties to use their leaders as their 'brand image', has led to the growth of personalized election campaigns in which the victorious leader comes to claim a personal mandate on the basis of their electoral success. This has led to the growth of 'spatial leadership'; that is, the tendency of leaders to distance themselves from their parties and governments either by presenting themselves as 'outsiders', or by developing a personal ideological stance.

However, significant though these trends may be, it is difficult to argue that they have rebalanced the structural dynamics of the UK's parliamentary executive. Although Blair's decision in 2003 was, in itself, a remarkable example of prime-ministerial power, it cast a dark shadow over the rest of his premiership, ultimately leading to the end of his political career. After 2003, Blair's poll ratings plummeted, and Labour's majority in the 2005 general election was slashed from 166 to just 65. A mood of restiveness and unease took hold on Labour's backbenches and was expressed in increasingly frequent backbench revolts. Tensions also grew within the cabinet, especially as Gordon Brown and his allies became more open about pursuing their political ambitions. Shortly before the 2005 election, Blair became the first prime minister to, in effect, pre-announce his own resignation. He did this by promising that, if he were re-elected for a third term in office, he would not seek a fourth term. This promise was duly carried out when he resigned in June 2007. Presidential tendencies may have allowed Blair to make the fateful 2003 decision in the first place, but the fact that UK prime ministers are always forced to operate within a cabinet and parliamentary system meant that he was unable to escape the consequences of that decision.

Focus on . . .
Cabinet government: advantages and disadvantages

Cabinet government is characterized by two central features. First, the cabinet constitutes the principal link between the legislative and executive branches of government; its members are drawn from and accountable to the parliament, but also serve as the political heads of the various government departments. Second, the cabinet is the senior executive organ, and policy-making responsibility is shared within it, the prime minister being 'first' in name only. This system is usually underpinned by collective responsibility – all the cabinet ministers are required to 'sing the same song' and support official government policy.

The virtues of cabinet government are the following:

- It encourages full and frank policy debate within the democracy of cabinet meetings, subjecting proposals to effective scrutiny.
- It guarantees the unity and cohesion of government, since the cabinet makes decisions collectively and collectively stands by them.

However, cabinet government has been criticized for the following reasons:

- It acts as a cloak for prime-ministerial power because it forces dissenting ministers to support agreed government policy in public.
- It means that government policy becomes incoherent and inconsistent, as decisions are based on compromises between competing ministers and departmental interests.

The relative weakness of John Major's premiership, particularly in the 1992–97 period, stemmed less from his personal inadequacies and more from the greater difficulties his government had to face. Chief amongst these was a combination of the Conservatives' diminished parliamentary majority and the party's deepening rift over Europe. In contrast, Tony Blair benefited not only from his large majorities and the electoral decline of the Conservative Party, but also from the fact that, after 18 years in opposition, the Labour Party was initially more responsive to demands for strong leadership and unity. Gordon Brown's premiership, 2007–10, was blighted by both his personal limitations as a political communicator and by the severe recession that was triggered by the 2007–09 global financial crisis, which effectively destroyed Brown's and Labour's reputation for economic competence.

Cabinets

Virtually all political executives feature a cabinet of some sort. In France, the cabinet is known as the 'Council of Ministers' and, in China, it is called the 'Politburo'. A cabinet is a committee of senior ministers who represent the various government departments or ministries. This term is not to be confused with '*cabinet*', as used in France and the EU to denote small groups of policy advisers who support individual ministers. The widespread use of cabinets reflects the political and administrative need for collective procedures within the political executive. In the first place, cabinets enable government to present a collective face to assemblies and the public. Without a cabinet, government

CONCEPT

Core executive

The core executive is a network of institutions and people who play key roles in the overall direction and coordination of government policy. It usually encompasses the prime minister, senior policy advisers, leading cabinet members, cabinet committees, and staff in strategically important government departments. The core executive model gets away from the simplistic 'prime minister versus cabinet' debate, by acknowledging that these bodies operate within an institutional context. It also acknowledges the extent to which policy influence is exerted through the building up of alliances and coalitions of support.

could appear to be a personal tool wielded by a single individual. Second, cabinets are an administrative device designed to ensure the effective coordination of government policy. In short, in the absence of a cabinet, government would consist of rival bureaucratic empires each bent on self-aggrandisement, rather as occurred in the Hitler state in Nazi Germany.

The precise role and political importance of cabinets vary from system to system and state to state. In presidential systems such as the USA's, the cabinet exists to serve the president by acting as a policy adviser, rather than a policy-maker. Indeed, in the second half of the twentieth century, executive growth in the USA occurred largely at a non-cabinet level, in the form of the construction of the Executive Office of the President (discussed in Chapter 16). In contrast, the cabinet, in theory at least, is the apex of the executive in states that respect the principle of cabinet government, such as the UK, most of the Commonwealth and several European countries (including Italy, Sweden and Norway).

It is, nevertheless, difficult in practice to find examples of collective executives that operate through a cabinet or equivalent body. In theory, a form of collective leadership operates in China, reflecting the Marxist–Leninist belief that the Communist Party (CCP), rather than a single leader, is the leading and guiding force in Chinese society. In practice, the leadership system in China has been dominated by a paramount individual. In the cases of Mao Zedong, during 1949–76, and Deng Xiaoping, during 1978–97, they wielded such supreme power that they retained their position until they died. More recent Chinese leaders have combined their position with the posts of general secretary of the CCP and president of the People's Republic of China. In Germany, and commonly throughout continental Europe, a tradition of departmental special-ization discourages ministers from seeing themselves as 'team players', and so counters any tendency towards cabinet government. Even in the UK system, supposedly the archetypal example of cabinet government, it is difficult to see the cabinet as a decision-making body, let alone as a democratic forum.

Not only has the rise of prime-ministerial power subverted the collective nature of UK government, but the growth in the range and complexity of government policy has also ensured that most decisions are effectively made elsewhere, and thus reach the cabinet in a prepackaged form. This highlights the important contribution that government departments make to policy formula-tion, as well as the impact of cabinet committees and, indeed, subcommittees. In the UK and elsewhere, the full cabinet is merely the hub of a cabinet system, comprising committees of subject specialists able to examine policy proposals in greater detail and depth than is possible in the cabinet itself. This system weakens the cabinet both because it strengthens the levers of control that are available to the prime minister, who sets up and staffs committees, and because full cabinets usually lack the time and expertise to challenge proposals that emanate from committees. The complex relationships that result from this have been explained by some commentators in terms of the idea of a 'core executive' (Rhodes and Dunleavy, 1995).

On the other hand, it would be a mistake to dismiss cabinets as merely 'digni-fied' institutions. Many prime ministers, for example, have paid a high price for ignoring the collective element within modern government. German chancellors are generally considered to be even stronger than UK prime ministers because

CONCEPT

Leadership

Leadership can be understood either as a pattern of behaviour, or as a personal quality. As a pattern of behaviour, leadership is the influence exerted by an individual or group over a larger body to organize or direct its efforts towards the achievement of desired goals. As a personal attribute, leadership refers to the character traits that enable the leader to exert influence over others; leadership is thus effectively equated with charisma (see p. 83). In both respects, however, leadership requires 'followership'. For a claim to leadership to be upheld, others, the followers, must recognise and act on that claim.

they can be removed only by a vote of 'constructive no confidence'. This means that the *Bundestag* can remove a government only by approving an alternative one, not merely by withdrawing support from the existing one (as occurs in the UK). Nevertheless, Chancellor Schmidt was forced to resign in 1982 when the small Free Democratic Party withdrew from his Social-Democrat-led coalition cabinet to join forces with the Christian Democrats, led by Helmut Kohl. Coalitions certainly add to the difficulties of cabinet management, as Italian prime ministers have regularly discovered, but a single-party cabinet can also cause problems for chief executives.

Although cabinets generally remain loyal to prime ministers for fear that divisions in a party's senior leadership spell the likelihood of election defeat, prime ministers are sometimes removed as a result of pressure from within the cabinet, or from senior party figures. Margaret Thatcher interpreted her fall in 1990 in precisely these terms. Thatcher claimed to have been ousted by a cabinet *coup* through the withdrawal of ministerial support once she had failed to secure re-election as party leader on the first ballot (Thatcher, 1993). Kevin Rudd's removal as Australian prime minister in 2010 reinforced the lesson that parliamentary leaders cannot long survive without the support of senior party figures. Faced with the declining popularity of his government and growing dissatisfaction with his own leadership, Rudd stood down as prime minister and Labor Party leader in favour of his deputy, Julia Gillard, becoming the first Australian prime minister to be removed from office by his own party during his first term in office.

THE POLITICS OF LEADERSHIP

In some respects, the subject of political leadership appears to be outdated. The division of society into leaders and followers is rooted in a predemocratic culture of deference and respect in which leaders 'knew best' and the public needed to be led, mobilized or guided. Democratic politics may not have removed the need for leaders, but it has certainly placed powerful constraints on leadership; notably, by making leaders publicly accountable and establishing an institutional mechanism through which they can be called to account and removed. In other respects, however, the politics of leadership has become increasingly significant, helping to contribute to the establishment of a separate discipline of political psychology, whose major concerns include a study of the psychological make-up and motivations of political leaders (Kressel, 1993).

This growing focus on leadership has occurred for a number of reasons. For instance, to some extent, democracy itself has enhanced the importance of personality by forcing political leaders, in effect, to 'project themselves' in the hope of gaining electoral support. This tendency has undoubtedly been strengthened by modern means of mass communication (especially television), which tend to emphasize personalities, rather than policies, and provide leaders with powerful weapons with which to manipulate their public images. Furthermore, as society becomes more complex and fragmented, people may increasingly look to the personal vision of individual leaders to give coherence and meaning to the world in which they live. Ironically, then, leadership may never have been so important, but also so difficult to deliver.

Friedrich Nietzsche (1844–1900)

German philosopher. A professor of Greek at Basel by the age of 25, Nietzsche became increasingly interested in the ideas of Schopenhauer (1788–1860) and the music of Wagner (1813–83). Growing illness and insanity after 1889 brought him under the control of his sister Elizabeth, who edited and distorted his writings. Nietzsche's complex and ambitious work stressed the importance of will, especially the 'will to power', and it anticipated modern existentialism in emphasizing that people create their own worlds and make their own values. He attacked conventional values based on God, truth and morality, and sought to replace these with new values and a new ideal of the human person. His best known writings include *Thus Spake Zarathustra* (1883/84), *Beyond Good and Evil* (1886) and *On the Genealogy of Morals* (1887).

Theories of leadership

The question of political leadership is surrounded by controversy. To what extent is leadership compatible with freedom and democracy? Does personalized leadership inspire and motivate, or does it subdue and repress (see p. 305)? Are strong leaders to be admired or feared? At the heart of these disagreements lie differing views about the nature of political leadership. What does the phenomenon of leadership comprise? Where does leadership come from? Four contrasting theories of leadership can be identified. Leadership can be understood as:

- a natural gift
- a sociological phenomenon
- an organizational necessity
- a political skill.

A natural gift

The traditional view of leadership sees it as a rare but natural gift. As Aristotle (see p. 6) put it, 'men are marked out from the moment of birth to rule or be ruled'. From this perspective, leadership is strictly an individual quality, manifest in the personalities of what were traditionally thought of as 'men of destiny'. The most extreme version of this theory is found in the fascist 'leader principle' (*Führerprinzip*). This is based on the idea of a single, supreme leader (always male), who alone is capable of leading the masses to their destiny. Such an idea was, in part, derived from Friedrich Nietzsche's notion of the *Übermensch* (the 'overman' or 'superman'), who rises above the 'herd instinct' of conventional morality and so achieves self-mastery. In a more modest form, this theory of leadership is embodied in the idea of charisma, generally understood to mean the power of personality. The classic examples of charismatic leaders are usually seen as forceful personalities (such as Hitler, Castro, Nasser and Thatcher), although the more modest, but no less effective, 'fireside chats' of F. D. Roosevelt and the practised televisual skills of almost all modern leaders also exemplify charismatic qualities. However, unfortunately, leaders who exhibit genuine moral authority are rare.

CONCEPT

Cult of personality

A cult of personality (or cult of leadership) is a propaganda device through which a political leader is portrayed as a heroic or God-like figure. By treating the leader as the source of all political wisdom and an unfailing judge of the national interest, the cult implies that any form of criticism or opposition amounts to treachery or lunacy. Cults of personality have typically been developed in totalitarian regimes (first by Stalin) through the exploitation of the possibilities of modern means of mass communication, and the use of state repression to cultivate a form of ritualized idolatrization.

Modern political psychology adopts a similar view of leadership, in that it analyses it in terms of human personality. One of the earliest attempts to do this was the collaboration in the late 1920s between the Austrian psychologist Sigmund Freud (1856–1939) and US diplomat William C. Bullitt on a controversial study of President Woodrow Wilson (Freud and Bullitt, 1967). Harold Lasswell's ground-breaking *Psychopathology and Politics* (1930) suggested that leaders are motivated largely by private, almost pathological, conflicts, which are then rationalized in terms of actions taken in the public interest. A widely discussed modern analysis of political leadership has been advanced by James Barber (1988). Focusing on what he called 'presidential character', Barber categorized US presidents according to two key variables: first, whether they were 'active' or 'passive' in terms of the energy they put into their jobs; and, second, whether they were 'positive' or 'negative' in terms of how they felt about political office. He therefore identified four character types:

- active-positive
- active-negative
- passive-positive
- passive-negative.

Examples of active-positive presidents would include Kennedy, Clinton and Obama. Active-negative presidents would include Harding and Reagan. Nixon is an example of a passive-positive president, while Coolidge and Eisenhower were passive-negative. Nevertheless, the limitations of Barber's analysis are demonstrated by the way that George W. Bush was transformed from a passive-positive president into a much more assertive and active one by the terrorist attacks on the USA on 11 September 2001.

A sociological phenomenon

An alternative view of leadership sees it as a sociological, rather than psychological, phenomenon. From this perspective, in other words, leaders are 'created' by particular socio-historical forces. They do not so much impose their will on the world as act as a vehicle through which historical forces are exerted. This is certainly the approach adopted by Marxists, who believe that historical development is structured largely by economic factors, reflected in a process of class struggle. The personalities of individual leaders are, thus, less important than the broader class interests they articulate. Marx, nevertheless, acknowledged that **Bonapartism** was an exception. This was a phenomenon based on Louis Bonaparte's *coup d'état* in France in 1851, through which a personal dictatorship was established in conditions in which the bourgeoisie had lost power, but the proletariat was not sufficiently developed to seize it. Even in this case, however, Marx insisted that the Bonapartist dictatorship reflected the interests of the numerically strongest class in France, the smallholding peasantry. Similarly, in analysing Stalinism in the USSR, Trotsky (see p. 369) emphasized the degree to which Stalin's power was rooted in the dominance of the state bureaucracy (Trotsky, 1937). Sociological factors have also provided the basis for the very different idea that political leadership is largely a product of collective behaviour. In his seminal *The Crowd* ([1895] 1960), Gustav Le Bon analysed the dynamics

● **Bonapartism**: A style of government that fuses personal leadership with conservative nationalism; for Marxists, it reflects the relative autonomy of the state.

of crowd psychology, arguing that leaders are impelled by the collective behaviour of the masses, not the other way round.

An organizational necessity

The third theory of leadership sees it in largely technical terms as a rational, or bureaucratic, device. In this view, leadership is essentially an organizational necessity that arises from the need for coherence, unity and direction within any complex institution. Leadership therefore goes hand-in-hand with bureaucracy (see p. 361). Modern large-scale organizations require specialization, which, in turn, gives rise to a hierarchy of offices and responsibilities. This bureaucratic leadership conforms to what Weber (see p. 82) called legal-rational authority, in that it is essentially impersonal and based on formal, usually written, rules. The rise of constitutional government has undoubtedly invested political leadership with a strongly bureaucratic character by ensuring that power is vested in a political office, rather than the individual office-holder. This, nevertheless, conflicts with democratic pressures that force political leaders to cultivate charisma and emphasize personal qualities in order to win and retain power.

A political skill

The final theory of leadership portrays it very much as an artefact; that is, as a political skill that can be learned and practised. Political leadership, in this sense, is akin to the art of manipulation, a perhaps inevitable feature of democratic politics in an age of mass communications. This can be seen most graphically in the cults of personality that have been constructed to support the dictatorial leaderships of figures such as Mao Zedong (see p. 304), Colonel Gaddafi and Saddam Hussein. Indeed, many of the classic examples of charismatic leadership can, in practice, be seen as forms of manufactured leadership. Stalin, for example, bolstered his own popularity by building up an elaborate cult of Lenin in the 1920s; he erected statues, renamed streets and towns, and placed Lenin's embalmed body in a mausoleum in Red Square. During the 1930s, having carefully linked himself to Lenin's heritage, Stalin transferred this cult to himself. Similarly, Hitler's performances at the Nuremburg rallies were carefully stage-managed by Albert Speer. His every word and gesture were carefully rehearsed and choreographed; the whole event was designed to build up emotional tension that would be released by Hitler's appearance.

Modern democratic politicians have no less strong a need to project themselves and their personal vision, though the skills appropriate to the television age tend to be refined and sophisticated compared with those suitable for mass rallies and public demonstrations. The heightened optimism that greeted Barack Obama's first election victory in 2008 and his inauguration the following year, and his unusually successful early period in office (especially over the issue of health care reform), were often linked to his capacity to deploy two important leadership skills. First, an astute and highly fluent public speaker, Obama was able to convey professionalism and gravitas whilst also, as appropriate, using humour and self-deprecation. Second, he demonstrated strong **emotional intelligence**, the capacity that, according to Greenstein (2009), is the key to establishing a successful leadership style. Emotional intelligence reflects the

• **Emotional intelligence:** The ability to handle oneself and to build successful relationships, based on an understanding of one's own and others' feelings.

Mao Zedong (Mao Tse-tung) (1893–1976)

Chinese Marxist theorist and leader of the People's Republic of China, 1949–76. Mao was the son of a peasant farmer in Hunan. He initially worked as a librarian and teacher. In 1921, he helped to found the Chinese Communist Party and, in 1935, became its leader. As a political theorist, Mao adapted Marxism–Leninism to the needs of an overwhelmingly agricultural and still traditional society. His legacy is often associated with the Cultural Revolution (1966–70), a radical egalitarian movement that denounced elitism and 'capitalist roaders' (these inclined to bow to pressure from bourgeois forces), and that resulted in widespread social disruption, repression and death. Maoism is usually understood as an anti-bureaucratic form of Marxism that places its faith in the radical zeal of the masses.

ability to draw on four key competences or skills: self-awareness (the ability to read one's own emotions), self-management (the ability to control one's emotions and marshall positive emotions), empathy (the ability to sense, understand and react to others' emotions) and relationship management (the ability to use these skills in combination to have the greatest impact in any situation) (Goleman, 2005). In Obama's case, these skills were used in an attempt to balance a commitment to bipartisanship against support for an underlying vision of the federal government as an agent of social justice that harked back to Franklin Roosevelt's 'New Deal' and Lyndon Johnson's 'Great Society'. However, a possible drawback of such 'soft' leadership skills (in many ways, these are akin to 'soft' power (see p. 428)) is that they may so increase levels of hope and expectation that eventual disillusionment with the leader becomes inevitable.

Styles of leadership

A style of leadership refers to the strategies and behavioural patterns through which a leader seeks to achieve his or her goals. Quite simply, leaders are not all alike: leadership can be exercised in a number of different ways. The factors that shape the adoption of a particular leadership strategy or style are, of course, numerous. Amongst the most obvious are the personality and goals of the leader, the institutional framework within which he or she operates, the political mechanisms by which power is won and retained, the means of mass communication available, and the nature of the broader political culture. Three distinctive styles of leadership have been identified (Burns, 1978):

● *laissez-faire* leadership
● transactional leadership
● transformational leadership.

The chief feature of *laissez-faire* leadership is the reluctance of the leader to interfere in matters outside his or her personal responsibility. Such leaders have a 'hands off' approach to cabinet and departmental management. An example of such leadership could be found in the Reagan White House, and the relatively

Debating . . .
Should personalized leadership always be feared?

Questions about leadership become particularly controversial when leaders draw less on their office and its formal powers and more on their own personal qualities and characteristics. When leadership becomes more an individual rather than an institutional phenomenon, does it become sinister or threatening? Or is personalized leadership more meaningful, even inspiring, than 'bureaucratic' forms of leadership?

YES

Recipe for authoritarianism. The fact that, as democracy has advanced, political leadership has increasingly been 'depersonalized' (by being subject to constitutional and institutional constraints) is no coincidence. When a leader's authority derives more from his or her personality than his or her office, government power is apt to be abused. This reflects the longstanding concern that as charisma (charm, or the power of personality) is not based on formal rules or procedures, potentially, it has no limit. In line with Lord Acton's warning that 'absolute power corrupts absolutely', leaders may also become more greedy, selfish and insensitive to the views of others to the extent that they feel they can manipulate them.

Infantilizing society. Personalized leadership may not only affect leaders but also followers, the public at large. Charismatic leadership has a near-mystical character, operating as it does through the belief that leaders possess special, even god-like qualities. As the relationship between leader and followers has a quasi-religious dimension, it generates uncritical loyalty, amounting perhaps to devotion. Personalized leaders are obeyed not because of what they say or do, but because of who they are. The rise of personalized leadership therefore infantilizes society, instilling a political passivity and unwillingness to engage in questioning, argument and debate that is incompatible with a healthy democracy.

Doomed to fail. Leaders who come to power largely as a result of personal gifts or qualities tend to be poor leaders whose political careers typically end in failure. Personalized leaders 'shine' in the theatre of politics, where their oratorical (and, often, televisual) skills are most in evidence, but their administrative and policy-making skills may be much less developed. Moreover, their capacity to engender optimism and enthusiasm may mean that they build up hope and expectation to a level that cannot be fulfilled, thereby making disappointment inevitable. Finally, when leaders believe they can persuade anyone of anything, they become susceptible to hubris and self-delusion.

NO

Charisma and democracy. The idea that charismatic leadership is irreconcilable with democracy is a gross over-statement. While no one would deny that charisma continues to be significant in the democratic age, its political character has changed fundamentally. Rather than being aloof, domineering and bombastic, modern charismatic leaders cultivate 'soft' qualities, hoping to be liked rather than feared and trying to resemble ordinary citizens rather than overlords. What is more, however attractive a leader's personality and however fluent and persuasive a communicator he or she may be, no modern leader has the capacity to use their personal skills to escape from the electoral and constitutional constraints of a democratic system.

Leadership with a human face. Leadership works only if it is personal. Leaders must move us: they must ignite our passions and inspire the best in us, and, in the process, help us recognize the potential of our society. They do this not simply because of the office that they hold, but because they are living, breathing human beings, who are capable of articulating a narrative that is meaningful precisely because it derives from the leader's life, values and sense of vision. Perhaps the foremost attribute of leadership in contemporary circumstances is the ability to formulate and, most importantly, communicate a message that resonates with large sections of the electorate.

Being above politics. Personalized leaders are able to distance themselves from the political and institutional context that may otherwise define them. This is most evident in relation to party politics and the danger that, being a party leader, a president or prime minister may use their position primarily to advance the interests of their party and its associated groups. Whereas party leadership entails partisanship, so leading to a one-sided approach to politics, personalized leadership opens up the possibility of bipartisanship, as the leader is able to rise above party divisions and appeal to a wider body of people and groups.

slight interest that Reagan took in the day-to-day workings of his administration. George W. Bush, similarly, was strongly inclined to delegate responsibilities to key advisers, but the so-called 'war on terror', launched in 2001, forced him to adopt a more forthright leadership style. A *laissez-faire* style is not irreconcilable with ideological leadership, but it certainly requires that ideological goals constitute only a broadly-stated strategic vision. The strengths of this approach to leadership are that, because subordinates are given greater responsibility, it can foster harmony and teamwork, and it can allow leaders to concentrate on political and electoral matters by relieving them of their managerial burdens. On the other hand, it can also lead to the weak coordination of government policy, with ministers and officials being allowed too much scope to pursue their own interests and initiatives. The Iran–Contra affair, for example, demonstrated how little President Reagan knew about the activities of the Central Intelligence Agency officers and White House officials for whom he was supposedly responsible.

In contrast, *transactional* leadership is a more 'hands-on' style of leadership. Transactional leaders adopt a positive role in relation to policy-making and government management, but are motivated by essentially pragmatic goals and considerations. Prominent amongst these are likely to be the maintenance of party unity and government cohesion, and the strengthening of public support and electoral credibility. Such leaders act as brokers who are concerned to uphold the collegiate face of government by negotiating compromises and balancing rival individuals, factions and interests against one another. In the USA, Lyndon Johnson and George Bush Sr could be seen as transactional leaders, as could Harold Wilson and John Major in the UK. This is, above all, a managerial, even technocratic, style of leadership, its advantage being that it is fiercely practical and allows scope for tactical flexibility. Its central drawback, however, is that such leaders may be seen as opportunistic wheeler-dealers who are devoid of firm principles or deep convictions. This was illustrated by George Bush's damaging admission during the 1992 US presidential election that he did not understand what he called 'the vision thing'.

In the third style of leadership, *transformational* leadership, the leader is not so much a coordinator or manager as an inspirer or visionary. Not only are such leaders motivated by strong ideological convictions, but they also have the personal resolution and political will to put them into practice. Instead of seeking compromise and consensus, transformational leaders attempt to mobilize support from within government, their parties and the general public for the realization of their personal vision. Howard Gardner (1996) suggested that a leader is 'an individual who creates a story'. The effectiveness of such a leader hinges on the degree to which the leader in question 'embodies' the story, and the extent to which the story resonates with the broader public.

General de Gaulle, for instance, recast the nature of political leadership in France as much by presenting himself as a 'father figure' and 'national leader' as by establishing a presidential system in the form of the Fifth Republic. A very similar style was adopted in the UK by Margaret Thatcher, whose avowed aim when coming into office was to run a 'conviction government'. The continued use of terms such as 'Gaullism' and 'Thatcherism' bears witness to the enduring impact of these leaders' ideological visions. Tony Blair in the UK also adopted a transformational stance by recasting the Labour Party as 'new' Labour, in the

Populism

Populism (from the Latin *populus*, meaning 'the people') has been used to describe both distinctive political movements and a particular tradition of political thought. Movements or parties described as populist have been characterized by their claim to support the common people in the face of 'corrupt' economic or political elites. As a political tradition, populism reflects the belief that the instincts and wishes of the people provide the principal legitimate guide to political action. Populist politicians therefore make a direct appeal to the people, and claim to give expression to their deepest hopes and fears.

process ensuring that his government pursued 'third way' rather than old-style socialist priorities. Not uncommonly, transformational leadership is linked to populism, reflecting the desire of such leaders to demonstrate that they are articulating the concerns and interests of 'the people'. Although the strength of transformational leadership is that it provides a basis for pushing through radical programmes of social, economic or political reform, it may also encourage a drift towards authoritarianism and lead to ideological rigidity. It is thus possible to see Thatcher herself as one of the casualties of Thatcherism, in that in 1990 she paid the price for her domineering leadership style and her unwillingness to change policy priorities, even when these had become electorally unpopular.

Regardless of the leadership style they adopt, there are reasons to believe that modern political leaders face greater challenges than their predecessors did. This is important, because attitudes towards leaders, and the perceived effectiveness of leadership, do much to influence people's general view of the political process. The first difficulty that leaders face is that modern societies have perhaps become so complex and enmeshed with global influences that politicians find it almost impossible to get things done. Leaders are therefore doomed to disappoint, to fail to live up to expectations. Indeed, virtually all political careers end in failure perhaps because would-be leaders can only rise by building greater expectations than they have the capacity to fulfil.

Second, leaders suffer because old ideological and moral certainties are breaking down, and this makes it more difficult to construct compelling narratives that have wide popular resonance. Third, modern societies are becoming more diverse and fragmented. Political leaders are therefore finding it increasingly difficult to construct a political appeal based on a common culture and a set of shared values. Fourth, and finally, a cultural gap has perhaps developed between the political and the non-political worlds. Political leaders are increasingly career politicians whose lifestyles, sensibilities and even language are remote from the concerns of private citizens. Far from being seen as providing inspiration and articulating popular hopes and aspirations, modern leaders tend to be viewed as self-serving and out of touch. To the extent that this is true, people become alienated from conventional politics, and perhaps look elsewhere for a source of political leadership.

SUMMARY

● The executive branch of government is responsible for the execution or implementation of policy. The political executive comprises a core of senior figures and is roughly equivalent to 'the government of the day' or 'the administration'. The bureaucratic executive consists of public officials or civil servants. However, the political/bureaucratic distinction is often blurred by the complexities of the policy-making process.

● Political executives act as the 'commanding heights' of the state apparatus and carry out a number of leadership roles. These include representing the state on ceremonial occasions, offering policy-making leadership in relation to strategic priorities, mobilizing popular support for the government or administration, overseeing the bureaucratic machine, and taking the initiative in the event of domestic or international crises.

● Presidential executives concentrate executive power in the hands of a president who combines the roles of head of state and head of government, but confronts an assembly that enjoys constitutional and political independence. Prime ministers in parliamentary systems operate through two key sets of relationships: the first is with their cabinets, ministers and departments; the second is with their parties and the assembly from which their power stems.

● The power of chief executives has been enhanced by the tendency of the media and electoral politics to focus on personality and image, by the opportunities to display statesmanship provided by international affairs and summitry, and by the need for political and ideological leadership within an increasingly large and complex executive branch. Their power is, nevertheless, checked by the importance of government and party unity, the need to maintain support in the assembly, and the difficulty of controlling the sprawling bureaucratic machine.

● Political leadership has been understood in various ways. It has been interpreted as a personal gift based on individual qualities such as charisma, as a sociological phenomenon in which leaders express particular socio-historical forces, as an organizational necessity rooted in the need for coherence and unity of direction, and as a political skill that can be learned by leaders intent on manipulating their colleagues and the masses.

● Leaders have adopted very different strategies to achieve their goals. *Laissez-faire* leadership attempts to foster harmony and teamwork by broadening the responsibilities of subordinates. Transactional leadership allows leaders to act as brokers, and balance rival factions and interests against each other. Transformational leadership places a heavy emphasis on the mobilization of support through the leader's capacity to inspire and to advance a personal vision.

Questions for discussion

● In what circumstances may heads of state play a significant political role?

● Is the only power that a chief executive possesses the power to persuade?

● Are presidents or prime ministers more powerful?

● Is collective cabinet government a principle worth preserving?

● Are leaders 'born' or 'made'?

● Is the task of leadership becoming easier or more difficult?

● Should strong leaders be admired or feared?

● Are cults of personality a feature of all political systems, not just dictatorial ones?

● Do we get the political leaders we deserve?

Further reading

Elgie, R., S. Moestrup and Yu-Shan Wu (eds), *Semi-Presidentialism and Democracy* (2011). A wide-ranging collection of essays that examine the workings and implications of semi-presidential systems.

Gardner, H., *Leading Minds* (1996). A fascinating exploration of the nature of leadership, and the skills and strategies deployed by leaders.

Helms, L., *Presidents, Prime Ministers and Chancellors: Executive Leadership in Western Democracies* (2004). A useful discussion of executive leadership that compares the USA, the UK and Germany.

Poguntke, T. and P. Webb., *The Presidentialization of Politics* (2007). A major examination of the 'presidential logic of governance', that also considers cross-national differences.

CHAPTER 14

Assemblies

'A Parliament is nothing less than a big meeting of more or less idle people.'

WALTER BAGEHOT, *The English Constitution* (1867)

PREVIEW   Assemblies (sometimes called 'parliaments' or 'legislatures') occupy a key position in the machinery of government. Traditionally, they have been treated with special respect and status as the public, even democratic, face of government. In written constitutions, for instance, they are usually accorded pride of place, being described before executives and judiciaries. Assemblies are respected because they are composed of lay politicians who claim to represent the people, rather than trained or expert government officials. Moreover, they act as national debating chambers, public forums in which government policies and the major issues of the day can be openly discussed and analysed. In most cases, they are also invested with formal law-making power, giving them some capacity to shape, or at least influence, public policy. Not all assemblies are alike, however. Their role and significance is crucially affected by wider constitutional and institutional factors – especially whether they operate within a parliamentary, presidential or semi-presidential system – as well as by their internal structures, including whether they comprise two legislative chambers or one. Nevertheless, it is widely alleged that, since the twentieth century, there has been a progressive weakening of parliamentary power reflected in a decline of assemblies relative, in particular, to executives. Although some may still play an important role in the policy process, many assemblies have been reduced to mere 'talking shops' that do little more than rubber-stamp decisions that have effectively, been made elsewhere. Others, however, claim that, for various reasons, recent decades have witnessed a revival of assembly power.

KEY ISSUES
- What is an assembly?
- How do parliamentary and presidential ones affect the role of the assembly?
- What are the main functions of assemblies?
- How are assemblies organized, and how do their internal structures differ?
- What are the principal determinants of parliamentary power?
- Why have assemblies declined? Does this decline matter?

CONCEPT

Parliamentary government

A parliamentary system of government is one in which the government governs in and through the assembly or parliament, thereby 'fusing' the legislative and executive branches. The chief features of a parliamentary system are as follows: (1) governments are formed as a result of assembly elections; (2) the personnel of government are drawn from the assembly; (3) the government rests on the assembly's confidence and can be removed if it loses that confidence; (4) the government can, in most cases, 'dissolve' the assembly; and (5) parliamentary executives are generally collective.

ROLE OF ASSEMBLIES

In practice, a bewildering variety of terms are used to describe political bodies with very similar functions: congress (USA), national assembly (France), house of representatives (Japan), parliament (Singapore), congress of deputies (Spain) and so on. Students of comparative politics usually classify such bodies as assemblies, legislatures or parliaments. An assembly, in its simplest sense, is a collection or gathering of people; as in, for example, a school assembly. As a political term, 'assembly' has come to be associated with representation and popular government, an assembly, certainly in the French tradition, being viewed as a surrogate for the people. For this reason, the term is sometimes reserved for the lower, popularly-elected chamber in a bicameral system (as, for instance, in Pakistan and France), or for the single chamber in a unicameral system (as in Egypt and Turkey). In this book, however, the term 'assembly' is used to refer to both houses or chambers, and is used interchangeably with the terms '**legislature**' and 'parliament'.

To see these bodies as legislatures is to classify them according to their primary function as law-making bodies. This view is seriously misleading, however. Institutions that are formally classified as legislatures rarely monopolize law-making power. For instance, executives (see p. 285) possess some ability to make law, through devices such as decrees or orders, and usually also have the capacity to influence, if not shape, the formal legislative process. Furthermore, the enactment of law is only one of the functions of legislatures, and not necessarily their most important.

The term 'parliament' (from the French *parler*, meaning 'to speak') is sometimes preferred because it avoids the limitations of the term 'assembly' and the confusion of the term 'legislature'. It nevertheless suggests that these bodies have a very particular character. It implies that their defining feature is that they are consultative or deliberative bodies. Regardless of their legislative powers and representative features, parliaments are, above all, debating chambers; that is, forums in which policies and political issues can be openly discussed and scrutinized.

Parliamentary, presidential and semi-presidential systems

One of the key features of any political system is the relationship between the assembly and the government and, therefore, the relationship between legislative and executive authority. In exceptional cases, a form of 'assembly government' may develop in which executive and legislative power is vested in the assembly, there being no separate executive body. Such a system, for example, emerged briefly under Robespierre and the Jacobins during the French Revolution, influenced by the radical democracy of Rousseau (see p. 97). In other cases, notably in orthodox communist regimes, both the legislative and the executive bodies have been subordinate to the unchallengeable authority of a 'ruling' party. However, assembly–executive relations more commonly conform to one of two institutional arrangements: parliamentary and presidential government (see p. 289).

Most liberal democracies have adopted some form of parliamentary government (see Figure 14.1). These are often Westminster-style systems, in that they are based on the model of the UK Parliament. Often portrayed as the 'mother of parliaments', the origins of the Westminster Parliament can be traced back to the

● **Legislature**: The branch of government whose chief function is to make laws, although it is seldom the only body with legislative power.

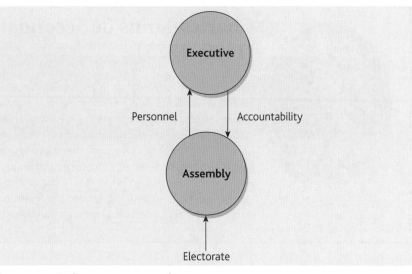

Figure 14.1 Parliamentary system of government

thirteenth century, when knights and burgesses were incorporated into the king's court. During the fourteenth century, separate chambers (the House of Commons and the House of Lords) were created to represent the knights and burgesses on the one hand, and the barons and churchmen on the other. Parliament's supremacy over the king was, nevertheless, not established until the Glorious Revolution of 1688, and its capacity to call government to account not recognized until the gradual emergence of a democratic franchise during the nineteenth century.

Similar parliamentary systems came into existence in states such as Germany, Sweden, India, Japan, New Zealand and Australia. The central feature of these systems is a fusion of legislative and executive power: government is parliamentary, in that it is drawn from and accountable to the assembly or parliament. The strength of this system is that it supposedly delivers effective but **responsible government**. Government is effective in that it rests on the confidence of the assembly and so can, in most cases, ensure that its legislative programme is passed. In short, parliamentary executives can get things done. However, responsible government is maintained because the executive can govern only as long as it retains the confidence of the assembly. In theory, the assembly has the upper hand because it has the ultimate power: the ability to remove the government.

Unfortunately, however, parliamentary systems often fail to live up to these high expectations. Certainly, there are examples such as Sweden in which, supported by strong norms of consultation and partnership, the assembly (the *Riksdag*) exerts a strong policy influence without threatening to immobilize the workings of government. However, parliamentary government is often associated with the problem of executive domination. This is the case in the UK, where a combination of strict party discipline and a disproportional electoral system (the simple plurality system) normally allows government to control Parliament through a cohesive and reliable majority in the House of Commons. This encouraged Lord Hailsham (1976) to dub UK government an '**elective dictatorship**'. Ironically, therefore, parliamentary systems may allow parliaments

● **Responsible government**: A government that is answerable or accountable to an elected assembly and, through it, to the people.

● **Elective dictatorship**: An imbalance between the executive and the assembly that means that, once elected, the government is only constrained by the need to win subsequent elections.

Charles-Louis de Secondat Montesquieu (1689–1775)

French political philosopher. Montesquieu came from an aristocratic family and became an advocate before establishing his literary reputation with the publication of *Persian Letters* (1721). After settling in Paris in 1726, he travelled throughout Europe studying political and social institutions. Montesquieu's masterpiece, *The Spirit of the Laws* ([1748] 1949), is a long and rambling comparative examination of political and legal issues. He championed a form of parliamentary liberalism that was based on the writings of Locke (see p. 31) and, to some extent, a misreading of English political experience. Montesquieu emphasized the need to resist tyranny by fragmenting government power, particularly through the device of the separation of powers.

to become little more than 'talking shops', and may reduce their members to mere '**lobby fodder**'.

Parliamentary systems have also been linked with weak government and political instability. This usually occurs when the party system is fractured, and it is often associated with highly proportional electoral systems. In the French Fourth Republic during 1945–58, for instance, 25 governments came and went in little over 12 years. During this period, no French government could command a stable majority in the National Assembly, in which both the Communists on the left and the Gaullists on the right were implacably opposed to the regime itself. Similar problems afflicted post-World War II Italian politics. A polarized multiparty system led to the establishment of no fewer than 59 governments between 1945 and 2001. Such apparent **immobilism** may, however, be misleading. In Italy, for example, changes in government typically involve a reshuffling of ministerial personnel, not a political upheaval, and only occasionally result in general elections.

The principal alternative to parliamentary government is a presidential government (see Figure 13.1). Presidential systems are based on the strict application of the doctrine of the separation of powers (see p. 313), associated with Montesquieu. This ensures that the assemblies and executives are formally independent from one another and separately elected (see Figure 14.2). The classic example of this is found in the USA, where the so-called 'founding fathers' were particularly anxious to prevent the emergence of an over-strong executive, fearing that the presidency might assume the mantle of the British monarchy. The resulting system therefore incorporated a network of **checks and balances**. Congress, the US presidency and the Supreme Court are separate institutions, in the sense that no overlap of personnel is permitted but, nevertheless, possess the ability to constrain one another's power. Thus, while Congress has the ability to make law, the president can veto it; but Congress can, in turn, override this veto with a two-thirds majority in both houses. In the same way, although the president has the power to make senior executive and judicial appointments, these are subject to confirmation by the upper house, the Senate.

● **Lobby fodder**: A pejorative term denoting assembly members who vote consistently and unquestioningly as their parties dictate.

● **Immobilism**: Political paralysis stemming from the absence of a strong executive, caused by multiple divisions in the assembly and (probably) society.

● **Checks and balances**: Internal tensions within the governmental system that result from institutional fragmentation.

Separation of powers

The separation of powers, is the principle that each of the three functions of government (legislation, execution and adjudication) should be entrusted to a separate branch of government (the legislature, the executive and the judiciary) (see Figure 14.2) Its purpose is to fragment government power in such a way as to defend liberty and keep tyranny at bay. In its formal sense, it demands independence, in that there should be no overlap of personnel between the branches. However, it also implies interdependence, in the form of shared powers to create a network of checks and balances.

Outside the USA, US-style presidential systems have been confined largely to Latin America. However, a 'hybrid', or semi-presidential, system was established in France during the Fifth Republic. In this system, there is a 'dual executive' in which a separately elected president works in conjunction with a prime minister and cabinet drawn from, and responsible to, the National Assembly. How such a system works in practice depends on a delicate balance between, on the one hand, the personal authority and popularity of the president and, on the other, the political complexion of the National Assembly. A similar semi-presidential system operates in Finland, in which the president is concerned largely with foreign affairs and leaves the burden of domestic responsibilities in the hands of the cabinet. Semi-presidential systems have become more common in recent decades, particularly due to their adoption by many post-communist states. However, they range from forms of 'balanced' semi-presidentialism, in which the parliament exercises effective constraint over the presidency, to forms of 'asymmetrical' semi-presidentialism, in which the parliament lacks independence and is routinely controlled by the presidency. In Russia, this imbalance is so severe that the system can be described as an example of '**superpresidentialism**'.

The principal virtue of presidential systems is that, by separating legislative power from executive power, they create internal tensions that help to protect individual rights and liberties. As Hobbes (see p. 61) put it, 'liberty is power cut into pieces'. In the USA, for instance, the danger of executive domination is protected against by the range of powers vested in the Congress. For instance, Congress has the right to declare war and raise taxes, the Senate must ratify treaties and confirm presidential appointments, and the two houses can combine to charge and impeach the president. Such fragmentation, however, may also have drawbacks.

In particular, presidential systems may be ineffective and cumbersome because they offer an 'invitation to struggle' to the executive and legislative branches of government. Critics of the US system, for example, argue that, since it allows the president to propose and Congress to dispose, it is nothing more than a recipe for institutional deadlock, or 'government gridlock'. This may be more likely when the White House (the presidency) and Capitol Hill (Congress)

● **Superpresidentialism**: A president-heavy constitutional order in which the presidency is invested with great power and the assembly or parliament operates as a mere 'rubber stamp'.

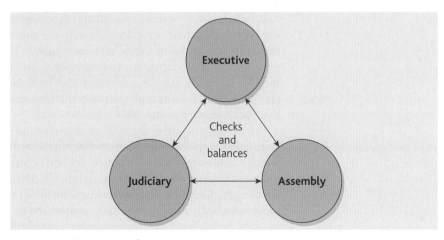

Figure 14.2   Separation of powers

are controlled by rival parties, but can also occur, as the Carter administration of 1977–81 demonstrated, when both branches are controlled by the same party. A similar problem occurs in semi-presidential systems in the form of cohabitation when the president is forced to work with a hostile prime minister and assembly.

Functions of assemblies

To classify assemblies simply as legislatures, debating chambers or representative bodies obscures their true significance. Although the role of the assembly varies from state to state and from system to system, in every case it fulfils a complex of functions. Above all, assemblies provide a link between government and the people, a channel of communication that can both support government and help to uphold the regime, and force government to respond to public demands and anxieties. The principal functions of assemblies are:

- legislation
- representation
- scrutiny
- political recruitment
- legitimacy.

Legislation

Legislation is often seen as the key function of assemblies, as is clearly implied by their common classification as legislatures. Assemblies or parliaments are typically vested with legislative power in the hope that the laws thus made will be seen to be authoritative and binding. This applies for two reasons. First, an assembly is a forum in which proposed laws can be openly discussed and debated. Second, assemblies are constituted so as to suggest that the people (or, in pre-democratic days, the major interests in society) make the laws themselves. However, the idea that assemblies possess the formal legislative authority is often deeply misleading. As pointed out, assemblies rarely monopolize legislative authority. Constitutional law is usually placed beyond the competence of the assembly. In Ireland, for example, the constitution is amended by referendums and, in Belgium, by special constitutional conventions. Executive officers, such as the French president, are often able to make law by decree, or, like the US president, can veto laws when they have been passed. The European Parliament is not a legislature at all, European law being enacted largely by the Council. Even in the UK, where Parliament is invested with legal sovereignty (see p. 58), ministers routinely make law through statutory instruments that are subject to little effective parliamentary scrutiny.

More significantly, assemblies exercise little *positive* legislative power. Legislative proposals and programmes emanate, in the main, from the executive, which has the organizational coherence and access to specialist advice and information necessary for policy formulation. UK MPs, for instance, still have a residual capacity to initiate legislation in the form of private member's bills, but these are debated only if the government is prepared to make time for them alongside its own legislative programme. Approximately 80 per cent of the legislation considered by the US Congress, the most independent and strongest assembly in

Responsibility

Responsibility can be understood in two contrasting ways. First, it means to act in a sensible, reasonable or morally correct fashion. A government may thus claim to be 'responsible' when it resists electoral pressures and risks unpopularity by pursuing policies designed to meet long-term public interests. Second, responsibility means accountability or answerability. This implies the existence of a higher authority to which an individual or body is subject, and by which it can be controlled. Government is 'responsible' in this sense, if its actions are open to scrutiny and criticism, particularly by the assembly.

● **Pork barrel politics:** Government projects whose only, or primary, purpose is to bring money or jobs to a representative's district or constituency.

the developed world, now stems from presidential initiatives. The *negative* legislative power of assemblies – that is, their ability to reject or amend proposed laws – is also limited. In cases such as the Dutch States-General, up to half of all legislative measures are significantly redrafted as a result of parliamentary consultations. However, in the UK, government defeats in the House of Commons are usually rare events. All too often, legislation is passed *through* assemblies, rather than *by* assemblies.

Representation

Assemblies play an important representative role in providing a link between government and the people. In the eighteenth century, this was expressed by the slogan adopted by the 13 American colonies that rebelled against British rule: 'no taxation without representation'. The extension of the franchise and the eventual achievement of universal adult suffrage turned assemblies into popular forums, bodies that 'stood for' the people themselves. For this reason, the power of an assembly within the political system is usually seen as an important index of democratic government. However, it is less clear how this representative function is carried out in practice.

Representation (see p. 197) is a complex principle that has a number of contrasting implications. For example, Westminster-style parliamentary systems based on UK traditions have often portrayed representatives as trustees whose prime responsibility is to exercise their own judgement and wisdom on behalf of their constituents. However, this Burkean notion of representatives as independent actors conflicts sharply with the strict party discipline now found in most assemblies, particularly those in parliamentary systems. The alternative theory of representation, the doctrine of the mandate (see p. 200), views parties, not assemblies, as the central mechanism through which representation takes place.

In other states, the idea of constituency representation takes pride of place. This applies particularly to the US Congress, as a result of its relatively weak party system and the unusually short two-year terms of Representatives. The primary concern of both Representatives and Senators is to 'bring home the bacon'. Congress is therefore commonly dominated by what is called "**pork barrel' politics**', pushed through by a form of cooperation amongst individual legislators known as 'log rolling'. However, it is the very effectiveness of Congress in its representative function that makes it an unsuitable policy-maker; it is better able to block the president's programme than to propose a coherent alternative of its own.

In the USSR and other communist states, in the absence of electoral choice and party competition, representation was often based on the degree to which assemblies resembled the larger society. The Supreme Soviet thus came far closer to being a microcosm of Soviet society (in terms of gender, nationality, occupation and so on) than assemblies in the developed West have ever done. Such a concern with descriptive representation continues to apply to China's National People's Congress, the largest parliament in the world, where attempts are made to ensure consistent levels of female and ethnic-minority representation. Finally, assemblies are often mechanisms of interest representation. This is particularly the case when they are seen to exert a significant degree of policy influence, and party systems are sufficiently relaxed to offer interest groups a point of access. Once again, the USA provides the prime example, with, for the first time in US history, more than $1 billion being raised in 2008 by candidates for the presidency, mainly from business sources.

Scrutiny and oversight

While the legislative and representative roles of assemblies have declined in significance, greater emphasis has been placed on the ability of assemblies to constrain or check executive power. Assemblies have increasingly become scrutinizing bodies, the principal role of which is to deliver responsibility (see p. 315) or accountability. Most assemblies have developed institutional mechanisms designed to facilitate this role. Parliamentary systems, for example, usually subject ministers to regular oral or written questioning, the classic example being Question Time in the UK House of Commons. This allows the prime minister to be cross-examined once a week, and subjects other senior ministers to similar scrutiny about once a month. Germany and Finland use the practice of 'interpellation', a process of oral questioning followed by a vote to establish the confidence of the assembly in the answers given. Since questioning and debate on the floor of a chamber inevitably tend to be generalized, much of the scrutinizing work of assemblies is carried out by committees (see p. 322) set up for this purpose. The powerful **standing committees** of the US Congress have served as a model for many other assemblies in this respect.

However, assemblies are not always effective in calling executives to account. In the National People's Congress in China, for example, control by a monopolistic party has turned the assembly into a mere propaganda weapon, with government policy nearly always being approved by unanimous votes. Party discipline also constrains parliamentary scrutiny elsewhere. For instance, it can be argued that, in Westminster-style systems, the principal function of the assembly is to uphold and support government, since the majority of the members of the assembly belong to the governing party. The job of scrutiny thus passes to the opposition parties, which, as long as the government retains majority control, have no power to remove it.

A further key factor is the ability of the assembly to extract information from the executive. Knowledge is power; without full and accurate information, meaningful scrutiny is impossible. In the USA, France, the Netherlands, Canada and Australia, for instance, formal freedom of information acts have been passed to establish a general right of public access to government information and records. Finally, oversight of the executive requires that parliamentary representatives be well resourced and have access to research services and expert advice. Here, the contrast is dramatic, ranging from the lavish funding and large personal staffs provided for the members of the US Congress to the less well-paid, inadequately resourced and sometimes overworked UK MPs.

Recruitment and training

Assemblies often act as major channels of recruitment, providing a pool of talent from which leading decision-makers emerge. This applies less in authoritarian

● **Standing committee**: A permanent committee within a legislative chamber, which considers bills and oversees executive activities.

states, where rubber-stamp assemblies seldom attract serious politicians, and less in presidential systems, in which a separation of powers prevents executive office from being filled by current members of the assembly. However, although the trend of late has been for US presidents to have been former state governors, presidents such as Kennedy, Nixon and Obama first cut their teeth as members of Congress. In parliamentary systems, however, service in the assembly is a required career path for ministers and prime ministers, who then continue to hold their assembly seats alongside their executive offices. In many developed and developing states, assemblies recruit and train the next generation of political leaders, thus giving them experience of political debate and policy analysis.

On the other hand, assemblies can also be inadequate in this respect. Parliamentarians certainly gain experience of politics as **rhetoric**, or what is derogatorily known as 'speechifying', but they have few opportunities to acquire the bureaucratic and managerial skills required to run government departments and oversee the process of policy formulation. Moreover, it is sometimes argued that assemblies 'corrupt' politicians by socializing them into norms and values that distance them from the needs of their constituents and the instincts of grass-roots party workers. Parliamentary socialists, for example, may thus come to subscribe more passionately to the ideals of parliamentarianism than they do to the principles of socialism (Miliband, 1972).

Legitimacy

The final function of assemblies is to promote the legitimacy (see p. 81) of a regime by encouraging the public to see the system of rule as 'rightful'. This is why most authoritarian and, even, totalitarian states tolerate assemblies; though, of course, those that have no legislative independence or policy-making power. The ability of assemblies to mobilize consent depends largely on their ability to function as popular conventions, endorsing laws and policies in the name of the public, as well as in their interest. In addition to having propaganda value, assemblies may also perform more creditable educational functions. Parliamentary debates can help to inform and instruct citizens about the affairs of government and the major issues of the day. Thus, reactions in the UK to the Argentine invasion of the Falklands in 1982 were clearly influenced by the rare Saturday sitting of the House of Commons, and what the US public knew of the Iran–Contra affair in 1988 was based largely on the hearings of the Senate Committee on Intelligence.

To a growing extent, however, the propaganda/educational role of assemblies has been taken over by the mass media (see p. 179). The rise of the electronic media in the form of radio and, particularly, television, and more recently of digitally-based new media, has given government direct access to literally millions of voters, instead of having, as before, to rely on the reporting of parliamentary debates and discussions. As a result, the status that assemblies enjoy increasingly depends less on their constitutional position and more on the media attention they receive. This helps to explain why assemblies have been increasingly anxious for their proceedings to receive television coverage. The public impact of US congressional committees has long been enhanced by the televising of their hearings. In the case of the UK, television cameras were not allowed into the House of Commons until 1989, shortly after they were first introduced in the Soviet parliament.

● **Rhetoric**: The art of using language to persuade or influence; rhetoric can imply high-sounding but essentially vacuous speech.

STRUCTURE OF ASSEMBLIES

Assemblies differ in a number of respects. For example, their members may be elected or appointed, or they may contain both elected and appointed members. When members are elected, this may be on the basis of population (in the form of equal-sized constituencies), or through regions or states. The franchise may be restricted or universal, and various electoral systems may be used (see pp. 206–13). The sizes of assembly also vary considerably. The tiny republic of Nauru, in the West Central Pacific, has an assembly of 18 members, each of whom represents approximately 518 people. At the other extreme, there is the almost 3,000-member National People's Congress in China, in which one member represents over 433,000 people. However, the principal structural differences between assemblies are whether they comprise one chamber or two, and the nature and role of their committee systems.

Unicameralism or bicameralism?

Although Yugoslavia once experimented with a five-chamber assembly and, from 1984 to 1994, South Africa had a three-chamber assembly, the vast majority of assemblies have either one or two chambers. Single-chamber, or unicameral, assemblies have been common in much of Africa, in communist states such as China, and in postcommunist states that have maintained an earlier tradition of **unicameralism**. Indeed, there was a clear trend towards unicameralism in the post-World War II period. For instance, in 1948 Israel established a single-chamber parliament (the Knesset), and second chambers were abolished in New Zealand (1950), Denmark (1953), Sweden (1970) and Iceland (1990), although Morocco (1996) moved in the opposite direction. Such developments support the view that unicameral assemblies are more streamlined and effective than bicameral ones, especially in terms of responding to the needs of small and relatively cohesive societies. In the famous remark of the Abbé Sieyès in 1789: 'if the second Chamber agrees with the first it is unnecessary; if it disagrees it is pernicious'. Nevertheless, about half the world's states retain two-chamber, or bicameral, assemblies (see p. 320).

In terms of strengthening checks and balances within assemblies and between executives and assemblies, **bicameralism** has usually been seen as a central principle of liberal constitutionalism (see p. 337). This was the case in the debates amongst the 'founding fathers' who drew up the US constitution in 1787. Whereas earlier second chambers, such as the UK House of Lords, had developed as vehicles through which powerful economic and social interests could be represented in government, delegates such as James Madison saw the US Senate as a means of fragmenting legislative power and as a safeguard against executive domination.

The representative advantages of bicameralism are particularly important in federal states, where the sharing of sovereignty creates a constant danger of irreconcilable conflict between the centre and the periphery. All of the world's 16 fully federal states thus have bicameral legislatures, and in 14 of them the second chamber represents the provinces or component states. These may enjoy equal representation, as in Australia, Switzerland and the USA, or they may be represented according to the size of their populations, as in Austria and Germany.

● **Unicameralism**: The principle or practice of having an assembly composed of a single legislative chamber.

● **Bicameralism**: The principle or practice of fragmenting legislative power through the establishment of two (in theory, co-equal) chambers in the assembly.

James Madison (1751–1836)

US statesman and political philosopher. A Virginian delegate to the Constitutional Convention of 1787, Madison was a strong proponent of US nationalism and a keen advocate of ratification. He later served as Jefferson's Secretary of State (1801–09) and was the fourth president of the USA (1809–17). Usually regarded as a leading supporter of pluralism and divided government, Madison urged the adoption of federalism, bicameralism and the separation of powers. However, when in government, he was prepared to strengthen the power of national government. His best-known political writings are his contributions, with Alexander Hamilton and John Jay, to *The Federalist Papers* (Hamilton *et al.*, [1787–89] 1961).

Second chambers in some non-federal states are also used to resolve regional differences. In France, most members of the second chamber, and in the Netherlands all members, are elected indirectly via local government.

Most second chambers are constitutionally and politically subordinate to first chambers, which are usually seen as the locus of popular authority. This is particularly the case in parliamentary systems, in which government is generally responsible to and drawn, largely or wholly, from the lower house. In Norway, the Netherlands and Fiji, all **bills** must be introduced in the first chamber, as is the case with money bills in India, Canada and the UK. Second chambers may also be denied veto powers. The Japanese first chamber, the House of Representatives, is thus able, by a two-thirds majority, to override the House of Counsellors. The UK House of Lords only has the power to delay non-financial legislation for a single year.

Not uncommonly, such weaker versions of bicameralism reflect the restricted representative basis of the upper house. Indirect elections are used in Germany, Austria and India, for example, and a combination of election and appointment is used in Belgium, Malaysia and Ireland. The Canadian Senate and the UK House of Lords are wholly nominated; indeed, until their right of attendance was removed in 1999, the majority of the members of the House of Lords were hereditary peers. A stronger version of bicameralism is found in assemblies with two chambers that have broadly equal powers. The Italian Chamber of Deputies and the Italian Senate, for example, are both elected by universal adult suffrage, and are legislatively co-equal. An electoral college representing both chambers elects the president, and the prime minister and council of ministers are collectively responsible to the whole assembly. The US Congress is perhaps the only example of an assembly that has a dominant upper chamber. Although all tax legislation must be introduced in the House of Representatives, the Senate alone exercises ratification and confirmation powers.

One of the greatest drawbacks of legislative fragmentation is the possibility of conflict between the two chambers. When the houses have broadly equal powers, a device is needed to resolve differences and prevent institutional immobilism. The most common mechanism is that used in the US Congress, in which a special joint congressional committee, composed of senior figures from both chambers,

● **Bill**: Proposed legislation in the form of a draft statute; if passed, a bill becomes an act.

Debating . . .
Are two legislative chambers better than one?

Although there is wide agreement that assemblies play a vital role in upholding democracy and accountable government, there is considerable disagreement about whether these tasks are better discharged by bicameral assemblies or unicameral ones. Do second chambers protect political freedom and strengthen links between government and the people? Or do they merely get in the way, increasing the chances of legislative stalemate and political stagnation?

YES	NO

Stronger checks and balances. The key advantage of having a second legislative chamber, or upper house, is that it serves as a check on both the first chamber and the government of the day. Bicameralism thus acknowledges that the best way of preventing government tyranny is through a system of fragmented government, making power a check on power. A fragmented assembly disperses legislative power and prevents the domination of a single chamber or, in practice, of the majority party or parties within that chamber. More importantly, fragmented assemblies enhance executive oversight because two chambers, not one, are charged with responsibility for exposing the flaws and failings of government.

Wider representation. So long as they are elected, second chambers establish stronger channels of communication between government and the people. The role of second chambers in providing representation for constituent provinces or states in federal systems, or in countries that are geographically expansive and possess large populations, is generally acknowledged. Bicameral assemblies, nevertheless, bring wider representative benefits. By using different electoral systems, the two chambers can articulate a different range of views and interests; by adopting different electoral terms, elections are held more frequently and government becomes more responsive. Indeed, such considerations may be becoming increasingly pressing as society itself becomes more diverse.

Better legislation. Second chambers ensure that legislation is more thoroughly scrutinized, while also relieving the legislative burden on the first chamber and rectifying its mistakes and oversights. Although this makes the legislative process longer and more complex, it greatly improves the quality of the resulting legislation. This applies even in cases of weak or asymmetrical bicameralism, where second chambers often operate as 'revising chambers', using their expertise and experience to deal with legislative details that first chambers, more concerned about broad principles, tend to neglect.

Recipe for institutional conflict. Bicameral assemblies often result in government gridlock. Fragmenting legislative power can simply lead to delays and disagreement, especially as the two chambers are, of necessity, composed in different ways and, therefore, have different political complexions. In contrast, unicameral assemblies are more streamlined and efficient. Moreover, when bicameral assemblies are gripped by inter-chamber conflict, there is no guarantee that this will produce better-considered outcomes; instead, conflicts are typically resolved by joint committees, significantly narrowing access to policymaking. At a larger level, a strong second chamber may simply make the assembly over-powerful, leading to government immobilism and political stagnation.

Reduced accountability. The great advantage of a unicameral assembly is that legislators cannot blame the other chamber if legislation fails to pass, or if it proves to be unpopular. When some or all members of the second chamber are non-elected or indirectly elected, by challenging the first chamber, democratic accountability is weakened. When second chambers are fully elected this merely creates confusion about the location of democratic authority. Ultimately, public accountability requires that, over the major issues of the day in particular, a single view is expressed that claims to represent the national interest. This can only be done if the assembly is a single, coherent body, comprising a single chamber.

Conservative bias. Second chambers often tip the balance within political systems in favour of conservatism and against radical change. For instance, as second chambers are often seen, formally or informally, as a custodian of the constitution, they are typically circumspect about proposals for constitutional reform. Second chambers are also often composed of members of the political and social establishment. This occurs when, through appointment or indirect election, their members are drawn from the ranks of senior figures in politics, business, the academic world and public life generally.

is authorized to produce a compromise agreement. In Germany, although the lower chamber (the *Bundestag*) is, in most cases, legislatively dominant, the upper chamber (the *Bundesrat*) enjoys considerable veto powers in relation to constitutional questions and matters related to the *Länder*. When disputes occur, they are referred to a joint *Bundestag–Bundesrat* conciliation committee, the members of which are drawn from the two chambers in equal proportions.

Committee systems

Almost all assemblies have a committee system of some sort. Indeed, the trend towards the use of committees, in assemblies and elsewhere, is often seen as one of the distinctive features of modern politics. Committee systems have increasingly been portrayed as the power houses of assemblies, the very hub of the legislative process; whereas parliamentary chambers are for talking, committees are for working. As Woodrow Wilson ([1885] 1961) put it: 'Congressional government is committee government. Congress in session is Congress on public exhibition. Congress in its committee-rooms is Congress at work'. It is therefore not surprising that assemblies are often classified according to their committees. In crude terms, strong assemblies have strong committees, and weak assemblies have weak committees.

Assembly committees usually have one of three functions. First, they may carry out detailed consideration of legislative measures and financial proposals. They thus not only help to relieve the legislative burden on chambers, but also engage in more thorough and exacting examination than is possible on the floor of a house. This task is usually carried out by standing committees, which may be broad and flexible, as in the UK and France, or permanent and highly specialized, as in Germany and the USA. Second, committees may be set up to scrutinize government administration and oversee the exercise of executive power. Such committees must be permanent and specialized, because, to be effective, they have to rival the executive in terms of detailed knowledge and expertise. In the US Congress, for example, legislative and scrutinising responsibilities are vested in standing committees, whereas, in the UK Parliament and the French National Assembly, separate departmental select or supervisory committees are set up. Third, *ad hoc* committees may investigate matters of public concern. Some of the most important examples of investigatory committees have been found in the USA, notably the Irvin Committee on the Watergate scandal, and the House Un-American Activities Committee, which became a vehicle for **McCarthyism** in the 1950s.

If powerful committees mean a powerful assembly, what makes committees powerful? It is generally agreed that the US Congress has the most powerful committees found anywhere in the world, and these provide a model that many other assemblies have tried to adopt. Their power certainly stems from their specialist responsibilities, permanent membership and lavish support in terms of funding and access to advice. This allows them to match the expertise of the bureaucracy (see p. 361). Moreover, their role in the legislative process is crucial. Whereas in the UK, France and Japan bills reach committees having been debated and approved in principle by the floor of the house, in Congress, committee scrutiny comes first. This means that many bills are completely redrafted, and others never see the light of day.

● **McCarthyism**: The use of witch hunts and unscrupulous investigations, as practised in the 1950s against 'communists' by US Senator Joseph McCarthy.

Focus on . . .
Committees: advantages and disadvantages

A committee is a small work group composed of members drawn from a larger body and charged with specific responsibilities. Whereas *ad hoc* committees are set up for a particular purpose and disbanded when that task is complete, permanent or standing committees have enduring responsibilities and an institutionalized role. Committee structures have become increasingly prominent in legislative and executive branches of government, as deliberative and consultative forums and also as decision-making bodies.

Amongst the advantages of committees are the following:

- They allow a range of views, opinions and interests to be represented.
- They provide the opportunity for fuller, longer and more detailed debate.
- They encourage decisions to be made more efficiently and speedily by restricting the range of opposing opinions.
- They make possible a division of labour that encourages the accumulation of expertise and specialist knowledge.

However, committees have been criticized for the following reasons:

- They can easily be manipulated by those who set up and staff them.
- They encourage centralization by allowing a chairperson to dominate proceedings behind a mask of consultation.
- They narrow the range of views and interests that are taken into account in decision-making.
- They divorce their members from the larger body, creating a form of sham representation.

Most importantly, however, Congress has a relatively weak party system, which allows its committees considerable independence from the presidency. Where stricter party discipline operates, as in Australia, New Zealand and the UK, committees are effectively neutered by the fact that the majority of their members owe an overriding loyalty to the government of the day. Germany is an exception in this respect. Although Germany has an effective party system, it also possesses strong legislative committees, largely as a consequence of the need for coalition governments (see p. 239) to conciliate the assembly in order to maintain the support of two or more parties.

In an attempt to strengthen Parliament in the UK against the executive, a system of departmental select committees was established in 1979. These were consciously modelled on the US example, and the system sought to promote open government (see p. 362) by allowing for the examination of government papers and the cross-examination of ministers and senior civil servants. It was hoped that these committees would become effective watchdogs that would be capable of influencing government policy. However, the experiment has proved disappointing, for a number of reasons. First, the hoped-for less partisan character of committees has failed to materialize, as the government has ensured that party disciplines intrude into the work of committees. Second, the select committees are inadequately resourced and have limited powers. Although they can send for 'persons, papers and records', they cannot force particular civil servants or ministers to attend; neither can they ensure that their questions are fully answered. Third, no alternative career structure has developed around the committees; MPs still look to advance their careers through jobs in government, and so tend to be more sensitive to party pressures than parliamentary ones.

PERFORMANCE OF ASSEMBLIES

Do assemblies make policy?

The difficulty with assessing the performance of assemblies is that they carry out such a wide range of functions. Should they be judged on the quality of the legislation they pass, their effectiveness in mobilizing consent, the degree to which they represent public opinion, or what? The greatest political concern, however, relates to the policy impact of assemblies; that is, their capacity to shape, or at least influence, what governments actually do. Do assemblies have power, in the sense that they affect the content of public policy, or are they merely talking shops that draw attention away from where the real business of government happens? The key issue here is the nature of assembly–executive relations and the distribution of power between the two major branches of government. On this basis, the assemblies of the world can be classified into three broad categories:

- policy-making assemblies, which enjoy significant autonomy and have an active impact on policy
- policy-influencing assemblies, which can transform policy but only by reacting to executive initiatives
- executive-dominated assemblies, which exert marginal influence or merely rubber-stamp executive decisions.

Policy-making assemblies are rare. To exert a positive influence on the policy process, an assembly has to fulfil three criteria. First, it must command significant constitutional authority and respect. Second, it must enjoy meaningful political independence from the executive, and, third, it must possess sufficient organizational coherence to undertake concerted action. As far as the UK Parliament is concerned, these conditions were perhaps fulfilled only during its so-called 'golden age', the period between the Great Reform Act of 1832 and the Second Reform Act of 1867. In this period, Parliament, its authority enhanced by the extension of the franchise but not yet hampered by the emergence of effective party discipline, changed governments, forced the removal of individual ministers, rejected government legislation, and initiated significant measures.

In the modern period, the best (and, some would argue, the only) example of a policy-making assembly is the US Congress. Congress is perhaps unique, in that it enjoys an unusual combination of advantages. The separation of powers invests Congress with constitutional independence and an impressive range of autonomous powers. Relatively weak party cohesion deprives the president of the usual means of exerting legislative control, and Congress may, anyway, be controlled by the opposition party. A powerful committee system guarantees the organizational effectiveness of Congress. Finally, Congress has had the staffing

Focus on . . .

Adversary politics: for or against?

Adversary politics is a style of politics characterized by an antagonistic relationship between major parties that turns political life into an ongoing electoral battle. Parliamentary debate thus becomes a 'continuous polemic' before what is seen as the 'bar of public opinion'.

Adversarialism has been defended on the following grounds:

- It offers voters clear alternatives, thus promoting electoral choice and democratic accountability.

- It checks government power by ensuring that there is opposition and scrutiny.

Its dangers, nevertheless, include the following:

- It discourages sober and rational debate, and precludes compromise.
- It fosters polarization, which, as governments change, gives rise to political instability.

and informational resources to operate without depending on the executive branch for assistance.

Nevertheless, despite these advantages, Congress has lost some of its influence during the modern period. Since the time of the New Deal, the US public – and, for that matter, Congress itself – has increasingly looked to the White House (the presidency) for political leadership (see p. 300). The main burden of Congress's work is therefore to examine the president's legislative programme. This has weakened Congress's role as a policy initiator, and has led to a situation in which 'the president proposes and Congress disposes'. Indeed, growing anxiety about the subordination of Congress was expressed in the 1960s in fears about the emergence of a so-called 'imperial presidency'. In the aftermath of the Watergate scandal, however, a resurgent Congress adopted a more assertive attitude towards presidential power, and initiated a series of reforms in the committee and seniority systems. The most striking example of Congress seizing control of public policy occurred after the 1994 elections, when the Republican Congress, led by the then-Speaker of the House Newt Gingrich, pushed through a radical programme of tax and spending cuts under the slogan 'Contract with America'. Nevertheless, when the Republicans controlled the White House and both houses of Congress during 2002–6, few checks were imposed on presidential power, particularly over foreign issues.

In parliamentary systems, assemblies have generally played a *policy-influencing* role, rather than one of policy-making. Where exceptions have occurred, as in the Italian assembly and the National Assembly of the Fourth French Republic, this has usually been a consequence of weak coalition government and a fragmented party system. More commonly, assembly–executive relations are structured by party divisions. This is most clearly the case when majoritarian or weakly proportional electoral systems invest a single party with majority control of the assembly, as has traditionally occurred in the UK, New Zealand and Australia. In such cases, the central dynamic of the parliamentary system is an antagonistic relationship between the government and the opposition, usually termed 'adversary politics'. Government governs in the sense that it is responsible for formulating, and later implementing, a legislative programme, while the assembly plays an essentially reactive role.

The scope that the assembly has to influence policy in these circumstances depends largely on two factors: the strength in the assembly of the governing party, and the party's ability to maintain internal unity. The Blair government dominated the UK House of Commons because of the landslide parliamentary majorities it won in 1997 and 2001, and because the Labour Party had succeeded in resolving its deepest ideological divisions before it returned to power. Nevertheless, governments in parliamentary systems must remain constantly sensitive to the morale of their backbenchers. Margaret Thatcher, for example, discovered this to her cost in November 1990, when she was abruptly removed as Conservative party leader, and therefore prime minister, despite still commanding a substantial Commons majority. Other assemblies that exert a strong influence on policy are the German *Bundestag* and the Swedish *Riksdag*. However, in both these cases parliamentary influence stems less from adversary politics than from ingrained habits of negotiation and compromise fostered both by the political culture and by long experience of coalition government.

Parliamentary systems that have become accustomed to prolonged domination by a single party often have assemblies that are weak or *executive-dominated*. A deliberate attempt was made in the Fifth French Republic to weaken parliamentary power so as to avoid the conflict and obstructionism that had undermined the Fourth Republic. A system of 'rationalized parliamentarianism' came into existence in the form of semi-presidentialism. This allowed the French president to dominate government largely through party control, but also through his power to dissolve the National Assembly in order to gain a new majority, as de Gaulle did in 1962 and 1968, and Mitterrand did in 1981 and 1988. De Gaulle also reduced the National Assembly's powers of political control, and limited its legislative competence by creating the *Conseil Constitutionnel* to ensure that its laws conform to the constitution. However, the end of Gaullist domination in 1981 created opportunities for a greater degree of parliamentary influence, particularly when the Socialists lost control of the assembly and Mitterrand was forced into cohabitation with a Gaullist government under Jacques Chirac. The same applied after 1997, when President Chirac was confronted by a Socialist-led government under Jospin.

The Japanese Diet (*Kokkai*) is another example of a traditionally subordinate assembly. Until the 1980s, the Diet was required to do little more than ratify the decisions of the executive: this was a consequence of the unbroken domination of the Liberal Democratic Party after 1955. Rival parties were eternal outsiders, and factional divisions within the LDP were generally played out away from the Diet. However, the progressive decline in the sizes of LDP majorities led, by the 1970s, to a less adversarial and more conciliatory attitude towards parliamentary opposition. For instance, the membership of standing committees was broadened to include minority parties as the LDP started to relax its grip on the parliamentary process. A full system of parliamentary scrutiny and oversight finally emerged in Japan following the LDP's defeat in the 1993 election.

Less ambiguous examples of marginal assemblies have been found in communist regimes and developing states. In the former, tight control by 'ruling' communist parties and the practice of non-competitive elections ensured that assemblies did little more than provide formal approval for the government's programme. Significant levels of executive-domination have also sometimes continued into the postcommunist era. The weakness of the Russian parliament has encouraged some to view it as a mere 'rubber stamp' (see p. 327). In the developing states of Africa and Asia, assemblies have played a largely integrative role, rather than one of policy-influencing. Their central function has been to strengthen legitimacy and so assist in the process of nation-building. It is a back-handed compliment to assemblies that the establishment of military rule has usually been accompanied by their suspension or abolition. This occurred in Chile, Pakistan and the Philippines in the 1970s, and in Turkey and Nigeria in the 1980s.

Why are assemblies in decline?

There is nothing new about the 'decline of assemblies' debate. Since the late nine-teenth century, anxiety has been expressed about the strengthening of executives, and particularly bureaucracies, at the expense of assemblies. This anxiety has been heightened by the fact that, since the days of Locke (see p. 31) and Montesquieu, assemblies have been seen as the principal vehicles for delivering responsible and representative government. The notion that good government requires a strong assembly is questionable, however. Assembly power can certainly become 'excessive', especially when it leads to immobilism and policy stalemate. The model of the US Congress, for instance, has as many critics as it has admirers. There is, nevertheless, general agreement that, during the twenti-eth century, the power and status of assemblies changed, and usually for the worse. Whether this amounts to a general decline of assemblies, or, rather, a shift in their purpose or function, is another matter. The principal factors that have brought about these changes are the following:

- the emergence of disciplined political parties
- the growth of 'big' government
- the organizational weaknesses of assemblies
- the rise of interest-group and media power.

Disciplined political parties

The emergence from the late nineteenth century onwards of mass-membership parties weakened assemblies in a number of respects. In the first place, the tran-sition from loose factions (see p. 223) to disciplined party groupings under-mined the ability of individual members to represent constituents as trustees by exercising their own judgement and conscience. Parties, rather than assemblies, thus became the principal agents of representation, operating through the doctrine of the mandate. Party loyalty also weakened assemblies in terms of their function as debating chambers. However articulate, impassioned or persuasive parliamentary oratory may be, it has little or no impact on voting in party-dominated assemblies, which means that debate becomes sterile or ritualized. As Richard Cobden (1804–65) commented about the UK House of Commons, 'In this House I have heard many a speech that moved men to

POLITICS IN ACTION . . .

Russia's parliament: a 'rubber stamp' assembly?

Events: In November 2008, in his first annual address to the Russia's Federal Assembly, President Dimitry Medvedev (who had recently replaced Vladimir Putin in office, the latter becoming prime minister) proposed a change to the Russian constitution, extending the president's electoral term from four years to six years. The reform created the possibility that Putin, who had stood down after eight years in office due to the constitutional ban on presidents serving more than two consecutive terms, could return and, potentially, serve for a further twelve years as president. Some of his opponents warned that such a development created the prospect of a 'Putin dictatorship'. The constitutional amendment was, nevertheless, approved in less than two months. Needing a two-thirds majority in the lower chamber, the State Duma, the amendment was passed by 393 votes to 57. In the upper chamber, the Federation Council, where a three-quarter's majority is needed to pass a constitutional amendment, the measure was passed by 144 votes to just 1. In September 2011, Putin announced his intention to run once again for the presidency, which he successfully did in March 2012, Medvedev replacing him as prime minister.

Significance: Russia's Federal Assembly came into existence in dramatic circumstances. Following the break-up of the USSR, President Yeltsin was confronted by a parliament (the holdover Supreme Soviet of the Russian Federation) largely unsympathetic to the liberal reforms his administration attempted to advance. Growing tensions between the president and the parliament led in October 1993 to the military seizure of the White House, the site of the Russian Supreme Soviet, and the imposition of presidential rule. Under Yeltsin's new constitution, a semi-presidential system of government was established, and the Supreme Soviet was replaced by the bicameral Federal Assembly. The Federal Assembly is formally designated as the supreme representative and legislative body of the Russian Federation, and, on the face of it, the powers of the State Duma parallel those of the US House of Representatives. Both houses, for instance, can initiate the impeachment of the president and override the president's legislative veto. In addition, the State Duma is vested with the power to bring the government down and to confirm the president's appointment of a prime minister, while, in return, the president can dissolve the State Duma.

However, Russia's semi-presidential system is highly unbalanced. Not only does the president have a wide-ranging ability to legislate by issuing decrees and executive orders, but the fact that only the executive, and not the State Duma, can initiate money bills, means that the president also controls the disposal of most of the government's resources. Nevertheless, the chief weakness of the Federal Assembly is its lack of meaningful political independence from the executive. Apart from the 1993 and 1995 parliamentary elections, forces opposed to the Kremlin have rarely been allowed to gain significant influence. Once Yeltsin stood down in favour of Putin in 1999, the success of the United Russia party, strongly aligned to Putin and Medvedev, has played a major role in ensuring the subordination of the State Duma to the Kremlin. United Russia achieved a peak of 64 per cent of the vote in the 2007 Duma elections, and, even though its vote fell to 49 per cent in 2011, the party retained majority control of the chamber. The latter elections provoked the first anti-Kremlin protests of the Putin era, giving voice to allegations of electoral irregularities, including ballot stuffing. Critics of Russia's 'superpresidential' system have argued that the weakness of its parliament has been a significant factor in the growth of arbitrary government, as insufficient checks have been placed on the drift towards corruption, the intimidation of opponents of the regime, and the manipulation of the Russian media.

tears – but never one that turned a vote'. More important, however, is the tendency of party unity to facilitate executive domination. In parliamentary systems in particular, loyalty to party means, for the majority of parliamentarians, loyalty to the government of the day, which is formed, after all, from the leading members of their own party. Far from checking or even embarrassing the executive, many assemblies have therefore come to function as its willing accomplices or doughty defenders.

'Big' government

The growth in the role of government, especially in the areas of social welfare and economic management, has usually been associated with a redistribution of power from assemblies to executives. This occurs for three reasons. First, it leads to an increase in the size and status of bureaucracies, which are responsible for administering government policy and overseeing an ever-widening range of public services. Second, it places greater emphasis on the process of policy initiation and formulation. Although individual assembly members can initiate policy in specific areas, the task of developing broad and coherent government programmes is quite beyond them. During the twentieth century, most assemblies therefore adjusted to the loss of positive legislative power by accepting that their central role was to scrutinize and criticize, rather than to make policy. Third, 'big' government has meant that government policy is increasingly complex and intricate. This, in turn, has placed a higher premium on expertise, a quality more abundantly possessed by 'professional' bureaucrats than by 'amateur' politicians.

Lack of leadership

By virtue of their function as representative forums and debating chambers, assemblies suffer from a number of organizational weaknesses. In particular, they usually comprise several hundred members, who enjoy formal equality, in the sense that they can all vote and contribute to debates. Although advantageous in other respects, the egalitarian and fragmented character of assemblies weakens their capacity to provide leadership and take concerted action. This problem has become more acute in an age in which the public looks to government to solve social problems and deliver sustained prosperity, and in which states have no choice but to participate in international affairs and global politics. Party-organized assemblies are certainly better able to adopt clear and coherent domestic and foreign policies, but, in these cases, leadership tends to be provided *by* parties and only *through* assemblies. As discussed in Chapter 13, it has generally been political executives, rather than assemblies, that have been able to respond to this need for leadership, by virtue of their greater organizational coherence and the fact that they are headed by a single individual, usually a president or prime minister.

Interest group and media power

Not only have power and public attention shifted from assemblies to executives, but they have also been lost to interests and groups external to government. The rise of interest groups (see p. 247) has threatened assemblies in a number of respects. The first is that the groups have provided the public with an alternative mechanism of representation. Often set up specifically for this purpose, interest groups tend to be more effective than assemblies in taking up popular griev-ances, and giving expression to the concerns and aspirations of particular groups. Single-issue groups, for instance, now engage in, and promote, the kind of public debate that previously took place only in parliamentary chambers. Second, while assemblies have increasingly been excluded from the process of policy formulation, organized interests have become more prominent both as representatives of 'affected groups', and as sources of expert advice and informa-tion. Third, the susceptibility of assemblies to lobbying has undermined their legitimacy, not least because of the growing perception that assembly members are motivated more by self-interest than by a sense of public service. Finally, the media, and particularly television and new forms of electronic communication, have also helped to make assemblies appear redundant. This has occurred because newspapers and television have displaced assemblies as the major forums for political debate, and because political leaders increasingly wish to deal with the public via the media, rather than indirectly through assemblies.

The rise of assemblies?

Many argue that the above analysis paints an over-gloomy picture. To some extent, the 'decline of assemblies' is too sweeping a notion, since it conceals the perhaps more important fact that the role of assemblies in the political process has fundamentally changed. Whereas their decline as legislatures and as policy-shaping bodies can hardly be doubted, many agree with Blondel (1973) that, if anything, they have become more important as 'communicating mechanisms'. The willingness of a growing number of assemblies to open up their proceedings to television cameras and to provide growing amounts of web-based informa-tion has certainly helped to raise their public profiles and strengthen them as arenas of debate and agencies of oversight. In other words, the media can upgrade assemblies, as well as downgrade them. Similarly, there is a trend towards the professionalization of assembly work. Following the example of the US Congress, this has seen the adoption and strengthening of specialized committees, and an improvement in the staff and resources available to individ-ual assembly members.

More broadly, there is evidence in the UK and elsewhere of assemblies becoming more critical and independent as a result of the decline of parties as tightly disciplined blocs. Not only may better-informed voters expect more of individual assembly members, but also better-educated and better-resourced members may be less willing to defer to a party line and act as 'lobby fodder'. If nothing else, general recognition that the legitimacy and stability of a political system is linked to the perceived effectiveness of its assembly guarantees that, whenever assembly power is weakened, voices will be raised in protest. Ultimately, however, the desirable balance between the assembly and the execu-tive boils down to a normative judgement about the need for representation and accountability, on the one hand, and for leadership and strong government, on the other.

SUMMARY

● The terms 'assembly', 'legislature' and 'parliament' are usually used interchangeably. The term 'assembly' suggests that the body is a surrogate for the people, as it is composed of lay politicians who claim to represent the people rather than of trained or expert government officials. The term 'legislature' is misleading, because assemblies never monopolize law-making power. The term 'parliament' draws attention to the importance within assemblies of debate and deliberation.

● A parliamentary system is one in which government governs in and through the assembly or parliament, the executive being drawn from, and accountable to, the assembly. A presidential system is based on a separation of powers between the assembly and the executive. This establishes a relationship characterized by a combination of independence and interdependence between the two branches.

● Assemblies provide a link between government and the people: that is, a channel of communication that can support government and uphold the regime, and force government to respond to popular demands. The chief functions of an assembly are to enact legislation, act as a representative body, oversee and scrutinize the executive, recruit and train politicians, and assist in maintaining the political system's legitimacy.

● Assemblies generally comprise either one or two chambers. The attraction of bicameralism is that it strengthens checks and balances and broadens representation, which is particularly useful in federal systems. Its disadvantage is that, in this type of system, there is a tendency towards immobilism and government gridlock. Committee systems are increasingly important in the legislative process; strong assemblies usually have strong committees, weak ones have weak committees.

● Assemblies rarely make policy. More usually, they influence policy or are executive-dominated. The amount of power an assembly has is determined by a variety of factors. These include the extent of the assembly's constitutional authority, its degree of political independence from the executive, the nature of the party system, and the assembly's level of organizational coherence.

● The decline of assemblies provokes anxiety because it is linked to the health of responsible and representative government. Assemblies have declined because of the emergence of disciplined political parties, the growth in the role of government, the executive's greater capacity to formulate policy and provide leadership, and the increasing strength of interest groups and the mass media.

Questions for discussion

● Why have assemblies been seen as vital to the democratic process?

● Does the widespread adoption of parliamentary government reflect the system's success and efficiency?

● Why is the separation of powers considered to be such an important liberal-democratic principle?

● What conditions are most conducive for the promotion of responsible government?

● Do committees bolster legislative power or narrow parliamentary debate?

● Are two chambers always better than one?

● In complex modern societies, are assemblies doomed to lose out to executives?

● Does the decline of assemblies necessarily weaken representation and accountability?

Further reading

Davidson, R., W. Oleszek and F. Lee, *Congress and Its Members* (2009). A useful discussion of the role of the US Congress and shifts in congressional power.

Fish, S. and M. Kroenig, *The Handbook of National Legislature: A Global Survey* (2011). A thorough survey of the powers and characteristics of legislature worldwide, best used as a reference book.

Lijphart, A. (ed.), *Parliamentary Versus Presidential Government* (1992). A wide-ranging collection of essays that reflect on the merits of parliamentarianism and presidentialism.

Strøm, K., W. Müller and T. Bergman (eds), *Delegation and Accountability in Parliamentary Democracies* (2006). A comprehensive account of the institutions of democratic delegation in Western European parliamentary democracies.

CHAPTER 15

Constitutions, Law and Judges

'Government without a constitution is power without right.'

THOMAS PAINE, *The Rights of Man* (1791–2)

PREVIEW

In the 1950s and 1960s, the study of constitutions and constitutional issues became distinctly unfashionable. Political analysts turned instead to what were seen as deeper political realities, such as political culture, and the distribution of economic and social power. To be interested in constitutions was to perpetuate an outdated, legalistic and, frankly, boring approach to politics, to focus on how a political system portrays itself, rather than on how it actually works. Since the 1970s, however, constitutional questions have moved to the centre of the political stage. Developed and developing states have adopted new constitutions, and political conflict has increasingly been expressed in terms of calls for constitutional reform. This has occurred because constitutional change has far-reaching implications, affecting not just how decisions are made within government but also the balance of political forces that shape these decisions. Nevertheless, there is considerable debate about how constitutions should be configured and about the nature and extent of their political significance. Such issues, in turn, have had major implications for the role of law and the position of judges. Law has widely been seen as a vital guarantee of public order, but disagreement about the relationship between law and morality, and especially about the extent to which law should uphold individual freedom, have long been core themes in political theory. As far as the position of judges is concerned, although the courts have usually been viewed as strictly separate from politics, in practice, in many parts of the world, they have acquired a growing capacity to shape public policy. This has encouraged a search for a revised balance between judicial, executive and legislative power, and also led to calls for the reform of the courts and the judiciary.

KEY ISSUES

- What is a constitution, and what forms can it take?
- What is the purpose of a constitution?
- To what extent do constitutions shape political practice?
- What is the relationship between law and politics?
- What is the political significance of the courts?
- Can judges keep out of politics? Should judges keep out of politics?

CONCEPT

Constitution

A constitution is, broadly, a set of rules, written and unwritten, that seek to establish the duties, powers and functions of the various institutions of government; regulate the relationships between them; and define the relationship between the state and the individual. The balance between written (legal) and unwritten (customary or conventional) rules varies from system to system. The term 'constitution' is also used more narrowly to refer to a single, authoritative document (a 'written' constitution), the aim of which is to codify major constitutional provisions; it constitutes the highest law in the land.

CONSTITUTIONS

Constitutions: their nature and origins

Traditionally, constitutions have been associated with two key purposes. First, they were believed to provide a description of government itself, a neat introduction to major institutions and their roles. Second, they were regarded as the linchpin of liberal democracy (see p. 270), even its defining feature. Sadly, neither view is correct. While constitutions may *aim* to lay down a framework in which government and political activity are conducted, none has been entirely successful in this respect. Inaccuracies, distortions and omissions can be found in all constitutions. Similarly, although the idea of constitutionalism (see p. 337) is closely linked to liberal values and aspirations, there is nothing to prevent a constitution being undemocratic or authoritarian. In the case of communist states and some developing states, constitutions have, indeed, been profoundly illiberal. Why then bother with constitutions? Why include in an account of the machinery of government a discussion of constitutions? The reason is that the objective of constitutions is to lay down certain meta-rules for the political system. In effect, these are rules that govern the government itself. Just as government establishes ordered rule in society at large, the purpose of a constitution is to bring stability, predictability and order to the actions of government.

The idea of a code of rules providing guidance for the conduct of government has an ancient lineage. These codes traditionally drew on the idea of a higher moral power, usually religious in character, to which worldly affairs were supposed to conform. Egyptian pharaohs acknowledged the authority of *Ma'at* or 'justice', Chinese emperors were subject to *Ti'en* or 'heaven', Jewish kings conformed to the Mosaic Law and Islamic caliphs paid respect to *Shari'a* law. Not uncommonly, 'higher' principles were also enacted in ordinary law, as seen, for example, in the distinction in the Athenian constitution between the *nomos* (laws that could be changed only by a special procedure) and the *psephismata* (decrees that could be passed by a resolution of the assembly). However, such ancient codes did not amount to constitutions in the modern sense, in that they generally failed to lay down specific provisions relating to the authority and responsibilities of the various institutions, and rarely established authoritative mechanisms through which provisions could be enforced and breaches of the fundamental law punished.

Constitutions are thus best thought of as a relatively recent development. Although the evolution of the British constitution is sometimes traced back to the Bill of Rights of 1689 and the Act of Settlement of 1701, or even to the Magna Carta (1215), it is more helpful to think of constitutions as late eighteenth-century creations. The 'age of constitutions' was initiated by the enactment of the first 'written' constitutions: the US constitution in 1787 and the French Declaration of the Rights of Man and the Citizen in 1789. The examples of the USA and revolutionary France not only provided in form and substance a model for later constitution-makers to follow, but also shed light on why and how constitutions come about.

The enactment of a constitution marks a major breach in political continuity, usually resulting from an upheaval such as a war, revolution or national independence. Constitutions are, above all, a means of establishing a new polit-

CONCEPT

Convention

A convention, in everyday language, is either a formal political meeting, or an agreement reached through debate and negotiation. A constitutional convention, however, is a rule of conduct or behaviour that is based not on law, but on custom and precedent. These non-legal rules are upheld either by a sense of constitutional propriety (what is 'correct'), or by practical circumstances (what is 'workable'). Conventions of this sort exist in all constitutional systems, usually providing guidance where formal rules are unclear or incomplete, but they are particularly significant in 'unwritten' constitutions.

ical order following the rejection, collapse or failure of an old order. In this light, the revival of interests in constitutions since the 1970s (with new constitutions being adopted in countries such as Portugal, Spain, Canada, Sweden and the Netherlands, and the issue of constitutional reform becoming more prominent in, for example, the UK, India, Canada, New Zealand and Australia) indicates growing disenchantment, even disillusionment, with existing political systems. In general, it can be said that political conflicts assume a constitutional dimension only when those demanding change seek to redraw, and not merely readjust, the rules of the political game. Constitutional change is therefore about the reapportionment of both power and political authority.

Classifying constitutions

Constitutions can be classified in many different ways. These include the following:

- the form of the constitution and *status* of its rules (whether the constitution is written or unwritten, or codified or uncodified)
- the ease with which the constitution can be *changed* (whether it is rigid or flexible)
- the degree to which the constitution is *observed* in practice (whether it is an effective, nominal or façade constitution)
- the *content* of the constitution and the institutional structure that it establishes (whether it is, for example, monarchical or republican, federal or unitary, or presidential or parliamentary).

Traditionally, considerable emphasis has been placed on the distinction between written and unwritten constitutions. Written constitutions are, in theory, constitutions that are enshrined in laws, while unwritten constitutions are supposedly embodied in custom and tradition (see p. 82). The former are human artefacts, in the sense that they have been 'created', while the latter have been seen as organic entities that have evolved through history. This system of classification, however, has now largely been abandoned. In the first place, an overwhelming majority of states now possess basic written documents that lay down major constitutional provisions. Only three liberal democracies (Israel, New Zealand and the UK) continue to have unwritten constitutions, together with a handful of non-democratic states such as Bhutan, Saudi Arabia and Oman. Moreover, the classification has always been misleading. No constitution is entirely written, in the sense that all its rules are formal and legally enforceable. Few constitutions, for instance, specify the roles of, or even mention, political parties and interest groups. Similarly, no constitution is entirely unwritten, in the sense that none of its provisions have any legal substance, all of them being conventions, customs or traditions.

Every constitution, then, is a blend of written and unwritten rules, although the balance between these varies significantly. In countries such as France and Germany, in which constitutional documents act as state codes, specifying in considerable detail the powers and responsibilities of political institutions, the emphasis is clearly on written rules. The US constitution (the world's first written constitution) is, however, a document of only 7,000 words that confines itself, in the main, to broad principles, and so lays down only a loose framework for government. US institutions of undoubted constitutional significance, such as congressional committees, primary elections (see p. 228) and the bureaucracy (see p. 361), have simply evolved over time. Other constitutions, although not entirely unwritten, place considerable stress on conventions. For example, the ability of UK ministers to exercise the powers of the Royal Prerogative (technically, the monarch's powers) and their responsibility, individually and collectively, to Parliament is based entirely on convention.

The worldwide trend, however, is to favour the adoption of written and formal rules. Not only has the number of unwritten constitutions diminished, but also, within them, there has been a growing reliance on legal rules. Although respect for the Torah, the Jewish book of holy law, encouraged the Israelis to establish an independent state in 1948 without an authoritative constitutional document, within two years the Knesset had voted to adopt such a constitution by evolution over an unspecified period of time. The publication in the UK of documents such as *Questions on Procedure for Ministers* has given detailed formal substance to practices that were previously covered by ill-defined conventions. The passage in New Zealand of the Constitution Act 1986 (which consolidated previously scattered laws and principles), and the adoption in 1990 of a bill of rights (see p. 340), has been interpreted by many commentators as indicating that New Zealand should no longer be classified amongst the ranks of states with unwritten constitutions.

More helpful (and more accurate) than the written/unwritten distinction is the contrast between codified and uncodified constitutions. A **codified constitution** is one that is based on the existence of a single authoritative document. As pointed out above, most constitutions can be so classified, even though they may differ in the degree to which constitutional detail is specified and the extent to which other provisions are unwritten. The significance of codification is, nevertheless, considerable.

First, in a codified constitution, the document itself is *authoritative*, in the sense that it constitutes 'higher' law; indeed, the highest law of the land. The constitution binds all political institutions, including those that enact ordinary law. The existence of a codified constitution thus establishes a hierarchy of laws. In unitary states, a two-tier legal system exists, in which the constitution stands above **statute law**. In federal states, there is a third tier, in the form of 'lower' state or provincial laws. Second, the status of the codified document is ensured by the fact that at least certain of its provisions are *entrenched*, in the sense that it is difficult to amend or abolish them. The procedure for establishing the constitution, and for subsequently revising it, must therefore be in some way more complex and difficult than the procedure for enacting ordinary statute laws. Finally, the logic of codification dictates that, as the constitution sets out the duties, powers and functions of government institutions in terms of 'higher' law, it must be *justiciable*, meaning that all political bodies must be subject to the authority of the courts and, in particular, a supreme or constitutional court. This substantially enhances the importance of judges, or at least senior judges, who become, in effect, the final arbiters of the constitution, and thereby acquire the power of judicial review (see p. 347).

Uncodified constitutions, although few in number, have very different characteristics. The UK constitution, which is properly thought of as an uncodified but partly-written constitution, draws on a variety of sources. Chief amongst

● **Codified constitution**: A constitution in which key constitutional provisions are collected together in a single legal document, popularly known as a 'written constitution' or 'the constitution'.

● **Statute law**: Law that is enacted by the legislature.

● **Uncodified constitution**: A constitution that is made up of rules drawn from a variety of sources, in the absence of a single authoritative document.

Focus on . . .
A codified constitution: strengths and weaknesses

The strengths of a codified or written constitution include the following:

- Major principles and key constitutional provisions are entrenched, safeguarding them from interference by the government of the day.
- The power of the legislature is constrained, cutting its sovereignty (see p. 58) down to size.
- Non-political judges are able to police the constitution to ensure that its provisions are upheld by other public bodies.
- Individual liberty is more securely protected, and authoritarianism is kept at bay.
- The codified document has an educational value, in that it highlights the central values and overall goals of the political system.

The drawbacks or weaknesses of codification include the following:

- A codified constitution is more rigid, and may therefore be less responsive and adaptable than an uncodified one.
- Government power may be more effectively constrained by regular elections than by a constitutional document.
- With a codified constitution, constitutional supremacy resides with non-elected judges, rather than with publicly accountable politicians.
- Constitutional provisions enshrined in custom and convention may be more widely respected because they have been endorsed by history and not 'invented'.
- Constitutional documents are inevitably biased, because they endorse one set of values or principles in preference to others, meaning that they may precipitate more conflicts than they resolve.

these are statute law, which is made by Parliament, **common law**, conventions, and various works of authority that clarify and explain the constitution's unwritten elements. The absence of a codified document implies, most importantly, that the legislature enjoys sovereign or unchallengeable authority. It has the right to make or unmake any law whatsoever, no body having the right to override or set aside its laws. By virtue of their legislative supremacy, bodies such as the UK Parliament and the Knesset in Israel are able to function as the ultimate arbiters of the constitution: the constitution means what they say it means.

In the UK in particular, this has stimulated deep controversy and widespread criticism. Parliamentary sovereignty (see p. 336) has been held responsible for what Lord Hailsham (1976) termed 'elective dictatorship'; that is, the ability of a government to act in any way it pleases as long as it maintains majority control of the House of Commons. The concentration of power in the hands of the executive to which this leads, and the consequent threat that it poses to individual rights and liberties, has encouraged some to argue that the UK has no constitution at all. If governments can, once elected, act in whatever way they wish, they are surely at liberty to enlarge their own powers at will, and are thereby unconstrained by constitutional rules of any kind. In Griffith's (2010) phrase, the constitution in the UK is 'what happens'. Such concerns fuelled, in the 1980s and 1990s, a growing campaign in the UK for radical constitutional reform, which,

● **Common law**: Law based on custom and precedent; law that is supposedly 'common' to all.

Parliamentary sovereignty

Parliamentary sovereignty refers to the absolute and unlimited authority of a parliament or legislature, reflected in its ability to make, amend or repeal any law it wishes. Parliamentary sovereignty is usually seen as the central principle of the UK constitution, and results from (1) the absence of a codified constitution, (2) the supremacy of statute law over other forms of law, (3) the absence of rival legislatures, and (4) the convention that no parliament can bind its successors. Parliamentary sovereignty is a strictly legal, and not political, form of sovereignty (see p. 58).

together with the Labour Party's long period in opposition (1979–97), eventually converted the party to the reformist cause. From 1997 onwards, the Blair government reshaped important aspects of the UK's constitutional landscape. Devolution (see p. 390) was introduced in Scotland, Wales and Northern Ireland; referendums (see p. 201) and proportional electoral systems were more widely used; the European Convention on Human Rights (1950) was incorporated into UK law through the Human Rights Act (1998); most hereditary peers were removed from the House of Lords; and freedom of information legislation was passed. Although this programme stops short of codification, some have argued that it has brought about a shift from parliamentary sovereignty to **popular sovereignty** (Hazell, 2008).

An alternative form of classification distinguishes between rigid and flexible constitutions. What procedures exist for amending a constitution? How easily does the constitution adapt to changing circumstances? On the face of it, codified constitutions are likely to be relatively inflexible because their provisions are in some way entrenched in 'higher' law. By the same token, uncodified ones appear to be flexible and adaptable, because laws of constitutional significance can be changed through the ordinary legislative process and conventions are, by their nature, based on conduct and practice. However, there is no simple relationship between written constitutions and rigidity, or unwritten ones and flexibility.

Various degrees of flexibility are possible, and, surprisingly, the flexibility of a constitution is not directly proportional to the formality of its procedures and rules. Whereas the US constitution has endured, albeit with amendments, since 1787, France has had, over the same period, no fewer than 17 constitutions. Similarly, amendment procedures may be more or less complex or difficult. In Australia, Denmark, Ireland and Spain, for example, referendums are used to obtain the public's approval for constitutional amendments or to ratify those endorsed by the legislature. In other cases, special majorities must be achieved in the legislature, as in the requirement in Germany's Basic Law (1949) that amendments must have two-thirds support in both the *Bundestag* and the *Bundesrat*. In the USA, in addition to two-thirds majorities in both houses of Congress, constitutional amendments must be ratified by three-quarters of the 50 states. This requirement has meant that a mere 27 constitutional amendments have been passed, with 10 of these (the so-called 'Bill of Rights') having been introduced in the first two years of the constitution's existence.

The seeming rigidity this produces is, however, misleading. Although the words of the US constitution and other codified documents may change little, their meanings are subject to constant revision and updating through the process of judicial interpretation and reinterpretation. The role of the judiciary in this respect is examined in the final main section of this chapter. Just as written provisions can allow for flexibility, unwritten ones can, at times, be rigid. While, in the UK, the conventions of ministerial responsibility have proved to be so adaptable they can almost be reshaped at the convenience of the government of the day, other conventions are so deeply engrained in the political culture and in popular expectations that their abandonment or modification is virtually unthinkable. This certainly applies in the case of conventions that restrict the political role of the monarchy and prevent monarchs challenging the authority of Parliament.

A third system of classification takes account of the relationship between constitutional rules and principles, on the one hand, and the practice of

● **Popular sovereignty**. The principle that there is no higher authority than the will of the people, directly expressed.

CONCEPT

Constitutionalism

Constitutionalism, in a narrow sense, is the practice of limited government ensured by the existence of a constitution. Constitutionalism can, thus, be said to exist when government institutions and political processes are effectively constrained by constitutional rules. More broadly, constitutionalism is a set of political values and devices that fragment power, thereby creating a network of checks and balances. Examples of such devices include codified constitutions, bills of rights, the separation of powers, bicameralism, and federalism.

government (the 'working' constitution), on the other. As early as 1867, Walter Bagehot in *The English Constitution* ([1867] 1963) distinguished between the 'dignified' parts of the constitution (the monarchy and the House of the Lords), which promoted popular allegiance but exercised little effective power, and its 'efficient' parts (the cabinet and the House of Commons). An effective constitution is one that fulfils two criteria. First, in major respects at least, the practical affairs of government correspond to the provisions of the constitution. Second, this occurs because the constitution has the capacity, through whatever means, to limit governmental behaviour.

An effective constitution therefore requires not merely the existence of constitutional rules, but also the capacity of those rules to constrain government and establish constitutionalism. As we shall see below, however, all constitutions are violated to a greater or lesser extent; the real issue is thus the significance and regularity of such violations. Some constitutions can be classified as *nominal*, in that their texts or principles may accurately describe governmental behaviour but fail to limit it. For instance, the 1982 Chinese constitution acknowledges that China is 'a socialist state under the people's dictatorship', but the constitution lacks significance because the judiciary, charged with interpreting the constitution, is kept under firm party control. Other states have sham or façade constitutions. These differ substantially from political practice and tend to fulfil, at best, only a propaganda role. This is particularly the case in dictatorial or authoritarian states, where the commitment to individual rights and liberties extends little further than the content of the state's constitutional documents.

Constitutions have also been classified in terms of their content and, specifically, by the institutional structure they underpin. This enables a number of distinctions to be made. For example, constitutions have traditionally been categorized as either monarchical or republican. In theory, the former invest constitutional supremacy in a dynastic ruler, while, in the latter, political authority is derived from the people. However, the emergence of constitutional monarchies (see p. 292), in which power has effectively been transferred to representative institutions, has meant that, apart from in the surviving absolute monarchies in states such as Swaziland, Oman and Saudi Arabia, this distinction is no longer of central importance. More widely used, though, is the distinction between unitary and federal constitutions (discussed more fully in Chapter 17); that is, the difference between constitutions that concentrate sovereignty in a single national body and ones that divide it between two levels of government.

Yet another approach is to differentiate between what are seen as parliamentary constitutions and presidential constitutions. The key here is the relationship between the executive and the assembly. In parliamentary systems, the executive is derived from and accountable to the assembly; in presidential systems the two branches of government function independently on the basis of the separation of powers (see p. 313). These different systems are examined in Chapters 13 and 14. Finally, pluralist constitutions can be contrasted with monopolistic ones. The former are characteristic of liberal democracies, in that they ensure that political power is dispersed, usually through guarantees of participatory rights and party competition. The latter are more commonly found in communist or authoritarian states where the unquestionable authority of a 'ruling' party or supreme leader is formally entrenched, thus demonstrating that a constitution and liberal constitutionalism do not necessarily go hand-in-hand.

The purpose of a constitution

Not only do the vast majority of states have constitutions, but also most institutions and organized groups have rules that have some kind of constitutional effect. This applies in the case of international bodies such as the United Nations and the European Union, and is also true of regional and provincial government, political parties, interest groups, corporations, churches, clubs and so on. The popularity of these constitutional rules draws attention to the fact that constitutions somehow play a vital role in the running of organizations. Why is it difficult, and perhaps impossible, for states and other organized bodies to function without a constitution? The difficulty with answering this question is that constitutions do not have a single or simple purpose. Rather, they have a number of functions and are used in a variety of ways. The most important of these are to:

- empower states
- establish unifying values and goals
- provide government stability
- protect freedom
- legitimize regimes.

Empowering states

Although the popular image of constitutions is that they limit government power, a more basic function is that they mark out the existence of states and make claims concerning their sphere of independent authority. The creation of new states (whether through the overthrow of colonialism, the fragmentation of larger states, or the unification of smaller ones) is invariably accompanied by the enactment of a constitution. Indeed, it can be argued that such states exist only once they have a constitition, since without one they lack formal jurisdiction over a particular territory, or a governing apparatus that can effectively exercise that jurisdiction.

The state of India can thus be said to have come into existence in the period between the granting of independence in 1947 and the adoption of its federal constitution in 1950: during this time, a UK-appointed Governor General continued to exercise supervision. In the same way, the American Declaration of Independence in 1776 initiated the process through which the USA achieved statehood, but this was not completed until the US constitution was ratified in 1789. The need for empowerment also applies to subnational and supranational bodies. In federal systems, for example, constituent provinces or states have their own constitutions in order to guarantee their sphere of authority relative to that of central government. Although the idea of a formal EU constitution was abandoned in 2005, following its rejection by the Netherlands and France, a collection of treaties – including the Treaty of Rome (1957), the Single European Act (1986) and the Treaty of European Union (1993) and the Treaty of Lisbon (2009) – have constitutional effect, in that they authorize EU bodies to intervene in various ways in the affairs of member states. This highlights the fact that, although **treaties** differ from constitutions, the former can constitute part of the latter. EU law and treaties, for instance, serve as a source of the constitution for each EU member state.

● **Treaty**: A formal agreement between two or more states, on matters of peace, trade or some other aspect of international relations.

Freedom

The term 'freedom' (or liberty) means, in its broadest sense, the ability to think or act as one wishes. A distinction is nevertheless often made between 'negative' and 'positive' liberty (Berlin, 1958). *Negative* freedom means non-interference: the absence of external constraints on the individual. Freedom, in this sense, is a private sphere within which individuals are 'at liberty' to act as they wish. *Positive* freedom is linked to the achievement of some identifiable goal or benefit, usually in the sense of personal development, self-realization, or self-mastery.

Establishing values and goals

In addition to laying down a framework for government, constitutions invariably embody a broader set of political values, ideals and goals. This is why constitutions cannot be neutral; they are always entangled, more or less explicitly, with ideological priorities. The creators of constitutions therefore seek to invest their regime with a set of unifying values, a sense of ideological purpose and a vocabulary that can be used in the conduct of politics. In many cases, these aims are accomplished explicitly in preambles to constitutional documents, which often function as statements of national ideals. These ideals can vary from a commitment to democracy, freedom or the welfare state to a belief in socialism, federalism or Islam. The 1982 Turkish constitution is dedicated to 'the concept of nationalism as outlined by Atatürk', the founder of the republic, while Germany's Basic Law states a determination to 'serve the peace of the world'.

In other cases, however, these values and ideological priorities are largely implicit. Charles Beard (1913), for example, argued that the provisions of the US constitution were shaped essentially by economic interests, in particular the desire to defend property against the rising power of the propertyless masses. Similarly, it can be argued that, while the Fourteenth Amendment and Fifteenth Amendment to the US constitution acknowledge the significance of racial divisions, the constitution effectively conceals divisions that arise from social class or gender. In the case of the UK constitution, the doctrine of parliamentary sovereignty has been interpreted as a means of discouraging, or even discrediting, forms of extraparliamentary political action.

Providing government stability

In allocating duties, powers and functions amongst the various institutions of government, constitutions act as 'organizational charts', 'definitional guides' or 'institutional blueprints'. As such, they formalize and regulate the relationships between political bodies and provide a mechanism through which conflicts can be adjudicated and resolved. The Indian constitution, for instance, contains a highly detailed description of institutional powers and relationships in a lengthy document containing almost 400 articles. Despite varying in their degree of specificity and their effectiveness, all constitutions fulfil the vital function of introducing a measure of stability, order and predictability to the workings of government. From this point of view, the opposite of constitutional government is random, capricious or arbitrary government. This is precisely why constitutions go hand-in-hand with organization. Complex patterns of social interaction can be maintained only if all concerned know the 'rules of the game' and, therefore, who can be expected to do what.

Protecting freedom

● **Limited government**: Government operating within constraints, usually imposed by law, a constitution or institutional checks and balances.

In liberal democracies, it is often taken for granted that the central purpose of a constitution is to constrain government with a view to protecting individual liberty. This is why constitutions tend to be viewed as devices for establishing and maintaining **limited government**. Certainly, constitutions lay down the relationship between the state and the individual, marking out the respective

CONCEPT

Bill of rights

A bill of rights is a constitutional document that specifies the rights and freedoms of the individual, and so defines the legal extent of civil liberty (see p. 404). Entrenched bills of rights can be distinguished from statutory ones. An *entrenched* bill of rights is enshrined in 'higher' law and, thus, provides the basis for constitutional judicial review (see p. 347). A *statutory* bill of rights, or statute of rights, can be amended or repealed through the same processes as other statute laws. Unlike an entrenched bill of rights, it does not breach parliamentary sovereignty (see p. 336).

spheres of government authority and personal freedom. They do this largely by defining civil rights and liberties, often through the means of a bill of rights. The impact of liberal constitutionalism has ensured that, in many cases, 'classic' or traditional civil liberties (see p. 404), such as freedom of expression, freedom of religious worship, freedom of assembly and freedom of movement, are recognized as 'fundamental' in that they are constitutionally guaranteed. These so-called '**negative rights**' have a liberal character in that, because the state is thus prevented from encroaching on the individual, they mark out a sphere of government *in*activity.

A growing number of states have, in addition, entrenched a range of economic, social and cultural rights, such as the right to health care, the right to education and, even, the right to work. These **positive rights**, however, have caused controversy, because they are linked to the expansion, not contraction, of government, and because their provision is dependent on the economic and social resources available to the state in question. Can these rights and freedoms be thought of as 'fundamental' when there is no practical way of guaranteeing their delivery? In the Indian constitution, this is acknowledged through the qualification that the right to work, for example, is secured 'within the limits of economic capacity and development'.

Legitimizing regimes

The final function of a constitution is to help build legitimacy (see p. 81). This explains the widespread use of constitutions, even by states with constitutions that are merely nominal or a complete façade. This legitimation process has two dimensions. In the first place, the existence of a constitution is almost a prerequisite for a state's membership of the international community and for its recognition by other states. More significant, however, is the ability to use a constitution to build legitimacy within a state through the promotion of respect and compliance amongst the domestic population. This is possible because a constitution both symbolizes and disseminates the values of the ruling elite, and invests the governmental system with a cloak of legality. To make the constitution more effective in this respect, attempts are often made to promote veneration for the constitution itself, either as a document of historical importance or as a symbol of national purpose and identity.

Do constitutions matter?

The value of a constitution is often taken for granted. The existence of a constitution, so the assumption goes, provides benefits such as political stability, limited government, and guaranteed rights and liberties. Nowhere is this faith in a constitution more developed than in the USA, where it amounts, in Louis Hartz's (1955) words, to 'the cult of constitution worship'. Of course, this faith has been severely tested, not least by allegations during the Watergate crisis that President Richard Nixon had helped to cover up illegal acts by senior White House officials during the 1972 election campaign. Nevertheless, Nixon's resignation in 1974 enabled his successor, Gerald Ford, to declare that 'our constitution works', reiterating the classic sentiment of constitutionalism: 'we have a government of laws, not of men'. However, the mere existence of a constitution

● **Negative rights**: Rights that mark out a realm of unconstrained action, and thus check the responsibilities of government.

● **Positive rights**: Rights that make demands of government in terms of the provision of resources and support, and thus extend its responsibilities.

does not ensure that a government is constitutional. Indeed, there is little evidence that a constitution is a major guarantee against tyranny, still less that it offers a 'ticket to Utopia'.

Constitutions 'work' in certain circumstances. In other words, they serve their various purposes only when they are supported by a range of other cultural, political, economic and social conditions. In particular, constitutions must correspond to and be supported by the political culture; successful constitutions are as much a product of the political culture as they are its creator. This is why so many of the model liberal-democratic constitutions bequeathed to developing states by departing colonial rulers failed to take root. Constitutional rules guaranteeing individual rights and political competition may be entirely irrelevant in societies with deeply entrenched collectivist values and traditions, especially when such societies are struggling to achieve basic economic and social development.

In the same way, the various Soviet constitutions not only enshrined 'socialist' values that were foreign to the mass of the people, but also failed to develop popular support for such values during the 74 years of the USSR's existence. In the USA, as a result of widespread and institutionalized racism, the constitutional guarantees of civil and voting rights for black Americans enacted after the Civil War were often not upheld in Southern states until the 1960s. On the other hand, the 1947 Japanese constitution, despite the fact that it was imposed by the occupying USA and emphasized individual rights in place of the more traditional Japanese stress on duty, has proved to be remarkably successful, providing a stable framework for postwar reconstruction and political development. As in postwar Germany, however, the Japanese constitution has had the advantage of being sustained by an 'economic miracle'.

A second key factor is whether or not a constitution is respected by rulers and accords with the interests and values of dominant groups. Germany's Weimar constitution (1919), for example, despite the fact that it enshrined an impressive array of rights and liberties, was easily set aside in the 1930s as Hitler constructed his Nazi dictatorship. Not only did the competitive democracy of the Weimar regime conflict with the ambitions of the Nazis and conservative elites in business and the military, but it was also poorly supported by a population facing economic crisis and little accustomed to representative government. In India, under Indira Gandhi during 1975–77, and in Pakistan, under General Zia ul-Haq during 1977–81, major provisions of the constitutions were abrogated by the declaration of '**states of emergency**'. In these cases, the support of the military leadership proved to be far more crucial than respect for constitutional niceties. The UK's uncodified constitution is often said to provide unusual scope for abuse because it relies so heavily on the self-restraint of the government of the day. This became particularly apparent as the Conservative governments of the 1980s and 1990s exploited the flexibility inherent in parliamentary sovereignty to alter the constitutional roles of institutions such as the civil service, local government and the trade unions, and, some argued, substantially undermined civil liberties.

The final factor is the adaptability of a constitution and its ability to *remain* relevant despite changing political circumstances. No constitution reflects political realities, and few set out specifically to do so. Generally, successful constitutions are sufficiently flexible to accommodate change within a broad and

● **State of emergency**: A declaration by government through which it assumes special powers, supposedly to allow it to deal with an unusual threat.

enduringly relevant framework; those that are infinitely flexible are, strictly speaking, not constitutions at all. The US constitution is particularly interesting in this respect. Its 'genius' has been its concentration on broad principles and the scope it therefore provides to rectify its own deficiencies. US government has thus been able to evolve in response to new challenges and new demands. The formal amendment process, for example, allowed US institutions to be democratized and, in the twentieth century, judicial interpretation made possible the growth of presidential powers, a shift of authority from state to federal government and, in certain respects, a widening of individual rights.

Such changes, however, can be said to have occurred *within* the constitution, in that core principles such as the separation of powers, federalism and individual liberty have continued to be respected, albeit in renewed form. The same is true of the reforms the Blair government introduced in the UK's uncodified constitution after 1997. In contrast, the constitution of the Fourth French Republic proved to be unworkable, because the emphasis it placed on the National Assembly tended to produce a succession of weak and unstable governments. As the constitution offered no solution to this impasse, the result was a new constitution in 1958, inaugurating the Fifth Republic, which broadened presidential power according to a blueprint devised by General de Gaulle.

THE LAW

Law, morality and politics

The relationship between law and morality is one of the thorniest problems in political theory. On the surface, law and morality are very different things. Law is a distinctive form of social control, backed up by the means of enforcement; it defines what *may* and what *may not* be done. Morality, on the other hand, is concerned with ethical questions and the difference between 'right' and 'wrong'; it prescribes what *should* and what *should not* be done. Moreover, while law has an objective character, in that it is a social fact, morality is usually treated as a subjective entity; that is, as a matter of opinion or personal judgement. Nevertheless, natural law theories that date back to Plato (see p. 13) and Aristotle (see p. 6) suggest that law is, or should be, rooted in a moral system of some kind. In the early modern period, such theories were often based on the idea of God-given 'natural rights'. This assertion of a link between law and morality became fashionable again as the twentieth century progressed, and it was usually associated with the ideas of civil liberties or human rights.

However, the rise in the nineteenth century of the 'science of positive law' offered a very different view of the relationship between **law** and morality. Its purpose was quite simply to free the understanding of law from moral, religious and mystical assumptions. John Austin (1790–1859) developed the theory of '**legal positivism**', which defined law not in terms of its conformity to higher moral or religious principles, but in terms of the fact that it was established and enforced: the law is the law because it is obeyed. This approach was refined by H. L. A. Hart in *The Concept of Law* (1961). Hart suggested that law stemmed from the union of 'primary' and 'secondary' rules, each of which had a particular function. Primary rules regulate social behaviour and can be thought of as the

● **Law**: A set of public and enforceable rules that apply throughout a political community; law is usually recognized as binding.

● **Legal positivism**: A legal philosophy in which law is defined by the capacity to establish and enforce it, not by its moral character.

Debating...
Is the central purpose of law to protect freedom?

At the heart of questions about the relationship between law and morality is the issue of freedom and the proper balance between those moral choices that should be made by society and enforced through law, and those that should be reserved for the individual. While liberals have typically argued that laws are only justifiable if they enlarge, rather than contract, the sphere of freedom, conservatives and others have claimed that law serves interests beyond those of the individual.

YES

Personal and social development. The classic liberal belief is that law and freedom are intrinsically related. Freedom is only possible 'under the law' (because each citizen is a threat to every other citizen) but, at the same time, the sphere of law should not extend beyond the protection of freedom (otherwise law is non-legitimate). In *On Liberty* ([1859] 1982), J. S. Mill (see p. 198) thus asserted that, 'Over himself, over his own body and mind the individual is sovereign'. Mill was prepared to accept the legitimacy of law only when it was designed to prevent 'harm to others'. This so-called 'harm principle' can be justified in two ways. First, it reflects the fact that human beings will only grow or develop if they enjoy the widest possible scope for unconstrained action, allowing them to make their own moral decisions. Second, a wider sphere for freedom promotes healthy debate and discussion, so advancing the cause of reason and promoting social progress.

Fundamental freedoms. An alternative defence for liberty-based law derives from attempts to establish freedom as a fundamental value. In Immanuel Kant's (see p. 410) view, freedom consists in being bound by laws that are, in some sense, of one's own making, as individuals should be treated as 'ends in themselves'. However, in modern political debate the notion of human beings as autonomous agents is most commonly grounded in the doctrine of human rights. Human rights are rights to which people are entitled by virtue of being human. They are therefore 'fundamental' rights, in that they are inalienable: they cannot be traded away or revoked. The doctrine of human rights implies that civil liberties – especially classic civil liberties such as freedom of speech, freedom of the press and freedom of movement and assembly – are fundamental entitlements, which are upheld for all people and in all circumstances. To treat such rights and freedoms, not as moral absolutes, but as matters of convenience, is to leave the door open to tyranny and oppression.

NO

Order over freedom. The flaw in the liberal theory of law is a failure to recognize that law exists, primarily, not to defend freedom, but to uphold order; and that, by widening freedom, order can be put at risk. In this view, liberals can only argue that the protection of freedom should be set above other considerations because they embrace an optimistic model of human nature in which people are portrayed as rational and moral creatures. Citizens can thus be endowed with freedom because they can be trusted, in normal circumstances, not to use and abuse their fellow citizens. Conservatives, in contrast, adopt a pessimistic, even Hobbesian, view of human nature, but one which they argue is more realistic. As individuals are greedy, selfish and power-seeking creatures, orderly existence can only be maintained through strict laws, firm enforcement and, where necessary, harsh penalties. 'Soft' laws or the treatment of civil liberties as fundamental freedoms threaten to bring about a descent into crime and delinquency.

Enforcing morality. Instead of promoting personal and social development, unrestrained freedom may damage the fabric of society. At issue here is the moral and cultural diversity which Mill's view permits, or even encourages. A classic statement of this position was advanced by Patrick Devlin in *The Enforcement of Morals* (1968), which argues that there is a 'public morality' which society has the right to enforce through the instrument of law. Underlying this position is the belief that society is held together by a 'shared' morality, a fundamental agreement about what is 'good' and what is 'evil'. In particular, Devlin argued that Mill's notion of harm should be extended to include 'offence', at least when actions provoke what Devlin called 'real feelings of revulsion', rather than simple dislike. The central theme of such arguments is that morality is simply too important to be left to the individual. Where the interests of society and those of the individual conflict, law must always take the side of the former.

CONCEPT

Rule of law

The rule of law is the principle that the law should 'rule', in the sense that it establishes a framework to which all conduct and behaviour must conform. This requirement applies equally to all the members of society, be they private citizens or government officials. As such, rule of law is a core liberal-democratic principle. In continental Europe, it has often been enshrined in the German concept of the *Rechtsstaat*, a state based on law. In the USA, the rule of law is closely linked to the status of the constitution as 'higher' law and the doctrine of 'due process'. In the UK, it is grounded in common law and implies that a codified constitution is not needed.

'content' of the legal system: criminal law is an example. Secondary rules, on the other hand, are rules that confer powers on the institutions of government. They lay down how primary rules are made, enforced and adjudicated, thus determining their validity.

In view of the crucial role that law plays in regulating social behaviour, no one can doubt that it has immense political significance. Nevertheless, questions about the actual and desirable relationship between law and politics – reflecting on the nature of law, and its function and proper extent – have provoked deep controversy. Much of our understanding of law derives from liberal theory. This portrays law as the essential guarantee of civilized and orderly existence, drawing heavily on social-contract theory (see p. 62). In the absence of the state and a system of law – that is, in the 'state of nature' – each individual is at liberty to abuse or threaten every other individual. The role of law, then, is to protect each member of society from his or her fellow members, thereby preventing their rights and liberties from being encroached on. However, the notion that the central purpose of law is to protect freedom has provoked deep controversy (see p. 343).

As this protection extends throughout society and to every one of its members, law has, liberals insist, a neutral character. Law is therefore 'above' politics, and a strict separation between law and politics must be maintained to prevent the law favouring the state over the individual, the rich over the poor, men over women, the ethnic majority over ethnic minorities, and so on. This is why liberals place such a heavy emphasis on the universal authority of law, embodied in the principle of the rule of law. This view of law also has significant implications for the judiciary, whose task it is to interpret law and adjudicate between parties to a dispute. Notably, judges must be independent, in the sense that they are 'above' or 'outside' the machinery of government and not subject to political influence.

THE JUDICIARY

The judiciary is the branch of government that is empowered to decide legal disputes. The central function of judges is therefore to adjudicate on the meaning of law, in the sense that they interpret or 'construct' law. The significance of this role varies from state to state and from system to system. However, it is particularly important in states with codified constitutions, where it extends to the interpretation of the constitution itself, and so allows judges to arbitrate in disputes between major institutions of government, or between the state and the individual.

The significance of the judiciary has also been enhanced by the growing importance of international law. The International Court of Justice in the Hague (formally known as the World Court) is the judicial arm of the United Nations. It provides a forum in which disputes between states can be settled, although, as international law respects the principle of sovereignty, this requires the consent of all parties. The International Criminal Court (ICC) has revived the idea established by the 1945–46 Nuremberg trials of **war crimes** or 'crimes against humanity'. The ICC has indicted and arrested a number of people for mass crimes including, in 2001, the former Yugoslav president, Slobodan Milosevic. In

● **War crimes**: Acts that violate international conventions on the conduct of war, usually involving either aggressive warfare or atrocities carried out against civilians or prisoners of war.

Neutrality

Neutrality is the absence of any form of partisanship or commitment; it consists of a refusal to 'take sides'. In international relations, neutrality is a legal condition through which a state declares its non-involvement in a conflict or war. As a professional principle, applied to the likes of judges, civil servants, the military and other public officials, it implies, strictly speaking, the absence of political sympathies and ideological leanings. In practice, the less exacting requirement of impartiality is usually applied. This allows that political sympathies may be held as long as these do not intrude into, or conflict with, professional or public responsibilities.

addition, there are international courts with regional jurisdiction, such as the EU's European Court of Justice in Luxembourg and the (unrelated) European Court of Human Rights in Strasbourg.

One of the chief characteristics of the judiciary – in liberal-democratic systems, its defining characteristic – is that judges are strictly independent and non-political actors. Indeed, the ability of judges to be 'above' politics is normally seen as the vital guarantee of a separation between law and politics. However, this image of the judiciary is always misleading. The judiciary is best thought of as a political, not merely a legal, institution. As central figures in the legal process, judges play a vital role in such undeniably political activities as conflict resolution and the maintenance of state authority. Although judges are clearly political, in the sense that their judgements have an undeniable political impact, debate about the political significance of the judiciary revolves around two more controversial questions. First, are judges political in that their actions are shaped by political considerations or pressures? Second, do judges make policy in the sense that they encroach on the proper responsibilities of politicians?

Are judges political?

Certain political systems make no pretence of judicial neutrality or impartiality. For example, in orthodox communist regimes, the principle of 'socialist legality' dictated that judges interpret law in accordance with Marxism–Leninism, subject to the ideological authority of the state's communist party. Judges thus became mere functionaries who carried out the political and ideological objectives of the regime itself. This was most graphically demonstrated by the 'show trials' of the 1930s in the USSR. The German courts during the Nazi period were similarly used as instruments of ideological repression and political persecution. In other states, however, judges have been expected to observe strict political neutrality. In states that subscribe to any form of liberal constitutionalism, the authority of law is linked to its non-political character, which, in turn, is based on the assumption that the law is interpreted by independent and impartial judges.

External bias

Judges may be political in two senses: they may be subject to external bias or to internal bias. External bias is derived from the influence that political bodies, such as parties, the assembly and government, are able to exert on the judiciary. Internal bias stems from the prejudices and sympathies of judges themselves, particularly from those that intrude into the process of judicial decision-making. External bias is supposedly kept at bay by respect for the principle of **judicial independence**. In most liberal democracies, the independence of the judiciary is protected by their security of tenure (the fact that they cannot be sacked), and through restrictions on the criticism of judges and court decisions. However, in practice, the independence of judges may be compromised because of the close involvement of political bodies in the process of judicial recruitment and promotion.

Judges in the USA supposedly hold office for life on condition of 'good behaviour'. Supreme Court judges, however, are appointed by the US president, and these appointments are subject to confirmation by the Senate. This process has,

● **Judicial independence:** The constitutional principle that there should be a strict separation between the judiciary and other branches of government; an application of the separation of powers.

since F. D. Roosevelt's battles with the court in the 1930s, led to a pattern of overt political appointment. Presidents select justices on the basis of party affiliation and ideological disposition, and, as occurred to Robert Bork in 1987, the Senate may reject them on the same grounds. The liberal tendencies of the Warren Court (1954–69), and the more conservative inclinations of the Burger Court (1969–86), the Rehnquist Court (1986–2005) and the Roberts Court (since 2005), have thus been brought about largely through external political pressure.

Politics may also intrude into the US judiciary due to the practice found in most states of choosing some, most or all of their judges through contestable popular elections, some of which are openly partisan. Supporters of this practice argue that democracy requires that the electoral principle should apply as much to those who interpret law as to those who make law. Otherwise, judges are accountable to no one, being able to act according to their own views and preferences, rather than those of the public. On the other hand, critics of elected judges point out not only that elections inevitably draw judges into partisan politics, and so make judicial neutrality impossible, but also that selecting judges on the basis of popularity may compromise their expertise and specialist knowledge.

UK judges were traditionally appointed by the government of the day, senior judges being appointed by the prime minister on the advice of the Lord Chancellor. However, the 2005 Constitutional Reform Act not only removed the appointment of judges from the political arena by establishing a Judicial Appointments Commission, but also significantly strengthened judicial independence through the creation, in 2009, of the UK Supreme Court, in place of the appellate committee of the House of Lords. The *Conseil Constitutionnel* (Constitutional Court) in France, which is empowered to examine the constitutionality of laws and can, thus, restrain both the assembly and the executive, is subject to particularly marked political influence. Its members have, in the main, been politicians with long experience, rather than professional judges. The French president and the presidents of the National Assembly and the Senate each select one-third of the members of the Court, party affiliation often being a significant factor.

In Japan, the Supreme Court is effectively appointed by the cabinet, with the high judges being selected by the emperor on the nomination of the cabinet. Prolonged Liberal-Democratic Party (LDP) domination in the post-World War II period meant, however, that the LDP packed the Court with its own supporters, ensuring that it remained firmly subordinate to the Diet. One of the consequences of this was that, despite widespread **gerrymandering** in favour of the LDP in rural districts, the Supreme Court was never prepared to nullify election results, even when, as in 1983, elections were declared to be unconstitutional because of the disproportionate allocation of seats (Eccleston, 1989).

Internal bias

● **Gerrymandering**: The manipulation of electoral boundaries so as to achieve political advantage for a party or candidate.

Judicial independence is not the only issue; bias may creep in through the values and culture of the judiciary as easily as through external pressure. From this perspective, the key factor is not so much *how* judges are recruited, but *who* is recruited. A long-standing socialist critique of the judiciary holds that it articulates the dominant values of society, and so acts to defend the existing political

Judicial review

The power of judicial review is the power of the judiciary to 'review', and possibly invalidate, the laws, decrees and the actions of other branches of government. In its classical sense, the principle stems from the existence of a codified constitution and allows the courts to strike down as 'unconstitutional' actions that are deemed to be incompatible with the constitution. A more modest form of judicial review, found in uncodified systems, is restricted to the review of executive actions in the light of ordinary law using the principle of *ultra vires* (beyond the powers) to determine whether a body has acted outside its powers.

and social order. This tendency is underpinned by the social exclusivity of judges and by the peculiar status and respect that the judicial profession is normally accorded. Griffith (2010) argued that this conservative bias is particularly prominent in the UK's higher judiciary, and that it stems from the remarkable homogeneity of senior judges, who are overwhelmingly male, white, upper-middle-class, and public school and 'Oxbridge' educated. Similar arguments have been used to suggest that judges are biased against women, racial minorities, and, indeed, any group poorly represented within its ranks.

Although the US Supreme Court has included a nominal black judge since the 1950s and in 2012 contained three female judges, its membership has generally been dominated by white Anglo-Saxon Protestants drawn from the USA's middle and upper-middle classes. On the other hand, in states such as Australia attempts have been made to counter such tendencies by making the judiciary more socially representative. For instance, since the 1980s, Australian judges have been recruited from the ranks of academics, as well as lawyers. Nevertheless, even critics of the judiciary recognize that there is a limit to the extent to which judges can be made socially representative. To achieve a judiciary that is a microcosm of the larger society, it would be necessary for criteria such as experience and professional competence to be entirely ignored in the appointment of judges.

Do judges make policy?

The image of judges as simple appliers of law has always been a myth. Judges cannot apply the so-called 'letter of the law', because no law, legal term or principle has a single, self-evident meaning. In practice, judges *impose* meaning on law through a process of 'construction' that forces them to choose amongst a number of possible meanings or interpretations. In this sense, *all* law is judge-made law. Clearly, however, the range of discretion available to judges in this respect, and the significance of the laws that they invest with meaning, vary considerably. Two factors are crucial here. The first is the clarity and detail with which law is specified. Generally, broadly-framed laws or constitutional principles allow greater scope for judicial interpretation. The second factor is the existence of a codified or 'written' constitution. The existence of such a document significantly enhances the status of the judiciary, investing it with the power of judicial review. In the case of the US Supreme Court, it has turned the court into, as Robert Dahl (1956) put it, 'a political institution, an institution, that is to say, for arriving at decisions on controversial questions of national policy'.

The Supreme Court's significance as a policy-maker has been evident throughout US history. In the late nineteenth century and early twentieth century, for example, Supreme Courts wedded to *laissez-faire* principles used the doctrine of **due process** to strike down welfare and social legislation: in particular, the court blocked much of Roosevelt's New Deal programme in the early 1930s. It was only after the so-called 'court revolution' of 1937, following the appointment of pro-New Deal judges such as Hugo Black and William O'Douglas, that the shift to economic and social intervention gained judicial endorsement. During the 1950s and 1960s, the court, under Chief Justice Earl Warren, made landmark liberal decisions such as *Brown* v. *Board of Education* (1954), which rejected segregation in schools as unconstitutional, and *Baker v Carr* (1962), which required that legislative constituencies in the USA be of uniform size.

● **Due process:** Conduct of legal proceedings strictly in accordance with establised rules and principles, linked to ensuring a fair trial.

Bush v Gore: the US Supreme Court substitutes itself for the electorate?

Events: The 2000 US presidential election, held on 7 November, was contested between Vice President Al Gore, the Democratic candidate, and Texas Governor George W. Bush, for the Republicans. Having initially conceded defeat in a close-fought election, Gore retracted his concession in the early hours of 8 November, as uncertainty grew over the result of the election in Florida, whose 25 electoral college votes would have given either candidate the overall majority needed to win. Doubts of various kinds had surfaced about the accuracy of the count, not least linked to the working of the punch-card ballots used in Florida. In these circumstances, Gore requested hand recounts of votes in four of Florida's counties, and the Florida Supreme Court eventually ordered a state-wide recount of ballots. The US Supreme Court heard two cases, both known as *Bush v Gore*. In the first, the Court granted a temporary delay in enforcing the Florida Supreme Court's order and, in the second, which concluded on 12 December, the Court ordered that the Florida recount be stopped. Gore, as a result, withdrew his objections to the electoral outcome and Bush duly became the 43rd president of the USA. It is generally believed that had the state-wide recount gone ahead, Gore would have won Florida and the presidential election.

Significance: The Supreme Court's capacity to terminate the election of 2000 and, in essence, deliver the presidency to George W. Bush derives from the system of judicial review that operates in the USA. The US constitution makes no mention of judicial review, but, arguably, embodies the logic that made its emergence inevitable. As the constitution laid down legal standards for the behaviour of government institutions, these needed to be supervised or policed, and the judiciary (more specifically, the Supreme Court) was the only institution equipped for this purpose. In the case of *Bush v Gore*, the Supreme Court determined that the actions of the Florida Supreme Court were not compatible with the US constitution because they did not afford Bush the 'equal protection of the laws', as stipulated in the Fourteenth Amendment. The judgement has been defended on the grounds that, in a context of deep and continuing uncertainty, the matter simply had to be resolved. In blocking the Florida recounts, the Supreme Court was acting to bring an end to a damaging period of political insecurity. The exceptional nature of the case was acknowledged in the ruling itself, which stipulated that it should not be used as a precedent for future cases.

However, the Supreme Court has been accused of 'judicial misbehaviour' on at least three grounds. First, many have argued that the Court simply overreached itself. Not only has its interpretation of the equal protection clause of the Fourteenth Amendment been questioned, but a belief in states' rights, embodied in the Tenth Amendment, would suggest that the matter should have been settled not by the US Supreme Court, but by the Florida Supreme Court. Second, given the profound implications of the judgement and the deep controversy surrounding it, the Court demonstrated worrying divisions, the split decision, 5–4, meaning that the outcome was determined by a single vote. Previous landmark judgements have usually been decided unanimously. Third, and most seriously, it has been claimed that the ruling was motivated by considerations of partisan political advantage. Each of the five Justices who supported it had been appointed by Republican presidents and were judicial conservatives, who usually supported states' rights and, above all, judicial restraint. Critics have therefore suggested that these Justices had either acted to promote the advantage of a particular political party, or that, by installing a Republican rather than a Democrat in the White House, they were increasing the chances of further conservative appointments to the Court in the future.

In many cases, the Supreme Court was ahead of Congress and the presidency, often paving the way for later legislation, as in the case of the civil rights reforms of the mid-1960s. Similarly, the Supreme Court upheld the constitutionality of abortion in *Roe* v. *Wade* (1973), at a time when elective institutions refused to address such a deeply controversial issue. Although the **judicial activism** of this period subsequently subsided, reflecting the impact of the conservative appointments of Republican presidents such as Nixon, Reagan and George Bush Sr, the Court continued to exert influence; for instance, in allowing the gradual reintroduction of capital punishment and growing restrictions on the right to abortion. Nevertheless, perhaps the most politically significant of Supreme Court judgments came in December 2000, when the court effectively resolved the disputed presidential election in favour of George W. Bush (see p. 348).

If judges are policy-makers, they must operate as part of the broader machinery of government and within constraints established by the political culture and public opinion. The difficulties the judiciary may encounter in fulfilling its role as guardian of the constitution were demonstrated by the battle between Indira Gandhi and the Indian courts in the 1970s. Despite its written constitution, the balance between US-style judicial review and Westminster-style parliamentary sovereignty in India has never been fully resolved. Amid mounting criticism of Prime Minister Gandhi's autocratic leadership style, in June 1975 the Indian High Court declared her guilty of electoral malpractice and disqualified her from political office for five years. Although the Indian Supreme Court suspended the disqualification pending an appeal, within days Gandhi declared a 'state of emergency', allowing for the arrest of hundreds of her political opponents and for the introduction of stiff censorship. Even though the judiciary was able to restore its authority after the lifting of the emergency in March 1977, it has subsequently practised greater self-restraint and has been reluctant to challenge the government of the day so openly again.

The view that judges are policy-makers is less persuasive in the absence of a codified constitution. Where the constitution is unwritten, judges lack a legal standard against which to measure the constitutionality of political acts and government decisions. The UK Parliament is therefore sovereign, and the judiciary is subordinate to it. Before the Glorious Revolution of 1688 in the UK, judges were prepared to set aside acts of Parliament when they violated common law principles, as occurred in *Dr. Bonham's Case* (1610). The revolution, however, established the supremacy of statute law (law made by Parliament), a principle that has only subsequently been challenged by the courts in relation to the higher authority of EU law. The power of judicial review can, nevertheless, be applied in a narrower sense in the case of executive powers that are derived from enabling legislation. In such cases, the principle of *ultra vires* can be used to declare actions of ministers, for instance, unlawful. Indeed, since the 1980s there has been a marked upsurge in judicial activism in the UK, highlighting the growing political significance of judges. This growing activism reflects both the spread of a 'human rights culture' within the UK judiciary and anxiety about the misuse of executive power that flows from the absence of effective constitutional checks and balances in the UK. The Human Rights Act (1998) has bolstered this trend by widening judges' capacity to protect civil liberties in relation to terrorism and other issues, often leading to clashes with ministers.

● **Judicial activism**: The willingness of judges to arbitrate in political disputes, as opposed to merely saying what the law means.

● *Ultra vires*: (Latin) Literally, beyond the powers; acts that fall outside the scope of a body's authority.

SUMMARY

- A constitution is a set of rules that seek to establish the duties, powers and functions of the institutions of government and define the relationship between the state and the individual. Constitutions can be classified on the basis of the status of their rules, how easily their rules can be changed, the degree to which their rules are observed in practice, and the content of their rules and the institutional structure that they establish.

- Constitutions do not serve a single or simple purpose. Amongst their functions are that they empower states by defining a sphere of independent authority, establish a set of values, ideals and goals for a society, bring stability, order and predictability to the workings of government, protect individuals from the state, and legitimize regimes in the eyes of other states and their people.

- There is an imperfect relationship between the content of a constitution and political practice. Constitutions 'work' in certain conditions, notably when they correspond to, and are supported by, the political culture, when they are respected by rulers and accord with the interests and values of dominant groups, and when they are adaptable and can remain relevant in changing political circumstances.

- Questions about the actual and desirable relationship between law and politics are deeply controversial. Liberal theory, sensitive to civil liberties and human rights, tends to emphasize the limited province of law operating simply as a means of guaranteeing orderly existence. The conservative view, however, emphasizes the link between law and social stability, acknowledging that law has an important role to play in enforcing public morality.

- The separation of law from politics is accomplished through attempts to make the judiciary independent and impartial. Judicial independence, however, is threatened by the close involvement of political bodies in the process of judicial recruitment and promotion. Judicial impartiality is compromised by the fact that nowhere are judges representatives of the larger society. In western polyarchies, for instance, they are overwhelmingly male, white, materially privileged and relatively old.

- As judges impose meaning on law, they cannot but be involved in the policy process. The extent of their influence varies according to the clarity and detail with which the law is specified and the scope available for judicial interpretation, and according to the existence or otherwise of a codified or written constitution, which invests in judges the power of judicial review.

Questions for discussion

- How useful is a constitution as a guide to political practice?
- What factors determine the level of respect that rulers show for their constitution?
- Are uncodified constitutions doomed to be ineffective?
- Do codified constitutions and bills of rights merely lead to the tyranny of the judiciary?
- Should law be rooted in 'higher' moral principles?
- Is it desirable that law be separate from politics, and if so, why?
- How scrupulously is judicial independence maintained in practice?
- Does it matter that the social composition of the judiciary does not reflect that of society at large?
- Should judges be elected?

Further reading

Alexander, L. (ed.), *Constitutionalism: Philosophical Foundations* (2001). Stimulating reflections on theories and ideas that underpin constitutionalism.

Griffith, J. A. G., *The Politics of the Judiciary* (2010). A stimulating and provocative study of why the judiciary cannot act neutrally, from a UK standpoint.

Lane, J.-E., *Constitutions and Political Theory* (2011). A thorough and coherent discussion of key debates related to constitutions and constitutionalism.

Shapiro, M. and A. Stone Sweet, *On Law, Politics and Judicialization* (2002). An authoritatve analysis of the causes and consequences of the 'judicialization of politics' in a wide range of empirical settings.

CHAPTER 16

Public Policy and the Bureaucracy

'Bureaucracy is a giant mechanism operated by pygmies.'

HONORÉ DE BALZAC, *Epigrams*

PREVIEW

In a sense, policy is the aspect of politics that concerns most people. In crude terms, policy consists of the 'outputs' of the political process. It reflects the impact of government on society; that is, its ability to make things better or make things worse. Indeed, since the 1960s and 1970s a distinctive area of study has developed: policy analysis. This sets out to examine how policy is initiated, formulated and implemented, and how the policy process can be improved. At a deeper level, policy analysis reflects on how and why decisions are made, the policy process being, in effect, a linked series of decisions, or bundles of decisions. Particular debate nevertheless surrounds the extent to which these decisions are rationally-based. However, studying the policy process often means, in practice, studying the bureaucracy, the massed ranks of civil servants and public officials who are charged with the execution of public policy. As government has grown and the breadth of its responsibilities has expanded, bureaucracies have come to play an increasingly important role in political life. No longer can civil servants be dismissed as mere administrators or policy implementers; instead, they may dominate the policy process, and even, sometimes, *run* their countries. A reality of 'rule by the officials' may thus lie behind the façade of representation and democratic accountability. The control of bureaucratic power is therefore one of the most pressing problems in modern politics, and one that no political system has found easy to solve. Concern about how bureaucracies are organized has also become more acute as the image of bureaucratic efficiency and rationality has been challenged by critics who allege that civil servants are motivated primarily by career self-interest. This charge has led to radical attempts to restructure the administrative state.

KEY ISSUES

- How are decisions on public policy made?
- What are the key stages in the policy process, and what is their significance?
- What are the functions of bureaucracies?
- How are bureaucracies organized? How should they be organized?
- Why are bureaucrats so powerful?
- How, and how successfully, are bureaucracies controlled?

CONCEPT

Policy

A policy, in a general sense, is a plan of action. To designate something as a 'policy' implies that a formal decision has been made, giving official sanction to a particular course of action. Public policy can therefore be seen as the formal or stated decisions of government bodies. However, policy is better understood as the linkage between intentions, actions and results. At the level of *intentions*, policy is reflected in what government says it will do. At the level of *actions*, policy is reflected in what government actually does. At the level of *results*, policy is reflected in the impact of government on the larger society.

THE POLICY PROCESS

The policy process relates to the mechanisms through which public (government) policy is made. Policy-making is a *process* in two senses. First, it involves a linked series of actions or events. These commence with the germination of ideas and the initiation of proposals; continue with some form of debate, analysis and evaluation; and conclude with the making of formal decisions and their implementation through designated actions. Policy-making is therefore similar to the process of digestion in the human body: it links certain 'inputs' to particular 'outputs'. Second, it is a process in the sense that it distinguishes the 'how' of government from the 'what' of government; that is, it focuses on the way in which policy is made (process), rather than on the substance of policy itself and its consequences (product). The first section of this chapter considers how decisions are made, and examines the significance of the various stages in the policy process. The subsequent sections reflect on the role and significance of bureaucracies in the policy process.

Theories of decision-making

The making of **decisions**, and specifically of bundles of decisions, is clearly central to the policy process. Although policy-making also relates to the acts of initiation and implementation, the making of decisions and reaching of conclusions is usually seen as its key feature. However, it may be difficult to establish how and why decisions are made. Decisions are undoubtedly made in different ways by individuals and by groups, within small bodies and within large organizations, and within democratic and authoritarian structures. Nevertheless, a number of general theories of political decision-making have been advanced. The most important of these are the following:

- rational actor models
- incremental models
- bureaucratic organization models
- belief system models.

Rational actor models

Decision-making models that emphasize human rationality have generally been constructed on the basis of economic theories that have themselves been derived from utilitarianism (see p. 353). Such ideas provide the basis for public-choice theories (see p. 252), developed by thinkers such as Anthony Downs (1957), and enthusiastically taken up by the New Right. At the heart of such theories lies the notion of so-called 'economic man', a model of human nature that stresses the self-interested pursuit of material satisfaction, calculated in terms of **utility**. In this light, decisions can be seen to be reached using the following procedures:

- The nature of the problem is identified.
- An objective or goal is selected on the basis of an ordering of individual preferences.

● **Decision**: An act of choice; a selection from a range of options.

● **Utility**: A measure of satisfaction, based on the quantity of pleasure over pain (usually) derived from material consumption.

Utilitarianism

Utilitarianism is a moral philosophy that was developed by Jeremy Bentham (see p. 96) and James Mill (1773–1836). It claimed to propound a reliable, even scientific, ethical theory by equating 'good' with pleasure or happiness, and 'evil' with pain or unhappiness. Individuals are thus assumed to act so as to maximize pleasure and minimize pain, these being calculated in terms of utility, or use value. A principle of general or social utility can be used to evaluate laws, institutions and political systems in the form of 'the greatest happiness for the greatest number'.

● The available means of achieving this objective are evaluated in terms of their effectiveness, reliability, costs and so on.

● A decision is made through the selection of the means most likely to secure the desired end.

This type of process assumes both that clear-cut objectives exist, and that human beings are able to pursue them in a rational and consistent manner. For this to occur, utility must be homogeneous: it must be possible to compare the amount of satisfaction (pleasure or happiness) that each action would bring with that which would result from any other action.

The rational actor model is attractive, in part, because it reflects how most people believe decisions *should* be made. Certainly, politicians and others are strongly inclined to portray their actions as both goal-orientated, and the product of careful thought and deliberation. When examined more closely, however, rational calculation may not appear to be a particularly convincing model of decision-making. In the first place, the model is more easily applied to individuals, who may have an ordered set of preferences, than it is to groups, within which there are likely to be a number of conflicting objectives. Organizations may therefore be said to make rational decisions only if they are highly centralized and possess a strict command structure.

A second problem is that, in practice, decisions are often made on the basis of inadequate and, sometimes, inaccurate information, and the benefits of various actions may, in any case, not be comparable. Is it possible, for instance, to compare the 'costs' of raising taxes with those of reducing health care provision? Such difficulties encouraged Herbert Simon (1983) to develop the notion of 'bounded rationality'. This acknowledges that, as it is impossible to analyse and select all possible courses of action, decision-making is essentially an act of compromising between differently valued and imprecisely calculated outcomes. Simon described this process as 'satisficing'. The final drawback of rational actor models is that they ignore the role of perception; that is, the degree to which actions are shaped by beliefs and assumptions about reality, rather than by reality itself. Little or no importance is thus attached to the values and ideological leanings of decision-makers.

Incremental models

Incrementalism is usually portrayed as the principal alternative to rational decision-making. David Braybrooke and Charles Lindblom (1963) termed this model 'disjointed incrementalism', neatly summed up by Lindblom (1959) as the 'science of muddling through'. This position holds that, in practice, decisions tend to be made on the basis of inadequate information and low levels of understanding, and this discourages decision-makers from pursuing bold and innovative courses of action. Policy-making is therefore a continuous, exploratory process: lacking overriding goals and clear-cut ends, policy-makers tend to operate within an existing pattern or framework, adjusting their position in the light of feedback in the form of information about the impact of earlier decisions. Indeed, incrementalism may suggest a strategy of avoidance or evasion, policy-makers being inclined to move away from problems, rather than trying to solve them.

● **Incrementalism:** The theory that decisions are made not in the light of clear-cut objectives, but through small adjustments dictated by changing circumstances.

Lindblom's case for incrementalism is normative, as well as descriptive. In addition to providing a more accurate account of how decisions are made in the real world, he argued that this approach also has the merit of allowing for flexibility and the expression of divergent views. In this sense, it has a distinctly anti-utopian character and is well-suited to policy-making in pluralist democracies: 'muddling through' at least implies responsiveness and flexibility, consultation and compromise. However, the model has also been criticized as profoundly conservative, in that it justifies a bias against innovation and in favour of inertia. Policy-makers who embrace incrementalism are more likely to be concerned with day-to-day problems than with indulging in long-term visionary thinking. Their energy is channelled into keeping the ship on course, not into reflecting on where that course is leading.

A further difficulty is that incrementalism sheds little light on those political decisions that are radical, even revolutionary, in character. For instance, Stalin's decision to launch the USSR's First Five Year Plan in 1928, Castro's decision to seize power in Cuba in 1959, and even Thatcher's decision to 'roll back the state' in the UK in the 1980s, can hardly be described as incremental adjustments. In view of such difficulties, Amitai Etzioni (1967) proposed the idea of '**mixed scanning**', which attempts to bridge the gap between the rational approach and incrementalism. Mixed scanning allows for decision-making being carried out in two distinct phases. First, decision-makers broadly evaluate, or scan, all the available policy options in terms of their effectiveness in meeting pre-existing objectives. Then, a narrower and more incremental approach is adopted as the details of a selected policy option are reviewed. In this way, for example, a broad decision to cut public spending must be accompanied by a series of more narrowly focused decisions relating to the specific areas or programmes that may be affected.

Bureaucratic organization models

Both rational actor and incremental models are essentially 'black box' theories of decision-making; neither pays attention to the impact that the structure of the policy-making process has on the resulting decisions. Bureaucratic or organizational models, on the other hand, try to get inside the black box by highlighting the degree to which process influences product. This approach was pioneered by Graham Allison (1971) in his examination of US and Soviet decision-making during the Cuban Missile Crisis of 1962. Two contrasting, but related, models emerged from this study. The first, usually called the 'organizational process' model, highlights the impact on decisions of the values, assumptions and regular patterns of behaviour that are found in any large organization. Rather than corresponding to rational analysis and objective evaluation, decisions are seen to reflect the entrenched culture of the government department or agency that makes them. The second theory, the 'bureaucratic politics' model, emphasizes the impact on decisions of bargaining between personnel and agencies each pursuing different perceived interests. This approach dismisses the idea of the state as a monolith united around a single view or a single interest, and suggests that decisions arise from an arena of contest in which the balance of advantage is constantly shifting.

Although these models undoubtedly draw attention to important aspects of decision-making, they also have their drawbacks. In the first place, the organiza-

● **Mixed scanning**: A way of making decisions that uses rationalistic, or high-order, processes to set a basic direction before incremental processes are employed.

(see p. 300)
tional process model allows little scope for political leadership to be imposed from above. It would be foolish, for example, to suggest that all decisions are shaped by organizational pressures and perceptions, for this would be to ignore the personal role played by F. D. Roosevelt in initiating the New Deal, or Hitler's influence on Germany's decision to invade Poland. Second, it is simplistic to suggest, as the bureaucratic politics model does, that political actors simply hold views that are based on their own position and on the interests of the organizations in which they work. Although the aphorism 'where you stand depends on where you sit' may often be applicable, personal sympathies and individual goals cannot be altogether discounted. Finally, to explain decisions entirely in terms of black-box considerations is to fail to give any weight to the external pressures that emanate from the broader economic, political and ideological context.

Belief system models

Models of decision-making that place an emphasis on the role of beliefs and ideology (see p. 28) highlight the degree to which behaviour is structured by perception. What people see and understand is, to an extent, what their concepts and values allow them, or encourage them, to see and understand. This tendency is particularly entrenched because, in most cases, it is largely unconscious. Although decision-makers may believe that they are being rational, rigorous and strictly impartial, their social and political values may act as a powerful filter, defining for them what is thinkable, what is possible, and what is desirable. Certain information and particular options are therefore not appreciated, or even considered, while other pieces of information and other courses of action feature prominently in the calculus of decision-making. Indeed, Kenneth Boulding (1956) underlined the vital importance of this process by pointing out that, without a mechanism to filter information, decision-makers would simply be overwhelmed by the sheer volume of data confronting them.

However, there are different views about the origin and nature of this filtering process. Robert Jervis (1968), for instance, drew attention to evidence of consistent misperception on the part of decision-makers in international affairs. In his view, this stemmed largely from ethnocentrism. The inclination of Anthony Eden and the UK government to view General Nasser as a 'second Hitler' during the 1956 Suez Crisis, and the tendency of the USA in 1959 to regard Fidel Castro as a Marxist revolutionary, may be examples of this phenomenon. Irving Janis (1972), on the other hand, suggested that many decisions in the field of international relations could be explained in terms of what he called 'groupthink'. This helps to explain how and why contrary or inconvenient views may be squeezed out of consideration.

An attempt to combine different approaches to decision-making that takes account of the impact of belief systems has been made by Paul Sabatier (1988). Sabatier's principal concern was to explain how policy changes occur. In particular, he drew attention to the role of 'policy subsystems'; that is, collections of people who in some way contribute to influencing policy in a particular area. A policy system may include not only interlocking groups of politicians, civil servants and interest groups, but also researchers, academics and journalists concerned with that area, sometimes seen as an **epistemic**

CONCEPT

Ethnocentrism

Ethnocentrism has two related meanings. First, it refers to a personality type characterized by a rigid, implicitly authoritarian belief in the superiority of his or her own group or people. Ethnocentrism in this sense overlaps with racialism (see p. 120). Second, it refers to a mode of understanding in which the actions and intentions of other groups or peoples are understood through the application of values and theories drawn from the observer's own culture. In this sense, ethnocentrism is a (typically unconscious) bias that results from a failure to appreciate the significance of cultural differentiation.

● **Groupthink**: The phenomenon in which psychological and professional pressures conspire to encourage a group of decision-makers to adopt a unified and coherent position.

● **Epistemic community**: A network of professionals who are recognized to possess expertise and policy-relevant knowledge in a particular issue area.

community. Sabatier maintained that, within policy subsystems, 'advocacy coalitions' emerge that comprise collections of individuals who share broadly similar beliefs and values. These beliefs, nevertheless, operate on three different levels:

- deep core beliefs (fundamental moral or philosophical principles)
- near-core beliefs (policy preferences)
- secondary beliefs (views about implementation or application).

The importance of such beliefs is that they provide what Sabatier called the 'glue' of politics, binding people together on the basis of shared values and preferences. However, while core beliefs are highly resistant to change, a greater measure of disagreement and flexibility is usually found at the near-core and secondary levels. Using this framework, Sabatier proposed that policy change could be understood largely in terms of the shifting balance of forces within a policy subsystem, in particular through the dominance of one advocacy coalition over others. This process may, nevertheless, be seen to be rational insofar as debate within a belief system, and rivalry between belief systems, promotes 'policy-orientated learning'.

In the hands of Marxists and feminists, however, such ideas can be used to draw very different conclusions (Hann, 1995). Marxists have argued that the core beliefs within any policy subsystem – or, indeed, amongst policy-makers and opinion-formers at large – are structured by ruling-class ideology and so favour the interests of dominant economic interests. Feminists, for their part, may argue that a preponderance of men amongst policy-makers ensures that the 'glue' of politics is provided by patriarchal ideas and values. This results in policy biases that help to sustain a system of male power.

Stages in the policy process

Policy-making cannot be understood simply in terms of how decisions are made. Policy involves not only clusters of decisions, in the sense of a number of related decisions concerning a particular policy area, but also different *kinds* of decisions. For instance, in the first place, there is the 'decision to make a decision'. Such decisions arise from the perception that there are problems to solve and **issues** to address: in short, 'something must be done'. The policy process then moves on to a different set of decisions about exactly *what* should be done, *how* it should be done, and *when* it should be done. The matter does not stop there, however. Even when the 'doing' has been done and the decisions have been put into effect, other questions emerge and other decisions must be taken. These relate to whether policy outcomes match policy intentions, and whether the content of policy, as well as the process of decision-making, can be improved in the future. The policy process can thus be broken down into four distinct stages:

● **Issue**: A matter recognized as part of the policy agenda, over which there is public debate or disagreement.

- policy initiation
- policy formulation
- policy implementation
- policy evaluation.

Policy initiation

Where does policy come from? How do policy proposals arise in the first place? Such questions are significant not only because policy must start somewhere (without initiation there can be no formulation, implementation, and so on), but also because this stage in the policy process structures all subsequent debate, discussion and decision-making. Policy initiation, then, is crucial, in that it sets the political agenda both by defining certain problems as issues and by determining how those issues are to be addressed. Why, for example, did environmental protection, largely ignored up to that point, arise on the political agenda in the 1980s, and how did this occur? Also, why has unemployment, commonly understood in the 1950s and 1960s to imply a need to boost public spending, come to be linked with ideas such as labour flexibility and the weakening of trade union power? Why do other political options (for example, the extension of workers' self-management) fail to become issues at all?

The difficulty of studying policy initiation is that policy can originate in literally any part of the political system. Policy can stem 'from above' – that is, from political leaders, cabinets, government agencies and so forth; and it can arise 'from below', through pressure from public opinion, the mass media (see p. 179), political parties (see p. 222), interest groups (see p. 247), 'think tanks' and the like. In the form of political leadership, policy initiation consists of mobilizing support for initiatives emanating from the personal vision of the leader, or the ideological priorities of a ruling party or group. This is most clearly seen in cases of transformational leadership (exemplified by Lenin and the Bolsheviks in Russia, Hitler and the Nazis in Germany, as discussed in Chapter 13).

However, political leaders are rarely original thinkers and are seldom the source of genuine policy innovation. It is in this area that writers, academics and philosophers seemingly unconnected with the world of practical politics may play a vital role in the process of policy initiation by developing 'core' values and theories, later developed into specific policy proposals by leaders and parties. Much of the economic policy in developed western states during the early post-World War II period emanated from the ideas of John Maynard Keynes (see p. 137). Similarly, New Right policies aimed at 'rolling back the state', reducing taxes, targeting welfare spending and so on, originally sprang from the writings of, for example, Friedrich von Hayek (see p. 37) and Milton Friedman (see p. 138).

Policy initiation 'from below' is significant in all political systems. As the UK prime minister, 1957–63, Harold Macmillan replied, when asked about the decisive factors in political life, 'Events, dear boy, events'. These events can range from strikes, riots and natural disasters to stock market crashes in foreign states and investment decisions made by transnational corporations. As a general rule, however, the more democratic and pluralistic the political system, the more significant are bottom-up pressures on policy initiation. Public opinion clearly plays a significant role in this process, insofar as regular and competitive elections force aspiring leaders to form policy proposals that take account of popular concerns and aspirations. However, these concerns and aspirations often remain shapeless and unformed until they are articulated by groups claiming to represent sections of the public.

The media undoubtedly make a major contribution to this, both by selecting and prioritizing the information available to the public, and by digesting and

CONCEPT

Policy network

A policy network (or policy community) is a systematic set of relationships between political actors who share a common interest or general orientation in a particular area. These relationships typically cut across formal institutional arrangements and the divide between government and non-governmental bodies, and are particularly significant in the process of policy initiation. A policy network may therefore embrace government officials, key legislators, well-placed lobbyists, sympathetic academics, leading journalists and others.

● **Agenda setting**: The ability to structure policy debate by controlling which issues are discussed or establishing a priority amongst them.

interpreting it through the process of editorialization. Political parties and interest groups also play a key role in **agenda setting**. Opposition parties, for example, do not merely criticize government policy; they also develop alternative policies in an attempt to appear to be viable parties of government. Interest groups, for their part, highlight a broad array of grievances and concerns, promote causes and ideals, and give expression to the interests of diverse groups and sections of society. Since the 1970s, researchers have tended to play down the role of formal, representative institutions, and to give greater prominence to the informal processes through which policy is initiated and developed. This highlights the importance of policy networks.

Policy formulation

Once an issue, or set of issues, is on the political agenda, a process of detailed elaboration and analysis is required to develop systematic policy proposals. Conventionally seen as the most crucial stage in the policy process, policy formulation entails not only the translation of broad proposals into specific and detailed recommendations, but also the filtering out of proposals, and perhaps even the fundamental recasting of the issue under consideration. In their analysis of the policy cycle, Hogwood and Gunn (1984) identified a number of stages in the formulation process. The first stage involves decisions about how to decide; that is, decisions about which mechanisms or procedures and which political actors should be involved in the analysis and elaboration of policy. These decisions are clearly vital, as they determine the sympathies and interests that will be brought to bear on the policy as it is developed and discussed. The second stage involves issue definition and forecasting. This stage allows considerable scope for reinterpretation, as those who formulate policy may view 'the problem' very differently from those who raised the issue in the first place. Third, there is the setting of objectives and priorities. Although public opinion and the concerns of bodies such as the media, political parties and interest groups are likely to influence objective setting, there is, of course, no guarantee that the priorities identified by priority formulators will be the same as those advanced by policy initiators.

Finally, there is the analysis and review of the policy options, leading to the selection of a preferred option. This, in effect, means that an authoritative decision is taken. Various factors are likely to be taken into account at this stage in policy formulation, the political and electoral ramifications of particular options being no less important than considerations of administrative efficiency and effectiveness. It is important to note, however, that the final decision, which brings the formulation process to an end, may be little more than a formality, decisive argument and debate having happened at a much earlier stage. Cabinets, legislatures and international summits thus often ratify or 'rubber stamp' decisions that have effectively been *made* elsewhere.

It would be foolish to imply that the task of formulation has the same character in different systems and different states. Richardson (1984) attempted to unravel different policy-formulation processes by identifying contrasting national 'policy styles'. In particular, he drew attention to two main dimensions: whether policy formulation is based on consultation or imposition, and whether governments engage in long-term planning or react to events on a more or less day-to-day basis. In this light, Sweden and Japan can perhaps be classified as states with policy styles that broadly favour both consultation and long-term planning. In both cases, there is an elaborate and formalized system of group consultation orientated around a widely agreed set of policy objectives and priorities. On the other hand, in the USA, although the fragmented nature of the federal government requires a high level of consensus for policy to be accepted, it also virtually rules out longer-term planning, and so entrenches a reactive, 'fire brigade' policy style.

A key feature of formulation, regardless of differences in national policy styles, is that it substantially reduces the range of actors involved in the policy process. While a broad variety of interests, groups and movements may play a role in policy initiation, policy formulation is the job of 'insiders' (government officials, key advisers, politicians and consulted groups), those who are either part of the machinery of government or have institutionalized access to it. This has left the formulation process open to a number of criticisms. One of these arises from the undue influence that civil servants supposedly exert by virtue of their role as policy advisers, examined in more detail later in the chapter. Other criticisms suggest that the tendency towards group consultation has meant that policy is shaped by powerful sectional interests, rather than by the broader public good (Olson, 1982), and that, although elected politicians oversee the policy process and make the final decisions, the process itself often guarantees that their contribution is marginal.

Policy implementation

One of the major advances made in the discipline of policy analysis has been to underline the importance of the implementation stage. Traditionally, implementation was taken for granted, being seen as an aspect of administration (see p. 363), not as a feature of politics. Analyses of the Great Society programme in the USA in the mid-1960s, however, destroyed illusions about the politics–administration divide, and graphically illustrated how far policy 'outputs' may differ from the intentions of policy-makers. For this reason, Wildavsky (1980) described policy analysis as 'speaking truth to power'. The conditions required to achieve 'perfect' implementation, in the sense of ensuring that policy is delivered exactly as intended, were outlined by Hood (1976) as follows:

- a unitary administrative system with a single line of authority to ensure central control
- uniform norms and rules that operate throughout the system
- perfect obedience or perfect control
- perfect information, perfect communication and perfect coordination
- sufficient time for administrative resources to be mobilized.

In view of the difficulty of achieving any of these conditions, let alone all of them, it is not surprising that the gap between decision and delivery is often a gulf. Indeed, not only may central control and strict obedience be unfeasible, they may also be undesirable. Although those who make policy may enjoy democratic legitimacy, those who implement it (civil servants, local government officers, teachers, doctors, police officers and so on) may have a better 'street-level' understanding of what will work and what will not work. Such considerations have led to a 'bottom-up' tradition of policy analysis that stresses the need for flexibility, as well as the value of leaving discretion in the hands of policy executors. This contrasts with the more conventional 'top-down' view of implementation that emphasizes uniformity and control. Most commentators, however, now recognize the trade-off between central control and flexibility in application as the major dilemma in the area of policy implementation (Barrett and Fudge, 1981).

Although perfect implementation may be neither possible nor desirable, most of the concerns expressed about policy implementation have focused on the dangers of flexibility in application. This was underlined by Pressman and Wildavsky's (1973) pioneering study of implementation, subtitled *How Great Expectations in Washington Are Dashed in Oakland Or Why It's Amazing That Federal Programs Work At All. . . .* Flexibility may arise for a number of reasons. One of these is that those who execute policy may not merely be anxious to use their experience and 'street-level' knowledge to ensure that implementation is effective, they may also, as public-choice theorists point out, wish to protect their career and professional interests. Civil servants and public-sector professionals will then have an obvious incentive to filter out or reinterpret aspects of public policy that seem to be threatening or inconvenient.

Other concerns about policy implementation arise less from the inadequacy of political control from above and more from the absence of consumer pressure from below. From this perspective, poor implementation, especially in the delivery of public services, results from the fact that government typically operates outside the market mechanism and is usually a monopoly supplier of its 'goods'. Civil servants, local government officers and public-sector workers can, in general, afford to be sloppy and inefficient because, unlike in private businesses, they do not have to keep the customer satisfied. An important response to this has been the emergence of the new public management (see p. 367).

Policy evaluation

The policy process culminates with the evaluation and review of policy, leading, in theory at least, to decisions being made about the maintenance, succession or termination of the policy in question. This stage completes the policy cycle, in the sense that information acquired through evaluation can be fed back into the initiation and formulation stages. This process can throw up new policy proposals, and help to refine and improve existing ones (see Figure 16.1).

As well as addressing substantive issues related to the appropriateness or effectiveness of public policy, typically carried out through the use of **cost–benefit anaylsis**, evaluation may also shed light on procedural issues, such as how the formulation stage is organized, who is consulted and when, and how implementation is controlled. However, unfortunately, despite its manifest importance, governments have usually been reluctant to allocate funds for policy evaluation. In the USA in the late 1970s, President Carter's insistence that 1 per cent of the funds for any project should be devoted to evaluation may have been a bold innovation, but it generated an enormous amount of paperwork without bringing about a noticeable improvement in either the policy process or its products. The only states that take policy evaluation seriously are the few, usually consensual, democracies that are geared to long-term planning.

● **Cost–benefit analysis**: A technique to evaluate the feasibility of a project or plan, or the impact of a policy, by quantifying its costs and benefits.

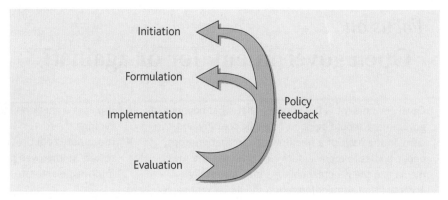

Figure 16.1   Policy-feedback process

CONCEPT

Bureaucracy

Bureaucracy (literally, 'rule by officials') is, in everyday language, a pejorative term meaning pointless administrative routine, or 'red tape'. In the social sciences, the concept of bureaucracy refers to phenomena as different as rule by non-elected officials, the process of public administration, and a rational mode of organization. According to Max Weber (see p. 82), bureaucracy is characterised by rationality, rule-governed behaviour and impersonal authority. In the field of comparative government, the term refers to the administrative machinery of the state, bureaucrats being non-elected state officials or civil servants.

Academics have taken more interest in evaluation through policy output studies, widely undertaken, especially in the USA, since the late 1960s. Empirical research is used to examine both what government does, in terms of laws, taxes, programmes and so on (outputs), and the consequences or impact of such policies (outcomes). As Dye (1995) put it, this form of policy analysis is concerned with 'who gets what'.

What is clear is that the outcomes of the policy process are often very different from what was intended by those who formulated or made policy decisions. There are many examples of this. Welfare policies designed to alleviate poverty and enable all citizens to participate in the life of the community have led, according to Le Grand (1982), to the cushioning of the middle classes, or, in the view of Murray (1984), to the growth of a welfare-dependent underclass. In their case study of the poll tax in the UK, Butler *et al.*, (1994) highlighted a catalogue of failures and oversights in government, the cabinet and Parliament that allowed a policy primarily designed to control local government spending to result in widespread civil unrest. Similarly, in the USA, the Bush administration's decision to invade Iraq in 2003 as part of the 'war on terror' (see p. 401) led to an ongoing counter-insurgency war and, in some respects, strengthened militant Islam. For many, such policy failures highlight the pressing importance of open government (see p. 362) and public accountability. For the policy process to work effectively in translating inputs into appropriate outputs, it must be open, at all times, to scrutiny and criticism. All too frequently, a culture of secrecy merely conceals incompetence, and provides scope for arbitrary and self-serving behaviour.

ROLE OF THE BUREAUCRACY

On the face of it, bureaucracies fulfil a single, but vital, function. Their primary concern is policy implementation: the execution and enforcement of the laws made by the legislature and the policies decided by the political executive. Indeed, while other functions of government (such as representation, policy-making and interest articulation) are carried out by a variety of institutions, policy implementation is solely the responsibility of civil servants, albeit working

Focus on . . .

Open government: for or against?

Open government is the principle that what happens in government should be open to public scrutiny and criticism on the basis of a free flow of information from public bodies to representative institutions, the mass media and the general public. As it is universally accepted that some information should be kept secret (on the grounds of national security, privacy and so on), open government is normally understood to imply a bias in favour of the public's 'right to know'. This is usually enshrined in a freedom of information act that forces the government to defend secrecy before the courts.

The advantages of open government include the following:

- It places a check on incompetence, corruption and tyranny.
- It promotes political argument and debate, and results in improved policy outcomes and a better-informed electorate.

Its drawbacks include the following:

- It hampers the efficiency of policy-making by exposing the formulation process to the glare of publicity.
- It discourages the consideration of unpopular, but nevertheless important, ideas and proposals.

under their political masters. Moreover, in Max Weber's (see p. 82) model of bureaucracy as a reliable, predictable and, above all, efficient means of social organization, there is a strict separation between the administrative world and the political world. According to this view, bureaucrats are simply cogs in a machine, administrators operating within a fixed hierarchy and according to clearly-defined and rational rules. Indeed, Weber warned that the strict emphasis within bureaucracy on rationality may trap people in an 'iron cage', meaning that bureaucrats become 'specialists without spirit, sensualists without heart' (Weber, 1904–5). The reality is very different, however. Despite their formal subordination and impartiality, bureaucrats exert considerable influence on the policy process, and thus fulfil a number of key functions in any political system. The most important of these are the following:

- carrying out administration
- offering policy advice
- articulating and aggregating interests
- maintaining political stability.

Functions of the bureaucracy

Administration

The core function of the bureaucracy is to implement or execute law and policy: it is thus charged with administering government business. This is why the bureaucracy is sometimes referred to as 'the administration', while the political executive is termed 'the government'. This distinction implies that a clear line can

Administration

The term administration is used in a number of ways. It can be used to refer collectively to the senior personnel in the executive branch, as in the 'Obama administration'. More generally, it means the task of coordinating and executing policy. More narrowly, administration means dealing with information and maintaining control. In this sense, it refers to the managerial duties of senior officials, as opposed to the day-to-day job of execution. 'Public administration' refers either to the mechanisms and institutions through which public policy is put into effect, or to the academic discipline that studies these mechanisms.

be drawn between the policy-making role of politicians and the policy-implementing role of bureaucrats. Certainly, the vast majority of the world's civil servants are engaged almost exclusively in administrative responsibilities that range from the implementation of welfare and social security programmes to the regulation of the economy, the granting of licences, and the provision of information and advice to citizens at home and abroad. The sizes of bureaucracies are therefore closely linked to the broader responsibilities of government. Civil service employment in the UK expanded in proportion to the role of government throughout the twentieth century. It reached a peak of 735,000 in the 1970s, but then contracted to 440,000 by 2012, owing to the pursuit of neoliberal policies from the 1980s onwards. The federal bureaucracy in the USA expanded significantly as a result of the New Deal and has now grown to approximately 2.7 million strong; and the USSR's central planning system eventually required 20 million state officials to administer it.

Nevertheless, the image of bureaucrats as mere functionaries who apply rules and carry out orders issued by others can be misleading. In the first place, since much administrative detail is, of necessity, left to officials, civil servants may be allowed significant discretion in deciding precisely how to implement policy. Second, the degree of political control exercised over the bureaucracy varies greatly from state to state. Whereas state officials in China are subject to strict and continuous party supervision, in France and Japan their high status and reputation for expertise guarantee them a considerable degree of autonomy. Third, in their capacity as policy advisers, senior civil servants at least have the ability to shape the policies that they are later required to administer.

Policy advice

The political significance of the bureaucracy stems largely from its role as the chief source of the policy information and advice available to government. This policy role helps to distinguish top-level civil servants (who have daily contact with politicians and are expected to act as policy advisers) from middle-ranking and junior-ranking civil servants (who deal with more routine administrative matters). Debate about the political significance of bureaucracies therefore tends to concentrate on this elite group of senior officials. In theory, a strict distinction can be drawn between the policy responsibilities of bureaucrats and those of politicians. Policy is supposedly *made* by politicians; bureaucrats simply offer *advice*. The policy role of civil servants therefore boils down to two functions: outlining the policy options available to ministers, and reviewing policy proposals in terms of their likely impact and consequences. The policy influence of senior officials is further restricted by the fact that they are either required to be politically neutral, as in the UK, Japan and Australia, or are subject to a system of political appointment, as in the USA.

However, there are reasons to believe that the policy role of civil servants is politically more significant than is suggested above. For instance, there is no clear distinction between making policy and offering policy advice. Quite simply, decisions are made on the basis of the information available, and this means that the content of decisions is invariably structured by the advice offered. Moreover, as the principal source of the advice available to politicians, bureaucrats effectively control the flow of information: politicians know what civil servants tell

Debating ...
Can civil servants ever be politically impartial?

Apart from political systems in which the state is committed to an explicit set of ideological goals, all or most civil servants are expected to be politically impartial, in the sense that they do not allow their own views and preferences to affect their professional activities. But is neutrality in this sense possible? Can administration be kept separate from politics, or may political impartiality be a mere pretence, concealing the pursuit of self-interest or other biases?

YES

Civil servants as rational actors. Civil servants differ fundamentally from politicians, in that they are primarily concerned with the rational and efficient organization of society, not the pursuit of partisan advantage. According to Max Weber, bureaucracy is a reliable, predictable and, above all, efficient means of social organization. Bureaucratic organization offers civil servants very little scope for personal discretion because they operate within a firmly ordered hierarchy, in which lower offices are closely supervised by higher ones; an emphasis is placed on evidence-based, rational decision-making; and appointment and advancement are determined by strictly professional criteria.

Permanence and its implications. For civil servants, permanence and professionalism go hand-in-hand. Except where spoils systems are in operation, incoming governments are confronted by the same body of officials who served the outgoing government. In these circumstances, civil servants are forced to become political chameleons, able to work loyally for whichever government happens to be in power, regardless of its political complexion or ideological leanings. Otherwise, their careers will be seriously damaged. In practice, political neutrality therefore means that any personal preferences that civil servants may have are never so strongly held that they prevent them from faithfully serving any political master.

Public service ethos. Civil servants, in the main, do not need to be forced to be politically impartial; it is something that is inculcated by the way civil servants are recruited, trained and operate. This occurs in a number of ways. People are drawn to public service by a concern for the larger interests of the state and society, a motivation clearly different from both the partisan passions that drive politicians and the self-interested concerns of those in private business. A public service ethos is also inculcated by the arrangements though which civil servants are recruited and trained, with a strong emphasis on cultivating expertise and specialist knowledge.

NO

Bureaucratic self-interest. For public-choice theorists (see p. 252), civil servants are primarily motivated by career self-interest and, thus, seek the expansion of the agency or department in which they work and an increase in its budget (Niskanen, 1971). This is because bureaucratic growth guarantees job security, expands promotion prospects, improves salaries, and brings top officials at least greater power, patronage and prestige. Supporters of the New Right therefore often explain the trend towards 'big' government in terms of the policy influence exerted by civil servants acting as 'nature's social democrats'. In order to advance free-market policies successfully, bureaucratic power must be checked or circumvented.

Conservative power bloc. Socialists, and particularly Marxists, highlight class biases that run through the state bureaucracy, turning senior civil servants into a conservative veto group that dilutes, even blocks, the radical initiatives of socialist governments (Miliband, 2009). This happens, in part, because top civil servants share the same educational and social background as industrialists and business managers, and so share their values, prejudices and general outlook. Higher civil servants also work closely with the world of corporate capitalism, leading, amongst other things, to the 'revolving door' through which bureaucrats are increasingly recruited from the private sector, and civil servants are offered lucrative employment opportunities when they retire.

Departmental culture. Government agencies are not impersonal administrative machines (as suggested by Weber), but social institutions within which develop a set of shared (and usually unquestioned) beliefs, values and assumptions. Such 'groupthink' exerts a powerful influence over politicians, who are encouraged to 'go native' by the fact that they are both vastly outnumbered by officials and generally recognize that officials possess greater knowledge and expertise than they do themselves. Not uncommonly, a department's culture is also shaped by the nature and interests of the client groups it serves.

them. Information can thus be concealed, or at least 'shaped' to reflect the preferences of the civil service. The principal source of bureaucratic power is, nevertheless, the expertise and specialist knowledge that accumulates within the bureaucracy. As the responsibilities of government expand and policy becomes more complex, 'amateur' politicians almost inevitably come to depend on their 'professional' bureaucratic advisers.

CONCEPT

Corruption

Corruption, in a general sense, is a condition of depravity or moral defilement. Power is thus said to corrupt, in that it breeds an appetite for domination and an insensitivity to the sufferings of others. More specifically, corruption is a quasi-legal term meaning a person's failure to carry out his or her 'proper' or public responsibilities due to the pursuit of private gain. In most cases, corruption has a material or narrowly financial character, its most common political manifestations being bribery or 'sleaze'. Political corruption can, broadly, be associated with the abuse of office.

Articulating interests

Although by no means one of their formal functions, bureaucracies often help to articulate, and sometimes aggregate, interests. Bureaucracies are brought into contact with interest groups through their task of policy implementation, and their involvement in policy formulation and advice. This has increased as a result of corporatist (see p. 251) tendencies that have blurred the divisions between organized interests and government agencies. Groups such as doctors, teachers, farmers and business corporations thus become 'client groups', serviced by their respective agencies, and also serve as an invaluable source of information and advice. This **clientelism** may benefit the political system, insofar as it helps to maintain consensus (see p. 8). By virtue of having access to policy formulation, it is more likely that organized interests will cooperate with government policy. On the other hand, clientelism may also interfere with the public responsibilities and duties of civil servants. This, for instance, occurs when US regulatory agencies end up being controlled by the industries they supposedly regulate, a tendency that is also found in other countries. When group interests coincide with those of the bureaucracy, a policy nexus may develop that democratic politicians find impossible to break down.

Political stability

The final function of bureaucracies is to provide a focus of stability and continuity within political systems. This is sometimes seen as particularly important in developing states, where the existence of a body of trained career officials may provide the only guarantee that government is conducted in an orderly and reliable fashion. This stability depends very largely on the status of bureaucrats as permanent and professional public servants: while ministers and governments come and go, the bureaucracy is always there. The Northcote–Trevelyan reforms of 1870 that created the modern UK civil service were based on the principles of impartial selection, political neutrality (see p. 345), permanence and anonymity. Even in the USA, where senior officials are appointed politically through a so-called '**spoils system**', the mass of federal bureaucrats are career civil servants.

However, continuity can also have its disadvantages. In the absence of effective public scrutiny and accountability, it can undoubtedly lead to corruption, a problem that is found in many developing states, where it is compounded by widespread poverty and disadvantage. In other cases, permanence may breed in civil servants either a tendency towards arrogance and insularity, or a bias in favour of conservatism. Career civil servants can come to believe that they are more capable of defining the common good or general will than are elected politicians. They may, therefore, feel justified in resisting radical or reformist political tendencies, seeing themselves as custodians of the state's interest.

● **Clientelism**: A relationship through which government agencies come to serve the interests of the client groups they are responsible for regulating or supervising.

● **Spoils system**: A system in which the ability to make appointments is a reward for achieving political office, leading to the preferment of friends or supporters.

Organization of the bureaucracy

One of the limitations of Weber's theory of bureaucracy is that it suggests that the drive for efficiency and rationality will lead to the adoption of essentially similar bureaucratic structures the world over. Weber's 'ideal type' (see p. 20) of bureaucracy thus ignores the various ways in which bureaucracies can be organized, as well as differences that arise from the political, social and cultural contexts in which bureaucracies operate. The organization of bureaucracies is important for two reasons. It affects the degree to which public accountability and political control over the bureaucracy can be achieved and, as has been increasingly recognized since the 1980s, it influences its efficiency and effectiveness, and so has major implications for the performance and cost of public services.

All state bureaucracies are in some way organized on the basis of purpose or function. This is achieved through the construction of departments, ministries and agencies charged with responsibility for particular policy areas: education, housing, defence, drug control, taxation and so forth. Of course, the number of such departments and agencies varies over time and from state to state, as do the ways in which functional responsibilities are divided or combined. For example, after the September 11 attacks on the USA in 2001, President Bush established the White House Office of Homeland Security. This is a super-department that combines the departments of immigration, customs and domestic security, and is designed to ensure a fully coordinated response to the threat of terrorism.

The most significant feature of these functionally defined bureaucracies is the degree of centralization or decentralization within them. The systems found in the remaining communist regimes, such as China, which are subject to strict party control and supervision at every level, are amongst the most centralized bureaucratic systems in the world. Nevertheless, the sizes and complexity of communist bureaucracies have also provided considerable scope for bureau and departmental independence. Despite the formal 'leadership' of the CPSU, the Soviet bureaucracy, for example, functioned as a labyrinthine mechanism for interest articulation and aggregation, amounting to a form of 'institutional pluralism' (Hough, 1977). The most centralized liberal-democratic bureaucracy has traditionally been that in France. Whereas bureaucracies in states such as the UK and Germany have developed through a process of reform and adaptation, the French system was constructed on the basis of the Napoleonic model of administration. This emphasized the importance of a highly centralized and hierarchically structured body of technical experts, wedded to the long-term interests of the French state. The *Conseil d'État* (Council of State) is the supreme administrative body in France; it advises on legislative and administrative matters, and acts as the highest administrative court. The *École Nationale d'Administration* and the *École Polytechnique* function as training schools for civil servants, giving the so-called '*grands corps*' (senior administrators and technical experts) unrivalled prestige.

The USA, in contrast, is an example of a decentralized bureaucracy. The federal bureaucracy operates under the formal authority of the president as chief administrator. However, it is so diffuse and unwieldy that all presidents struggle to coordinate and direct its activities. One reason for this fragmentation is that the responsibilities of the federal government overlap with those of state and local governments, whose cooperation is required to ensure effective implemen-

CONCEPT

New public management

New public management (NPM) stands broadly for the use of private sector management techniques in government and for the transfer of government functions to private bodies. The philosophy of NPM is that government should 'steer' (decide policy) while private bodies should 'row' (deliver services), and that public bodies should be imbued with the 'entrepreneurial spirit'. Examples of the latter include the use of performance-related pay, short-term contracts and open recruitment strategies. NPM is based on assumptions about the inherent inefficiency and unresponsiveness of public bodies.

● **Executive agency**: A body that (usually) operates within a government department but enjoys a significant measure of managerial and budgetary independence.

tation. A second reason is the impact of the separation of powers (see p. 313). While executive departments and agencies operate under presidential authority via their cabinet secretaries or directors, a bewildering array of independent regulatory commissions have been created, and are funded, by Congress. Although presidents appoint the members of these commissions, they cannot dismiss them or interfere with their responsibilities as laid down by Congress. A third reason is that there is tension between permanent civil servants and the much smaller number of political appointees in so-called 'Schedule C' posts. While the latter can be expected to make loyalty to the administration their priority, the former may be more committed to the growth of their bureaux or the continuance of their services and programmes.

The conventional structure of government bureaucracies has come under particular scrutiny and pressure since the 1980s. In extreme cases, this has led to attempts to restructure the administrative state. For instance, the Clinton administration in the USA, was deeply impressed by the ideas developed in Osborne and Gaebler's *Reinventing Government* (1992). The key idea suggested that the job of government is to 'steer' not to 'row'; in other words, that government works best when it concerns itself with policy-making and leaves the delivery of services or policy implementation to other bodies acting as agents of the state. In theory, such an approach need not necessarily be linked to the contraction of state responsibilities, but its most enthusiastic advocates have undoubtedly come from the New Right, which has embraced this analysis as part of its broader attack on 'big' government.

These ideas have been influential in the USA and a number of other western countries. The construction of a 'skeletal state', based on what is called the 'new public management', has been taken furthest in New Zealand, but this thinking has also affected the UK, through the civil service reforms introduced by Thatcher and Major, and further developed by Blair. A significant step in this process was taken with the launching in 1988 of the Next Steps initiative, which began dismantling a unified national administration by restricting ministries to their 'core' policy functions and handing over responsibility for implementation to **executive agencies**, as occurs in Sweden. In 2009, the Cabinet Office estimated that there were 752 so-called Arm's-Length Bodies in the UK, spending over £80 billion and employing over 300,000 staff.

Attempts to compensate for alleged inefficiency and unresponsiveness in public administration have also led to the wider use of performance targets and quality measurement. The Blair government, 1997–2007, attempted to extend a culture of target-setting and performance review across the UK public sector, linking target fulfilment to funding and being willing publicly to expose 'underperformance'. Such innovations were also accompanied by a substantial increase in the role of quangos (see p. 368) in the administration of services such as health, education, urban development and regulation. In 1996, there were an estimated 5,207 quasi-governmental bodies in the UK, spending over £60 billion a year (35 per cent of total public spending) and employing 60,000 staff.

As governments struggle to keep public spending under control, such developments, especially the divorce between policy advice and policy implementation, are likely to become more common. However, the drive to streamline administration, promote efficiency and cut costs carries political costs. The most obvious of these is the weakening of public accountability and the emergence of

Focus on . . .

Quangos: advantages and disadvantages

'Quango' is an acronym for quasi-autonomous non-governmental organization. This is a notoriously loose and confusing term. In its most general sense, 'quango' refers to any body carrying out government functions that is staffed by appointees, rather than by ministers or civil servants. Quangos thus include bodies with executive functions of various kinds, as well as advisory committees and tribunals. The quasi-autonomous status of quangos means that they are part of 'arm's-length' government; their non-governmental character means that they are part of the 'non-elected state'.

The benefits of quangos include the following:

- They allow government to call on the experience, expertise and specialist knowledge of outside advisers.

- They reduce the burden of work of 'official' government departments and agencies.

Quangos have been criticized for the following reasons:

- They expand the range of ministerial patronage and so contribute to the centralization of political power.
- They weaken democratic accountability by reducing the ability of representative institutions to oversee the workings of government.
- They foster **balkanization** by making public administration more disjointed and less systematic.

a 'democratic deficit'. The creation of semi-independent executive agencies and, above all, quangos tends to mean that elected politicians no longer take responsibility for day-to-day administrative or operational matters. A second problem is that the introduction of management techniques, structures and, increasingly, personnel from the private sector may weaken the public-service ethos that state bureaucracies have striven over the years to develop. The civil service culture in states as different as Japan, India, France and the UK may be criticized for its aloofness, even arrogance, but it is at least linked to ideas such as public service and the national interest, rather than private gain and entrepreneurialism. A third disadvantage is that, although this type of reorganization tends to be associated with the rolling back of the state, it may, in practice, lead to greater centralization and government control. This occurs because, as government relinquishes direct responsibility for the delivery of services, it is forced to set up a range of new bodies to carry out funding and regulatory functions.

BUREAUCRATIC POWER: OUT OF CONTROL?

Sources of bureaucratic power

● **Balkanization**: The fragmentation of a political unit into a patchwork of antagonistic entities (as has often occurred in the Balkans).

Despite their constitutional image as loyal and supportive public servants, bureaucrats have widely been seen as powerful and influential figures who collectively constitute a 'fourth branch of government'. Theorists as different as Weber, J Robert

Leon Trotsky (1879–1940)

Russian Marxist political thinker and revolutionary. An early critic of Lenin's theory of the party and the leader of the 1905 St Petersburg Soviet, Trotsky joined the Bolsheviks in 1917, becoming Commissar for Foreign Affairs and, later, Commissar for War. Isolated and out-manoeuvred after Lenin's death in 1924, he was banished from the USSR in 1929, and assassinated in Mexico in 1940 on the instructions of Stalin. Trotsky's theoretical contribution to Marxism consists of his theory of 'permanent revolution', his consistent support for internationalism, and his analysis of Stalinism as a form of 'bureaucratic degeneration'. His major writings include *Results and Prospects* (1906), *History of the Russian Revolution* (1931) and *The Revolution Betrayed* (1937).

Michels (1911), James Burnham (1941) and Leon Trotsky have drawn attention to the phenomenon of bureaucratic power and the degree to which politicians are subordinate to it. For instance, while Michels explained this in terms of the 'iron law of oligarchy' (see p. 232), Trotsky argued that Russia's workers state had degenerated through the transformation, under Stalin, of the communist party into a bureaucratic dictatorship (Trotsky, 1937). Japanese civil servants, especially those in the once prestigious Japanese MITI, have often been viewed as the 'permanent politicians' who masterminded the Japanese 'economic miracle' of the 1950s and 1960s (see p. 372). Kellner and Crowther-Hunt (1980) dubbed the UK's civil service 'Britain's ruling class'. Similarly, there is a perception that the driving force in the EU behind monetary and political union is the Brussels-based administrative staff of the European Commission, the so-called 'Eurocrats'.

Concern about bureaucratic power has been particularly acute amongst those on the political left and the political right who have dismissed the conventional notion of civil service neutrality. Marxists have traditionally argued that class interests operate through the bureaucracy, tending, in particular, to dilute radical policy initiatives by socialist governments. The New Right, for its part, insists that self-interested public officials foster state growth and are, thus, inclined to resist neoliberal or free-market policies. However, it is important to remember that the nature of bureaucratic power is, perhaps inevitably, shrouded in mystery and conjecture. This is both because, if civil servants exert power, they do so through private dealings with ministers that are not subject to public scrutiny, and because, in view of the myriad other pressures bearing on ministers, the influence of the civil service cannot be quantified. Nevertheless, three key sources of bureaucratic power can be identified:

- the strategic position of bureaucrats in the policy process
- the logistical relationship between bureaucrats and ministers
- the status and expertise of bureaucrats.

Strategic position

The policy process in all modern states is structured in a way that offers considerable scope for civil service influence. Most crucially, in their capacity as policy advisers, civil servants have access to information and are able to control its flow to their ministerial bosses. In government departments, knowledge is undoubtedly power, and it is officials who decide what ministers know and what they do not know. Policy options can thus be selected, evaluated and presented in such a way as to achieve a desired decision. This need not, of course, imply that bureaucrats are deliberately manipulative or openly political, but merely that their preferences – conscious or unconscious – significantly structure policy debate and so can influence the content of decisions made.

Links that develop between the bureaucracy and organized interests further strengthen their position. As the major interface between government and business, labour, professional and other groups, the bureaucracy can build up powerful alliances and play a crucial role in formulating and reviewing policy options. This has led to the emergence of policy networks, which tend to be relatively impervious to influence from the public or elected politicians. Needless to say, bureaucratic power does not cease to play a role once policy decisions have been made. Whereas politicians can seek alternative sources of policy advice, they are compelled to leave policy implementation in the hands of the bureaucracy, whether organized as a unified entity, or as a series of semi-independent agencies. Control of implementation gives civil servants the opportunity to reinterpret the content of policy, as well as to delay, or even thwart, its introduction.

Logistical relationships

The second source of bureaucratic power is the operational relationship and distribution of advantage between ministers and civil servants. Ostensibly, ministers are political masters and appointed bureaucrats are loyal subordinates. However, there are reasons to believe that this relationship may be different, even reversed, in practice. The first of these is that politicians are heavily outnumbered by leading bureaucrats. For example, in the USA, even if only top-level political appointees (those who require Senate approval) are considered, US presidents, aided by a cabinet of fewer than 20 secretaries, confront more than 600 senior officials. A second factor is the different career structures of civil servants and elected politicians. Except where 'spoils systems' operate, as in the USA, civil servants are permanent, in the sense that they remain in office while governments come and go. In contrast, ministers are only temporary, and in parliamentary systems such as the UK's where reshuffles are frequent, may remain in office for only about two years on average. The third advantage enjoyed by civil servants is that they are full-time policy advisers, while ministers are only part-time departmental bosses. The other demands on their time and energy include cabinet and cabinet-committee duties, sometimes parliamentary responsibilities and constituency work, media appearances, attendance at ceremonial and public functions, and foreign visits and summitry. However dedicated, tenacious and resourceful ministers may be, their role is therefore restricted to the offering of strategic guidance, knowing that much of the detail of policy and operational matters must be left to appointed officials.

Status and expertise

The final source of bureaucratic power is the status and respect that is often accorded to civil servants. This stems principally from their expertise and

Departmentalism

Departmentalism refers to centrifugal pressures within a governmental structure that strengthen the identity of individual departments and agencies. Agencies are thus able to pursue their own separate interests, and resist both political control and broader administrative disciplines. The distinctive culture of a government agency is shaped by factors such as its policy responsibilities, the collective interests of its body of officials, and the interests of the client groups that it serves. Departmentalism also operates through the tendency of ministers and senior officials to 'go native', by being absorbed into the department's culture.

● **Maladministration**: Bad administration; the improper use of powers, biased application of rules, failure to follow procedures, or simple incompetence.

specialist knowledge. In many systems, senior bureaucrats are regarded as a meritocratic elite, and are invested with responsibility for the national interest. This is certainly reflected in an emphasis on merit and achievement in the recruitment and training of civil servants. Top German civil servants, for instance, are recruited by competitive examination from the ranks of university graduates, usually in law, and then endure a rigorous three-year training programme followed by a second state examination. In France, the *École Nationale d'Administration* was set up specifically to recruit and train the nation's top generalist civil servants, thus supplementing the work of schools such as the *École Polytechnique*, which turns out technical experts. Similarly, the status of the UK civil service has been linked with a traditional reliance on Oxbridge candidates and the rigours of the fast-stream entrance procedure.

In comparison, governments and ministers often come into office ill-prepared, and in need of advice and support. Although governments are formed on the basis of party programmes and manifestos, they depend on civil servants to translate broad policy goals into practical and workable legislative programmes. This problem is particularly acute because of the mismatch between the skills and attributes required to win elective office and those needed to run an effective administration. In parliamentary systems in particular, ministers are appointed from an unusually small pool of talent (the members of the majority party or parties in the assembly), and it is rare for them to have either specialist knowledge of their departmental remit, or previous experience of administering a large-scale organization.

How can bureaucrats be controlled?

The perceived need to control the bureaucracy reflects a wide range of concerns. Most importantly, unchecked bureaucratic power spells the demise of representative and responsible government. For political democracy to be meaningful, appointed officials must in some way be accountable to politicians who, in turn, are accountable to the general public. Indeed, one of the long-standing criticisms of liberal democracy is that, behind the façade of party competition and public accountability, lies the entrenched power of bureaucrats who are responsible to no one. Guarantees against corruption, **maladministration** and the arbitrary exercise of government power must therefore be established.

Political control is also required because of the need to promote efficiency in a bureaucracy that may be bent on maintaining its professional comforts and material security, and because of the need for administrative coordination to resist the centrifugal pressures of 'departmentalism'. Bureaucrats themselves may argue that external control is unnecessary in view of the self-discipline imposed by strict professional standards and a deeply ingrained public service ethos, especially in permanent civil services such as those found in Germany, France, India and the UK. On the other hand, such a civil service culture may be part of the problem, rather than part of the solution: it may entrench a lofty arrogance based on the belief that 'bureaucrats know best'. The principal forms of control over bureaucracies can be classified as follows:

● the creation of mechanisms of political accountability
● the politicization of the civil service
● the construction of counter-bureaucracies.

The Japanese 'economic miracle': bureaucratic rule that works?

Events: Japan entered into the post-World War II world defeated and with its economy seemingly shattered. In 1950, Japan's GDP was roughly equal to that of Ethiopia and Somalia, and 40 per cent lower than India's. And yet, during the 1950s and 1960s, Japan enjoyed a period of spectacular economic growth, often called an 'economic miracle'. Japanese growth peaked in 1964 at 13.9 per cent and, from 1968 until 2010 (when it was superseded by China) Japan was the world's second largest economy. Having initially been based on 'heavy' industries, the crucial shift to exporting came in the 'Golden Sixties', with consumer goods and car manufacturing becoming increasingly prominent. From the 1970s onwards, Japan's economy was reorientated around knowledge-based products such as computers and electronic goods. By the 1980s, Japan's export-orientated growth model was increasingly adopted elsewhere in East Asia. The period of growth, however, came to an end with the bursting of the Japanese asset price bubble in 1991. Ongoing stagnation during the 1990s led to the period being dubbed Japan's 'lost decade', with little subsequent improvement in Japan's economic performance.

Significance: The Japanese economic miracle has provoked debate about, amongst other things, the unusually prominent role that the relatively unpurged Japanese bureaucracy played in the process, especially through the MITI, established in 1949 (Johnson, 1982). Japan's top civil servants are credited, in particular, with having brought about the close government–big business relationship that underpinned Japan's 'mixed' economic model. This model of indicative planning sought to stimulate and guide market forces, rather than either allowing markets to rule or subordinating markets to the state. The MITI was especially influential in advancing Japan's export-based strategy for growth by identifying and supporting the industries of the future, a policy often dubbed 'picking winners'. The Japanese bureaucracy exerted its influence not through formal powers (which remained meagre), but through its elite status, which was maintained by an examination system that recruited only 1 candidate in 40, and by the preponderance of Tokyo University entrants, who provided 70 per cent of senior civil servants. Moreover, by encouraging competition within the bureaucracy, at individual, inter-ministerial and central-local governmental levels, Japan's civil service was nimble, efficient and creative, quite the opposite of the traditional image of a lethargic bureaucracy (Kim *et al*, 1995).

However, this image of technocratic economic efficiency has been questioned on a number of grounds. For instance, Japan's economic recovery was significantly brought about by external factors, notably massive US aid designed to create a counterweight to communist influence in East Asia. Similarly, the high status and extensive influence of the Japanese bureaucracy compromised Japan's transition to democracy, in some senses. By transferring power to a tightly-knit nexus of conservative politicians (invariably from the ruling Liberal-Democratic Party), senior officials and business leaders, Japan was establishing a political elite that would, over time, become more concerned with maintaining its own power and privileges than with responding to popular pressures. Finally, Japan's civil servants were seen to be too influential for the long-term good of the country's economy. This, allegedly, was because 'top-down' planning and 'picking winners' created inflexibility and made the Japanese economy insufficiently responsive to market pressures, especially in an age of globalization. The once-mighty MITI thus went into decline, weakened by the perception that it had become a vehicle for protecting the interests of a small number of export-orientated conglomerates. Having been the architect of Japan's industrial policy for five decades, the MITI was taken over by the newly-created Ministry of Economic Trade and Industry in 2001.

CONCEPT

Ministerial responsibility

The doctrine of ministerial responsibility ('individual' responsibility) defines the relationship between ministers and their departments. The doctrine is observed in most parliamentary systems, and has two key features. First, ministers are responsible for the acts and omissions of their departments, maintaining the fiction that ministers themselves make all the decisions taken in their name. Second, ministers are accountable to the assembly, in the sense that they are answerable for anything that goes on in their departments, and are removable in the event of mistakes made by their civil servants.

Political accountability

State bureaucracies can be made accountable to the political executive, the assembly, the judiciary, or the public. The political executive is easily the most important of these bodies, because of its overall responsibility for government administration and its close working relationship with the civil service. The most elaborate system of executive control has been found in state socialist regimes such as China, where a hierarchically structured network of party organs has been constructed to run parallel to, and exercise supervision over, the state administration. However, so complex and extensive is the machinery of government in such regimes that even the pervasive influence of a 'leading' party fails to prevent the bureaucracy from developing interests of its own, or acting as conduits through which economic, social and regional interests are expressed.

In liberal democracies, especially those with parliamentary executives, political control depends largely on respect for the doctrine of ministerial responsibility. This holds that ministers alone are responsible *to* the assembly *for* the actions of their officials and the policies pursued by their departments. Ministerial responsibility has been developed in its most extreme form in the UK, where it is taken to imply that civil servants have an exclusive responsibility to their minister and, therefore, to the government of the day. The ability of this doctrine to deliver political control is, nevertheless, hampered by three factors. First, as discussed above, the expertise, size and complexity of modern bureaucracies make effective ministerial oversight virtually impossible. Second, ministers have been unwilling to sacrifice their political careers by resigning as a result of blunders made by officials (or themselves), and prime ministers have been reluctant to encourage resignations that will attract adverse publicity. Third, assemblies usually lack the expertise and political will to subject either ministers or civil servants to effective scrutiny.

Legislative oversight may also help to ensure that bureaucrats are politically accountable. The decision in the UK in 1979 to allow the newly-created departmental select committees to cross-examine senior civil servants, as well as ministers, was an implicit acknowledgement of the failings of the system of ministerial responsibility. Effective legislative control is tied up with the supply of money, however. The US Congress scrutinizes the presidential budget and has the constitutional authority to provide funds for the various executive departments and agencies. This gives congressional committees the opportunity to probe and investigate the workings of each department, scrutinize their estimates, and expose cases of maladministration and misappropriation. Congressional oversight may, nevertheless, allow powerful alliances to form, as in the so-called 'iron triangles'.

Judicial scrutiny of the bureaucracy is, in particular, found in systems in which **administrative law** is established as a separate branch of public law. In many continental European states, this leads to the creation of a network of administrative courts and tribunals empowered to resolve disputes between the government bureaucracy and private citizens. In France, the *Conseil d'État* is the supreme administrative court. It exercises general supervision over all forms of French administration, but may also weaken political control by protecting civil servants from unwarranted interference by their political masters.

Bureaucrats can be made accountable to the public in a number of ways, formal and informal. One method – Scandinavian in origin, but later extended

● **Administrative law**: Law that defines the power and functions of the executive organs of the state.

CONCEPT

Ombudsman

Ombudsman is a Scandinavian word that has no exact English equivalent. An ombudsman is an officer of the state who is appointed to safeguard citizens' rights in a particular sector and investigate allegations of maladministration, (ranging from the improper use of powers to the failure to follow procedures) and simple incompetence. The role of an ombudsman is to supplement, not replace, normal avenues of complaints such as administrative courts or elected representatives. However, ombudsmen's investigations and findings seldom have the force of law.

in different variations to countries such as New Zealand, Australia, the UK and France – is the ombudsman system. Although the ombudsman system offers a means through which individual grievances can be redressed, ombudsmen rarely operate with the force of law, and generally lack direct means of enforcing their decisions. The UK Parliamentary Commissioner for Administration is particularly ineffective, since complaints cannot be made directly by the public, but only on referral from an MP, and because there is widespread public ignorance about the office and its function.

Amongst the informal pressures on the bureaucracy are those exercised by the media and well-organized interest groups. Bureaucrats recognize that, regardless of the mechanisms of formal accountability, their status and public standing can be damaged by the exposure of scandals, corruption and administrative ineptitude. The publicity given to the Watergate affair in the USA in the 1970s thus led to tighter oversight of US government agencies such as the Central Intelligence Agency (CIA) and the Federal Bureau of Investigation (FBI). Similarly, the French newspaper *Le Monde* played a significant role in exposing the sinking in 1985 of the Greenpeace ship the *Rainbow Warrior*, thus contributing to the resignation of the defence minister. On the other hand, such investigations can be severely hampered by the culture of secrecy that usually pervades state administration, and by the absence of open government.

Politicization

One of the most common ways of exercising political control is to recruit the senior bureaucracy into the ideological enthusiasms of the government of the day. This effectively blurs the distinctions between politics and administration, and between politicians and public officials. Control is overtly accomplished through a system of political appointments. A spoils system was institutionalized in the USA by Andrew Jackson in the nineteenth century, when he replaced about 20 per cent of the federal civil service with his own men. When there is a new US president, the administration changes. Some 3,000 top posts are filled by political appointees, mostly in a rush between the election in November and the inauguration of the new president in January. Fewer than 200 of these appointments are likely to be made by the president personally; the others are made by senior executive officers, subject to presidential approval.

In Germany, although the formal scope for making ministerial appointments is limited, the *Berufsverbot* (literally, the 'denial of access to a profession') system allows incoming ministers and governments to discard unwanted officials by retiring them on full pay and appoint more sympathetic ones in their place. However, covert politicization is more widespread. In the UK, the abolition of the Civil Service Department in 1981 allowed prime ministers to take a closer interest in the appointment of senior civil servants. Although this has led to allegations of crude partisanship (evident in Margaret Thatcher's well-publicized criterion for preferment: are they 'one of us'?), its impact has usually been more subtle as civil servants have recognized that career progress is likely to be advanced if they evince clear support for the goals and objectives of the government of the day. Creeping politicization has also become a feature of French administration. Approximately 500 senior posts are now filled at the discretion of leading government figures, and, since the 1980s, those appointed have usually had a highly partisan profile, or have been linked personally or politically with senior politicians. The French higher civil service therefore now resembles a patchwork of politicized clans, rather than a unified body standing above party politics.

The attraction of a politicized senior bureaucracy is plainly that it ensures that there is a higher level of loyalty and commitment in such a group than would be likely amongst politically impartial civil servants. Moreover, those observers who believe that neutrality is always a myth, arguing that some kind of political bias is inevitable in the state bureaucracy, generally hold that a system of overt politicization is preferable to one of covert politicization. However, political commitment also brings serious disadvantages. In the first place, politicization strikes at the very heart of the idea of a professional and permanent civil service. Once bureaucrats are selected on political grounds by the government of the day, or encouraged to share their ideological sympathies, their appointments become as temporary as those of their political masters. This, in turn, means that knowledge and experience are not accumulated over a number of governments, and, as in the USA, that a change in administration brings about a major breach in the continuity of government.

Furthermore, it is difficult to have both political commitment and meritocracy within the civil service. In a politicized service, not only are appointments made on the basis of political affiliation and personal loyalty, rather than ability and training, but it may also be more difficult to attract high-calibre staff to work in temporary positions that offer no form of job security. A more insidious danger is that ideological enthusiasm may blind civil servants to the drawbacks and disadvantages of policy proposals. From this point of view, the virtue of neutrality is that it establishes an 'arm's length' relationship between bureaucrats and politicians, allowing the former to see the weaknesses, as well as the strengths, of the policy options they are required to examine.

Counter-bureaucracies

The final mechanism of political control is through structures designed to support or assist politicians, or to act as a counterweight to the official bureaucracy. The simplest such system is the use of political advisers or 'outsiders', which is now a feature of almost all modern states. More significantly, institutions of various kinds have been established to share ministers' workloads and provide them with personal advisory staff. In the UK, this role is largely played by the Prime Minister's Office, which is composed of a collection of senior officials and political advisors (numbering over 100) who advise the prime minister about policy and implementation, communications, party management and government relations. Of more general application is the device of the *cabinet ministériel*. These have long been established in France and have been taken up in states such as Italy and Austria, as well as by the EU. *Cabinets* are ministers' personal teams of advisers (in France, usually 15–20 strong) that help to formulate policy, assist in supervising departmental activities, and help ministers to carry out their various other responsibilities. The idea of a counter-bureaucracy has been most elaborately developed in the USA, in the form of the Executive Office of the President (EOP). This was established in 1939 by President Roosevelt following the Brownlow Committee's declaration that 'the President needs help'. The EOP is the president's personal bureaucracy. It consists of a growing number of councils and offices, and employs about 1,400 staff. Its key agencies include the White House Office, which comprises the president's closest political advisers; the Office of Management and Budget, which assists in the preparation of budgetary and legislative proposals; the National Security Council (NSC), which advises on defence and foreign affairs issues; and the Council of Economic Advisors, which provides the president with professional advice on economic policy.

The purpose of counter-bureaucracies is to compensate for the imbalance in the relationship between amateur, temporary and outnumbered politicians and their expert, permanent and professional officials. However, this form of political control has its drawbacks. In the case of the EOP, it leads to the duplication of government agencies, and so causes jurisdictional conflicts and a measure of bureaucratic in-fighting. This has been particularly evident in the often fraught relationship between the National Security Council and the State Department. A further difficulty is that allowing politicians to surround themselves with hand-picked advisers creates the danger that they will cut themselves off from political reality and be told only what they want to hear. This problem was highlighted in the USA by both the Watergate and the Iran–Contra affairs, when the respective presidents, Nixon and Reagan, became overdependent on EOP advisers, partly because they believed that they could neither trust nor control an essentially hostile federal bureaucracy.

SUMMARY

- Public policy is made through a series of linked decisions. Decisions can be explained in terms of the goal-directed behaviour of rational actors, incremental judgements made in the light of changing circumstances, the bureaucratic or organizational factors that shape the decision-making process, and the beliefs and values held by decision-makers.

- There are four stages to the policy process. In the initiation stage, policy proposals are originated and the policy agenda is set. In the formulation stage, broad policy proposals are developed into specific and detailed recommendations. The implementation stage consists of the processes through which policy decisions are put into effect. The evaluation stage takes the form of critical reflection on policy outputs designed to improve the policy process in the future.

- The core function of the bureaucracy is to implement or execute law and policy through the administration of government business. However, civil servants also play a significant role in offering policy advice to ministers, in articulating and aggregating interests (especially through links to client groups), and in maintaining political stability and continuity when there is a change of government or administration.

- Bureaucracies have traditionally been organized on the basis of purpose or function: hence their division into departments, ministries and agencies. The degree of centralization or decentralization within them varies considerably. Modern trends, however, are towards the divorce of policy-making from policy implementation, and the incorporation of private-sector management techniques, if not outright privatization.

- There is concern about bureaucratic power because of the threat it poses to democratic accountability. The principal sources of bureaucratic power include the ability of civil servants to control the flow of information and, thus, determine what their political masters know, the logistical advantages that they enjoy as permanent and full-time public officials, and their status as experts and custodians of the national interest.

- Control is exerted over bureaucracies in a number of ways. Mechanisms of public accountability to ministers, assemblies, the courts or ombudsmen can be established. The civil service can be politicized so that it shares the ideological enthusiasms of the government of the day. Counter-bureaucracies can be constructed to provide an alternative source of advice and to strengthen the hands of elected politicians.

Questions for discussion

- Do people generally make decisions in a rational and calculated fashion?
- Can 'groupthink' be avoided, and how could this best be achieved?
- What is the most important stage in the policy process, and why?
- Why do governments usually allocate insufficient funds to policy evaluation?
- Can a clear distinction be drawn between making policy and offering policy advice?
- Are public bureaucracies inherently inefficient?
- Do bureaucrats really 'run' their countries?
- Do the benefits of a politically committed civil service outweigh the costs?
- What are the most effective mechanisms for controlling bureaucratic power?

Further reading

Birkland, T., *An Introduction to the Policy Process: Theories, Concepts and Models of Public Policy Making* (2011). A clear and comprehensive primer in the policy process that balances theoretical issues against practical ones.

Knoepfel, P., C. Larrue, F. Varone and M. Hill, *Public Policy Analysis* (2007). An accessible and insightful introduction to policy analysis and how it should be approached.

Peters, Guy B., *The Politics of Bureaucracy* (2009). An encyclopaedic exploration of the political and policy-making role of bureaucracies.

Raadschelders, J., T. Toonen and F. Van de Meer (eds), *The Civil Service in the 21st Century: Comparative Perspectives* (2007). A comparative study of civil service systems that explores regional variations and developments worldwide.

CHAPTER 17

Multilevel Politics

'All politics is local.'

Favourite saying of former Speaker of the US House of Representatives
THOMAS ('TIP') O'NEILL JR

PREVIEW   The nation-state has traditionally been viewed as the natural, and perhaps only
legitimate, unit of political rule. Domestic politics therefore centred on the activities
of the national government, while, in international politics, nation-states have been
treated as discreet and unified entities. However, globalization and other developments have contributed to a process through which political authority has been
both 'sucked up' and 'drawn down', creating what is called 'multilevel governance'.
States have always incorporated a range of internal divisions and levels of power;
most significantly, territory-based divisions between central or national government
and various forms of provincial, city or local government. These divisions are
crucially shaped by a state's constitutional structure; that is, by whether it has a
federal or unitary system of government. Although each provides a distinct framework within which centre–periphery relationships can be conducted, both have
been subject in recent years to a combination of centrifugal and centripetal pressures. At the same time, a trend towards transnational regionalism has emerged out
of the fact that states are increasingly confronted by challenges that even the most
powerful state struggles to meet on its own. This has created the spectre of an
emerging 'world of regions'. In this view, regionalism is both the successor to the
nation-state and an alternative to globalization. Without doubt, the most advanced
example of regionalism found anywhere in the world is the European Union, but
this raises questions about whether the EU regional model is exportable and
whether it is viable.

KEY ISSUES
- Why does politics always have a territorial dimension?
- What is multilevel governance?
- How successfully do federal and unitary systems of government recon-
  cile territorial and other differences?
- Why has transnational regionalism grown in prominence?
- How does regionalism in Europe differ from regionalism in other parts
  of the world?

POLITICS, TERRITORY AND MULTILEVEL GOVERNANCE

Geopolitics

Geopolitics is an approach to foreign policy analysis that understands the actions, relationships and significance of states in terms of geographical factors such as location, climate, natural resources, physical terrain and population. Key exponents of geopolitics include Alfred Mahan (1840–1914), who argued that the state that controls the seas would control world politics, and Halford Mackinder (1861–1947), who suggested that control of the land mass between Germany and central Siberia is the key to controlling world politics. The advance of globalization is sometimes seen to have made geopolitics obsolete.

Politics has always had a spatial, or **territorial**, dimension. As political rule involves making and enforcing general rules over a particular population, this must imply taking account of where those people live, even if their location is imprecise or shifting (as in the case of a nomadic tribe). The association between politics and territory became more formalized and explicit from the sixteenth century onwards, as a result of the emergence of the modern state. For example, as the Peace of Westphalia (1648) defined sovereignty (see p. 58) in territorial terms, states were seen to be defined by their ability to exercise independent control over all the institutions and groups that live within their territorial borders. Two further developments consolidated the importance of territory. The first of these was the emergence of nationalism from the late eighteenth century onwards. As nationalist doctrines spread, so did the idea that national communities are, in part, forged by their sense of having a 'homeland'. As states evolved into nation-states, territory therefore became a matter not just of legal jurisdiction, but also one of identity and emotional attachment. The second development was the strengthened association between national power with territorial expansion that was brought about by imperialism (see p. 4270). Political power is always linked to the control of territory because it allows rulers both to extract resources and to control geographically-defined populations. However, the European 'struggle for colonies' in Africa and Asia during the nineteenth century was motivated by a heightened sense of this link, encouraging some to argue that the destiny of states is essentially determined by geographical factors. This gave rise to the discipline of 'geopolitics'.

Nevertheless, the unity and coherence of established nation-states, as well as their ability to maintain territorial sovereignty, have both been compromised in recent decades. Although the expansion of the state's economic and social responsibilities during much of the twentieth century had helped to fuel political **centralization**, during the 1960s and 1970s countervailing forces emerged, particularly through the tendency to redefine identity on the basis of culture or ethnicity (see p. 160), as discussed in Chapter 7. This was evident in the emergence of secessionist groups and forms of ethnic nationalism that sprang up places such as Quebec in Canada, Scotland and Wales in the UK, Catalonia and the Basque area in Spain, Corsica in France, and Flanders in Belgium. As the pressure for political **decentralization** grew, major constitutional upheavals were precipitated in a number of states (as discussed later in the chapter). In Italy, the process did not get under way until the 1990s with the rise of the Northern League in Lombardy. There have been similar manifestations of ethnic assertiveness amongst the Native Americans in Canada and the USA, the aboriginal peoples in Australia and the Maoris in New Zealand. In the latter two cases, at least, this has brought about a major reassessment of national identity, suggesting, perhaps, that nationalism was being displaced by multiculturalism (see p. 167).

The process through which political authority has been 'pulled down' within the state has been complemented by a tendency for political authority also to be 'sucked up' beyond the state, especially through the creation, or strengthening, of regional organizations. This has occurred, first, through a substantial growth in

● **Territory**: A delimited geographical area that is under the jurisdiction of a governmental authority.

● **Centralization**: The concentration of political power or government authority at the national level.

● **Decentralization**: The expansion of local autonomy through the transfer of powers and responsibilities away from national bodies.

CONCEPT

Multilevel governance

Multilevel governance is a complex policy process in which political authority is distributed at different levels of territorial aggregation. The 'vertical' conception of multilevel governance takes account of the interdependence of actors in the policy process at subnational, national and transnational levels, creating a fluid process of negotiation. Much of the complexity of multilevel governance derives from 'horizontal' developments such as the growth of relationships between states and non-state actors, and the emergence of new forms of public–private partnership.

● **Transnational**: A configuration, which may apply to events, people, groups or organizations, that takes little or no account of national government or state borders.

● **Federal system**: A system of government in which sovereignty is shared between central and peripheral levels (see p. 382).

● **Unitary system**: A system of government in which sovereignty is located in a single national institution, allowing the centre to control the periphery.

● **Confederation**: A qualified union of states in which each state retains its independence, typically guaranteed by unanimous decision-making.

cross-border, or **transnational**, flows and transactions – movements of people, goods, money, information and ideas. In other words, state borders have become increasingly 'porous', a development particularly associated with 'accelerated' globalization (see p. 142) since the 1980s. The second development, linked to the first, is that relations among states have come to be characterized by growing interdependence (see p. 433) and interconnectedness. Tasks such as promoting economic growth and prosperity, tackling global warming, halting the spread of weapons of mass destruction and coping with pandemic diseases are impossible for any state to accomplish on its own, however powerful it may be. States, in these circumstances, are forced to work together, relying on collective efforts and energies. The combination of these processes, through which an increasing burden of political decision-making has been made both 'above' and 'below' the national level, has helped to reshape territorial politics and generate interest in the phenomenon of multilevel governance. This could best be examined by looking, respectively, at the governance processes that operate at the subnational level and at the transnational level.

SUBNATIONAL POLITICS

All modern states are divided on a territorial basis between central (national) and peripheral (regional, provincial or local) institutions. The balance between centralization and decentralization is shaped by a wide range of historical, cultural, geographical, economic and political factors. The most prominent of these is the constitutional structure of the state, particularly the location of sovereignty in the political system. Although modified by other factors, the constitutional structure provides, as a minimum, the framework within which centre–periphery relationships are conducted. The two most common forms of territorial organization found in the modern world are the **federal** and **unitary** systems. A third form, **confederation**, has generally proved to be unsustainable. As confederations establish only the loosest and most decentralized type of political union by vesting sovereign power in peripheral bodies, it is not surprising that their principal advocates have been anarchists such as Pierre-Joseph Proudhon (see p. 381). The confederal principle is, in fact, most commonly applied in the form of intergovernmentalism (see p. 395), as embodied in international organizations such as the North Atlantic Treaty Organization (NATO), the United Nations (UN), the African Union (AU) and the Commonwealth of Nations. Examples of confederations at the nation-state level are, however, far rarer. The USA was originally a confederation, first in the form of the Continental Congresses (1774–81), and then under the Articles of Confederation (1781–89). The most important modern example of a confederal state is the Commonwealth of Independent States (CIS) which, in 1991, formally replaced the USSR. The CIS was established by 11 of the 15 former Soviet republics (only Georgia and the three Baltic states refused to join). However, it lacks executive authority and therefore constitutes little more than an occasional forum for debate and arbitration. Indeed, the evidence is that, in the absence of an effective central body, confederations either, as in the USA, transform themselves into federal states, or succumb to centrifugal pressures and disintegrate altogether, as has more or less occurred in the case of the CIS.

Pierre-Joseph Proudhon (1809–65)

French anarchist. A largely self-educated printer, Proudhon was drawn into radical politics in Lyons before settling in Paris in 1847. As a member of the 1848 Constituent Assembly, Proudhon famously voted against the constitution 'because it was a constitution'. He was later imprisoned for three years, after which, disillusioned with active politics, he concentrated on writing and theorizing. His best-known work, *What is Property?* ([1840] 1970), developed the first systematic argument for anarchism, based on the 'mutualist' principle; it also contained the famous dictum 'property is theft'. In *The Federal Principle* (1863), Proudhon modified his anarchism by acknowledging the need for a minimal state to 'set things in motion' (although by 'federal' he meant a political compact between self-governing communities – in effect, confederalism).

Federal systems

Federal systems of government have been more common than confederal systems. Over one-third of the world's population is governed by states that have some kind of federal structure. These states include the USA, Brazil, Pakistan, Australia, Mexico, Switzerland, Nigeria, Malaysia and Canada. Although no two federal structures are identical, the central feature of each is a sharing of sovereignty between central and peripheral institutions. This ensures, at least in theory, that neither level of government can encroach on the powers of the other (see Figure 17.1). In this sense, a federation is an intermediate form of political organization that lies somewhere between a confederation (which vests sovereign power in peripheral bodies) and a unitary state (in which power is located in central institutions). Federal systems are based on a compromise between unity and regional diversity, between the need for an effective central power and the need for checks or constraints on that power.

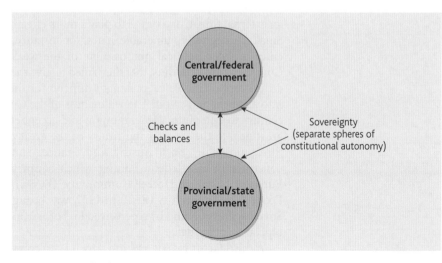

Figure 17.1   Federal states

CONCEPT

Federalism

Federalism (from the Latin *foedus*, meaning 'pact', or 'covenant') usually refers to legal and political structures that distribute power territorially within a state. Nevertheless, in accordance with its original meaning, it has been taken to imply reciprocity or mutuality (Proudhon), or, in the writings of Alexander Hamilton and James Madison (see p. 319), to be part of a broader ideology of pluralism. As a political form, however, federalism requires the existence of two distinct levels of government, neither of which is legally or politically subordinate to the other. Its central feature is therefore shared sovereignty.

Why federalism?

When a list of federal states (or states exhibiting federal-type features) is examined, certain common characteristics can be observed. This suggests that the federal principle is more applicable to some states than to others. In the first place, historical similarities can be identified. For example, federations have often been formed by the coming together of a number of established political communities that nevertheless wish to preserve their separate identities and, to some extent, their autonomy. This clearly applied in the case of the world's first federal state, the USA. Although the 13 former British colonies in America quickly recognized the inadequacy of confederal organization, each possessed a distinctive political identity and set of traditions that it was determined to preserve within the new, more centralized, constitutional framework.

The reluctance of the former colonies to establish a strong national government was demonstrated at the Philadelphia Constitutional Convention of 1787, which drafted the US constitution, and by the ensuing debate over ratification. The 'nationalist' position, which supported ratification, was advanced in the so-called 'Federalist Papers', published between 1787 and 1789. They emphasized the importance of establishing a strong centralized government while, at the same time, preserving state and individual freedoms. Ratification was finally achieved in 1789, but only through the adoption of the Bill of Rights and, in particular, the Tenth Amendment, which guaranteed that powers not delegated to the federal government would be 'reserved to the states respectively, or to the people'. This provided a constitutional basis for US federalism. A similar process occurred in Germany. Although unification in 1871 reflected the growing might of Prussia, a federal structure helped to allay the fears of central control of the other 38 Germanic states that had long enjoyed political independence. This tradition of regional autonomy, briefly interrupted during the Nazi period, was formalized in the constitution of the Federal Republic of Germany, adopted in 1949, which granted each of the 11 *Länder* (provinces or states) its own constitution. Their number was increased to 16 as a result of the reunification of Germany in 1990.

A second factor influencing the formation of federations is the existence of an external threat, or a desire to play a more effective role in international affairs. Small, strategically vulnerable states, for instance, have a powerful incentive to enter broader political unions. One of the weaknesses of the US Articles of Confederation was, thus, that they failed to give the newly-independent US states a clear diplomatic voice, making it difficult for them to negotiate treaties, enter into alliances and so on. The willingness of the German states in the nineteenth century to enter into a federal union and accept effective 'Prussification' owed a great deal to the intensifying rivalry of the great powers, and, in particular, the threat posed by both Austria and France. Similarly, the drift towards the construction of a federal Europe, which began with the establishment of the European Coal and Steel Community (ECSC) in 1952 and the European Economic Community (EEC) in 1957, was brought about, in part, by a fear of Soviet aggression and by a perceived loss of European influence in the emerging bipolar world order.

A third factor is geographical size. It is no coincidence that many of the territorially largest states in the world have opted to introduce federal systems. This was true of the USA, and it also applied to Canada (federated in 1867), Brazil (1891), Australia (1901), Mexico (1917) and India (1947). Geographically large states tend to be culturally diverse and often possess strong regional traditions. This creates greater pressure for decentralization and the dispersal of power than can usually be accommodated within a unitary system. The final factor encouraging the adoption of federalism is cultural and ethnic heterogeneity. Federalism, in short, has often been an institutional response to societal divisions and diversities. Canada's ten provinces, for instance, reflect not only long-established regional traditions, but also language and cultural differences between English-speaking and French-speaking parts of the country. India's 25 self-governing states were defined primarily by language but, in the case of states such as Punjab and Kashmir, also take religious differences into account. Nigeria's 36-state federal system similarly recognizes major tribal and religious differences, particularly between the north and south-east of the country.

Features of federalism

Each federal system is unique, in the sense that the relationship between federal (national) government and state (regional) government is determined not just by constitutional rules, but also by a complex of political, historical, geographical, cultural and social circumstances. In some respects, for example, the party system is as significant a determinant of federal–state relationships as are the constitutionally allocated powers of each level of government. Thus, the federal structure of the USSR, which unlike the USA granted each of its 15 republics the right of secession, was entirely bogus given the highly centralized nature of the 'ruling' Communist Party, to say nothing of the rigidly hierarchical central-planning system. A similar situation was found in Mexico, where the once dominant Institutional Revolutionary Party (PRI) effectively counteracted a federal system that was consciously modelled on the US example. In the USA, Canada, Australia and India, on the other hand, decentralized party systems have safeguarded the powers of state and regional governments.

There is a further contrast between federal regimes that operate a 'separation of powers' (see p. 313) between the executive and legislative branches of government (typified by the US presidential system), and parliamentary systems in which executive and legislative power is 'fused'. The former tend to ensure that government power is diffused both territorially and functionally, meaning that there are multiple points of contact between the two levels of government. This leads to the complex patterns of interpenetration between federal and state levels of government that are found in the US and Swiss systems. Parliamentary systems, however, often produce what is called 'executive federalism', most notably in Canada and Australia.

Nevertheless, certain features are common to most, if not all, federal systems:

● **Executive federalism**: A style of federalism in which the federal balance is largely determined by the relationship between the executives of each level of government.

● **Two relatively autonomous levels of government:** Both central government (the federal level) and regional government (the state level) possess a range of powers on which the other cannot encroach. These include, at least, a measure of legislative and executive authority, and the capacity to raise revenue; thus enjoying a degree of fiscal independence. However, the specific fields of jurisdiction of each level of government, and the capacity of each to influence the other, vary considerably. In Germany and Austria, for instance, a system of 'administrative federalism' operates in which central government is the key policy-maker, and provincial government is charged with the responsibility for the details of policy implementation.

- **Written constitution:** The responsibilities and powers of each level of government are defined in a codified or 'written' constitution. The relationship between the centre and the periphery is therefore conducted within a formal legal framework. The autonomy of each level is usually guaranteed by the fact that neither is able to amend the constitution unilaterally; for example, in Australia and Switzerland amendments to the constitution must also be ratified by an affirmative referendum (see p. 201).

- **Constitutional arbiter:** The formal provisions of the constitution are interpreted by a supreme court, which thereby arbitrates in the case of disputes between federal and state levels of government. In determining the respective fields of jurisdiction of each level, the judiciary in a federal system is able to determine how federalism works in practice, inevitably drawing the judiciary into the policy process. The centralization that occurred in all federal systems in the twentieth century was invariably sanctioned by the courts.

- **Linking institutions:** In order to foster cooperation and understanding between federal and state levels of government, the regions and provinces must be given a voice in the processes of central policy-making. This is usually achieved through a bicameral legislature, in which the second chamber or upper house represents the interests of the states. The 105 seats in the Canadian Senate, for example, are assigned on a regional basis, with each of the four major regions receiving 24 seats, the remainder being assigned to smaller regions.

Assessment of federalism

One of the chief strengths of federal systems is that, unlike unitary systems, they give regional and local interests a constitutionally guaranteed political voice. The states or provinces exercise a range of autonomous powers and enjoy some measure of representation in central government, usually, as pointed out above, through the second chamber of the federal legislature. On the other hand, federalism was not able to stem the general twentieth-century tendency towards centralization. Despite guarantees of state and provincial rights in federal systems, the powers of central government have expanded, largely as a result of the growth of economic and social intervention, and central government's own greater revenue-raising capacities.

The US system, for instance, initially operated according to the principles of 'dual federalism'. From the late nineteenth century onwards, this gave way to a system of 'cooperative federalism' that was based on the growth of 'grants in aid' from the federal government to the states and localities. State and local government therefore became increasingly dependent on the flow of federal funds, especially after the upsurge in economic and social programmes that occurred under the New Deal in the 1930s. From the mid-1960s, however, cooperative federalism, based on a partnership of sorts between federal government and the states, was replaced by what has been called 'coercive federalism'. This is a system through which federal government has increasingly brought about the compli-

● **Administrative federalism:** A style of federalism in which central government is the key policy-maker, and provincial government is charged with responsibility for policy implementation.

● **Dual federalism:** A style of federalism in which federal and state/provincial government occupy separate and seemingly indestructible spheres of policy power.

ance of the states by passing laws that pre-empt their powers, and imposing restrictions on the states and localities in the form of mandates.

A second advantage of federalism is that, in diffusing government power, it creates a network of checks and balances that helps to protect individual liberty. In James Madison's (see p. 319) words, 'ambition must be made to counteract ambition'. Despite a worldwide tendency towards centralization, federal systems such as those in the USA, Australia and Canada have usually been more effective in constraining national politicians than have been unitary systems. However, structures intended to create healthy tension within a system of government may also generate frustration and paralysis. One of the weaknesses of federal systems is that, by constraining central authority, they make the implementation of bold economic or social programmes more difficult. F. D. Roosevelt's New Deal in the USA, for example, was significantly weakened by Supreme Court decisions that were intended to prevent federal government from encroaching on the responsibilities of the states. In the 1980s, Ronald Reagan deliberately used federalism as a weapon against 'big' government, and specifically against the growing welfare budget. Under the slogan 'new federalism', Reagan attempted to staunch social spending by transferring responsibility for welfare from federal government to the less prosperous state governments. In contrast, the dominant pattern of cooperative federalism in Germany has facilitated, rather than thwarted, the construction of a comprehensive and well-funded welfare system. Nevertheless, since the 1990s the USA has increasingly relied on **fiscal federalism**, federal grants to state and local government having risen steadily under a succession of presidents.

Finally, federalism has provided an institutional mechanism through which fractured societies have maintained unity and coherence. In this respect, the federal solution may be appropriate only to a limited number of ethnically diverse and regionally divided societies but, in these cases, it may be absolutely vital. The genius of US federalism, for instance, was perhaps less that it provided the basis for unity amongst the 13 original states, and more that it invested the USA with an institutional mechanism that enabled it to absorb the strains that immigration exerted from the mid-nineteenth century onwards. The danger of federalism, however, is that by breeding governmental division it may strengthen centrifugal pressures and ultimately lead to disintegration. Some have argued, as a result, that federal systems are inherently unstable, tending either towards the guaranteed unity that only a unitary system can offer, or towards greater decentralization and ultimate collapse. Federalism in Canada, for example, can perhaps be deemed a failure, if its chief purpose were to construct a political union within which both French-speaking and English-speaking populations can live together in harmony (see p. 114).

Unitary systems

● **Fiscal federalism**: A style of federalism in which the federal balance is largely determined by funding arrangements, especially transfer payments from the centre to the periphery.

The vast majority of contemporary states have unitary systems of government. These vest sovereign power in a single, national institution. In the UK, this institution is Parliament, which possesses, at least in theory, unrivalled and unchallengeable legislative authority. Parliament can make or unmake any law it wishes; its powers are not checked by a codified or written constitution; there are no rival UK legislatures that can challenge its authority; and its laws outrank all other forms of English and Scottish law. Since constitutional supremacy is vested with the centre in a unitary system, any system of peripheral or local government exists at the pleasure of the centre (see Figure 17.2). At first sight, this creates the spectre of unchecked centralization. Local institutions can be reshaped, reorganized and even abolished at will; their powers and responsibilities can be contracted as easily as they can be expanded. However, in practice, the relationship between the centre and the periphery in unitary systems is as complex as it is in federal systems – political, cultural and historical factors being as significant as more formal constitutional ones. Nevertheless, two distinct institutional forms of peripheral authority exist in unitary states: local government and devolved assemblies. Each of these gives centre–periphery relationships a distinctive shape.

Local government

Local government, in its simplest sense, is government that is specific to a particular locality; for example, a village, district, town, city or county. More particularly, it is a form of government that has no share in sovereignty, and is thus entirely subordinate to central authority – or, in a federal system, to state or regional authority. This level of government is, in fact, universal, being found in federal and confederal systems, as well as in unitary systems. In the USA, for instance, there are over 86,000 units of local government that employ 11,000,000 people, compared with a total of fewer than 8,000,000 staff at federal and state levels. However, what makes local government particularly important in unitary systems is that, in most cases, it is the only form of government outside the centre.

It would, nevertheless, be a mistake to assume that the constitutional subordination of local government means that it is politically irrelevant. The very ubiquity of local government reflects the fact that it is both administratively necessary and, because it is 'close' to the people, easily intelligible. Moreover, elected local politicians have a measure of democratic legitimacy (see p. 81) that enables them to extend their formal powers and responsibilities. This often means that central–local relationships are conducted through a process of bargaining and negotiation, rather than by diktat from above. The balance between the centre and the periphery is further influenced by factors such as the political culture (particularly by established traditions of local autonomy and regional diversity) and the

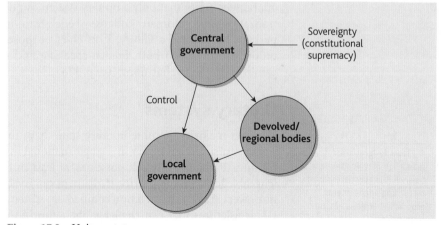

Figure 17.2   Unitary states

nature of the party system. For instance, the growing tendency for local politics to be 'politicized', in the sense that national parties have increasingly dominated local politics, has usually brought with it greater centralization. In the absence of the kind of constitutional framework that federalism provides, the preservation of local autonomy relies, to a crucial extent, on self-restraint by the centre. This tends to mean that the degree of decentralization in unitary systems varies significantly, both over time and from country to country. This can be illustrated by the contrasting experiences of the UK and France.

The UK traditionally possessed a relatively decentralized local government system, with local authorities exercising significant discretion within a legal framework laid down by Parliament. Indeed, respect for **local democracy** was long seen as a feature of the UK's unwritten constitution. However, the pattern of local–central relationships was dramatically restructured in the 1980s and 1990s, as the Conservative governments of that period saw local government as an obstacle to the implementation of their radical market-orientated policies. Central control was thus strengthened as local authorities were robbed of their ability to determine their own tax and spending policies. Local authorities that challenged the centre, such as the Greater London Council and the metropolitan county councils, were abolished – their functions being devolved to smaller district and borough councils, and a variety of newly-created **quangos**. The ultimate aim of these policies was fundamentally to remodel local government by creating 'enabling' councils, whose role is not to provide services themselves, but to supervise the provision of services by private bodies through a system of contracting-out and privatization. Although later governments re-established a London-wide council, in the form of the Greater London Authority (2000), and supported the introduction of elected mayors for towns and cities, the overall shift in power from local to central government in the UK has not been reversed. Very different policies were nevertheless adopted in France over the same period. During the 1980s, President Mitterrand sought to dismantle the strict administrative control in regional government that operated largely through prefects (appointed by, and directly accountable to, the Ministry of the Interior), who were the chief executives of France's 96 *départements*. The executive power of the prefects was transferred to locally elected presidents, and the prefects were replaced by *Commissaires de la République*, who are concerned essentially with economic planning. In addition, local authorities were absolved of the need to seek prior approval for administrative and spending decisions. The net result of these reforms was to give France a more decentralized state structure than it had had at any time since the 1789 revolution. Underpinning these developments was faith in the benefits of decentralization, reflecting the belief that political decisions should be made at the lowest possible level (see p. 388).

Devolution

Devolution (see p. 390), at least in its legislative form, establishes the greatest possible measure of decentralization in a unitary system of government – short, that is, of its transformation into a federal system. Devolved assemblies have usually been created in response to increasing centrifugal tensions within a state, and as an attempt, in particular, to conciliate growing regional, and sometimes nationalist, pressures. Despite their lack of entrenched powers, once devolved

● **Local democracy**: A principle that embodies both the idea of local autonomy and the goal of popular responsiveness.

● **Quango**: An acronym for quasi-autonomous non-governmental organization: a public body staffed by appointees, rather than politicians or civil servants (see p. 368).

Debating . . .
Should political decisions be made at the lowest possible level?

Although all modern states are divided on a territorial basis, there is considerable debate about where the balance should lie between centralization and decentralization. Supporters of decentralization tend to argue that it is a core principle of democratic rule. But may local power only be achieved at the cost of efficient government and, maybe, social justice?

YES

Boosting participation. Local or provincial government is a more effective agent of participation than central government. This is because far more people hold office at the local level than the national level, and even more are involved in standing for election or campaigning generally. By making political participation more attractive, devolving decision-making responsibility to lower levels helps to narrow the gap between the politically 'active' few and the 'passive' many.

Greater responsiveness. By being, quite literally, 'closer' to the people, peripheral bodies are more sensitive to their needs. This both strengthens popular accountability and ensures that government responds not merely to the general interests of society, but also to the specific needs of particular communities. There is certainly a much greater chance that local or provincial politicians will have a personal knowledge of, and perhaps live in, the community they serve, bolstering their responsiveness.

Increased legitimacy. Physical distance from government affects the acceptability or rightfulness of political decisions. Decisions that are made at a local or provincial level are likely to be seen as intelligible, and therefore legitimate, whereas geographical remoteness engenders a sense of political remoteness, so weakening the binding character of political decisions. This is especially the case as centralized decision-making can only treat the public as an amorphous mass, rather than as a collection of different groups and different communities.

Upholding liberty. Decentralization and localism help to deter tyranny and, therefore, protect individual freedom. This happens because, as liberals emphasize, corruption increases as power becomes more concentrated, as there are fewer checks on politicians' self-seeking inclinations. As political decisions are devolved to lower and lower levels, power is more widely dispersed and a network of checks and balances emerges. Strong peripheral bodies are more effective in checking central government power, as well as one another.

NO

National disunity. Central government alone articulates the interests of the whole of society, rather than its various parts. While a strong centre ensures that government addresses the common interests and shared concerns, a weak centre allows people to focus on what divides them, creating rivalry and discord. Shifting political decision-making to lower levels risks fostering parochialism and will make it more difficult for citizens to see the political 'big picture'.

Uniformity threatened. Only central governments can establish uniform laws and public services that, for instance, help people move more easily from one part of the country to another. Geographical mobility, and therefore social mobility, are likely to be restricted to the extent that political decentralization results in differing tax regimes and differing legal, educational and social-security systems across a country. A lack of uniformity may also threaten the nationwide growth of businesses.

Inhibiting social justice. Devolving political decisions from the centre has the disadvantage that it forces peripheral institutions increasingly to rely on the resources available in their locality or region. Only central government can rectify inequalities that arise from the fact that the areas with the greatest social needs are invariably those with the least potential for raising revenue, and only central government has the resources to devise and implement major programmes of welfare provision. Decentralization therefore puts social justice at risk.

Economic development. Centralization and economic development invariably go hand-in-hand. Because of its greater administrative capacity, central government can perform economic functions that are beyond the capacity of local bodies. These include managing a single currency, controlling tax and spending, and providing an infrastructure in the form of roads, railways, airports and so on. Centralization also promotes efficiency because it allows government to benefit from economies of scale.

assemblies have acquired a political identity of their own, and possess a measure of democratic legitimacy, they are very difficult to weaken and, in normal circumstances, impossible to abolish. Northern Ireland's Stormont Parliament was an exception. The Stormont Parliament was suspended in 1972 and replaced by direct rule from the Westminster Parliament, but only when it became apparent that its domination by predominantly Protestant Unionist parties prevented it from stemming the rising tide of communal violence in Northern Ireland that threatened to develop into civil war.

One of the oldest traditions of devolved government in Europe is found in Spain. Although it has been a unitary state since the 1570s, Spain is divided into 50 provinces, each of which exercises a measure of regional self-government. As part of the transition to democratic government following the death of General Franco in 1975, the devolution process was extended in 1979 with the creation of 17 autonomous communities. This new tier of regional government is based on elected assemblies invested with broad control of domestic policy, and was designed to meet long-standing demands for autonomy, especially in Catalonia and the Basque area. The French government has also used devolution as a means of responding to the persistence of regional identities, and, at least in Brittany and Occitania, to the emergence of forms of ethnic nationalism. As part of a strategy of 'functional regionalism', 22 regional public bodies were created in 1972 to enhance the administrative coordination of local investment and planning decisions. These, however, lacked a democratic basis and enjoyed only limited powers. In 1982, they were transformed into fully-fledged regional governments, each with a directly elected council. The tendency towards decentralization in Europe has, however, also been fuelled by developments within the European Union (EU), and especially by the emergence since the late 1980s of the idea of 'Europe of the Regions'. Regional and provincial levels of government have benefited from the direct distribution of aid from the European Regional Development Fund (1975), and have responded both by seeking direct representation in Brussels and by strengthening their involvement in economic planning and infrastructure development.

The UK was slower in embracing devolution. The revival of Scottish and Welsh nationalism since the late 1960s had put devolution on the political agenda, but devolved bodies were not established until 1999. A system of 'asymmetrical' devolution was established. Legislative devolution operated in Scotland, through the Scottish Parliament's ability to vary income tax by up to three pence in the pound and its **primary legislative power**; administrative devolution operated in Wales, as the Welsh Assembly had no control over taxation and only **secondary legislative power**; and so-called 'rolling' devolution was established in Northern Ireland, as the powers of the Northern Ireland Assembly were linked to progress in the province's 'peace process'. At the same time, England, with 84 per cent of the UK's population, remained entirely outside the devolution process. Nevertheless, devolution in the UK quickly developed into a form of '**quasi-federalism**', having gone beyond the simple handing down of power by a still sovereign Westminster Parliament. This has occurred because, although the Scottish, Welsh and Northern Irish bodies lack constitutional entrenchment, they enjoy a significant measure of democratic legitimacy by virtue of being popular assemblies that were set up following affirmative referendums. Moreover, the asymmetrical nature of UK devolution

● **Primary legislative power**: The ability to make law on matters which have been devolved from a central authority.

● **Secondary legislative power**: The ability to vary some laws devolved from a central authority that retains ultimate legislative control.

● **Quasi-federalism**: A division of powers between central and regional government that has some of the features of federalism without possessing a formal federal structure.

CONCEPT

Devolution

Devolution is the transfer of power from central government to subordinate regional institutions. Devolved bodies thus constitute an intermediate tier of government between central and local government. However, devolution differs from federalism in that devolved bodies have no share in sovereignty. In *administrative* devolution, regional institutions implement policies that are decided elsewhere. In *legislative* devolution (sometimes called 'home rule'), devolution involves the establishment of elected regional assemblies that have policy-making responsibilities.

● **Security regionalism**: Forms of transnational regional cooperation that are designed primarily to protect states from their enemies, both neighbouring and distant ones.

● **Political regionalism**: Attempts by states in the same area to strengthen or protect shared values, thereby enhancing their image, reputation and diplomatic effectiveness.

creates pressures for the ratcheting-up of devolved powers: the Welsh and Northern Irish assemblies have aspired to the powers of the Scottish Parliament, and the Scottish Parliament has, in turn, been encouraged to expand its powers in order to maintain its superior status. The Welsh Assembly thus acquired primary legislative powers in 2011, and, when the Scottish National Party (SNP) gained majority control of the Scottish Parliament in 2011, it committed itself to holding a referendum on Scottish independence, due to take place in 2014.

TRANSNATIONAL REGIONALISM

Regionalism: its nature and growth

Types of regionalism

In general terms, regionalism is a process through which geographical regions become significant political and/or economic units. Regionalism has two faces, however. In the first place, it is a subnational phenomenon, a process of decentralization that takes place *within* countries, and is closely associated, as already discussed, with federalism and devolution. The second face of regionalism is transnational, rather than subnational. In this, regionalism refers to a process of cooperation or integration *between* countries in the same region of the world. An ongoing problem with regionalism has nevertheless been the difficulty in establishing the nature and extent of a region. What is a 'region'? On the face of it, a region is a distinctive geographical area. Regions can therefore be identified by consulting maps. This leads to a tendency to identify regions with continents, as applies in the case of Europe (through the EU), Africa (through the African Union, or AU) and America (through the Organization of American States). However, many regional organizations are sub-continental, such as the Association of Southeast Asian Nations (ASEAN), the Southern African Customs Unions and the Central American Common Market, while others are transcontinental, such as Asia-Pacific Economic Cooperation (APEC) and the North Atlantic Treaty Organization (NATO). An alternative basis for regional identity is socio-cultural, reflecting similarities of region, language, history, or even ideological belief amongst a number of neighbouring states. Cultural identity is particularly important in the case of bodies such as the Arab League and the Nordic Council, and it may also apply in the case of the EU, where membership requires an explicit commitment to liberal-democratic values.

Regionalism has taken a number of forms and been fuelled by a variety of factors. **Security regionalism** emerged in the early post-1945 period through the growth of regional defence organizations that gave expression to the new strategic tensions that were generated by the Cold War. NATO and the Warsaw Pact were the most prominent such organizations, although other bodies, such as the Southeast Asian Treaty Organization (SEATO), were also formed. **Political regionalism** has witnessed the construction of organizations such as the Arab League, which was formed in 1945 to safeguard the independence and sovereignty of Arab countries; the Council of Europe, which was established in 1949 with the aim of creating a common democratic and legal area throughout the continent of Europe; and the Organization of African Unity (OAU), which was

CONCEPT

Regionalism

Regionalism is the theory or practice of coordinating social, economic and political activities within a geographical region, which may either be part of a state (subnational regionalism) or comprise a number of states (transnational regionalism). On an *institutional* level, regionalism involves the growth of norms, rules and formal structures through which coordination is brought about. On an *affective* level, regionalism implies a realignment of political identities and loyalties from the state to the region.

● **Economic regionalism**: Forms of cooperation amongst states in the same region that are designed to create greater economic opportunities, usually by fostering trading links.

● **Pooled sovereignty**: The sharing of decision-making authority by states within a system of international cooperation, in which certain sovereign powers are transferred to central bodies.

● **Functionalism**: The theory that social and political phenomena can be explained by their function within a larger whole, implying that regional integration occurs because it has functional advantages over state independence.

founded in 1963 to promote self-government and social progress throughout the African continent, and was replaced by the African Union (AU) in 2002. The most significant impetus towards transnational regionalism has undoubtedly been economic, however. **Economic regionalism** is therefore the primary form of regional integration and has become more so since the advent of so-called 'new' regionalism in the early 1990s.

Regionalism and globalization

'New' regionalism is manifest in the growth of regional trade blocs and the deepening of existing trade blocs (see p. 392). This surge has continued unabated, so that, by 2005, only one member of the World Trade Organization – Mongolia – was not party to a regional trade agreement. These agreements usually establish free trade areas through the reduction in internal tariffs and other barriers to trade; but, in other cases, they may establish customs unions, through the establishment of a common external tariff, or common markets (sometimes called 'single markets'), areas within which there is a free movement of labour and capital, and a high level of economic harmonization. The advent of 'new' regionalism has nevertheless highlighted the complex, and sometimes contradictory, relationship between regionalism and globalization. As Bhagwati (2008) put it, regional trade blocs can operate as both 'stumbling blocks' or 'building blocks' within the global system. Economic regionalism can be essentially defensive, in that regional organizations have sometimes embraced protectionism as a means of resisting the disruption of economic and, possibly, social life through the impact of intensifying global competition. This gave rise to the idea of the region as a fortress, as indeed evinced by the once-fashionable notion of 'fortress Europe'. Nevertheless, regional trade blocs have also been motivated by competitive impulses, and not merely protectionist ones. In these cases, countries have formed regional blocs not so much to resist global market forces but, rather, to engage more effectively with them. Although states have wished to consolidate or expand trade blocs in the hope of gaining access to more secure and wider markets, they have rarely turned their back on the wider global market, meaning that regionalism and globalization are usually interlocking, rather than rival, processes.

Explaining regionalism

Wider explanations have also been advanced for the rise of regionalism. The earliest theory of regional, or even global, integration was federalism, drawing inspiration from its use in domestic politics. As an explanation for transnational regionalism, federalism relies on a process of conscious decision-making by political elites, attracted, in particular, by the desire to avoid war by encouraging states to transfer at least a measure of their sovereignty to a higher, federal body. This is often referred to as **'pooled' sovereignty**. However, although a federalist vision is often said to have inspired the early process of European integration, federalism has had relatively little impact on the wider process of regional integration. Instead, even in the case of the European project, federalist thinking has had less impact than a **functionalist** road to integration. In the functionalist view, regional cooperation reflects the recognition that specific activities can be performed more effectively through collective action than by states acting indi-

Focus on . . .
Regional economic blocs

- **North American Free Trade Agreement (NAFTA):** This was signed in 1993 by Canada, Mexico and the USA. NAFTA was formed, in part, as a response to the growing pace of European integration, and is intended to provide the basis for a wider economic partnership covering the whole western hemisphere.
- **European Union (EU):** This was formed in 1993, developing out of the European Economic Community (founded in 1957). The EU has expanded from 6 to 27 members, and now includes many former communist states. It is the most advanced example of regional integration at an economic and political level.
- **Asia-Pacific Economic Cooperation (APEC):** This informal forum was created in 1989 and has expanded from 12 member states to 21 (including Australia, China, Russia, Japan and the USA); collectively, these states account for 40 per cent of the world's population and over 50 per cent of global GDP.

- **Association of South-East Asian Nations (ASEAN):** This was established in 1967 by Brunei, Indonesia, Malaysia, Philippines, Singapore and Thailand, with Brunei, Vietnam, Laos, Myanmar and Cambodia joining subsequently. ASEAN has attempted to promote a free-trade zone that would help south-east Asian states maintain their economic independence.
- **Mercosur:** The Mercosur agreement (1991) links Argentina, Brazil, Venezuela, Paraguay and Uruguay with Chile, Colombia, Ecuador, Peru and Bolivia as associate members. It is Latin America's largest trade bloc, and operates as a free-trade union.
- **Free Trade Area of the Americas (FTAA):** This is an agreement made at the 1994 Miami Summit of the Americas to build a free-trade area to extend across the Americas, as a proposed extension to NAFTA. The FTAA has 34 provisional members, but it is dominated by the USA and Canada.

vidually. This also helps to explain why regional integration has a predominantly economic character, as this is the area in which the functional benefits of co-operation are most evident. The weakness of functionalism is, however, that it overemphasizes the willingness of states to hand over responsibilities to functional bodies, especially in areas that are political, rather than technical. Furthermore, there is little evidence that regional bodies are capable of acquiring a level of political allegiance that rivals that of the nation-state, regardless of their functional importance. As a result of these deficiencies, a growing emphasis has been placed what is called '**neofunctionalism**'. Neofunctionalism has been particularly influential in explaining European integration, the most advanced example of regional integration found anywhere in the world.

European regionalism

What is the EU?

● **Neofunctionalism:** A revision of functionalism that recognizes that regional integration in one area generates pressures for further integration in the form of 'spillover'.

The 'European idea' (broadly, the belief that, regardless of historical, cultural and language differences, Europe constitutes a single political community) was born long before 1945. Before the Reformation in the sixteenth century, common alle-

Focus on . . .

How the European Union works

- **The European Commission:** This is the executive-bureaucratic arm of the EU. It is headed by 27 commissioners (one from each of the member states) and a president (José Manuel Barroso's term of office as president began in 2004). It proposes legislation, is a watchdog that ensures that EU treaties are respected, and is broadly responsible for policy implementation.

- **The Council:** This is the decision-making branch of the EU, and comprises ministers from the 27 states who are accountable to their own assemblies and governments. The presidency of the Council of Ministers rotates amongst member states every six months. Important decisions are made by unanimous agreement, and others are reached through qualified majority voting or by a simple majority.

- **The European Council:** Informally called the 'European Summit', this is a senior forum in which heads of government, accompanied by foreign ministers and two commissioners, discuss the overall direction of the Union's work. The Council

meets periodically and provides strategic leadership for the EU.

- **The European Parliament:** The EP is composed of 754 Members of the European Parliament (MEPs), who are directly elected every five years. Originally a scrutinizing assembly rather than a legislature, the passage of the Lisbon Treaty means that the EP now decides on the vast majority of EU legislation. The Parliament is a co-legislator with the Council over matters including agriculture, energy policy, immigration and EU funds, with the Parliament having the last say on the EU budget.

- **The European Court of Justice:** The ECJ interprets, and adjudicates on, European Union law. There are 27 judges, one from each member state, and 8 advocates general, who advise the court. As EU law has primacy over the national law of EU member states, the court can 'disapply' domestic laws. A Court of First Instance handles certain cases brought by individuals and companies.

giance to Rome invested the Papacy with supranational authority over much of Europe. Even after the European state-system came into existence, thinkers as different as Rousseau (see p. 97), Saint-Simon (1760–1825) and Mazzini (see p. 116) championed the cause of European cooperation and, in some cases, advocated the establishment of Europe-wide political institutions. However, until the second half of the twentieth century aspirations to achieve this through consent (as opposed to military power, as in the case of Charlemagne and Napolean) proved to be hopelessly utopian. Since World War II, Europe has undergone a historically unprecedented process of integration, aimed, some argue, at the creation of what Winston Churchill in 1946 called a 'United States of Europe'. Indeed, it is sometimes suggested that European integration provides a model of political organization that will eventually be accepted worldwide as the deficiencies of the nation-state become increasingly apparent.

It is clear that this process was precipitated by a set of powerful, and possibly irresistible, historical circumstances in post-1945 Europe. The most significant of these were the following:

- The need for economic reconstruction in war-torn Europe through cooperation and the creation of a larger market.

Jean Monnet (1888–1979)

French economist and administrator. Monnet was largely self-taught. He found employment during World War I coordinating Franco-British war supplies, and he was later appointed Deputy Secretary-General of the League of Nations. He was the originator of Winston Churchill's offer of union between the UK and France in 1940, which was abandoned once Pétain's Vichy regime had been installed. Monnet took charge of the French modernization programme under de Gaulle in 1945, and in 1950 he produced the Schuman Plan, from which the European Coal and Steel Community and the European Economic Community were subsequently developed. Although Monnet rejected intergovernmentalism in favour of supranational government, he was not a formal advocate of European federalism.

- The desire to preserve peace by permanently resolving the bitter Franco-German rivalry that caused the Franco-Prussian War (1870–71), and led to war in 1914 and 1939.
- The recognition that the '**German problem**' could be tackled only by integrating Germany into a wider Europe.
- The desire to safeguard Europe from the threat of Soviet expansionism, and to mark out for Europe an independent role and identity in a bipolar world order.
- The wish of the USA to establish a prosperous and united Europe, both as a market for US goods and as a bulwark against the spread of communism.
- The widespread acceptance, especially in continental Europe, that the sovereign nation-state was the enemy of peace and prosperity.

To some extent, the drift towards European integration was fuelled by an idealist commitment to internationalism (see p. 117) and the belief that international organizations embody a moral authority higher than that commanded by nation-states. However, more practical consideration, not least linked to economic matters, ultimately proved to be of greater significance. The European Coal and Steel Community (ECSC) was founded in 1952 on the initiative of Jean Monnet, adviser to the French foreign minister, Robert Schuman. Under the Treaty of Rome (1957), the European Economic Community (EEC) came into existence. The ECSC, EEC and Euratom (the body concerned with the peaceful use of nuclear energy) were formally merged in 1967, forming what became known as the European Community (EC). Although the community of the original 'Six' (France, Germany, Italy, the Netherlands, Belgium and Luxembourg) was expanded in 1973 with the inclusion of the UK, Ireland and Denmark, the 1970s was a period of stagnation. The integration process was relaunched, however, as a result of the signing in 1986 of the Single European Act (SEA), which envisaged an unrestricted flow of goods, services and people throughout Europe (a 'single market'), to be introduced by 1993. The Treaty of European Union (the TEU or Maastricht treaty), which became effective in 1993, marked the creation of the European Union (EU). This committed the EU's then-15 members (Greece, Portugal, Spain, Austria, Finland and Sweden having joined)

● **German problem**: The structural instability in the European state system caused by the emergence of a powerful and united Germany.

Inter-governmentalism, supranationalism

Intergovernmentalism refers to any form of interaction between states that takes place on the basis of sovereign independence. This includes treaties and alliances as well as leagues and confederations. Sovereignty is preserved through a process of unanimous decision-making that gives each state a veto, over vital national issues.

Supranationalism is the existence of an authority that is 'higher' than that of the nation-state and capable of imposing its will on it. It can therefore be found in international federations, where sovereignty is shared between central and peripheral bodies.

● **Political union**: Although the term lacks clarity, it refers to the coming together of a number of states under a common government; can imply supranational governance.

● **Monetary union**: The establishment of a single currency within an area comprising a number of states.

● **Veto**: The formal power to block a decision or action through the refusal of consent.

● **Qualified majority voting**: A system of voting in which different majorities are needed on different issues, with states' votes weighted (roughly) according to size.

to the principles of **political union** and **monetary union** (although Sweden, Denmark and the UK opted not to participate in monetary union). The centre-piece of this proposal was the establishment of a single European currency, the euro, which took place in 1999, with notes and coins being circulated in 2002. In 2004, the EU began its most radical phase of enlargement, as ten countries of Central and Eastern Europe and the Mediterranean joined, bringing about the reunification of Europe after decades of division by the Iron Curtain. Bulgaria and Romania joined in 2007, with negotiations for membership under way with Croatia, Macedonia and Turkey, and with Albania, Bosnia-Herzegovina, Montenegro and Serbia all potential candidate countries.

The EU is a very difficult political organization to categorize. In strict terms, it is no longer a confederation of independent states operating on the basis of intergovernmentalism (as the EEC and EC were at their inception). The sovereignty of member states was enshrined in the so-called 'Luxembourg compromise' of 1966. This accepted the general practice of unanimous voting in the Council, and granted each member state an outright **veto** on matters threatening vital national interests. As a result of the SEA and the TEU, however, the practice of **qualified majority voting**, which allows even the largest state to be outvoted, was applied to a wider range of policy areas, thereby narrowing the scope of the national veto. This trend has been compounded by the fact that EU law is binding on all member states, and that the power of certain EU bodies has expanded at the expense of national governments. The result is a political body that has both intergovernmental and supranational features; the former evident in the Council, and the latter primarily in the European Commission and the Court of Justice. The EU may not yet have created a federal Europe, but because of the superiority of European law over the national law of the member states, it is perhaps accurate to talk of a 'federalizing' Europe. An attempt was made to codify the EU's various constitutional rules, particularly in the light of enlargement, through the introduction of the Constitutional Treaty, commonly known as the 'EU Constitution'. This failed because of referendum defeats in the Netherlands and France in 2005 but, although many elements of the Constitutional Treaty were incorporated into the 2009 Lisbon Treaty, the episode highlights the extent to which, despite decades of institutional 'deepening', EU member states continue to function as states, still orientated around issues of national interest.

As an economic, monetary and, to a significant extent, political union brought about through voluntary cooperation amongst states, the EU is a unique political body: the world's only genuine experiment in supranational governance. The transition from Community to Union, achieved via the TEU, not only extended cooperation into areas such as foreign and security policy, home affairs and justice, and immigration and policing, but also established the notion of EU citizenship through the right to live, work and be politically active in any member state. This level of integration has been possible because of the powerful, and, some would argue, exceptional combination of pressures in post-1945 Europe that helped to shift public attitudes away from nationalism and towards cooperation, and to convince elites that national interests are ultimately better served by concerted action, rather than independence. Where such pre-requisites were weak, as in the case of the UK, often dubbed Europe's 'awkward partner', participation in the integration process has tended to be either reluctant

The eurozone crisis: regionalism beyond its limits?

Events: The euro officially came into existence on 1 January 1999. Of the EU's then-15 members, only the UK, Sweden and Denmark chose not to join the currency. The eurozone subsequently expanded to 17 members. The new currency achieved parity with the US dollar by November 2002 and increased steadily thereafter, peaking at a value of $1.59 in July 2008. However, the onset of the 2007–09 global financial crisis and a global recession created deepening problems. As growth slowed and tax revenues contracted, concern built about the heavily-indebted countries in the eurozone; notably, Portugal, Ireland, Greece, Spain and, to some extent, Italy. The crisis in Greece was so severe that, in May 2010, it led to a massive German-led eurozone bailout, backed by the IMF, with a further bailout being agreed in July 2011. Similar bailouts were agreed for Ireland in November 2010 and Portugal in May 2011, amid fears that 'contagion' might spread to Spain, Italy and beyond. In each of these countries severe austerity measures were introduced in the hope that spending cuts and increased taxation would reduce budget deficits and so restore the confidence of financial markets.

Significance: A single European currency had been seen as an important way of bolstering growth and prosperity within the EU. The key attraction of the euro was that its introduction promised to boost trade by reducing the costs and risks involved in transactions. Cross-currency transactions incur costs because of the need to buy or sell foreign currency. Such transactions involve risk and uncertainty because unanticipated exchange rate movements may make trade either more expensive or less expensive than expected. A single currency would therefore complete the single market, and help to ensure unrestricted labour and capital mobility. What is more, much had been done already to ensure the success of the euro, as many barriers to the free movement of goods and peoples within the EU had been removed by the Single European Act (1986) and the Treaty of European Union (1993). This encouraged the view that the EU constituted an optimal currency area, with confidence that, over time, the workings of the single currency would foster greater economic harmonization. An additional advantage was that a single currency would bring with it helpful economic disciplines; notably, limits on the size of budget deficits and national debts, as laid out in the 1997 Stability and Growth Pact.

The eurozone crisis, nevertheless, highlights the limitations and flaws in the single currency project. Some even argue that monetary union was, in principle, economically unfeasible and stretched European regionalism beyond its proper limits. Any transnational currency area is likely to contain such disparate economies, operating according to different business cycles, that it may be doomed to fail. A particular concern is that monetary union prevents an underperforming eurozone member from using one of the three traditional strategies for boosting growth: devaluation, reducing interest rates, and Keynesian-style deficit budgeting. For some, the chief problem with the eurozone is that monetary union was established in the absence of fiscal union, or 'fiscal federalism'. A major step to rectifying this, acknowledging that the Stability and Growth Pact has simply proved to be unenforceable, was the Fiscal Stability Treaty, or 'fiscal pact', signed by 25 EU states in March 2012. However, the fiscal pact has at least two key drawbacks. First, in substantially strengthening political union it may precipitate a backlash once populations recognize that losing 'fiscal sovereignty' is more significant than losing 'monetary sovereignty'. Second, the terms of the fiscal pact are designed to restore the confidence of financial markets, but their net effect may be to generate EU-wide austerity and make economic growth impossible to achieve.

or faltering (the UK rejected an invitation to join the EEC in 1957, and negotiated an opt-out from monetary union in 1991).

Nevertheless, although the EU has done much to realize the Treaty of Rome's goal of establishing 'an ever closer union', moving well beyond Charles de Gaulle's vision of Europe as a confederation of independent states, it stops far short of realizing the early federalists' dream of a European 'superstate'. This has been ensured, partly, by respect for the principle of **subsidiarity**, embodied in the TEU, and by the pragmatic approach to integration adopted by key states such as France and Germany. Decision-making within the 'New Europe' is increasingly made on the basis of multilevel governance, in which the policy process has interconnected subnational, national, intergovernmental and supranational levels, the balance between them shifting in relation to different issues and policy areas. This image of complex policy-making is more helpful than the sometimes sterile notion of a battle between national sovereignty and EU domination.

The EU in crisis?

Despite the progress it has made, the EU is confronted by a number of problems. For some, the failure of the EU has just been a matter of time. In this view, the level of diversity within the EU, in terms of history, traditions, language and culture, means that the EU can never match the capacity of the nation-state to engender loyalty and a sense of civic belonging, or to act effectively on the world stage. Tensions have been particularly intense over the long-term viability of the euro, with some arguing that the eurozone crisis since 2010 has shown that Euro-regionalism has gone too far, while others believe that it has not gone far enough (see p. 396).

Challenges have also arisen from the process of enlargement, especially the eastward expansion of the EU during 2004–07. This saw the EU grow from an organization of 15 members to one of 27 members. In some respects, the 2004–07 enlargements were the crowning achievement of the EU, in that they underpinned – and, in a sense, completed – the politico-economic transformation of Central and Eastern Europe, marking the Europe-wide triumph of liberal democracy (see p. 270). However, progressive enlargements have created tension between the EU's 'widening' and 'deepening' agendas. As a larger number of states and interests become involved in the EU policy process, decision-making becomes more difficult and threatens to become impossible. This created pressure for the adoption of an EU Constitution but, despite the resurrection of some of the elements of the rejected Constitutional Treaty through the Treaty of Lisbon, the EU continues to face the prospect of institutional sclerosis. Finally, there is the problem of the EU's so-called 'democratic deficit'. This is usually understood to mean the EU's lack of democratic accountability, resulting from the fact that its only directly elected body, the European Parliament, remains relatively weak, despite being bolstered by the Treaty of Lisbon. This, indeed, may merely highlight a deeper deficiency in all forms of transnational governance, which is that, as the locus of policy-making becomes more remote from the people, political legitimacy is compromised, perhaps fatally.

● **Subsidiarity**: The principle that decisions should be taken at the lowest appropriate level.

SUMMARY

● Politics has always had a spatial, or territorial, dimension, but this became more formalized and explicit with the emergence of the idea of territorial sovereignty. However, territorial politics have been reconfigured by a shift in political decision-making to bodies both 'above' and 'below' national government, giving rise to multi-level governance and the establishment of a complex policy process in which political authority is distributed vertically and horizontally.

● The most common forms of subnational territorial organization are federal and unitary systems. Federalism is based on the notion of shared sovereignty, in which power is distributed between the central and peripheral levels of government. Unitary systems, however, vest sovereign power in a single, national institution, which allows the centre to determine the territorial organization of the state.

● Other factors affecting territorial divisions include the party system and political culture; the economic system and level of material development; the geographical size of the state; and the level of cultural, ethnic and religious diversity. There has been a tendency towards centralization in most, if not all, systems. This reflects, in particular, the fact that central government alone has the resources and strategic position to manage economic life and deliver comprehensive social welfare.

● Regionalism is a process through which geographical regions become significant political and/or economic units, serving as the basis for cooperation and, possibly, identity. Transnational regionalism takes different forms depending on whether the primary areas for cooperation are economic, security related or political. The main theories of regional integration are federalism, functionalism and neofunctionalism.

● Regional integration has been taken furthest in Europe. The product of this process, the EU, is nevertheless a very difficult political organization to categorize, having both intergovernmental and supranational features. Amongst the challenges confronting the EU are tensions between the goals of 'widening' and 'deepening', continuing anxieties about the EU's 'democratic deficit' and the crisis in the eurozone which may threaten the long-term viability of monetary union.

Questions for discussion

● Why, and to what extent, is politics linked to territory?

● Is the federal principle applicable only to certain states, or to all states?

● What are the respective merits of federalism and devolution?

● Is the tendency towards centralization in modern states resistable?

● Why has economic regionalism made more progress than security regionalism or political regionalism?

● Does regionalism have the capacity to replace nationalism?

● What is the relationship between regionalism and globalization?

● What kind of political body is the EU?

● Is the process of European integration in danger of unravelling?

Further reading

Burgess, M., *Comparative Federalism: Theory and Practice* (2006). A comprehensive and accessible introduction to the study of federalism and federations.

Denters, B. and L. E. Rose (eds), *Comparing Local Governance: Trends and Developments* (2005). A useful examination of the nature and extent of transformation of local governance, which looks across Europe as well as at New Zealand, Australia and the USA.

Fawn, R. (ed.) *Globalising the Regional, Regionalising the Global* (2009). An authoritative collection of essays that examine theoretical and thematic approaches to regionalism, including six regional case studies.

McCormick, J., *Understanding the European Union: A Concise Introduction* (5th edn) (2011). A concise, lively and readable introduction to the workings and development of the EU, and the implications of European integration.

CHAPTER **18** # Security: Domestic and International

'The condition of man . . . is a condition of war against everyone.'

Thomas Hobbs, *Leviathan* (1651)

PREVIEW Security is the deepest and most abiding issue in politics. At its heart is the question: How can people live a decent and worthwhile existence, free from threats, intimidation and violence?' The search for security is therefore linked to the pursuit of order; and for the establishment of relative peace and stability amongst individuals and groups with different needs and interests. These concerns are commonly thought to resolved in the domestic realm by the existence of a sovereign state, a body capable of imposing its will on all the groups and institutions within its borders. Nevertheless, domestic security raises important issues, particularly about the roles of the institutions of the 'coercive state'; the police and the military. However, the issue of security is often considered to be especially pressing in international politics because the international realm, unlike the domestic realm, is anarchical, and therefore threatening and unstable by its nature. There has been fierce theoretical debate about whether this implies that international conflict and war are inevitable features of world affairs, and about the extent to which states are able to keep war at bay through cooperation. These debates have become increasingly pressing due to the advent of new challenges to international security, such as the rise of transnational terrorism and the proliferation of nuclear weapons. Finally, growing interest in the concept of 'human security' has shifted attention from the security of the state to the security of the individual, and, in the process, widened the notion of security to include, for instance, economic security, food security and personal security.

KEY ISSUES
- In what ways does civil policing differ from political policing?
- What mechanisms are used to make police forces publicly accountable?
- When, and in what ways, does the military intervene in domestic politics?
- What are the key theories of international security?
- How has the international security agenda changed in recent years?
- What are the implications of the notion of human security?

CONCEPT

Order

As a political principle, order refers to stable and predictable forms of behaviour and, above all, to those that safeguard personal security. Nevertheless, order has two very different political associations. Most commonly, it is linked with political authority and is thought to be achievable only if imposed 'from above' through a system of law. 'Law and order' thus become a single, fused concept. The alternative view links order to equality and social justice, and emphasizes that stability and security may arise naturally 'from below', through cooperation and mutual respect.

SECURITY BEYOND BOUNDARIES?

Although **security**, as the absence of danger, fear or anxiety, has a common character, a distinction is conventionally drawn between the maintenance of security in the domestic sphere and the maintenance of security in the international sphere. This implies that the domestic/international, or 'inside/outside', divide (discussed in Chapter 1) is of particular importance when it comes to security matters. From the 'inside' of politics, security refers to the state's capacity to maintain order within its own borders, using the instruments of the coercive state, the police and, at times, the military. Security, in this sense, deals with the relationship between the state and non-state actors of various kinds, ranging from criminal gangs to dissident groups and protest movements. In this respect, the state enjoys the great advantage that, in most cases, its sovereign power allows it to stand above all other associations and groups in society, ultimately by virtue of possessing a monopoly of the means of what Max Weber (see p. 82) called 'legitimate violence'.

From the 'outside' of politics, security refers to the capacity of the state to provide protection against threats from beyond its own borders, especially the ability of its armed forces to fight wars (see p. 415) and resist military attack. Security, in this sense, has traditionally dealt with the state's relationships with other states, reflecting the conventional assumption that only states possess the material and military resources to engage in warfare and, thereby, exert significant coercive influence on the international stage. However, whereas state sovereignty (see p. 58) supports the maintenance of security 'inside', it makes the maintenance of security 'outside' deeply problematic. As sovereignty means that there is no authority higher than the state, international politics is conducted in an environment that is anarchical, in the sense that it lacks enforceable rules or a pre-eminent power. It is commonly argued that this creates a bias in international affairs in favour of insecurity, rather than security.

Nevertheless, the 'inside/outside' divide in security matters has become increasingly difficult to sustain. This has been a result of recent trends and developments, not least those associated with globalization (see p. 142), which have seen a substantial growth in cross-border, or transnational, movements of people, goods, money, information and ideas. State borders may not have become irrelevant, but, in a technological age, they have certainly become more fragile or 'porous'. This was dramatically demonstrated by the terrorist attacks on New York and Washington on 11 September 2001, commonly dubbed 9/11. If the world's greatest power could be dealt such a devastating blow to its largest city and its national capital, what chance did other states have? Furthermore, the 'external' threat in this case came not from another state but from a non-state actor, a terrorist organization that operated more as a global network than as a nationally-based organization. For some, September 11 marked the point at which security ceased to be either a domestic issue or an international issue, but became instead a global issue.

Moreover, the blurring of the domestic/international divide has widened the opportunities available to governments to frame security issues in ways that are politically or ideologically advantageous. Within days of the 9/11, for instance, President George W. Bush portrayed the attacks as part of the 'war on terror' (see p. 401), a term that dominated subsequent discourse about both the nature of

● **Security**: the condition of being safe from harm or threats, usually understood as 'freedom from fear', implying physical harm.

Focus on . . .

The 'war on terror'

The 'war on terror' (or the 'war on terrorism'), known in US policy circles as the Global War on Terror, or GWOT, refers to the efforts by the USA and its key allies to root out and destroy the groups and forces deemed to be responsible for global terrorism. Launched in the aftermath of 9/11, it supposedly mapped out a strategy for a 'long war' that addresses the principal security threats to twenty-first-century world order. It aims, in particular, to counter the historically new combination of threats posed by non-state actors and especially terrorist groups, so-called 'rogue' states, weapons of mass destruction and the militant theories of radicalized Islam. Critics of the 'war on terror' have argued both that its inherent vagueness legitimizes an almost unlimited range of foreign and domestic policy interventions, and that, in building up a climate of fear and apprehension, it allows the USA and other governments to manipulate public opinion and manufacture consent for (possibly) imperialist and illiberal actions. Others have questioned whether it is possible to have a 'war' against an abstract noun.

the attacks themselves and how the USA and others should respond to them. By presenting 9/11 as an act of 'war', as opposed to a 'crime', it was lifted out of a domestic security frame and presented within an international frame. This, perhaps, served to prepare US public opinion, as well as the wider international community, for a response that had a clear international dimension, namely military intervention in Afghanistan and, for that matter, against any other country claimed to be implicated with 'terror'. To have portrayed 9/11 as a criminal act would have been to suggest a more modest and focused response: namely, a police action against accused international murders.

DOMESTIC SECURITY

The police and politics

The police force lies at the heart of the coercive state. The central purpose of a police force is to maintain domestic order. Police forces came into existence in the nineteenth century, largely as a result of the higher levels of social unrest and political discontent that industrialization unleashed. For instance, in the UK, a paid, uniformed, full-time and specially trained police force was established by Robert Peel in London in 1829 following the Peterloo Massacre of 1819 in Manchester, when cavalry had been used to break up a large but peaceful working-class demonstration. This type of police system was introduced throughout the UK in 1856 and was later adopted by many other countries. Although police forces and militaries are similar, in that they are both disciplined, uniformed, and (if to different degrees) armed bodies, important differences can be identified.

In the first place, whereas the military's essentially external orientation means that it is called into action only rarely (for example, in times of war, national

> ### CONCEPT
>
> ## Crime
>
> A crime is a breach of criminal law, which is law that establishes the relationship between the state and the individual. Criminals (persons convicted of a crime) are usually seen as being motivated by self-gain of some kind, rather than broader political or moral considerations, as in the case of civil disobedience (see p. 259). However, the causes of, and remedies for, crime are hotly contested. The general divide is between those who blame individual corruption and place their faith in punishment, and those who blame deprivation and thus look to reduce crime through social reform.

emergency, and national disaster), the police force's concern with domestic order means that it has a routine and everyday involvement in public life. The police force is also more closely integrated into society than is the military: its members and their families usually live in the communities in which they work, although, as discussed below, a distinctive police culture often develops. Furthermore, the police typically use non-military tactics: because of their reliance on at least a measure of consent and legitimacy, they are either usually unarmed (as in the UK), or their arms are primarily a form of self-defence. To some extent, however, modern developments have tended to blur the distinction between the police and the military. Not only have armed forces been called in to deal with domestic disorder, as during the Los Angeles riots of 1992, but police forces have also tended to develop an increasingly paramilitary character. This is reflected in their access to progressively more sophisticated weaponry and, in many states, in their adoption of a quasi-military mode of operation.

There are three contrasting approaches to the nature of policing and the role that it plays in society:

- The *liberal* perspective regards the police as an essentially neutral body, the purpose of which is to maintain domestic order through the protection of individual rights and liberties. In this view, police forces operate within a broad consensus and enjoy a high measure of legitimacy, based on the perception that policing promotes social stability and personal security. The police are principally concerned with protecting citizens from each other. As policing is strictly concerned with upholding the rule of law (see p. 344), it has no broader political function.
- The *conservative* perspective stresses the police's role in preserving the authority of the state and ensuring that its jurisdiction extends throughout the community. This view, which is rooted in a more pessimistic view of human nature, emphasizes the importance of the police as an enforcement agency capable of controlling social unrest and civil disorder. In this light, police forces are inevitably seen as mechanisms of political control.
- The *radical* perspective advances a much more critical view of police power. This portrays police forces as tools of oppression that act in the interests of the state, rather than of the people, and serve elites, rather than the masses. In the Marxist version of this theory, the police are seen specifically as defenders of property and upholders of capitalist class interests.

The role of the police force is also shaped by the nature of the political system in which it operates and the ways in which the government uses the police. Civil policing tends to be distinguished from political policing, and divisions are usually identified between liberal states and so-called 'police states'.

Role of the police

Civil policing is the aspect of police work with which the general public is usually most familiar and which dominates the public image of the police force: the police force exists to 'fight crime'. This process increasingly has an international character, brought about by the advent of major transnational criminal organizations associated, in particular, with drug-trafficking and people-trafficking. However,

● **Civil policing**: The role of the police in the enforcement of criminal law.

the routine process of maintaining civil order is very different when undertaken in, say, rural India than in modern cities such as New York, Paris and St Petersburg. It is widely accepted that, while small and relatively homogeneous communities are characterized by a significant level of self-policing, this changes as societies become more fragmented (socially and culturally), and as large-scale organization depersonalizes relationships and interaction. The spread of industrialization in the twentieth century therefore brought about a measure of convergence in police organization and tactics in different parts of the world. Police forces everywhere tend to confront similar problems in the form of, for example, traffic infringements, car theft, burglary, street crime and organized crime.

However, contrasting styles of civil policing have been adopted. On the one hand, there is the idea of **community policing**. This system has traditionally operated in Japan. Japanese police officers are expected to know and visit the various families and workplaces that fall within their area of jurisdiction, operating either from police boxes (*koban*) or from residential police stations (*chuza-isho*). The success of this method, however, depends on the police being regarded as respected members of the local community and on citizens accepting that their lives will be closely monitored. Pressure for efficiency and cost cutting led to the phasing out of community policing in the UK and elsewhere in the 1960s and 1970s, with a shift towards what is called 'fire brigade' policing. This emphasizes the capacity of the police to react to breaches of law when they occur, in the hope that crime will be prevented by the effectiveness of the police response. Fire-brigade policing, or reactive policing, requires the adoption of harder, even paramilitary, tactics, and a greater emphasis on technology and arms. Pioneered in the early 1990s in New York, 'zero tolerance' policing, or positive policing, has been widely adopted, formally or informally, in many parts of the world. Based on the so-called **'broken windows theory'**, this relies on a strategy of strict enforcement in relation to minor offences (hence 'zero tolerance') in order to reduce levels of serious crime. It works on the basis that unrestrained petty crime creates the impression that 'no one is in control'.

Policing can, nevertheless, be 'political' in two senses. First, policing may be carried out in accordance with political biases or social prejudices that favour certain groups or interests over others. Second, policing may extend beyond civil matters and impact on specifically political disputes. The first concern has traditionally been raised by radicals and socialists, who dismiss the idea that police forces (or any other state body) act in a neutral and impartial fashion. From this perspective, the training and discipline of the police force and the nature of police work itself tend to breed a culture that is socially authoritarian and politically conservative. The working classes, strikers, protesters, women and racial minorities are therefore likely to be amongst the groups treated less sympathetically by the police.

Despite mechanisms of public accountability and protestations of impartiality, there is undoubtedly evidence to support these allegations, at least in particular circumstances. For instance, the US National Advisory Commission on Civil Disorders, set up by Lyndon Johnson to investigate the urban unrest that broke out in the USA during the 'long hot summer' of 1967, found that many of the disturbances were linked to the grievances of black ghetto dwellers about abusive or discriminatory police actions. The attack on Rodney King by four white Los Angeles police officers, whose acquittal in 1992 sparked two days of rioting, kept

● **Community policing:** A style of policing in which a constant police presence in the community seeks to build trust and cooperation with the public.

● **Broken windows theory:** The theory that minor offences (broken windows) that are not speedily dealt with advertise that an area is not cared for and so lead to more, and more serious, offenses.

CONCEPT

Civil liberty

Civil liberty refers to a private sphere of existence that belongs to the citizen, not the state. Civil liberty therefore encompasses a range of 'negative' rights, usually rooted in the doctrine of human rights, which demand non-interference on the part of government. The classic civil liberties are usually thought to include the rights to freedom of speech, freedom of the press, freedom of religion and conscience, freedom of movement and freedom of association. These key freedoms are generally seen as vital to the functioning of liberal-democratic societies.

● **Institutional racism:** A form of racism that operates through the culture or procedural rules of an organization, as distinct from personal prejudice.

● **Police state:** A state that relies on a system of arbitrary and indiscriminate policing in which civil liberties are routinely abused.

this image alive. Similarly, in the UK, the Macpherson Report (1999) into the murder of Stephen Lawrence concluded that the Metropolitan Police were guilty of **institutional racism**.

The level of political policing, meaning the use of the police as a political, rather than civil, instrument, has increased as societies have become more complex and fragmented. Some observers challenge the very distinction between civil and political areas of police work, arguing that all crime is 'political', in the sense that it springs from, and seeks to uphold, the established distribution of wealth, power and other resources in society. The neutrality of the police force in the eyes of the public is particularly compromised when it is used to control strikes, demonstrations and civil unrest that stem from deep divisions in society. The threat of terrorism (see p. 416), especially since the events of 11 September 2001, has drawn policing into some particularly difficult areas. Not only have many states strengthened national security legislation, and in the process extended the powers of the police but, in the USA, the UK and elsewhere, policing strategies have been adapted so as to take better account of particular threats posed by terrorism. Both of these developments have led to allegations that civil liberties have been compromised through the emergence of a national security state.

Police states

However, the widening of police powers has been taken further in so-called 'police states'. In a police state, the police force operates outside a legal framework and is accountable to neither the courts nor the general public. Police states have totalitarian (see p. 269) features, in that the excessive and unregulated power that is vested in the police is designed to create a climate of fear and intimidation in which all aspects of social existence are brought under political control. However, a police state is not run by the police force in the same way as a military regime is controlled by the armed forces. Rather, the police force acts as a private army that is controlled by, and acts in the interests of, a ruling elite.

This was clearly the case in Nazi Germany, which spawned a vast apparatus of political intimidation and secret policing. The SA (*Sturm Abteilung*), or 'Brownshirts', operated as political bullies and street fighters; the Gestapo was a secret police force; the SD (*Sicherheitsdienst*) carried out intelligence and security operations; and the SS (*Schutzstaffel*) developed, under Himmler, into a state within a state. Russia also relied heavily on the activities of the secret police. Lenin formed the *Cheka* in 1917 to undermine his political opponents, and this mutated into the OGPU, then the NKVD (Stalin's personal instrument of terror), in 1953 the KGB and, since 1991, the Federal Security Service (FSB).

At the same time, some states usually classified as 'liberal' have also found a role for the secret police. The CIA in the USA has certainly engaged in a range of covert external operations, including the 1973 Pinochet *coup* in Chile, several attempted assassinations of the Cuban leader Fidel Castro, and the supply of arms to Contra rebels who are fighting against the Sandinista government in Nicaragua in the 1980s. It has also been subject to allegations of interference in domestic affairs, not least in the form of the still unsubstantiated claim that it played a role in the assassination of President Kennedy in 1963. Terroristic policing was used in

Northern Ireland in the late 1960s in the form of the B-Specials. This was an aux-iliary unit of the Royal Ulster Constabulary formed to control civilian demonstra-tions and fight the Irish Republican Army (IRA). The B-Specials engaged in partisan and routine intimidation of the Catholic community and were disbanded in 1969, but only as the British army took on a more prominent role in policing 'the troubles'.

The military and domestic politics

The development of modern armed forces can be traced back to the period following the Middle Ages when European powers started to develop a stan-dardized form of military organization, usually based on a standing army. During the nineteenth century, the military became a specialized institution with a professional leadership separate from the rest of society. European colo-nialism, in turn, ensured that this military model was adopted all over the world, turning the military into a near-universal component of state organiza-tion. Costa Rica is sometimes identified as the classic exception to this rule, but its lack of armed forces is possible only because of the security provided by the US military.

The military is a political institution of a very particular kind. Four factors distinguish the military from other institutions and give it a distinct, and at times overwhelming, advantage over civilian organizations. First, as an instru-ment of war, the military enjoys a virtual monopoly of weaponry and substan-tial coercive power. As the military has the capacity to prop up or topple a regime, its loyalty is essential to state survival. Second, armed forces are tightly organized and highly-disciplined bodies, characterized by a hierarchy of ranks and a culture of strict obedience. They are, thus, an extreme example of bureau-cracy (see p. 361) in the Weberian sense. Third, the military is invariably char-acterized by a distinctive culture and set of values, and an *esprit de corps* that prepare its personnel to fight, kill and possibly die. Sometimes portrayed as implicitly right-wing and deeply authoritarian (by virtue of its traditional emphasis on leadership, duty and honour), military culture can also be grounded in creeds such as revolutionary socialism (as in China), or Islamic fundamentalism (as in Iran). Fourth, the armed forces are often seen, and generally regard themselves, as being 'above' politics, in the sense that, because they guarantee the security and integrity of the state, they are the repository of the national interest.

The character of particular armed forces is nevertheless shaped by internal and external factors. These include the history and traditions of the military and specific regiments or units, and the nature of the broader political system, the political culture and the values of the regime itself. For example, the political orientation of the People's Liberation Army (PLA) in China is deeply influenced by the decisive role it played in establishing the communist regime in 1949 and by strict party control at every level of the Chinese military. In Israel, the military enjoys an unusual position of trust and respect, based on its role in absorbing and socializing immigrants, and on its record of safeguarding the security of the Israeli state. Finally, although all militaries serve as instruments of war (examined later in the chapter), some militaries also play a major role in domes-tic politics.

Guarantee of domestic order

Although military force is usually directed against other political societies, it may also be a decisive factor in domestic politics. However, the circumstances in which militaries are deployed, and the uses to which they are put, vary from system to system and from state to state. One of the least controversial non-military tasks that armed forces may be called on to undertake is to act as an emergency service in the event of natural and other disasters. This type of involvement in domestic affairs is exceptional and is usually devoid of political significance. However, the same cannot be said of circumstances in which the armed forces are used to police domestic civil disturbances or disputes.

US troops, for instance, were deployed to implement federal racial desegregation orders during the civil rights struggles of the 1950s and 1960s. Similarly, in the UK in the 1970s and 1980s, the army was brought in during industrial disputes to provide emergency fire and ambulance services. Such actions provoke criticism, not only because the military is used in ways that encroach on responsibilities that usually belong to the police, but also because they compromise the traditional neutrality of the armed forces. This highlights the difficulty of distinguishing between the domestic use of the military as a 'public' instrument serving the national interest and its use as a 'political' weapon furthering the partisan goals of the government of the day. This distinction becomes still more blurred when the military is used to quell civil unrest or counter popular insurrection.

Certain states confront levels of political tension and unrest that are quite beyond the capacity of the civilian police to contain. This occurs particularly in the case of serious religious, ethnic or national conflict. In such circumstances, the military can become the only guarantee of the integrity of the state, and may even be drawn into what may amount to a civil war to achieve this end. In 1969, UK troops were dispatched to Northern Ireland, initially to defend the beleaguered minority Catholic community, but increasingly to contain a campaign of sectarian terror waged by the IRA and opposing 'loyalist' groups such as the Ulster Defence Association (UDA) and the Ulster Defence Force (UDF). The Indian army has been used on a number of occasions to counter civil unrest and restore political order. These have included the eviction of Sikh separatists from the Golden Temple at Amritsar in 1984 at the cost of 1,000 lives, and the seizure of Ayodhya from Hindu fundamentalists in 1992 following the destruction of the ancient Babri mosque. Russian troops were dispatched to the republic of Chechnya in 1994 to thwart its bid for independence in an operation that turned into a full-scale war, later developing into an ongoing guerrilla struggle.

In cases in which political legitimacy has collapsed altogether, the military may become the only prop of the regime, safeguarding it from popular **rebellion** or revolution. When this occurs, however, all semblance of constitutionalism (see p. 337) and consent is abandoned, as the government becomes an outright dictatorship. Thus, in May 1989, the survival of the Chinese communist regime was maintained only by the military assault on Tiananmen Square, which effectively neutralized the growing democracy movement. Such circumstances place a heavy strain on the loyalty of officers and the obedience of troops required to inflict violence on civilian demonstrators. Trouble was taken to deploy in Beijing only PLA divisions brought in from the countryside whose political loyalty could be counted on. During the Egyptian revolution in 2011, the unwillingness of the

● **Rebellion**: A popular uprising against the established order, usually (unlike a revolution) aimed at replacing rulers, rather than the political system itself.

military to take action against rioters in Cairo and elsewhere eventually forced President Mubarak to step down and turn power over to the Supreme Council of the Armed Forces, which prepared for the calling of elections.

Alternative to civilian rule

The military's capacity to intervene directly in domestic politics can lead, in extreme cases, to the establishment of military rule (as discussed in Chapter 12). Just as the military can prop up an unpopular government or regime, it can also remove and replace the governing elite, or topple the regime itself. The defining feature of military rule is that members of the armed forces displace civilian politicians, meaning that the leading posts in government are filled on the basis of the person's position within the military chain of command. One version of military rule is the military junta. Most commonly found in Latin America, the military junta is a form of collective military government centred on a command council of officers whose members usually represent the three services (the army, navy and air force). In its classic form, for example in Argentina in 1978–83, civilians are excluded from the governing elite, and trade union and broader political activity is banned. However, rivalry between the services and between leading figures usually ensures that formal positions of power change hands relatively frequently. In other cases, a form of military dictatorship emerges as a single individual gains pre-eminence within the junta, as with Colonel Papadopoulos in Greece in 1967–74, General Pinochet in Chile after the 1973 *coup*, and General Abacha in Nigeria, 1993–98.

It is difficult, however, for military rule to exist in a stable and enduring political form. While military leaders may highlight the chronic weakness, intractable divisions and endemic corruption (see p. 365) of civilian government, it is unlikely that military rule will provide a solution to these problems, or that it will be perceived as legitimate, except during temporary periods of national crisis or political emergency. This is why military regimes are typically characterized by the suspension of civil liberties and the suppression of all potential sources of popular involvement in politics. Protest and demonstrations are curtailed, opposition political parties and trade unions are banned, and the media are subjected to strict censorship. As a result, the military often prefers to rule behind the scenes and exercise power covertly through a civilianized leadership. This occurred in Zaire under Mobutu, who came to power in a military *coup* in 1965, but later allowed the army to withdraw progressively from active politics by ruling through the Popular Movement of the Revolution, founded in 1967. In the 1960s and 1970s, Egypt's transition from military government to authoritarian civilian rule was achieved under Gamal Nasser and Anwar Sadat, both military figures. The appointment of civilian cabinets and the emergence of parties and interest group politics not only strengthened the regime's legitimacy, but also gave Nasser and Sadat a greater measure of freedom from their own militaries.

● **International security**: Conditions in which the mutual survival and safety of states is secured through measures taken to prevent or punish aggression, usually within a rule-governed international order.

INTERNATIONAL SECURITY

International security occupies a central position in the broader academic discipline of international relations (IR). Indeed, a recurrent theme in IR has

CONCEPT

Realism

Realism is a theory of international politics whose core theme can be summed up as: egoism plus anarchy equals power politics. Some, nevertheless, argue that this formulation betrays a basic theoretical fault line within realism, dividing it into two schools of thought. *Classical realism* explains power politics largely in terms of human selfishness or egoism, suggesting that, as states prioritize self-interest and survival, the international realm tends towards unending conflict. *Neorealism* (or structural realism) explains power politics in terms of the structural dynamics of an anarchic international system that forces states to rely on military self-help.

● **Power politics**: An approach to politics based on the assumption that the pursuit of power is the principal human goal; the term is sometimes used descriptively.

● **Egoism**: Greater concern with one's own interests or well-being, or selfishness; the belief that one's own interests are morally superior to those of others.

● **National interest**: Foreign policy goals, objectives or policy preferences that supposedly benefit a society as a whole (the foreign policy equivalent of the 'public interest').

been the search for ways of countering the risk, uncertainty and deep insecurity that are sometimes believed to be rooted in the international system itself. As pointed out above, such thinking is based on the principle of state sovereignty, which, in the domestic realm, implies order and stability (as no group or body can challenge the supreme authority of the state), but in the international realm implies disorder and possibly chaos (as no body stands above the state and can impose order upon it). However, the issue of security in the international realm has been the subject of considerable theoretical debate, with quite different approaches to the prospects for international security being advanced by realist, liberal and critical theorists. Moreover, since the end of the Cold War a series of new security challenges have emerged that are particularly problematic, because, in various ways, they exploit the greater interconnectedness of the modern world. These include the shift from traditional, inter-state war to so-called 'new' wars, the rise of transnational terrorism and an increase in nuclear proliferation. A further, and linked, development has been the tendency to rethink the concept of security at a still deeper level, usually through a concern with what has been called 'human security' (see p. 418), in contrast to 'national' or 'state' security.

Approaches to international politics

Realist approach

Realism (sometimes called 'political realism') has been the dominant perspective on international politics since World War II. It claims to offer an account of international politics that is 'realistic', in the sense that it is hard-headed and, as realists see it, devoid of wishful thinking and deluded moralizing. For realists, international politics is, first and last, about power and self-interest. This is why it is often portrayed as a '**power politics**' model of world affairs. As Hans Morgenthau (1948) put it, 'Politics is a struggle for power over men, and whatever its ultimate aim may be, power is its immediate goal and the modes of acquiring, maintaining and demonstrating it determine the technique of political action'.

The theory of power politics is based on two core assumptions. The first is that people are essentially selfish and competitive, meaning that **egoism** is the defining characteristic of human nature. This is an idea that provides the foundation for the political theories of Niccolò Machiavelli (see p. 5) and Thomas Hobbes (see p. 61). However, whereas Machiavelli and Hobbes were primarily concerned to explain the conduct of individuals or social groups, realist international theorists have been concerned, above all, with the behaviour of states, seen as the most important actors on the world stage. The fact that states are composed of, and led by, people who are inherently selfish, greedy and power-seeking means that state behaviour must exhibit the same characteristics, human egoism implying state egoism. State egoism leads to international conflict, and possibly war, because each state pursues its own **national interest**, and these are, by their nature, incompatible.

From the 1970s onwards, new thinking within the realist tradition started to emerge which was critical of 'early' or 'classical' realism. Under the influence of Kenneth Waltz (see p. 409), 'neorealists' or 'structural' realists started to explain the behaviour of states on the basis of assumptions about the structure of the

Kenneth Waltz (born 1924)

US international relations theorist. Waltz's initial contribution to international relations, outlined in *Man, the State, and War* (1959), adopted a conventional realist
approach and remains the basic starting point for the study of war. His *Theory of
International Politics* (1979) was the most influential book of international relations
theory of its generation. Ignoring human nature and the ethics of statecraft, Waltz
used system theory to explain how international anarchy effectively determines the
actions of states, with change in the international system occurring through changes
in the distribution of capabilities between and amongst states. Waltz's analysis was
closely associated with the Cold War, and the belief that bipolarity provides a better
guarantee of peace and security than does multipolarity.

international system and, in particular, the fact that, in the absence of world
government, the international system is characterized by anarchy. Being, in
effect, an international 'state of nature', the system tends towards tension, conflict
and the unavoidable possibility of war because states are forced to ensure
survival and security by relying on their own capacities and resources, rather
than any form of external support. This leads to the creation of a 'self-help'
system in which states inevitably prioritize the build-up of military power as the
only strategy that promises to ensure survival.

The realist approach to international politics has important implications for
security. Indeed, Waltz (1979) presented security as the 'highest end' of international politics. From the realist perspective, states have primary responsibility for
maintaining security, as reflected in the notion of '**national security**'. The major
threats to security therefore come from other states. In this way, the threat of
violence and other forms of physical coercion are intrinsically linked to the
prospects of inter-state war. National security is, thus, closely linked to the
prevention of such wars, usually through the build-up of military capacity to
deter potential aggressors. However, the fact that states are inclined to treat other
states as enemies does not inevitably lead to bloodshed and open violence.
Rather, realists believe that conflict can be contained by the **balance of power**.
Classical realists have thus advocated that the balance of power be embraced as
a policy which uses diplomacy, or possibly war, to prevent any state from achieving a predominant position in the international system. Neorealists, for their
part, view the balance of power as a system, rather than as a policy; that is, as a
condition in which no one state predominates over others, tending to create
general equilibrium and discourage any state from pursuing hegemonic ambitions.

● **National security**:
Conditions in which the survival
and safety of a particular
nation or state is secured,
usually through the build up of
military capacity to deter
aggression.

● **Balance of power**: A
condition in which no one state
predominates over others,
tending to create general
equilibrium and curb the
hegemonic ambitions of states.

Liberal approach

The key ideas and themes of liberal ideology are examined in Chapter 2.
However, liberalism has also had a major impact on the discipline of international relations. This draws on a much older tradition of so-called 'idealist' theo-

Immanuel Kant (1724–1804)

German philosopher. Kant spent his entire life in Königsberg (which was then in East Prussia), becoming professor of logic and metaphysics at the University of Königsberg in 1770. His 'critical' philosophy holds that knowledge is not merely an aggregate of sense impressions; it depends on the conceptual apparatus of human understanding. Kant's political thought was shaped by the central importance of morality. He believed that the law of reason dictated categorical imperatives, the most important of which was the obligation to treat others as 'ends', and never only as 'means'. Kant's most important works include *Critique of Pure Reason* (1781), *Critique of Practical Reason* (1788) and *Critique of Judgement* (1790).

rizing which dates back, via Kant's belief in the possibility of 'universal and perpetual peace', to the Middle Ages and the ideas of early '**just war**' thinkers such as Thomas Aquinas (1225–74). Liberalism offers an optimistic vision of international politics, based, ultimately, on a belief in human rationality and moral goodness (although liberals also believe that humans are naturally self-interested creatures). This inclines them to believe that the principle of balance or harmony operates in all forms of social interaction. Individuals, groups and, for that matter, states may pursue self-interest, but a natural equilibrium will tend to assert itself. Just as, from a liberal perspective, natural or unregulated equilibrium emerges in economic life (Adam Smith's (see p. 130) 'invisible hand' of capitalism), a balance of interests develops amongst the states of the world. This inclines liberals to believe in internationalism (see p. 117) and to hold that realists substantially underestimate the scope for cooperation and trust to develop within the international system (see p. 412).

Nevertheless, liberals do not believe that peace and international order simply arise entirely on their own. Instead, mechanisms are needed to constrain the ambitions of sovereign states, and these take the form of **international 'regimes'** or international organizations. This reflects the ideas of what is called 'liberal institutionalism'. The basis for such a view lies in the 'domestic analogy', the idea that insight into international politics can be gained by reflecting on the structures of democratic politics. Taking particular account of social contract theory, as developed by thinkers such as Hobbes and John Locke (see p. 31), this highlights the fact that only the construction of a sovereign power can safeguard citizens from the chaos and barbarity of the 'state of nature'. If order can only be imposed 'from above' in domestic politics, the same must be true of international politics. This provided the basis for the establishment of an international rule of law, which, as US President Woodrow Wilson (1856–1924) put it, would turn the 'jungle' of international politics into a 'zoo'. Liberals have therefore generally viewed the trend towards global governance (see p. 432) in positive terms (as discussed in Chapter 19). Against realist support for national security, they have also supported the idea of 'collective security' (see p. 411), the notion that underpinned the construction of the League of Nations and, later, the United Nations.

● **Just war:** A war that in its purpose and content meets certain ethical standards, and so is (allegedly) morally justified.

● **International regime:** Sets of norms or rules that govern the interactions of states and non-state actors in particular issue areas.

Collective security

The idea of collective security, simply stated, is that aggression can best be resisted by united action taken by a number of states. It suggests that states, as long as they pledge themselves to defend one another, have the capacity either to deter aggression in the first place, or to punish the transgressor, if international order has been breached. Successful collective security depends (1) on states being roughly equal, (2) on all states being willing to bear the cost of defending one another, and (3) on the existence of an international body that has the moral authority and military capacity to take effective action.

● **Security paradox:** The paradox that a build up of military capacity designed to strengthen national security may be counter-productive, in that it encourages other states to adopt more threatening and hostile postures.

Critical approaches

Since the late 1980s, the range of critical approaches to international politics has expanded considerably. Until that point, Marxism had constituted the principal alternative to mainstream realist and liberal theories. What made the Marxist approach distinctive was that it placed its emphasis not on patterns of conflict and cooperation between states, but on structures of economic power and the role played in world affairs by international capital. It thus brought international political economy, sometimes seen as a sub-field within IR, into focus. However, hastened by the end of the Cold War, a wide range of 'new voices' started to influence the study of world politics, notable examples include constructivism (see p. 16), critical theory, poststructuralism, postcolonialism, feminism and green politics. In view of their diverse philosophical underpinnings and contrasting political viewpoints, it is tempting to argue that the only thing that unites these 'new voices' is a shared antipathy towards mainstream thinking. However, two broad similarities can be identified. The first is that, albeit in different ways and to different degrees, they have tried to go beyond the positivism of mainstream theory, emphasizing instead the role of consciousness in shaping social conduct and therefore world affairs. Second, critical theories are 'critical' in that, in their different ways, they oppose the dominant forces and interests in modern world affairs and so contest the international status quo, usually by aligning themselves with marginal or oppressed groups. Each of them, thus, seeks to uncover inequalities and asymmetries that mainstream theories tend to ignore.

The critical theories that have most clearly addressed the issue of security are constructivism and feminism. Constructivism has been the most influential post-positivist approach to international theory, and has gained significantly greater attention since the end of the Cold War. Constructivists who follow in the tradition of Alexander Wendt (1999), argue that interactions between states are mediated by beliefs, values and assumptions that structure both how states see themselves and how they understand, and respond to, the structures within which they operate. This implies, for instance, that state behaviour is not determined, as neorealists assert, by the structural dynamics of international anarchy, but by how they *view* that anarchy. As Wendt (1992) put it, 'anarchy is what states make of it'. While some states view anarchy as dangerous and threatening, others may see it as the basis for freedom and opportunity. An 'anarchy of friends' is thus very different from an 'anarchy of enemies'. Constructivists argue that this leaves open the possibility that states may transcend a narrow conception of self-interest and embrace the cause of global justice, even cosmopolitanism (see pp. 51–2). Feminists, on the other hand, have criticized the realist view of security on two other grounds. In the first place, it is premised on masculinist assumptions about rivalry, competition and inevitable conflict, arising from a tendency to see the world in terms of interactions amongst a series of power-seeking, autonomous actors. Second, feminists have argued that the conventional idea of national security tends to be self-defeating as a result of the **security paradox**. This creates what has been called the 'insecurity of security'. For many feminists, the gendered nature of security is also reflected in the gendered nature of war and armed conflict, as highlighted by, amongst others, Jean Bethke Elshtain (see p. 413).

Debating...
Is peace and cooperation amongst states destined to remain elusive?

International relations is centrally concerned with the balance between cooperation and conflict in world affairs, traditionally linked to the issues of war and peace. While realists argued that the tendency towards international conflict and, probably, war are ultimately irresistible, liberals and others highlight the possibility of trust and cooperation amongst states. Why are state relations so often characterized by fear and hostility, and can this fear and hostility ever be overcome?

YES

Absence of world government. The tragedy of international politics is that the only way of ensuring enduring peace and order – the establishment of world government – is either starkly unrealistic (states will never sacrifice their sovereignty to a higher body), or profoundly undesirable (it will lead to global despotism). As neorealists point out, international anarchy tends towards conflict because states are forced to survive through military self-help, and this is only contained by a fortuitous, but always temporary, balance of power. For 'offensive' realists (who believe that states seek to maximize power and not merely security), when the balance of power breaks down, war is the likely outcome (Mearsheimer, 2001).

The security dilemma. Conflict and, even, war are inevitable because relations between states are always characterized by uncertainty and suspicion. This is best explained through the security dilemma. This is the dilemma that arises from the fact that a build-up of military capacity for defensive reasons by one state is always liable to be interpreted as aggressive by other states. The irresolvable uncertainty about these matters leads to arms races and a ratcheting-up of tension between states, especially because states are likely to assume that the actions of other states are aggressive because misperception in this respect risks national disaster.

Relative gains. International conflict is encouraged by the fact that the primary concern of states is to maintain or improve their position relative to other states; that is, to make 'relative' gains. Apart from anything else, this discourages cooperation and reduces the effectiveness of international organizations because, although all states may benefit from a particular action or policy, each state is actually more worried about whether other states benefit more than it does. In this view, international politics is a zero-sum game: states can only improve their position within the power hierarchy at the expense of other states.

NO

An interdependent world. Realism's narrow preoccupation with the military and diplomatic dimensions of international politics, the so-called 'high politics' of security and survival, is misplaced. Instead, the international agenda is becoming broader with greater attention being given to the 'low politics' of welfare, environmental protection and political justice. Of particular importance is the growing tendency for states to prioritize trade over war, recognizing both that this opens up a non-military route to state progress and, by deepening economic interdependence, makes war perhaps impossible. States are concerned with making 'absolute' gains, engaging in cooperation in order to be better off in real terms, rather than a self-defeating struggle for 'relative' gains.

International society. The realist emphasis on power politics has been modified by the recognition that interacting states constitute a 'society' and not merely a 'system'. To a growing degree, international society is rule-governed and biased in favour of order and predictability, rather than risk and uncertainty. This occurs because, as states interact with one another, they develop norms and rules enabling trust and cooperation to emerge, a tendency supported by international law, diplomacy and the activities of international organizations.

Democratic peace thesis. Liberals have long argued that state relations are structured as much by the internal, constitutional structure of the state as they are by external factors such as the structural dynamics of the international system. In particular, strong empirical evidence that democratic states do not go to war against one another suggests a link between peace and democracy. 'Democratic peace' is upheld by the fact that public opinion normally favours the avoidance of war; that democracies are inclined to use non-violent forms of conflict resolution in all of their affairs; and that cultural ties develop amongst democracies, encouraging them to view each other as friends not enemies.

Jean Bethke Elshtain (born 1941)

US political philosopher. Elshtain's *Public Man, Private Woman* (1981) made a major contribution to feminist scholarship in examining the role of gender in fashioning the division between public and private spheres in political theory. In *Women and War* (1987), she discussed the perceptual lenses that determine the roles of men and women in war, interweaving personal narrative and historical analysis to highlight the myths that men are 'just warriors' and women are 'beautiful souls' to be saved. In *Just War Against Terror* (2003), Elshtain argued that the 'war on terror' was just, in that it was fought against the genocidal threat of 'apocalyptic' terrorism, a form of warfare that made no distinction between combatants and non-combatants.

New security challenges

From traditional wars to 'new' wars

International security has usually implied a search for the conditions in which traditional, inter-state wars can be ended or prevented. Since the birth of the modern international system through the Peace of Westphalia (1648), war has been seen as an instrument of state policy, a means through which states gained ascendancy over one another, or sought to resist other states' bid for ascendancy. As the Prussian general and military theorist Karl von Clausewitz (1780–1831) put it, 'War is merely a continuation of politics (or policy) by other means'. However, war and warfare have changed. Since World War II, the number of inter-state wars with 20 or more deaths per year rose to 9 in 1987, then dropped to 1 in 2002, 2 in 2003 and zero in 2004. Starting with the tactics employed in the 1950s and 1960s by national liberation movements in places such as Algeria, Vietnam and Palestine, and then extending to conflicts in countries such as Somalia, Liberia, Sudan and the Congo, a new style of warfare has developed, possibly even redefining war itself. Following the break-up of the USSR and Yugoslavia in the 1990s, such 'new' wars occurred in Bosnia and in the Caucasus, particularly Chechnya, as well as in Iraq and Afghanistan, often seen as part of the larger 'war on terror'.

'New' wars tend to be **civil wars**, rather than inter-state wars. About 95 per cent of armed conflicts since the mid-1990s have occurred within states, not between states. Civil wars have become common in the postcolonial world, where colonialism (see p. 122) has often left a heritage of ethnic or regional rivalry, economic underdevelopment and weakened state power; hence the emergence of 'quasi-states' or 'failed states' (see p. 76). These states are weak, in that they fail the most basic test of state power: they are unable to maintain domestic order and personal security, meaning that civil strife, and even civil war, become routine. This is the point, however, where domestic security becomes entangled with international security, as the only effective protection for the domestic population may come from external sources in the form of humanitarian intervention (see p. 424). The complex and problematic nature of such interventions can be examined through the example of intervention in Libya in 2011 (see p. 414).

● **Civil war**: An armed conflict between politically organized groups within a state, usually fought to gain (or retain) control over the state, or to establish a new state.

Intervention in Libya: a responsibility to protect?

Events: In February 2011, a popular uprising erupted against President Gaddafi, as part of the Arab Spring (see p. 88). However, unlike earlier events in Tunisia and Egypt, the Gaddafi regime launched a brutal crackdown and pro-Gaddafi forces started to push eastward, threatening the rebel stronghold of Benghazi. Fearing a bloodbath, the international community responded swiftly. By the end of February, the UN Security Council had placed sanctions, an arms embargo and an asset freeze on Libya, and referred Gaddafi's crimes against humanity to the International Criminal Court in the Hague. On 17 March, the Security Council passed Resolution 1973, which mandated that 'all necessary measures' be taken to protect civilians'. Two days later, a US-led coalition launched air and missile strikes against Libyan forces, responsibility for what was dubbed Operation Unified Protector quickly being transferred to NATO. In policing the arms embargo and patrolling the no-fly zone over Libya through aerial attacks on pro-Gaddafi forces and military equipment, NATO's intervention helped to tip the balance in the conflict in favour of the Libyan opposition. By early October, the Libyan National Transitional Council had secured control over the entire country and rebels had captured and killed Gaddafi. 'Operation Unified Protector' ended on 31 October, 222 days after it had begun (Daalder and Stavridis, 2012).

Significance: The fact that major humanitarian interventions had not occurred since Kosovo and East Timor in 1999, and Sierra Leone in 2000 had encouraged some to believe that the era of humanitarian intervention was over, a reflection of the unusual set of circumstances that prevailed during the early post-Cold War period. The USA's involvement in prolonged counter-insurgency wars in Iraq and Afghanistan also served to highlight the danger of states getting bogged down in military interventions, especially as, sooner or later, the so-called 'body bag effect' tends to weaken domestic support. The 2011 Libyan intervention, nevertheless, went ahead for two main reasons. First, the political leaderships in the USA, France and the UK, the key supporters of intervention, feared the political cost of being seen to stand passively by while widespread slaughter took place in Libya, particularly as they had given such clear support to earlier Arab Spring uprisings. Second, and crucially, the intervention was deemed to be militarily feasible, both because of the relative weakness of the pro-Gaddafi forces once they were deprived of their aerial capacity, and in view of the calculation that intervention could be accomplished with minimal NATO losses, as a land invasion ('boots on the ground') could be avoided.

The key moral justification for the Libyan intervention arose from the principle of the 'responsibility to protect' (R2P), even though the notion was not specifically cited in Resolution 1973. The core theme of R2P is that the international community is bound by a humanitarian imperative to intervene to protect civilians in the event of either an actual or apprehended large-scale loss of life, or large-scale ethnic cleansing, if the resources exist to do so and the cost is not disproportionate. As moral responsibilities extend, potentially, to the whole of humanity, we have an obligation to 'save strangers'. In the case of Libya, this moral justification was bolstered by the legitimacy the intervention derived from its authorization by the Security Council and the support of key regional bodies such as the Arab League and the Gulf Cooperation Council. Critics of the intervention have nevertheless portrayed Libya as an example of neocolonialism, on the grounds that it was significantly motivated by the desire to gain control of oil and other resources, and also reflected a continuing attempt by western powers to control the destiny of developing states. In this light, R2P merely provides a moral cloak for self-seeking behaviour, and it is invoked only when it suits the purposes of western powers. In cases such as Syria during 2011–12 it is conveniently ignored. Others have portrayed the Libyan intervention as a violation of international law, in that it violated the principle of state sovereignty.

War

War is a condition of armed conflict between two or more parties (usually states). The emergence of the modern form of war as an organized and goal-directed activity stems from the development of the European state-system in the early modern period. War has a formal or quasi-legal character, in that the declaration of a state of war need not necessarily be accompanied by the outbreak of hostilities. In the post-Cold War era it has been common to refer to 'new' wars. These have been characterized, variously, by intra-state ethnic conflict, the use of advanced military technology, and the use of terrorist and guerrilla strategies.

However, 'new' wars often pose a wider and more profound threat to civilian populations than did the inter-state wars of old. The civilian/military divide – which had been symbolized by the fact that traditional wars were fought by uniformed, organized bodies of men (national armies, navies and air forces) – has been blurred in a variety of ways. The wide use of **guerrilla** tactics and the emphasis on popular resistance, or **insurgency**, has given modern warfare a diffuse character. As it tends to involve a succession of small-scale engagements, rather than set-piece, major battles, the conventional idea of a battlefield has become almost redundant. War has developed into 'war amongst the people' (Smith, 2006), a tendency that has been deepened by the 'collateral damage' that has sometimes been caused by counter-insurgency operations. The blurring has also occurred because civilian populations have increasingly been the target of military action (through the use of landmines, suicide bombs, vehicle bombs and terrorism generally), its objective being to create economic and social dislocation, and to destroy the enemy's resolve and appetite for war. Modern warfare is therefore often accompanied by a refugee crisis in which thousands, and sometimes millions, of displaced people seek shelter and security, either on a temporary or permanent basis.

The civilian/military divide has been further blurred by the changing nature of armies and security forces. Guerrilla armies, for instance, consist of irregular soldiers or armed bands of volunteers, and insurgency often comes close to assuming the character of a popular uprising. Finally, 'new' wars have often been more barbaric and horrific than old ones, as the rules that have constrained conventional inter-state warfare have commonly been set aside. Practices such as kidnapping, torture, systematic rape and indiscriminate killings that result from landmines, car bombs and suicide attacks have become routine features of modern warfare. This is sometimes explained in terms of the implications of militant identity politics, through which the enemy is defined in terms of their membership of a particular group, rather than in terms of their role or actions. An entire people, race or culture may therefore be defined as 'the enemy', meaning that they are seen as worthless or fundamentally evil, and that military and civilian targets are equally legitimate.

Transnational terrorism

During much of the post-1945 period, terrorism generally had a nationalist orientation. In the 1940s and 1950s, it was associated with Third World anti-colonial struggles in Africa, Asia and the Middle East, later being taken up by national liberation movements such the Palestine Liberation Organization (PLO) and groups such as Black September. Terrorism was also used by disaffected national or ethnic minorities in developed western societies, notably by the IRA in Northern Ireland and on the UK mainland, by ETA (*Euzkadi ta Askatsuna*) in the Basque region of Spain and by the FLQ (*Front de libération du Québec*) in Quebec. Nevertheless, the September 11 terrorist attacks convinced many people that terrorism had been reborn in a new and more dangerous form, leading some to conclude that it had become the principal threat to international peace and security.

The most obvious way in which terrorism has become more significant is that has acquired a transnational, even global, dimension. Although the interna-

● **Guerrilla war**: (Spanish) Literally, 'little war'; an insurgency or 'people's' war, fought by irregular troops using tactics that are suited to the terrain and emphasize mobility and surprise, rather than superior fire power.

● **Insurgency**: An armed uprising, involving irregular soldiers, which aims to overthrow the established regime.

Terrorism

Terrorism, in its broadest sense, is a form of political violence that aims to achieve its objectives by creating a climate of fear, apprehension and uncertainty. The most common forms of terrorist action include assassinations, bombings, hostage seizures and plane hijacks, although 9/11 and the advent of terrorism with a global reach has threatened to redefine the phenomenon. The term is highly pejorative and tends to be used selectively (one person's terrorist is another's freedom fighter). Often portrayed as a specfically anti-government activity, some portray the use by governments of terror against their own or other populations as 'state terrorism'.

● **Weapons of mass destruction:** A category of weapons that covers nuclear, radiological, chemical and biological weapons, which have a massive and indiscriminate destructive capacity.

tional character of terrorism can be traced back to the advent of airplane hijackings in the late 1960s, carried out by groups such as the PLO, 9/11 and other al-Qaeda, or al-Qaeda-linked, attacks in Madrid, London and elsewhere have taken this process to a new level. Transnational terrorism is generally associated with the advance of globalization, in that it takes advantage of increased cross-border flows of people, goods, money, technology and ideas, and thereby creates the impression that terrorists can strike anywhere, at any time. Such terrorism has also been dubbed 'catastrophic' terrorism or 'hyper-terrorism', highlighting its radical and devastating impact, as well as the greater difficulties experienced in counteracting it.

This applies for at least three reasons. First, an increased emphasis has been placed on terrorist tactics that are particularly difficult to defend against, notably, suicide terrorism. How can protection be provided against attackers who are willing to sacrifice their own lives in order to kill others? This contributes to the idea that, although it may be possible to reduce the likelihood of terrorist attacks, the threat can never be eradicated. Second, the potential scope and scale of terrorism has greatly increased as a result of modern technology, and particularly the prospect of **weapons of mass destruction** (WMD) falling into the hands of terrorists. Since 9/11, governments have been trying to plan for the possibility of terrorist attacks using chemical or biological weapons, with the prospect of nuclear terrorism no longer being dismissed as a fanciful idea. Third, it is sometimes argued that modern terrorists not only have easier access to WMD, but also have a greater willingness to use them. This, allegedly is because they may be less constrained by moral and humanitarian principles than previous generations of terrorists. In the case of Islamist terrorism, this is supposedly explained by the radical politico-religious ideology which inspires it, in which western society and its associated values are viewed as evil and intrinsically corrupt, an implacable enemy of Islam.

Upholding international security in an age of transnational terrorism has been a particularly difficult task. Three main counter-terrorism strategies have been employed in the modern period. The first strategy involves the revision and strengthening of arrangements for state security, usually by extending the legal powers of government. States, for example, have asserted control over global financial flows; immigration arrangements have been made more rigorous, especially during high-alert periods; the surveillance and control of domestic populations, but particularly members of 'extremist' groups or terrorist sympathizers, has been significantly tightened; and, in many cases, the power to detain terrorist suspects has been strengthened. However, state security measures have often had an extra-legal or, at best, quasi-legal character. In the early post-9/11 period, the Bush administration in the USA took this approach furthest, notably by establishing the Guantánamo Bay detention centre in Cuba, and by practices such as 'extraordinary rendition'.

The second strategy is the use of force-based or repressive counter-terrorism, which, in recent years, has been associated with the 'war on terror'. Military responses to terrorism have been designed to deny terrorists the support or 'sponsorship' of regimes that had formerly given them succour (such as Sudan and Afghanistan), or to launch direct attacks on terrorist training camps and terrorist leaders. Nevertheless, as demonstrated by the US-led 'war on terror', military repression may sometimes be counter-productive, especially when military action against terrorism is seen to be insensitive to human rights and the interests of civilian populations. The third strategy is the use of political deals to encourage terrorists to abandon violence by drawing them into a process of negotiation and diplomacy. Although this is sometimes seen as an example of appeasement, a moral retreat in the face of intimidation and violence, the fact is that most terrorist campaigns have political endings. In part, this is because leading figures in terrorist movements tend to gravitate towards respectability and constitutional politics once they recognize that terrorist tactics are generally ineffective.

Nuclear proliferation

The 'nuclear age' was born on 6 August 1945, when the USA dropped an atomic bomb on the Japanese city of Hiroshima. A second bomb was dropped three days later on Nagasaki. The unprecedented destructive potential of **nuclear weapons** explains why the issue of nuclear proliferation has been at the forefront of the international security agenda since World War II. During the Cold War period, sometimes dubbed the 'first nuclear age', nuclear proliferation was primarily 'vertical' (the accumulation of nuclear weapons by established nuclear states) rather than 'horizontal' (the acquisition of nuclear weapons by more states or other actors). The 'nuclear club' contained only the five permanent members of the UN Security Council (the USA, the USSR, China, France and the UK), but, during this period, the USA and the USSR built up the capacity to destroy the world many times over. By 2002, the joint US and Russian nuclear capacity amounted to 98 per cent of all nuclear warheads that had been built. This nuclear arms race was fuelled, in particular, by the profound **deterrence** value of nuclear weapons. In view of the devastating potential of nuclear weapons, an attack on a nuclear power is almost unthinkable. A nuclear balance of power therefore developed in which both the USA and the USSR acquired so-called 'second-strike' nuclear capabilities that would enable them to withstand an enemy's attack and still destroy major strategic targets and population centres. By the early 1960s, both superpowers had an invulnerable second-strike capability which ensured that nuclear war would result in **Mutually Assured Destruction** (MAD), sometimes seen as a 'balance of terror'.

However, although the end of the Cold War and the cessation of East–West rivalry produced early, optimistic expectations or declining concerns about nuclear proliferation, the 'second nuclear age', has proved, in certain respects, to be more troubling than the first. For one thing, established nuclear powers continue to use nuclear strategies. Thus, even though the new START Treaty, signed in 2010 by the USA and Russia, agreed to reduce the number of strategic nuclear missile launchers by half, both countries would still possess 1,550 nuclear warheads. The greatest concern has, nevertheless, arisen over further horizontal nuclear proliferation, fuelled by regional rivalries and the fact that, particularly since the break-up of the USSR, nuclear weapons and nuclear technology have become more readily available. India and Pakistan joined the 'nuclear club' in 1998, as did North Korea in 2006. Israel has been an undeclared nuclear power, possibly since 1979, and it is widely believed that Iran is in the process of developing an independent nuclear capacity.

Anxieties over proliferation have intensified because of the nature of the states and other actors that may acquire nuclear capabilities. This particularly

---

● **Nuclear weapons:** Weapons that use nuclear fission (atomic bombs) or nuclear fusion (hydrogen bombs) to destroy their targets, through the effect of blast, heat and radiation.

● **Deterrence:** A tactic or strategy designed to prevent aggression by emphasizing the scale of the likely military response (the cost of an attack would be greater than any benefit it may bring).

● **Mutually Assured Destruction:** A condition in which a nuclear attack by either state would only ensure its own destruction, as both possess an invulnerable second-strike capacity.

CONCEPT

Human security

Human security refers to the security of individuals, rather than of states. As such, it embraces the notions of both 'freedom from fear' and 'freedom from want'. Human security, nevertheless, has a variety of dimensions. These include *economic security* (having an assured basic income), *food security* (access to basic food) *health security* (protection from disease and unhealthy lifestyles), *environmental security* (protection from human-induced environmental degradation), *personal security* (protection from all forms of physical violence), *community security* (protection for traditional identities and values), *political security* (the maintenance of political rights and civil liberties).

● **Rogue state**: A state whose foreign policy poses a threat to neighbouring or other states, through its aggressive intent, build-up of weapons, or association with terrorism.

● **Human development**: A standard of human well-being that takes account of people's ability to develop their full potential, and lead fulfilled and creative lives in accordance with their needs and interests.

applies in the case of so-called '**rogue states**', in which military-based dictatorial government combines with factors such as ethnic and social conflict, and economic underdevelopment, to dictate an aggressive foreign policy, particularly in the context of regional instability. North Korea is widely portrayed as a potential rogue nuclear state, which poses a threat not only to South Korea, but also to Japan and even the USA. The acquisition of nuclear weapons by Iran has been seen as a profound threat to international security for a number of reasons. These include the possibility that Israel may launch a pre-emptive nuclear attack against Iran before it acquires nuclear capability; that Iran itself may launch an unprovoked nuclear attack on Israel; and that Iran's acquisition of nuclear weapons may spark a destabilizing nuclear arms race across the entire Middle East, with increased pressure on states such as Saudi Arabia and Turkey to acquire nuclear weapons. However, others have argued that such concerns are alarmist and that the acquisition of nuclear weapons tends to foster caution, even statesmanship, based on the sense of security and national prestige that they bring, rather than nuclear adventurism. According to Waltz (2012) a nuclear Iran would bring stability to the Middle East, as Israel and Iran would then deter each other, without giving other countries in the region a greater incentive to acquire their own nuclear capability.

Human security

The post-Cold War period has not only seen the emergence of new threats to international and global security, but it has also witnessed the emergence of new thinking about the nature of security, as such. The key shift has been from viewing security as essentially an attribute of a state (as in 'state security' or 'national security') to viewing it as a matter for the individual, as implied by the idea of 'human security'. Human security has recast the concept of security by taking on board the idea of **human development**, which has been used in the UN's Human Development Reports since 1994. This switched attention from economic-based conceptions of poverty (for example, using an income of 'a dollar a day' as a standard of poverty) to conceptions built around human capabilities, such as the ability to acquire knowledge, access resources, achieve gender equality and so forth. Human security thus takes account not only of the extent to which threats posed by armed conflict have changed and, in some senses, intensified (as discussed earlier, in relation to 'new' wars), but also the degree to which modern armed conflict is entangled with issues of poverty and underdevelopment. Economic disruption and widening inequality, which stem, amongst other things, from disparities in the global trading system, are seen to heighten the vulnerability of states to civil war, terrorism and warlord conflict, while, at the same time, armed conflict disrupts economies and trade and leads to other forms of human misery. In addition, human security takes account of non-military sources of insecurity, bringing issues such as the lack of an assured basic income, inadequate access to basic food and environmental degradation within the international security agenda.

A growing concern about human security has also, at times, encouraged the international community to assume a more interventionist stance. This can be seen in a greater willingness to undertake humanitarian interventions since the early 1990s, and in support for the establishment of international tribunals and, since 2002, the International Criminal Court (ICC). The conviction of Charles Taylor – the former president of Liberia, who was found guilty in 2012 of aiding and abetting murder, rape, enslavement and the use of child soldiers by the Special Tribunal for Sierra Leone – was thus meant to ensure that other heads of government or state would be less likely to act in such ways in the future. The Landmines Treaty (1997) was, similarly, designed to deter the use, stockpiling, production and transfer of anti-personnel mines.

However, the concept of human security has also been criticized. Some have argued, for instance, that human security has deepened and widened the concept of security to such an extent that it has become virtually meaningless. This particularly applies as it extends security beyond the conventional idea of 'freedom from fear' to include the much broader notion of 'freedom from want'. Furthermore, the notion may create false expectations about the international community's capacity to banish violence and insecurity. In other cases, however, intervention by the international community intended to promote human security has proved to be highly controversial, not uncommonly provoking charges of 'neocolonialism'. As of 2012, for example, the ICC had arrested only Africans.

SUMMARY

● The central role of the police is to enforce criminal law and maintain civil order. The police force may nevertheless have a political character if social or other biases operate within it, if it is deployed in the event of civil unrest or political disputes, and if there is a police state in which the police force is turned into a private army that serves only the interests of the ruling elite.

● The key purpose of the military is to be an instrument of war that can be directed against other political societies. However, the military may also help to maintain domestic order and stability when civilian mechanisms are unable or unwilling to act, and it may, in particular circumstances, displace civilian government with a form of military rule. Military regimes, nevertheless, tend to be short-lived because they rely on coercive power in the absence of legitimacy.

● Realists advance a power politics model of world affairs in which security is primarily understood in terms of 'national security' and war is kept in check by the balance of power. The liberal belief in interdependence and balance in world affairs inclines them to place their faith in 'collective security', while critical theorists have either emphasized the extent to which state interactions are mediated by beliefs, values and assumptions, or exposed masculinist biases in the conventional realist paradigm.

● A variety of new security challenges have arisen in the post-Cold War era. These include: the shift from traditional, inter-state war to 'new' wars, in which the civilian/military divide is typically blurred; the advent of transnational terrorism which threatens to strike anywhere, at any time, and possibly with devastating effect; and increased horizontal nuclear proliferation, especially linked to fears about nuclear weapons getting into the 'wrong' hands.

● The concept of 'human security' has shifted thinking about security away from the state and towards the individual. By extending the notion of security beyond 'freedom from fear' to include 'freedom from want', it has deepened and widened the notion of security, and thereby, potentially, extended the responsibilities of the international community. Critics, however, argue that this risks making the concept of security virtually meaningless, and creates false expectations about the international community's capacity to banish violence and insecurity.

Questions for discussion

● Why did the USA respond to 9/11 with a 'war on terror' rather than a police action against international murderers?

● Is all policing political?

● If all states rest on coercive power, why do armed forces so rarely intervene directly in politics?

● When, if ever, is it justifiable to use the military as an instrument of domestic policy?

● Which approach to international politics provides the soundest basis for understanding the prospects for international security?

● Are 'new' wars really more barbaric and horrific than traditional wars?

● Is transnational terrorism a greater threat to international security than nuclear proliferation?

● What have been the implications of thinking about security in 'human' terms?

Further reading

Brewer, J., A. Guelke, I. Hume, E. Moxon-Browne and R. Wilford, *The Police, Public Order and the State* (1996). A good comparative introduction to the role of the police in eight states.

Kaldor, M., *Human Security: Reflections on Globalization and Intervention* (2007). A wide-ranging and stimulating discussion of human security in the context of the changing nature of economic relations and armed conflict.

Silva, P. (ed.) *The Soldier and the State in South America: Essays in Civil–Military Relations* (2001). A collection of essays that examine the political impact of the military in South America in the past and the present.

Smith, M. E., *International Security: Politics, Policy, Prospects* (2010). A clear and comprehensive account of modern threats to international security and how such threats are managed.

CHAPTER 19

World Order and Global Governance

'We shall have world government whether or not you like it, by conquest or consent.'

Statement by the US Council on Foreign Relations, February 1950

PREVIEW

The issue of world order is central to an understanding of international politics. The shape of world order affects both the level of stability within the global system and the balance within it between conflict and cooperation. However, since the end of the Cold War, the nature of world order has been the subject of significant debate and disagreement. Early proclamations of the establishment of a 'new world order', characterized by peace and international cooperation, were soon replaced by talk of a unipolar world order, with the USA taking centre stage as the world's sole super-power. This 'unipolar moment' may nevertheless have been brief. Not only did the USA's involvement in difficult and protracted counter-insurgency wars following September 11 strengthen the impression of US decline, but emerging powers, notably China, started to exert greater influence on the world stage. The notion that unipolarity is giving way to multipolarity has, moreover, been supported by evidence of the increasing importance of international organizations, a trend that is sometimes interpreted as emerging 'global governance'. Of particular importance in this respect have been the major institutions of global economic governance – the International Monetary Fund, the World Bank and the World Trade Organization – and the centrepiece of the global governance system, the United Nations. Although some argue that the trend in favour of global governance reflects the fact that, in an interdependent world, states must act together to address the challenges that confront them, others dismiss global governance as a myth and raise serious questions about the effectiveness of international organizations.

KEY ISSUES

- What were the implications for world order of the end of the Cold War?
- Is the USA a hegemonic power, or a power in decline?
- How is rising multipolarity likely to affect world politics?
- Is global governance a myth or a reality?
- How effective is the system of global economic governance?
- Is the UN an indispensable component of the modern international system?

Superpower

A superpower (a term first used by William Fox in 1944) is a power that is greater than a traditional 'great power'. For Fox, superpowers possessed great power 'plus great mobility of power'. As the term tends to be used specifically to refer to the USA and the USSR during the Cold War period, it is of more historical than conceptual significance. Nevertheless, superpowers are generally assumed to have: (1) a global reach, allowing them to operate anywhere in the world; (2) a predominant economic and strategic role within an ideological bloc or sphere of influence; and (3) preponderant military capacity, especially in terms of nuclear weaponry.

● **World order**: The distribution of power between and amongst states and other key actors, giving rise to a relatively stable pattern of relationships and behaviours.

● **Bipolarity**: The tendency of the international system to revolve around two poles (major power blocs).

TWENTY-FIRST-CENTURY WORLD ORDER

The 'new world order' and its fate

Although there is considerable debate about the nature of twenty-first-century **world order**, there is considerable agreement about the shape of world order during the Cold War period. Its most prominent feature was that two major power blocs confronted one another, a US-dominated West and a Soviet-dominated East. In the aftermath of the defeat of Germany, Japan and Italy in World War II, and with the UK weakened by war and suffering from long-term relative economic decline, the USA and the USSR emerged as 'superpowers'. Cold War **bipolarity** was consolidated by the formation of rival military alliances – the North Atlantic Treaty Organization (NATO) in 1949 and the Warsaw Pact in 1955, and was reflected in the division of Europe – symbolized by the Berlin Wall, erected in 1961. Although the Cold War remained 'cold', in the sense that the adversaries avoided direct confrontation, the period was characterized by a by protracted – and, at times, extreme – tension, reflected both in covert operations and proxy warfare and, most dramatically, in the build up by both parties of massive armouries of nuclear weapons, creating a 'balance of terror'.

However, when the Cold War came to an end, the end was dramatic, swift and quite unexpected. Over seventy years of communism collapsed in just two years, 1989–91, and where communist regimes survived, as in China, a process of radical change took place. During the momentous year of 1989, communist rule in Eastern Europe was rolled back to the borders of the USSR by a series of popular revolutions; in 1990, representatives of NATO and the Warsaw Pact met in Paris formally to end the Cold War; and, in 1991, the USSR itself collapsed. While most explained these developments in terms of the structural weaknesses of Soviet-style communism, emphasis has also been placed on the disruption caused in the USSR by the accelerating programme of economic and political reform, initiated by President Gorbachev from 1985 onwards, and on President Reagan's so-called 'second Cold War' in the 1980s, when increased military spending put massive pressure on the fragile and inefficient Soviet economy.

The end of the Cold War produced a burst of enthusiasm for the ideas of liberal internationalism (see p. 117). The idea that the post-Cold War era would be characterized by a 'new world order' had first been mooted by Gorbachev in a speech to the UN General Assembly in 1988. In addition to proposing a strengthening of the United Nations and a reinvigoration of its peacekeeping role, Gorbachev called for the 'de-ideologization' of relations amongst states to achieve greater cooperation and reduce the use of force in international affairs. In his 'Towards a New World Order' speech to Congress in September 1990, President Bush Sr outlined his version for the post-Cold War world – its features included US leadership to ensure the international rule of law, a partnership between the USA and the USSR including the integration of the latter into the world economic bodies, and a check on the use of force by the promotion of collective security. This post-Cold War world order appeared to pass its first series of major tests with ease. Iraq's annexation of Kuwait in August 1990 led to the construction of a broad western and Islamic alliance that, through the Gulf

Focus on . . .
Humanitarian intervention

Humanitarian intervention is military intervention that is carried out in pursuit of humanitarian rather than strategic objectives. The growth in humanitarian intervention reflects the wider acceptance of universalist doctrines such as human rights (see p. 342) and the fact that democratic support for warfare can increasingly be mobilized only on the basis of a moral cause. Supporters of humanitarian intervention see it as evidence of the inability of states in a global age to restrict their moral responsibilities to their own people.

Humanitarian intervention has been seen as justified in the following circumstances:

- In the case of gross abuses of human rights (such as the expulsion or extermination of large numbers of defenceless people).
- When such abuses threaten the security of neighbouring states.

- When the absence of democracy weakens the principle of national self-determination.
- When diplomatic means have been exhausted and the human cost of intervention is less than that of non-intervention.

Critics of humanitarian intervention, however, make the following points:

- Any violation of state sovereignty weakens the established rules of world order.
- Aggression has almost always been legitimized by humanitarian justification (examples include Mussolini and Hitler).
- Military intervention invariably leaves matters worse, not better, or draws intervening powers into long-term involvement.

War of 1991, brought about the expulsion of Iraqi forces. The advent of a new moral consciousness in foreign affairs was also evident in the wider use of 'humanitarian intervention', notably in NATO's campaign of aerial bombing that removed Serb forces from Kosovo in 1999.

However, the wave of optimism and idealism that greeted the post-Cold War world did not last long. Many were quick to dismiss the 'new world order' as little more than a convenient catchphrase, and one that was certainly not grounded in a developed strategic vision. Much of how this 'new world' would work remained vague. Moreover, alternative interpretations of the post-Cold War world order were not slow in emerging. Some heralded the rise not of a new world order but, rather, a new world *dis*order. The reason for this was the release of stresses and tensions that the Cold War had helped to keep under control. By maintaining the image of an external threat (be it international communism or capitalist encirclement), the Cold War had served to promote internal cohesion and given societies a sense of purpose and identity. However, the collapse of the external threat helped to unleash centrifugal pressures, which usually took the form of ethnic, racial and regional conflict. This occurred in many parts of the world, but was particularly evident in Eastern Europe, as demonstrated in the prolonged bloodshed in the 1990s amongst Serbs, Croats and Muslims in the former Yugoslavia. Far from establishing a world order based on respect for justice and human rights, (see p. 342), the international community stood by in former Yugoslavia and, until the Kosovo crisis, allowed Serbia to wage a war of expansion and perpetrate **genocidal** policies reminiscent of those used in World War II.

- **Genocide:** An attempt to eradicate a people – identified by their nationality, race, ethnicity or religion – through acts including mass murder, forced resettlement, and forced sterilization.

Nevertheless, the greatest weakness of the idea of an emerging liberal world order was a failure to take account of the shifting role and status of the USA. The main significance of the end of the Cold War was the collapse of the USSR as a meaningful challenger to the USA, leaving the USA as the world's sole super-power, a **hyperpower** or 'global hegemon'. Indeed, talk of a 'new world order' may have been nothing more than an ideological tool to legitimize the global exercise of power by the USA. In other words, the 'liberal moment' in world affairs turned out to be the '**unipolar** moment'. However, the implications of a unipolar world order only emerged over a period of time.

The 'war on terror' and beyond

September 11, 2001 is often seen as a defining moment in world history, the point at which the true nature of the post-Cold War era was revealed and the beginning of the period of unprecedented global strife and instability. In that sense, the advent of the 'war on terror' (see p. 401), rather than the collapse of communism, marked the birth of the 'real' twenty-first century. On the other hand, it is possible to exaggerate the impact of 9/11. As Robert Kagan (2004) put it, 'America did not change on September 11. It only became more itself'.

A variety of theories have been advanced to explain the advent of global, or transnational, terrorism (see p. 416) and the nature of the 'war on terror'. The most influential and widely discussed of these is Samuel Huntington's (see p. 425) theory of a **clash of civilizations**. Huntington argued that the major civi-lizations (western, Chinese, Japanese, Hindu, Islamic, Buddhist, Latin American and Orthodox Christian) would become, in the absence of the East–West ideo-logical conflict and in reaction to globalization (see p. 142), the principal actors in world affairs. Such an analysis contrasted sharply with the expectation of 'end of history' theorists such as Francis Fukuyama (see p. 271) that politico-cultural divisions would narrow and ultimately evaporate as all parts of the world converged around support for liberal-democratic values and systems. Huntington particularly warned about the likelihood of conflict between China (wedded to distinctive Sinic cultural values, despite rapid economic growth) and the West, and between the West and Islam.

Huntington's thesis has nevertheless been widely criticized. The most common criticism is that it fails to recognize the extent to which globalization and other forces have already blurred cultural differences in many parts of the world. For instance, the notion of an 'Islamic civilization' or a 'western civiliza-tion' fails to take account of either the extent of political, cultural and social divi-sion within each 'civilization', or the extent to which Islam and the West have influenced one another, and continue to do so. Moreover, the link between cultural difference and political antagonism is, at best, questionable, as most wars take place between states from the same, rather than different, civilizations. Finally, conflict between civilizations may be more an expression of perceived economic and political injustice than of cultural rivalry. The rise of political Islam, for instance, may be better explained by tensions and crises (in the Middle East in general and the Arab world in particular) linked to the inheritance of colonialism, the unresolved Israeli–Palestinian conflict, the survival of unpopu-lar but often oil-rich autocratic regimes, and urban poverty and unemployment, than by cultural incompatibility between western and Islamic value systems.

● **Hyperpower:** A power that commands much greater power than any of its potential rivals, and so dominates world politics.

● **Unipolarity:** An international system in which there is one pre-eminent state; the existence of a single great power.

● **Clash of civilizations thesis:** The theory that twenty-first century conflict would not primarily be ideological or economic, but rather cultural: it would be conflict between nations from 'different civilizations'.

Samuel P. Huntington (1927–2008)

US academic and political commentator. Huntington made influential contributions in three fields: military politics, strategy and civil–military relations; US and comparative politics; and political development and the politics of less-developed societies. In *The Third Wave* (1991) he coined the notion of 'waves of democratization' and linked the process of democratization after 1975 to two earlier waves, in 1828–1926 and 1943–62. His most widely discussed work, *The Clash of Civilizations and the Making of World Order* (1996), advanced the controversial thesis that, in the twenty-first century, conflict between the world's major civilizations would lead to warfare and international disorder.

Alternative explanations highlight the significance of changes in world order. According to Robert Cooper (2004), the East–West confrontation of the old world order has given way to a world divided into three parts:

- In the 'premodern' world, by which Cooper meant those post-colonial states that have benefited neither from political stability nor from economic development, chaos reigns. Examples of such states include Somalia, Afghanistan and the Democratic Republic of the Congo, sometimes seen as 'weak states', 'failed states' (see p. 76) or rogue states.
- In the 'modern' world, states continue to be effective and are fiercely protective of their own sovereignty (see p. 58). Such a world operates on the basis of a balance of power, as the interests and ambitions of one state are only constrained by the capabilities of other states.
- In the 'postmodern' world, which Cooper associated primarily with Europe and the European Union (EU), states have evolved 'beyond' power politics, and have abandoned war as a means of maintaining security in favour of multilateral agreements, international law and global governance (see p. 432).

This view of the emerging world order, however, highlights a range of challenges and new security threats. Not the least of these arises from the proliferation of weapons of mass destruction (WMD), which, in the premodern world, can easily get into the hands of 'rogue' states or non-state actors (such as terrorist organizations). Particular concern has been expressed about nuclear proliferation, the membership of the so-called 'nuclear club' having expanded from five (the USA, Russia, China, France and the UK) to nine, with the acquisition of nuclear weapons by India, Pakistan, Israel and North Korea, and with other countries, such as Iran, thought to be close to developing them (as discussed in Chapter 18). Although Europe may be a 'zone of safety', outside Europe there is a 'zone of danger and chaos' in which the instabilities of the premodern world threaten to spill over into the modern – and even the postmodern – worlds. Cooper (2004) acknowledged that a kind of 'new' imperialism (see p. 427) may be the only way of bringing order to chaos. Such an analysis overlaps at significant points with the neoconservative (or 'neo-con') ideas that had a particular

CONCEPT

Pre-emptive attack

A pre-emptive attack (or preventative war) is military action that is designed to forestall or prevent likely future aggression – 'getting your retaliation in first'. The attractions of pre-emptive attack include that greater destruction may be avoided and that military action is taken before a potential aggressor becomes too strong to be challenged. Its drawbacks include that calculations about future actions or threats may be flawed and that the notion may simply be a cloak for aggression. Pre-emptive attack is almost certainly illegal under the UN Charter, which authorizes war only in the case of self-defence.

● **Bush doctrine:** The doctrine, outlined by President George W. Bush in 2002, that the USA had a right to treat states that harbour, or give aid to, terrorists as terrorists themselves.

impact on the Bush administration in the USA in the years following 9/11, and which were reflected in what came to be known as the **Bush doctrine**. Neoconservatives thus sought to preserve and reinforce what was seen as the USA's 'benevolent global hegemony' (Kristol and Kagan, 2004). Its key features included a build-up of the USA's military strength to achieve a position of 'strength beyond challenge' and an assertive, interventionist foreign policy that set out to promote liberal-democratic governance through a process of 'regime change', achieved by military means if necessary.

After 9/11, the USA's approach to the 'war on terror' quickly started to take shape. Its opening act was the US-led military assault on Afghanistan that toppled the Taliban regime within a matter of weeks. The 'war on terror', however, moved in a more radical and controversial direction as it became clear that 'regime change' in Saddam Hussein's Iraq was the Bush administration's next objective. This led to the 2003 Iraq War, fought by the USA and a 'coalition of the willing'. What made the Iraq War controversial was that, whereas the attack on Afghanistan had been widely seen as a form of self-defence (Afghanistan had provided al-Qaeda with the closest thing to a home base), the war against Iraq was justified using the doctrine of pre-emptive attack. Although the Bush administration alleged (with little substantiation) that there were links between the Saddam regime and al-Qaeda, and asserted (contrary to subsequent evidence) that Iraq was in possession of WMD, the central justification was that a 'rogue' regime such as Saddam's that actively sought, and may have acquired, WMD could not be tolerated in the twenty-first century.

In both Afghanistan and Iraq, despite early dramatic successes (the overthrow of the Taliban and Saddam regimes), the USA and its allies found themselves fighting wars that proved to be more problematic and protracted than anticipated. Both developed into complex counter-insurgency wars against enemies whose use of the tactics of guerrilla warfare, terrorism and suicide bombings highlighted the limitations of preponderant US military power. As in the Vietnam War (1959–76), guerrilla warfare tactics proved to be highly effective against a much more powerful and better resourced enemy, but the use of military means had also weakened the USA's 'soft' power (see p. 428) and damaged its reputation across the Middle East. In that sense, the USA was in danger of creating the very 'arc of extremism' that it had set out to destroy. In addition, the strategy of imposing 'democracy from above' had proved to be naïve at best – failing, in particular, to recognize the difficulties involved in the process of 'state-building' (as discussed in Chapter 3).

Significant shifts occurred in the 'war on terror' once President Obama was inaugurated in January 2009, building on a drift towards multilateralism (see p. 435) during Bush's second term in office, 2005–09. In line with the advice of soft-power theorists for the USA to 'learn to cooperate, and to listen' (Nye, 2004), Obama altered the tone of the USA's engagement with world affairs generally, and with the Muslim world in particular. In a keynote speech in Cairo in June 2009, he called for a 'new beginning' between the USA and Muslims around the world, acknowledging that 'no system of government can and should be imposed upon one nation by another'. However, even though the rhetoric of the 'war on terror' was quickly toned down and soon abandoned, and the strategic approach to it was revised, military engagement continued to play an important role under Obama. This was reflected in a significant shift of

Imperialism

Imperialism is, broadly, the policy of extending the power or rule of a state beyond its borders. In its earliest usage, imperialism was an ideology of conquest and expansion, designed either to extend dynastic authority or to further nationalist ambitions. The term is now more commonly used to describe any form of external domination, and includes both the imposition of direct political control through colonialism (see p. 122) and economic exploitation in the absence of political rule, or neocolonialism. Marxists and realists disagree over whether imperialism is essentially an economic or a political phenomenon.

● **Hegemon**: A leading or paramount power.

● **Multipolarity**: An international system in which there are three or more power centres, creating a bias in favour of fluidity and, perhaps, instability.

● **Imperial over-reach**: The tendency for imperial expansion to be unsustainable as wider military responsibilities outstrip the growth of the domestic economy.

emphasis from Iraq to Afghanistan and Pakistan in the form of what became known as the 'Af-Pak' policy. Thanks to the success of the 'surge' in US troops, which started in 2007, in reducing levels of civil strife and civilian deaths in Iraq, responsibility for maintaining security in Iraqi towns and cities was passed from US and allied troops to Iraqi forces in 2009, and the USA's combat mission in Iraq ended in August 2010. Under Obama's redrawn battle strategy for Afghanistan, a similar 'surge' was initiated in early 2010, in an attempt to refocus and re-energize NATO's deeply problematic mission there. At the same time, July 2011 was set as the date that US forces in Afghanistan would start to withdraw, with a commitment that by the end of 2014 the USA's 'combat' mission will have ceased.

From unipolarity to multipolarity?

The wars in Afghanistan and Iraq raised major questions about the nature and extent of the USA's global leadership. In sharp contrast to the image of the USA as the 'indispensable nation', a benevolent **hegemon** whose widening influence brought peace and prosperity, radical theorists such as Noam Chomsky (see p. 181) portrayed the USA as a 'rogue superpower', the principal source of terrorism and violence across the globe. Whether its hegemony (see p. 174) was benevolent or malign, the difficulty the USA experienced in achieving its military and political goals through the 'war on terror' convinced many that its global leadership was faltering, a conclusion supported by the 2007–09 global financial crisis (as discussed in Chapter 6). These developments, indeed, have been seen as part of a wider process; namely, a significant redistribution of global power, with unipolarity giving way to **multipolarity**. Rising multipolarity has been associated with three main trends:

● the decline of the USA
● the rise of China and other 'emerging powers'
● the changing nature of power and power relations.

Decline of the USA?

Debates about the decline of the USA's global hegemony are nothing new. They date back to the late 1950s and the launch by the USSR of the Sputnik satellite. During the 1970s and 1980s, it became fashionable to proclaim that the USA had been eclipsed by resurgent Japan and Germany, the USA succumbing to a tendency, common amongst earlier great powers, to **imperial over-reach** (Kennedy, 1989). However, the issue has resurfaced with renewed force in the early twenty-first century. Although judgements about a state's ranking within a hierarchy are bedevilled by the complex and multifaceted nature of global power (see p. 428), the idea of US decline has been linked to a number of developments. The USA's military dominance over the rest of the world is, undeniably, huge. By 2007, the USA accounted for 46 per cent of the world's military spending, and had a nine-fold lead over China, the second largest military spender. The USA has some 700 military bases in over 100 countries, as well as an unchallengeable lead in hi-tech weaponry and airpower. Yet, preponderant military power may no longer be a secure basis for hegemony. There is a huge gap between the

Focus on . . .
Dimensions of global power

There is no agreement about the precise factors that allow states and other key actors to exert influence on the world stage. Nevertheless, global power can be seen to have a number of dimensions:

- **Military power**: For many commentators, power in international politics boils down to military capacity. Realist theorists, for example, have traditionally favoured a 'basic force' model of power, on the grounds that military capacity enables a country both to protect its territory and people from external aggression, and to pursue its interests abroad through conquest and expansion. Key factors are therefore the size of the armed forces; their effectiveness in terms of morale, training, discipline and leadership; and, crucially, their access to advanced weaponry and equipment. Nevertheless, military capabilities may not translate into genuine political efficacy, as the 'unusability' of nuclear weapons in most circumstances demonstrates.

- **Economic power**: The 'weight' of states in international affairs is closely linked to their wealth and economic resources. This applies, in part, because economic development underpins military capacity, as wealth enables states to develop large armies, acquire modern weapons, and wage costly or sustained wars. Modern technology and a vast industrial base also gives states political leverage in relation to trading partners, especially if their national currency is so strong and stable that it is used as a means of international exchange. Liberals tend to argue that, in an age of globalization, trade had displaced war as the chief currency of international politics.

- **'Soft' power**: Thinking about global power has conventionally focused on 'hard' power – the ability to affect the behaviour of others through the use of inducements (carrots) or threats (sticks); in effect, a combination of economic and military power. 'Soft' power is 'co-optive power'; it rests on the ability to shape the preferences of others by attraction, rather than coercion (Nye, 2004). Whereas hard power draws on resources such as force, sanctions, payments and bribes, soft power operates largely through culture, political ideals and foreign policies (especially policies imbued with moral authority). However, soft power strategies are seldom effective on their own – hard and soft power typically reinforcing one another through what has been called 'smart power' (Nye, 2008).

- **Structural power**: Structural power is the power to decide 'how things are done', reflected in the ability to shape the frameworks within which states relate to one another, relate to people, or relate to corporate enterprises (Strange, 1996). Of particular significance, in this respect, is the influence states exert through their participation within regimes and international organizations, allowing them to have a wider, if less tangible, impact on matters ranging from finance and trade to security and development. Nevertheless, structural power usually operates alongside 'relational' power (the direct influence one actor has on another actor), providing alternative ways of explaining how outcomes in international politics are determined.

- **Asymmetrical war**: War fought between opponents with clearly unequal levels of military, economic and technological power, in which warfare strategies tend to be adapted to the needs of the weak.

destructive capacity of the US military machine and what it can achieve politically. The forced withdrawals of the USA from Lebanon in 1984 and Somalia in 1993, and the difficulty of winning **asymmetrical wars** in Iraq and Afghanistan, demonstrate how the use of terrorist, guerrilla and insurrectionary tactics can thwart even the most advanced power.

A major component of the debate about US power is the focus on its relative economic decline. Although the USA remains the world's largest economy, its competitors, notably China and India, have been growing much more quickly in recent decades, with the Chinese economy being predicted to outstrip the US economy, perhaps by 2020. The 2007–09 global financial crisis may have further weakened the USA, exposing the flaws of the US economic model and bringing the dollar's position as the world's leading currency into question. On the other hand, the USA continues to account for about 40 per cent of world spending on research and development, giving it an almost unassailable technological lead over other countries and ensuring high productivity levels. China is generations away from rivalling the USA in the technologically advanced sectors of the economy. Moreover, just as the British Empire remained a global hegemon until the mid-twentieth century, despite being overtaken in economic terms by the USA and Germany in the late nineteenth century, the USA may continue to retain global leadership in a world in which it is no longer the economic number one.

US power, nevertheless, may have declined more in terms of 'soft' power than in terms of 'hard' power. This has happened in a number of ways. The USA's reputation has been damaged by its association with corporate power and by widening global inequality, with resentment developing against what has been seen as 'globalization-as-Americanization'. As discussed above, serious damage has also been done to the USA's moral authority by the 'war on terror' generally and the Iraq War in particular, made worse by the treatment of prisoners at Abu Ghraib and in the Guantánamo detention camp. Such developments are nevertheless counterbalanced by the USA's continued and unrivalled structural power. The USA exercises disproportional influence over the institutions of global economic governance (see p. 436) and over NATO. Despite the growing influence of the developing world and of emerging economies, no country is close to challenging the USA's influence over global economic decision-making. Indeed, although – as demonstrated by the 2011 intervention in Libya (see p. 414) – the USA's global leadership is no longer so consistent or forthright, US involvement in matters related to intervention and economic, military or political affairs remains indispensable. Without the USA, nothing happens.

Rise of China and 'the rest'

Of all the powers that may rival, or even eclipse, the USA, the most significant is undoubtedly China. Indeed, many predict that the twenty-first century will become the 'Chinese century', just as the twentieth century had been the 'American century'. The basis for China's great power status is its rapid economic progress since the introduction of market reforms in 1978 under Deng Xiaoping (1904–97), the most dramatic phase of which began only in the 1990s. Annual growth rates of between 8 and 10 per cent for almost thirty years (about twice the levels achieved by the USA and other western states) meant that China became the world's largest exporter in 2009, and, in 2010, it overtook Japan to become the world's second largest economy. With the world's largest population (1.3 billion in 2007), China has a seemingly inexhaustible supply of cheap labour, making it, increasingly, the manufacturing heart of the global economy. China's emerging global role is evident in the influence it now exerts within the World Trade Organization (WTO) and the G20 over issues such as **climate change** in its burgeoning resource links with Africa, Australia and parts of the Middle East and Latin America. An often neglected aspect of China's growing

● **Climate change**: A shift in long-term or prevalent weather conditions; the term is almost always used to refer to the phenomenon of 'global warming'.

influence is the extraordinary rise of its 'soft' power. This reflects both the significance of Confucianism (see p. 278) in providing a cultural basis for cooperation in Asia, and the attraction of its anti-imperialist heritage in Africa and across much of the global South.

Nevertheless, the rise of China is often seen as part of a larger shift in the balance of global power from West to East, and specifically to Asia, and maybe from the USA to the **BRICs countries**, sometimes dubbed 'the rest'. Initial predictions of the growing economic might of the BRICs countries suggested that they would exceed the combined strength of the industrialized G7 countries by the middle of the twenty-first century, although this has been repeatedly revised and could occur as early as 2021. An alternative scenario is that the twenty-first century will not so much be the 'Chinese century' as the 'Asian century', with India, Japan and South Korea also being key actors. The transformation of India into an emerging power has been based on economic growth rates only marginally less impressive than China's. It is estimated that, if recent trends persist, by 2020 China and India will jointly account for half of the world's GDP.

However, the continued forward march of a Chinese-led Asia, or the BRICs countries, cannot be taken for granted. In addition to showing signs of an economic slowdown in 2011 and 2012, the Chinese economy remains heavily dependent on supplies of cheap labour, and a transition to a more highly-technologized economy based on advanced skills and production techniques has yet to be achieved. The most serious challenge facing China, however, may be how it reconciles tensions between its political and economic structures. While the Chinese political system remains firmly Stalinist, based on single-party rule by the Chinese Communist Party (CCP), its economic system is increasingly market-orientated and firmly embedded in the global capitalist system. Although authoritarianism (p. 277) may have advantages in terms of managing large-scale economic change and, for instance, pushing through audacious infrastructure programmes, it may be unable to cope with the pluralizing and liberalizing pressures generated by a market capitalist system.

Moreover, neither China nor any of the other BRICs countries shows a capacity for, or willingness to demonstrate, political or diplomatic leadership by openly challenging the USA. This is both because they recognize that US hegemony has a variety of advantages (not least that the USA contributes disproportionately to maintaining the international frameworks through which they increasingly exert influence) and because their desire for economic development takes precedence over geopolitical leadership. Finally, the capacity of the BRICS countries to act as a single entity is severely restricted by political, ideological and economic differences among its members. Indeed, the principal significance of the BRICS countries may be less that they reflect the common interests of 'the rest' and more that they represent a device through which China can bolster its position in relation to the USA, without risking a direct confrontation that may endanger its 'peaceful rise' (see p. 431).

● **The BRICs countries:** A collective term for the four large, fast-growing economies of Brazil, Russia, India and China.

Changing nature of power and power relations

Multipolar trends are not evident only in the decline of old powers and the growth of new powers, but also in the wider diffusion of power beyond the control of any state. This has been evident in globalization's tendency to

Debating ...
Will China's rise continue to be peaceful?

China's emergence is customarily referred to by Chinese authorities as a its 'peaceful rise'. This confounds the conventional expectation that emerging powers become great powers largely by building up military power and through the use of war. In this view, major shifts in world order are seldom accomplished peacefully, suggesting that war, in particular between 'rising' China and the 'declining' USA, is likely, if not inevitable. Is China a rising power of a different kind? Has military power become redundant in world affairs?

YES

Implications of interdependence. The key reason why China's rise has been, and will continue to be, peaceful is that it is taking place within an international system shaped by globalization. Globalization reduces the incidence of war in two main ways. First, rising states such as China no longer need to make economic gains by conquest because globalization offers a cheaper and easier route to national prosperity, in the form of trade. Second, by significantly increasing levels of economic interdependence, globalization makes a Chinese recourse to war almost unthinkable. This is because of the economic costs that war would involve – destroyed trade partnerships, lost external investment, and so on.

'Soft' balancing. Neorealist theorists argue that, confronted by a rising or major power, other states will tend to 'balance' (oppose or challenge that power for fear of leaving itself exposed), rather than 'bandwagon' (side with that power; that is, 'jump on the bandwagon'). However, China's inclination to 'balance' against the USA will be confined to the adoption of 'soft' (non-military) balancing strategies, because the latter's huge military dominance is unlikely to be abandoned in the near future. Similarly, the likelihood that the USA will adopt 'hard' (military) balancing strategies against China has greatly reduced due to the difficulties it experienced in waging the 'war on terror'.

Sino–US bipolar stability. As the twenty-first century progresses, world order may be reshaped on a bipolar, rather than multipolar, basis. The military, economic and structural strengths of the USA are not going to fade soon, and China, already an economic superpower, is clearly not merely one of 'the rest'. Sino–US relations may, as a result, come to replicate US–USSR relations during the 'long peace' of the Cold War period. In other words, bipolarity will, once again, prove to be the surest way of preventing rivalry and hostility spilling over into aggression, as it provides the most favourable conditions for a stable balance of power.

NO

Multipolar instabilities. China's rise is part of a wider restructuring of world order, in which global power is being distributed more widely. Neorealists argue that such multipolarity creates conditions that are inherently prone to conflict and instability, making it increasingly unlikely that China will maintain its 'peaceful rise'. As multipolarity favours fluidity and uncertainty, shifting alliances and power imbalances, it creates opportunities (just as in the run-up to World War I and World War II) for ambitious states to make a bid for power through conquest and expansion. As states seek to maximize power, and not merely security, such circumstances make great powers prone to indiscipline and risk-taking (Mearsheimer, 2001).

Cultural and ideological rivalry. Sino–US bipolarity may pose a greater threat to global peace than did Cold War bipolarity. Whereas antagonism between the USA and the USSR was primarily ideological in character, in the case of 'liberal-democratic' USA and 'Confucian' China ideological differences are rooted in deeper cultural divisions. These may provide the basis for growing enmity and misunderstanding, in line with the 'clash of civilizations' thesis. The transfer of hegemony from the British Empire in the nineteenth century to the USA in the twentieth century may, thus, have remained peaceful only because of cultural similarities that allowed the UK to view the 'rising' USA as essentially unthreatening.

Flashpoints. There are various flashpoints that have the potential to turn tension and hostility into aggression. Chief amongst these is Taiwan, where US support for an independent and 'pro-western' Taiwan clashes with China's quest to incorporate Taiwan into 'greater China' (Carpenter, 2006). Other issues that may inflame Sino–US relations include Tibet, where Beijing's policy of aggressive 'Sinofication' conflicts with Washington's unofficial support for Tibetan independence; human rights generally, but especially China's treatment of 'pro-democracy' dissidents; and the future of disputed islands in the East and South China Seas.

CONCEPT

Global governance

Global governance refers to a broad, dynamic and complex process of interactive decision-making at the global level, involving formal and informal mechanisms, as well as governmental and non-governmental bodies. Global governance is characterized by *polycentrism* (different institutional frameworks and decision-making mechanisms operate in different issue areas), *intergovernmentalism* (states and national governments retain considerable influence within the global governance system) and *mixed actor* involvement (the public/private divide is blurred through the involvement of NGOs, TNCs and the like).

● **International organization**: An institution with formal procedures and a membership comprising three or more states, sometimes called an 'international governmental organization' (IGO).

strengthen the role of non-state actors. Transnational corporations (TNCs) (see p. 149), for example, increasingly dominate the global economy, accounting for about 50 per cent of world manufacturing production and over 70 per cent of world trade. Moreover, TNCs are able to elude political control because of the ease with which they can locate investment and production. Similarly, non-governmental organizations (NGOs) (see p. 248) have proliferated since the 1980s, coming to exercise powerful influence within **international organizations** such as the European Union and the United Nations.

As well as power being reapportioned amongst the states of the world, and between states and non-state actors of various kinds, there are reasons for thinking that the nature of power is changing in ways that make its concentration in a small number of hands increasingly difficult to sustain. This has happened in two main ways. First, due to technology, and in a world of global communications, and rising literacy rates and educational standards, 'soft' power has become as important as 'hard' power in influencing political outcomes. Military power, the traditional currency of world politics, has certainly not become irrelevant, but its use is greatly undermined when it is not matched by 'hearts and minds' strategies. For instance, the use of 'shock and awe' tactics by the US military in Iraq, and other demonstrations of US coercive power, have proved to be counter-productive, in the sense that they damaged the USA's reputation and its moral authority, particularly across the Arab and Muslim worlds.

Second, new technology has, in a number of ways, altered power balances both within and between societies, often empowering the traditionally powerless. For instance, al-Qaeda influence on world politics after 9/11 was out of all proportion to its organizational and economic strength, because modern technology, in the form of bombs and airplanes, had given its terrorist activities a global reach. Advances in communication technology, particularly the use of mobile phones and the internet, have also improved the tactical effectiveness of loosely organized groups, ranging from terrorist bands to protest groups and social movements. Finally, public opinion around the world, and thus the behaviour of governments, is affected by the near-ubiquitous access to television and the wider use of satellite technology. This ensures, for example, that pictures of devastation and human suffering – whether caused by warfare, famine or natural disasters – are shared across the globe almost instantaneously. (The political influence of new forms of information and communication technology is examined in greater detail in Chapter 8.)

GLOBAL GOVERNANCE

Rise of global governance

The issue of world order tends to focus on an image of international politics in which states are assumed to be the primary actors, world affairs largely being determined by the (sometimes shifting) distribution of power amongst states. However, this only gives us partial insight into the workings of the modern international system. A further major component is the framework of global governance, which, to a greater or lesser extent, helps to shape interactions amongst states. But what is global governance? Why has it developed, and how significant

CONCEPT

Interdependence

Interdependence' refers to a relationship between two parties in which each is affected by decisions that are taken by the other. Interdependence implies mutual influence, even a rough equality between the parties in question, usually arising from a sense of mutual vulnerability. Keohane and Nye (1977) advanced the idea of 'complex interdependence' as an alternative to the realist model of international politics. This highlights the extent to which (1) states have ceased to be autonomous international actors; (2) economic and other issues have become more prominent in world affairs; and (3) military force has become a less reliable and less important policy option.

● **Absolute gains**: Benefits that accrue to states from a policy or action regardless of their impact on other states.

● **Relative gains**: Benefits that improve a state's position relative to other states, promoting their position within a hierarchy.

is it? Global governance has been described as a 'collection of governance-related activities, rules and mechanisms, formal and informal, existing at a variety of levels in the world today' (Karns and Mingst, 2009). Global governance hovers somewhere between the traditional idea of international anarchy (in which states interact in the absence of a supranational authority) and the fanciful idea of world government (in which all of humankind is united under one common political authority). As such, global governance is a process of interactive decision-making that allows still-sovereign states to engage in sustained cooperation and, at times, undertake collective action. The growth in the number and importance of international organizations has certainly been a key factor in the emergence of a system of global governance, to such an extent that global governance is sometimes, in effect, used as a collective term describing the international organizations currently in existence. However, global governance and an international organization are not synonymous, as the former has mixed actor involvement, featuring (in addition to states and international organizations) NGOs, TNCs and other institutions of global civil society (see p. 106).

The rise of international organizations nevertheless provides an indication of the growing significance of global governance. The end of World War II marked the emergence of a global governance system with the creation of the United Nations and the institutions of the Bretton Woods system (examined in the next section). By 1949, the number of international organizations stood at 123, compared with 49 in 1914. By the mid-1980s, the total number of such bodies had reached 378, with the average membership per organization standing at over 40 (compared with 18.6 in 1945, and 22.7 in 1964). Although their number subsequently declined, largely due to the dissolution of the Soviet bloc organizations at the end of the Cold War, this masks a substantial growth in international agencies and other institutions, as the number of bodies spawned by international organizations themselves has continued to grow. Liberals such as Robert Keohane (see p. 434) tend to explain such developments in terms of growing interdependencies amongst states, associated with concerns about power politics, economic crises, human rights violations, development disparities and environmental degradation. International organizations are therefore a reflection of the extent of interdependence in the global system, an acknowledgement by states that, increasingly, they can achieve more by working together than by working separately. In this view, states will cooperate when each calculates that it will make '**absolute**' **gains** as a result.

Realists, in contrast, tend to explain the growth of global governance in terms of the emerging hegemonic role of the USA, which saw the pursuit of US national interests and the promotion of international cooperation as mutually sustaining goals. International organization is linked to hegemony because only a hegemonic state possesses the power to tolerate the '**relative**' **gains** that other states may make, so long as they make 'absolute' gains themselves. From this perspective, a hegemon needs not only to be able to enforce the 'rules of the game', but also to be committed to a system that brings benefit to the mass of states. Critical theorists, for their part, tend to view international organizations as devices constructed to serve the dominant interests of the global system – the hegemonic power; western industrialized states generally; TNCs and social, ethnic and gender elites across the global North. In this view, international organizations reflect and, to some degree, exist to consolidate global inequalities and asymmetries.

Robert Keohane (born 1941)

US international relations theorist. With his long-time collaborator, Joseph S. Nye, Keohane questioned some of the core assumptions of realist analysis in *Transnational Relations and Wold Politics* (1971), highlighting the increasing importance of non-state actors and of economic issues in world affairs. In *Power and Interdependence: World Politics in Transition* (1977), Keohane and Nye set out the theory of 'complex interdependence' as an alternative to realism. Since the publication of *After Hegemony* (1984), however, Keohane has attempted to synthesize structural realism and complex interdependence, creating a hybrid dubbed either 'modified structural realism' or 'neoliberal institutionalism'.

The extent to which the modern world conforms to the features of a global governance system is nevertheless a source of debate. Liberal theorists, in particular, not only argue that global governance is a meaningful development, providing an alternative to the international anarchy of old, but also claim that the trend in its favour is unmistakable and, perhaps, irresistible. This is based on two factors. First, thanks to globalization and the development of a generally more interconnected world, states are increasingly confronted by challenges that are beyond their capacity to deal with when acting alone. In short, global problems require global solutions. Second, the growth of international organizations fosters further cooperation by strengthening trust (see p. 87) amongst states, accustoming them to rule-governed behaviour. This suggests that the trend in favour of global governance generates an internal momentum, making it difficult to reverse. However, the extent to which the world as a whole has become orderly and norm-governed should not be exaggerated. It is more accurate to refer to an *emerging* global governance process, rather than an *established* global governance system. Moreover, the norms and rules of global governance are better established in some parts of the world than in others. For instance, Europe has been portrayed as the heart of the so-called 'postmodern' world, by virtue of the EU's success in 'pooling' sovereignty and banishing balance-of-power politics (Cooper, 2004). Europe, nevertheless, is an exception and many parts of the world are still little-affected by international norms and rules, as demonstrated by the existence of 'rogue' states and **pariah states**.

Global economic governance

Evolution of the Bretton Woods system

The trend towards global governance has been particularly evident in the sphere of economic policy-making. This is because economics is the most obvious area of interdependence amongst states, and the area where the failure of international cooperation can cause the clearest damage. Since 1945, a system of global economic governance has emerged through a thickening web of multilateral agreements, formal institutions and informal networks, with the most important institutions being those established by the Bretton Woods agreement, negotiated

● **Pariah state**: A state whose behaviour places it outside the international community, leading to diplomatic isolation and widespread condemnation.

Multilateralism

Multilateralism can broadly be defined as a process that coordinates behaviour amongst three or more countries on the basis of generalized principles of conduct (Ruggie, 1992). For a process to be genuinely multilateral, it must conform to three principles. These principles are *non-discrimination* (all participating countries must be treated alike), *indivisibility* (participating countries must behave as if they were a single entity, as in collective security (see p. 411)) and *diffuse reciprocity* (obligations amongst countries must have a general and enduring character, rather than being examples of one-off cooperation).

● **Exchange rate**: The price at which one currency is exchanged for another.

● **Washington consensus**: A policy package that sought to reduce intervention in the market through measures of deregulation, privatization and fiscal constraint.

● **Structural adjustment programmes**: Devices used to bring about market-orientated 'structural adjustment' of economies through 'conditionalities' attached to loans made by the IMF and the World Bank.

just before the end of World War II. Known, in due course, collectively, as the 'Bretton Woods system', these bodies were:

● The International Monetary Fund (IMF)
● The International Bank for Reconstruction and Development (IBRD), better known as the World Bank
● The General Agreement on Tariffs and Trade (GATT), which was replaced in 1995 by the World Trade Organization (WTO).

The Bretton Woods agreement is a clear example of the multilateralism that was to become increasingly prominent in the post-1945 period. However, it would be a mistake to portray Bretton Woods simply in terms of multilateralism and the recognition of mutual interests. This would be to ignore the crucial role played by the USA, which emerged from World War II as the world's predominant military and economic power, and which linked its continuing prosperity to the establishment of an open and stable international economic system. At the centre of the Bretton Woods system was a new monetary order, overseen by the IMF, which sought to maintain stable **exchange rates**. This was achieved by fixing all currencies to the value of the US dollar, which acted as a 'currency anchor', with the US dollar being convertible to gold at a rate of $35 per ounce. For at least two decades, the Bretton Woods system appeared to be a remarkable success. Instead of the end of World War II, and the consequent drop in military expenditure, bringing back, as some had feared, the dark days of the Great Depression, it heralded the onset of the 'long boom' of the postwar period, the longest period of sustained economic growth the world economy had ever experienced.

However, the 'golden age' of the 1950s and 1960s was followed by the 'stagflation' of the 1970s, in which economic stagnation and rising unemployment was linked to high inflation. In this context, and with the US economy struggling to cope with spiralling spending of home and abroad, in 1971 the USA abandoned the system of fixed exchange rates – signalling, in effect, the end of the Bretton Woods system in its original form. The advent of 'floating' exchange rates initiated a major policy and ideological shift. In policy terms, it gave rise to the **Washington consensus**. In ideological terms, the IMF, GATT and the World Bank were converted during the 1970s and 1980s to the idea of an international economic order based on free-market and free-trade principles. The replacement of GATT by the World Trade Organization in 1995 strengthened the free trade agenda and helped to accelerate the advance of economic globalization.

Evaluating global economic governance

In its initial mission, as the guarantor of exchange rates stability, the IMF was highly successful for at least two decades. Nevertheless, the IMF became an increasingly controversial institution from the 1980s onwards. This was because it linked the provision of loans to developing and transition countries to conditions for '**structural adjustment**' that reflected an unqualified faith in free markets and free trade. Supporters of the IMF argue that, despite short-term instability and insecurities, an adjustment to an open and market-based

Focus on . . .
Global economic governance

- **The International Monetary Fund (IMF)**: The IMF was set up to oversee the global rules governing money in general and, in particular, to maintain currency stability through a system of fixed exchange rates. Since 1971, the IMF has embraced a neoliberal economic model, and requires countries to carry out stringent market-based reforms as a condition for receiving assistance. The IMF has grown from its original 29 members to 188 members. Its headquarters are in Washington.
- **The World Bank**: The World Bank (formerly the International Bank for Reconstruction and Development) was designed to reduce the element of risk in foreign lending, thereby underpinning economic stability. Since the 1980s the Bank has geared its lending to 'structural adjustment', the

reorientation of economies around market principles and their integration into the global economy. The World Bank's headquarters are in Washington.
- **The World Trade Organization (WTO)**: The WTO was established in 1995, replacing the General Agreement on Tariffs and Trade (GATT). Created by the 'Uruguay round' of negotiations (1986–95), the WTO has wider and stronger powers than those of the GATT. The WTO's mission is to 'liberalize' world trade and create an 'open' global trading system. However, the 'Doha round', which started in 2001, broke down in 2006 because of disagreements between developed and developing states. The WTO had 157 members in 2012, with a further 27 countries applying to join. Its headquarters are in Geneva.

economy is the only reliable road to long-term economic success. Other strengths of the IMF are that it will often provide loans to countries that can find no other source of finance, and that its interest rates may be more competitive than those otherwise available. However, critics have seen the IMF, and global economic governance generally, as the political arm of neoliberal globalization, forcing poor and vulnerable countries to accept a US business model that better caters to the needs of western banks and corporations than it does to long-term development needs. The fact that IMF intervention has often caused more problems than it has solved stems, critics allege, from its flawed development model, which fails to recognize the possibility of market failure or the drawbacks of economic openness. In the wake of the 2007–09 global financial crisis, the IMF was roundly criticized for not having prevented the crisis by highlighting the instabilities and imbalances that had produced it. This led to calls for the reform of the IMF, particularly with a view to strengthening its ability to regulate the global financial system. However, this has so far resulted in little more than a minor adjustment of voting rights in favour of developing states.

In the early period, the World Bank concentrated on promoting postwar reconstruction. However, over time, promoting development became the principal focus of its work. During the 1970s, under the presidency of Robert McNamara, 1968–81, the Bank placed an increased emphasis on poverty reduction. This involved, for example, promoting projects in rural development and concentrating on meeting basic needs. From the early 1980s onwards, and in conjunction with the IMF, the Bank embraced a strategy of 'structural adjustment'. The market reforms that its programmes sought to promote were

CONCEPT

Free trade

Free trade is a system of trading between states not restricted by tariffs or other forms of protectionism. In line with the theory of 'comparative advantage', liberals argue that international trade benefits all countries that participate in it, not least through greater specialization. The political case for free trade is that, in deepening economic interdependence and fostering international exchange, it makes war less likely and, perhaps, impossible. Critics point out that free trade widens economic inequalities by giving dominant powers access to the markets of weak states, while having little to fear themselves from foreign competition.

designed to re-establish as quickly as possible the credit-worthiness of developing countries in order to allow them to focus once again on the fight against poverty. During the 1990s, in face of growing criticism and the failure of many of its structural adjustment programmes, the Bank started to place less emphasis on macro-economic reform and greater emphasis on the structural, social and human aspects of development. This new strategy has been dubbed the 'post-Washington consensus'. Supporters of the World Bank highlight its success in transferring resources, through development projects, from wealthy countries to poorer ones. However, critics argue, variously, that its financing of development is insufficient; that its record of reducing poverty has often been poor; and that, together with the IMF and the WTO, it tends to uphold the imbalances and disparities of the global economic order, rather than challenge them.

In many ways, the emergence of the WTO was a response to the changing imperatives of the international trading system in the 1980s. The triumph of neoliberalism (see p. 144) and the acceleration of globalization created stronger pressure to advance the cause of free trade through a more powerful trade organization with broader responsibilities. The WTO is seen by some as a global economic government in the making. Its supporters argue that, in encouraging trade liberalization, it has made a major contribution to promoting sustainable growth in the world economy. Such a view is largely based on the belief that free and open trade is mutually beneficial to all the countries that engage in it. Trade liberalization is, thus, seen to sharpen competition, foster innovation and breed success for all. Nevertheless, the WTO has been no less controversial an organization than the IMF and the World Bank.

Many of the WTO's critics focus on its basic principles, arguing that, far from bringing benefit to all, trade liberalization is responsible for structural inequalities and the weakening of workers' rights and environmental protection. Furthermore, although decision-making within the WTO is based on consensus-building (as opposed to the system of weighted votes used by both the IMF and the World Bank, which are biased in favour of the USA and industrialized countries generally), it is widely argued that consensus decision-making favours states that have sizeable, well-resourced and permanent representation in the WTO's Geneva headquarters. A final criticism highlights the weakness of the WTO, and specifically its inability to reconcile strongly-held opposing views. This is evident in the near-collapse of the Doha Round of trade negotiations, which commenced in 2001. Negotiations have stalled because of disagreements, mainly over agricultural subsidies, between, on the one hand, developing countries and emerging economies, including China, and developed countries on the other hand. Such a failure has enabled the USA and the EU to maintain agricultural protectionism, while penalizing developing countries and the world's poor, who would benefit most from reducing barriers and subsidies in farming.

The United Nations

Role of the United Nations

The United Nations is, without doubt, the most important international organization created to date and the heart of the emerging system of global governance. Established through the San Francisco Conference of 1945, it is the only

Focus on . . .

How the United Nations works

- **The Security Council:** This is the most significant UN body. Its key purpose is to ensure the maintenance of international peace and security, and so it is responsible for the UN's role as a negotiator, observer and peacekeeper. The Security Council has 15 members, but it is dominated by the P-5, its permanent 'veto powers' (the USA, Russia, China, the UK and France), which can block decisions made by other members of the Council.

- **The General Assembly:** This is the main deliberative organ of the UN, sometimes dubbed the 'parliament of nations'. The Assembly consists of all members of the UN, each of which has a single vote. The Assembly can debate and pass resolutions on any matter covered by the Charter, but it has no legislative role and does not oversee or scrutinize, in any meaningful sense, the Security Council or the Secretariat.

- **The Secretariat:** This serves the other principal organs of the UN and administers the programmes and policies laid down by them. At its head is the Secretary-General (since 2007, Ban Ki-moon), who functions as the public face of the UN, as well as its chief administrative officer. The main activities of the Secretariat take place in the UN's headquarters in New York.

- **The Economic and Social Council:** The ECOSOC consists of 54 members elected by the General Assembly. Its chief role is to coordinate the economic and social work of the UN. This involves overseeing the activities of a large number of programmes, funds and specialized agencies, such as the International Labour Organization (ILO) and the World Health Organization. Its main areas of concern are human rights, development and poverty reduction, and the environment.

- **The International Court of Justice:** The ICJ is the principal judicial organ of the UN. Its primary role is to settle, in accordance with international law, legal disputes submitted to it by states. Located in The Hague, Netherlands, the ICJ is composed of 15 judges elected by the General Assembly and the Security Council, voting separately.

truly global organization ever constructed, having a membership of 193 states and counting. The UN is, nevertheless, a sprawling and complex organization, described by its second Secretary-General, Dag Hammarskjöld, as 'a weird Picasso abstraction'. Beyond its five major organs, it encompasses the so-called 'three sisters' – the World Bank, the IMF and the WTO – and also bodies such as the World Health Organization (WHO), the United Nations Children's Fund (UNICEF), the United Nations Educational, Scientific and Cultural Organization (UNESCO), and the United Nations High Commission for Refugees (UNHCR). Although this has created an organization that is highly cumbersome, often conflict-ridden and, some say, inherently inefficient, it also enables the UN to respond to myriad interests and to address an ever-widening global agenda.

The principal aims of the UN, spelled out by its founding Charter, are as follows:

- To safeguard peace and security in order 'to save succeeding generations from the scourge of war'.
- To 'reaffirm faith in fundamental human rights'.
- To uphold respect for international law.
- To 'promote social progress and better standards of life'.

Maintaining peace and security

The chief purpose of the UN is to maintain international peace and security, with responsibility for this being vested in the Security Council. Indeed, the performance of the UN can largely be judged in terms of the extent to which it has saved humankind from deadly military conflict. It is, nevertheless, difficult to assess the extent of the UN's contribution to ensuring that the two world wars of the twentieth century have not been followed by World War III when other factors, not least the 'balance of terror' between the USA and the USSR, have also contributed. However, what is clear is that, being a creature of its members, the UN's capacity to enforce a system of collective security (see p. 411) is severely limited. It can do no more than its member states, and particularly the permanent members of the Security Council, permit. As a result, its role has essentially been confined to providing mechanisms that facilitate the peaceful resolution of international conflicts. During the Cold War, the UN was routinely paralyzed by superpower rivalry that led to deadlock in the Security Council. The UN, therefore, was a powerless spectator when the USSR invaded Hungary (1956), Czechoslovakia (1968) and Afghanistan (1979), and it failed to curtail the USA's escalating military involvement in Vietnam during the 1960s and 1970s. A further weakness is that the UN has never been able to develop an armed force of its own, so that it has always had to rely on troops supplied by individual member states.

The end of the Cold War, however, produced optimism about the capacity of an activist UN to preside over the 'new world order'. The UN approved the US-led expulsion of Iraq from Kuwait in the 1991 Gulf War, and, in a few short years, the number of UN peacekeeping operations had doubled, and the annual budget for peacekeeping had quadrupled. Hopes for a more effective UN in the post-Cold War period were nevertheless dashed, both by a declining willingness of states, freed from East–West rivalry, to accept neutral, multilateral intervention, and by the eroding support, financial and military, of the USA. Despite some genuine successes in peacekeeping (such as in Mozambique and El Salvador) and in peace-building (East Timor), the UN's reputation was badly damaged by its failure to prevent large-scale slaughter in the mid-1990s in Rwanda and Bosnia.

Economic and social development

As the membership of the UN expanded as a result of decolonization in the 1950s and 1960s, giving the developing world much greater influence over the General Assembly, the promotion of economic and social development became an increasingly prominent UN concern. The main areas of UN economic and social responsibility are human rights, development and poverty reduction, and the environment. In the case of human rights, the centrepiece of the international regime that has developed since World War II to promote and protect such rights has been the UN's Universal Declaration of Human Rights, adopted in 1948. The incorporation of the Declaration into a legally-binding codification of human rights – in effect, human rights law – was achieved through the adoption in 1966 of the International Covenants on Civil and Political Rights, and on Economic, Social and Cultural Rights. Collectively, the 1948 Declaration and the two covenants are commonly referred to as the 'International Bill of Human Rights'. However, the UN's record of standing up to dictators, condemning human rights violations and intervening to prevent genocide and other compa-

POLITICS IN ACTION . . .

Tackling climate change: doomed to failure?

Events: The 1992 Rio 'Earth Summit' (the UN Conference on Environment and Development) was the first international conference to give significant attention to the issue of climate change. It did so by establishing the Framework Convention on Climate Change (FCCC), and by calling for greenhouse gases to be stabilized at 'safe' levels. Although it was accepted by 181 governments, the FCCC was no more than a framework for further action and contained no legally binding targets. The Kyoto Protocol to the FCCC, negotiated in 1997, went further, in that, for the first time, legally binding targets were set (for the period to 2012) for states to limit or reduce their greenhouse gas emissions. Its chief limitation was that the USA (the world's largest emitter) failed to ratify the treaty. In addition, as targets were only set for developed states,

emerging powers such as China (which, in 2008, overtook the USA to become the world's largest emitter) and India were excluded. In 2009, the UN Climate Change Conference was convened in Copenhagen to develop a successor to the Kyoto Protocol. The conference, nevertheless, merely agreed to 'take note of' the so-called 'Copenhagen Accord'. This pledged to prevent rises in global temperature of more than 2°C above pre-industrial levels, but failed to create any new legally binding obligations on any country to cut emissions, or even to set a global target for emissions cuts. The final opportunity to extend the Kyoto process came with the 2012 Doha conference.

Significance: Some have argued that Rio, Kyoto and Copenhagen mark a record of steady, if unspectacular, international progress on the issue of climate change. Rio created a framework within which the issue could be addressed; Kyoto set binding targets for the developed world; and Copenhagen, for all its limitations, moved beyond Kyoto in that it was marked by the participation of the two biggest players, the USA and China. Yet, the dominant response to these events has been one of frustration and disappointment, with some warning that the failure of the international community to take robust action over climate change will ultimately have catastrophic implications. Why, when some argue that climate change is the most urgent and important challenge currently confronting the international community, has international cooperation over the issue been so difficult to achieve?

A number of obstacles stand in the way of concerted international action over climate change. First and foremost, although all states acknowledge the threat posed by climate change, tackling the issue imposes major costs on individual states, in terms of investment in sometimes expensive strategies, and accepting lower levels of economic growth. In such circumstances, states are encouraged to be 'free riders', enjoying the benefits of a healthier environment without having to pay for them. A second obstacle is tension between developed and developing states, based on what the FCCC refers to as their 'common but differentiated responsibilities and respective capabilities'. Many in the developing world believe that targets should be set to reflect the fact that developed countries have a historic responsibility for the accumulated stock of carbon emitted since the beginning of the industrial age, which has provided the basis for their level of economic growth and prosperity. Attempts by the developed world to ensure that the costs of tackling climate change are shared globally, are, therefore, seen as morally unfounded and a denial of the developing world's right to prosperity. Finally, many in the green movement trace increased emissions levels, or 'carbon industrialization', back to the spread of materialist and consumerist values that ensure that economic and political systems have come to be geared towards growth and rising living standards. Unless this ideological and cultural dimension of the problem is addressed, international action is destined to remain weak and ineffective.

rable acts has been poor – a product, perhaps, of the moral relativism (see p. 453) that has taken hold as the UN's membership has expanded.

In the case of development and poverty reduction, the principal vehicle has been the UN Development Programme (UNDP), created in 1965. The UNDP has a presence in some 177 countries, working with them on their own solutions to global and national development challenges, and also helps developing countries to attract and use aid effectively. By focusing on the notions of 'human development' and 'human security' (see p. 418), the UNDP has fostered innovative thinking about poverty and deprivation, moving away from a narrowly economic definition of poverty. In the case of the environment, the UN's Conference on the Human Environment in Stockholm in 1972 laid the foundations for environmental action at an international level and prepared the way for the launch of the UN's Environmental Programme (UNEP). Over time, the issue of climate change has come to dominate the UN's environmental agenda, as a succession of high-profile conferences on the issue has been convened, albeit often with disappointing outcomes (see p. 440).

An indispensable body?

The UN is no stranger to controversy and criticism. Some, indeed, regard it as fundamentally flawed. In this view, the UN is a proto-world government, and has all the drawbacks of a would-be world government – a lack of legitimacy, accountability and democratic credentials. Not only does the UN interfere in the affairs of states, thereby eroding their sovereignty, but it also disrupts the workings of the balance-of-power system, thus endangering the very peace and stability that it was set up to maintain. Others decry the UN's ineffectiveness, rather than its capacity to meddle in world affairs. As is commonly pointed out, there have been more wars since the creation of the UN than there had been before, and the organization is routinely sidelined as major world events unfold, not least because the Security Council can be so easily paralyzed by conflict amongst the 'Big Five'. Further criticisms highlight the dysfunctionality of a body that functions as 'two UNs', one of which serves as a voice for the great powers and operates through the Security Council, while the other articulates the interests of the developing world and operates through the General Assembly. While the former has huge potential power but seldom exercises it, the latter acts as little more than a debating society.

For all its flaws and failings, one central fact must be borne in mind: the world is a safer place with the UN than it would be without it. Although the UN will never be able to prevent all wars and resolve all conflicts, it provides an indispensable framework for cooperation, should the international community choose to use it. The UN serves, however imperfectly, to increase the chances that international conflict can be resolved without a resort to war and that, if war breaks out, military conflict will quickly lead to peacemaking and peace-building. Moreover, the UN did not fossilize around its initial mission but, rather, succeeded in redefining itself in the light of new global challenges. Not only has the UN developed into the leading organization promoting economic and social development worldwide, but it has also helped to shape the agenda as far as new global issues are concerned, ranging from climate change and gender equality to population control and dealing with pandemics. In short, if the UN did not exist, it would have to be invented.

SUMMARY

● The end of the Cold War led to proclamations about the advent of a 'new world order'; however, this new world order was always imprecisely defined, and the idea quickly became unfashionable. Instead, bipolarity came to be seen to have been replaced by unipolarity – the USA, as the sole remaining superpower, having become a 'global hegemon'.

● The implications of US hegemony became particularly apparent following September 11, as the USA embarked on the so-called 'war on terror'. This, nevertheless, drew the USA into deeply problematic military interventions, which highlighted the limitations of the USA's unrivalled military strength.

● Twenty-first century world order increasingly has a multipolar character. This is evident in the relative decline of the USA and rise of so-called 'emerging powers', notably China; however, it is also a consequence of wider developments, including the advance of globalization and global governance, and the growing importance of non-state actors.

● Global governance is a broad, dynamic and complex process of interactive decision-making at the global level. Liberal theorists argue that there is an unmistakable (and perhaps irresistible) trend in favour of global governance, reflecting growing interdependence and a greater willingness of states to engage in collective action. However, the USA's role in promoting global governance for reasons of national interest has also been significant.

● The trend towards global governance has been particularly prominent in the economic sphere, where it has been associated with three bodies: the International Monetary Fund, the World Bank and the World Trade Organization. These bodies have, nevertheless, each, in their different ways, been drawn into controversy through their association with neoliberal globalization.

● The United Nations is the only truly global organization ever constructed, and it operates as the heart of the emerging global governance system. Its principal aims have been to maintain international peace and security, and to promote economic and social development. Although the UN has been no stranger to controversy and criticism, it is widely regarded as an indispensable framework for cooperation, should the international community choose to use it.

Questions for discussion

● Was the idea of a 'new world order' merely a tool to legitimize US hegemony?

● How has the 'war on terror' affected the global status of the USA?

● Is China in the process of becoming the next global hegemon?

● Is tension between the USA and 'the rest' a growing fault line in world politics?

● Should emerging multipolarity be welcomed or feared?

● How far does modern world politics operate as a functioning global governance system?

● Why is global governance most advanced in the economic sphere?

● How effective has the UN been in maintaining peace and security?

● What impact has the UN had on economic and social issues?

Further reading

Parmar, I. and M. Cox (eds) *Soft Power and US Foreign Policy* (2010). A wide-ranging and insightful collection of essays on the role of soft power in affecting the balances of world order.

Weiss, T. G. *What's Wrong with the United Nations (and How to Fix it)* (2009). A stimulating diagnosis-and-cure approach that considers why the United Nations and its system of related agencies seem to be perpetually in crisis.

Whitman, J. (ed.) *Global Governance* (2009). An authoritative and incisive collection of essays that examine the nature and implications of global governance.

Young, A., J. Duckett and P. Graham (eds) *Perspectives on the Global Distribution of Power* (2010). A collection that reviews the shifting global distribution of power and examines the changing power resources of key protagonists.

CHAPTER 20

A Crisis in Politics?

'Politics is a strong and slow boring of hard boards'

MAX WEBER, 'Politics as a vocation' (1919)

PREVIEW   In this concluding chapter, we return to some of the themes discussed in Chapter 1, and, in the process, draw together some of the themes set out at different points in the book. This is done by examining the nature and health of politics itself, taking particular account of how and why politics – and especially conventional, or 'mainstream', politics – has been subject to increasing criticism. Of course, there is nothing new about politics being viewed in a negative light – the term has long been used as a 'dirty' word, implying an activity that is distasteful, even demeaning – but criticism seems to have risen to unprecedented levels in recent decades. Politicians, needless to say, have usually borne the brunt of these attacks, with popular associations with 'politician' commonly including 'liar', 'corrupt', 'careerist' and 'untrustworthy'. Politics, moreover, appears to be losing its ability to engage and enthuse, as witnessed by declining levels of voter turnout and falling party membership – trends that are most pronounced in mature democracies and particularly affect younger people. However, this may be a deeply misleading picture. Anxieties about growing civic disengagement, for instance, may ignore the extent to which political participation is not declining but changing, through, amongst other things, the rise of protest movements of various kinds or the spread of internet-based activism. It is also far from clear that the trends mentioned above can be laid at the door of politics and politicians; other possible culprits include the media and, perhaps, the public themselves. Nevertheless, dissatisfaction with politics may have a deeper, even philosophical, dimension, in the form of confusion about what, exactly, politics is 'for', and how the performance of political systems should be judged. These questions, however, touch on some of the most intractable normative debates within the discipline of itself.

KEY ISSUES
- Is civic engagement in crisis?
- What do the phenomena of 'new politics' and 'anti-politics' tell us?
- Who, or what, is to blame for civic disengagement?
- What are the most important outcomes of the political process?
- How do different political systems perform in relation to these outcomes?

CONCEPT

Political participation

Political participation is the act of taking part in the formulation, passage or implementation of public policies, regardless of whether these acts are successful or effective. However, political participation takes place at very different levels. Citizens have been divided into 'apathetics' (who do not engage in formal politics), 'spectators' (who rarely participate beyond voting) and 'gladiators' (who fight political battles) (Milbrath and Goel, 1977). Conventional participation comprises a number of 'modes', notably voting, party campaigning, communal activity and contacting a representative or official about a particular personal matter (Verba, Nie and Kim, 1978).

● **Civic engagement**: The participation of citizens in the life of their community, although this may range from formal political participation to wider communal activities or even 'civic-mindedness'.

POLITICS UNDER ASSAULT?

On the face of it, it seems odd to suggest that politics is in crisis. In some respects, politics has never been healthier. Dramatic demonstrations of 'people power' have brought authoritarian regimes to their knees, as occurred in the Eastern European Revolutions of 1989–91 and the Arab Spring (see p. 88), and the seemingly remorseless advance of democratization (see p. 272) has led to a major expansion of political and civic rights. Insofar as politics (in the sense of compromise and consensus-building, see pp. 8–9) constitutes a distinctively non-violent means of resolving conflict, the long- and short-term decline in violence that has occurred mainly, but not only, in western societies (Pinker, 2011) surely provides evidence of both the effectiveness of politics and its wider use. Yet, in other respects, a heavy cloud hangs over politics. In particular, growing numbers of people appear to be disengaging from the political process, or expressing disenchantment with it. Why is politics coming under attack? Has politics become a problem, rather than a solution?

Declining civic engagement?

It has long been assumed that the level of **civic engagement** is an indication of the health of a political system. Democratic theorists have certainly argued that one of the key strengths of democratic rule (examined more fully in the final section of this chapter) is that it offers wider opportunities for popular participation than any other form of rule, ensuring not merely government *for* the people, but also government *by* the people. Yet, however hard-won the rights of political participation may have been, especially the right to vote in free and fair elections, there is evidence (from mature democracies in particular) that citizens are becoming less interested in using these rights.

For instance, in the period 1945–97, average voter turnout in UK general elections usually remained above 75 per cent, with a postwar high of 84 per cent being achieved in 1950. The turnout in the 2001 general election nevertheless fell to 59 per cent, the lowest figure since 1918. Although the turnouts in 2005 and 2010 rose marginally (to 61 per cent and 65 per cent, respectively), these figures were still more than 10 per cent below the 1945–97 average, and occurred despite the wider use of postal voting (in 2005) and the first use of televised leaders' debates (in 2010). In Canada, voter turnout in federal elections plummeted during the 1990s from levels, once again, usually above 75 per cent to an average of 61.5 per cent in the elections held between 2000 and 2011. As elsewhere, declining voter turnout in Canada has been particularly evident amongst younger voters, creating a situation in which only about one third of first-time voters now actually vote, half the rate of a generation ago. Similar trends can be found across Western Europe, in Japan and in parts of Latin America, leading to the estimate that voter turnout has decreased globally by about 5 percentage points since the 1950s (Lijphart, 1996).

Civic disengagement goes well beyond non-voting, however. As discussed in Chapter 10, political parties in many parts of the world appear to be failing in their traditional role as agents of popular mobilization and political participation. This has been evident at a number of levels. Fewer people 'identify' with political parties than they once did, in the sense of having a psychological attach-

Citizenship

Citizenship is a relationship between the individual and the state in which the two are bound together by reciprocal rights and duties. Citizens differ from subjects and aliens in that they are full members of their political community or state by virtue of their possession of basic rights. Liberals advance the principle of a 'citizenship of rights' that stresses private entitlement and the status of the individual as an autonomous actor. Communitarians, in contrast, advance the principle of a 'citizenship of duty' that highlights the role of the state as a moral agency and the importance of community or social existence.

ment or loyalty towards a party. This trend is called partisan dealignment (see p. 217), and has been associated with more volatile voting behaviour and a growing willingness to vote for 'fringe' parties. There is also evidence of a major long-term decline in party membership across established democracies. During the 1980s and 1990s, party membership dropped by one million or more in Italy, France and the UK, around half a million in Germany, and close to half a million in Austria. Norway and France have lost well over half their party members since the 1980s, while fewer than 1 per cent of adults in the UK belong to political parties, down from 7 per cent some fifty years ago.

Declines in party membership are also matched by declines in levels of party activism. Party members have increasingly become 'cheque book members', who are prepared to pay their membership fees but are less inclined to attend regular meetings or, in particular, get involved in canvassing or campaigning. Civic disengagement may nevertheless go beyond conventional forms of political participation, such as voting, party membership and campaigning, and affect wider civic participation, in the form of church attendance, membership of professional societies, sports clubs, youth groups and parent-teacher associations, and the like. Robert Putnam (see p. 176) has interpreted such trends as evidence of declining 'social capital' (see p. 175) in the USA and, by extension, other industrialized countries, and of the emergence of a 'post-civic' generation.

However, the notion that modern societies suffer from a 'participation crisis' has also been criticized. The problem may not be so much that the overall level of political participation has fallen, but that there has been a shift from one kind of participation to another. In particular, as disillusionment and cynicism with **mainstream politics** has grown, there has been an upsurge in interest in pressure group politics, protest movements and the use of 'new media' to facilitate political debate and activism (see p. 190). The rise of what has been called the 'new politics' – reflecting more fluid, participatory, non-hierarchical and, possibly, more spontaneous styles of political participation – has been linked, variously, to the emergence of post-industrial societies (as discussed in Chapter 7) and to the spread of 'postmaterialist' values (as discussed in Chapter 8). As such, it may reflect a shift from a traditional conception of citizenship to a kind of 'reflexive' citizenship, through which citizens seek a more critical and reciprocal relationship with the structures of power.

The politics of 'anti-politics'

The perception that politics is in crisis arises not merely from concerns about civic disengagement, but also from evidence of growing cynicism about, and even anger towards, mainstream political parties and politicians. What appears sometimes to be a breakdown in trust (see p. 87) between the public and the political class in general, sometimes seen as the rise of 'anti-politics', does not simply encourage citizens to turn away from politics and retreat into private existence. Instead, it has spawned new forms of politics, which, in various ways, seek to articulate resentment or hostility towards conventional political structures. Although such hostility is based on a common perception that established political elites are 'out-of-touch', 'privileged', 'corrupt' or 'self-serving', anti-political groups and movements have taken very different forms. Certain forms of anti-politics clearly overlap with 'new politics', as in the case of the upsurge in

● **Mainstream politics**: Political activities, processes and structures that are regarded as normal or conventional; the dominant trend in politics.

Debating...
Should political participation be widened and deepened whenever possible?

Although the link between political participation and democratic rule is widely accepted, there is significant debate about the desirable level of citizens' engagement with politics. Why have some seen virtues in low-participation societies, and even warned against the dangers of 'excessive' political participation? But why, also, have exponents of 'participatory democracy' viewed participation as a good in itself, and called for political participation to be widened and deepened whenever this is possible?

YES

Making better citizens. Political participation is often defended on educational or developmental grounds. Participatory democrats, such as J. S. Mill (see p. 198) and, more recently, Pateman (1970), argue that the great benefit of citizens becoming directly involved in making political decisions is that it extends their moral, social and political awareness, and even their intellectual development. As people participate in the life of their community, they not only acquire a better appreciation of their own and others' civic rights and responsibilities; they are also encouraged to reflect on often complex moral issues and to gain a better understanding of how their society works.

Meaningful democracy. A direct link can be made between the level of political participation and the health of a democratic system. This is based on the instrumental argument in favour of participation, which is that participation is a means of promoting or defending the interests of ordinary citizens. Quite simply, the more people participate in politics, the louder their voice becomes. A strong participatory culture therefore forces politicians to act in line with the public interest. By the same token, low levels of participation lead to a 'hollowed-out' democratic system, in which politicians become self-serving and, increasingly, heedless of public opinion.

Common good before private good. Political participation can also be justified on communitarian grounds. By participating in making collective decisions on behalf of their community, people acquire a stronger sense of social belonging, recognizing that there is more to life than their own narrow or selfish existence. Such arguments can be traced back to Aristotle's (see p. 6) assertion that human beings are 'political animals', who can only live the 'good life' as members of a political community. In Rousseau's (see p. 97) view, the direct and continuous participation of all citizens in political life helps to bind the state to the common good.

NO

Virtues of apathy. High levels of popular participation may be a recipe for discord, incivility and the breakdown of social order. This is because as people become more involved in politics, they take their loyalties and allegiances more seriously and pursue their views with greater passion and determination. A high-participation society may, therefore, be a society of political zealots. The great virtue of apathy and political passivity is, thus, that they increase the likelihood that citizens will 'put up with' political decisions with which they disagree, or which conflict with their interests, something that is essential to any stable and peaceful political system.

Manageable democracy. Democratic systems may function best when political participation extends little beyond the act of voting every few years. For theorists such as Schumpeter (see p. 202), the essence of democracy is not popular participation, but a competition for leadership that forces those in power to act broadly in accordance with the public interest. Similar thinking is evident in the 'sleeping dogs' theory of democratic culture, which implies that low participation indicates broad satisfaction with government (Almond and Verba, 1989). Thus, as the performance of government improves, not least through the promotion of economic growth, participation rates are likely to fall.

The right to disengage. Low-participation or non-participation is not a cause for concern because it results from choices made by free individuals. Non-voting, for instance, may be perfectly rational, as it reflects the fact that a single vote is highly unlikely to affect the outcome of an election. Infrequent and brief civic engagement, what has been called 'attention deficit democracy' (Berger, 2011), may occur simply because people calculate that they have better things to do with their time and energy than engage in politics. While 'private' life is seen as vibrant and stimulating, 'public' activities are deemed to be worthy but essentially boring.

anti-capitalist or anti-globalization protests since the late 1990s. The anti-capitalist movement has embraced an activist-based, theatrical style of politics that is sometimes called the 'new' anarchism. Its attraction, particularly to young people, is its resistance to compromise for the sake of political expediency, borne out of a suspicion of structures and hierarchies of all kinds (including governmental arrangements and conventional parties), and the fact that it offers a form of politics that is decidedly 'in the moment'.

However, anti-politics has also been articulated though a range of right-wing groups and movements that have arisen in recent decades. In many parts of Europe, for example, far right or 'neo-fascist' groups have emerged that mix an appeal based on opposition to immigration, multiculturalism (see p. 167) and globalization (see p. 142) with avowed support for the 'common man' in the face of 'corrupt' economic and political elites. Similar tendencies have been evident in the Tea Party movement in the USA, which has emerged since 2009–10. Taking its name from the 1773 Boston Tea Party (a political protest against colonial British tax policies, in which tea was thrown into Boston Harbour), the Tea Party has built a separate and distinct political identity for itself around the commitment to tax cuts, reductions in federal government's spending, support for unregulated markets, limited government and a strictly literal interpretation of the US constitution. The overwhelming target of the Tea Party's lobbying and agitation has been 'Washington', represented both by the Obama administration and its supposed imposition of 'big government', and 'weak willed', mainstream conservatives in the Republican Party, in both Congress and the states. Nevertheless, there has been disagreement about the extent to which the Tea Party should be viewed as a genuine spontaneous, grass-roots 'anti-political' movement, or as the creation of wealthy interests, intent on using populism (see p. 307) to further the agenda of a small number of rich individuals in the USA.

Explaining civic disengagement

Although there is ongoing, and possibly irresolvable, debate about whether the overall level of political participation has declined, evidence of voter **apathy** cannot be lightly dismissed. As all modern democracies are representative democracies, elections lie at their very core. The level of voter turnout must, therefore, be an important indication of the health of the larger democratic system. But who, or what, is to blame for declining participation rates and, in particular, for falling voter turnout? A number of possible culprits have been identified, as follows:

- politics
- politicians and parties
- the media
- the public
- modern society.

● **Apathy**: The absence of interest in or enthusiasm for things that are generally considered to be interesting.

Blame politics

Although it is common for civic disengagement to be laid at the feet of politicians – they, after all, are the target of most of the criticism and abuse – the chief culprit may be politics itself. It is easy to defend politics as a beautiful and civilizing activity, as, following Aristotle (see p. 6), political thinkers have done through the ages. Apart from its other virtues, politics allows people to live together in, at least, relative peace despite their differing views, values, ideas and interests. When politics fails, the result is likely to be fear, death, destruction and tyranny. Despite this, politics is 'consistently disappointing' (Dunn, 2000). Politics is doomed to disappoint: as the activity through which people make, preserve and amend the general rules under which they live, compromise – and, therefore, dissatisfaction – lie at its very heart. Indeed, politics may be most effective when this dissatisfaction is universalized, no group in society getting exactly what it wants. Moreover, the political process, the process through which competing claims and demands are discussed and assessed, is necessarily messy and cumbersome. Nevertheless, although this may help to explain why politics can be dismissed as boring, even as distasteful, it fails, at least in itself, to explain the trend in favour of civic disengagement, as the nature of politics has not changed over time. Other factors, then, must be considered.

Blame politicians and parties

Although the reputation of politicians may be tainted by the frustrations and disappointments that inevitability attaches to politics as an activity, there are at least three further reasons why politicians are held in low regard. The first and, in a sense, 'classical' attack on politicians stresses the link between power and corruption, famously expressed in Lord Acton's aphorism: 'Power tends to corrupt, and absolute power corrupts absolutely' (quoted in Lazarski (2012).

But how does power corrupt? According to Blaug (2010), it corrupts by distorting people's perceptions in ways that include a:

- growing *personal aggrandisement*, arrogance and loss of control
- progressive *contempt* for subordinates, suspicion and arbitrary cruelty
- gradual *separation* from others and a choice of advisors who always agree
- total *lack of awareness* that any corruption is happening.

For Acton, the association between power and corruption followed naturally from liberal assumptions about human nature. Human beings are, first and foremost, individuals, inclined to place their own interests ahead of anyone else's interests. If placed in a position of power, they will therefore use their post or office to benefit themselves, in all likelihood at the expense of others. In simple terms, egoism plus power equals corruption. According to Acton's logic, corruption will grow as the span of a politician's power increases. This analysis suggests that all politicians, but especially political leaders, are not to be trusted, and that government is, as Thomas Paine (see p. 199) put it, a 'necessary evil'. Our only protection from politicians comes from constitutional devices that fragment or check political power. Anarchists take such thinking further than liberals, in viewing all forms of political rule, including constitutional rule, as nakedly tyrannical.

Second, politicians cannot avoid having 'dirty' hands. This is because they make the difficult decisions that the public would rather not think about, and certainly not wish to make themselves. Decision-making in the political sphere invariably involves grappling with practical and moral dilemmas, and making trade-offs that are, at best, ethically imperfect (Flinders, 2012). So embedded in political life are hypocricy, deception and double-dealing, that the public is routinely left with a choice between, in Runciman's (2008) words, 'different kinds of lies and different kinds of truth'.

Third, democratic systems create further difficulties for politicians by forcing them to operate in a market in which each seeks to out-bid the others, inflating expectations and making disappointment yet more certain. In short, democratic politicians are always likely to promise more than they can deliver. In view of this, it is no surprise that attempts have sometimes been made to replace politics with **technocracy**, as has occurred in Italy (see p. 450). Once again, however, the unchanging nature of these tendencies and pressures suggests that they are not the cause of the modern trend towards civic disengagement. Nevertheless, there are a number of reasons why may be held in their public standing may have fallen even further in recent decades. These include the following:

- **Lack of vision.** The shift from programmatic political parties to so-called 'catch-all' or 'de-ideological' parties (as discussed in Chapter 10) helps to explain why modern politicians often appear to lack vision and a sense of moral purpose. As modern politicians and political parties increasingly seem to believe in nothing except getting elected, politics has become an end in itself, and being a politician has become just another professional career.
- **Age of 'spin'.** One of the consequences of the modern media-obsessed age is that politicians have become over-concerned about communication and news management (as discussed in Chapter 8). The growth of what is called 'spin' creates the impression that politicians are less trustworthy than before, and more willing to be 'economical with the truth'.
- **'All the same'.** The declining significance of the left/right divide and the emergence of managerial politics in place of ideological politics, means that, regardless of their party allegiance, all politicians have come to look the same and sound the same. The problem with this is both that, by abandoning major issues and 'big' choices, electoral battles have become less gripping and less meaningful, and that politicians have maintained their adversarial rhetoric by dramatically over-stating minor or technical divisions – a psychological tendency that Sigmund Freud referred to as 'the narcissism of small differences'.
- **'In it for themselves'.** The growth, in recent decades, of an industry of professional lobbying has focused greater attention on politicians' 'outside interests' and on their sources of revenue other than from politics. This has strengthened the image of politicians as self-serving and dishonest, and created anxiety, generally, about declining standards in public life.

Blame the media

As discussed in Chapter 8, the media is sometimes charged with having created a climate of cynicism amongst the public, leading to growing popular disenchantment with politics generally, and a lack of trust in governments and politicians of all complexions (Lloyd, 2004). This has occurred, in large part, because increasingly intense commercial pressures have forced the media to make their coverage of politics 'sexy' and attention-grabbing. Routine political debate and policy analy-

● **Technocracy**: Literally, 'rule by the skilled'; government or control by an elite of technical experts.

POLITICS IN ACTION . . .

Italian government: technocracy displaces politics?

Events: On 12 November 2011, Mario Monti was appointed prime minister of Italy, following the resignation of Silvio Berlusconi. Monti, however, was not a politician and had never held elective office. He was a respected economist who had been an EU Commissioner during 1994–2004, serving, in his final five years, as Competition Commissioner, one of the most powerful positions on the Commission. Monti went on to appoint a cabinet entirely composed of technocrats like himself. The Monti government, nevertheless, comfortably passed motions of confidence in both the Italian Senate and the Chamber of Deputies, with only members of the Northern League voting against. During December 2011, the Monti government outlined a package of austerity measures, which included increased taxes, pension reforms and steps to curtail tax evasion. In January 2012, a further package of measures, dealing in particular, with labour market flexibility were unveiled.

Significance: These exceptional events took place in highly pressured circumstances. Their backdrop was the 2007–09 global financial crisis, and the eurozone crisis (see p. 396) that it precipitated. With EU–IMF bailouts having already been agreed for Greece and Ireland, 10-year interest rates in Italy had risen above 7 per cent, creating the 'unthinkable' prospect of a bailout for the eurozone's third largest economy. In this context, a recourse to technocracy had a number of advantages. The key justification for Monti's appointment was, quite simply, that 'politics as normal' had ceased to work. Italy's highly-fragmented party system, long viewed as dysfunctional, had engendered such political paralysis (referred to by Monti as a 'deficiency of government') that the Berlusconi government was incapable of taking the bold measures thought necessary in the face of a mounting financial and economic crisis. At the same time, no alternative coalition of parties appeared to have enough popular support, or sufficient unity of purpose, to take its place. Monti's appointment calmed financial markets, reassured by the fact that, unlike an elected government, a technocratic government would do 'what had to be done', unhindered by political in-fighting and unconcerned about short-term unpopularity. Moreover, it highlighted the seriousness of the crisis that Italy faced, thereby helping to prepare the Italian public for the exceptional – and, inevitably, painful – political actions that were to come. Some have even suggested that technocracy may have the deeper advantage that, by pushing

popular delusions and the 'madness of crowds' to one side, it allows public policy to be informed by reason, rather than partisanship, ensuring that national interests prevail over party interests.

Nevertheless, serious concerns have been raised about Monti's appointment and Italy's substitution of technocracy for democracy. The most obvious of these was that the principles of popular control and public accountability were effectively abandoned. It is possible to see Monti's appointment as a kind of 'regime change' imposed on Italy by pressure from financial markets that were unchecked by the European Central Bank (ECB). In this view, the ECB orchestrated the fall of an elected political leader and, in the process, usurped the role of the Italian electorate. Lacking any democratic authority, the ECB went well beyond the legitimate role of a central bank, in acting to manipulate a stubborn citizenry. Furthermore, the notion that technocrats make decisions that are somehow more rational or enlightened than democratic politicians is highly questionable. If this were the case, technocrats and other experts would tend to think alike, their views converging around a set of agreed, wise beliefs. This, patently, is not the case, especially in the field of economics, a discipline notorious for disagreement over both theoretical and policy matters. What made Monti an attractive appointee from the perspective of the ECB and financial markets was not so much his expertise, as his support for the policy options they favoured; that is, bold austerity.

sis therefore receive less and less attention, as the media focuses instead on – or 'hypes' – scandals of various kinds and allegations of incompetence, policy failure or simple inertia. No longer are there 'problems', 'challenges' or 'difficulties' in politics; everything is a 'crisis'. Although the tabloid press in the UK is often seen as the most advanced example of a media-driven 'culture of contempt', similar trends are evident elsewhere. Healthy scepticism, which serves the interests of democracy and freedom, may, thus, have turned into corrosive and aggressive negativity.

Blame the public

Are 'we' the problem? Is civic disengagement a 'demand-side' problem (stemming from the attitudes and behaviour of the public), rather than a 'supply-side' problem (stemming from the performance of politics or politicians)? The argument that ordinary citizens bear much of the blame for civic disengagement is rooted in the allegation that consumerist attitudes and instincts, already widely evident in society at large, are increasingly being applied to politics. It is in the nature of consumerism (see p. 159) that people seek to acquire as much as possible, but pay as little as possible in return. Insofar as citizenship is in the process of being remodelled on consumerist lines, this implies that citizens are becoming ever-more demanding of politics and politicians whilst, at the same time, being less and less prepared to contribute to the maintenance of the political system in which they live. Are we becoming a society of politically-apathetic '**free-riders**', who enjoy all the benefits of citizenship (schools, roads, free speech, economic progress, public order and so forth) without accepting the associated costs, and, especially, without bothering to vote? If this is the case, it is difficult to see how the people can complain about the behaviour of politicians, or about allegedly declining standards in public life – we get the politicians we deserve. Those who explain civic disengagement in such terms, either wholly or in part, tend to advocate one of two solutions. Either they call for improved education (for example, compulsory citizenship classes in schools) to counteract consumerism, or they support ways in which political participation can be made easier and more convenient (such as postal voting or 'e-voting').

Blame modern society

The weakness in blaming the public for civic disengagement is that it suggests that popular attitudes and perceptions emerge in a vacuum, when they are, in important ways, shaped by the character of modern society. The social and economic circumstances of modern society may have fostered civic disengagement in two main ways. First, the spread of consumerist attitudes towards politics – and, for that matter, other things – is less a consequence of rational decision-making by independent citizens, and more a by-product of the growth of consumer capitalism combined with modern technology. The advance of neoliberal economic structures (as discussed in Chapter 6), which emphasize aspiration and individual self-striving, weaken people's capacity to think collectively and tend to make forms of communal activity – the basis of civic engagement – progressively less meaningful. The spread of neoliberalism (see p. 144) has, moreover, damaged the image of politics in at least two ways. First, by suggesting that political involvement in matters of economics and social

● **Free-rider**: A person or group that enjoys collectively-provided benefits without needing to pay associated costs, which are shouldered by others.

exchange is non-legitimate, it has forced political debate to revolve around technical or managerial issues, rather than major projects of social transformation. Second, it has associated politics with inefficiency and unwarranted interference, certainly by comparison with the supposedly 'higher' sphere of private enterprise. Modern information technologies have contributed to such tendencies, in particular by allowing communication to take place without the need for face-to-face interaction. Robert Putnam (2000), for instance, associated the decline of social capital with, in particular, the growth of television.

The second major social and economic trend that has been linked to civic disengagement is globalization. Globalization is often said to have contributed to the advance of a culture of consumer capitalism, which has, as discussed above, tended to 'hollow out' citizenship. Of no less significance, however, is the tendency of globalization to diminish the capacity of political actors to 'deliver the goods', leading to a profound crisis of both legitimacy and confidence in the process of political deliberation (Hay, 2007). National politicians have thus been placed in the uncomfortable position that, while they are confronted by rising demands and expectations on the part of the population at large, their ability to respond to these has shrunk, as domestic circumstances have increasingly been shaped by events that are beyond their control. The 'tyranny' that global markets appear to exercise over national economic decision-making may be the most obvious, but certainly is not the only, example of this.

ASSESSING POLITICAL PERFORMANCE

Anxieties about politics that stem from trends in civic engagement and questions about who, or what, may be responsible, reflect concern about the circumstances in which modern politics takes place. However, underlying these issues are deeper and abiding questions about the purpose of politics and, therefore, about how governments and political systems should be assessed. What, in short, is the political process 'for'? Such questions uncover some of the most intractable issues in political theory. For example, it is impossible to know what the political process is for without addressing issues such as the nature of justice and the desirable balance between freedom and authority – in other words, without having a vision of the 'good society'.

As views about such matters differ fundamentally, the standards against which political performance can be judged vary greatly. Four contrasting standards can, however, be identified, each shedding a very particular light on the purpose of politics and the assessment of political performance. These are as follows:

- stability and order
- material prosperity
- citizenship
- democratic rule.

Stability performance

It can reasonably be claimed that the maintenance of stability and order (see p. 400) is the most basic function of politics. With the exception of anarchists, who

CONCEPT

Relativism

Relativism is a position that denies the existence of objective or 'absolute' standards, and so holds that statements can be judged only in relation to their contexts. *Cultural* relativism is the belief that moral codes can only be understood in the context of the societies in which they operate. *Moral*, or normative, relativism refers to the belief that there are no authoritative ethical principles (usually because each individual is a morally autonomous being). *Cognitive*, or epistemological, relativism holds that different modes of knowing are equally valid, and thus dismisses the universalist pretensions of, say, science (see p. 12).

argue that social order will emerge from the spontaneous actions of free individuals, all political thinkers and philosophers have endorsed the political process, and especially government, as the only means of keeping chaos and instability at bay. In Thomas Hobbes's (see p. 61) words, in the absence of government, life would be 'solitary, poor, nasty, brutish and short'. From this perspective, the core purpose of government is to govern, to rule, to ensure stability through the exercise of authority. This, in turn, requires that government is able to perpetuate its own existence and ensure the survival of the broader political system. System performance can thus be judged on the basis of criteria such as longevity and endurance, as the simple fact of survival indicates a regime's ability to contain or reconcile conflict.

However, there are differing views about how this goal can best be achieved. These views fall into two broad categories. The first stems from the essentially liberal belief that a stable system of rule must be rooted in consensus (see p. 8) and consent. In this view, what ensures the long-term survival of a political system is its responsiveness to popular demands and pressures. This is expressed in the language of systems theory as the ability to bring the 'outputs' of government into line with the various 'inputs'. This capacity has often been identified as a particular strength of western liberal democracies. Advocates of liberal democracy (see p. 270) stress that, as it is based on consent, it embodies mechanisms that ensure that it is responsive, and so guarantees a high degree of systemic equilibrium. Government power is won through a competitive struggle for the popular vote, and can be lost when that support diminishes. A vigorous civil society also allows citizens to exert influence through autonomous groups and associations.

To some extent, it has been the ability of liberal democracy to generate political stability that explains the seemingly ever-wider adoption of liberal-democratic practices such as electoral democracy and party competition in the modern world. Nevertheless, liberal democracy also has its drawbacks in this respect. Chief amongst these is that responsiveness may generate instability, insofar as it heightens popular expectations of government and fosters the illusion that the political system can meet all demands and accommodate all 'inputs'. From this perspective, the central dilemma of stable government is that responsiveness must be balanced against effectiveness. Government must be sensitive to external pressures, but it must also be able to impose its will on society when those pressures threaten to generate irreconcilable conflict.

This latter fear underpins the alternative view of stability and order. Conservative thinkers have traditionally linked stability and order, not to responsiveness, but to authority. Thomas Hobbes presented this idea as a stark choice between absolutism (see p. 268) and anarchy, between the acceptance of an unquestionable and sovereign power and a descent into the chaos and disorder of the state of nature. However, conservatives have been particularly concerned to stress the degree to which political authority is underpinned by shared values and a common culture. In this view, stability and order are largely the product of social and cultural cohesion, underpinning the capacity of society to generate respect for authority and maintain support for established institutions.

This position is clearly reflected in neoconservative fears about permissiveness and moral and cultural relativism, leading to calls for the restoration of 'traditional', 'family' or 'Christian' values. It is also possible, from this perspective, to suggest that East Asian states that subscribe to some form of Confucianism (see p. 278), as well as Islamic states, have a greater capacity to maintain political

CONCEPT

Equality

Equality is the principle of uniform apportionment, but does not imply sameness. The term 'equality' has differing implications, depending on what is being apportioned. *Formal equality* means the equal distribution of legal and political rights, and is usually based on the assumption that human beings are 'born' equal. *Equality of opportunity* means that everyone has the same starting-point, or equal life chances, but may justify social inequality because talent and the capacity for hard work are unequally distributed. *Equality of outcome* refers to an equal distribution of income, wealth and other social goods.

stability than do western liberal-democratic systems. However, the weakness of this view of stability is that, since it relies on authority being exerted from above, it may not place effective constraints on the exercise of government power. If stability is seen as an end in itself, divorced from considerations such as democratic legitimacy, social justice and respect for human rights (see p. 342), the result may simply be tyranny and oppression. Saddam Hussein, after all, was able to perpetuate the existence of his Iraqi regime, despite economic sanctions and opposition from Shi'a Moslems and Kurds, largely through systematic terror and brutal repression, until US intervention brought the regime down in 2003.

Material performance

The idea that political systems can and should be judged by their material performance is a familiar one. Electoral politics, for example, is invariably dominated by economic issues and the so-called 'feel good' factor. Governments are usually re-elected in periods of growth and widening prosperity, and defeated during recessions and economic crises. Similarly, there can be little doubt that the success of the broader political system is linked to its capacity to 'deliver the goods'. Widespread poverty and low levels of economic growth in developing states have deepened social and ethnic tensions, fuelled corruption, and undermined attempts to establish constitutional and representative government. The collapse of the state socialist regimes of Eastern Europe and the USSR was also linked to the failure of central planning and, in particular, to its inability to deliver the levels of material prosperity and range of consumer goods that were available in the capitalist West. Moreover, it is no coincidence that advanced industrialized states have enjoyed both the greatest levels of political stability and the highest living standards in the world.

Considerable debate has taken place about the most reliable means of generating wealth and achieving material prosperity. In some senses, this debate reflects the traditional ideological divide between capitalism and socialism; the former places its faith in the market and competition, and the latter relies on nationalization and planning. However, the Eastern European revolutions of 1989–91 dramatically changed the terms of this debate by (apparently) undermining the validity of any form of socialism qualitatively distinct from market capitalism. In other words, even socialists came to accept that the market, or at least some form of market competition, is the only reliable mechanism for generating wealth. The 'capitalism or socialism?' debate has therefore developed into a 'what kind of capitalism?' debate, as examined in Chapter 5. However, this issue is not merely about how wealth can be *generated*, but also about how it is *distributed*; that is, it is about who gets what. As such, it is closely linked to debate about the desirable balance between the market and the state, and the degree to which government can, and should, modify market outcomes to achieve greater equality.

The central dilemma that arises from the use of material prosperity as a performance indicator is that economic growth must be balanced against fairness. This is the difficulty of being concerned both about the size of the cake and about how the cake is cut. Two contrasting views of this problem can be identified. The free-market view, advanced by theorists such as Friedrich von Hayek (see p. 37) and Milton Friedman (see p. 138), holds that general prosperity is best achieved by a system of unregulated capitalism. This is what Titmuss (1968) referred to as the 'industrial–achievement' performance model. From this perspective, economic growth is best promoted by material incentives that encourage enterprise and endeavour, and penalize laziness. The welfare state should therefore only act as a safety net that protects individuals from absolute poverty, in the sense that they lack the basic means of subsistence. Although this system is likely to increase social inequality, the theory suggests that it benefits even the less well-off, who receive a smaller proportion of a much larger cake, so ending up better off. Free-market economists refer to this theory as the 'trickle down' effect. Such policy priorities have guided New Right governments since the 1980s in their attempts to break away from the 'fiscal crisis of the welfare state'. In this view, burgeoning social budgets led to a growing tax burden that, in turn, hampered wealth generation.

The rival social-democratic view, which Titmuss called the 'institutional–redistributive' model, highlights the moral and economic benefits of equality. Not only is unregulated competition condemned for promoting greed and conflict, it is also seen as inefficient and unproductive. The virtue of social justice is that, by taking the distribution of wealth away from the vagaries of the market, it ensures that all citizens have a stake in society and that each of them has an incentive to contribute. In tolerating wide social inequality, free-market policies thus run the risk of promoting social exclusion, reflected in the growth of an underclass that is a breeding ground for crime and social unrest. Long-term and sustainable prosperity therefore requires that material incentives operate within a broader framework of fair distribution and effective welfare.

Citizenship performance

The idea that citizenship is the proper end of government can be traced back to the political thought of Ancient Greece. For instance, in 431 BCE, in his famous funeral oration, Pericles stated that:

> An Athenian citizen does not neglect the state because he takes care of his own household; and even those of us who are engaged in business have a very fair idea of politics. We alone regard a man who takes no interest in public affairs, not as harmless, but as a useless character; and if few of us are originators, we are all sound judges of policy.

A citizen is a member of a political community or state, endowed with a set of rights and a set of obligations. Citizenship is therefore the 'public' face of individual existence. People are able to participate in the life of their communities to the extent that they possess entitlements and responsibilities. Civil participation is, in turn, linked to the advance of constitutional government, as reflected in the extension of political rights and civil liberties (see p. 404).

In his classic contribution to the study of citizenship rights, T. H. Marshall (1950) distinguished between three 'bundles of rights': civil rights, political rights and social rights. Civil rights were defined by Marshall as 'rights necessary for individual freedom'. These include freedom of speech, freedom of assembly, freedom of movement, freedom of conscience, the right to equality before the law, and the right to own property. Civil rights are therefore rights that are exercised within civil society; they are 'negative' rights in the sense that they limit or check the exercise of government power. Political rights provide the individual with the opportunity to participate in political life. The central political rights are thus the right to vote, the right to stand for election, and the right to hold public office. The provision of political rights clearly requires the development of universal suffrage, political equality (see p. 90), and democratic government. Finally, and most controversially, Marshall argued that citizenship implies social rights that guarantee the individual a minimum social status and, in so doing, provide the basis for the exercise of both civil and political rights. Marshall defined these 'positive' rights, somewhat vaguely, as the right 'to live the life of a civilized being according to the standards prevailing in society'.

As the concept of citizenship is usually seen as a distinctively western invention, it is perhaps not surprising that liberal democracies have performed particularly well in this respect (previously discussed concerns about declining civic engagement notwithstanding). Civil and political rights clearly imply the form of constitutional and representative government commonly found in the industrialized West. The idea of social rights, however, has stimulated significant divisions, because it implies a level of welfare provision and redistribution that (as discussed earlier) classical liberals and the New Right regard as unjustifiable and economically damaging. Marxists and feminists have also criticized the idea of citizenship; the former on the grounds that it ignores unequal class power, and the latter because it takes no account of patriarchal oppression.

A major dilemma nevertheless confronts those who employ citizenship as a performance criterion: the need to balance rights against duties and, thereby, apportion responsibilities between the individual and the community. Since the early 1980s, this issue has been taken up in the growing debate between liberals and communitarians. Communitarian theorists such as Alisdair MacIntyre (1981) and Michael Sandel (1982) have dismissed the idea of an unencumbered self, arguing that the 'politics of rights' should be replaced by a 'politics of the common good'. In this view, liberal individualism (see p. 158), in effect, eats itself. By investing individuals with rights and entitlements, it simply breeds atomism and alienation, weakening the communal bonds that hold society together. From this perspective, non-western societies that may appear to perform poorly in relation to citizenship indicators (for example, having poor records on human rights) may nevertheless succeed in creating a strong sense of community and social belonging.

Democracy performance

Whereas stability, material prosperity and citizenship are all outcomes, or products, of the political process, democracy is concerned essentially with the process itself, with *how* decisions are made, rather than with *what* decisions are made. Democracy means popular rule – in crude terms, the widest possible dispersal of political power and influence. From the democratic perspective, the purpose of politics is to empower the individual and enlarge the scope of personal autonomy (see p. 457). Autonomy has been seen as both an end in itself and a means to an end. Classical theorists of democracy, such as J.-J. Rousseau (see p. 97) and J. S. Mill (see p. 198), portrayed political participation as a source of personal development and self-realization. Democracy is thus the stuff of freedom, or, as Rousseau put it, freedom means 'being one's own master'.

CONCEPT

Autonomy

Autonomy (from the Greek, meaning 'law unto oneself') literally means self-rule. States, institutions or groups can be said to be autonomous if they enjoy a substantial degree of independence, although autonomy in this connection is sometimes taken to imply a high measure of self-government, rather than sovereign independence. Applied to the individual, autonomy is closely linked to freedom (see p. 339). However, since it suggests being rationally self-willed, autonomy is classified as a form of positive freedom. By responding to inner or 'genuine' drives, the autonomous individual may be seen to achieve authenticity.

Taken to its logical extreme, the idea of popular self-government implies the abolition of the distinction between the state and civil society through the establishment of some form of direct democracy (see p. 92). For example, Athenian democracy (see p. 95) amounted to a form of government by mass meeting, in which citizens were encouraged to participate directly and continuously in the life of their *polis*, or city-state. Modern notions of democracy, however, have shifted away from this utopian vision and, instead, embrace democracy more as a means to an end. The more familiar machinery of representative democracy – universal suffrage, the secret ballot, and competitive elections – tends to be defended on the grounds that, for example, the existence of voting rights checks the abuse of government power, and party competition helps to generate social consensus. The ability of the people to 'kick the rascals out' therefore helps to ensure that government is limited and that there is, at least, a measure of public accountability.

However, most political systems fare poorly by the standards of personal autonomy and popular rule. What passes for democracy in the modern world tends to be a limited and indirect form of democracy: liberal democracy. This operates as an 'institutional arrangement for arriving at political decisions in which individuals acquire the power to decide by means of a competitive struggle for the people's vote' (Schumpeter, 1942). This 'institutional arrangement' has been criticized by radical democrats for reducing popular participation to a near meaningless ritual: casting a vote every few years for politicians who can be removed only by replacing them with another set of politicians. In short, the people never rule, and the growing gulf between government and the people is reflected, as we have seen, in the spread of inertia, apathy and a breakdown of community.

This perspective is, therefore, linked to calls for radical, even revolutionary, political and social change. For example, government power should be decentralized so as to bring power 'closer' to the people. This could, for instance, require the break-up of the nation-state, as it is difficult, in practical terms, to see how a community the size of a modern nation could govern itself through direct and continuous participation. Similarly, insofar as the democratic principle is applied in modern societies, it is confined to a narrowly 'political' set of decisions. If democracy is understood as self-mastery – the ability to shape decisions that affect one's life – surely economic power must also be democratized, presumably through the machinery of workers' control and self-management.

As with the performance criteria examined above, democracy also poses its own set of dilemmas. The most important of these is the need for a balance between the twin goals of government *by* the people and government *for* the people. This highlights the tension between the competing virtues of popular participation and rule in the public interest. The most fundamental objection to all forms of participatory democracy is simply that ordinary people lack the time, maturity and specialist knowledge to rule wisely on their own behalf. The earliest version of this argument was put by Plato (see p. 13), who advanced the idea of rule by the virtuous; that is, government by a class of philosopher kings. In this form, the case for government *for* the people amounts to an argument in favour of an enlightened despotism. The concern about the capabilities of ordinary people can, however, be dealt with more modestly, through the provision of representative processes that allow for a division of labour in political life. A further dilemma is that the empowerment of the individual must be balanced against the empowerment of the community. To give priority to personal autonomy is necessarily to place limits on public authority. However, to extol the virtues of popular rule is to risk subordinating the individual to the will of the public, or the majority. The tension between the individual and society not only raises major practical difficulties, but also highlights what some would argue has always been, and remains, the central issue in political theory.

SUMMARY

- Concerns about a crisis in politics stem largely from evidence of growing civic disengagement, reflected, in particular, in declining rates of voter turnout and falling levels of party membership and campaigning. However, such trends may not so much betoken a crisis in political participation, as indicate a shift from one kind of participation to another – as, for instance, protest movements rise in importance and 'new media' are more widely used to facilitate political debate and activism.

- Growing cynicism about, and even anger towards, mainstream political parties and politicians has been expressed in the phenomenon of 'anti-politics'. 'Anti-politics', nevertheless, does not encourage citizens to turn away from politics and retreat into private existence. Instead, it tends to spawn new groups and movements that express resentment or hostility towards established political structures, although these may range from anti-capitalist protests to far-right anti-immigration campaigns.

- Evidence of growing voter apathy cannot easily be disregarded, as modern democracies are all representative democracies, in which elections play a vital role. However, the task of explaining declining levels of formal political participation is fraught with difficulties, not least because of the number of possible culprits. The most significant of these are politics, politicians and parties, the public, the media and modern society.

- Political systems can be judged only in terms of their impact on the larger society, for good or ill. However, as this raises normative questions, there is no consensus about the desirable 'outcomes' of the political process. The most commonly used indexes of a government's or system's performance include its ability to maintain stability and order, deliver material prosperity, promote citizenship and foster democratic rule.

- Evaluating political systems is difficult because each performance indicator embodies complexities. Stability can be promoted through consent and popular responsiveness, or through a shared culture and greater respect for authority. The quest for material prosperity may be hampered by policies designed to ensure that wealth is more equally distributed. The spread of citizenship rights may undermine civic duty and weaken the sense of community. The extension of democratic rule may simply lead to a majoritarian despotism that places restrictions on individual freedom or personal autonomy.

Questions for discussion

- Is the 'participation crisis' in modern politics largely a myth?
- What is the significance of the rise of 'anti-political' groups and movements?
- Why is politics 'doomed to disappoint'?
- Do we get the politicians we deserve?
- Is there such a thing as a right of non-participation?
- Are consumerism and citizenship incompatible?
- Is there an inevitable tension between democracy and liberty?
- Are people the best judges of what is good for them?
- Which political system comes closest to achieving the 'good society'?

Further reading

Bauman, Z. *In Search of Politics* (1999). An examination of how a growing sense of transience and insecurity is undermining meaningful social bonds and threatening the 'private/public' space.

Flinders, M. *Defending Politics: Why Democracy Matters in the 21st Century* (2012). A fresh and engaging analysis of the nature of political rule, and a defence of politics against its key threats.

Hay, C. *Why We Hate Politics* (2007). An investigation into the origins of growing cynicism and negativity about politics, which focuses particularly on the impact of neoliberalism and globalization.

Stoker, G. *Why Politics Matters: Making Democracy Work* (2006). A stimulating analysis of why democratic politics is doomed to disappoint and how civic participation can be revived.

Bibliography

Abercrombie, W., S. Hill and B. Turner (1980) *The Dominant Ideology Thesis* (London: Allen & Unwin).

Albritton, R., B. Jessop and R. Westra (eds) (2010) *Political Economy and Global Capitalism* (London and New York: Anthem Press).

Albrow, M. (1970) *Bureaucracy* (London: Macmillan).

Alexander, L. (ed.) (2001) *Constitutionalism: Philosophical Foundations* (Cambridge and New York: Cambridge University Press).

Allison, G. (1971) *Essence of Decision* (Boston: Little, Brown).

Almond, G. (1989) *A Discipline Divided: Schools and Sects in Political Science* (Newbury Park, CA: Sage).

Almond, G. A. and S. Verba (1963) *The Civic Culture: Political Attitudes and Democracy in Five Nations* (Princeton: Princeton University Press).

Almond, G. A. and S. Verba (eds) (1980) *The Civic Culture Revisited* (Boston: Little, Brown).

Alter, P. (1989) *Nationalism* (London: Edward Arnold).

Anderson, B. (1983) *Imagined Communities: Reflections on the Origins and Spread of Nationalism* (London: Verso).

Anderson, J. (1984) *Public Policy-Making* (Orlando, FL: Holt, Rinehart & Winston).

Appiah, K. A. (2007) *Cosmopolitanism: Ethics in a World of Strangers* (London and New York: Penguin).

Arblaster, A. (1984) *The Rise and Decline of Western Liberalism* (Oxford: Basil Blackwell).

Arblaster, A. (1994) *Democracy* (2nd edn) (Milton Keynes: Open University Press; Minneapolis: University of Minnesota Press).

Arendt, H. (1958) *The Human Condition* (Chicago: University of Chicago Press).

Aristotle (1948) *Politics* (Oxford: Clarendon Press) (ed. E. Baker).

Arrow, K. (1951) *Social Choice and Individual Values* (New York: Wiley).

Axford, B. and R. Huggins (eds) (2001) *The New Media and Politics* (London and Thousand Oaks, CA: Sage).

Babbington, A. (1990) *Military Intervention in Britain*(London: Routledge).

Bachrach, P. and M. Baratz (1962) 'The Two Faces of Power', in F. G. Castles, D. J. Murray and D. C. Potter (eds) *Decisions, Organisations and Society* (Harmondsworth: Penguin).

Bagehot, W. ([1867] 1963) *The English Constitution* (London: Fontana).

Balaam, D. N. and M. Veseth (2001) *International Political Economy* (Basingstoke: Palgrave Macmillan).

Ball, A. and F. Millward (1986) *Pressure Politics in Industrial Societies* (London: Macmillan).

Ball, A. and G. Peters (2005) *Modern Politics and Government* (Basingstoke and New York: Palgrave Macmillan).

Barber, B. (1995) *Jihad ve McWorld: How Globalism and Tribalism Are Reshaping the World* (New York: Ballantine Books).

Barber, J. (1988) *Politics by Humans: Research on American Leadership* (Durham, NC: Duke University Press).

Barrett, S. and C. Fudge (1981) *Policy and Action* (London: Methuen).

Barry, Brian (2002) *Culture and Equality* (Cambridge: Polity Press).

Barry, N. P. (1987) *The New Right* (London: Croom Helm).

Bartle, J. and D. Griffiths (eds) (2001) *Political Communications Transformed: From Morrison to Mandelson* (Basingstoke: Palgrave Macmillan).

Bauman, Z. (2000) *Liquid Modernity* (Cambridge and Malden, MA: Polity Press).

Bauman, Z. (2004) *Identity* (Cambridge: Polity Press).

Baylis, J. and S. Smith (2005) *The Globalization of World Politics: An Introduction to International Relations* (Oxford and New York: Oxford University Press).

Beard, C. (1913) *Economic Interpretation of the Constitution of the United States* (New York: Macmillan).

Beck, U. (1992) *Risk Society: Towards New Modernity* (London: Sage).

Beck, U. and E. Beck-Gernsheim (2001) *Individualization: Institutional Individualism and its Social and Political Consequences* (London and Thousand Oaks, CA: Sage Publications).

Beer, S. (1982) *Britain Against Itself* (London: Faber).

Beetham, D. (1987) *Bureaucracy* (Milton Keynes: Open University Press).

Beetham, D. (1991) *The Legitimation of Power* (London: Macmillan).

Bekke, H., J. Perry and T. Toonen (eds) (1996) *Civil Systems in Comparative Perspective* (Bloomington, IN: Indiana University Press).

Bell, D. (1960) *The End of Ideology?: On the Exhaustion of Political Ideas in the 1950s* (New York: Free Press).

Bell, D.(1973) *The Coming of Post-Industrial Society: A Venture in Social Forecasting* (New York: Basic Books).

Bell, D. (1976) *The Cultural Contradictions of Capitalism* (London: Heinemann).

Bentham, J. ([1776] 1948) *Fragments on Government and an Introduction to the Principles of Law and Legislation* (Oxford: Blackwell) (ed. W. Harrison).

Bentley, A. ([1908] 1948) *The Process of Government* (Evanston, IL: Principia).

Berger, B. (2011) *Attention Deficit Democracy: The Paradox of Civic Engagement* (Princeton, NJ: Princeton University Press).

Berger, S. (ed.) (1981) *Organising Interests in Western Europe: Pluralism, Corporatism and the Transformation of Politics* (New York: Cambridge University Press).

Berlin, I. (1958) *Four Essays on Liberty* (Oxford: Oxford University Press).

Bernstein, E. ([1898] 1962) *Evolutionary Socialism* (New York: Schocken).

Bertsch, G., R. Clarke and D. Wood (1992) *Comparing Political Systems: Power and Policy in Three Worlds* (4th edn) (New York: Macmillan).

Bhagwati, J. (2008) *Termites in the Trading System* (Oxford: Oxford University Press).

Birch, A. H. (1972) *Representation* (London: Macmillan; New York: Praeger).

Birch, A. H. (2007) *The Concepts and Theories of Democracy* (London: Routledge).

Birkland, T. (2011) *An Introduction to the Policy Process: Theories, Concepts and Models of Public Policy Making* (Armonk, NY and London: M. E. Sharpe).

Blau, P. and M. Meyer (eds) (1987) *Bureaucracy in Modern Society* (3rd edn) (New York: Random House).

Blaug, R. (2010) *How Power Corrupts: Cognition and Democracy in Organisations* (Basingstoke: Palgrave Macmillan).

Blondel, J. (1973) *Comparative Legislatures* (Englewood Cliffs, NJ: Prentice Hall).

Bobbio, N. (1996) *Left and Right: The Significance of a Political Distinction* (Cambridge: Polity Press).

Bobbitt, P. (2002) *The Shield of Achilles: War, Peace and the Course of History* (Harmondsworth: Penguin).

Bodin, J. ([1576] 1962) *The Six Books of the Commonweal* (Cambridge, MA: Harvard University Press) (trans. R. Knolles).

Bogdanor, V. (1979) *Devolution* (Oxford: Oxford University Press).

Bogdanor, V. (ed.) (1988) *Constitutions in Democratic Politics* (Aldershot: Gower).

Bogdanor, V. and D. Butler (eds) (1983) *Democracy and Elections* (Cambridge: Cambridge University Press).

Bookchin, M. (1989) *Remaking Society* (Montreal: Black Rose).

Bottomore, T. (1991) *Classes in Modern Society* (London: Allen & Unwin).

Boulding, K. (1956) *The Image: Knowledge in Life and Society* (Ann Arbor, MI: University of Michigan Press).

Boulding, K. (1989) *Three Faces of Power* (Newbury Park, CA: Sage).

Brandt Commission (1980) *North–South: A Programme for Survival* (Cambridge, MA: MIT Press).

Brandt Commission (1983) *Common Crisis: North–South Cooperation for World Recovery* (London: Pan).

Braybrooke, D. and C. Lindblom (1963) *A Strategy of Decision: Policy Evaluation as a Political Process* (New York: Collier Macmillan).

Breitenbach, H., T. Burden and D. Coates (1990) *Features of a Viable Socialism* (London and New York: Harvester Wheatsheaf).

Bretherton, C. and G. Ponton (eds) (1996) *Global Politics: An Introduction* (Oxford: Blackwell).

Brewer, J., A. Guelke, I. Hume, E. Moxon-Browne and R. Wilford (1996) *The Police, Public Order and the State* (London: Macmillan).

Brittan, S. (1977) *The Economic Consequences of Democracy* (London: Temple Smith).

Brooker, P. (2009) *Non-Democratic Regimes: Theory, Government and Politics* (Basingstoke and New York: Palgrave Macmillan).

Brown, D. (2000) *Contemporary Nationalism* (London and New York: Routledge).

Brown, M. B. (1995) *Models in Political Economy: A Guide to the Arguments* (2nd edn) (Harmondsworth: Penguin).

Brownmiller, S. (1975) *Against Our Will* (New York: Simon & Schuster).

Bryson, V. (2003) *Feminist Political Theory: An Introduction* (Basingstoke: Palgrave Macmillan).

Budge, I. and D. Mackie (eds) (1994) *Developing Democracy* (London: Sage).

Bull, H. (2002) *The Anarchical Society* (Basingstoke: Palgrave Macmillan).

Burchill, S. and A. Linklater (2005) *Theories of International Relations* (3rd edn) (Basingstoke: Palgrave Macmillan).

Burgess, M. (2006) *Comparative Federalism: Theory and Practice* (Oxford and New York: Routledge).

Burgess, M. and A.-G. Gagnon (eds) (1993) *Comparative Federalism and Federation* (London and New York: Harvester Wheatsheaf).

Burke, E. ([1790] 1968) *Reflections on the Revolution in France* (Harmondsworth: Penguin) (ed. C. C. O'Brien).

Burke, E. (1975) *On Government, Politics and Society* (London: Fontana) (ed. B. W. Hill).

Burnham, J. (1941) *The Managerial Revolution* (Harmondsworth: Penguin).

Burns, J. M. (1978) *Leadership* (New York: Harper & Row).

Burton, J. (1972) *World Society* (Cambridge: Cambridge University Press).

Butler, D. and D. Stokes (1969) *Political Change in Britain* (2nd edn) (London: Macmillan).

Butler, D., H. Penniman and A. Ranney (eds) (1981) *Democracy at the Polls* (Washington, DC: American Enterprise Institute).

Butler, D., A. Adonis and T. Travers (1994) *Failure in British Government: The Politics of the Poll Tax* (Oxford: Oxford University Press).

Caldwell, C. (2009) *Reflections on the Revolution in Europe: Immigration, Islam and the West* (New York: Doubleday).

Calvocoressi, P. (2001) *World Politics 1945–2000* (London and New York: Longman).

Campbell, A., P. Converse, W. E. Miller and D. Stokes (1960) *The American Voter* (New York: John Wiley).

Capra, F. (1983) *The Turning Point: Science, Society and the Rising Culture* (London: Fontana).

Carothers, T. (2004) *Critical Mission: Essays on Democracy Promotion* (Washington, DC: Carnegie Endowment for International Peace).

Carpenter, T. G. (2006) *America's Coming War with China: A Collision Course over Taiwan* (Basingstoke: Palgrave Macmillan).

Carr, E. H. (1939) *The Twenty Years' Crisis, 1919–1939* (London: Macmillan).

Carr, N. (2008) 'Is Google Making Us Stupid?', *Atlantic Magazine,* July/August.

Carr, N. (2010) *The Shallows: What the Internet is Doing to our Brains* (New York: Norton).

Castells, M. (1996) *The Rise of Network Society* (Oxford: Blackwell).

Castle, B. (1980) *The Castle Diaries 1974–1976* (London: Weidenfeld & Nicolson).

Castles, F. and R. Wildmann (eds) (1986) *The Future of Party Government – Vol. 1* (Berlin: Gruyter).

Chamberlain, H. S. ([1899] 1913) *The Foundations of the Nineteenth Century* (New York: John Lane).

Charvert, J. (1982) *Feminism* (London: Dent).

Chomsky, N. (1994) *World Order, Old and New* (London: Pluto Press).

Chomsky, N. (2004) *Hegemony and Survival: America's Global Quest for Dominance (The American Empire Project)* (New York: Owl Books).

Chomsky, N. and E. Herman (2006) *Manufacturing Consent* (London: Vintage).

Chua, A. (2003) *World on Fire* (London: Heinemann).

Cigler, C. and B. Loomis (eds) (2011) *Interest Group Politics* (Washington, DC: Congressional Quarterly Press).

Clarke, S. (ed.) (1991) *The State Debate* (London: Macmillan).

Cohen, A. (1975) *Theories of Revolution: An Introduction*(London: Nelson).

Connolly, W. (ed.) (1984) *Legitimacy and the State* (Oxford: Blackwell).

Cooper, R. (2004) *The Breaking of Nations: Order and Chaos in the Twenty-first Century* (London: Atlantic Books).

Cox, A. (1987) *The Court and the Constitution* (Boston, MA: Houghton Mifflin).

Cox, R. (1987) *Production, Power and World Orde*r (New York: Columbia University Press).

Crewe, I. and D. Denver (eds) (1985) *Electoral Change in Western Democracies* (Beckenham: Croom Helm).

Crick, B. ([1962] 2000) *In Defence of Politics* (Harmondsworth and New York: Penguin).

Crosland, C. A. R. (1956) *The Future of Socialism* (London: Jonathan Cape).

Crossman, R. (1963) 'Introduction to W. Bagehot', in *The English Constitution* (London: Fontana).

Crossman, R. (1979) *The Crossman Diaries* (London: Methuen) (ed. A. Howard).

Crouch, C. (2009) 'Privatized Keynesianism: An Unacknowledged Policy Regime', *British Journal of Politics and International Relations*, 11(3).

Curran, J. and J. Seaton (2009) *Power Without Responsibility* (London: Routledge).

Daalder, I. and J. Stavridis (2012) 'NATO's Triumph in Libya', *Foreign Affairs* (March/April).

Dahl, R. (1956) *A Preface to Democratic Theory* (Chicago, IL: Chicago University Press).

Dahl, R. (1961) *Who Governs? Democracy and Power in an American City* (Newhaven, CT: Yale University Press).

Dahl, R. (1971) *Polyarchy: Participation and Opposition* (Newhaven, CT: Yale University Press).

Dahl, R. (1984) *Modern Political Analysis* (4th edn) (Englewood Cliffs, NJ: Prentice Hall).

Dahl, R. (1985) *A Preface to Economic Democracy* (Cambridge: Polity Press).

Dahl, R. (1991) *Democracy and its Critics* (New Haven, CT: Yale University Press).

Dahl, R. and C. Lindblom (1953) *Politics, Economics, and Welfare* (New York: Harper & Row).

Dalton, R. and D. Farrell (2011) *Political Parties and Democratic Linkage: How Parties Organize Democracy* (Oxford and New York: Oxford University Press).

Daly, M. (1978) *Gyn/Ecology: The Mathematics of Radical Feminism* (London: The Women's Press).

Davidson, R. (ed.) (1992) *The Post-Reform Congress* (New York: St Martin's Press).

Davidson, R., W. Oleszek and F. Lee (2009) *Congress and Its Members* (4th edn) (Washington, DC: Congressional Quarterly Press).

Davies, J. (1971) *When Men Revolt and Why* (New York: Free Press).

Davis, R. (2005) *Electing Justice: Fixing the Supreme Court Nomination Process* (Oxford and New York: Oxford University Press).

Decalo, S. (1976) *Coups and Army Rule in Africa* (Newhaven, CT: Yale University Press).

Denver, D., C. Carmen and R. Johns (2012) *Elections and Voters in Britain* (Basingstoke: Palgrave Macmillan).

Devlin, P. (1968) *The Enforcement of Morals* (Oxford: Oxford University Press).

Diamond, L., J. Linz and S. Lipset (eds) (1989) *Democracy in Developing Countries* (Boulder, CO: Lynne Rienner) (4 vols).

Dicey, A. V. ([1885] 1939) *Introduction to the Study of the Law of the Constitution* (London: Macmillan) (ed. E. C. S. Wade).

Djilas, M. (1957) *The New Class: An Analysis of the Communist System* (New York: Praeger).

Dobson, A. (1990) *Green Political Thought* (London: Routledge).

Downs, A. (1957) *An Economic Theory of Democracy* (New York: Harper & Row).

Drewry, G. (ed.) (1989) *The New Select Committees* (rev. edn) (Oxford: Oxford University Press).

Dryzek, J. and P. Dunleavy (2009) *Theories of the Democratic State* (Basingstoke: Palgrave Macmillan).

Duchacek, I. (1973) *Power Maps: The Politics of Constitutions* (Santa Barbara, CA: ABC Clio).

Duncan, G. (ed.) (1983) *Democratic Theory and Practice* (Cambridge: Cambridge University Press).

Dunleavy, P. (1991) *Democracy, Bureaucracy and Public Choice: Economic Explanations in Political Science* (Hemel Hempstead: Harvester Wheatsheaf).

Dunleavy, P. and C. Husbands (1985) *British Democracy at the Crossroads* (London: Allen & Unwin).

Dunleavy, P. and B. O'Leary (1987) *Theories of the State*(London: Macmillan).

Dunn, J. (ed.) (1992) *Democracy: The Unfinished Journey 508 BC to AD 1993* (Oxford: Oxford University Press).

Dunn, J. (2000) *The Cunning of Unreason: Making Sense of Politics* (London: HarperCollins).

Duverger, M. (1954) *Political Parties* (London: Methuen).

Dworkin, R. (1986) *Law's Empire* (London: Fontana).

Dye, T. (1995) *Understanding Public Policy* (London: Prentice Hall).

Easton, D. (1979) *A Framework for Political Analysis* (2nd ed.) (Chicago, IL: University of Chicago Press).

Easton, D. (1981) *The Political System* (3rd ed.) Chicago: University of Chicago Press).

Eccleston, B. (1989) *State and Society in Post-War Japan*(Cambridge: Polity Press).

Elgie, R. (1995) *Political Leadership in Liberal Democracies* (London: Macmillan).

Elgie, R., S. Moestrup and Yu-Shan Wu (eds) (2011) *Semi-Presidential Systems and Democracy* (Basingstoke: Palgrave Macmillan).

Engels, F. (1972) *The Origins of the Family, Private Property and the State* (London: Lawrence & Wishart).

Etzioni, A. (1967) 'Mixed Scanning: A Third Approach to Decision Making', *Public Administration Review*, vol. 27, pp. 385–92.

Etzioni, A. (1995) *The Spirit of Community: Rights Responsibilities and the Communitarian Agenda* (London: Fontana).

Eysenck, H. (1964) *Sense and Nonsense in Psychology* (Harmondsworth: Penguin).

Fanon, F. (1968) *The Wretched of the Earth* (Harmondsworth: Penguin).

Farrell, D. M. (2011) *Electoral Systems: A Comparative Introduction* (Basingstoke: Palgrave Macmillan).

Fawn, R. (2009) *Globalising the Regional, Regionalising the Global* (Cambridge: Cambridge University Press).

Fenton, S. (2003) *Ethnicity* (Cambridge: Polity Press).

Finer, S. (1975) *The Man on Horseback: The Role of the Military in Politics* (Harmondsworth: Penguin).

Finn, J. E. (1991) *Constitutions in Crisis: Political Violence and the Rule of Law* (New York: Oxford University Press).

Fish, M. Steven (2005) *Democracy Derailed in Russia: The Failure of Open Politics* (New York: Cambridge University Press).

Fish, M. Steven and M. Kroenig (2011) *The Handbook of National Legislatures: A Global Survey* (New York: Cambridge University Press).

Flinders, M. (2012) *Defending Politics: Why Democracy Matters in the 21st Century* (Oxford and New York: Oxford University Press).

Foley, M. (2000) *The British Presidency* (Manchester: Manchester University Press).

Forsyth, M. (1981) *Union of States: The Theory and Practice of Confederation* (London and New York: Leicester University Press).

Freud, S. and W. Bullitt (1967) *Thomas Woodrow Wilson: A Psychological Study* (Boston, MA: Houghton Mifflin).

Friedan, B. (1963) *The Feminine Mystique* (Harmondsworth: Penguin).

Friedman, M. (1962) *Capitalism and Freedom* (Chicago, IL: Chicago University Press).

Friedrich, C. J. and Z. Brzezinski (1963) *Totalitarian Dictatorships and Autocracy* (New York: Praeger).

Friedrich, C. J., M. Curtis and B. Barber (1960) *Totalitarianism in Perspective* (New York: Praeger).

Fromm, E. *The Fear of Freedom* (London: Ark).

Fukuyama, F. (1989) 'The End of History?', *National Interest*, Summer.

Fukuyama, F. (1992) *The End of History and the Last Man* (Harmondsworth: Penguin).

Fukuyama, F. (1996) *Trust* (Harmondsworth: Penguin).

Fukuyama, F. (2005) *State Building: Governance and World Order* (London: Profile Books).

Fukuyama, F. (2006) *After the Neocons: America at the Crossroads* (New York: Profile Books).

Fukuyama, F. (2011) *The Origins of Political Order: From Prehuman Times to the French Revolution* (London: Profile Books).

Galbraith, J. K. (1992) *The Culture of Contentment* (London: Sinclair Stevenson).

Gallagher, M. and P. Mitchell (2008) *The Politics of Electoral Systems* (Oxford and New York: Oxford University Press).

Gallie, W. B. (1955/56) 'Essentially Contested Concepts', *Proceedings of the Aristotelian Society*, vol. 56, pp. 167–97.

Gamble, A. (1981) *An Introduction to Modern Social and Political Thought* (London: Macmillan and New York: St Martin's Press).

Gamble, A. (1988) *The Free Market and the Strong State* (London: Macmillan).

Gardner, H. (1996) *Leading Minds* (London: HarperCollins).

Gellner, E. (1983) *Nations and Nationalism* (Ithaca, NY: Cornell University Press).

Gibbins, J. (ed.) (1989) *Contemporary Political Culture: Politics in a Post-Modern Age* (London: Sage).

Giddens, A. (1994) *Beyond Left and Right: The Future of Radical Politics* (Cambridge: Polity Press).

Giddens, A. (ed.) (2001) *The Global Third Way Debate* (Cambridge: Polity Press).

Gill, S. and D. Law (1988) *The Global Political Economy: Perspectives, Problems and Policies* (Brighton: Harvester Wheatsheaf).

Ginsberg, B. (1982) *The Consequences of Consent* (Reading, MA: Addison–Wesley).

Glazer, N. and D. Moynihan (1975) *Ethnicity: Theory and Experience* (Cambridge, MA: Harvard University Press).

Gobineau, J.-A. ([1855] 1970) *Gobineau: Selected Political Writings* (New York: Harper & Row) (ed. M. D. Biddiss).

Goleman, D. (2005) *Emotional Intelligence* (New York: Bantam Dell).

Graham, B. D. (1993) *Representation and Party Politics: A Comparative Perspective* (Oxford: Blackwell).

Graham, C. and T. Prosser (1988) *Waiving the Rules* (Milton Keynes: Open University Press).

Gramsci, A. (1971) *Selections from the Prison Notebooks* (Chicago, IL: International Publishing Corporation) (ed. Q. Hoare and G. Nowell-Smith).

Grant, W. (1989) *Pressure Groups, Politics and Democracy in Britain* (Hemel Hempstead: Philip Allan).

Gray, J. (1993) *Post-Liberalism: Studies in Political Thought* (London: Routledge).

Greenstein, F. (2009) *The Presidential Difference: Leadership Style from FDR to Barak Obama* (Princeton, NJ: Princeton University Press).

Greer, G. (1970) *The Female Eunuch* (New York: McGraw-Hill).

Griffen, R. (1991) *The Nature of Fascism* (London and New York: Pinter).

Griffith, J. A. G. (2010) *The Politics of the Judiciary* (5th ed.) (London: Fontana).

Groz, A. (1982) *Farewell to the Working Class* (London: Pluto Press).

Gurr, T. (1970) *Why Men Rebel* (Princeton, NJ: Princeton University Press).

Habermas, J. (1973) *Legitimation Crisis* (Boston, MA: Beacon).

Hague, R. and M. Harrop (2013) *Comparative Government and Politics: An Introduction* (9th edn) (Basingstoke and New York: Palgrave Macmillan).

Hailsham, Lord (1976) *Elective Dictatorship* (London: BBC Publications).

Hall, P. and D. Soskice (eds) (2001) *Varieties of Capitalism: The Institutional Foundations of Comparative Advantage* (Oxford and New York: Oxford University Press).

Halliday, F. (1986) *The Making of the Second World War* (2nd edn) (London: Verso).

Halpern, D. (2005) *Social Capital* (Cambridge: Polity Press).

Hamilton, A., J. Jay and J. Madison ([1787–89] 1961) *The Federalist Papers* (New York: New American Library) (ed. C. Rossiter).

Hampden-Turner, C. and F. Trompenaars (1993) *The Seven Cultures of Capitalism* (New York: Doubleday).

Hann, A. (1995) 'Sharpening up Sabatier: Belief Systems and Public Policy', *Politics*, February.

Harrop, M. and W. L. Miller (1987) *Elections and Voters: A Comparative Introduction* (London: Macmillan).

Hart, H. L. A. (1961) *The Concept of Law* (Oxford: Oxford University Press).

Hartz, L. (1955) *The Liberal Tradition in America* (New York: Harcourt Brace Jovanovich).

Hawksley, H. (2009) *Democracy Kills: What's So Good About the Vote?* (Basingstoke: Palgrave Macmillan).

Hay, C. (2002) *Political Analysis: A Critical Introduction* (Basingstoke and New York: Palgrave Macmillan).

Hay, C. (2007) *Why We Hate Politics* (Cambridge and Malden, MA: Polity Press).

Hay, C. (ed.) (2010) *New Directions in Political Science: Responding to the Challenges of an Interdependent World* (Basingstoke and New York: Palgrave Macmillan).

Hay, C., M. Lister and D. Marsh (2006) *The State: Theories and Issues* (Basingstoke and New York: Palgrave Macmillan).

Hayek, F. (1948) *The Road to Serfdom* (Chicago, IL: University of Chicago Press).

Hazell, R. (ed.) (2008) *Constitutional Futures Revisited: Britain's Constitution to 2020* (Oxford: Oxford University Press).

Heady, F. (1979) *Public Administration: A Comparative Perspective* (New York: Marcel Dekker).

Hearn, J. (2006) *Rethinking Nationalism: A Critical Introduction* (Basingstoke and New York: Palgrave Macmillan).

Hegel, G. W. F. ([1821] 1942) *The Philosophy of Right* (Oxford: Clarendon Press) (trans. T. M. Knox).

Heidenheimer, A., H. Heclo and C. T. Adams (1990) *Comparative Public Policy* (3rd edn) (New York: St Martin's Press).

Held, D. (1993) *Prospects for Democracy: North, South, East, West* (Oxford: Polity Press).

Held, D. (1995) *Democracy and the Global Order: From the Modern State to Global Governance* (Cambridge: Polity Press).

Held, D. (2006) *Models of Democracy* (3rd edn) (Oxford: Policy Press; Stanford, CA: Stanford University Press).

Held, D. and A. McGrew (eds) (2000) *The Global Transformation: An Introduction to the Globalization Debate* (Cambridge and Malden MA: Polity Press).

Helms, L. (2004) *Presidents, Prime Ministers and Chancellors* (Basingstoke and New York: Palgrave Macmillan).

Hennessy, P. (1986) *Cabinet* (Oxford: Blackwell).

Hennessy, P. (1990) *Whitehall* (rev. edn) (London: Fontana).

Herder, J. G. (1969) *J. G. Herder on Social and Political Culture* (Cambridge: Cambridge University Press) (ed. F. M. Barnard).

Herrnstein, R. and C. Murray (1994) *The Bell Curve: Intelligence and Social Class in American Life* (New York: Free Press).

Hertz, N. (2001) *The Silent Take-over: Global Capitalism and the Death of Democracy* (London: Heinemann).

Hess, S. (1988) *Organising the Presidency* (Brookings Institution).

Heywood, A. (2000) *Key Concepts in Politics* (Basingstoke: Palgrave Macmillan).

Heywood, A. (2004) *Political Theory* (3rd edn) (Basingstoke and New York: Palgrave Macmillan).

Heywood, A. (2011) *Global Politics* (Basingstoke and New York: Palgrave Macmillan).

Heywood, A. (2012) *Political Ideologies: An Introduction* (5th edn) (Basingstoke and New York: Palgrave Macmillan).

Hill, R. and P. Frank (1983) *The Soviet Communist Party* (London: Allen & Unwin).

Himmelveit, H. T., P. Humphreys and M. Jaeger (1985) *How Voters Decide* (Milton Keynes: Open University Press).

Hirst, P. and G. Thompson (1999) *Globalization in Question: The International Economy and the Possibilities of Governance* (Cambridge: Polity Press).

Hitler, A. ([1925] 1969) *Mein Kampf* (London: Hutchinson) (trans. R. Mannheim).

Hobbes, T. ([1651] 1968) *Leviathan* (Harmondsworth: Penguin) (ed. C. B. Macpherson).

Hobsbawm, E. (1983) 'Inventing Traditions', in E. Hobsbawm and T. Ranger (eds) *The Invention of Tradition* (Cambridge: Cambridge University Press).

Hobsbawm, E. (1993) *Nations and Nationalism since 1780* (2nd edn) (Cambridge: Cambridge University Press).

Hocking, B. and M. Smith (1995) *World Politics: An Introduction to International Relations* (London: Harvester Wheatsheaf).

Hogwood, B. and L. Gunn (1984) *Policy Analysis for the Real World* (Oxford: Oxford University Press).

Holden, B. (1993) *Understanding Liberal Democracy*) (2nd edn) (London and New York: Harvester Wheatsheaf).

Holmes, J. S. (2000) *Terrorism and Democratic Stability* (Manchester: Manchester University Press).

Hondrich, T. (1992) *Conservatism* (Harmondsworth: Penguin).

Hood, C. C. (1976) *The Limits of Administration* (London: John Wiley).

Hough, J. (1977) *The Soviet Union and Social Science Theory* (Cambridge, MA: Harvard University Press).

Huntington, S. (1957) *The Soldier and the State: The Theory and Practice of Civil–Military Relations* (Cambridge, MA: Harvard University Press).

Huntington, S. (1991) *Third Wave: Democratization in the late Twentieth Century* (Norman, OK and London: University of Oklahoma Press).

Huntington, S. (1996) *The Clash of Civilizations and the Making of World Order* (New York: Simon & Schuster).

Hutchinson, J. and A. D. Smith (eds) (1994) *Nationalism* (Oxford and New York: Oxford University Press).

Hutton, W. (1995) *The State We're In* (London: Jonathan Cape).

Hyman, H. (1959) *Political Socialisation: A Study in the Psychology of Political Behaviour* (New York: Free Press).

Inglehart, R. (1977) *The Silent Revolution: Changing Values and Political Styles Amongst Western Publics* (Princeton, NJ: Princeton University Press).

Inglehart, R. (1990) *Cultural Shift in Advanced Industrial Society* (Princeton, NJ: Princeton University Press).

Inter-Parliamentary Union (1986) *Parliaments of the World* (Aldershot: Gower) (2 vols).

Janis, I. (1972) *Victims of Groupthink* (Boston, MA: Houghton Mifflin).

Jenkins, H. and D. Thorburn (eds) (2004) *Democracy and New Media* (Cambridge, MA: MIT Press).

Jenkins, S. (1995) *Accountable to None* (Harmondsworth: Penguin).

Jervis, R. (1968) 'Hypotheses on Misperception', *World Politics*, vol. 20, pp. 454–79.

Jessop, B. (1982) *The Capitalist State* (Oxford: Martin Robertson).

Jessop, B. (1990) *State Theory: Putting Capitalist States in Their Place* (Oxford: Polity Press).

Johnson, C. (1966) *Revolutionary Change* (Boston, MA: Little, Brown).

Johnson, C. (1982) *MITI and the Japanese Miracle: The Growth of Industrial Policy, 1925–1975* (Stanford, CA: Stanford University Press).

Jones, G. (ed.) (1991) *Western European Prime Ministers*(London: Frank Cass).

Jordan, G. and W. Maloney (2007) *Democracy and Interest Groups: Enhancing Democracy?* (Basingstoke and New York: Palgrave Macmillan).

Kagan, R. (2004) *Paradise and Power: America and Europe in the New World Order* (London: Atlantic Books).

Kaldor, M. (2007) *Human Security: Reflections on Globalization and Intervention* (Cambridge and Malden, MA: Polity Press).

Kant, I. (1970) *Political Writings* (Cambridge: Cambridge University Press) (ed. H. Reiss).

Karns, M. and K. Mingst (2009) *International Organization: The Politics and Processes of Global Governance* (Boulder, CO: Lynne Rienner Publishers).

Katz, R. (1997) *Democracy and Elections* (Oxford & New York: Oxford University Press).

Katz, R. and W. Crotty (eds) (2006) *Handbook of Political Parties* (London and Thousand Oaks, CA: Sage Publications).

Keating, M. (1988) *State and Regional Nationalism: Territorial Politics and the European State* (London and New York: Harvester Wheatsheaf).

Kegley, C. W. and E. R. Wittkopf (2001) *World Politics: Trend and Transformation* (Boston, MA and New York: Bedford/St Martin's Press).

Keith, M. (1993) *Race Riots and Policing* (London: UCL Press).

Kellas, J. (1991) *The Politics of Nationalism and Ethnicity* (London: Macmillan).

Kellner, P. and Lord Crowther-Hunt (1980) *The Civil Servants* (London: Macdonald).

Kennedy, P. (1989) *The Rise and Fall of the Great Powers*(London: Fontana).

Keohane, R. and J. Nye (1977) *Power and Interdependence: World Politics in Transition* (Boston: Little Brown).

Key, V. O. (1966) *The Responsible Electorate* (New York: Vintage).

Keynes, J. M. ([1936] 1965) *The General Theory of Employment, Interest and Money* (San Diego, CA: Harcourt Brace).

Kim, H.-K., M. Muramatsu and T. J. Pempel (eds) (1995) *The Japanese Civil Service and Economic Development: Catalysts of Change* (New York: Oxford University Press).

King, A. (1975) 'Overload: Problems of Governing in the 1970s', *Political Studies*, vol. 23, pp. 284–96.

King, A. (ed.) (1985) *The British Prime Minister* (2nd ed.) (London: Macmillan).

Kirchheimer, O. (1966) 'The Transformation of the Western European Party Systems', in J. la Palombara and M. Weiner (eds) *Political Parties and Political Development* (Princeton, NJ: Princeton University Press).

Klein, N. (2000) *No Logo* (London: Flamingo).

Kneopfel, P., C. Larrue, F. Varone and M. Hill (2007) *Public Policy Analysis* (Bristol: The Policy Press).

Knott, J. and G. Miller (1987) *Reforming Bureaucracy: The Politics of Institutional Choice* (Englewood Cliffs, NJ: Prentice Hall).

Koh, B. (1989) *Japan's Administrative Elite* (Berkeley, CA: University of California Press).

Kolko, G. (1968) *The Politics of War* (London: Weidenfeld and Nicolson).

Kolko, G. (1988) *Restructuring the World Economy* (New York: Pantheon Books).

Kressel, N. J. (ed.) (1993) *Political Psychology: Classic and Contemporary Readings* (New York: Paragon House).

Kristol, I. (1983) *Two Cheers for Capitalism* (New York: Basic Books).

Kristol, W. and R. Kagan (2004) 'National Interest and Global Responsibility', in I. Stelzer *Neoconservatism* (London: Atlantic Books).

Kropotkin, P. (1912) *Fields, Factories and Workshops* (London: Nelson).

Kuhn, T. (1962) *The Structure of Scientific Revolutions* (2nd ed.) (Chicago, IL: Chicago University Press).

Kumar, K. (2004) *From Post-Industrial to Post-Modern Society: New Theories of the Contemporary World* (Oxford and Malden, MA: Blackwell).

Kymlicka, William (1995) *Multicultural Citizenship* (Oxford: Oxford University Press).

Laclau, E. and C. Mouffe (2001) *Hegemony and Socialist Strategy: Towards a Radical Democratic Politics* (London: Verso).

Lafont, R. (1968) *Sur la France* (Paris: Gallimard).

Lane, J. E. (2011) *Constitutions and Political Theory* (Manchester: Manchester University Press).

Laqueur, W. (ed.) (1979) *Fascism: A Reader's Guide* (Harmondsworth: Penguin; Berkeley, CA: University of California Press).

Lasswell, H. (1930) *Psychopathology and Politics* (New York: Viking).

Lasswell, H. (1936) *Politics: Who Gets What, When, How?* (New York: McGraw–Hill).

Lazarski, C. (2012) *Power Tends to Corrupt: Lord Acton's Study of Liberty* (Chicago, IL: Chicago University Press).

Le Bon, G. ([1895] 1960) *The Crowd* (New York: Viking Press).

Le Grand, J. (1982) *The Strategy of Equality: Redistribution and the Social Services* (London: Allen & Unwin).

LeDuc, L., R. G. Niemi and P. Norris (eds) (2010) *Comparing Democracies 3: Elections and Voting in the 21st Century* (London: Sage).

Lees, J. D. and M. Shaw (eds) (1979) *Committees in Legislatures: A Comparative Analysis* (Durham, NC: Duke University Press).

Leftwich, A. (ed.) (2004) *What is Politics? The Activity and Its Study* (Cambridge: Polity).

Lehmbruch, G. and P. C. Schmitter (1982) *Patterns of Corporatist Policy-Making* (London: Sage).

Leigh, D. and E. Vulliamy (1997) *Sleaze: The Corruption of Parliament* (London: Fourth Estate).

Lenin, V. I. ([1902] 1968) *What is to be Done?* (Harmondsworth and New York: Penguin).

Lenin, V. I. ([1916] 1970) *Imperialism: The Highest Stage of Capitalism* (Moscow: Progress).

Lichtheim, G. (1961) *Marxism* (London: Routledge & Kegan Paul).

Lijphart, A. (1990) 'Democratic Political Systems', in A. Bebler and J. Seroka (eds) *Contemporary Political Systems: Classifications and Typologies* (Boulder, CO: Lynne Reinner) pp. 71–87.

Lijphart, A. (ed.) (1992) *Parliamentary Versus Presidential Government* (Oxford: Oxford University Press).

Lijphart, A. (1996) 'Unequal Participation: Democracy's Unresolved Dilemma', *American Political Science Association,* 91(1).

Lijphart, A. (1999) *Democracies: Patterns of Majoritarian and Consensus Government in Thirty Six Countries* (New Haven, CT: Yale University Press).

Lijphart, A. and B. Grofman (eds) (1984) *Choosing an Electoral System* (New York: Praeger).

Lindblom, C. (1959) 'The Science of Muddling Through', *Public Administration Review*, vol. 19, pp. 79–88.

Lindblom, C. (1980) *Politics and Markets* (New York: Basic Books).

Lipset, S. and S. Rokkan (eds) (1967) *Party Systems and Voter Alignments* (New York: Free Press).

Little, R. and M. Smith (1991) *Perspective on World Politics* (London: Routledge).

Lively, J. (1975) *Democracy* (Oxford: Blackwell).

Lloyd, J. (2004) *What are the Media Doing to Our Politics?* (London: Constable).

Lloyd, J. and J. Seaton (eds) (2006) *What Can Be Done? Making the Media and Politics Better* (Oxford: Blackwell).

Locke, J. ([1690] 1965) *Two Treatises of Government* (New York: New American Library).

Loewenberg, F. and S. C. Patterson (1979) *Comparing Legislatures* (Boston, MA: Little, Brown).

Lovelock, J. (1979) *Gaia* (Oxford: Oxford University Press).

Lovelock, J. (2002) *Revenge of Gaia* (Santa Barbara, CA: Allen Lane).

Lukes, S. (2004) *Power: A Radical View* (Basingstoke and New York: Palgrave Macmillan).

Machiavelli, N. ([1531] 1961) *The Prince* (Harmondsworth: Penguin) (trans. G. Bau).

MacIntyre, A. (1981) *After Virtue* (Notre Dame, IL: University of Notre Dame Press).

Mackintosh, J. P. (1977) *The British Cabinet* (London: Stevens).

Macmillan, H. (1966) *The Middle Way* (London: Macmillan).

Macpherson, C. B. (1962) *The Theory of Possessive Individualism* (Oxford: Oxford University Press).

Macpherson, C. B. (1972) *The Real World of Democracy* (New York and Oxford: Oxford University Press).

Macpherson, C. B. (1977) *The Life and Times of Liberal Democracy* (Oxford: Oxford University Press).

Mair, P. (1990) *The West European Party System* (Oxford: Oxford University Press).

Mann, M. (1993) *The Sources of Social Power, Volume 2: The Rise of Classes and Modern States, 1760–1914* (Cambridge: Cambridge University Press).

Mao, Z. (1971) *Selected Readings from the Works of Mao Zedong* (Peking: Foreign Languages Press).

Marcuse, H. (1964) *One-Dimensional Man: Studies in the Ideology of Advanced Industrial Society* (Boston, MA: Beacon).

Marquand, D. (1988) *The Unprincipled Society* (London: Cape).

Marsh, D. and R. A. W. Rhodes (eds) (1992) *Policy Networks in British Government* (Oxford: Oxford University Press).

Marsh, D. and G. Stoker (eds) (2010) *Theory and Methods in Political Science* (Basingstoke: Palgrave Macmillan).

Marshall, P. (1991) *Demanding the Impossible: A History of Anarchism* (London: HarperCollins).

Marshall, T. H. (1950) 'Citizenship and Social Class', in T. Marshall (ed.) *Sociology at the Crossroads* (London: Heinemann).

Marty, M. E. and R. S. Appleby (1993) *Fundamentalisms and the State: Remaking Polities, Economies, and Militance* (Chicago, IL: University of Chicago Press).

Marx, K. ([1845] 1968) 'Theses on Feuerbach', in *Selected Works in One Volume* (London: Lawrence & Wishart), pp. 28–31.

Marx, K. ([1852] 1963) *The Eighteenth Brumaire of Louis Bonaparte* (New York: International Publishers).

Marx, K. ([1867, 1885, 1894] 1970) *Capital* (London: Lawrence and Wishart) (3 vols).

Marx, K. and Engels, F. ([1846] 1970) *The German Ideology* (London: Lawrence & Wishart) (ed. C. J. Arthur).

Marx, K. and Engels, F. ([1848] 1967) *The Communist Manifesto* (Harmondsworth: Penguin).

Mayes, P. (1986) *Gender* (London: Longman).

Mayo, H. (1960) *An Introduction to Democratic Theory* (New York: Oxford University Press).

McCauley, M. (1983) *The Origins of War* (London: Longman).

McCormick, J. (2011) *Understanding the European Union: A Concise Introduction* (Basingstoke and New York: Palgrave Macmillan).

McDowell, L. and R. Pringle (eds) (1992) *Defining Women: Social Institutions and Gender Divisions* (Cambridge: Polity Press).

McGrew, A. G. *et al.* (eds) (1992) *Global Politics: Globalisation and the Nation-State* (Oxford: Policy Press).

McKenzie, R. T. (1955) *British Political Parties* (London: Heinemann).

McLellan, D. (1986) *Ideology* (Milton Keynes: Open University Press; Minneapolis, MI: University of Minnesota Press).

McLennan, G., D. Held and S. Hall (eds) (1984) *The Idea of the Modern State* (Milton Keynes and Philadelphia, PA: Open University Press).

McQuail, D. (1992) *Media Performance* (London: Sage).

Mearsheimer, J. (2001) *The Tragedy of Great Power Politics* (New York: W. W. Norton).

Meinecke, F. ([1907] 1970) *Cosmopolitanism and the National State* (Princeton, NJ: Princeton University Press).

Menon, A. and M. A. Schain (2006) *Comparative Federalism* (Oxford and New York: Oxford University Press).

Meny, Y. and V. Wright (eds) (1985) *Centre–Periphery Relations in Western Europe* (London: Croom Helm).

Mezey, M. (1979) *Comparative Legislatures* (Durham, NC: Duke University Press).

Michels, R. ([1911] 1962) *Political Parties: A Sociological Study of the Oligarchical Tendencies of Modern Democracy* (New York: Collier).

Milbrath, L. and M. Goel (1977) *Political Participation: How and Why Do People Get Involved in Politics* (Chicago. IL: Rand McNally).

Miliband, R. (1972) *Parliamentary Socialism* (London: Merlin).

Miliband, R. ([1969] 2009) *The State in Capitalist Society* (London: Merlin).

Mill, J. S. ([1859] 1982) *On Liberty* (Harmondsworth: Penguin).

Mill, J. S. ([1861] 1951) *Considerations on Representative Government*, in H. B. Acton (ed.) *Utilitarianism, Liberty, and Representative Government* (London: Dent).

Millett, K. (1970) *Sexual Politics* (London: Granada).

Mills, C. W. (1956) *The Power Elite* (New York: Oxford University Press).

Modood, T. (2007) *Multiculturalism: A Civic Idea* (Cambridge: Polity Press).

Monbiot, G. (2001) *Captive State: The Corporate Take-over of Britain* (London: Pan).

Monbiot, G. (2004) *Age of Consent: A Manefesto for a New World Order* (London: Harper Perennial).

Montesquieu, C.-L. ([1748] 1949) *The Spirit of the Laws* (New York: Hafner) (trans. T. Nugent).

More, T. ([1516] 1965) *Utopia* (Harmondsworth: Penguin) (trans. P. Turner).

Morgenthau, H. (1948) *Politics Amongst Nations: The Struggle for Power and Peace* (New York: Knopf).

Mosca, G. ([1896] 1939) *The Ruling Class* (New York: McGraw–Hill) (trans. A. Livingstone).

Murray, C. (1984) *Losing Ground: American Social Policy (1950–80)* (New York: Basic Books).

Murray, C. and R. Herrnstein (1995) *The Bell Curve: Intelligence and Class Structure in American Life* (New York: Free Press).

Neumann, S. (1956) *Modern Political Parties* (Chicago, IL: University of Chicago Press).

Neustadt, R. (1991) *Presidential Power and the Modern President: The Politics of Leadership from FDR to Reagan* (New York: The Free Press).

Nietzsche, F. (1982) *Thus Spoke Zarathustra* (New York: Random House) (trans. R. J. Hollingdale).

Niskanen, W. A. (1971) *Bureaucracy and Representative Government* (Chicago, IL: Aldine–Atherton).

Nordlinger, E. (1977) *Soldiers in Politics: Military Coups and Governments* (Englewoods Cliffs, NJ: Prentice Hall).

Nordlinger, E. (1981) *On the Autonomy of the Democratic State* (Cambridge, MA: Harvard University Press).

Norton, A. (1994) *International Handbook of Local and Regional Government* (Aldershot and Brookfield, VT: Edward Elgar).

Norton, P. (ed.) (1990a) *Legislatures* (Oxford: Oxford University Press).

Norton, P. (ed.) (1990b) *Parliaments in Western Europe* (London: Frank Cass).

Norton, P. (1993) *Does Parliament Matter?* (London: Harvester Wheatsheaf).

Nove, A. (1983) *The Economics of Feasible Socialism* (London: Macmillan).

Nozick, R. (1974) *Anarchy, State and Utopia* (Oxford: Basil Blackwell).

Nugent, N. (1991) *The Government and Politics of the European Community* (2nd edn) (London: Macmillan).

Nye, J. (2004) *Soft Power: The Means to Succeed in World Politics* (New York: Public Affairs).

Nye, J. (2008) *The Powers to Lead: Soft, Hard and Smart* (New York: Oxford University Press).

Oakeshott, M. (1962) *Rationalism in Politics and Other Essays* (London and New York: Methuen).

Oates, S. (2005) 'Media and Political Communication', in S. White, Z. Gitelman and R. Sakwa (eds) *Developments in Russian Politics 6* (Basingstoke and New York: Palgrave Macmillan).

O'Brien, D. (2000) *Storm Center: The Supreme Court in American Politics* (5th edn) (New York: Norton).

O'Brien, R. and M. Williams (2010) *Global Political Economy* (3rd edn) (Basingstoke and New York: Palgrave Macmillan).

O'Donnell, G. (1999) *Counterpoints: Selected Essays on Authoritarianism and Democracy* (Notre Dame, IL: Notre Dame University Press).

OECD (1995) *Globalization: What Challenges and Opportunities for Governments?* (Paris: OECD)

Offe, C. (1984) *Contradictions of the Welfare State* (London: Hutchinson).

Ohmae, K. (1989) *Borderless World: Power and Strategy in the Interlinked Economy* (London: HarperCollins).

Olson, D. (1994) *Legislative Institutions: A Comparative View* (Armonk, NY: M. E. Sharpe).

Olson, M. (1974) *The Logic of Collective Action: Public Goods and the Theory of Groups* (Cambridge, MA: Harvard University Press).

Olson, M. (1984) *The Rise and Decline of Nations* (Newhaven, CT: Yale University Press).

Osborne, D. and T. Gaebler (1992) *Reinventing Government* (New York: Addison–Wesley).

Ostrogorski, M. (1902) *Democracy and the Organisation of Political Parties* (London: Macmillan).

O'Sullivan, N. (1976) *Conservatism* (London: Dent).

Paddison, R. (1983) *The Fragmented State: The Political Geography of Power* (New York: St Martin's Press).

Paine, T. ([1776] 1987) 'Common Sense', in M. Foot (ed.) *The Thomas Paine Reader* (Harmondsworth: Penguin).

Pakulski, J. (1990) *Social Movements: The Politics of Protest* (Melbourne: Longman).

Pape, R. A. (2005) 'Soft Balancing: How States Pursue Security in a Unipolar World', *International Security*, 30(1).

Parekh, B. (2006) *Rethinking Multiculturalism in Cultural Diversity and Political Theory* (2nd edn) (Basingstoke and New York: Palgrave Macmillan).

Parekh, B. (2008) *A New Politics of Identity: Political Principles for an Interdependent World* (Basingstoke and New York: Palgrave Macmillan).

Parmar, I. and M. Cox (eds) (2010) *Soft Power and US Foreign Policy* (London: Routledge).

Parry, G. and M. Moran (eds) (1994) *Democracy and Democratization* (London: Routledge).

Parsons, A. (1995) *From Cold War to Hot Peace: UN Interventions, 1945–1994* (London: Michael Joseph).

Parsons, W. (1995) *Public Policy: Introduction to the Theory and Practice of Policy Analysis* (Aldershot: Edward Elgar).

Pateman, C. (1970) *Participation and Democratic Theory* (Cambridge: Cambridge University Press).

Peele, G., C. Bailey, B. Cain and B. G. Peters (eds) (1994) *Developments in British Politics 2* (London: Macmillan).

Peters, B. Guy (2009) *The Politics of Bureaucracy* (London: Routledge).

Philo, G. (ed.) (1999) *Message Received* (London: Longman).

Pierson, C. (2000) *The New Politics of Welfare* (Oxford and New York).

Pierre, J. and B. Guy Peters (2000) *Governance, Politics and the State* (Basingstoke: Palgrave Macmillan).

Pinker, S. (2011) *The Better Angels of Our Nature: The Decline of Violence and Its Causes* (New York: Viking Penguin).

Pinkney, R. (1990) *Right-Wing Military Government* (London: Pinter).

Piore, M. J. and C. Sabel (1984) *The Second Industrial Divide: Possibilities for Prosperity* (New York: Basic Books).

Plant, R. (1991) *Modern Political Thought* (Oxford: Oxford University Press).

Plato (1955) *The Republic* (Harmondsworth: Penguin) (trans. H. D. Lee).

Poggi, G. (1990) *The State* (Cambridge: Polity Press).

Poguntke, T. and P. Webb (2007) *The Presidentialization of Politics: A Comparative Study of Modern Democracies* (Oxford and New York: Oxford University Press).

Polsby, N. (1963) *Community Power and Political Theory* Newhaven, CT: Yale University Press).

Poulantzas, N. (1968) *Political Power and Social Classes* (London: New Left Books).

Pressman, J. and A. Wildavsky (1973) *Implementation* (Berkeley, CA: University of California Press).

Proudhon, P.-J. ([1840] 1970) *What is Property?* (New York: Dover).

Przeworski, A. (1991) *Democracy and the Market: Political and Economic Reforms in Eastern Europe and Latin America* (Cambridge and New York: Cambridge University Press).

Pulzer, P. (1967) *Political Representation and Elections in Britain* (London: Allen & Unwin).

Putnam, R. (1993) *Making Democracy Work: Civic Traditions in Modern Italy* (Princeton, NJ: Princeton University Press).

Putnam, R. (1996) 'Who Killed Civic America?', *Prospect*, March, pp. 66–72.

Putnam, R. (2000) *Bowling Alone: The Collapse and Revival of American Community* (New York: Simon & Schuster).

Raadschelders, J., T. Toonen and F. Van der Meer (eds) (2007) *The Civil Service in the 21st Century: Comparative Perspectives* (London and New York: Palgrave Macmillan).

Randall, V. (ed.) (1988) *Political Parties in the Third World* (London: Sage).

Rawls, J. (1971) *A Theory of Justice* (Oxford: Oxford University Press).

Reiner, R. (1993) *The Politics of the Police* (2nd ed.) (Hemel Hempstead: Harvester Wheatsheaf).

Rex, J. and D. Mason (eds) (1992) *Theories of Race and Ethnic Relations* (Cambridge: Cambridge University Press).

Rhodes, R. (1996) 'The New Governance: Governing without Government', *Political Studies*, vol. 44, pp. 652–67.

Rhodes, R. and P. Dunleavy (eds) (1995) *Prime Minister, Cabinet and Core Executive* (London: Macmillan).

Rhodes, R. A. W. (1988) *Beyond Westminster and Whitehall* (London: Unwin Hyman).

Richardson, J. (ed.) (1984) *Policy Styles in Western Europe* (London: Allen & Unwin).

Richardson, J. (ed.) (1993) *Pressure Groups* (Oxford and New York: Oxford University Press).

Ritzer, G. (2000) *The McDonaldization of Society* (Thousand Oaks, CA: Pine Forge Press).

Roach, J. and J. Thomaneck (1985) *Police and Public Order in Europe* (London: Croom Helm).

Robins, L., H. Blackmore and R. Pyper (eds) (1994) *Britain's Changing Party System* (London and New York: Leicester University Press).

Rokkan, S. (1970) *Citizens, Elections, Parties* (New York: McKay).

Roler, E. (2005) *The Performance of Democracies* (Oxford and New York: Oxford University Press).

Rose, R. (ed.) (1980) *Challenge to Governance: Studies in Overloaded Politics* (London: Sage).

Rose, R. (1987) *The Postmodern Presidency: The White House Meets the World* (New York: Chartham House).

Roszak, T. (1994) *The Cult of Information: The Folklore of Computers and the True Art of Thinking* (London: Paladin Books).

Rousseau, J.-J. ([1762] 1913) *The Social Contract* (London: Dent) (trans. G. D. H. Cole).

Rowat, D. (ed.) (1988) *Public Administration in Developed Democracies: A Comparative Study* (New York: Marcel Dekker).

Ruggie, J. (1992) 'Multilateralism: The Anatomy of an Institution', *International Organization, 46*.

Runciman, D. (2008) *Political Hypocrisy: The Mask of Power from Hobbes and Orwell to Beyond* (Princeton, NJ: Princeton University Press).

Rush, M. (1992) *Politics and Society: An Introduction to Political Sociology* (Hemel Hempstead: Harvester Wheatsheaf).

Russell, M. (2000) *Reforming the House of Lords: Lessons from Overseas* (Oxford and New York: Oxford University Press).

Sabatier, P. (1988) 'An Advocacy Coalition Model of Policy Making and Change and the Role of Policy Orientated Learning Therein', *Policy Sciences*, vol. 1, pp. 129–68.

Said, E. (1978) *Orientalism: Western Conceptions of the Orient* (New York: Vintage Books).

Sandel, M. (1982) *Liberalism and the Limits of Justice* (Cambridge: Cambridge University Press).

Sartori, G. (1970) 'Guidelines for Conceptual Analysis', *American Political Science Review, 64*.

Sartori, G. (1987) *The Theory of Democracy Revisited* (Chatham, NJ: Chatham House).

Sartori, G. (2005) *Parties and Party Systems: A Framework for Analysis* (Cambridge: Cambridge University Press).

Saunders, P. (1990) *Social Class and Stratification* (London: Routledge).

Savage, S., R. Atkinson and L. Robins (1994) *Public Policy in Britain* (London: Macmillan).

Savigny, H. and L. Marsden (2011) *Doing Political Science and International Relations: Theories in Action* (Basingstoke and New York: Palgrave Macmillan).

Scammel, M. (2000) 'New Media, New Politics' in Dunleavy, P., A. Gamble, I. Holliday and G. Peele (eds) *Developments in British Politics 6* (Basingstoke: PalgraveMacmillan).

Schlesinger, A. (1974) *The Imperial Presidency* (New York: Popular Library).

Scholte, J. A. (2005) *Globalization: A Critical Introduction*, 2nd edn (Basingstoke and New York: Palgrave Macmillan).

Schumacher, E. F. (1973) *Small is Beautiful: A Study of Economics As If People Mattered* (London: Blond & Briggs).

Schumpeter, J. (1942) *Capitalism, Socialism and Democracy* (London: Allen & Unwin).

Schwarzmantel, J. (1991) *Socialism and the Idea of the Nation* (London: Harvester Wheatsheaf).

Schwarzmantel, J. (1994) *The State in Contemporary Society: An Introduction* (London and New York: Harvester Wheatsheaf).

Sedgemore, B. (1980) *The Secret Constitution* (London: Hodder & Stoughton).

Self, P. (1994) *Government by the Market? Politics of Public Choice* (London: Macmillan).

Seliger, M. (1976) *Politics and Ideology* (London: Allen & Unwin).

Sen, Amartya (2006) *Identity and Violence* (New York: W. W. Norton).

Sennett, R. (2004) *Respect: The Formation of Character in an Age of Inequality* (Harmondsworth and New York: Penguin).

Shapiro, M. and A. Stone Sweet (2002) *On Law, Politics and Judicialization* (Oxford: Oxford University Press).

Silva, P. (ed.) (2001) *The Soldier and the State in South America: Essays on Civil–Military Relations* (Basingstoke and New York: Palgrave Macmillan).

Simon, H. (1983) *Models of Bounded Rationality – Vol. 2* (Cambridge, MA: MIT Press).

Skocpol, T. (1979) *States and Social Revolutions* (Cambridge: Cambridge University Press).

Smith, A. ([1776] 1930) *The Wealth of Nations* (London: Methuen).

Smith, A. D. (1986) *The Ethnic Origins of Nations* (Oxford: Basil Blackwell).

Smith, B. C. (1985) *Decentralisation: The Territorial Dimension of the State* (London: Allen & Unwin).

Smith, M. (1995) *Pressure Groups* (Manchester: Baseline Books).

Smith, M. E. (2010) *International Security: Politics, Policy, Prospects* (Basingstoke and New York: Palgrave Macmillan).

Smith, R. (2006) *The Utility of Force: Theories, Actors, Cases* (Oxford: Oxford University Press).

Social Trends, 2005 (London: HMSO).

Sørenson, G. (2004) *The Transformation of the State: Beyond the Myth of Retreat* (Basingstoke and New York: Palgrave Macmillan).

Soros, G. (1998) *The Crisis of Global Capitalism: Open Society Endangered* (New York: BBS/Public Affairs).

Spencer, P. and H. Wollman (eds) (2005) *Nations and Nationalism* (Edinburgh: Edinburgh University Press).

Stilwell, F. (2011) *Political Economy: The Contest of Economic Ideas* (3rd edn) (Oxford: Oxford University Press.)

Stoker, G. (2006) *Why Politics Matter: Making Democracy Work* (Basingstoke and New York: Palgrave Macmillan).

Strange, S. (1986) *Casino Capitalism* (Oxford: Basil Blackwell).

Strøm, K., W. Müller and T. Bergman (eds) (2006) *Delegation and Accountability in Parliamentary Democracies* (Oxford and New York: Oxford University Press).

Suleiman, E. (ed.) (1984) *Bureaucrats and Policy Making* (New York: Holmes & Meier).

Sun Tzu (1963) *The Art of War* (New York: Oxford University Press) (trans. S. B. Griffith).

Talmon, J. L. (1952) *The Origins of Totalitarian Democracy* (London: Secker & Warburg).

Tarrow, S. (2011) *Power in Movement: Social Movements and Contentious Politics* (Cambridge and New York: Cambridge University Press).

Thatcher, M. (1993) *The Downing Street Years* (London: HarperCollins).

Tilly, C. (1975) 'Reflections on the History of European State-Making', in C. Tully (ed.) *The Formation of Nation-States in Europe* (Princeton, NJ: Princeton University Press).

Tilly, C. (1990) *Coercion, Capital and European States, AD 900–1990* (Oxford: Blackwell).

Titmuss, R. M. (1968) *Essays on the Welfare State* (London: Allen & Unwin).

Tocqueville, A. de ([1856] 1947) *The Old Regime and the French Revolution* (Oxford: Blackwell) (trans. M. W. Patterson).

Trotsky, L. (1937) *The Revolution Betrayed: What is the Soviet Union and Where is it Going?* (London: Faber).

Truman, D. (1951) *The Governmental Process* (New York: Knopf).

Verba, S., N. Nie and J. Kim (1978) *Participation and Political Equality: A Seven-Nation Comparison* (Cambridge and New York: Cambridge University Press).

Verheijes, T. and D. Coombes (eds) (1998) *Innovations in Public Management: Perspectives from East and West Europe* (Cheltenham & Northampton, MA: Edward Elgar).

Wachendorfer-Schmidt, U. (ed.) (2000) *Federalism and Political Performance* (London & New York: Routledge).

Waldron, J. (1995) 'Minority Cultures and the Cosmopolitan Alternative', in W. Kymlicka (ed.) *The Rights of Monority Cultures* (Oxford: Oxford University Press).

Wallerstein, I. (1984) *The Politics of the World Economy* (Cambridge: Cambridge University Press).

Waltman, J. and K. Holland (eds) (1988) *The Political Role of Law Courts in Modern Democracies* (New York: St Martin's Press).

Waltz, K. (1979) *Theory of International Politics* (Reading, MA: Addison-Wesley).

Waltz, K. (2012) 'Why Iran Should Get the Bomb', *Foreign Affairs* 91 (July/August).

Wattenberg, M. (2000) 'The Decline of Party Mobilization', in R. Dalton and M. Wattenberg (eds) *Parties without Partisans* (Oxford and New York: Oxford University Press).

Weber, M. (1904–5) *The Protestant Ethic and the Spirit of Capitalism* (London: Allen & Unwin).

Weber, M. (1948) *From Max Weber: Essays in Sociology* (London: Routledge & Kegan Paul).

Weiss, T. G. (2012) *What's Wrong with the United Nations (And How to Fix It)* (Cambridge and Maldon, MA: Polity Press).

Weller, P. (1985) *First Among Equals: Prime Ministers in Westminster Systems* (Sydney: Allen & Unwin).

Wendt, A. (1992) 'Anarchy is What States Make of It: The Social Construction of Power Politics', *International Organization*, 41.

Wendt, A. (1999) *Social Theory of International Politics* (Cambridge: Cambridge University Press).

White, S., J. Gardner, G. Schopflin and T. Saich (1990) *Communist and Postcommunist Political Systems* (London: Macmillan).

Whitman, J. (ed.) (2009) *Global Governance* (Basingstoke: Palgrave Macmillan).

Wildavsky, A. (1980) *Art and Craft of Policy Analysis* (London: Macmillan).

Wilkinson, R. and K. Pickett (2010) *The Spirit Level: Why Equality is Better for Everyone* (Harmondsworth: Penguin).

Willner, A. R. (1984) *The Spellbinders: Charismatic Political Leadership* (New Haven, CT: Yale University Press).

Wilson, G. (1990) *Interest Groups* (Oxford: Blackwell).

Wilson, W. ([1885] 1961) *Constitutional Government: A Study in American Politics* (New York: Meridian).

Wolinetz, S. (ed.) (1997) *Political Parties* (Aldershot and Brookfield, VT: Ashgate).

Wollstonecraft, M. ([1792] 1985) *A Vindication of the Rights of Women* (Harmondsworth: Penguin).

World Bank (2012) *World Development Report 2012* (Washington, DC: World Bank).

Wright, A. (1987) *Socialisms: Theories and Practices* (Oxford: Oxford University Press).

Wright, V., B. Guy Peters and R. Rhodes (eds) (2000) *Administering the Summit: Administration of the Core Executive in Developed Countries* (London: Macmillan).

Yergin, D. (1980) *Shattered Peace: The Origins of the Cold War and the National Security State* (Harmondsworth: Penguin).

Young, A., J. Duckett and P. Graham (2010) 'Perspectives on the Global Distribution of Power', Exceptional special edition of *Politics*, 30(1).

Zakaria, F. (1997) 'The Rise of Illiberal Democracy', *Foreign Affairs* 76 (November–December).

Zald, M. N. and J. D. McCarthy (1987) *Social Movements in an Organizational Society: Collected Essays* (Piscataway, NJ: Transactional Publishers).

Zimmerman, J. F. (1992) *Contemporary American Federalism* (London and New York: Leicester University Press).

Index

Notes: **bold** = reference to boxed items; *italic* = reference to marginal items.

476